Proto-Austronesian Phonology with Glossary

Volume I

John U. Wolff

Cornell Southeast Asia Program Publications
640 Stewart Avenue, Ithaca, NY 14850-3857

Volume I, ISBN: 978-087727-532-9
Volume II, ISBN: 978-087727-533-6

Table of Contents

List of Maps

Abbreviations

ACD	R. Blust (1995)
adj	adjective
An	Austronesian
aux	Auxiliary
C	consonant
Cauq	Cauquelin (Puyuma 1991)
CC	consonant cluster
conn	connected
dial	dialectic form
disylb	disyllable, disyllabic
E.	eastern or East
e.o.	each other
esp	especially
excl	exclusive
Form	Formosa, Formosan
G	Geraghty 1983
gen	genitive
H	Hardeland (Ngaju Dayak)
Hesp	Hesperonesian
incl	inclusive
Ind	Indonesia, Indonesian
inform	informant
instr	instrumental
K	informant for Amis (identification lost)
Kal	Kalimantan
k.o.	kind of
L-O	Lanyon-Orgill (Tolai)
lg, lgs	language(s)
lit.	literally
metath	metathesis, metathesize(d)
monosylb	monsyllable, monosyllabic
MP	Malayo-Polynesian
ms., mss.	manuscript(s)
N	nasalization, Bunun consultant
N.	northern or North
n.	number
n.d.	undated manuscript
Nih	Nihira 1988 (Bunun)
o.	one
Oc	Oceanic, Oceania
OC	Classical Chinese
o.s.	oneself
PAn	Proto-Austronesian
pass.	passive
p.c.	personal communication
pl	plural
Phil	Philippines
PMP	Proto-Malayo-Polynesian
POc	Proto-Oceanic
Polyn	Polynesian
PPn	Proto-Polynesian
R	Richardson (Malagasy)
r- or **R-**	reduplication
RPO	Ross, Pawley, and Osborn
RT	Li: Rukai Texts (I–IX)
S.	southern or South
sg	singular
s.o.	someone
sp., spp.	species, species (pl)
s.t.	something
S-T	Sino-Tibetan
Sul	Sulawesi
s.w.	somewhere
sylb	syllable
T-B	Tibeto-Burman
Tsuch	Tsuchida
unconn	unconnected
unk	unknown
V	vowel
W	Watuseke (Tondano)
W.	western or West
>	became
<	derives from
Z	Zoetmulder (OJv)

Alphabetical list of language abbreviations:

A-A	Are-Are	(S.E. Solomons)
Ach	Acheh	(N. Sumatra)
Akl	Aklanon	(Panay, Philippines)
Alas	Alas Batak	(Sumatra)
Am	Amiis	(Formosa [Taiwan])
Ars	Arosi	(SE. Solomons)
Asi	Asilulu	(Ambon, Moluku [Moluccas])
At	Atayal	(Formosa [Taiwan])
Ba	Pamona [Bare'e]	(Central Sulawesi)
Bag	Bagoʔbuʔ	(Mindanao, Philippines)
Bal	Balinese	(Bali)
Bau	Bauan	(Fiji)
Bd, RuBd	Rukai Budai	(Formosa [Taiwan])
Bgg	Banggai	(Central Sulawesi)
Bid	Bidayuh	(Sarawak)
Bil	Bilaan	(Mindanao, Philippines)
Bin	Bintulu	(Sarawak)
Bjr	Banjarese Ml	(S.E. Kalimantan)
Bkd	Bukidnon	(N. Luzon, Philippines)
Bkl	Bicolano	(S. Luzon)
Blw	Balangao	(N. Luzon, Phil)
BM	Bolaang Mongondow	(N. Sulawesi)
Bon	Bontoc	(N. Luzon, Philippines)
Bug	Bugis	(Sulawesi)
Bun	Bunun	(Formosa [Taiwan])
Buru	Buru	(Moluccas)
Cb	Cebuano	(Central Philippines)
Chmr	Chamorro	(Marianas, Oceania)
CtbMnb	Cotabato Manobo	(Mindanao, Phil)
Dgt	Dumagat	(N. Luzon, Phil)
Dib	Dibabawon	(Mindanao, Phil)
DPB	Dairi-Pakpak Batak	(Sumatra)
DY	Duke of York	(Bismark Archipelgo, New Britain)
EOc	Eastern Oceanic	
Fi	Fijian	(Oceania)
Fu	Futuna	(Oceania)
Gad	Gaddang	(N. Luzon, Phil)
Gdg	Gedaged	(N. New Guinea)
Gor	Gorontalo	(N. Sulawesi)
Han	Hanonoo	(Mindoro, Phil)

Hlg	Hiligaynon [Ilonggo]	(Negros and Panay, Phil)
Ibl	Ibaloi	(N. Luzon, Phil)
Ifg	Ifugao	(N. Luzon, Phil)
IfgA	Ifugao Aguinaldo	(N. Luzon, Phil)
IfgBt	Ifugao, Batad	(N. Luzon, Phil)
IfgK	Ifugao Kiangan	(N. Luzon, Phil)
Ilk	Iloko [Ilocano]	(N. Luzon, Phil)
Isg	Isneg	(N. Luzon, Phil)
Itb	Itbayatan	(Batanes Islands, Luzon, Phil)
Ivt	Ivatan	(Batanes Islands, Phil)
Ivt	Ivatan	(Batanes Islands, Luzon, Phil)
Jkt	Jakarta Ml	(Java)
Jv	Javanese	(Java)
Kan	Kankanay	(N. Luzon, Phil)
Kav	Kavalan	(E. Formosa [Taiwan])
Kay	Kayan	(N. Kalimatan)
KB	Kei Besar	(Moluccas)
KB	Karo Batak	(Sumatra)
Kdzn	Kadazan	(N. Kalimantan)
Kei	Kei	(Moluccas)
Kel	Kelabit	(Kalimantan)
Ken	Kendaya	(N. Kalimantan
KK	Kei Kecil	(Moluccas)
Kmb	Kambera	(Sumba)
Knn	Kanakanavu	(Formosa [Taiwan])
Kpp	Kapangpangan [Pampango]	(Central Luzon, Phil)
Ktg	Ketagalan	(NW. Formosa [Taiwan])
Leti	Leti	(Lesser Sundas)
Loin	Loin check	(Flores)
Long T	Long Teru	(Kalimantan)
Long W	Long Wat	(Kalimantan)
Mag	Magindano	(Mindanao, Phil)
Mar	Maranao	(Mindanao, Phil)
Mdr	Mandar	(SW. Sulawesi)
Mgg	Manggarai	(W. Flores)
Min	Minangkabau Ml	(Sumatra)
Mk	Makassar	(SW. Sulawesi)
Mkl_BS	Moklen check	(S.W. Thailand)
Mkl-BDC	Moklen check	(S.W. Thailand)
Mkln	Moklen	(S.W. Thailand)
Mkn-Dng	Moken check	(W. Thai-Burma border)
Mkn-Ks	Moken check	(S.W. Thailand)

Mkn-Lmp	Moken check	(S.W. Thailand)
Mkn-Rw	Moken Rawai	(S.W. Thailand)
Ml	Malay	(Malaysia, Indonesia)
Mlg	Malagasy	(Madagascar)
Mn	Mantauran (Rukai)	(Formosa [Taiwan])
Mnb	Manobo	(Mindanao, Philippines)
Mny	Maanyan	(S.E. Kalimantan)
Mok	Moken	(W. Thailand, S.W. Burma)
Motu	Motu	(Papua, New Guinea)
Msk	Mansaka	(Mindanao, Philippines)
Mu	Muna	(S.E. Sulawesi)
Muk	Mukah	(Kalimantan)
Mus	Mussau	(Admiralties)
Mx, AtMx	Mayrinax Atayal	(Formosa [Taiwan])
Nak	Nakanai (Lakalai)	(New Britain)
ND	Ngaju Dayak	(Central Kalimantan)
Ngad	Ngadha	(Flores)
Ngg	Nggela [Gela]	(S.E. Solomons)
NJv	New Javanese	(Java)
Num	Numfor	(N.W. New Guinea)
Ojv	Old Javanese	(Java)
Pai	Paiwan	(Formosa [Taiwan])
Pal	Palau	(Western Oceania)
Pau	Paulohi	(Moluccas)
Paz	Pazih	(N.W. Formosa [Taiwan])
Pgs	Pangasinan	(N. Luzon, Philippines)
Pu	Puyuma	(Formosa [Taiwan])
Rat	Ratahan	(N. Sulawesi)
Rej	Rejang	(Sumatra)
Ren	Rennellese	(Polynesia)
Rmb	Rembong	(Flores)
Rot	Rotuman	(E. Oceania)
Rov	Roviana	(Solomon Islands)
Ru	Rukai	(Formosa [Taiwan])
Sa	Sa'a	(S.E. Solomons)
Sal	Salayar	(S.W. Sulawesi)
Sam	Samoan	(Polynesia)
Sang	Sangir	(N. Sulawesi)
Sar	Saaroa	(Formosa [Taiwan])
Sas	Sasak	(Lombok)
Sbl	Sambal	(Central Luzon, Philippines)
Sed	Sediq	(Formosa [Taiwan])
Sik	Sika [Sikka]	(Sumba)

Skt	Sanskrit	(India)
SL	Samar-Leyte (Waray)	(Central Philippines)
Sm	Samoan	(Polynesia)
Snd	Sundanese	(W. Java)
Sob	Soboyo	(Moluccas)
Sq or AtSq	Squliq Atayal	(Formosa [Taiwan])
St	Saisiat	(NW. Formosa [Taiwan])
Tag	Tagalog	(Central Luzon)
Tar	Taroko Sediq	(Formosa [Taiwan])
TB	Toba Batak	(Sumatra)
Tbl	Tboli	(Mindanao, Philippines)
Tblu	Tombolu	(N. Sulawesi)
Tbw	Tagbanwa	(Mindanao, Philippines)
Tdn	Tondano	(N.Sulwesi)
Th	Thao	(Taiwan)
Tir	Tiruray	(Mindanao, Philippines)
TM	check	(Kalimantan)
To	Tongan	(W. Polynesai)
Tol	Tolai	(New Britain)
Tond, Tnd	Tondano	(N. Sulawesi)
Tse	Tonsea	(N. Sulawesi)
Ttb	Tontemboan	(N. Sulawesi)
Ttb Mtn	Tontemboan Matanai	(N. Sulawesi)
Ttb Mkl	Tontemboan Makelai	(N. Sulawesi)
UJ	Uma Juman	(Kalimantan)
Ul	Ulawa	(S.E. Solomons)
WBM	W. Bukidnon Manobo	(Mindanao, Philippines)
WOc	Western Oceanic	
Ymd	Yamdena	(Moluccas)

Acknowledgments

This monograph first began as a project to update Dempwolff's *Vergleichende Lautlehre* (1934–38), the cornerstone of the historical study of Austronesian languages. I was building on the work of my mentor I. Dyen, who had considerably revised Dempwolff's original phonology. I thus began with a considerable body of data and a tradition of analysis that was useful, but the research of two scholars published in the late seventies and early eighties provided ample data that could not be explained by Dempwolff's reconstructed phonology, even as revised by Dyen. These studies made it clear that it would be necessary to rethink each and every reconstruction and question the basic assumptions of the nature and location of the proto-language in order to accommodate the wealth of additional data they provided. First was the work of R. Blust 1980b, 1983, 1986, and 1989, who added geometrically to the the stock of reconstructed forms that had been published up to that time, and second, that of S. Tuschida 1976, who made accessible the crucial attestations from the Formosan languages. My first debt in the preparation of this monograph is to these four scholars, whose work formed the basis for my glossary and attestations. In addition to these, this study incorporates or takes into account a vast number of pieces of research, smaller and larger, as well as dictionaries, whose authors I can only acknowledge by a listing in the bibliography. I should however mention a few studies that were crucial in providing data that enabled me to make the reconstructions. For the Formosan languages, I relied heavily not only on Tsuchida 1976 but on the studies of the histories of the individual languages published under the auspices of the Academia Sinica, Taiwan, ROC, undertaken by Paul Li and other scholars from that institution. My data on Bugis and Salayar were substantiated and enhanced by the extensive materials for the languages of South Sulawesi presented by R. Mills 1975. For Oceanic Languages, the monumental work by M. Ross 1988 provided a wealth of data and the framework for understanding the subgrouping crucial to interpreting the complicated developments, especially in the Western Oceanic languages. In addition, for the Eastern Oceanic languages, there are two pieces of research that were particularly influential in the analysis presented in this study. They stand out among a multitude of fine dictionaries, grammars, and secondary studies on these languages. First is the work of P. Geraghty, whose in-depth study of the Fijian languages (1983) had an important part in shaping my thinking about the developments in the Eastern Oceanic languages. Second is the treasure-trove of attestations found in Pollex, which also had a substantial input into my analysis of the Eastern Oceanic data.

In addition to acknowledging the importance of these published materials, I also owe a debt of gratitude to the personal efforts of colleagues and institutions, without which I could not have produced this study. First I have had years and years of support from Cornell University, both the Southeast Asia Program and the Department of Linguistics, which not only provided me the opportunity of offering seminars in the subject matter of this study and giving me access to some absolutely first-rate students, but also provided me with summer stipends and research grants that enabled me to obtain clerical and editorial assistance and pay informants. In addition I profited greatly from three research fellowships abroad which afforded me facilities, stipends, and access to colleagues and informants: first, the International Institute for Asian Studies, Leiden, the Netherlands, where I spent three months in the fall of 1998, at the invitation of Professor Hein Steinhauer. Then in the summer of 2004 I received a fellowship from the Academia Sinica, Linguistics Department, under the sponsorship of Paul J. K. Li, which provided me the opportunity to visit several sites where Formosan languages are still spoken and paid all research and expenses. Because of the basic importance of these languages for historical studies of the Austronesian group, this fellowship was particularly important for enhancing the accuracy and quantity of my Formosan data. Finally, I had a six-week fellowship in from the Center for General Linguistics (ZAS), Berlin, at the invitation of Patrick Steinhauer in the winter of 2007, which afforded me the opportunity of writing portions of this manuscript and interacting with colleagues in Germany.

The collegiality and helpfulness of colleagues in the field have also had an important role in enabling me to carry out this study. For the first three introductory chapters I am indebted to the following people who read them and provided me with substantial commentary that enabled me to improve the presentation considerably and avoid some potentially embarrassing errors: K.A. Adelaar, L. Sagart, Martin Schell, Daniel Kaufman, and Matthew Amster. In fact, Sagart read almost the entire manuscript. I profited most prominently in my thinking about the first chapter of this study from the spring 2008 seminar that Sagart offered in Cornell University, the many hours of discussions that term, and the wealth of private unpublished data he supplied me with. Although my ignorance of Chinese and Tibeto-Birman linguistics rendered it impossible to incorporate these data directly into this study, the data were sufficient to inform my understanding of any number of reconstructions and in persuading me of the relationship of the Austronesian and the Sino-Tibetan languages and thus to shape the assumptions that underlie the analysis here presented. For the Formosan languages, I first and foremost owe a debt of gratitude to Paul Li for supplying me with all relevant publications produced at the Academica Sinica—off prints of articles, dictionaries, and compilations of texts, but also for arranging two visits, where I had first-hand access to the Formosan languages. I was also given much help by S. Tsuchida, who similarly supplied me with his data published and unpublished, including his extensive collection of data on the Bunun dialects. I also owe a debt of gratitude to M. Nojima, who accompanied me to the Bunun area and helped me understand the data gathered there. I should also mention the linguists who accompanied me in my month in Taiwan in 2005, P. Radetsky, C. Quinn, A. Tsukamoto, who not only interpreted my interaction with the informants but were helpful in gathering a large amount of data in a short time and making sense of it. For the Philippine languages I profited immensely in my discussions over the years with M. Charles and D. Zorc and from the large amount of data they had gathered and generously shared. For Ratahan I am indebted to N. Himmelmann, who spent many weeks together with me in Indonesia and with whom I collaborated in the investigating and preparing a monograph on the language. For the Minahassan languages I am indebted to F.K. Watuseke, who spent many hours discussing data from these languages and informing me on his native Tondano, drawing on a deep well of knowledge gained from a lifelong devotion to Minahassan studies. For my chapter on Bugis (§C6ff.) I profited greatly from a host of trenchant comments by U. Sirk, which not only informed my understanding of many of the attestations but also provided background material that explained the not inconsiderable disjunction between published materials and the material I gathered from informants during twelve weeks in Macassar. For Muna I had valuable feedback from R. van den Berg. For Malagasy, I had the benefit of careful and critical reading by W. Mahdi and K.A. Adelaar, both of whom provided me with commentary that strengthened my presentation considerably. For Kelabit I profited immensely from discussions with M. Amster, who with his active knowledge of the language, enabled me to solve some of the puzzles the data presented. For Moken I had the immensely good fortune of being able to conduct the field research together with P. Pittayaporn (Joe), who not only interpreted the interactions with the speakers, but also worked together with me in transcribing the data and making sense of them in terms of the published materials we had at our disposal. Joe also read Chapter One and the chapter on Moken (§E3ff.), and provided me with detailed commentary, which invariably was remarkably insightful and to the point. For Buru I had the benefit of a fairly lengthy correspondence with C. Grimes, whose thesis (1991), provided a context for the data provided by the dictionaries. Grimes' comments on my chapter on Buru (§E2ff.) rectified a number of misunderstandings by presenting additional data that led to an alternative solution. For Leti, I had the benefit of intensive contact with A. van Engelenhoven during my tenure as a fellow of IIAS in 1998. Although his two theses on Leti (1996b, 2004) are the key to understanding the complexities that the Leti data present, I would not have been able to present the history of this language in a lucid manner without the benefit of the many hours van Engelenhoven devoted to discussing and explaining the bewildering morphophonemics and their historical background. He was also instrumental in providing me the opportunity to contact the community of Kei speakers resident in the Netherlands and accompanied me to their settlement on several occasions. For Kei I also had help from E. Travis, who provided me with his draft dictionary of Kei, which considerably augmented the materials in the published dictionary and what I had been able to elicit from informants in the Netherlands. These were the people and institutions that remain in my memory as having made particularly important contributions to this study. I do not wish to imply that these scholars necessarily share all my conclusions, nor are they responsible for errors in this study. The errors herein are exclusively mine. There are many others who educated me, informed me on languages, discussed methodology, or commented on my talks or articles, and many others who encouraged me and gave me confidence that this was a project worth pursuing. I am grateful to each and every one of them, even if space limitations make it impossible to list them expressly. I praise God for the institutions and the many human beings that enabled me to undertake this lifelong study.

J.U.W.
August 2010

Foreword

I first met John Wolff in the lobby of a Waikiki hotel during the 6th ICAL conference, in 1990. A Chinese specialist, I was impatient to present my theory of a genetic relationship between Chinese and Austronesian to real-life Austronesianists. I was going to talk the next day, my abstract was in the conference booklet. I had not circulated my paper. A man came to me, introduced himself as John Wolff, and said "you know, I am going to take issue with your paper tomorrow". I replied that this was precisely what I was hoping for; that, not being an Austronesianist, I was hoping that criticism from specialists would either falsify the idea for good, or allow me to improve it. Then I added "and since you're going to take issue with my paper... why not read it ?". There was a flicker of amusement in his eye. We agreed that I would leave a copy for him at the reception desk. The next day after reading the paper his only comment to me was that I was "cooking with gas", meaning, I suppose, that he had not found any of the obvious methodological errors one expects to find in papers of that kind.

John Wolff, now an emeritus professor at Cornell University, has made the study of Austronesian languages the central interest of his life. After studying at Yale under Isidore Dyen and becoming an undisputed authority on Tagalog, Cebuano, Indonesian and Javanese, he has over the years offered a series of influential contributions to proto-Austronesian phonology, morphology and lexicon. This book, *Proto-Austronesian Phonology with Glossary*, is the first entirely devoted to the reconstruction of Proto-Austronesian phonology and lexicon since Dempwolff's *Vergleichende Lautlehre des Austronesischen Wortschatzes* (1934-1938): it brings Wolff's contributions together into a coherent system, adding a historical perspective which —I am gratified— arose out of the paper I left for him twenty years ago at the reception desk of that Waikiki hotel: one in which the Austronesian languages ultimately go back to a sister language of Proto-Sino-Tibetan spoken by a community of early rice and millet farmers in neolithic northern China.

We have before us a study of unprecedented proportions. Presentation of Wolff's Proto-Austronesian phonology is continued by thirty-seven *chapters* detailing the evolution of the system —regularities and irregularities— into as many languages (Dempwolff's eleven, plus twenty-six 'new' languages, including nearly all the Austronesian languages currently spoken in Taiwan; several known to him from personal fieldwork); this is followed by a Glossary of c. 2000 reconstructed etyma (about half of them assigned to a level above Malayo-Polynesian), with full supporting evidence, notes and cross-references to relevant sections in the Proto-Austronesian phonology chapter. The book ends with all the indexes, registers, and finder-lists the most exacting reader could wish for.

There are many uncertain aspects to Proto-Austronesian phonology and certainly no two linguists will agree on every part of its reconstruction. Wolff's Proto-Austronesian consonant system is notable for its simplicity and symmetry. This he achieves by rejecting certain phonemic contrasts, like the distinction between *C and *t, treated as stress-conditioned variants. He reconstructs contrastive stress in Proto-Austronesian based on stress-related facts in Philippine and Tsouic languages, although he admits that there are often inconsistencies between the two. This, at least, promises to be a controversial aspect of his reconstruction. What matters is the presentation by an experienced comparativist of a full set of interconnected, explicit hypotheses about Proto-Austronesian phonology, exemplified by a large number of cognate sets distributed over thirty-seven languages.

Treatment of phonological evolution into each language continues and makes explicit the tradition of study in each of the relevant geographical areas, while going into much finer detail than the simplified phoneme correspondence tables that can be found in the literature: Wolff identifies new sub-regularities, and exceptions to them. For instance, after stating the generally admitted fact that his Proto-Austronesian *ɣ (the phoneme conventionally identified as *R) normally goes to /r/ in Puyuma, he notes that final *ɣ becomes /n/ if there had been an *l or *n in the word. This regularizes forms like *vanin* 'board', *padamanan* 'dawn' , *vaṭinun* 'egg' and *unan* 'snake'.

Wolff assembles cognate sets based on the sound correspondences he has identified, also taking into account certain general processes, morphological or phonological, that interfere with regular phonological development, generating lexical doublets. Recognition and characterization of these processes allows him to unify forms that would otherwise be treated as independent. One of these is nasal substitution of the initial consonant in Formosan languages, for instance his Proto-Austronesian *taɣa 'wait' includes both Pazeh *taxa* and Atayal *naɣaʔ*. Another is unstressed vowel weakening and syllable loss in trisyllables: 'gall' is reflected as *apdo* in Tagalog, with syncope of the penultimate vowel, but as *peru* in Tondano, where the first syllable was lost. Wolff is surely on the right track there.

More than others Wolff pays attention to processes outside of neogrammarian mechanisms, like contamination: although his *aɣak 'lead by the hand' evolves regularly to Bunun *alak*, he claims the meaning of the Bunun form: 'bring with', has received semantic contamination from *alap 'take'. Another kind of contamination accounts for phonological irregularities: thus some of the reflexes of his *betíhec 'calf' (of leg) unexpectedly reflect *i in the first syllable due, in his view, to contamination from a word for 'shin wrestling'. Although the details in each case are open to discussion, Wolff is right to systematically seek explanations for irregular and unexpected developments rather than to limit cognate sets to their mechanically regular core.

The Glossary is a trove of new cognate sets: I particularly like *aci 'cooking fire', which explains Malay *nasi* 'cooked rice' by connecting it to a Puyuma word for 'fire'. More sets are expanded or raised to a higher level: Wolff found persuasive cognates to Dempwolff's *baǵah 'inform' in eight Formosan languages (see under *bágaq). His Glossary will be a major source of information to those interested in the evolution of the AN lexicon.

Phylogeny matters for reconstruction. Wolff explicitly accepts my numeral-based Austronesian subgrouping, where the West Formosan languages branch off before the East Formosan languages and Malayo-Polynesian belongs in a relatively low-order East Formosan subgroup. This is in contrast to Blust's subgrouping, where the Malayo-Polynesian languages are treated as a primary branch of the family, on the same level as nine primary branches spoken exclusively in Taiwan. Thus, Wolff relies less on Malayo-

Polynesian evidence than does Blust in reconstructing Proto-Austronesian. As an example, consider the word 'ear'. Dempwolff gave *taliŋaʿ based on Malayo-Polynesian evidence. Corresponding forms are found in Formosa: accordingly, Blust raised Dempwolff's reconstruction to Proto-Austronesian, as *Caliŋa (200 list). But there are also in Taiwan forms where the last two syllable onsets occur in the reverse order, for instance Pazeh *saŋira* 'ear'. Based on these forms, Wolff reconstructs the Proto-Austronesian word for 'ear' as *taŋila. He does so because even though *taŋila is not reflected in any Malayo-Polynesian language, it is in several Formosan languages including Pazeh, one of the earliest-branching languages. Wolff's interpretation further suggests a motivation for the metathesis: reversing the onsets of the penult and the final syllable in *taŋila aligns the word with other terms for paired or plural things with infixed *-al-, like *d-al-apa 'palms', *d-al-ukap 'soles', *b-al-aŋa 'pots'.

The great paucity of monosyllabic content words in Proto-Austronesian is noteworthy. At the same time, many Proto-Austronesian words appear to have a meaning-associated final syllable (a "root"), even though their initial syllable(s) are not readily analyzable. Wolff's treatment will, I believe, move the field forward. He argues that, far from being sound-symbolic strings of the kind of *gl-* in *gloom, glow, gleam* etc., Austronesian "roots" are the lost monosyllables of Proto-Austronesian: he identifies several processes which turned Proto-Austronesian monosyllables into disyllables: adding a prothetic vowel, "stretching" the nucleus (that is, gemminating the vowel and optionally inserting a glottal stop in the middle it, e.g. *taq > *taʔaq), reduplicating the root, and petrifying an affixed form. There may be others. The recognition of An roots as monosyllabic *morphemes* will be of the highest significance in establishing the outer connexions of Austronesian.

Wolff's *Proto-Austronesian Phonology* presents us with a detailed picture of the evolution of the Austronesian family in the past five millennia. It is a complex, economically-written book with many new explicitly-formulated hypotheses on phonology, morphology and the lexicon. Whether these hypotheses become part of the mainstream, as some undoubtedly will, or end up being falsified, most will inevitably fuel discussion, pushing the field forward. *Proto-Austronesian Phonology* is a major contribution to the enterprise of discovering the history of the Austronesians and their place in the linguistic landscape of East Asia.

Laurent Sagart
Senior Scholar
Centre National de la Recherche Scientifique, France

Preface

This work is the study of the history of words in the Austronesian (An) languages—their origin in Proto-Austronesian (PAn) or at later stages and how they developed into the forms that are attested in the current An languages. A study of their history entails the reconstruction of the sound system (phonology) of PAn and an exposition of the sound laws (rules) whereby the original sounds changed into those attested in the current An languages. The primary aim of this work is to examine exhaustively the forms that can be reconstructed for PAn and also for the earliest stage after the An languages began to spread southward from Taiwan. For the later stages—that is, forms that can be traced no further back than to the proto-languages of late subgroups, we do not attempt to be exhaustive but confine ourselves to only some of the forms that are traceable to those times, treating those that figure prominently in the literature on historical An linguistics or those that have special characteristics important for understanding in general how forms arose and the processes that led to change. In short, the aim of this study is not just to reconstruct protomorphemes and order the reflexes according to the entries[1] they fit under, but rather to account for the history of each form that is attested and explain what happened historically to yield the attestations.

Part A, the introduction, is composed of three chapters: Chapter One is a description of the geographical spread of the An languages and a summary of what is known about how these languages came to be located where they are now found; Chapter Two is a discussion of the assumptions and methodologies followed in this study; and finally, Chapter Three is a summary of PAn phonology, followed by a discussion of principles specific to a reconstruction of PAn phonology and of problems that affect phonological reconstruction of the whole family. Parts B–G deal with the history of each of the thirty-seven languages treated in detail in this study. Part H is the glossary, which gives the reconstructed protomorphemes and cites the attested reflexes in our thirty-seven languages and in other languages listed according to principles enunciated in §A1.2. Part I provides finder lists from the English translation and also from the reconstructions made by Blust ACD (1995b) and Dempwolff (1934–1938). These are followed by the finder lists for the 37 languages treated in detail. Part J gives the bibliography, and finally Part K provides an index of all topics discussed in Parts A–G.

[1] The term ENTRY refers to the entry under which the attestations are listed. The term PROTOMORPHEME refers to the reconstruction itself. Some of the entries refer to sequences that cannot be reconstructed. We require the concept of 'protomorphemes' as well as 'roots' because some of the entries refer not to roots, but to affixes. A few of the entries refer to stems consisting of an affix plus a root (which may or may not have occurred as words in PAn).

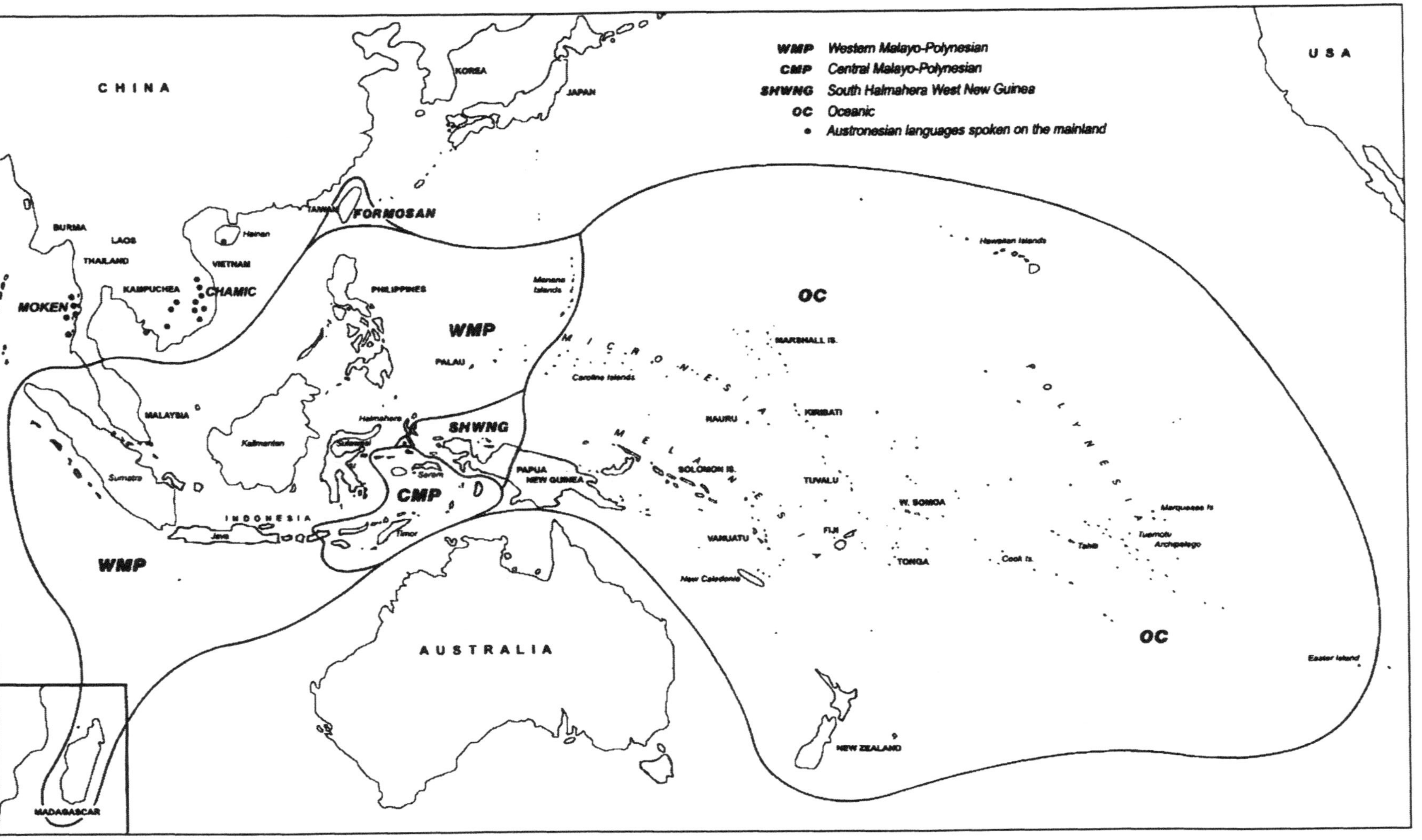

Map 1. The Austronesian languages.

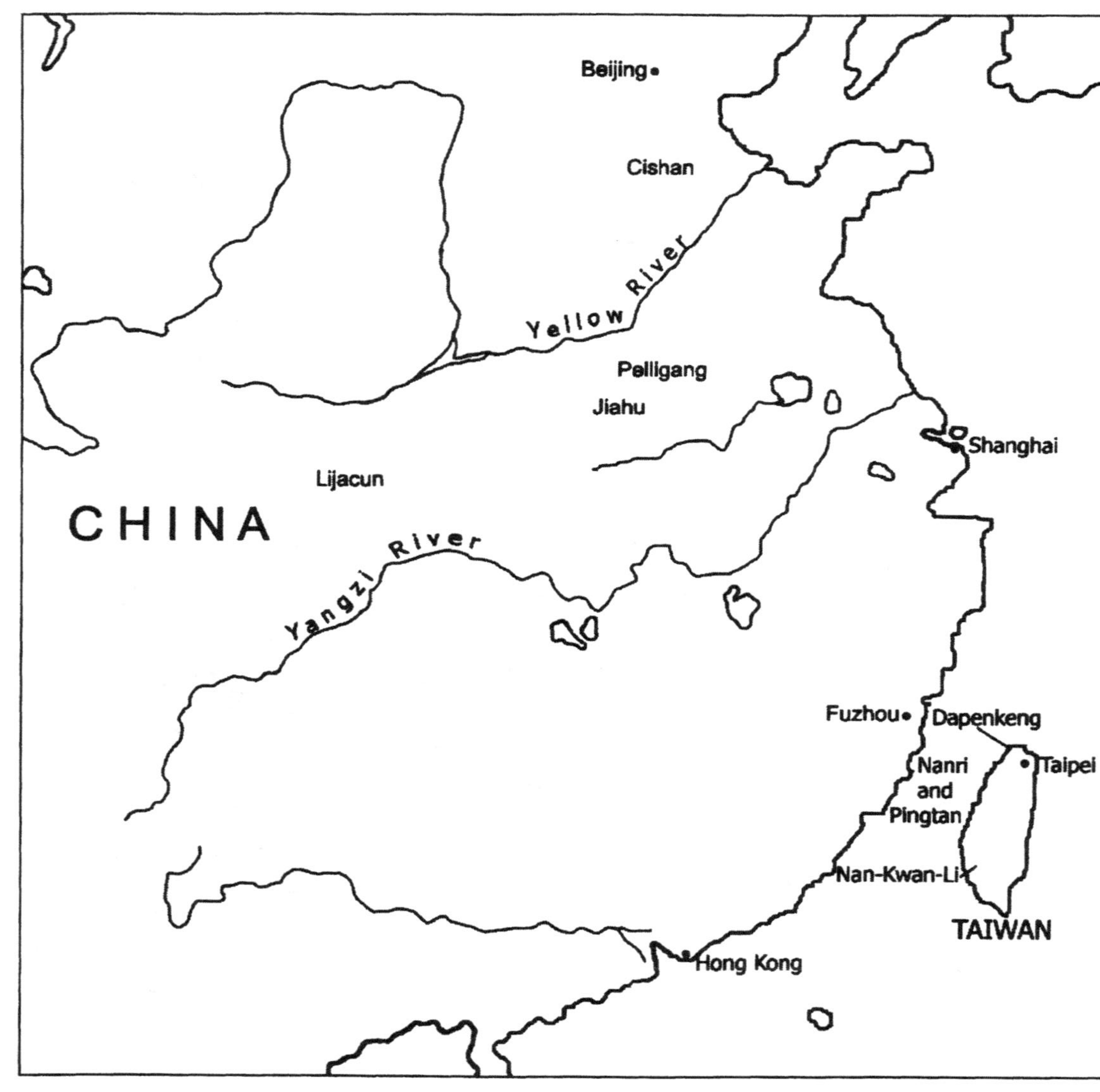

Map 2. China and sites yielding evidence for the development of agriculture.

CHAPTER ONE

The Austronesian Languages

A1.0 Languages that comprise the Austronesian group

The An languages are a family of languages located in the southern seas reaching from Madagascar on the west through island Southeast Asia and coastal areas eastward going through parts of Papua-New Guinea and from there throughout Oceania as far east as Easter Island and Hawaii. The An languages stretch as far north as and include Taiwan (Formosa) and reach as far south as the Australian subcontinent (but not anywhere on the subcontinent). On the southeast Asian mainland, An languages are spoken in Malaysia, on the west coast of Thailand, and in the mountains of Vietnam. In Thailand and Vietnam, the An languages are located in proximity to non-An languages and are in many cases in contact with them. In eastern Indonesia, Papua-New Guinea, and in western Oceania as far east as the Solomon Islands, both An and non-An languages are found. The An languages tend to be located near the coast. Inland areas mostly are peopled by communities that speak non-An languages, although some non-An languages are also found on the coast.

A1.1 The origin of the Austronesian languages and their spread: archeological evidence

It is thought that the major language groups of Southeast Asia originate some ten to fifteen thousand years ago in the area of central China stretching from south of the Yangzi to north of the Yellow River basin (Lu 2005:52). This was an area of widespread grasslands with an abundance of grain, and the populations speaking the ancestor or ancestors of the current languages increased as a result of the availability of grains as a staple food. The extensive spread of these languages took place as the population looked for grains to harvest. It is believed that rice cultivation developed in response to the increased population and climatic conditions (see below). With the development of agriculture came an even greater expansion of the population and movement in the search for new lands to cultivate. In short, the spread of the language families in Southeast Asia, the S-T, the Austronesian, the Kra-Dai, the Hmong Mien, and the Austroasiatic went hand in hand with the spread of rice cultivation.
The oldest remains of rice cultivation in the Yangzi River basin date to approximately 8,500 years ago.[1] Rice cultivation developed from domestication, a process where wild rice was tended and even planted but not in cultivated fields or with transplanted seedlings. It is thought that cultivation of rice in fields developed in response to cold

[1] Bellwood (2005a:114) gives the even earlier date of 7,000 BC. The account given in this paragraph is largely based on Sagart 2008.

conditions of the Younger Dryas, an era of cold lasting around a millennium more than ten thousand years ago. These climatic conditions necessitated careful tending of the rice plants and selection of seed that could survive cold. Within two or three centuries after the earliest cultivation of rice in the Yangzi river basin, this practice spread to the Yellow River basin, an area too cold for wild rice (that is, *Oryza sativa*) to occur naturally.[2] The areas of Lijacun and Jiahu between the Yangzi and the Yellow Rivers yield rice remains that date between 7,000 and 6,000 BC. In the area of Cishan and Peiligang in the Yellow River basin, with a culture very similar to that of Jiahu,[3] remains of both rice and millet cultivation have been found, dating to somewhat earlier than 6,000 BC. In this area foxtail millet occurs in the wild, and remains of both broomcorn millet and foxtail millet have been found in this region. The cultivation of millet was probably in response to the need to supplement the lower yields of rice in cooler regions.[4] As the populations increased and looked for new lands to cultivate, they spread eastward along the Yellow river and then southward along the coast, as archeological remains attest (Lu 2005:53–54). From the islands of Nanri and Pingtan on the coast of Fujian province, not far from Fuzhou and just opposite northwest Taiwan at its nearest point to the mainland, one can see Mt. Xueshan, the highest peak in northern Taiwan. It is thought that when the pre-Austronesians reached this area of the coast, they sailed in the direction of this mountain in their search for new lands to cultivate. These people brought the cultivation of foxtail millet and rice with them to Taiwan. This is proven by the discovery of remains of both rice and millet at the site of Nan-Kwan-Li on the west coast of Taiwan, halfway between the northeast and the southeast. These remains have been dated to no later than 2,500 BC but may possibly go back as far as 3,500 BC (Tsang 2005:71). Also the Dapenkeng culture in N.W. Taiwan, which has a pottery tradition that is clearly linked to finds of cultures located in the Yangzi basin, including the Yangzi delta, is dated as early as 3,500 BC (Bellwood 2005a: 124, 135–35). The Dapenkeng culture of Taiwan has other cultural traints in common with the neolithic Cisan and Peiligang cultures of the Yellow River Basin (Sagart 2008: §4.4). This makes it clear that Danpenkeng was also an agricultural society and probably engaged in both rice and millet production.

The people who migrated to Taiwan were the linguistic ancestors of all An language speakers. This is a hypothesis supported by linguistic evidence given in §A1.1.3ff. There is no early attestation of an An language on the mainland. In other words, although the origin was surely on the mainland, by the time of the PAn that is reconstructed here, this language had been brought from the mainland to Taiwan and was lost on the mainland (only to be reintroduced, possibly some two millennia later). Blust (1995a) dates PAn to 4,000 BC. This is only a few hundred years earlier than the earliest dating of the

---

[2] Presumably the rice cultivators looked for new lands to till to the north of the Yangzi and came upon ever cooler climates as they moved northward. As they moved further north, the seeds that survived would be from the plants most resistant to cold. In that way rice varieties tolerant to colder conditions were developed by the agriculturists as they moved northward toward the Yellow River basin.

[3] Lu (2005:54) states that there are substantial differences between the Jiahu culture and that of Cishan and Peiligang, so that the remains from these two areas come from different peoples. On the other hand, Bellwood points out the Chinese Neolithic evolved not from one small ancestral society, but "from within a region characterized by a high degree of communication and interaction, perhaps focusing on a chain of closely related ethnolinguitic populations" (Bellwood 2005a: 120).

[4] Bellwood believes that rice cultivation preceded millet and stimulated it as rice moved north (2205a: 119).

Dapenkeng culture (3,500 BC), discussed above, which is assumed to have been the culture of the earliest Austronesians.

The hypothesis then is that PAn was located on Taiwan, brought there from the mainland, with the earliest settlement on the west coast, toward the northwest coast of the island.[5] Over a period of a thousand years or more, the An speakers gradually moved southward in search of new lands and upon reaching the south coast began moving eastward and then northward up the east coast. I also hypothesize that the languages spoken currently or in the last couple of hundred years in the southwestern plains, in the south, and along the east coast are, or were, spoken by the descendants of the Austronesians who settled in these areas. We will discuss the linguistic evidence that indeed the homeland must have been on Taiwan and how the An languages spread in §A1.1.32, below. Prior to 1945 Taiwan was known as "Formosa", and the An languages of Taiwan are commonly referred to as the "Formosan languages", a practice we follow in this study, as well.

More than a thousand years after the first arrival of the Austronesians in Taiwan, they spread to the Philippines from the south coast of Taiwan. A similar type of culture to the Dapenkeng with its distinctive pottery and implements appears in very northern Luzon, remains that have been dated at 2,500–1,500 BC—i.e., at least a thousand years later than the earliest Taiwan remains. From the Philippines this Neolithic culture spread rapidly southeastward and southwestward. In summarizing archeological discoveries, Pawley (2002:257) says, "Neolithic assemblages appear more or less simultaneously in North Borneo, Sulawesi, Halmahera, Timor, the Bismarck Archipelago and various parts of Remote Oceania, with dates ranging from 1,500 to 1,000 BC and with assemblages carrying markers of close relationships."[6]

The earliest spread of the An languages eastward over Oceania is archeologically documented by a distinctive type of pottery called "Lapita".[7] This pottery is associated with implements, many of them having to do with fishing technology, and with distinctive architecture and settlement patterns, in the so-called "Lapita cultural complex". The earliest sites of the Lapita cultural complex, dating to 1,500 BC, are in the region of the St. Matthias Group, New Britain, and New Ireland. Within three or four centuries the Lapita culture spread widely across the southwest Pacific into Santa Cruz, New Caledonia, and Vanuatu. By 1,000-900 BC it had spread to Fiji and western Polynesia, and within another hundred years further to Samoa, Futuna, and Uvea. It was only after a gap of some one thousand years—i.e., after the fourth century AD, that eastern Polynesia was populated. Micronesia was settled by independent movements, the earliest being into Belau and the Marianas (probably from the Philippines or Indonesia), another movement to Yap, and a third by the "nuclear Micronesian language" community from elsewhere in Oceania, which occurred around 2,000 years ago.

---

[5] Sagart (2008: 145) reckons that if the earliest Austronesians sailing from Nanri or Pingtan were heading for Mt. Xueshan, they would make landfall on the N.W. coast near present-day Hsinchu or Miaoli.

[6] This sketchy outline of the spread of the An languages hardly does justice to the complexities and details, which are much in dispute and await a careful analysis of the data. It is possible that Kalimantan was settled directly from Taiwan without passing through the Philippines, and in fact the closeness of the Philippine languages to each other argues for a hypothesis that they do not derive from the language of the original settlement in northern Luzon, but rather from a language by a group that had left the Philippines and then reintroduced it at a later point.

[7] This account is based on Pawley (2002).

A1.1.1 Objections to the hypothesis that agriculture was the driving force that led to the development and spread of the An languages

This view of language dispersal associated with the spread of farming is not unquestioned (Oppenheimer 2004, Szabó and O'Connor 2004). The argument is that prehistoric rice agriculture has not been found in eastern Indonesia and in points east at the right dates, nor is it associated with the Lapita complex. Further, the Formosan languages reflect few of the reconstructed cognates referring to sailing technology, ceramics, or animal and plant domesticates reflected in the extra-Formosan languages (Blust 1985). Also genetic evidence that has been adduced to support this view is by no means unequivocal (Oppenheimer 2004: 595ff.).
Nevertheless, a hypothesis that the An languages spread southward and outward from Taiwan better accords with the linguistic evidence, and this view shapes the reconstructions of this study: (1) although rice cultivation may well not have accompanied the expansion of the An language, the cultivation of foxtail millet did do so, for archaeological remains at the right date have been found in eastern Indonesia (Glover 1977: 43), and the reconstructed name for this plant *betéŋ is reflected both in the Formosan languages and in eastern Indonesia (but not in between, where it has been mostly replaced by a loan of Indic origin *jawa); (2) the lack of cognates associated with sailing technology in the Formosan languages has to do with the paucity of information on these languages. Few of the aboriginal cultures oriented to the sea have survived, and the information we have on these languages comes mostly from communities not closely connected to the sea. In short, these terms may have well existed in the Formosan languages. As for the plant and animal domesticates, most of these forms are of secondary spread throughout the An languages—i.e., they were introduced after the original spread of the An languages.

A1.1.2 PAn terminology associated with agriculture

There are a number of terms associated with agriculture that can be reconstructed for PAn. These reconstructed terms together with the reconstructed terms for grain crops provide linguistic evidence that agriculture characterized the PAn civilization (Pawley 2002: 264). We may reconstruct the following forms for grain crops:

> *págay 'rice plant' *beɣác 'husked rice' (< *ɣac 'foodstuff') *betéŋ 'foxtail millet'

Associated with these are the following forms:

> *binesíq 'seed rice' *ɣik 'thresh' *iqetá 'rice husk' *ɬesúŋ 'mortar' *pacepac 'thresh by beating' *na 'wet ricefield' *qani 'harvest (usually rice)' *qáselu 'pestle' *tapés 'winnow' *juɣámi 'straw'

Pawley (2002:264) suggests that *buɣaw 'chase away' and *lepaw 'hut' are also associated with grain crops. There are other terms associated with gardening and garden crops:

> *qumáh 'cultivated area' *qútaɬ 'formerly cultivated land left to go wild' *talún 'fallow land' *taném 'plant'

Garden plants include :

*bíɣaq 'the giant taro: *Alocasia esculenta*' *qúbi 'k.o. yam: *Dioscorea alata*' *tali[8] 'taro' *tebús 'sugar cane'

A1.1.3 The linguistic evidence for the way the An languages spread

A1.1.31 The spread of the An languages in Formosa

The account given above of the way the An languages spread in Formosa is backed up to some extent by archaeology.[9] However, there is some remarkable evidence supplied by linguistics that make it all but inescapable that this pattern indeed characterized the movement of the An population after they came to Taiwan. This evidence was discovered by L. Sagart (2004).[10] This discovery was based on the fact that PAn had a quinary system of counting, such that the numerals 6–10 were additive, subtractive, or multiplicative, whereas the MP languages and Am, Pu, and Pai evince a decimal system.[11] The development to the decimal system was made on a step-by-step basis, one numeral at a time replacing the additive, subtractive, or multiplicative numbers. The remarkable fact is that the innovations to the quinary system were made in a nested way: if a language innovated '10' it has the innovated forms of '5'–'9' as well; [12] if a language innovated '9' but not '10', it has the innovated forms of '5'–'8' as well; if a language innovated '8' but not '9' (or '10'), it also has the innovated form of '5', '6', and '7 ' as well; if it has the innovated forms of '6', it also has the innovated forms of '5' and '7'; and if it has the innovated form of '5', it has '7' as well. This can be symbolized as follows:

'10' >> '9' >> '8' >> '6' >> '5' >> '7'

The innovations made were as follows: '7' was formed from the original word for '5' *ɣatep and *tusa 'two'; the old form of the word for '5' was replaced by the word for 'hand'; '8' was formed from *ɣatep and *telu 'three'; '9' by *ɣatep and '4'.[13] The innovations were made in exactly the same way in the languages that attest them, so that

---

[8] The Formosan languages reflect *táli for this plant, whereas the Malayo-Polynesian (MP) languages reflect *talec. It is certain that this plant was known to the PAn community, and *talec was an MP innovation. We make the general assumption, even when there is no other evidence, that when there are two or three reconstructed forms, the ones that are attested in the earliest languages (the languages located in the earliest area of An settlement, as discussed in §A1.1.31, below) are original and the forms in the later languages were innovations. This assumption may in some cases be in error. The early languages innovated as much as any other language, and some of the forms attested in the late languages, thought to be replacements of earlier forms, may possibly have been the original, and the attestations in the early languages were innovations that spread secondarily.

[9] Remains of pottery and other items from the Dapenkeng culture, which is thought to be the culture of the An speakers, have been found all around Taiwan (Tsang 2005). It is unclear if the dating of the remains conforms to the counterclockwise movement of peoples hypothesized.

[10] My conclusions here are, with small modification, directly taken from Sagart (2004). That article gives the original discovery that has played an important role in determining cases where one reconstructed form and meaning in the glossary, part H, is earlier and another is an innovation.

[11] Languages in Oceania innovated and replaced the decimal system with a quinary system, but that is totally independent of the original PAn quinary system.

[12] That is, the languages reflect *puluq '10' and *lima '5', *enem '6', *pitu 'seven', *walu '8', and *siwa 'nine'.

[13] The explanation of how each form developed from the additive forms is given in the commentary to *pitu, *walu, and *siwa. This is taken directly from Sagart (2004:§3, 415–420).

they could not have been made independently. The conclusion is inescapable that the languages that share the same innovation were the same or were in contact at the time the innovation was made. This conclusion clearly supports the account of the movements of the Austronesians in Taiwan, as given below. The following chart shows these forms.[14] The shaded cells show the innovated forms:

CHART ONE. THE NUMBERS IN THE FORMOSAN LANGUAGES[15]

PAn	*pitu '7'	*lima '5'	*enem '6'	*walu '8'	*siwa '9'	*puluq '10'
Luilang	innai	na-lup	na-tsulup	patulunai	satulunai	isit
Paz	xasebidusa	xasep	xasebuza	xasebaturu *or* xasebituru	xasebisupat	isit
St	ʃaybоʃii o ʔæhæ	haseb	ʃaybоʃii	kaʃpat	hæʔhæʔ	langpez
Favorlang	naito	achab	nataap	maaspat	tannacho	zchiett
Taokas	yweto	hasap	tahap	mahalpat	tanasu	(ta)isid
Thao	pitu	rima	katuru	kaʃpat	tanacu	maqcin
At (Mx)	mapituʔ	ima-ɣal	cziuʔ	spat	qeru	maɣal-pu
Papora	pitu	nema	(ne)nom	mahal[16]	(me)siya	(me)tsi
Hoanya	pito	Lima	(mi)num	(mi)alu	(a)sia	(miata)isi
Siraya	pittu	rima	nəm	kuixpa	matuda	saat kittian
Ru (Budai)	pito	lima	eneme	valo	vangate	poloko
Knn	u-pítu	u-líma	ánəm	aálu	u-sía	maanə
Sar	ú-pitu	ku-lima	ánəmə	ku-álu	ú-sia	ku-maaɬə
Bun	pituʔ	imaʔ	nuum	vauʔ	sivaʔ	masʔan
Kav	pitu	lima	nnem	waru	siwa	betin
Ketagalan	pitu	tsjima	anəm	wasu	ʃiwa	labatan
Pa	pitju	lima	unem	valu	siva	puluq
Pu	pitu	lima	enem	walu	iwa/siwa	pulufi
Am	pito	lima	enem	falo	siwa	polofi

This distribution of innovations fits in well with the location of these languages: the three languages that did not develop the decimal system (Luilang, Paz, and St) are the furthest northwest. This is where the Proto-Austronesians most likely first landed on Taiwan. It is the area closest to the mainland and the location of the highest peak on Taiwan, which is visible from the mainland. Pazeh, Saisiat, and Luilang developed in this area before the

[14] The citations from extinct languages come from the following sources: Favorlang: Ogawa (2003) and Happart (1842), Babuza Hoanya, and Luilang: Tsuchida (1982); Siraya and Basay: Tsuchida et al. (1991).

[15] Source: Sagart 2004: 414.

[16] Papora and Hoanya do in fact have reflexes of *walu and *siwa, but these forms show the loss of *w, an innovation made by Tsouic languages. The limited data available do not allow us know what the reflex of initial *w was in these languages, but we assume the words for 'eight' in hese languages are not inherited. We conclude then that these forms were borrowed into Hoanya and Papora from Tsouic at a recent time. Similarly, Ru *poloko* '10' is a late borrowing from Pai (as proven by the /k/ [cf. §B4.3.14]). In this respect this account differs slightly from Sagart 2004.

'7' innovation was made, and the community was directly descended from the earliest arrivals, who did not move far away. (See the map on p. 68 for the location of the Formosan languages.) Part of the community moved south. This group made the '7' innovation. After the '7' innovation had been made, a part of the community moved inland and south, leaving the Favorlang and Taokas behind, and this group made the '5' innovation. The '5' innovation also spread to the ancestor of Papora, which at that time probably was located further south than when it was documented in the last century. The Thao moved a bit inland and the ancestors of the Atayals moved further eastward and northward. The rest of the Austronesians at that point made the '6' innovation and filled the western plains. At that point they expanded through the south and eventually moved inland, where they made the '8' and the '9' innovations. At this point the area occupied by the remainder of the An was quite large, and Ru remained an island to which the innovation '9' did not spread. After the innovation '9', the remainder of the Austronesians filled the eastern plains. After the ancestors of the peoples later occupying the northeastern plains had departed, '10' developed among the peoples in the southeast probably among the pre-Amis and spread to the adjacent areas in the southeast—the area occupied by the pre-Paiwan, pre-Puyuma and the MP, prior to their departure from Taiwan.[17]

In short, this series of innovations in the numerals leads to a scenario whereby the Austronesians spread from their first landing in western Taiwan in a counterclockwise movement down the west coast around the south and then up to fill the eastern plains, with some groups moving inland at various points, and the MP peoples and possibly also the Kra-Dai moving out from a group living in the south.[18]

A1.1.32 The evidence that the extra-Formosan languages constitute a subgroup

It is thought that the An languages located outside Taiwan (the "Malayo-Polynesian:—MP languages) all originate from the An language that was spread southward, 'Proto-Malayo-Polynesian' (PMP). If it can be shown that these languages all descend from a protolanguage from which the other An languages (the Formosan languages) did not descend (that is, they form a "subgroup"), it follows that the community that spoke this protolanguage moved out of the area in which PAn was spoken. In short, if the MP languages form a subgroup, that would support the archeological evidence cited in §A1.1, above, and the scenario sketched in the previous section for the way that the An languages spread. Nevertheless, there is little by way of incontrovertible evidence that the MP languages do indeed form a subgroup, for the

---

[17] Sagart argues persuasively that the Kra-Dai languages are an offshoot of the An languages, and that their location at this time was also in southeast Taiwan, for the innovated numerals '5'–'10' have reflexes in some of the languages of this group (Sagart 2004:§5, 430–36). Cf. the further discussion in §A1.1.5.

[18] Note that I have not implied that these innovations provide proof of subgrouping. There is no doubt that in general the languages that individuated later are more closely related to each other than they are to the ones that individuated earlier. But the details of the subgrouping on a level of a small number of languages have not been determined and await further research. For some of these innovations in the numbering system can have spread secondarily after the languages individuated—and indeed such is demonstrably the fact in several cases. For this reason I cannot present a stammbaum: any that I might choose would necessarily need to make explicit priority of split from the main group and whether any given language split off from the main group together with another language or not. These are not facts that have been established up to now.

notion of "subgroup" is dependent on shared innovations. The argument is that if two related languages manifest an innovation from the protolanguage of the sort that is not likely to have been made independently, they must have made the innovation together at a time when they were a single language. The force of this argument is considerably weakened by several facts: first, many changes are the natural outcome of human articulatory capacities, and as such, they occur frequently in the history of languages spoken all over the world. Therefore, they may occur again and again independently. Such changes can give little evidence for the unity of the languages or dialects that share this change. Second, innovations made at any level—phonology, morphology, syntax or semantics, may spread across language boundaries to related or even unrelated languages. In short, when two languages evince a shared innovation, it is not necessarily the case that this innovation was made at a time when these two languages were one.

Most of the shared innovations of the MP languages manifest evidence not that they took place in a unified language, but that they spread through the MP languages after they were separated. The data suggest that PMP was not a unified protolanguage but rather a dialect linkage (Ross 1995:45–48), which did not necessarily derive from a single migration out of the area in which PAn was spoken, but possibly from a series of migrations over generations, in which the speakers of the various migrating communities spoke differentiated dialects or even different languages (Wolff 2007a). Nevertheless, even if the innovations occurred independently or spread secondarily, they can be shown to have spread starting after the MP community had separated from others (possibly from a community still located in Taiwan), moving on through the Philippines and thence southward and eastward. The evidence that the innovations that were shared by the MP languages and absent in Formosan languages were indeed made by a community moving away lies first in the nature of the change: the more conservative forms in features that underwent change are found among the Formosan languages. For example, [s] may change to [h], but except under very special circumstances [h] does not change to [s].[19] For the protophoneme *s, the reflex [s] is found among the Formosan languages but not further south. Further south we find [h] and subsequent loss. Similar considerations apply to the phoneme *h, which appears as [h] in a few languages of Taiwan, but outside is lost everywhere. (These changes are discussed in detail in the following paragraph.) This is prima facie evidence that the movement of the An peoples was southward from Taiwan and that it was not northward into Taiwan from the south. Second, there are innovations of a complexity such that they are unlikely to have been made independently. Although these innovations may indeed have spread secondarily (and there often is evidence that such is the case), the conservative forms, the ones that were not innovated, are found among the Formosan languages, and the innovated forms are found for the most part outside of Taiwan, in some cases in all the extra-Taiwan languages, and in other cases they are found more heavily in the Philippine and more western An languages and attested to a lessening degree as one goes eastward.

Now we will provide a detailed discussion on some of these innovations. The first innovation is the change of *s to [h] (and subsequent loss in some languages). This change is shared by Pu, Siraya, and the MP languages. Further, Sar, Knn, St, Thao, Paz,

---

[19] There must be an environment that would cause the [h] to develop additional friction (e.g., an adjacent [i]), but this condition did not exist in the case of the PAn phoneme that is reflected by /s/ in Formosa and /h/ in Malayo-Polynesian.

and Am change *s to /h/ in a few forms (cf. §A3.3.32). However, these changes in the Formosan languages are independent of the change manifested in the MP languages for three reasons: (a) in Sar, Knn, St, Thao, Paz, and Am the change is not carried through completely: *s > /h/and /s/ independent of any conditioning, a sign that the change was not carried through completely;[20] (b) the change of *s in Sar, Knn, St, Thao, Paz, and Am involves a merger with *h; (c) the change of *s > †h[21] caused two other important changes that affected the MP languages.[22]

Now let us look at the consequences of *s-loss in MP languages. As a result of this change the genitive of the second person singular pronoun *su is reflected differently in the languages of Taiwan and in the MP languages, as will be explained immediately. Note by way of introduction that there were two genitive markers in PAn: *m and *n. *m was probably the marker for the first and second person pronouns. The genitive of the second person singular thus would have been *msu in PAn. *msu developed differently in the Formosan and in the MP languages as a result of the developments of *s: in the Formosan languages *msu was simplified to *su*—that is, the Formosan languages lost *m (even Pu and Siraya, which also underwent the change of *s > *h [but after the loss of *m]). In short, the Formosan languages reflect *su. In the MP languages, *msu became †mhu. They lost the †h that had developed from *s. (They did not lose the *m and lost the *h only after the change of *s > †h.) Thus MP languages reflect †mu (< †mhu) (or sometimes †nu (< †nhu) from the other genitive marker *n).

Further, there is a shared innovation that is ascribable to PMP as a result of the loss of *-s: namely, the MP languages manifest metathesis of roots ending in *C_{-voice}Vs, where C_{-voice} is a voiceless stop. There are eight of them: *bukes 'hair', *daqis 'forehead', *liceqes 'nit', *nakis (*dakis) 'go up', *tapes 'winnow', *taqis 'sew', and *tuqas 'old'.[23] These forms in PMP can be reconstructed as †buhek, †liceheq, †nahik, †tahep, †tahiq, and †tuhaq, respectively.[24] Since syllables beginning with laryngeals were metathesized frequently (and even regularly in some environments in certain languages) over the range of the MP languages, it is likely that the metathesis is associated with the change of *s >

[20] There is poor correlation among these languages as to which forms reflect *s with /h/ and those that reflect *s with /s/ (cf. §A3.3.32).

[21] In this study we follow the tradition of marking inferred phonemes or forms with an asterisk. However, when the status of an inferred form as one inferred for PMP (but not PAn) is relevant, we mark the PMP form with a dagger ('†').

[22] This effect can of course be documented only in the languages that reflect the relevant forms.

[23] Blust described this phenomenon in the ACD and elsewhere. To these should be added †aɣuhuq '*Casuarina*' and †tuhuq 'true', which can be reconstructed for PMP but have not been attested in languages of Taiwan, and therefore cannot be proven to remount to PAn. The reflexes of these forms in most of the MP languages reflect a final syllable with the order †hVC, but there are reflexes of †aɣuhuq in some of the languages of the Philippines that reflect not that but †aɣuquh, and Moken *tokōʔ* reflects †tuquh and not †tuhuq. Further, Tag *to-toʔo* 'true' may reflect †tuquh, although that form may be metathesized from an earlier form *tuhuq that is attested in Cb *tuhuʔ* 'particle asserting that something is true'. In short, there may be unexplained exceptions to the rule.

[24] In the glossary forms are listed with the shape they would have in PAn as if they had continued PAn forms directly (whether or not they do indeed continue reconstructed PAn forms). That is, the PMP forms that can be reconstructed with PMP †h are quoted with *s, because that is the PAn origin of all PMP †h's. In this paragraph PMP forms are quoted with †h to make the relevant point clear.

†h. There are other forms that were metathesized in the MP languages but not in Formosan languages: *ɬawuŋ 'shade, shelter'.[25]

There is another factor connected with the change of *s > †h that sets this change apart from the analogous changes that occurred in Formosan languages: in final position, *-s disappears almost entirely in all MP languages, but not totally, for traces of *-s remain in reduplicated monosyllables in some Philippine languages. For example, the /h/ inCb *kukhu* 'scratch' (< *kuhkuh < *kuskus) developed from *s.[26]

The second innovation of the MP languages is the treatment of *ɬ: in the MP languages *ɬ had three outcomes, depending on the environment: it became a palatal nasal [ñ], lost its palatalization (merged with /n/), or merged with /l/. The complex details of the development of *ɬ in the MP languages make it clear that this innovation could not have happened independently in the languages that manifest them. (Cf. §A3.3.4 for examples.) This change affected all of the languages outside of Taiwan and none of the Formosan languages. To be sure, some of the Formosan languages also make this change *ɬ > /n/ (Bun, Knn, Kav, and the now extinct languages of northeast Taiwan). There is clear evidence that this change on Taiwan is quite independent of the change made by the MP languages: first, the Formosan languages carry the change out to all environments, whereas in the MP languages, there are environments in which *ɬ became a palatalized nasal, and further, there are environments in which *ɬ > /l/. Further, Knn makes the innovation *ɬ > /n/, but very closely related Sar does not, an indication that Knn made the innovation recently. It is true that there are many MP languages in which the PMP †ñ inherited from PAn *ɬ lost its palatization (merged with *n). But this innovation must be independent of the Formosan developments for the reason that *ɬ became both /ñ/ and /n/ in the MP languages (depending on the environment), and subsequently /ñ/ > /n/ in some languages. Further, the languages that retained /ñ/ are not in a subgroup nor are they geographically close. In fact, every region over the entire MP area has one or more languages that retain /ñ/. For example, most of the Philippine languages reflect *ɬ as /n/ in most environments, but Kapampangan reflects /ñ/ in some of the environments in which the other Philippine languages reflect /n/. Similarly, in Kalimantan, Sulawesi, and Sumatra, as well as Oceania, some languages reflect *ɬ with /ñ/ in some environments, whereas others show that the merger of *ñ with /n/ was carried to completion. In short, the change of *ɬ to /n/ happened independently in the various MP languages and has nothing to do with the change of * ɬ > /n/ in the Formosan languages.

The loss of the laryngeals is not evidence for the status of the MP languages as a subgroup as opposed to the Formosan languages.[27] First, the laryngeal *h is not retained in all of the Formosan languages. *h is retained as a separate phoneme only in At, Paz, St, and Am. The loss of *h could be taken to indicate that the Formosan languages that

[25] There are a number of other forms that are metathesized in most but not all of the MP languages: *púnuq, *taŋila, *paqegu, and others.

[26] Cb lost the final *-h that had developed from *-s, but other Phlippine languages retain it in reduplicated monosyllables, e.g., SL *kahkah* 'scratch' (probably a reformation of earler *kuhkuh). Blust (1974) also proposed that *-s affected medial voiced consonants in the languages of northern Sarawak, but the special consonants probably have a different explanation: namely, they are due to accentual characteristics (Zorc 1983: §8.3). Cf. the discussion of the Kelabit reflexes of the voiced consonants, part D, chapter 1, §D1.3.3.

[27] We reconstruct only one laryngeal *h, not several (§A3.3.1 [cf. Wolff 2009]).

underwent the loss of *h are in a subgroup with the MP languages (but not in the MP subgroup, for they do not make the other changes that the MP languages all made). That is, the languages that retain *h as a separate phoneme are direct descendants of the earliest stratum of PAn, and the other An languages descend from a language that moved away from that earliest stratum. That hypothesis is questionable for two reasons: the loss of [h] is such a commonly occurring event, that there is no reason to think that languages that lost *h did not do so independently. Further, it turns out that there is contradictory evidence. *h has left traces in the Philippine languages, including languages of northern Kalimantan and northern Sulawesi (§A3.3.3) and in Bun. The best hypothesis to accord with the retention of traces of *h in MP languages and loss of *h entirely in some languages of Taiwan is that the loss of *h began in post-PAn times, but *h had by no means disappeared entirely by PMP times. The Formosan languages that lost *h entirely did so independently—that is, at a time that PMP had split from them. The MP languages that lost traces of *h did so quite independently of the Formosan languages that underwent the same changes. The upshot of this is that the development of *h has no bearing on the question of whether or not the An languages of Taiwan apart from At, Paz, St, and Am are in a subgroup with the MP languages. The loss of *h in these languages was independent of the loss of *h in MP languages.

The merger of putative *C with *t (§A3.3.1, below) is cited as evidence that the MP languages comprise a subgroup (Ross 1995:51–53). However, *C did not exist. Rather, its reflexes evince an innovation in the languages of Taiwan that spread from language to language after the MP languages had left.

There is also evidence of shared morphological changes in the MP languages, but these are beyond the scope of this study. In addition there is a great deal of vocabulary shared across the range of the MP languages for which cognates have not been found in the Formosan languages. Although this MP vocabulary in many cases is probably a shared innovation in PMP, the case for this can be made only when there is internal evidence (§A1.1.4). There are many cases of forms that may be reconstructed for PMP, for which no attestations have been discovered in the Formosan languages. Lexical evidence for PMP innovations awaits a more thorough investigation of the vocabulary of the extant languages than has been done so far, but this kind of investigation is hampered by the lack of documentation: only four of the Taiwan languages have dictionaries (as opposed to word lists of a couple of thousand items or less), but they are of five thousand entries or less, not of the depth or detail necessary to discover all connections with MP languages.

A1.1.4 Assignments of reconstructions to PAn, PMP, or to a lower-order subgroup

Hypotheses on the location of PAn and the direction of its spread underlie the assumptions of protolanguage assignment of reconstructed protomorphemes. On the hypothesis of a PAn homeland on Taiwan and subsequent spread to the Philippines and thence southeastward and southwestward (§A1.1), we assume that reflexes attested both in the Formosan languages and outside of Taiwan derive from PAn. The earliest evidence of Malayo-polynesians in the Philippines comes from the discovery of East-Formosan-like ceramic remains in the Batanes Islands and northern Philippines, some one thousand years later than the earliest rice and millet agriculture in Taiwan. That means that what we call here PAn in fact covered a period of one thousand years. The earliest PAn is not distinguished here from forms that developed sooner or later in the course of those one thousand years. In the commentary to the individual entries an indication is given, where appropriate, as to which forms and meanings are innovated and which are earlier. For example, two words are reconstructed for 'moon': *bulaɬ and *qiɬas. *bulaɬ also means 'white', and a reflex of *qiɬas is attested only in Paz, St, At, and Pai, whereas a reflex of *bulaɬ 'moon' is attested across the gamut of the An languages. The best way to explain this distribution and the meaning 'white' as well as 'moon' is to hypothesize that the meaning 'moon' is derived from 'white'—i.e., 'moon' is 'the white one', and this metaphor spread in PAn times (before the departure of the MP community), but failed to reach two speech islands, the northern languages, St, Paz, and At and the southern Pai. These two areas maintained a reflex of *qiɬas, which the others had lost.[28] This example also shows how in cases where an innovated form drove out the older form, this replacement may have taken place in the course of the thousand-year time span before the MP speakers left Taiwan. That means that in those cases, if there is evidence, a PAn form may be reconstructed that is not reflected in an MP language.

The example of this distribution of the word for 'moon' is one kind of evidence that a form attested only among the Formosan languages but not among the MP languages can be determined to remount to PAn. Another source of evidence is cognation with a Sino-Tibetan (S-T) form.[29] Although a definitive list of cognates between S-T forms and An forms has not been established, but outlines of the sound laws have been worked out (Sagart 2005a), and sufficient evidence has been published to enable us to establish cognation with a fair amount of certainty among a small number of forms (Sagart 2005a). This allows us to say without speculation that a given An form has a cognate in S-T. Some of these forms have reflexes only in the Formosan languages and nowhere else (and sometimes only among the northwest Formosan languages). These Formosan forms must remount to the protolanguage that engendered the An and S-T languages and therefore remount to PAn, as well. (Cf. the further commentary in the introduction to Part B, chapter 1, on the importance of evidence provided by Paz, St, Th, and Atayalic.) Forms that are ascribable to PAn are marked with an asterisk ('*') in the glossary.

We assume that reflexes that are not attested in Taiwan but are attested in the Philippines or anywhere in Hesperonesia[30] and in Oceania derive minimally from PMP. They could possibly have existed in PAn, but without an attestation from Taiwan, there is no way to know that.[31] This assumption cannot be correct in each and every case of attestation in Hesperonesia and Oceania, for it is obviously the case that forms may have spread secondarily through Hesperonesia and into Oceania in post-MP times, and further, forms originating in Oceania have spread westward into Hesperonesia and even beyond. Forms that have spread secondarily betray themselves by their phonology: they evince irregular

---

[28] This hypothesis was suggested by L. Sagart (p.c.).

[29] Cf. The discussion in §A1.1.5, immediately following, on the relationship of the An and the Sino-Tibetan languages.

[30] We include in Hesperonesia the Austronesian areas starting from and including the Philippines, Sulawesi, and the Lesser Sundas westward. The account that we assume here is that the An languages spread from the Philippines both southwestward and southeastward at the same time. That implies that the Hesperonesian languages, as defined here, do not make up a subgroup.

[31] Entries that are not ascribable to PAn but are ascribable to PMP are marked with '†' in the glossary (but usually with asterisk in the text). Forms that are not ascribable to PMP or PAn but occur in a subgroup and are ascribable to the protolanguage of the subgroup are marked with '††'. Entries that cannot be reconstructed for any protolanguage are placed in square brackets ('[ ]').

correspondences, and they may also betray themselves by an unusual shape. For example, *kangkung*, which refers to a leafy vegetable, *Ipomoeia aquatica*, betrays its non-An origin by the unique phonetic shape of being a doubled monosyllabic root with different vowels in each of the monosyllabic components. We know that it spread secondarily, even though the correspondences are regular in most of the languages ranging over the entire An area. There is confirmation that this word cannot be reconstructed for PAn or PMP because it can be shown that the plant and name originate in South Asia, and the name is attested in languages of India and Sri Lanka, as well as in An languages as far east as New Britain (and also in non-An languages of Eastern Indonesia and Papua-New Guinea).

Further, distribution of forms that do not accord with the direction of the spread of An hypothesized here may well betray secondary spread, even in cases where the comparable attestations do evince regular correspondences. An example of this is the form *muntay 'citrus', which is spread from the area of Mindanao-Borneo westward to languages in Sumatra (but is not found north or east of Mindanao).

A large portion of the forms that have an irregular distribution or that give evidence of secondary spread refer to flora and fauna.

Another question arises with forms attested only sporadically. It is a matter of weighing probabilities, and decisive proof regarding which of these developed from PAn and which were spread secondarily is not always available. In the case of names of fishes and sea creatures that are well attested in Oceania but otherwise may appear in only one or two Hesperonesian languages,[32] we assume that the name originated in the east and moved westward secondarily. An example is Cb *muʔung*, 'cardinal fish', which is attested nowhere else west of Oceania, but a corresponding form is nearly ubiquitous in Oceania. In some cases there is phonological corroboration that the form is secondary. An example is Cb *saluwakiʔ* 'sea urchin', which in Oceania has noncorresponding shapes: Fi *caawaki*, Takia *sarwag* (Fi ∅ and Takia /r/ do not correspond to Cb /l/).

In some cases, there is evidence that the lone attestation in Hesperonesia is indeed cognate with forms attested further east. For example, the reflexes of the word for foxtail millet *betéŋ are attested in Sar and Ru on Taiwan and otherwise only in eastern Indonesia. In this case we can be pretty much assured that these forms are cognate and not connected through secondary spread because they have been replaced in the languages between Ru/Sar and eastern Indonesia by an Indic loan word *jawa. In the case of †nati 'pasture animal', reflexes of which are attested only in the southern Philippines and in the WOc languages, it is simply improbable that this word spread secondarily to Oceania from the Philippines (and even more improbable that it spread westward from Oceania). We assume here that it goes back minimally to PMP. It is of course an important word for establishing the culture of the peoples that migrated eastward beginning from the Philippines.

---

[32] The lack of attestation may well be a function of the dictionaries available—i.e., Cb *muʔung*, discussed immediately below, for which cognates are attested only in Oc languages, in fact may occur in many languages, but it has not been documented anywhere but in Cb. The names for more important plants that are likely to be registered even in a short word-list are well attested in Hesperonesia. Some of these plants and their names originate in Oceania. An example is the name for the sago palm that corresponds regularly to *ɣambiya throughout Oceania. This name (and probably the plant) spread westward to a large portion of the Hesperonesian languages, but there the names evince all sorts of irregularities in phonology.

A1.1.5 Relationships between An and other language families

As stated above, the major language groups of Southeast Asia all originate with people living in the central grasslands of China, and it is quite possible that their ancestors, who had expanded in these grasslands before the development of agriculture, were all at one time speakers of a single language that diversified. There is a small amount of evidence that scholars have been able to adduce to connect the Austroasiatic and Austronesian (Reid 2005). The best of this is a small amount of morphology that can be reconstructed and looks similar in both groups. Proof of a relationship of PAn with Proto-Austroasiatic in the form of cognate vocabulary with recurrent correspondences remains to be worked out. There is little consensus as to where Proto-Austroasiatic was spoken, but clearly it must have been considerably south of where Proto-S-T and PAn were spoken. It is thought that the date of Proto-Austroasiatic precedes PAn and Proto-S-T by at least a millennium. (This is an educated guess. Dates for Proto-Austroasiatic are unknown.) The Austroasiatic peoples also expanded with the development of rice cultivation, but their development of rice agriculture was independent of the Austronesian development. Thus it is not surprising that no agricultural vocabulary in common between the Austroasiatic and the An languages has been found.[33] As for the Hmong-Mien languages, little has been published so far to show a connection with An. In the case of S-T and Kra-Dai (formerly called Tai-Kadai), there is a great deal of lexical evidence (Ostapirat 2005). A number of sound laws that relate the Kra-Dai correspondences with Austronesian have been persuasively worked out, but the greatest part of the rules remains unknown—mainly because Kra-Dai has not been well reconstructed and even for Proto-Tai there is much that is not clearly understood. Be that as it may, there is enough in Kra-Dai that is clearly connected with An that it surely will be possible to establish thorough-going correspondence sets once Proto-Kra-Dai or even Proto-Tai have been better worked out.

We are in a better position to understand connections between S-T and An. The An homeland is on Taiwan, but its origin is in the Yellow River basin, approximately the same area where S-T originated.[34] Indeed there is good evidence for the relationship between S-T and An. Although the S-T vocabulary has not been entirely reconstructed—that is, only parts of the roots have been definitively reconstructed, evidence can be adduced from classical Chinese of 2,500 years ago (three thousand years after Proto-S-T) and from current Tibeto-Burman languages. This evidence consists of reconstructed items of basic vocabulary and items pertaining to agriculture in classical Chinese or attested in current Tibeto-Burman languages that evince regular correspondences with

---

[33] This argument has been made by L. Sagart (2003)

[34] There is no consensus that this is exactly the same area in which S-T originated (cf. Van Driem [2005: Map 6.3]). Sagart (2008: 124) argues on the basis of cognition of the PAn and Proto S-T words for 'foxtail millet' (PAN *beteŋ), that the PAn and Proto-S-T communities originate in an area where the earliest remains of foxtail millet have been found. This is over two wide areas, with one area located near Tibet and the other along the Yellow River, but Sagart argues that it is an artefact of the archeological record that the areas are not contiguous, and we may assume that the two, PAn and Proto-S-T, remount to a single earlier cultural complex. Belwood similarly points out the likelihood that PAn and Proto-S-T were part of a single cultural complex. (Cf. footnote 3, above.) The word for 'millet' by itself cannot prove the relationship of PAn and Proto-S-T languages. However, numerous other cognates that correspond systematically have been found This firmly establishes the relationship between the two families.

PAn forms. In addition there is a certain amount of morphology that can be reconstructed for S-T that closely resembles PAn morphology both in form and function (Sagart 2005).

A1.2 Languages treated in this study

In this study thirty-seven languages are chosen for which we list reflexes and describe their phonological history—relating the reflexes to the PAn reconstruction. The choice of languages for detailed treatment is based on the hypothesis for the PAn homeland and how the An languages spread. Therefore, we have endeavored to have a language from each of the large geographical areas, choosing those languages for which we have access to the best data. In some cases we have chosen a language on the basis of having had an opportunity to work first hand with native speakers of the language. Also we treat all of the languages studied by Dempwolff (1934–38) except that we quote OJv, rather than NJv, and for Fi we quote Wayan rather than Bauan (the dialect of Fi used as the national language). Since Taiwan was the homeland and offers evidence for the existence of a given form in PAn, we list attestations from all of currently spoken An languages from Taiwan except Tsou, even though for many of these languages data are scanty.
Data from the following languages are listed exhaustively in the glossary—i.e., every possible reflex of a PAn or PMP reconstruction in these languages has been listed and taken account of.

Taiwan: Pazih (Paz), Saisiat (St), Thao (Th), Atayal (At)—mostly the Mayrinax (Mx) dialect, Kanakanavu (Knn), Saaroa (Sar), Rukai (Ru)—usually Budai dialect (RuBd), Bunun (Bun), Amis (Am), Kavalan (Kav), Puyuma (Pu), Paiwan (Pai)
Philippines: Tagalog (Tag)
Sulawesi: Tondano (Tdn), Ratahan (Rat), Baree or Pamona (Ba), Bugis (Bug), Salayar (Sal), Muna (Mu)
Eastern Indonesia: Manggarai (Mgg), Buru, Leti, Kei
Western Indonesia and mainland southeast Asia: Old Javanese (OJv) or New Javanese (NJv), Kelabit (Kel), Ngaju Dayak (ND), Malay (Ml), Toba Batak (TB), and Moken (Mok)
Madagascar: Malagasy—Merina dialect (Mlg)
Oceania: Chamorro (Ch), Tolai (Tol), Motu, Sa'a (Sa), Fiji (Fi), Samoan (Sm), Tongan (To)

Where a reflex from a given PAn or PMP reconstruction does not occur in a certain one of the above languages, but if a reflex is attested in another language in that same geographical region, we quote that form. For example, where Tag fails to evince a reflex for a reconstructed PAn or PMP form, we quote from Cebuano (Cb) or Ilocano (Ilk) or from another Philippine language if a reflex occurs in one of those languages. We also quote forms from geographically close languages if one of our given languages has lost a contrast that a geographically close language maintains. Unless a note is made for the source in the citation in the glossary, it may be assumed that the citation comes from the dictionary or word list given in the bibliography. The exception is the case of citations based on my own work with native speakers as discussed in §A1.3, 3rd¶.

A1.3 Work on the history of the An languages heretofore and sources for this study

Since the eighteenth century it has been known that there is a connection between Ml, Mlg, and the languages of Oceania,[35] and in the nineteenth century the first attempts were made to compare some of the An languages with each other to draw conclusions about their history. In the period 1860–70 H. N. van der Tuuk investigated selected consonant correlations among Philippine and Indonesian languages. Beginning a decade later Hendrik Kern extended this work to include more sounds and languages of the Pacific. The first to attempt a reconstruction of PAn phonology was Renward Brandstetter in a series of articles published between 1906 and 1916. Brandstetter dealt only with languages of Indonesia and the Philippines, and his work was overshadowed by Otto Dempwolff's *Vergleichende Lautlehre des austronesischen Wortschatzes* (1934–38). Dempwolff's work became the cornerstone on which subsequent studies of An historical phonology were built.

The years since the publication of Dempwolff's work have seen a geometric increase in the amount of material readily available. Further, a great deal of good scholarship has been done that enables us to understand the nature of PAn and its developments to a depth and detail that was impossible in Dempwolff's time. The first important work was that of Dyen (1947, 1951, 1953) in which Dempwolff's materials were reworked to clarify PAn phonology considerably. Specifically Dyen reinterpreted correspondences that comprised the voiced dental and palatal stops (or *d and *j [§A3.3.2]) and the phonemes that were thought to have been laryngeals (our *s and *q). Subsequently, Dyen (1965) drew on data from the Formosan languages to expand the PAn inventory. Later in my own work I showed that if we take loan words into consideration, the correspondences assigned to four of Dempwolff's reconstructed phonemes were in fact reflexes of other well-established phonemes (Wolff 1975, 1982, 1997).

Beginning in the 1970s, both in the area of the Formosan languages and in Oceania, important scholarship was published to bring order and make sense out of obscure and difficult-to-interpret data. A large portion of the accessible data on the Formosan languages was gathered and analyzed by Paul Li and Shigeru Tsuchida and their colleagues. Their work not only made data accessible but also solved or pointed a way to the solution of the major portion of the knotty problems that the data from the Formosan languages present. Their work provided key information for the reconstruction of PAn and is largely responsible for enabling me to reach the conclusions drawn in this study. Another source of progress was the work done by Robert Blust in expanding the list of possible cognates (Blust 1980b, 1983, 1986, 1989, and 1995b). Blust's work was possible because of the many first-rate dictionaries that appeared beginning in the 1960s and also because it had become possible to do firsthand data gathering in areas formerly remote and inaccessible. Blust's published work and his sharing of some of the data in the unpublished ACD (Blust 1995b) enabled me to recognize many connections that I might not have seen otherwise and add considerably to my list of attestations. I. Dyen, in unpublished work that was partially put on disk and made available to the public through

[35] The first printed notice that we have of similarities between languages of the Philippines and the Pacific was that of Hadrian Reland in a 1706 pamphlet entitled *Dissertatio de linguis insularum quarundam orientalium*. His source for the Oceanic data were accounts of the voyages of Willem Schouten and Jacob Le Maire in 1616.

the efforts of Margaret Sharp, also has been an important source of attestations as well.[36] The secondary literature on various An languages or subgroups has also proven to be a source for recognizing connections, enabling me to enrich the citation of attestations and increase the number of protomorphemes.

Many of the data in this study have come from secondary sources—dictionaries and historical scholarship. However, the best analysis and most reliable citations come from languages with which I have had firsthand contact and where I had some connection to the speech community. I have had long-term and intensive contact with Tag, Cb, Ml (Indonesian) and NJv and have active control of them. I have done firsthand work over a period of months with speakers of SL, Tnd, ND, Rat, Sal, and Bug. I have worked briefly with speakers of Ba and Mok and in Taiwan with speakers of At (Kinhakul and Mayrinax), Sar, Knn, St, and Bun.

A quick comparison of the reconstructions here offered and those of Blust and Dempwolff, which are also cited, will reveal that there is a fair difference between those given here and those of Blust's and even more so of Dempwolff's. To facilitate comparison, finder lists of Dempwolff's reconstructions and Blust's reconstructions have been appended in part I.

I have endeavored to make this study more than a compilation of material published elsewhere. The data are examined anew, and the phonology is built up from scratch with no preconceptions as to the inventory or even how the similar forms presented in the data should be arranged by entries. That led me to arrive at a phonology that was new and different from that traditionally assumed. The new reconstruction shows that many of the traditional reconstructions reflect spurious phonemes: either the reconstructed morphemes that manifest them cannot in fact be reconstructed (the listed attestations are not cognate; they are loan words; or they are unconnected entirely) or they are indeed protomorphemes, but they can be reconstructed by other valid phonemes that substitute for the spurious ones (Wolff 1975, 1982, 1991, 1993a). Cf. Chart One in §A3.1 for the inventory and Chart Two in that section for a comparison between the inventory here assumed and that widely assumed in the literature as exemplified by Blust 1995b (ACD). At times, forms that were placed under the same entry in the literature turn out to belong under different entries, and what is much more frequent, forms that in the literature had been placed under different entries can, by the new phonology, be assigned to the same headword.

The new phonology enables us to account for the innovations that have taken place in a natural way—that is, the changes can be presented as the result of plausible articulatory processes of the sort that are paralleled in documented changes in languages belonging to any number of language families located in all parts of the world: assimilation, weakening, simplification, and so forth. The new phonology also enables us to separate

---

[36] All the attestations cited here have been checked in the sources as indicated in the bibliography. I also looked through the sources in order to find cognates. In the process of looking for cognates, not surprisingly I noticed many connections that turned out to be among the forms pointed out by Blust or Dyen. It is hard to know what portion of the citations would not have come to my attention if I had not had access to Blust's or Dyen's work. Since I had access to only a portion of the total number of forms they had examined, it is well possible that the forms that seem to me to be totally new in this study have already been identified but are not yet available to me. In any case, without Blust's or Dyen's work, there is no doubt that the number of protomorphemes here reported would have been smaller and the number of citations fewer.

more accurately forms that are directly inherited from the protolanguage from those of secondary spread (§A2.5).

This study has focused not only on the inventory, but also regards the PAn phonology in terms of the phonetic, phonological, and psychological processes that have driven its development to the attested forms. First is the reconstruction of stress. PAn stress has had a decisive influence in the development of the post-PAn phonology, not only in providing the environment for explaining phoneme splits (§§A3.3.1 and A3.3.4) but also for its role in weakening of vowels, loss of distinctive features, and loss of vowels and consonants (§A3.5.1). The reconstruction of stress provides evidence that PAn had monosyllabic, disyllabic, and trisyllabic roots. PAn roots were not predominantly disyllabic as previously supposed (Dempwolff 1937: 27–28). There was, however, a strong tendency in most of the daughter languages to disyllabize the monosyllabic and trisyllabic roots (and this tendency continues in some of the currently attested An languages). Most important is the case of the PAn monosyllabic roots. There are several alternative ways for disyllabization to take place (§A3.6.2, last paragraph). The upshot of this fact is that it can be shown that totally diverse attestations are derived from the same PAn monosyllabic root by alternative means of disyllabization.[37] Similarly, the trisyllabic roots were disyllabized by the loss of the antepenult, the penult, or (rarely) the final syllable in different daughter languages.

Second, root structure and canonical form also determined the development of PAn roots. Consideration of these factors brings to light cognation among forms that could otherwise not be connected. Third, sound symbolism has been an influence stronger than heretofore acknowleged in the developent of PAn morphemes. This has provided an explanation for numerous hitherto unexplained irregularities of correspondence . (Cf. the further discussion in §§A3.6 and A3.8.)

Finally, this study reexamines questions of semantic development. An effort has been made to ascertain the meaning of each protomorpheme and how it developed in the various daughter languages at various stages in those cases where the reflexes of a given protomorpheme attest to a wide semantic diversity. This has led to some divergence from the earlier published historical literature on the assignment of the attestations to a given entry. In a few cases, forms in different languages that were heretofore thought to be cognate are here not considered cognate with each other but rather are considered to be reflexes of different protomorphemes. In the case where several reconstructions can be made for the same meaning, an analysis has been made on the basis of the age of the attestations according to the spread of the An peoples as outlined in §A1.1.31 to determine which reconstruction of meaning is older and which was innovated in PAn or later times.

---

[37] Blust (1988) recognizes monosyllabic roots, and there is, in fact, a literature dealing with them. The contribution here is in analyzing the alternative processes of disyllabization and showing how the diverse reflexes, hitherto unexplained, in fact result from alternative means of disyllabization of what was originally a single monosyllabic root.

CHAPTER TWO

Considerations of Theory and Methodology

A2.1 Methodology[38] and assumptions

The aim of a reconstruction is to find a single form that explains all attested reflexes. The explanation comes in terms of sound laws that have no exceptions. However, the reality is that a large portion of the attested forms do not reflect a reconstructed form by a sound law that has no exceptions. Analogical changes and secondary spread lead to developments that show irregular reflexes. Therefore, the task of the historical linguist is to hypothesize the phonology, give the sound laws, and then show how the sound laws explain the development of each attested form believed to be cognate with forms in other languages of the family. Where the sound laws cannot do so—that is, where there are exceptions, the task of the historical linguist is to explain them in terms of secondary spread or analogical developments. To put this another way: the phonology is hypothesized, and the hypothesized phonology is borne out by the attested forms—i.e., the attested forms can be shown to derive by sound laws from the hypothesized phonology. In terms of the nitty-gritty of historical analysis, this means that the hypothesis is changed by the analyst in the process of dealing with data—nonconforming data lead to the reformulation of the phonology when there is no explanation in terms of analogical change or secondary spread.

---

[38] It is useful to borrow terms from linguistics that were generally part of the normal vocabulary of the 1950s, as in elaborated in Hockett 1958. The term ALLOMORPH refers to the form a certain morpheme has in a particular phonological environment. Another word for that concept that was widely adopted ALTERNANT. I use these terms in distinction to VARIANT. This term is widely used in sociolingustics, e.g. by Labov 1994. A variant of X is a synonym of X that has a similar phonological makeup to X, is dialectally distributed, or is found in the same dialect with X but is in competition with it. Thus, we often speak about cases such a the following as involving ALLOMORPHS: Tagalog *walaʔ* 'there is not' (< *wada 'there is') occurs as /walaʔ/ in most environments. But before the suffix *-an* this morpheme has the allomorph /wal/, as in *na-wal-an* 'have lost s.t.'. On the other hand in a case such as the following, we speak of VARIANTS: the form *buwan* 'month, moon' (< *bulaɬ) has a variant *buʔan*, which has no substantive meaning different from that of *buwan* (though surely has a different connotative or social meaning). The two mark speech of a certain area within the Tagalog speech area. One and the same speaker may use both *buwan* and *buʔan* and in that case, *buwan* and *buʔan* are in competition. The term DOUBLET is used in the case of a two forms that are variants of each other.

Furthermore, in most cases, any given attestation can be explained by a number of different protoforms. Which of the alternative protoforms is the correct one depends on which of the alternatives explains all of the cognates in the family. An example of this process is the term for 'egg'. Three reconstructions can connect Tag *itlóg* and Ml *telur:* *teluɣ, *iteluɣ, or *qiteluɣ. In the case of *teluɣ, the Ml reflex would have come down unchanged, and the Tag reflex could be explained as metathesis involving the first syllable *teluɣ > *tiluɣ (PAn *e > Tag /i/) > *itluɣ (metathesis) > *itlóg*. (There are other Tag cases in which C_1 C_2 > C_2 C_1.) This hypothesis is proven false in light of data from other Philippine languages, e.g., Cb *itlug* cannot derive directly from *teluɣ because in Cb *e > /u/ (not /i/). Further, data from other MP languages prove that the form in the protolanguage had three syllables, e.g., OJv *hanteluu*. The OJv form additionally proves that the form in the protolanguage had initial *q. Therefore, *qiteluɣ is the reconstructed form, and this reconstructed form can explain all of the MP reflexes and most of those in languages from Taiwan. However, this reconstruction cannot account for Tsou *fcuru*, Am *fitaʔol,* and Pu *vetsinun*. These forms can be explained by a protoform *qiteluɣ prefixed with *bV-, the V being reconstructed on the assumption that no vowelless morphemes occurred in the protolanguage and that the V has been lost in all attestations without a trace. Therefore, to account for all of the attested forms, we might reconstruct *bVqiteluɣ, assuming that *bV- was lost everywhere but in Ts, Am, and Pu. An alternative explanation (adopted here) is that the prefix *bV- is an innovation for Ts, Am, and Pu. This hypothesis is supported by the fact that these languages (and others on Taiwan) evince prefixes (of unknown meaning) with several other reconstructed PAn roots. Further, St and Th, which are descended from an earlier stratum than Ts, Am, and Pu (§A1.1.31), as well as Knn, manifest reflexes of *qiteluɣ without the *bV- prefix.

Not only are there several possible protoforms that explain each one of most of the attested forms, but also there is more than one reconstructed phonological system that can explain the attested forms. There is a best one, however. We have adopted four principles that we believe will lead to the best system—the best hypothesis to explain all attested forms. First, a minimum of variation is hypothesized for the roots of the protolanguage. Second, the phonology should have maximum simplicity. In the case of the An languages, this means that the phonology should be close to the kind of phonology that is found in the more conservative of the attested languages (as opposed to languages that can be shown to have innovated strongly in the course of their history). Third, the explanations of sound changes should be natural—that is, they should: (a) conform to kinds of articulatory changes that have been observed all over the world and that could well occur in terms of the way phones are articulated; (b) be well motivated, that is, internally consistent in terms of the total pattern of the phonology of the language at the stage at which the innovation was made (effect classes of phones, conform to rhythmic and other articulatory characteristics of the phonology); (c) be well established (not unique, exemplified by only one case).

Finally, we have made assumptions as to how sound change takes place—namely, that sound change proceeds on a word-by-word basis and is not completed until all forms with the phoneme in a given environment have been replaced by the innovation. These assumptions are based on the discovery by Labov and others in studying ongoing changes in English (Labov 1994: parts C and D) that sound change proceeds morpheme by morpheme within a community as part of the process of creating social structure. The change does not begin by replacement of an entire phoneme or allophone, but by the creation of an alternative pronunciation of individual items, which then competes with the original and often (but not always) replaces it. In other words, sound changes usually begin on a word-by-word basis. This implies that a sound change that took place in a particular phoneme may currently be reflected only in some forms and not in all forms that had the particular phoneme. Normally, the connotation implied by the form with a certain sound change gets extended to the whole class of sounds.[39] The new sound becomes a variable that is then in competition with the unchanged sound. Variables are in competition, and in most cases, one of them eventually wins out. If the innovated variable wins out, the sound change has been completed.

This way of looking at sound change is a considerable refinement to the principle enunciated more than one hundred years ago by the Neo-grammarians that "sound-laws admit of no exceptions". We can now say that they admit of no exceptions when they have been completed, but when they remain uncompleted, they show exceptions in the form of changes that were never made. Although some historians of the An languages adhere strictly to the Neo-grammarian principles that sound changes admit of no exceptions, in fact much of the literature accepts implicitly, if not explicitly, that indeed there are changes that have exceptions.

A2.1.1 Indeterminate reconstructions

When the reconstructions are indeterminate as to the protoform—i.e., when for a given protomorpheme, only reflexes that have lost a contrast are attested and no reflex is attested in a language that maintains the contrast, the reconstruction here somewhat arbitrarily assigns the more commonly occurring protophoneme. For example, * -h is distinguished only by At, Paz, St, and Am. Everywhere else, final *-h is lost without a trace. Thus for forms reconstructed with final vowel for which there is no At, Paz, St, or Am reflex, it is perfectly possible that the PAn form had *-h. However, rather than write the hundreds of forms reconstructed with an indeterminate final vowel—making a notation something like *(-h, -Ø), we have chosen just to write the most commonly occurring phoneme (or its loss, as in this case). Similarly, for the final *-j/*-d contrast, which is only retained in Javanese and Ml among the languages here treated in detail, we write *-d when no Javanese or Ml reflex is attested. Other contrasting pairs, where the contrast may not be reflected in any of the attestations, are as follows. We write the first of the pair in citing reconstructions because the first of the pairs is the more common: *n/*ɬ; *l-/ɬ-; *-q-/*-h-; Ø/*q; *k-/*g-; *-n/*-ŋ; *-p/*-b; *-t/*-d; *-k/*-g.

A2.2 Conditions for reconstructing a contrast

When two reflexes are attested for what was thought to be a single protophoneme or sequence, the first step is to ascertain phonological conditioning for the two reflexes. If this cannot be found, an explanation in analogy must be sought. There are many cases of basic vocabulary that show more than one set of reflexes of a single protophoneme or of a

[39] Labov (1960) has a good example of sound change underway in Martha's Vineyard in which the social connotation of the variant was not in the lexical item but in the class of sounds. In this speech community /aw/ was developing centralized allophones. The degree and extent of centralization was correlated with attitude. Among speakers with strong ties to the community and whose values affirmed a positive attitude to life on the island, the centralization was far more advanced and widespread than among speakers with loose ties and whose values reflected a rejection of island life.

sequence. There are also many protomorphemes throughout the An group, not basic vocabulary but with well-attested reflexes, where the attestations show more than one set of phonemic reflexes. In many of these cases, no phonological condition can be ascertained and no analogical process can provide a reasonable account for the different reflexes. The tradition of historical phonology in the An world in such cases has been to reconstruct two phonemes or different sequences for these different reflexes. However, this methodology does not invariably result in a reasonable account of the sound changes that took place. Many of these differing reflexes are cases of borrowing (dialect mixture or borrowing from another An language), and others are double reflexes (sound changes not carried to completion). Only under specific conditions do the different reflexes of what was thought to be a single protophoneme or sequence in fact result from a contrast in the protolanguage.

These conditions are outlined here: in the case of a protophoneme or sequence *p, this protophoneme or sequence in fact must be reconstructed as two phonemes (or two different phonemic sequences), *p_1 and *p_2, when two conditions hold: (1) there are two daughter languages A and B, not in a subgroup or more closely related to each other than they are to other An languages, and A shows two correspondences for protophoneme or sequence *p, and language B also shows two correspondences for *p, and (2) the two sets of reflexes in A are correlated with the cognate forms in B—that is, the reflexes of *p_1 in A are in the same reconstructed morphemes that show the reflexes of *p_1 in B, and the reflexes of *p_2 in A are in the same reconstructed morphemes that show the reflexes of*p_2 in B.[40] However, when these conditions are not met, then it is a case of double reflexes or borrowing—that is, there was borrowing/dialect mixture or a case of double reflexes for a single PAn phoneme when in a given language there are two sets of correspondences of a particular phoneme or sequence that correlate with only one set of correspondences for the same phoneme in other An languages, not very closely related to the given language.[41]

An example of this phenomenon is from Bun (northern and central dialects). We assume here that these dialects reflect *-Ø in two ways: /-ʔ/ and /-Ø/—i.e., a pre-Bun stem with a final vowel may be reflected in Bun with a final vowel or be closed with a glottal stop. But is the assumption correct that /-ʔ/ and /-Ø/ reflect one PAn ending, *-Ø? May it not be that there were two endings in pre-Bun and in fact in PAn? Other languages manifest a very similar phenomenon (but none of the other Formosan languages do so). For example, Iban has /-ʔ/ and /-Ø/, where other Ml dialects have only /-Ø/, and where Banjarese Ml has only /-ʔ/. Now /-ʔ/ and /-Ø/ in Bun and Iban would reflect a PAn contrast if it were the case that there were a good correspondence between Iban and Bun—that is, in cognate stems in which Iban manifests /-ʔ/, Bun also manifests /-ʔ/ and vice-versa, and where Iban manifests /-Ø/, Bun also manifests /-Ø/ and vice-versa. But

---

[40] It goes without saying that there must be more than two or three attestations of reflexes of *p in language A and B (or in other languages that evince the same phenomenon). An example of where there are two reflexes of a sequence in daughter languages, but where a contrast cannot be reconstructed for PAn is the reconstruction of *ay, discussed in §A3.4.

[41] In the case of laryngeal phonemes, double reflexes and borrowing are not the only possible explanations. Laryngeals may develop spontaneously. For example, many of the Philippine languages have developed a stem final /-ʔ/ in vowel-final stems when a vowel-initial suffix was added. Subsequently, the stem with /-ʔ/ was generalized throughout the paradigm—i.e., a sequence *pq split into /pq_1/ and /pq_2/ (cf. §C1.1.42).

that is decidedly not the case. The data attest all possible combinations and no correlation predominates. The only conclusion is that Bun and Iban both developed /-ʔ/ independently. (Cf. §§B4.1.4 and D4.3.1, footnote, for a discussion of these phenomena in Bun and Ml.)[42]

A2.3 Dialect mixture/borrowing vs. double reflexes

The difference between dialect mixture/borrowing and double reflexes is as follows: dialect mixture and borrowing come from code switching in which a form of the loaning language (or dialect) is adopted in the receiving language or arises when a speech community adopts another language (often closely related) and carries with it vocabulary and articulatory habits from the old language—i.e. results from a substratum (cf. §A2.3.1, immediately following). Double reflexes come about through sound changes that have not been carried through. (Cf. §A2.1, 3rd¶ for a discussion of how a sound change is introduced and spread.)

An example of double reflexes is found in the history of OJv. An important change in the development of OJv is the merger of PAn *d and *g as /r/. Only it is not a complete merger. Some forms with *d change to /r/; some become retroflexed /ḍ/ (that is, remain unchanged); and a good proportion of these develop doublets, forms with /r/ and variants with /ḍ/ (e.g., *deŋeɣ 'hear' > OJv *ḍengö* and *rengö*). (Cf. §E1.3.32.) These are cases of double reflexes. Now in the case of this particular OJv development, scholars have suggested language contact phenomena to explain the double reflexes (Dyen 1947: 229). OJv was in contact with Ml and was strongly influenced by Ml throughout its known history. Ml reflects PAn *d as /d/, and OJv borrows with a retroflexed /ḍ/ forms that in Ml had /d/. In this way it is possible to maintain that OJv "borrowed" the forms with /d/ and adhere strictly to the neo-grammarian hypothesis.

However, there is much to indicate that a hypothesis of borrowing does not hold water in the OJv case. There are three factors that mitigate against the hypothesis of Ml borrowing as a source of OJv /ḍ/ These three factors do not rule this hypothesis out, they only speak against it. First, there are about as many forms that reflect *d with retroflexed /ḍ/ as those that reflect this phoneme with /r/, and there is nothing about their semantic characteristics that would induce borrowing of them. Second, a number of these forms do not occur currently in Ml, so that to say that the forms with /ḍ/ in OJv were borrowings would entail the assumption that forms that no longer exist at this time did exist at an older stage of the Ml with which OJv was in contact or alternatively the assumption of a process of Malayanization—that is, the creation of hybrid forms of OJv origin in which /ḍ/ had been substituted for the original /r/ to make the form sound more 'Malay'. Third, many of the forms with /ḍ/ in OJv evince other changes that Ml did not participate in, e.g., OJv *ḍengö* 'hear' < *deŋeɣ reflects the change of *eɣ > /ö/, which did not take place in Ml (cf. Ml *dengar* 'hear'). In short, Ml influence can explain the OJv forms with retroflexed /ḍ/ only by making a hypothesis about the development of hybrid forms in OJv (forms that were Malayanized by substituting /ḍ/ for /r/).

Malayanization may indeed be the explanation of the /ḍ/ in *ḍengö* and some of the other attestations of /ḍ/ in place of /r/, but not of all of them, for there is further evidence that

---

[42] A detailed examination of these phenomena is given in Wolff 2009.

there must have been two reflexes of *d. The evidence comes from the fact that OJv /r/ may have origins other than *d, and the OJv /r/ from other origins is never in competition with /ḍ/, as would be the expected case if any OJv form with an /r/ could be Malayanized by substituting /ḍ/ for /r/. OJv /r/ may originate from PAn *g or it may occur in forms of Indic provenience. In other words, among all the OJv forms with /r/ of Indic provenience or that come from a PAn form with *g, not one is in competition with a form containing /ḍ/ in place of /r/. A hypothesis that the change of *d to /r/ remained incomplete, very much like the incomplete changes that Labov adduces for English, is the best explanation for the double reflex.[43] Languages from throughout the An area from west to east evince similar phenomena of double reflexes that can be laid to sound changes that spread to some but not all of the vocabulary.

Some of our languages have spread widely beyond the original speakers and have been adopted by communities speaking other languages: the show a substratum effect (§A2.3.1, immediately following). Such cases are recognizable by the fact that the items manifresting the alternative reflex often show other irregularities, whereas in the case of sound changes that were not carried to completion, the forms showing the aternative reflex do not normally show other irregularities.

A.2.3.1 Relexification and substratum

The term RELEXIFICATION refers to massive borrowing from another dialect or language. Although this term is used traditionally to refer to word replacement, as a process it is no different in kind from borrowing of morphemes and syntactic constructions, which may in fact also occur on a large scale. Languages that underwent relexification may have borrowed syntax and morphology on a large scale in addition to vocabulary. What is left over—what was not relexified or features of syntax and morphology that had not been borrowed is the SUBSTRATUM.

When a community adopts a second language that eventually replaces the original language of the community, the process by which this takes place is tantamount to the process of relexification and borrowing of syntax and morphology on a massive scale. Processes of language replacement have happened continuously throughout the history of the An languages, and almost all, if not all, of the languages here discussed have come down to the current time after having been adopted by communities that had originally spoken other languages (often closely related) or dialects. Accordingly, in the discussion of the development of the individual languages (parts B–G) frequent exceptions to the rules will be unexplainable. Often these unexplained exceptions are the result of the influence of a substratum. For example, Bugis *lima* 'hand' clearly comes from *qalíma 'hand'. Now apocope of an unstressed antepenult in trisyllabic roots is a widely occurring sound change, and many of the languages with which Bugis was in contact evince this change. However, Bugis itself does not evince this change in other trisyllables. We assume that Bugis *lima* actually originates from the substratum in a community that had taken on Bugis after speaking another language and that it spread to the rest of the Bugis speech community. (Cf. part C, chapter 6, where the development of Bugis is discussed.)

[43] Dempwolff's explanation of the reflexes /r/ and /ḍ / was tantamount to our hypothesis here: he attributes the double reflexes to a "Tendenz zur Lautverschiebung"—tendency for sound shift' (1934: 90).

A2.4 Variation in the protolanguage

Dempwolff made liberal use of alternative reconstructions (*Nebenformen*) to account for discrepant reflexes that could not be explained by environmental conditioning, analogical processes, or by borrowing, and this tradition has continued in the historical An literature. Indeed, no language is without variation, and PAn and PMP must have had it. In fact, we assume so in espousing the hypothesis that sound change takes place in the process of creating social structure (§A2.1, middle). Nevertheless, the methodology we follow here is to exhaust all other explanations, including reconstruction of a new contrast, before positing an alternative protoform. In short, it is only when a given irregular reflex cannot be accounted for as a borrowing, or as a failure to carry through on a sound change, or as having undergone change by analogy, and the conditions for reconstructing a contrast (§A2.2) are not met, is it possible (and in fact necessary) to reconstruct doublets.

There is a good reason for making avoidance of reconstruction of variation a methodological principle. Namely, for those languages where we have attested historical traditions, it turns out that a large portion of variations in those languages disappears with time: there is competition between two forms, and only one wins out. The kind of variation in the protolanguage that is reflected in the daughter languages is at the systemic, not often at the lexical level. For example, protolanguage phonological variation can be reflected as a change that took place in the phonology of one daughter language but not in another. However, variation of individual lexical items in most cases dies out.

There are cases where we are constrained to reconstruct two alternative individual forms in a protolanguage. An example of a situation in which two doublets must be reconstructed for the protolanguage is the word for 'sleep', *tiduɣ and *tuduɣ. Although reflexes of *tiduɣ are found only in languages of Indonesia and the Philippines, whereas reflexes of *tuduɣ are found across the board from Taiwan through Oceania, nevertheless the distribution of forms with /i/ in the penult (that is, reflexes of *tiduɣ) is totally capricious and has nothing to do with subgrouping among the languages that evince †tiduɣ. In short, at the level of Proto-Philippines/Indonesia we must reconstruct ††tiduɣ as well as *tuduɣ (but at the PAn level, only *tuduɣ).[44]

Most of the cases of reconstruction of doublets are monosyllabic roots that have been disyllabized in two different ways. For example, the root *biɣ 'lip-like extension' has reflexes of *bibíɣ (disyllabization by prefixing the initial syllable without the final consonant) and *biɣebiɣ (disyllabization by doubling the root).[45] Since reflexes occur in languages that allow consonant clusters but show no medial cluster (e.g., Tag *bibíg* 'mouth'), it is necessary to reconstruct *bibiɣ. Further, some languages that preserve the final consonant of monosyllabic roots show reflexes of *biɣebiɣ (e.g., Bun *bilbil* 'lips').

---

[44] In fact, reflexes of *tuduɣ only have the meaning 'sleep' in MP languages. In Formosan languages the reflexes refer to dozing or napping, whereas the word for 'sleep' in Formosa is in many languages expressed by reflexes of *qiseɫep, which later developed other meanings in some of the MP languages (but remains 'sleep' in others).

[45] We reconstruct a medial /e/, assuming that /e/ is epenthesized, on the hypothesis that PAn had no consonant clusters (§A3.6.1).

Since neither the reflexes of *biɣebiɣ nor those of *bibiɣ are found in languages that can be subgrouped, we reconstruct doublets *bibiɣ and *biɣebiɣ.[46]

There are many cases of forms in various languages with corresponding phonemes, save for one or at most two phonemes, that have a semantic component in common. Most of these are cases of forms that reflect monosyllabic roots—i.e., the final syllables correspond, but the initial syllables do not. These are discussed further in §A3.6.3. There are a few cases where the discrepancy is not in the initial syllable, but rather in the final syllable. In most of those cases, contamination has probably taken place, and these forms cannot supply evidence for PAn or PMP variation. Some good examples are the forms listed under †butu, ††butud, ††butuɣ in the glossary. It is impossible to reconstruct the PMP etymon for these forms because there has been a great deal of contamination among the forms of similar meaning and sound in various languages. It is likely that the forms under those entries are descended from something in PMP, but it is only possible to reconstruct a part of the root.

A2.5 Loan words

A great number of attestations are forms of secondary spread—that is, they moved from one language to another after the breakup of the An and MP languages. For a large portion of these, the origin is known: they come from Sanskrit or another Indic language and spread via Ml or they are Ml forms that have spread. These forms are for the most part not listed in this study. There has also been a great deal of borrowing between other languages in contact, and these forms are in the great majority of cases readily identifiable. They can be recognized by two criteria: (1) they have irregular reflexes—that is, their phonemic make-up does not correspond with the reflexes of the inventory of phonemes as reconstructed by the principles enunciated in §§A2.1, A2.2; (2) their reference is to cultural items of a sort that is most frequently borrowed from one community by another. Clearly it is an art and not a science to determine whether a putative irregularity in an attestation is the reflection of an undiscovered contrast in the phonology of the protolanguage or is the result of secondary spread (borrowing in post-protolanguage times).[47] Under a large portion of the entries listed here, there are attested forms that are not directly inherited from a protomorpheme but are the result of secondary spread—i.e., they are loan words. The reconstructions are based on the attestations that are not of secondary spread.

There are forms found throughout the range of the An languages from Taiwan to Oceania that surely spread secondarily, but these forms manifest regular reflexes. It is difficult, if not impossible, to recognize them as forms spread by borrowing. An example is a word referring to a kind of flute reconstructed as *lali. Aside from the fact that this form refers to a cultural item readily subject to borrowing, the only other evidence that this form is spread by borrowing is that it often appears not alone, but with an unexplainable sequence preceding it or as part of a 'cranberry morph' (a compound one part of which is not an otherwise existing morpheme). The following forms are attested in our data:

---

[46] Since only the Formosan languages reflect *biɣebiɣ unequivocally, it is tempting to hypothesize that the creation of *bibiɣ was a PMP innovation. However, this is not possible because some MP attestations come from languages that simplify CC's—i.e., these attestations could as well reflect *biɣebiɣ as *bibiɣ.

[47] Dyen 1956 is a classic study that enunciates the principles for distinguishing loan words from inherited forms in ND.

Ru *ba-lali* 'flute' Pai *lali-ngedan* 'nose flute' Ilk *tu-láli* 'flute' Tboli *se-loli* 'flute-like instrument' Gor *tu-lali* 'flute' Ba *tu-yali* 'flute' Fi *ndu-lali* 'nose flute'.

Most of the forms that were spread by borrowing but cannot be readily recognized as loan words refer to flora or fauna.

A2.6 Reality of reconstructed forms

It is not always certain that a given reconstructed form was actually part of the same language that contained the other reconstructed forms. In the first place, PAn and probably PMP both covered a period of many hundred years, and there is good evidence that some of the forms that can be reconstructed for PAn in fact came into existence after the time that the Austronesians arrived in Formosa and replaced earlier forms of the same meaning. An example is the term for 'moon', where *bulaɬ 'white' came to mean 'moon' and replaced earlier *qiɬas 'moon'. *bulaɬ 'moon' is reconstructed for PAn, but it came into being well after the earliest Austronesian settlement of Taiwan. Cf. the discussion in §A1.1.4.

Second, in some cases analogical creations of roots were made independently in many languages within a given group, such that the attestations give the appearance of having derived from the protolanguage of the group, whereas in fact the attestations came into existence at a later time independently in several languages. This is exemplified by the reconstructions of *luŋ, *luk, *kuŋ, *kuk. They all can be reconstructed for PMP, but it is not certain which of these in fact existed in PMP times, as some of the forms that reflect these reconstructions were created by analogy, and it is impossible to know which ones. Cf. the discussion in §A3.8.

Finally, in parts B–G, in the discussions of the development of forms from PAn or later stages to the currently attested forms, we often give a series of steps whereby the given form developed. Most of these steps involve several changes, and it is not always possible to know the order in which the changes occurred. Accordingly, in many cases we may cite reconstructed forms that show changes that had in fact not taken place at that stage, or fail to show changes that had already taken place. For example, in the following Kav development in §B62.1.11, we illustrate the loss of the antepenult. To explain how the form /qipit/ evolved from *kepit we posited five stages:

*kepit + *ise- > *qipit* 'hold under arm' (< *kipit < *ekipit < *ikepit < *isekepit)

This notation is spelled out as follows: (a) the addition of a petrified prefix creating a stem of four syllables (> *isekepit), (b) loss of *s onset to a syllable to the left of the penult of a stem of three or more syllables and contraction of the abutting vowels to create a trisyllabic root (> *ikepit), (c) metathesis of the vowels of the antepenult and penult (> *ekipit), (d) loss of the antepenult (> *kipit), and finally (e) change of *k to /q/. It is clear that step (a) had to precede the other changes, (d) must have taken place after (a), (b), and (c), and it is very likely that the step (e) took place very recently in Kav history (§B62.3.13). However, it is not at all sure that stage (b) preceded stage (c). It is arbitrary that we decide that metathesis took place after loss of *s, and we could have as well presented an account whereby metathesis preceded the loss of *s.[48] However, where

[48] I have reconstructed the prefix in this root as *ise-, but there is evidence for an alternative reconstruction of *si- (§A3.5.4, 5th ¶). Both metathesis of *i and *e in the penult and antepenult and loss of *s to the left of the penult of a root of three or more syllables are innovations made by many languages in Formosa, but it is

it does not otherwise matter, we have not endeavored to find evidence for the chronological order of the various changes in each language. In most of the accounts, we have chosen a likely chronology, but it is not always known if the chronology is correct. What is known to be correct, however, is the overall account of the origin and changes that took place to produce the attested form, even if it is not always known in what order these changes took place.

---

not determinable in which order these changes took place, and it is not known which of these innovations were made together by certain languages and which are independent (cf. §A3.5.4).

CHAPTER THREE

Inventory of PAn Phonemes and Other Issues of Phonology

A3.1 The PAn consonants

We begin by hypothesizing an inventory of phonemes according to the principles enumerated in chapter 2, above. After giving the inventory (§§A3.1, A3.4) and discussing the pronunciation (§§A3.2ff.), we will discuss issues affecting the reconstructions that apply to large numbers of languages (§§A3.5, A3.6ff.). Problems peculiar to specific languages or groups of languages will be discussed in the sections dealing with the groups and individual languages (parts B–G). Those affecting specific lexical items will be discussed in the glossary under the entry containing the item with the problem. A summary of the reflexes in each of the thirty-seven languages discussed in parts B–G is given individually in the chapters dealing with the developments in each of these languages.

CHART ONE. PAN CONSONANTS

voiced consonants[49]	b	j[50]	d	g	ɣ
voiceless stops	p	c	t	k	q
nasals	m		n	ŋ	
laterals		ɬ	l		
semivowels	w	y			
sibilants			s		h

The relation between the system I posit and the transcription found in much of the current literature, as exemplified by Blust 1995b,[51] is given here in Chart Two.

[49] This series consists of stop consonants except in the case of the *ɣ which is post-velar, a position in which voiced stops are rare. The reflexes of *ɣ are spirants (or developments from spirants) in all languages except in the languages in which *g merged with *d or *j or with *ɣ, in which case the reflex has a sound [g], for there was room for *ɣ to move to an articulation further forward in the mouth.

[50] Note that for the series *j, *c, and *ɬ the tongue tip was further front than for the series *d, *t, *n, *l, and *s (§§A3.2.2ff., A3.2.3).

[51] Blust ACD (1995c) does not distinguish *L and *N, nor *z and *Z, as is done in much of the historical literature. Blust considers these two correspondences to represent one protophoneme, as I do, implicitly in the

CHART TWO. WOLFF'S AND BLUST'S TRANSCRIPTIONS

Wolff	Blust	Wolff	Blust
p	p	ɣ	R
t	C, t	m	m
k	k	n	n
none	T, c	ɬ	ñ, N, L
q	q	ŋ	ŋ
b	b	l	l
none	d	none	r
d	D	c	s
j	z	s	S
none	Z	h	H_1 (H_2)
g	j	w	w
none	g	y	y

A.3.2 Articulations

The reflexes of the protophonemes allow us to determine the nature of their articulation, for we assume that sound changes proceed in a natural way.

A3.2.1 Voiceless consonant articulation

The voiceless series *p, *c, *t, *k, *q were all stops. *p and *k are fairly stable and are retained as bilabial and velar stops respectively in languages spread over the entire Austronesian area. *t was an apico-alveolar stop with the tongue tip further back than for *c. *t was stable outside of Taiwan—i.e., in most of the MP languages, but in some of the Formosan languages it developed affricate allophones, which subsequently became contrastive, as discussed in §A3.3.1, below. *c was an apico-dental stop very far front (like *j and *ɬ, see below in §A3.2.2), probably affricated or possibly even an interdental spirant [θ]. *c is reflected as [c], an apico-dental affricate in many of the Formosan languages and in scattered languages of Indonesia. It became a spirant [s] (that is, with the tongue tip further back) independently in many languages across the entire Austronesian area. In some languages, this spirant [s] subsequently and independently became weakened to [h] and later in some languages became lost as well. In a few languages, *c became (or remained) an interdental spirant [θ]. In Pai and independently in other languages scattered across the entire An area, *c lost its affrication and became [t], mostly an apico-dental stop. In Pai this occurred after *t had become palatalized or affricated (depending on stress patterns—§A3.3.1). *q is retained as a post-velar voiceless stop in only a few languages, all on Taiwan.

---

case of *L and *N and explicitly in the case of *z and *Z (Blust 1995c: the end of the commentary to the word for 'rain' *quzaN [here *qujaɬ]). Further ACD lists only one *H. In the case of *g, some of my initial *g-'s are in the same protomorphemes as listed in the ACD, but I consider many of the ACD entries with *g- not to be reconstructible for PAn (cf. Wolff 1982).

Otherwise, it weakened (and often got lost entirely) or it moved forward and merged with *k. These developments occurred independently in languages across the board. When *q was weakened, it sometimes became (1) [ʔ], as happened independently in languages in Taiwan, in the Philippines, and in Oceania and subsequently was lost in many of these languages, or (2) it became a spirant [x] and then weakened further to [h] and often also was subsequently lost. In one of the languages discussed in detail in this work, Muna, *q became a voiceless spirant [x] and then weakened further to a voiced spirant [ɣ].

A3.2.2 Voiced consonant articulation

The voiced stops continued to be pronounced as voiced stops in most of the languages west of Oceania.[52] In Oceania the voiced and voiceless series fell together when the voiced consonants were not protected by a nasal. (Cf. further discussion in §G.0.) In OJv lenition replaced voicing as the distinctive feature that marks this series off from other stop consonants. In almost all of the An languages the labials remain labials and the consonants that are articulated in the front of the mouth continue to be articulated in the front. The voiced velars *g and the post-velar *ɣ tended to be unstable and changed their points of articulation in many of the An languages. (Cf. detailed discussion in §A3.3.2, end, below.) The post-velar consonant *ɣ was in all probability a voiced spirant: it is reflected frequently as a liquid [r] or [l] or as a voiced spirant, or as a voiceless spirant [x] (as, for example, in Paz). [x] may then undergo lenition [h] (as, for example, in Rat of a hundred years ago) and subsequently it may further be lost (e.g., in contemporary Rat). The change of *ɣ to [r] and [l] involves a change widespread in the world's languages, where a voiced velar spirant becomes a uvular trill and subsequently a tongue-tip trill, which may then merge with /l/. *ɣ also became [l] in other ways. For example, in Bun *ɣ moved forward and became lateralized when the inherited lateral had changed into something else (or in St *ɣ moved forward and merged with the palatalized lateral, the reflex of ɬ). In languages in which the articulation of *g moved forward (merging with *d or *j), there was space for *ɣ to occupy, and in a few languages it changed to /g/ (e.g., in many of the Philippine languages). In OJv and Pai, *b, *d, and *ɣ developed in entirely analogous and natural ways, where *b and *d lost the occlusive feature entirely and become fricatives or taps, and *ɣ became lost altogether.[53] Similar developments characterize the reflexes of the voiced stops in many of the other languages discussed in detail in this study. Although not all voiced stops are weakened in all positions, there is a palpable consistency in this development that allows us to be secure in the conclusion that these stops were in fact voiced stops. Further, it is unequivocal that points of articulation implied by the symbols of the chart are in fact the distinctive features of the PAn consonant inventory.

---

[52] In Bun and in languages of eastern Indonesia, the voiced stops *b, *j, and *d became glottalized or imploded. It is possible that the implosion is original and did not develop—that is, these are remnants of the earliest articulation that had changed to a voiced stop without implosion in the course of development of the An languages. We ignore this issue here and speak of the series as 'voiced'.

[53] OJv in fact had double reflexes of *b and *d: one a weakened continuant and the other a pharyngealized stop (§§A2.3, 2nd¶, E1.3.21, E1.3.22).

A3.2.21 Articulation of *j, *c, and *ɬ

We begin with *j and discuss its articulation vis-à-vis *d. In OJv, Ru, and some of the Pai dialects,*d is reflected as a back retroflexed apical stop [ḍ] and *j is reflected as a tongue-tip front [d]. In other languages that retain the *d –*j distinction, *j is reflected as a voiced affricate and *d is reflected with a [d] made in the front of the mouth—it is even apico-dental in Ml dialects. Ross (1992:36–37) argued that the nature of the distinction in PAn was one of apico-dental versus apico-alveolar or retroflex because this is the distinction found in two widely separated languages. However, languages in which the contrast is manifested as a palatalized versus a nonpalatalized reflex are not entirely contiguous either. Nevertheless, Ross's conclusions are surely correct. In all languages in which the *j –*d contrast is reflected, the reflex of *j is pronounced further forward in the mouth than *d. Since the reflexes of *d are not articulated further back than the alveolar ridge, PAn *d was no further back either. Thus *j must have been very far front, perhaps even interdental. If *j was a very forward voiced stop, the blade of the tongue would naturally be raised, implying a palatal coarticulation. This palatalization could become distinctive in many languages independently. However, in many languages, both in those among the MP and among the Formosan languages, *j and *d fell together.

We assume a parallelism of development between the voiced and the voiceless series—that is, between *j vs. *c and *d vs. *t: if *j is distinguished from *d mainly by being further forward, so *c should be distinguished from *t by being further forward. The Oceanic languages bear out this parallelism: in Oceania *j merged with *c and did not merge with *d, and in most Oceanic languages, reflexes of *d are articulated further back in the mouth than the reflexes of *j and *c. In general over the range of the An languages, the reflexes of *c are no further back than the reflexes of *t, and in many cases, especially in the languages spoken in the area of the earliest settlement in Taiwan (§A1.1.31), the reflexes of *c are dental or even interdental. We assume a similar parallelism in the liquid/nasal series: *ɬ was further forward than *l or *n, and the reflexes of *ɬ bear this out (§A3.2.3, immediately following).

A3.2.3 Articulation of the continuants

*h was a pharyngeal spirant [h] and survives with this articulation in only four languages of Taiwan. However, although *h disappeared in the MP languages, it left traces in some of them (§A3.3.31).

*s was an apical sibilant that is pronounced as a sibilant in most of the Formosan languages. Outside of Taiwan and in some Formosan languages as well, *s weakened to [h]. Subsequently, it was independently lost in some of these languages.

The nasals *m, *n, and *ŋ were bilabial, apico-alveolar, and velar respectively. They are stable except that in a few languages of western Formosa *n and *ŋ merged. *ɬ was a lateral, articulated far forward with a point of articulation analogous to *c and *j. The argument for the more forward articulation of *ɬ as opposed to *l and *n is that the reflexes of the former are always more forward than the reflexes of the latter two—i.e., the same argument as that reflexes of *j and *c were articulated more to the front than reflexes of *d and *t. *ɬ was probably a lateral rather than a nasal. The reasons for believing that to be the case are as follows: the reflexes of *ɬ are or were laterals in the languages of the area of the earliest settlement and, in fact, everywhere in Formosa that *ɬ did not merge with /n/ (see the second-to-last sentence of this paragraph). Also *ɬ is reflected as a lateral in the MP

languages in certain environments (§A3.3.4). On the other hand. there is conflicting evidence that this phoneme was a nasal: namely, the process termed "nasalization" (§A3.7.1) involves this phoneme *ɬ as well as the nasals *m, *n, and *ŋ.
Although the symbol *ɬ* suggests that palatalization was a distinctive feature of *ɬ, in fact palatalization was concomitant, entailed by the far forward position of tongue tip, as was probably the case of *j and *c. In some of the Formosan languages, *ɬ became palatalized and in several of them became devoiced. In Tsou the devoiced *ɬ subsequently changed to [h] (as discussed in §A3.3.4). In other Formosan languages, *ɬ remained a lateral but lost palatalization (or never developed it). Finally, in a number of languages adjacent to each other (Bun, Knn, Kav, and the extinct languages of northeast Taiwan), ɬ lost its lateralization and moved back to an alveolar position, falling together with *n.[54] In the MP languages, depending on the environment, *ɬ became a palatal nasal [ñ], became [n], or became [l], articulated further back in the mouth than we hypothesize to have been the case for PAn *ɬ. The development of *ɬ is discussed in §A3.3.4, below.

A3.3 Issues of reconstruction of consonants affecting large sets of languages

The reconstruction of the consonants is on the whole straightforward and uncomplicated. However, there are some reconstructions that offer problems and for which it is necessary to make assumptions, which are laid out in the following subsections.

A3.3.1 Voiceless stops

The voicless stops are *p, *c, *t, *k, and *q. Of these only *t offers problems in reconstruction: in the Formosan languages spoken in the northwestern and southeastern portions of the island, *t has affricate or sibilant reflexes in some roots and apico-alveolar (or dental) stop reflexes in other roots. There are two interpretations possible for these facts: (1) (as is widely expressed in the literature, first by Dyen 1965) that there were two PAn phonemes *C and *t, which fell together in southwestern and northeastern Taiwan and in the MP (extra-Taiwan) languages, but were retained as two contrasting phonemes in the southeastern and northwestern languages.[55] Further, by this hypothesis *C and *t fell together in all other Austronesian languages. The other possibility is (2) that there was one protophoneme *t (as proposed in Wolff 1991), which split in one language and spread through the southeastern and northwestern languages but did not spread to the other An languages. Here we take hypothesis (2) to be the case. There are some facts that support the hypothesis that there was one phoneme *t, which had two outcomes in some of the Formosan languages. Namely, some of the languages that have two outcomes for *t evince an affricate reflex in certain items for which the other languages evince a stop. This is most strongly manifested in the Atayalic languages,[56] less strongly so in Tsou and Ru, and sporadically in

---

[54] We assume that the change of *ɬ to /n/ spread from one language to another. In fact this change spread to Kanakanavu but not to the very closely related Saaroa nor to Tsou.

[55] The following languages show affricated reflexes (or further development into sibilants) and are termed here the 'southeastern and northwestern languages': Paz, St, Th, Atayalic, Sar, Knn, Tsouic, Ru, Pu, and Pai, as well as the extinct Favorlang/Babuza and some of the other extinct languages of the western plains. The following languages of Taiwan reflect only *t for this phoneme or these phonemes and are here termed the 'southwestern and northeastern languages': Am, Bun, Kav, the now extinct Siraya, Basay, Trobiawan, and PMP.

[56] In some Atayalic dialects *-t is always reflected with an affricate (§B2.3.12, 5th¶).

the other northwestern and southeastern languages.[57] In final position, there is even less agreement as to the forms that evince the affricate or spirant reflex (cf. the last paragraph of this section).

This fact provides some support (but by no means conclusive support) for the hypothesis that there was only one phoneme *t. Stronger support is given by a hypothesis that stress was the environment that determined the development of an affricate allophone of *t that subsequently merged with the reflexes of *c or became a separate phoneme in the northwestern and southeastern languages. Since the reconstruction of stress is equivocal in many items in the PAn glossary (§A3.5), it is not possible to determine without a shadow of doubt the stress pattern of the root that led or did not lead to the development of an affricate (or later a sibilant) in the northwestern and southeastern languages.

In any case, the hypothesis developed in Wolff 1991 is here taken to be essentially correct—that this development took place in roots of iambic stress pattern in disyllabic roots or in the first two syllables of trisyllabic roots. These rules can be restated as follows: the change of *t to an affricate is a weakening. Initial *t developed affricate allophones [ts] before a vowel that was unstressed in Post-PAn.[58] Note that we assume that word stress was on the long vowel furthest to the right and on the final syllable if the word contained no long vowel. Thus an allophone [ts] developed initially before an unstressed (short) vowel and medially before a stressed vowel (a vowel that was long or was final). In other words, tVCV́ >tsVCV́ and CVtV́ > CVtsV́ (where V is a short vowel, V́ is a stressed vowel, and C is a consonant): e.g., *taŋíla 'ear' > Post-PAn [tsaŋíla], *bitúka 'stomach' > Post-PAn [bitsúka], *tałém 'bury' > Post-PAn [tsałém], *matá 'eye' > Post-PAn [matsá]. On the other hand, tV́CV > tV́CV and CV́tV> CV́tV (where V́ is a stressed or long vowel): *tápis 'skirt' remains Post-PAn [tápis]', PAn *gíta 'see' remains Post-PAn [gíta]. Monosyllabic roots that occurred alone in Post-PAn affricate any *t: PAn *taw > Post-PAn *tsawú.[59] On the other hand, initial *t in doubled monosyllabic roots did not affricate: PAn *táketak[60] 'cut down' remains Post-PAn *táketak. In final position, *t remained *t, but in a few cases that evince unstressed penults, the *t became affricated. We assume that the affricates developed in affixed forms of the root—that is, when the root was followed by a suffix or an enclitic and the stress was shifted from the final syllable of the root to the suffix or enclitic. This implies that among the languages that undergo the process of affrication of *t, the affrication did not necessarily affect the reflexes

[57] The following list gives forms that manifest affricates or spirants in some of the southeastern and northwestern languages, and stops in others: *łateŋ, *tali, *talis, *tałeq, *taŋic, *taqi, *tasiq, *tebus, *tiŋas. It should be noted that there are forms not reflexes of reconstructible PAn etyma that manifest this correspondence in various Formosan languages (cf. Tusch 1976: 147–152). Further, in final position there are a great number of forms reconstructed with *-t that show a stop in some Formosan languages and an affricate or spirant in others (cf. the immediately preceding footnote).

[58] It is impossible to state exactly when this change took place. It must have spread through the languages in Formosa after the island had been occupied, and the change affected some languages spoken by groups that had migrated to the south and inland from there (Ru, Pai, and Pu). On the other hand, this change did not affect Bun, which split off from the main group earlier (§A1.1.31), nor did it affect Siraya, a group that had split off much earlier, and it does not affect the languages of groups that had spread up the east coast (Am, Kav, and the extinct languages of the northeast) and PMP.

[59] Presumably monosyllabic roots were pronounced with two morae with the stress falling on the second mora, and thus behaved like disyllabic roots with a short penult: e.g., *taw 'person' was probably pronounced *[taú].

[60] Epenthetic /e/ is assumed in roots consisting of reduplicated monosyllables (§A3.6.1), but the first syllable of the doubled root retained the stress and because the penultimate syllable was marginal—it was metrically part of the initial syllable, the *t was metrically before a long vowel.

of *-t in the same roots, for either the affricated allophone could be spread from the affixed stem to the unaffixed form, or the the unaffricated allophone cound be spread from th unaffixed form to the affixed stem. In fact, *-t in southern languages undergo this process more frequently than in the northern languages. An example is *kaɣát 'bite'. Root final stress should lead to affrication, but it does so only in some of the languages that undergo this process. It fails to do so in Paz and in some Atayalic dialects (but in others, stress does lead to affrication of *t).

AtMx *kaat* AtSkikun *kac* Tsou *b-orcə* St *kalas* Ru *kaacə* Puy *kaɣaţ* Pai *kats*'bite' Paz *kaxat* 'whittle' Tag *kagát* Fi *kat-i* 'bite'

A3.3.2 Voiced stops

The distinction between *d and *j is poorly attested in final position. It is not attested in any of the Formosan languages. Only three of our languages manifest different reflexes of these phonemes in final position: TB, Ml, OJv. In OJv contact with Ml probably is the source for this contrast—i.e., OJv in fact merged *-d and *-j. TB is also very much influenced by Ml. Further, TB and Ml are clearly in a subgroup as opposed to other MP languages.[61] It is possible that the contrast between *d and *j was neutralized in PAn and only developed again in the protolanguage that gave rise to TB-Ml or arose in Ml and was introduced into TB through borrowings.[62] The hypothesis we adopt here is that *-d > /r/ in TB and Ml and *-j > /-t/. Here we write *-j only for those protomorphemes that have a TB or Ml reflex with /-t/. Otherwise we list the protomorphemes with *-d if they have reflexes of voiced dentals in the other An languages that reflect them (§A2.1.1).

The phoneme *g offers problems for reconstruction, as it was unstable.[63] The voiced velar *g frequently loses voicing, merging with *k, when onset of the penult or earlier or when onset of a monosyllabic root. This merger must have taken place independently many times, for the languages that retain /g-/ as a reflex of initial *g- are found over the entire range of languages from Taiwan to western Indonesia. The following languages retain reflexes of initial *g- contrasting with *k- among those treated in detail here: Ru, Pu, Pai, ND, Ml, TB, Mok, OJv. The following languages manifest a scattering of forms that attest /g/contrasting with /k/ as a reflex of initial *g-, but these are not the normal reflexes of *k-, and they probably represent borrowings from other languages in the neighborhood: Chmr, Tag,[64] Bug, Sal, Mgg, Leti. In medial position *-g- is reflected as /g/ only in Ru and TB among our languages.[65] Otherwise it has shifted, in many cases merging with other phonemes. In the Formosan languages other than the Ru languages, the reflexes of *-g- moved forward and in some cases merged with *-d- (see the discussion of the individual languages in part B for details). In Kav and Am, as well as in the extinct Siraya, *-g- developed nasalized allophones, which then became /-n-/— that is, moved forward to merge with the reflexes of *-n-. In most of the Hesperonesian

---

[61] Nothofer (1975) did not include Batak in his subgroup "Malayo-Javanic", but if it is not in a subgroup with them, it is in a subgroup of MP that developed shortly prior to "Malayo-Javanic" as opposed to languages further afield.

[62] There is no explanation how this distinction could have arisen in Ml, and we assume here that the distinction is inherited from PAn, even though it is reflected in only two closely related languages.

[63] If initial *b-, *d-, *j- had imploded reflexes (as suggested in §A3.2.2, footnote), it is not surprising that *g- was unstable, for velar imploded stops are inherently unstable and regularly change if they develop.

[64] Some of the languages of the Philippines retain the contrast, e.g., Ilk and Kpp.

[65] *-g- is also reflected as /g/ in many languages of Luzon in the Philippines.

languages *-g- also moved forward, in many (but not all) cases merging with *-d- (and also with *-j- in those languages that merged *d and *j).[66] In Proto-Oceanic *-g- merged with *-j-, subsequently losing its voicing and merging with *-c- in most Oceanic languages (§G.0). *g merged with *j in Proto-Oceanic because *d had changed to [r], and this change allowed the tongue tip to move back to the alveolar ridge or velum in articulating *j without interference of *d.

L. Sagart (2004: 429) suggests that *g was in fact a palatal nasal [ñ]. This hypothesis would jibe with our reconstruction of *ɬ as a very front or interdental [ɬ] (as reflected in many Formosan languages) and not articulated at the alveolar ridge or velum. Sagart's reasoning is based on the fact that this phoneme is reflected as a nasal both in Siraya and in Am and Kav. Sagart makes three arguments: first, the account of the spread of An in Formosa prior to the split of the MP languages (to which I also subscribe [§A1.1.31]) makes it virtually impossible that Siraya should be in a subgroup with Am and Kav. In short, this nasal reflex cannot be a shared innovation between Siraya and those two languages. Second, Siraya was not contiguous to Am or Kav such that an innovation of *g > *ñ could have spread from one to the other two. Third, it is also impossible that the same innovation was made independently in Siraya and in Am and Kav, for it was a complex innovation and can only have happened once. To wit, a change of *g > *ñ would have involved two steps: a moving forward of [g] and a subsequent nasalization. The combination of these two steps is not something that could have taken place twice, independently. On these grounds Sagart concludes that Siraya and Am/Kav are remnant areas and that the innovation was denasalization—*ñ > *g, which spread to the other An languages (at a time when all of them were located on Taiwan). Under Sagart's hypothesis this correpondence must be reconstructed as a *ñ and not as *ŋ for the reason that this phoneme merged with *n in Am and Kav and not with *ŋ. The phoneme *ŋ is reflected as /ŋ/ in both Am and Kav (§§B61.3.43, B62.3.44). If this set were to have derived from a back nasal, then it should not have merged with *n but rather with *ŋ. In summary, a reconstruction of *ñ in place of my older *g would explain the reflex /n/ in Kav, Am, and extinct Siraya. Sagart points out the following (in discussion): this reconstruction entails that the PAn voiced series lacked *g, a typologically plausible inventory, especially if the voiced series were in fact imploded (as suggested in §A3.2.2, footnote). Further, the fact that /t/ and/d/ are pronounced with different tongue-tip placement in Bun and Ru (and perhaps other Formosan languages—although we do not have data) supports a view that the voiced series was originally imploded. I may adduce one more development to support the view that what I here reconstruct as *g was in fact a palatal nasal: namely, in Sar and Tsou among the Tsouic languages and in Th, the phoneme I reconstruct as *g merges with the phoneme I reconstruct as *ɬ (§§B13.3.33, B13.3.41, B31.3.33, B31.3.41). The referenced sections give an explanation for this merger other than that *g was in fact a nasal, but the merger would be very plausible in articulatory terms if we were to espouse Sagart's view that my *g was in fact a palatal nasal.

However, we do not here espouse this hypothesis and assume rather that medial *g was indeed [g]. The reason for that is that it is not a great leap of faith to assume that Siraya expanded and moved around the south of the island to become adjacent to Am and

[66] In OJv the merger is almost complete in that both *g and *d > /r/ in medial and final positions. However, since medial *-d- alternatively may become /-ḍ-/ as well as /-r-/ (cf. §A2.3), but *-g- always becomes /-r-/, the merger is not complete.

influenced it.[67] By this hypothesis the ancestors of Pai, Pu, and Ru were located further inland and only later came to separate Siraya from Amis. This scenario jibes well with the fact discussed above, that Pai, Pu, and Ru participated in the split of *t (§A3.3.1, 3rd ¶), whereas Siraya and the east coast languages did not. That is less questionable than to explain one failure to make an innovation that would be entailed by assuming that my *g was in fact a palatalized [ñ]—to wit, why did this [ñ] not fall together with the /n/ that arose from *ɬ in Bun, Knn, Kav, and the extinct northeast languages (§A3.3.4)? Further, we would have to assume denasalization and depalatalization of the putative reconstructed [ñ] and a merger with *d in a host of languages. This indeed is possible, for the assumption of [ñ] for this correspondence set means that there is a gap in the voiced series—namely, no *g was reconstructed. If the original PAn voiced series was imploded, at a later point most of the An languages lost implosion and the lack of *g was a gap waiting to be filled. Under this scenario [ñ] would have filled the gap—i.e., [ñ] > [g], and this [g] remained so in Ru and TB, but moved forward, as explained earlier in this section.

If this correspondence set reflects an original*ñ, a further question arises. Namely, why is there no reflex of this putative *ñ in initial position? On the other hand, if we reconstruct this set as *g, there is no such gap in initial position. In initial position there is clear evidence to reconstruct *g-, for the reflexes are universally /k/ or /g/ (or derived from /k/ in recent times). It makes sense to say that an unstable *g occurred not only initially but also medially and finally and became a nasal medially and finally in the languages of the coast of Formosa from the southwest around to the northeast. This hypothesis is more likely on typological grounds than that there was a *g- initial that failed to occur medially and finally, and that there was a nasal medially and finally that failed to occur inititally.

A3.3.3 Spirants

A3.3.31 *h

The reflexes of *h have not been clearly understood heretofore. The reconstruction of this phoneme is presented here in detail.[68] *h is directly reflected in only four Formosan languages: At, St, Paz, and Am. It is reflected indirectly in many of the languages of the Philippines and northern Sulawesi.

In initial position no form attests *h-. Forms that appear in At, St, Paz, or Am with /h-/ all turn out to have a cognate with a reflex of *s in one or another language—i.e., those attestations of /h-/ reflect PAn *s and not *h. (Cf. §A.3.3.32, immediately following, for a discussion of /h-/ as a reflex of *s in Formosan languages.)[69]

---

[67] In fact, Tsuchida et al. (1991) identify a fair number of items of the Taivoan dialect of Siraya as being of Am origin.

[68] Zorc (1982) summarized all that had been established previously and added considerable data from the Philippine languages. This study reconstructed a second laryngeal on the basis of [ʔ] and [h] that occur in Bun and Iban, but these sounds in fact to do not correspond regularly and provide no evidence for *ʔ (Wolff 2009).

[69] *h- is reconstructed by Tsuchida (1976:131–37) with initial *h- in *hulec 'clothing', as it appears in the Formosan languages with *h-, and nowhere is there an attestation with *s-. However, the reflexes of this root in the Formosan languages are irregular, and clearly the forms have been spread secondarily. The cognates of this form in the MP languages evince regular correspondences and can be taken to descend from a PMP form †hulec or †qulec. Further, Tsuchida reconstructs *h in *uɣat (1976: 137), but Amis *olat* 'vein' has no trace of an initial consonant, and Tsou *vrocə* 'vein' retains a trace of initial V-

In medial position*-h- is reflected as /h/ in Paz, St, Atayalic, and Am, but in Am not when it is the onset of the final syllable in trisyllabic roots (§B61.3.21). In some of the languages of the Philippines, *-h- leaves a trace: after *-h- was lost, hiatus developed in disyllabic roots and when *-h- had been the onset of the final syllable in trisyllabic roots. (But hiatus did not develop when *h had been the onset of the penult in trisyllabic roots.) Subsequently [ʔ] developed in the hiatus except in the sequence *ia, *ua, *ai, and *ui where a glide developed instead.[70] In most cases syllable loss and contractions have obscured the development of *-h-.

> *bahaɬiɣ > St *baɬihœh* Bun *banhil* 'cypress'[71] Ru *baaɬi* 'cypress' Am *fahɬil* 'cedar'; *buhet 'squirrel > Paz *buhut* St *kabhœt* At *buhut* Am *fohet* 'squirrel' Tag *búʔot* 'rabbit';[72] *láhuj 'seaward' > Paz *rahut* 'seaward' St *lœhœr* 'downhill' Cb *lawud* 'sea, seaward';[73] *ɣabihi > Am *lafii*[74] 'midnight' Cb *gabíʔi* 'night'.

*-h is reflected as /-h/ in At, Paz, St, and Am. Elsewhere *-h is lost without a trace.

> *baɣah > Paz *bahah* 'charcoal' St *bœlœh* 'embers' At *baɣah* 'charcoal' Am *valah* 'glowing coals'; *baqeɣuh > At (Squliq) *bah* Am *fahɬoh* 'new'; *buŋuh > Am *fongoh* 'head'; *capuh > Paz *sapuh* St *sapœh* At *sapuh* 'sweep'; *áɬih > Paz *alih* St *ʔaɬ-ʔaɬih-an* Sed (Tar) *d-alex* (/dalih/) 'near'; *qumah Paz *umamah* 'farm, field' St *ʔœmah* 'land in one's possession' At *me-qomah* 'till' Am *omah* 'field, farm'; *tuɬúh > St *soɬœh* 'roast right on the fire' Am *toɬoh* 'roast' *nunuh > Paz *nunuh* 'breast' Sed (Trunun) *nunuh* 'breast, nipple'

*-h- may also be reconstructed on the basis of the indirect evidence of /-ʔ-/ from hiatus in Philippine languages, even when no cognate is attested in one of the four Formosan languages that retain overt reflexes of *-h-. This is the case when two conditions are fulfilled: (1) /ʔ/ occurs in a Philippine language intervocalically[75] or, what is more common, originally in intervocalic position but in the current language abutting on a consonant because of loss of unstressed penults in forms of three or more syllables—(§A3.5.1) and (2) the root does not reflect *q—i.e., is not attested with a reflex of *q in languages that reflect *q with something other than [ʔ]. Thus we may reconstruct a medial *h in the following forms and in many others as well: *betehus 'come forth, appear', *betíhec 'calf of leg', *buheni 'k.o. skin infection', *kanuhec 'squid' (cf. the citations in the glossary).

---

[70] The Philippine languages do not permit vowel sequences. In vowel sequences that developed from loss of *-h- or from any other process, in Tag and many other Philippine languages a glide was inserted between high and low vowels and a glottal stop is inserted in other cases. An example is *kan 'eat', which disyllabized in many Philippine languages by stretching the nucleus to two morae—i.e., *kan > *kaan or *kaen. In between the vowel sequences that had developed, the Philippine languages inserted [ʔ]: SL *kaʔen* 'eat', BM *kaʔan* 'eat'.

[71] Bun manifests /h/ as a reflex of *h only in this and two other words. It is probably a loan word in Bun (§§B5.1.5, B5.3.22).

[72] Tsou has *buhetsi* 'squirrel', a borrowing from an unknown source in which PAn *-h- was reflected as /h/.

[73] *h is replaced by glide between high and low vowels (cf. the statement in the immediately preceding paragraph of this section).

[74] In Am *h was lost in trisyllabic roots when it was the onset of the final syllable.

[75] Western Bukidnon Manobo evinces /h/ instead of /ʔ/ in this position in at least one form *bahi* 'female'. It is almost certain that this /h/ developed as a transitional phenomenon and did not come down from PAn: first, other Manobo languages evince /÷/ in cognates; second, WBM develops /h/ when a vowel-initial affix is added to a stem ending in a vowel: *edbevaha* 'will carry it' (< *ed-* + *bava* + *-a*) (Elkins 1970: 54).

A3.3.32 *s

As many as eight different protophonemes have been reconstructed for *s in the literature (symbolized *S_1, *S_2, *S_3, etc.). For the most part the correspondences that lead to the hypotheses of these protophonemes involve at most two or three forms that are not systematically attested—that is, the same irregularities are not reflected in all (that is, in both or all three) of the attestations in the same languages. There is no reason to assume that these correspondences reflect a feature of PAn. They are surely the result of later developments (contact phenomena or analogical changes). There are two correspondence sets, however, that are more systematic and need to be examined in detail, although at the end of the day they do not constitute evidence for another contrast and are surely also due to contact phenomena. First is the correspondence that Tsuchida (1976:159ff.) symbolizes *S_6. The second is discussed in §A3.3.33, immediately following. Tsuchida posits *S_6 on the basis of Sar reflexes. PAn *s is normally reflected in Tsou and Knn with /s/ but in Sar with both Ø and /s/ (§B31.3.22). Tsuchida considers Ø to be the normal reflex of *S_6. In fact several Formosan languages, mostly from northwest Taiwan show Ø or /h/ instead of /s/ as reflexes of *s. The following chart shows the languages and correspondences. It should be noted that, for a few of the sets of cognates that reflect the irregular correspondences, one or two languages of Taiwan other than these nine may also reflect /h/ or Ø.[76]

CHART THREE. CORRESPONDENCES OF *S IN CERTAIN FORMOSAN LANGUAGES

PAn	At	Sed	Tsou	Knn	Sar	Thao	Paz	St	Am
s (normal reflex)	s	s	s	s	s, Ø	ʃ	s	ʃ	s
irregular reflex	h	h	Ø	Ø	Ø	Ø/ʔ	h	h	h

Chart Four, immediately following, lists the forms that in at least one of these languages show the irregular reflex. The forms underlined in the chart evince the normal rather than the irregular reflex. Italicized forms evince other irregularities.

[76] Bun also manifests a small number of cases in which *s is reflected with Ø instead of the normal /s/: *kasiw > *kawi* 'tree, wood' *sema > *ma-ma* 'tongue' (< *ema) *seyup > *ma-ʔiup* 'blow'.

CHART FOUR. IRREGULAR REFLEXES OF *S

	Paz	St	Thao	Atayal[77]	Tsou	Sar[78]	Knn	Am
*busat 'lift'			mubuhat					fohat 'open'
*gusam 'thrush'							su-kúam-a	
*iseyup 'blow'	hihium	hiup	iup	iyup				*ʔiyof*
*iseci 'flesh, content'				hi-hihiʔ		maa-is-an-a	ʔa-isi-	
*isu 'you (sing)'	siu	ʃoʔo	ihu	isu	suu		íika-su	k-iso
*kaɬuskus 'nail, hoof'[79]		kakɬokœh				ʔaɬuku	ʔanuka	kanoos
*kasiw 'tree'	kahuy	kæhœy	kawi	kahuy	evi	kaalu	kiuʔu	kasoy
*ɬisebic 'thin'[80]	ha-lipit	ɬihpih-an			hipsi	ma-ɬipii	ma-nipi	ko-hpic
*(qaɬi)sipec 'roach'	hipet	hipih		ha-hipux				ɬaɬipic
*qusalipan 'milliped'	haripan	alongæhip an			r-erpa			
*qusaw 'thirsty			uqaw (< *quaw)					soʔaw
*qusuŋ 'mushroom'			qun	qihung	ungo	uʔunga	uúngo	
*sakut 'transport'	hakus							
*saweni 'short while'	uhuni (also sasaunan)			saoni	osni		sauni	i-soni
*sema 'tongue'		kæ-hma	zama	hema				sma
*suɣ 'string beads'		sœ-hœl		lu-hug			cuuru	
tumes 'body louse'	sumah	somæh	tumbuʃ	lumiq				tomes
*suni 'soft noise'	huni		ʃmaʃuni		m-uni		umáuni	soni

First, it should be noted that there are only eighteen forms that evince this irregular correspondence among the forms that have cognates in the MP languages. (More of these irregular correspondences would show up if complete data on these languages were available and if forms that have no cognates outside of the Formosan languages were to be included.) Second, each of these languages has reflexes of only about half of the forms. All of these languages (except Sar) have regular reflexes in a quarter to a third of the attestations of these forms. In fact Am has regular reflexes in most of them but then has /h/ as a reflex of *s in a few forms not on the list in Chart Four, above. The following facts make it clear that the

[77] Here At (Mx) is quoted.

[78] If a form shows *∅* in Saaroa and the normal reflex of *s in other languages, I do not consider this to be an example of the irregular correspondence that Tsuchida called $*S_6$, for I consider *∅* to be the normal reflex of *s in Saaroa (but there are cases where *s is reflected a /s/ in Sar, cf.§B31.3.22). In other words, the Sar forms quoted in this chart are regular.

[79] Note that *kuskus 'scrape', from which this protomorpheme is derived, is based on attestations that manifest the normal reflexes of *s: St *koʃkoʃ* 'shave'.

[80] In Tsou the /s/ is the same as the majority reflex. In Paz the *s is lost entirely in this root instead of becoming /h/, presumably because it is in a cluster.

weaker reflexes (Ø and /h/) are innovations rather than retention of a contrast in PAn: first is the very number of forms that failed to make the innovation in one or another of these languages; second is the fact that the reflexes of the same protomorpheme in one language fail to show the innovation (i.e., show the regular reflex of *s) in the reflex of that protomorpheme in another language—the innovation affects different reflexes of different protomorphemes in the eight languages; third is the distribution of the innovated forms (there are more in Sar and Knn than in Tsou, with which these languages are thought to group); fourth, in a handful of instances, one of these languages evinces both the regular and the irregular reflex; fifth, the irregularity is sporadically attested in Bun and even further afield; sixth, Am evinces the same change in reflexes of at least six protoforms, but only two of the six are the same as those listed for the other languages in Chart Four. In short, these innovations must have resulted from the spread of an innovation across language boundaries. The comparatively small numbers of items involved and the poor attestations in these languages make any further conclusions little more than informed speculations. However, these limited statistics allow us to say tentatively that the innovation began in Sar and spread to the other languages. Further, we believe that the innovation is the change of *s to [h], which subsequently was lost in some of the languages. The change began in a language that had lost PAn *h (e.g., Sar), so that *s was free to change to /h/ without resulting in a merger. From there, the forms with /h/ spread to other languages on an item by item basis. If the change began in one of the currently attested languages other than Sar, it was not carried through. It very likely began in a language or a dialect that is now lost.[81] Alternatively, L. Sagart has suggested (p.c.) that in fact the forms on this chart originally contained *h and that the *h developed palatalization and subsequently merged with *s in the environment of *i in the forebears of the MP languages and the Formosan languages not listed in the chart (Pai, Pu, Ru, Bun, Am, Kav, and the extinct languages of northeast Taiwan). This is a possibility, for most of the forms on the chart are adjacent to /i/and are not in the final syllable of the root. However, some examples have /h/ not in the environment of /i/, but they do have a corresponding /s/ in Kav or Pai, and so forth. Further, there are forms with *h adjacent to an /i/, not in the final syllable of the root, that have not changed the *h > /s/ in Pai and Kav (nor are they reflected with /h/ in the Philippines). An example of this is *bahi 'female'. (This does not have an /s/ anywhere, nor an /h/ in the Philippine languages.)[82] These forms present countercases that make it certain that these aberrant reflexes of *s are indeed aberrant.

A3.3.33 *c

For the phoneme we here reconstruct as *c Tsuchida (1976:127ff.) posited two protophonemes: *s and *θ. This putative additional phoneme is based on data from Knn and Sar compared to data from the Ru languages.[83] Knn and Sar reflect *c sometimes as /s/ and

---

[81] We know from forms cited by Ogawa (2006) that Sar, for example, was dialectally diverse in the early years of the twentieth century, although now with only a handful of speakers left, traces of aberrant dialects have been nearly lost.

[82] The WBM cognate *bahi* 'female' has developed an /h/ in this root as a transitional phenomenon. This /h/ is not carried down from PAn *h. (Cf. the 6th footnote to §A3.3.31)

[83] Tsuchida (1976:127) also states that the difference in the two correspondence sets of Ru, Knn, and Sar corresponds systematically with differences in the reflexes of the same forms in Mlg and Maanyan. This is simply not the case. The number of forms with reflexes of *c found in these languages and also in Sar, Knn, and Ru is small: there are less than thirty, and of those thirty many of them are attested in only one of the Formosan languages, so that it is impossible to draw definitive conclusions. In any case there is no correlation between the

sometimes as ∅ (mostly, but not entirely in the same items). Three of the Ru languages (Maga, Tona, and Budai) sometimes reflect *c with *s*, sometimes with ∅, and sometimes with /θ/. /θ/ does not always occur in all three of these languages when one of them reflects a /θ/. In a couple of cases one or another of the Ru languages has /θ/ where the other two have /s/, e.g., Bud *iθa*'one' Maga *se-sáa.* (For details see §B4.3.23.) To return to Tsuchida's reconstruction of two protophonemes, *s and *θ, where we reconstruct *c: Tsuchida believes that Sar reflects /s/ whenever one of the Ru dialects shows /θ/ and that accounts for the second phoneme, *θ. However, there are only two examples where Sar reflects /s/ and a Ru dialect reflects /θ/. There are other examples of Ru /θ/, but for them no Sar cognate is attested. Further, there are countercases where Knn reflects /s/ in forms cognate with Ru forms with /s/ (rather than /θ/):[84]

**qaceŋ* Knn *maʔasəŋgə*, Budai *b-asəŋgə* (but Sar *maəŋgə* 'sneeze')

As there are only two items that manifest the correspondence of /θ/ in Ru and ∅ in Sar and Knn, the evidence for a protophoneme is slender, all the more so since there are countercases. Tsuchida's reconstruction of two phonemes becomes all the more improbable in view of the fact just mentioned that /θ/ is not consistently reflected over the Ru languages. A final point is that in several cases where Sar and Knn have ∅, Ru languages also have ∅. In short it is highly unlikely that Ru, Sar, and Knn give evidence for another PAn phoneme. Here we hypothesize that the reflex ∅ for *c (as well as /s/) in Sar and Knn, is a sound change not carried through. This hypothesis is strengthened by the fact that, in Sar and Knn, *c and *s fell together and *c is reflected as ∅ in some forms and /s/ in others as much as *s is (§A3.3.32, above). (Cf. §§B31.3.22, B31.3.23, B32.3.22, B32.3.23 for discussion on the development of *s and *c in Sar and Knn.) The question of the origin of /θ/ in Ru is independent of the other two reflexes of *c in Ru. The irregular distribution of /θ/ in the Ru languages could possibly be a retention of an old phoneme *c that had a pronunciation [θ], which in most forms was replaced by /s/ or ∅. The reasoning behind this hypothesis is the articulation of PAn *c: there is evidence that it was pronounced far forward in the mouth (§§A3.2.1, A3.2.2). Since [θ] is further forward than [s], we hypothesize that [θ] reflects the older sound (§B4.3.23). In any case all three Ru phonemes /θ/, /s/, and ∅, reflect only one protophoneme.

A3.3.4 Liquids and nasals

We reconstruct two laterals: a very front lateral *ɬ and a lateral further back, *l, and three nasals *m, *n, and *ŋ. Only the reconstruction of *ɬ requires commentary. In the southwestern and northeastern languages of Taiwan *ɬ falls together with *n, the exception being Am. (See the first note to §A3.3.1, above, for an enumeration of the southwestern and

---

two outcomes of *c in Ru, Sar, and Knn and those in Mlg and Maanyan. Further, Tsuchida goes on to subdivide *s into two further protophonemes, *s and *s_1. *s_1 is solely based on the reflexes of the word for 'nine', here reconstructed as *siwa and *ciwa. The explanation for the existence of two forms is explained in the commentary to *siwa in the glossary, part G.

[84] Both Knn and Sar have two reflexs of *c: ∅ and /s/. Further, the same forms that evince ∅ in Knn also evince ∅ in Sar, and the same forms that evince /s/ in Knn also evince /s/ in Sar. Hence, a correspondence Knn /s/ with Ru /s/ contradicts Tsuchida's hypothsis.

northeastern languages and the southeastern and northwestern languages.) In Am and in the southeastern and northwestern languages, the *ɬ is retained as a separate phoneme: it is changed to a palatalized lateral and develops further from that to a voiceless lateral, and in Tsou, further to /h/. In some dialects *ɬ remained nonpalatal (or lost its palatalization [§A3.2.3, end]). Outside of Taiwan—that is, in the MP languages, the development of *ɬ is complex and requires an elaborated description.

We begin with the easiest case, the final position, and from there proceed to the medial, and then to the initial position, which evinces the most complications. First, final position: *-ɬ falls together with *-n in all MP languages: *bulaɬ 'moon' > Ml *bulan* 'moon, month'. Cf. Th *furaz* 'moon, month', which shows that the final C was *-ɬ.

Second, medial position in the MP languages: *-ɬ- becomes /-ñ-/ in roots with stressed penults, whereas medial *-ɬ- > /-n-/ if the penult is unstressed (short). Compare *qáɬuj and *aɬák: Ml *hanyut* Tag *ánod* (proving a long/stressed penult) 'drift, be carried by the current' but Ml *anak* 'offspring' Tag *anák* 'child' Pu *alak* 'child' (proving *-ɬ-).

Third, initial *ɬ-: *ɬ- becomes †ñ- before a stressed vowel and in a monosyllabic root.[85] It changes before an unstressed vowel, as described in the following paragraph.

> *ɬámuɣ > Ru *ɬamo* 'dew' Ml *nyamur* 'dew drop'; *ɬam 'tasty' > Th *zamzam* 'tasty' Ml *nyam-an* 'tasty' Tag *mali-namnam* 'tasty'.[86]

Further in initial position: *ɬ- in roots with unstressed penults becomes /l-/. There are numerous exceptions to the development of /l-/, and indeed, the further east in the MP languages, the fewer the reflexes of *ɬ with /l-/. However, there are clear cases in which *ɬ is reflected by /l/ in all the MP languages that have reflexes, and these are forms of a character that makes spread by borrowing improbable. An example is the reflexes of *ɬawúŋ. The segmental phonemes can be reconstructed with certainty:

> Th *laun*, St *ɬaong*, Bun *navung*, Pai *ɬaung* 'shadow'.

This same PAn root is reflected in MP languages with metathesis of the onset of the first two syllables:

> Cb *álung* 'cast shadow'[87] Sas *along* 'screened, shaded' Sob *kamalong* 'shadow' Fi *malu* 'be shaded', Sm *malu* 'shade, shelter'

Because of the instability of stress (§A3.5), there are numerous cases of alternative stress patterns in roots that contain initial *ɬ-. This instability yields a reflex of initial /l-/ in some

---

[85] There is some evidence that *ɬ in monosyllabic roots > /l/ in the MP languages under unidentified circumstances. One possibility is that the accent of the monosyllabic root was the determining factor as to whether *ñ >/l/ there or not. For example, *leb and *ɬeb may in fact both be continuations of earlier *ɬeb. The meanings of the attestations are compatible—that is, the meanings reconstructed for *ɬeb and *leb are similar or perhaps identical. Am *loflof* 'inside of house' looks connected with *leb, but has the wrong vowel and is therefore not connected. (See the glossary for attestations.)

[86] As mentioned in §A1.1.32, 4th¶, above, PMP †ñ, which had developed in the environments discussed here, remained /ñ/ in some languages, but changed to /n/ in others. The change to /n/ happened many times independently, for /ñ/ is reflected in only a few languages, but these few languages are found in all the major subgroups across the board.

[87] Evidently Cb moved the stress to the penult when forming a verb from the original nominal root, for the reflex of initial *ɬ as /l/ normally developedf with end stress (cf. the preceding paragraph). Evidently the [w] onset of the original final syllable was weak, so that it was not reflected after being metathesized to initial onset.

languages and initial /ñ-/ or /n-/ in others. For example, *łúka (with stressed penult) produced Cb *núka* 'infected wound' and *łuká (with stressed final syllable as reflected by Tsou *hʔohʔo* 'wound') produced Ml *luka* 'wound'.

The PMP †ñ that developed changed to /n/ (merged with /n/ the reflex of †n) in many languages independently over the entire range of the MP languages:

*qałuj > †qañuj > Tag *ánod* Ml *hanyut* Sal *m-anyuʔ* To *ma-ʔanu* 'drift, be carried by current'

A3.4 The reconstruction of vowels and diphthongs

PAn had four vowels *i, *u, *a, *e. *e was a central vowel [ə]. There were four diphthongs *ay, *aw, *iw, and *uy. The reconstruction of the vowels is straightforward. *i, *u, and *a have very largely remained [i], [u], and [a] in languages located all over the An area except that in many languages they become weakened (centralized) in unstressed position (§A3.5ff, immediately following). Also *i and *u often split into two and even three phonemes apiece from lower allophones. *e remains [ə] in many of the languages outside of Oceania. In Oceania and in many of the western languages, *e migrates to the front or to the back (and sometimes both to the front and the back), becoming [e] and/or [o]. In many cases [e] and [o] merged with the /e/ and /o/ that developed from *ay and *aw respectively. In other languages outside of Oceania, *e independently merged with /i/ or with /a/ or with /u/. The reconstruction of *ay and *aw offers some problems. The question arises whether there were two more diphthongs, *ey and *ew contrasting with *ay and *aw respectively (Ross 1995:72). Evidence for putative *ey and *ew comes from a small subset of languages of Indonesia, certainly in a subgroup as opposed to larger groupings. In Ml, OJv, and ND and also in the closely related languages not studied in detail in this monograph, Sundanese, Madurese, and Balinese, there are multiple correspondences for the set that we may reconstruct for *ay and multiple correspondences for the one we may reconstruct with *aw. Each of these languages manifests only two or at most three reflexes, but they do not match up with each other. That is, OJv, Sundanese, and Balinese reflect *ay as /e/ and /i/, Ml reflects *ay as /ay/ and /i/, ND reflects *ay as /ey/, /e/, and /i/. Since these various reflexes are attested only in a subgroup of western languages, Malcolm Ross (1995:72) and Robert Blust (1995b under *buRaw) independently suggested that it would not be correct to assign the contrast to PAn: it must have developed within the subgroup. However, there is a stronger reason for these reflexes not to be evidence for a PAn contrast. Namely, /i/ is not manifested in the same lexical items in all five languages. Items that reflect /e/ in OJv may reflect /i/ in one or more of the other languages, and mutatis mutandis items that reflect /i/ in OJv may reflect /e/ in one of the other languages or /ai/ in Ml. Although there are a fairly large number of forms that show these correspondences in these languages, only nine can be reconstructed for PAn.[88] Of these, *bahi 'female',[89] *ɣuqáłay 'male', *tay 'dead', *págay 'rice', and *beɣáy 'give' are reflected with final /i/ in all of these languages. *qatáy 'liver' is reflected with final /i/ in three and with final /e/ in Madurese and Sundanese. *áłay 'termite'

[88] There are more than nine forms reconstructed with *ay in these materials, but only nine are attested in these languages.

[89] The reconstruction of this form in PMP must be †bai and when affixed, †-bay. Even though this form is reflected with /i/ in these languages, it is unquestionable that the PMP form was †-bay and not hypothetical †-bey because the PAn reconstruction is without question *bahi. (See the comment under the lemma *bahi.)

is reflected with final /ai/ in Ml and ND with /i/ in OJv. These are very basic forms, well attested throughout the An area, and we take /i/ to be the normal reflex of *ay in Ml, OJv, and ND. For forms that reflect /e/ in all these languages or /ai/ in Ml, there is only one that clearly reflects a PAn etymon: *bay 'hang'. There are two other forms with /e/ and /ai/ in all these languages that are attested throughout the range of the PMP languages: *balay 'building' and a bird name *kanaway. There are numerous other forms found only in languages of Indonesia and the Philippines showing /e/ or /ay/. These have been largely spread by borrowing. Although *bay, and *ałay can be reconstructed for PAn, and *baláy and probably *kanáway , for PMP, the forms with irregular reflexes of *ay are loan words in the languages that have these irregularities.
The hypothesis that there was a contrast of *ew as opposed to *aw is based on data from the same languages as those that provide evidence for the putative reconstruction of *ey and also Chamorro, but there are only two forms of PAn provenience and two not attested in the Formosan languages but widely attested in the MP languages that could provide evidence for this contrast. Normally Ml reflects *aw as /au/ and OJv and Ch reflect it as /o/, but in the following forms /u/ is attested in some of these languages instead:

> *búɣaw > Ml *buru* 'chase' Tag *búgaw* 'chase away' Ch *pugaw* 'cause a flock to scatter', *dánaw 'lake' OJv *ranu* Tag *dánaw* 'lake, pond', †lakáw 'go' Ml *laku* 'for goods to sell', NJv *laku* 'go' Ch *lahu* 'go' Cb *lakáw* 'go, walk', †pánaw OJv *panu* Ml *panaw* 'white splotches on skin' Bkl *pánaw* 'k.o. skin ailment'[90]

/aw/ and /o/ are the normal reflexes of *aw in these languages and when /u/ is attested, there is an explanation in terms of secondary developments (borrowing) but no evidence for the establishment of a contrasting diphthong *ew.

A3.5 Stress and its effects

PAn had roots of one, two, or three syllables. Forms reconstructed with more than three syllables are stems consisting of an affixed root. The stress was free: it could fall on the final syllable, on the penult, or in the case of the trisyllabic roots, on the antepenult. The monosyllabic roots are most often reflected disyllabized (§A3.6.2). In their disyllabic attestation they may reflect end stress or penultimate stress, but there is no basis for assigning the attested stress pattern to a feature of the monosyllabic root of the protolanguage. The same root may appear with penultimate stress (or a reflection of this) in one language and final stress in another, or even with two different stress patterns in the same language. Stress is reconstructed on the basis of stressed reflexes or on the basis of vowel weakening or loss (§A3.5.1, immediately following this section).

A3.5.1 Vowel weakening and syllable loss

Most of the An languages evince syllable weakening or loss as the result of stress. Over the entire range of the An languages from Taiwan through Oceania (but not in all of them), the majority of the reflexes of stems of three or more syllables show a reduction by one syllable. Stems of three or more syllables lose a syllable in one of three ways: (1) loss of the V of the penultimate syllable (the most frequently attested development), (2) loss of the first syllable of the stem, (3) loss of sonority in the final syllable (not frequently attested). An

---

[90] ND, which normally reflects *aw as /aw/, manifests /u/ in *ambu* 'high, top', the second syllable of which reflects *baw.

example of all three processes is the root *paqegu (the reflexes here quoted retain the reconstructed meaning 'gall'): Tag *apdo* (exhibiting the first process), Tdn *peru* (exhibiting the second), and Bun *paqav* (exhibiting the third).[91] In the Philippine languages, the general rule is that the medial syllable is lost if unstressed.

A3.5.2 Reconstruction of stress on the penult or the final syllable

It is unknown to what extent 'stress' consisted of length as well as force of articulation. Since stress is reflected by syllable loss or weakening in languages across the board at some point in their history, force of articulation was certainly a component. However, the An languages differ greatly from one another as to the extent of the syllable weakening that they undergo. As far as is now known, PAn stress is systematically reflected as stress or length only in some of the languages of the Philippines and in Knn among the Formosan languages. In none of the other An languages is PAn stress continued as such systematically. Other languages show a small amount of contrastive stress that is a remnant of PAn stress, but in most cases of languages that have contrastive stress, that stress does not continue stress patterns of PAn uninterruptedly except in marginal cases.[92] Nevertheless, some Formosan languages provide evidence of stress that has been lost, and in many cases that evidence can be compared with cognates in the Philippines and Knn to yield reliable conclusions about the stress pattern of the PAn root.

That said, we must also note that it is impossible to reconstruct stress unequivocally for adjectival and verbal roots for the following reason: stress shift from the penult to the final syllable or from the final to the penult is part of the inflectional/derivational morphology of adjectival and verbal roots in the Philippine languages that have contrastive stress. Stress shift affects nominal roots less than verbal or adjectival roots, but nevertheless nominal roots do in a fairly large number of cases in many languages manifest stress shifts on the basis of analogy. In any case, stress shift led to the analogical creation of roots with a new stress pattern in cases where the stress-shifted form was generalized. For that reason an unequivocal reconstruction of stress is not possible in every case.

As for the evidence of PAn stress from the Formosan languages: the effects of an inherited stress contrast are retained in at least one language in the form of weakened or lost syllables, Tsou. In Tsou the penult is lost if it was unaccented in Post-PAn, but a long penult is retained.[93] An example with short penult in PAn: *ɬaŋúy: Tag *langóy* Tsou *ruu-hngu* 'swim', where Tsou shows loss of the penult in the inherited root. Unfortunately, it is impossible to reconstruct PAn stress on the basis of these rules, for the attestations show inconsistencies: the stress patterns reflected by the Tsou reflexes often do not agree with those of the Philippine cognates. An example is *batu 'stone'. The Philippine languages evince final stress, Tag *bató*, but Tsou *fatu* clearly reflects penultimate stress: *bátu. In the case of *dapaɬ 'foot', the Philippine languages reflect final stress: Ilk *dapán* 'foot'. Tsou reflects

---

[91] Cf. §A3.6.1, 2nd¶, for an account of the development of Bun *paqav*.

[92] TB, for example, has an overwhelming tendency for penultimate stress. However, adjectives as a class have final stress, and in view of the fact that shift of stress to the final syllable is a morpheme marking statives in languages of the Philippines (e.g., Tag *bútas* 'hole, make a hole' *butás* 'perforated'), we may conclude that TB continues a pattern of PMP, and possibly a pattern that remounts to PAn.

[93] The general rule of which this rule is a corollary is as follows: in roots with short penults, every even-numbered syllable counting from the end is lost (the second-to-last, the fourth-to-last, etc.). In roots with long penults, the third to last syllable and every odd-numbered syllable preceding the penult is lost.

penultimate stress: Tsou *caphə* 'sole of foot'. In short, there are many cases in which PAn stress cannot be unequivocally reconstructed.
In most of the An languages, stress is determined by the word. If the word has a one-syllable suffix, the stress moves a syllable to the right, and if the word has a two syllable suffix, the stress moves two syllables to the right. This rule holds, whether stress is contrastive or predictable. Here are three examples, one from Ml, which has no contrastive stress, one from Tsou, which also has no contrastive stress but preserves traces in syncopation, and Tag, which has contrastive stress:[94]

Ml: *mákan 'eat'* + *-an* > *makánan* 'food' Tsou: *mongsi* 'cry' (< *tmongsi, reflecting *táŋic—the final /i/ is an echo vowel), and *tngisi* 'bewail', reflecting *taŋíci (from *taŋic + *i), Tag: *alípin* 'slave' + *-in* > *alipínin* 'enslave' *higáʔ* 'lie down' + *-an* > *higaʔán* 'bed'

A3.5.3 Reconstruction of stress in trisyllabic roots

The stress patterns of trisyllabic roots require special comment. Stress is reconstructed on the final syllable if the attestations in the Philippine languages reflect final stress. When a trisyllabic root had final stress, most An languages also reflect vowel weakening or syllable loss either of the antepenult or of the penult and occasionally of both the penult and the antepenult. If the Philippine languages do not reflect the root or the Philippine cognate has a closed penult (in which case stress contrast is neutralized), vowel weakening provides evidence for final stress placement.[95] For example, *binesíq 'seed' undergoes vowel weakening in the antepenult and subsequent elision of the penult in Bkl, Ml, and many other languages. This is evinced by a [ə] (or a reflex of *e) in the antepenult (which became penult of the attestation): Ml *benih* Bkl *banhiʔ* 'seed rice, seedling'. In the Formosan languages and in many of the MP languages, the antepenult of *binesíq was not weakened, but the penult underwent elision (and subsequent CC simplification in the MP languages) before the antepenult could be weakened. This is evinced by /i/ in the penult of the attestations.

Th *finfiq* 'seed rice' St *binfiq* 'seed' Bun *binsiq* 'millet seed' Pu *vini* 'seed' Rat *βine* 'rice seed' Bug *binee* 'seed' Muna *wine* 'seed, seedling' Mgg *wini* 'seed' ND *biñi* 'seed rice'.[96]

Other examples of trisyllabic roots with final stress are found in the glossary. Here is a partial list of them:

---

[94] In Tagalog the stress pattern of an affixed form may differ from that of the unaffixed form—i.e., stress may be shifted to the right or the left as part of the affix, in which case the rule for stress movement here described is not adhered to.

[95] Languages of areas covering parts of Kalimantan and northern and central Sulawesi do not provide evidence for the reconstruction of antepenultimate stress as opposed to final stress because these languages shifted the antepenultimate stress of trisyllabic roots to the end and then weakened the antepenult.

[96] It could be argued that this root in fact originally had antepenultimate stress and that the Ml and Philippine forms evince stress shift to the final syllable. This is indeed assumed for a number of trisyllabic roots in languages of the Philippines, but there are no roots in Ml for which we assume a shift of stress to the final syllable. If this were to be assumed for Ml, it would be the only example of a Ml form reflecting a trisyllabic root that gives evidence of having undergone stress shift to the final syllable. For this reason we assume that this root had final stress in PAn.

†baheɣát 'heavy' *beɣekéc 'tie into a bundle' *biɣeŋí 'night' *caheɬáɣ 'shine (sun)' *icebú 'urine' *iceɣáb 'yesterday' ††iceɣéd 'shift position, budge, scoot over' ††iceŋét 'sharp, stinging' *iqetáh 'rice husk' iqebéd 'fly' *isecí 'contents *isekám 'weave a mat' *isepí 'dream' *iseyúp 'blow' ††lahuwén 'long time' ††lasuwék 'mix food with staple' *leqacém 'sour' *paheɣáw 'hoarse' *qitelúɣ 'egg' *sehapúy 'fire' *siyuɬúq 'beads' *taquwéɬ 'year' *upiyá 'good'

Stress on the penult of trisyllabic roots is reflected by stressed penults in the languages of the Philippines[97] and often by weakened or lost antepenultimate vowel *e or *a (but not *i or *u). The following list gives some of the trisyllabic roots with stressed penults:

*betíhec 'calf' †buqáya 'crocodile' *daqáɬi 'daytime' *ɣuqáɬay 'man, male' *qalíma 'hand' *sináwa 'breath' *taŋíla 'ear'

Stress is reconstructed in the antepenult with an *a or *e nucleus, if the antepenult is not reflected as weakened in those languages that weaken the antepenult when the stress falls on the end. That is, failure to weaken the antepenult in those languages is an indication that stress originally fell on the antepenult.[98] In the following examples the Fi reflex with /a/ reflects stress on the antepenult, for otherwise the antepenult would have been weakened to /o/ (< *[ə] [§§G3.1.21]):

*bánuwa 'land, place where there is something' Fi *vanua* 'land, region, community'
*jáqewis[99] 'far' Fi *e-sau* 'outside'

The reconstruction of stress of trisyllabic roots in the protolanguage is not without complication. There was a tendency to shift the stress away from the antepenult in all of the daughter languages, and many of the attestations reflect weakening in the antepenult in some languages (reflecting a shift of stress away from the antepenult) or weakening of the penult in others. These changes took place independently in various languages, and not all languages evince the same forms that are weakened, nor the same kinds of weakening. For example, *báqeɣuh 'new' in the languages of Sulawesi, eastern Indonesia and in Moken is reflected with disyllabization and a weakened penult (formerly the antepenult), but languages of Taiwan, Philippines, western Indonesia, and Oceania retain the antepenult unweakened. The stress shifted to the end in the languages that weakened the antepenult (which became the penult when the root disyllabized).

(with retained antepenult, reflecting *báqeɣuh) Tsou *farva* Th *fahɬu* Bun *baqlu* Bkl *baʔgu* Ml *bahru*

(with weakened or lost antepenult, reflecting *baqeɣúh) Tdn *weru* Ba *woʔu* Mgg *weru* Mok *keloy* 'new'

---

97 However, there are cases where Philippine penultimate stress reflects PAn stress on the antepenult. See the discussion at the end of this section.

98 However, as stated in footnote 92, above, some languages of Kalimantan and those of northern and central Sulawesi do not provide evidence because they shifted stress to the end and weakened the antepenultimate vowel subsequently.

99 The weakening of the last syllable in reflexes from all over the MP area is also a reflection of antepenultimate stress:

Tag *ma-láyoʔ* Rat *raw* Ml *jauh* OJv *dwah* 'far'

†láqeya 'ginger' reflects a weakened antepenult in the Philippines as well as in Sulawesi and parts of Kalimantan, but not elsewhere. In a few cases in which the languages of the Philippines manifest penultimate stress, the protoform had stress on the antepenult. In those examples, we conclude that originally the stress had been on the antepenult and then shifted to the penult in the Philippine languages on the basis of the fact that some languages reflect a penult that was elided but others do not and that the antepenult was not lost anywhere. For example, the BM, SL, and Mok citations following evince elision of the penult (reflecting a short penult), whereas there are attestations from the Philippine languages that manifest long penults where the original antepenult is not weakened:

> ††búsaŋin 'sand spit' > Tag *buhángin* 'sand' BM *bungin* 'sandbank at the mouth of a river', *ɣábihi 'night' Cb *gabíʔi* 'night' SL *gabʔi* 'night', *káwayan 'k.o. bamboo' Tag *kawáyan* Mok *kaʔūn* 'bamboo', *qáɬitu 'evil spirit' Cb *anítu* 'benevolent spirit' Mok *katoy* 'evil spirit' (< *qantu)

The following list gives other trisyllabic roots reconstructed with stress on the antepenult where some of the daughter languages evince stress shift:

> *bítuqan/*bítuqen 'star' *líceqes 'louse egg' *páqegu 'gall' *qáɣicam 'plant with reed-like stem' *qáɬegaw 'day, sun' *pálisi 'taboo' *túqelaɬ 'bone'

A3.5.4 Metathesis

Metathesis was an active process in PAn, continuing after the An ancestors began moving around the island and also affecting PMP. There are also processes of metathesis active at the PMP stage that affect the MP languages across the board (cf. §A1.1.32, 3rd¶), and metathesis continues in many languages. The most active language in carrying out metathesis is Leti, but this process is also very widely attested in other near-by languages, including some of Timor.

The most notable case of PAn metathesis was in cases of the verbal affixes *um-,*is-, and *in-. At laest *um- and *is- and possibly also *in- were originally prefixes, and they are reflected as metathesized in all branches of the An family that retain them or traces of them. It should be emphasized that metathesis was not automatic, but that it took place independently in dialects of PAn and in languages of the subgroups after the split-up of PAn. The motivation for metathesis was the accentual pattern of the stem to which the affix was added. Before a monosyllabic root or before a stressed syllable these affixes continued to be prefixes probably with an added epenthetic vowel after the coda to preserve the open syllabic structure of PAn. However, before an unstressed syllable, these prefixes metathesized: *is- > /si-/ and *um- became an infix.[100] *ni- became an infix /-in-/ in some languages. Since the

[100] *-um-* is an infix in so many forms in so many languages (it is a productive part of the verbal inflectional system in many languages) that it is normally assumed to have been an infix in PAn. However, there are petrified cases of *um- as a prefix, and here we assume that *um- was original for the reason that a change of *um- to an infix by metathesis is natural and to be expected. A prefix *um-* violates the canonical form of syllables (§A3.6.1), whereas there is no motivation for the change of an infixed *-um-*to a prefixed *um-*, and certainly no motivation to create a form that violates rules of canonical syllable shape. A similar argument can be made for the primacy of *is- over *si-. Further evidence is given by the fact that in the daughter languages, roots beginning with /p-/ and, in some languages, with /b-/ as well do not occur normally with /-um-/. Instead they substitute /m-/ for the initial /p-/ or /b-/ as an allomorph of this affix (cf. §A3.7.1, 6th¶). Moken happens to provide additional evidence, because the affix *um- played a significant role in the evolution of the Moken root.

affixes were verbal affixes, there was a tendency to generalize one or the other outcome, regardless of the accentual pattern of the root. In the case of *is-, most of the languages of Taiwan reflect /si-/ across the paradigm, but in petrifactions where there is no felt connection with the verbal affix, the accentual rules determine the reflex: e.g., Bun *iskaan* 'fish (lit., the viand, eaten together with the food)' (< *is- + *kan). In the Philippines, on the other hand, the form not metathesized was generalized—that is, the widespread instrumental passive prefix *i-* originates with *is-. Reflexes of *is- that had been metathesized to *si- are sporadically retained in petrified form or even as part of the paradigm in some Philippine languages: e.g., the instrumental passive prefix *hi-* of SL, which occurs with the potential prefixes, e.g., *mahisásaka* 'can be carried up' (= *ma-* 'potential prefix' + *hi-* 'instrumental passive prefix' + reduplication[101] 'future' + *saka* 'go, bring upward').

Similarly, wherever reflexes of *um- have been retained as part of the verbal conjugation, the attested forms show metathesis *(-um-* is an infix), having been spread to the accentual environment where metathesis did not take place. However, in petrified forms where the affix has lost its force, *um- may be reflected as a prefix. The best examples are monosyllabic roots that have become disyllabized by reinterpreting the affix *um- as part of the root, e.g., *pan + *um- > Ml *umpan* 'bait'. Often the nasal cluster that constituted the coda of the prefix plus the initial root consonant gets simplified: *um +*cek > Cb *úsuk* 'drive a stake in' Uma *unco?* 'enter' (*m > /n/ before /c/).

It is the phonology and not the morphology that determines metathesis: the sequence *is- in initial position is widely metathesized under the propitious accentual conditions, whether it is a morpheme or a sequence occurring in another morpheme. The rule is as follows: *is- > /si/ when *s- came to occur before a consonant (as happened when an unstressed *e was lost by elision (§A3.5.1), e.g., *isepi > pre-Paz *ispi > Paz *sipi* 'dream'. Metathesis in this situation does not happen in all languages (because unlike PAn, most of the daughter languages permit consonant clusters). E.g., St *iʃpi* 'dream' reflects elision but no metathesis. Sometimes the antepenult was weakened and lost before the penult was elided—i.e., the *i of the antepenult was lost, leaving a disyllabic root. For example, Pai *sepi 'dream'* reflects the weakening of the antepenult and subsequent loss before elision in the penult had a chance to take place: *isepi > *esepi > *sepi*. Another example is *iseguŋ 'nose', where Tag reflects loss of the penult and simplification of *-sg- (*iseguŋ > *isguŋ > *iguŋ > *ilúng*), whereas Malayo-Javanic languages reflect metathesis (*iseguŋ > *esiguŋ > *siguŋ > OJv *hirung* Ml *hidung*).

This rule of metathesis applies not just to *s, but to all spirants, including those that developed from *c.[102] An initial sequence *ic- was also metathesized before an *e that was lost by sycope. *icebu 'urine' is reflected in Tsou as *sifu* 'urine' (< *ecibu) but is reflected as

---

The shape of the PAn morpheme *um- and its development in Moken are discussed and exemplified more extensively in part E, chapter 3, §§E3.1.211–E3.1.213.

[101] The term REDUPLICATION, abbreviated 'R' in this study refers specifically to the repetition of the first syllable of the root or stem. This is in contrast to the term DOUBLING, which we use here to refer specifically to the repetition of the entire stem or root. E.g., Tag reduplication: *pá-pásuk* 'will enter' (R + *pásuk*); doubling: *dala-dala* 'bringing' (root: *dala* 'bring').

[102] In fact we have not reconstructed any examples of *ih- before a root beginning with a consonant, but there is no reason to believe that *h- behaved differently from the other spirants.

St *-hbœ?* 'urine' (where the loss of the vowel of the penult reflects an earlier *e—i.e., *icebú > *ecebú > *cbu > *hbœ?*).[103]
These phonological rules decisively support the hypothesis that the instrumental passive prefix *is- was the original form and *si- the metathesized allomorph. There is counterevidence, however: namely, this prefix occurs also as a verbal root in At and Ts, as a reflex of *si: At *sumi* (= *-um-* + *si*) 'put' Tsou *mosi* 'put'. (< *um- + *si*). The verbal function of this morpheme is surely prior to its function as an affix. Therefore, we must reconstruct *is for the verb as well as for the affix. This presents an unresolved paradox: why did the verb root *is metathesize to /si/ in Atayalic and Tsou? There is no motivation for metathesis of the verb as there is for the prefix, for there are no suffixes beginning with a consonant. Yet the order *is must be the original, and as the root of a verb it metathesized to /si/.[104]

A3.6 Canonical forms

Canonical form—the canonical shape of the root and syllable, play an important role in the development of PAn phonology in the daughter languages. Not only is a community constrained to make forms conform to existing phonological patterns, but there is a tendency for a community to change infrequent but permissible patterns or shapes to conform to ones that are more frequent (Hay et al. 2003).

A3.6.1 Syllable types

The evidence for syllable types is unequivocal in the case of root-initial and root-final syllables. The case of the medial syllables requires discussion. Root-initial syllables had the shape (C)V—that is, they had open coda and may or may not have C onset. Root-medial syllables likewise had open codas but obligatorily had C onset. Final syllables likewise had obligatory C onset and could either be open or end in a consonant. A disyllabic root thus had a structure (C)VCV(C) and a trisyllabic root had a structure (C)VCVCV(C). A corollary of this is that there were no consonant and no vowel sequences within the root.[105] However, because of the process of syllable elision, discussed in §A3.5.1, the daughter languages largely show medial consonant clusters. In other words, if a CC is reflected in the daughter languages, we hypothesize that that reflects *CVC—i.e., that a vowel had been lost, and that the cluster was not inherited from the protolanguage. If a cognate of the attestation with CC manifests CVC, we hypothesize that the attestation with CVC continues the PAn structure. For example, here we reconstruct *paqegú 'gall'. Should this have been reconstructed *paqgu?—i.e., was the /e/ of Ml *hampedú* 'gall' inserted by epenthesis or is it inherited? and

---

[103] It is remotely possible that the trisyllabic roots that we recontruct with initial *i- and with *e as the penultimate vowel in fact contained a prefix *i- and that the forms reflecting /e/ in the penult are reflexes of the unaffixed root, whereas the forms reflecting /i/ in the penult are reflexes of the affixed root. This is only a remote possibility because I have not been able to identify this prefix. *icebu discussed here is an example: St *-hbœ?* 'urine' reflects *cebu, but Tsou *sifu* reflects *icebu.

[104] One possible answer is that the verb *is typically occurred in a phrase consisting of two verbs—i.e., was the first word of a serial-verb phrase, and as such may have been procliticized and may most commonly have occurred before a root beginning with a consonant.

[105] A glance at the glossary will give the impression that nasal clusters did in fact exist. But this is only the case for PMP, not for PAn. None of the forms listed in the glossary with a nasal cluster have a cognate reflex in the Formosan languages, and therefore, a nasal cluster cannot be reconstructed for PAn. Further, many forms with a medial nasal cluster developed in PMP—that is, many PAn forms developed nasal clusters in one or more of the MP languages (§A3.7.2, below). Nasal clusters also developed in some of the languages of Taiwan. Bun, Thao, and St have roots with nasal clusters (as well as other clusters).

does Tag *apdó* 'gall' reflect loss of the medial penultimate vowel or was the root disyllabic in PAn? The question arises in the cases where the medial vowel of the penult was *e or if it was *i before *y or *u before *w, and also it arises in the case of doubled monosyllabic roots. If the vowel of the penult of trisyllabic roots was other than *e, the penultimate vowel of the root not subject to elision in at least some of the daughter languages. The middle part of the root is reflected as CVC in the daughter languages (CV́C in the Philippine languages that continue PAn stress patterns).

The best support for our hypothesis—i.e., the best evidence for reconstructing trisyllabic roots with short medial vowels rather than CC's comes from the process of vowel weakening in the antepenult (§A3.5.1). Reflexes that manifest consonant sequences in some daughter languages are cognate with reflexes in other daughter languages where the vowel of the first syllable is weakened. Thus Ml has weakened the vowel of the first syllable in the following example: *banuwá > Ml *benúa* 'continent' [106] Cb *bánwa* 'fatherland, town'. In some cases a reflex of the penultimate *e is retained because the final syllable has lost its sonority, e.g., *paqegu > Bun *paqav* 'gall' (*paqegú > *paqeú > *paqáu > *páqav*). Similarly, doubled monosyllabic roots had an *e inserted between the repeated monosyllables (as is still the case in the Tsouic, Atayalic and Ru languages). In Ml, this is reflected by the fact that the first syllable of Ml reflexes of doubled monosyllabic roots with /a/ are weakened: *tacetác > Ml *tetas* 'slitting, ripping up' Tag *tastás* 'undone (stiches)'. The weakening of the vowel of the first syllable of the root in Ml indicates an earlier *tacetác. It is not likely that the *tacetác that preceded Ml *tetas* developed from an earlier disyllabic and then underwent epenthesis of [ə]. The reason for this is that in several of the Formosan and Philippine languages, there are cases in which the medial vowel between the doubled monosyllabic elements fails to get lost. In the languages that have retained stress contrasts, an epenthetic vowel in doubled monosyllabic forms is always stressed. An example of this is *sapésap Bun *sapsap* 'grope' SL *hapúhap* 'look for by groping'. (Cf. examples in parts B–G in the discussion of developments of the reduplicated monosyllabic roots in the histories of the individual languages.)

We also reconstruct /w/ and /y/ glides between front and back vowels. There is no evidence for a contrast between a glide and its absence in PAn. We assume that there were no front-back or back-front vowel sequences because no other vowel sequences can be reconstructed.[107] No clusters are reconstructed initially or finally in a root, nor is there any evidence that would lead to the reconstruction of such sequences.

---

[106] Weakening of the antepenultimate vowel is the general rule in Ml, but if that vowel was protected by a nasal (intercalated by the process described in §A3.7.2), it was not weakened. For example, *i and *a are not weakened in the following cases: *bituqén >*bíntuqen > *bíntang* 'star', *paqegú > *hampedú* 'gall' (< *qapegu).

[107] PAn did not contrast the presence and absence of a glide between a front and a back vowel—i.e., between [awu] and [au], [ayi] and [ai], [uwa] and [ua], etc. We assume here that PAn sequences involving front and back vowels had glides phonemically—i.e., sequences involving front and back vowels should be reconstructed with *awu, *ayi, *uwa, etc. However, there is some evidence to throw doubt on this point. The form *ɬawuŋ 'shade' is reflected with metathesis in the MP languages, but the metathesized form has initial /a/—i.e., *ɬawuŋ > *Øaɬuŋ, an indication that the correct reconstruction must have been *ɬaØuŋ [*ɬauŋ]. Here we reject this conclusion—i.e., assume no syllables with vocalic onset. Rather we hypothesize that the *-w- was lost in metathesis (cf. §A3.3.4, 3rd footnote). The reason for this assumption is that, in the languages of the Philippines and Taiwan with which I have worked firsthand, the w-glide is clearly audible in forms containing /a/ adjacent to /u/ and a y-glide is audible in forms containing /a/ adjacent to /i/. Articulatory characteristics of such a wide range of languages belonging to different primary subgroups surely also characterized PAn.

A3.6.2 Root shapes

PAn had roots of one, two and three syllables. Protoforms consisting of more than three syllables in fact contained affixes. Many of the trisyllabic roots in the glossary are composed of a disyllabic root plus a petrified affix, and a number of the disyllabic roots are composed of a monosyllabic root plus a petrified affix (cf. §A3.6.3). The tendency in the development of the daughter languages across the board with only sporadic exceptions[108] is to form disyllabic roots, and since this phenomenon is spread throughout the area, it must be concluded that this tendency existed also in PAn—that is, the forces that led to the formation of disyllabic roots from longer or shorter roots were present in PAn. Some of the daughter languages located on Taiwan and among the western MP languages developed canonical trisyllabic roots when they developed open syllables by accreting echo vowels after syllable final consonants.[109]

First, we discuss monosyllabic roots. In a few cases, monosyllabic roots have been inherited in some of the daughter languages. For example, *lum 'ripe' is inherited in most cases as a monosyllabic root and has doubtlessly never been disyllabized in the languages that attest it as a monosyllabic root:

> *lum 'ripe Ru(Bd) *ma-ləmə* 'ripe' (the final /-ə/ is an echo vowel automatically added to all word endings [§B4.1.3]) Pu *ma-rum* 'dry' Pai *ma-lum* 'ripe' Ml *lum* in *masak lum* 'overripe'

*lum was also disyllabized by stretching the nucleus as in Ilk *na-luʔum* 'ripe'

Similarly OJv *gem* 'hold' is probably derived directly from a PAn monosyllabic root, although most attestations show disyllabization. However, not every monosyllabic reflex of a monosyllabic root in a daughter language was directly inherited. Most of these had been disyllabized and subsequently changed back to a monosyllabic root. This is widely attested in the Oceanic languages as a result of the process of weakening the first syllable of a disyllabic root consisting of a reduplicated syllable. If there is no attestation of a monosyllabic reflex in a language outside of Oceania, we assume that the Oceanic monosyllabic root developed from a disyllabic root. For example, *bacebac$_2$ 'strike' is reflected in Sm as *fas-i* 'beat (a child), kill an animal' but outside of Oceania, as a doubled syllable, e.g., Am *facfac* 'beat'. The monosyllabic root in Sm developed by shortening the reflex of *bacebac.

There are three processes that affected monosyllabic roots to disyllabize them: (1) adding a prothetic vowel or stretching the nucleus, (2) doubling the root or reduplicating it, or (3) petrifying an affixed form. The root *cek 'crammed in, squeezed into a recess' shows all three processes (and is also widely retained as a monosyllabic root): (1) Sal *osso?* 'crowded together with little room'. This form derives from *ecek with a prothetic vowel added to the monosyllabic root. Cb disyllabized the root by stretching the vowel nucleus. Subsequently a

[108] An exception among the languages studied here in detail are the Tsouic languages, which, although they disyllabize monosyllabic roots (§§B31.1.1 and B32.1.1), retain trisyllabic roots as such and in fact tend to add a syllable to disyllabic roots.

[109] The languages in which this occurred are not contiguous, nor is there reason to think that they constitute a subgroup. A partial listing: Tsouic languages, the Ru languages, many of the Sangiric languages, Gor, languages of southeast Sulawesi, Mlg. It is possible that this phenomenon in the Formosan languages is in fact an inheritance of a characteristic of PAn, rather than a development, for we posit open syllables for PAn (§A3.6.1, above). However, in the MP languages there is internal evidence that the open syllables developed in post-PAn times. It must also be mentioned that open syllables developed in many languages by the loss of syllable final consonants (simplification of C sequences internally and loss of word-final consonants).

glottal stop was inserted between the two moras: *suʔúk* 'remote corner, being deep inside' (2) Am and Ml disyllabize this root by doubling it and in the case of Ml, subsequently simplifying the CC that had developed: Am *cekcek* 'stab' Ml *sesak* 'crammed full, packed tight'. Various languages disyllabize the monosyllabic root by adding an affix that was subsequently petrified and made part of the root. Here are three examples of well-attested affixes added to *cek to form disyllabic roots in the current languages. The semantic force of the affix is clear from the meaning that the attested root has: Am *pacek* 'nail' (< *cek plus a petrified occurrence of the causative affix *pa-), Ttb *isek* 'press down to make compact' (< *cek plus a petrified occurrence of the instrumental passive affix *is-), Cb *úsuk* 'drive stakes into the ground' (< *um- 'active dynamic verb affix' added to *cek).[110] The hypothesis that assumes formation of the disyllabic root by stretching the nucleus is amply supported by the large number of semantically related forms that manifest this process. It is this process, for example, that accounts for various reflexes of *kan (cf. the glossary under *kan and the immediately following entries for complete illustration): Cb *káʔun*, Bun *kaʔun,* Tdn *kaʔan* 'eat', all of which independently stretched the vowel nucleus (in different ways producing otherwise noncorresponding vowels)[111] and intercalated a glottal stop between the vowel sequence that had developed. These reflexes can be related to forms that reflect a monosyllabic root and those that reflect a root plus petrified affixation: Ml *makan* (from *kan to which prefixes that are now no longer productive in Ml, *um- plus *pa-, had been added) and To *kai* 'eat' (from *-i added to *ka-, which developed when the root-final C was lost).[112]

A3.6.3 Reconstruction of the second syllable of a root where the first syllable is unknown

There are numerous cases of attested forms that resemble each other in meaning but correspond only in the final syllable (Blust 1988, Wolff 2007b). In some cases, the first syllable corresponds to a well-attested prefix, e.g., *tay 'die', which is attested reflecting *pa-, *ma- (< *um- + *pa- [§A3.7.1, 6th ¶, below]), as well as other affixes. There are other cases where the initial syllables of the roots cannot be reconstructed as the reflex of a PAn prefix—i.e., data simply have not come to light that would attest to petrified prefixes. In most such cases, no such data will ever come to light, for the attested forms have been created by the analogical process whereby an existing form is reshaped to conform to another form of

[110] Stress on the penult of Cb *úsuk* indicates that the origin of the first syllable is the prefix *um- rather than a prothetic vowel. The loss of the *m of this prefix is normal over the entire An language range. In fact this affix rarely retains the *m when added to monosyllabic roots. The semantics strongly support the hypothesis that the first syllable of this Cb root derives from *um-: the monosyllabic root had a stative meaning 'crammed, packed tight'. When *um- is added to this, the result would mean 'to pack tight'. This became specialized in Cb to mean 'drive stakes'. Further support is given by the Uma cognate *uncuk* 'push through a crowd', which preserves the nasal coda of the prefix.

[111] This root is commonly referred to in the literature as having two variants in PAn, *kan and *kaen, or it is assumed that the PAn form was *kaen and that contraction took place independently in the various daughter languages. However, two factors speak against the reconstruction of *kaen: first, nucleus stretching is manifested in many, many languages and in many roots; second, stretching takes place in different ways—that is, the nucleus is stretched to [aa] as well as to [ae]. Accordingly, one would have to reconstruct *kaan as well as *kaen to account for the different reflexes of this root in the languages of Taiwan, Philippines, and Sulawesi. The only reasonable conclusion is that the root was *kan and the process of nucleus stretching took place independently in languages of Taiwan and in languages further south.

[112] The following list gives some of the other entries for which daughter languages reflect nucleus lengthening: *cuk, *ɣiq, *lit₁, *kut, *luk, *lum, *pan, *pit, *tan, *tun.

similar meaning or by sound symbolism (§A3.8, below).[113] In almost all of these cases, there is independent evidence that the final syllable is descended from a monosyllabic root: there are reflexes cognate with these cases that manifest one of the processes described in §A3.6.2 above. An example is the root *pit, which has a reflex in Cb *piʔút* 'narrow'. (This root developed in Cb by stretching the nucleus of the monosyllabic root.) Hence the following forms contain a final syllable inherited from PAn even though the first syllables of these forms are not connectable:

> Bug *seppi* 'be pressed between' Ml *sempit* 'narrow' Kav *sipit* 'pinch between the fingers and twist' Rat *sipiʔ* 'pinch off'[114] Ml *sumpit* 'chopsticks' Tag *lápit* 'near' Ml *jepit* 'nip' Am *ʔalapit* 'tweezers', etc.

These forms do not derive directly from a PAn disyllabic root. They were probably formed in post-PAn times. Possibly some were formed by the addition of affixes that became petrified, but the majority were probably created by sound symbolism—i.e., they were created by the analogical processes whereby an existing form is changed to make it conform phonologically to a word with a similar meaning (§A3.8, below). For example, Ml *jepit* derives from an earlier *kepit, which is no longer attested in Ml, but which is reflected widely over the MP area and probably derives from *pit plus a weakened form of the well-reconstructed prefix *ka-. In this case the earlier *kepit became changed to *jepit* under the influence of other words beginning with an affricate referring to pinching and the like: *cubit, cebit, cepit* 'pinch', *jemput* 'pick up in the fingers'. *pit was clearly a monosyllabic root, and other forms were derived from it by analogical processes or by the disyllabization processes described above.

In most of these cases, independent evidence has turned up for the existence of the second syllable as a monosyllabic root, but there are a few cases for which no such evidence has turned up (but even in these cases, evidence is waiting to be discovered). How such sequences may be formed by analogy is discussed below (§A3.8, 2nd¶). The reconstructed form *kec is an example of a monosyllabic element that is well attested as the second syllable and has a connectable meaning all across the range of the An languages, but there is no evidence that this was a monosyllabic root. None (or practically none) of the attested first syllables are descended from a known PAn prefix, and the second syllable occurs in no form that indicates descent from a monosyllabic root: there is no example of root lengthening (by prothesis or nucleus stretching) and no doubling or reduplication. All of these forms have a meaning of 'bind around' in common:

> Am *fakec* 'belt' Cb *bakús* 'belt' Savu *wake* 'tie around waist' Mlg *vahy* 'plants used for winding, making into rope' Cb *gakús* 'embrace' Bun *malukus* 'tie up' Tag *bigkis* 'bundle' Ml *berkas* 'bundle' Tdn *waʔkes* 'bundle' Sa *hoʔosi* 'bind' Am *takec* 'embrace', Kadazan *tagkos* 'bundle', etc.

---

[113] It is also possible that some of these forms descend from old compounds or even phrases. The extreme reduction of complex forms consisting of several morphemes in the case of *pitu '7', *walu '8', and *siwa '9', as discussed in the glossary under these entries, is evidence that extreme reduction of complex forms was an active process over the span of PAn times. In other words, in some of these cases of disyllabic roots resembling each other only in the final syllables, the first syllables may well have developed from independent roots. No evidence for an example of this process has been discovered, but it is very possible that a more careful examination of attestations, especially in the Formosan languages, will reveal examples of this phenomenon.

[114] Kav *sipit* and Ru *sipiʔ* may in fact contain a petrifaction of the instrumental passive prefix *ise- metathesized to *si- (§A3.5.4, 4th¶).

Normally a correspondence of final syllables with a semantic element in common in various daughter languages is taken to be sufficient for reconstructing a monosyllabic protoroot if one of two conditions are met: (1) when the first syllable of the attestations can be connected with an attested prefix or (2) when there is evidence that the process of disyllabization, as described in §A3.6.2, above, has taken place in one or more of the daughter languages. If these conditions are not met, but the second syllable is widely attested, as is the case of *kec, the form is listed in the glossary with brackets rather than with an asterisk or dagger, an indication that the monosyllabic root never existed (or at lest, no evidence has been discovered for its existence), but that the forms reflecting the monosyllabic element were created by some sort of analogy.[115]

There are times when there is a good possibility that the corresponding final syllable came into being independently in various languages and is therefore not traceable to a protolanguage. Such forms are not listed in the glossary. These are cases of onomotopoeia, where the form is iconic of the reference. Examples are as follows (from Blust 1988): *geng* 'hum, buzz', *ger* 'shake, shiver, tremble', *gik* 'shrill throaty sound', *guk* 'deep, throaty sound', *gung* 'deep, resounding sound', etc.

A3.6.31 Forms of three or more syllables in which only the penult and the final syllable correspond

Just as there are attested roots for which only the final syllable corresponds in various languages, so are there forms of more than two syllables for which only the final two syllables correspond. Again, these initial sequences may be petrified prefixes or remnants of an independent root compounded with the root attested by the final two syllables, but in most cases there are no data that provide evidence indicating that these sequences are prefixes or independent morphemes. Such forms are listed in the glossary preceded by a dash. An example is the word for 'thin' *-sebic, which occurs across the range of the An languages with a prefix *ɬi-, and also with the same meaning in Am with a prefix *ko-*, as well as with a variety of other prefixed sequences to form roots with closely related meanings. Another example is the word for 'egg' *-iteluɣ the reflexes of which in three languages from Taiwan reflect a prefixed sequence *bV- (discussed in §A2.1, 1st¶, above).

In many cases of this sort, however, there is a good possibility that the forms spread secondarily—that is, came into the daughter languages in post-PAn times and did not necessarily exist in the protolanguage. Most of these terms refer to flora and fauna, but some refer to cultural items. An example is *lali 'flute'(§A2.5), which often shows up together with an unexplained prefix or other unexplained sequences, even though *lali itself is regularly reflected in languages across the board from Taiwan to Oceania.

A3.7 Morphophonemic processes that influence the development of roots

A3.7.1 Nasalization and the affix *um-

PAn had a morphophonemic process of nasalization of the initial consonant of the root—that is, the substitution of an initial homorganic nasal for an initial stop consonant of

[115] Another example of how these monosyllabic elements may develop by analogical processes is the syllable *ɣet, discussed in §A3.8, 3rd¶, below.

the root.[116] This process after a prefix *pa-* is currently productive in many of the languages of the Philippines and in languages of Indonesia located in Sulawesi and westward. (The prefix *pa-* often is attested as part of a portmanteau morph that contains other morphemes.) Further east and in Oceania, nasalization is well attested in petrified form. For example, the root *kan 'eat' is widely reflected with a prefix *pa-* plus nasalization of the first consonant of the root, *paŋan: OJv *pangan* 'eat, food', Sa *hanga* 'eat', To *fanga* 'feed'. In the languages of Taiwan, traces of this process are extremely rare. Attestations that reflect this phenomenon for certain are listed for the following roots:

> *kayaw: Pu *mangayaw* 'head hunting', *qetaq: At *qataq* 'eat raw' Ru *mangeta* Am *mangtaq* 'raw' *simantaq* 'eat raw',*taɣa: At *mnaɣa* 'wait' Sed *tmaga* 'wait' St *may-nala?* 'wait' Paz *taxa* 'wait' Bun *mi-tala* 'ambush', *taqu: Pu *manaqu* 'see' (cf. Ml *tahu* 'know'), and *tukub: Kav *mnukub* 'cover' Bun *matukub* 'cover'.

This process also occurs without *pa-* and is important for the reconstruction of PAn in order to attest to the cognation between roots with initial stops and roots with initial nasals. Roots with a nasal cognate with a root having a nonnasal are listed together in the glossary with the nonnasal form first. Here are some examples of disyllabic roots with nasalization without *pa-*.

> *cabuq and *ɬábuq/ɬabúq: Kadazan *savu* 'anchor' Wolio *sabu* 'jump down, drop' Fi *savu* 'fall like a waterfall' To *hafu* 'trickle down', and Kpp *nabuq* 'fall' BM *labuq* 'fall' Uma *nawuq* 'fall' Ml *labuh* 'anchor' Mok *labuk* 'fall down' Buli *nawu* 'fall'

> *ceɣab and ɬeɣab:[117] At *hira?* Th *tiɬa* Kav *sirab* 'yesterday' Ifg *k-ugab* 'evening meal' and Kadazan *ko-niab* Bantik *ka-nehab-a?* Fi (Bauan) *ena-noa* Sa *no-nola* 'yesterday'

The following roots of two or more syllables are attested with nasalization. The nasalization may be attested in any of the An languages. In some cases the majority of the attestations reflect nasalization, but in some cases the nasalization is confined to forms in only a few languages.

> *cacuk and *ɬacuk 'boil', *camuk and *ɬamuk 'mosquito', *ceket and *ɬeket 'stick', *dagam and *ɬagam 'tame',[118] *dakis and *nakis 'up', *damaɣ 'light, torch' and *ɬamaɣ 'fire, burn', *ipen and *ŋipen 'tooth',[119] *iseguŋ 'nose' and *ŋiseguŋ 'nose', *qagan and

---

[116] The PAn process can be reconstructed to be very similar to that current in the Philippines: *p, *b > *m; *t, *d > *n; *c > *ɬ; *k, *q, and vowel initial > *ŋ. *s is nasalized as *ɬ in forms that can be traced to PAn, but roots with reflexes of *s that cannot be traced to PAn are nasalized with *ŋ. (We have found no examples containing the other phonemes with nasalization.) Note that the term "nasalization" here is used rather broadly to include a change to a lateral in the case of *c and *s. The 'nasalization' of *c amounts to the change to a nasal in most of the currently spoken An languages, but in PAn and in most of the Formosan languages the nasalization process results in a lateral.

[117] Some of the attestations reflect *iceɣab and *iɬeɣab—i.e., the locative preposition *i was prefixed to the root, and the resulting form was subsequently metathesized. See §A3.5.4, 4th¶ for an explanation for the reflex of *i in the first syllable in some languages and *e in others.

[118] Only Paz and Favorlang from northwest Taiwan reflect *d-. All other attestations reflect nasalization. Remarkably, the nasalization results in *ɬ in most languages rather than the expected *n. However, in Am, Pu, and Pai, the initial nasal is /n/. The explanation of these irregular reflexes is that the nasalized forms spread secondarily. *damaɣ also has a nasalized alternant with *ɬ.

[119] Inexplicably several roots with initial vowel or *qV- show nasal phonemes other than /ŋ/ in some of their reflexes: *ipen > Paz *lepeng* Kel *lipen* Mok *lèpan* 'tooth' (< *ɬipen) To *nifo* 'tooth' (< *nipen), *uda > Am

> *ŋagan 'name', *qaluɬ and *ŋaluɬ 'wave', *useɣ and *ŋuseɣ 'nasal mucus', *uda and *ŋuda 'young'

This process is also attested with monosyllabic roots:

> *paq and *mamaq (*ma-maq): Am *paʔpaʔ* 'chew' Cb *paʔpaʔ* 'take hold with teeth' OJv *se-pah* 'chewed food, quid', and Cb *mamáʔ* Ml *mamah* 'chew quid' Fi *mama* 'chew'

> *pec and *mec: Pu *t-pec* 'deflated, as a balloon' Pai *se-pet* 'wring out' Bal *tepes* 'squeeze, press, pinch' and Am *mecmec* 'crumple (like a piece of paper)' Kan *mesmes* 'press, squeeze' Leti *ko-mas* 'squeeze'

> *dem and *nem: Ru *ki-ḍəmə-ḍmə* 'think, worried' Pu *demdem* 'heart, feelings' Cb *dumdum* 'remember' Ml *dendam* 'yearning from love or spite' Nggela *ando* 'think' and Kav *anem* 'mind, heart' Pai *ki-nemnem* 'think' Ilk *pa-nemnem-en* 'consider it' Kei *fang-nan* 'remember' Mota *nonom* 'think'

Other examples of monosyllabic roots that are subject to nasalization are the following: *cep/*ɬep, *pak/*mak, *pek/*mek, *puŋ/*muŋ, *teŋ/*neŋ (cf. the attestations in the glossary).

There is a similar process involving the affix *um-. Namely, reflexes of *um- in the daughter languages have a special allomorph when it is added to roots with /p-/ and in some languages also to roots with /b-/: when *um- is added to a root or stem beginning with /p-/ (or /b-/), the /p-/ (or /b-/) is replaced by /m-/:

> PAn *patay 'dead' + *um- 'verb-forming affix' > *matay 'die'; Tag *palíguʔ* + *-um-* > *malíguʔ* 'bathe'; BM *bayaʔ* + *-um-* > *mayaʔ* 'go'

Thus, the alternations between initial *p- and *m- as discussed immediately above may in fact involve the affix *um- rather than the nasalization process. There is another upshot of this morphophonemic process: namely, when the affix *um-* is added to a root with an initial vowel, the affix has the alternate form /m-/. The *u has become lost by elision—§A3.5.1. Consequently, a form beginning with /m-/ may contain a root with an initial vowel or an initial /p-/. This is the basis for the analogical process that allows the addition of /p-/ to a root beginning with a vowel. An example of this process that took place early (in the protolanguage of nearly all, if not all, An languages):

> *uɬa and *puɬa: Paz ulah 'go first' St minsaʔ-ɬaʔ 'first' Tag úna 'go first' Leti una 'begin' Ral mun 'first, formerly'

> (reflecting *puɬa) BM punang 'source, origin, cause' ND puna 'actually, the real thing' Ral vuna 'beginning, source' Sm puna 'spring, source'

A3.7.2 Nasal accretion of medial consonants

The two processes of nasalization discussed in §A3.7.1, above, should not be confused with nasal accretion (tantamount historically to prenasalization) that affects medial consonants in the An languages of Indonesia and the Philippines, nor with the nasal accretion of Oceanic languages (§G0.1). Many attested forms in the western MP languages manifest

---

moraʔ 'immature' Ml *muda* Buru *mura-n* 'young', *useɣ > SL *muhúg* 'nasal mucus', *qagan > Chmr *naʔan* 'name'.

nasal accretion before the medial consonant in one or more languages, where the cognate reflex in other An languages shows no nasal. The attestation of nasalization is sporadic and most widespread in OJv in our languages, but it is found widely in the other MP languages of the western group that we study here. It is assumed here that the nasal accretion arises from subphonemic nasalization of the vowel carried over into the articulation of the initial C of the succeeding syllable. Examples of this process are noted in the glossary with a reference to this section. In languages of eastern Indonesia and further east, nasal accretion also may affect word-initial syllables.

A3.8 Sound symbolism

Sound symbolism had an important role in the development of the An languages. There are two aspects of this: first is 'contamination'—the notion that forms similar in meaning tend to influence each other. Thus, for example, ND *jela* 'tongue' has initial /j/ instead of the expected /d/ (if it is to correspond with Ml *lidah* 'tongue' or Ru *uḍila* 'lick'). The explanation is that it is contaminated by (or influenced by) *jelap* 'play with the tongue'. Second, is onomotopoeia. Certains sounds are iconic: they represent their reference directly. For example, *tuketuk refers to the sound of tapping 'tuk'. Similarly, a form with a higher vowel may refer to something lesser (smaller, weaker) or sharper and more focused than a similar form that has a lower vowel in place of the higher vowel. Thus, for example, *pikepik 'sound of patting or tapping' was developed from *pakepak 'the sound of flapping or slapping'. *pikepik refers to a smaller, higher-pitched sound than *pakepak. Simlarly the form *ɬikeɬik 'stinging insect' developed from *ɬekeɬek 'midge, gnat'. The insect referred to by *ɬikeɬik produced a sharp, penetrating, focused pain as opposed to the *ɬekeɬek that was a broader, less-sharp, less-focused nuisance.

Contamination accounts for many of the forms attested in the An languages that resemble each other in the second syllable, but not in the first (§A3.6.3, above). For example, Cb *pukáng* (a euphemism for *púki?* 'vagina') was formed from *pukí?* on the analogy of other roots that end in /kang/ that refer to the area between the legs: Cb *bakáng* 'bow-legged', *kangkang* 'spread the legs', *lákang* 'step across', *tikangkang* 'lie or lean on back and spread the legs'. Although we have hypotheses to account for a portion of the creations of this sort that are found in the data, for the vast majority of these analogical creations, the research has not been done to uncover the source of the creations. In some cases the data are probably unrecoverable.

An example of how sequences that resemble monosyllabic roots may develop by analogical processes in the first syllable is the sequence *ɣet. No root [ɣet] can be reconstructed for PAn. The starting point for this syllable was *keɣet 'cut off', well attested from northern Taiwan to the Solomons. Other forms ending in a reflex of *ɣet were developed on the basis of *keɣet. For example, Cb *punggut* 'cut off head' developed on the influence of the many Cb forms beginning in /pung/ that have a meaning of 'sever, cut off', e.g., *púngal* 'break off s.t. firmly attached', *pungdul* 'blunt ended', *punggak* 'knock off from attachment', *pungkul* 'amputated, amputee'. There can be no doubt that this is the origin of Cb *punggut* even though no reflex of *keɣet is found in Cb, for *keɣet has reflexes in other languages of the Philippines, e.g., Bontoc *kelet* 'cut hair'. Cases of similar processes are widespread over the range of the An languages.

A monosyllabic root may be the starting point for the creation of a 'quasi-prefix', as exemplified by Cb /pung/ in the paragraph immediately preceding. An example of the creation of such a quasi-prefix is the syllable /le-/. This sequence is found in a dozen or more forms that occur in languages of an early subgroup. For example, ††lekaŋ 'become separated', reconstructed for Proto-Hesperonesian; †lekaq 'split open', reconstructed for PMP; and *lepac 'get free', reconstructed for PAn. There is also a form [letas] 'separate', which, as far as I know, does not have cognates outside of the Philippines and probably was formed on analogy to *lepac. One of these forms (possibly *lepac) provided the model whereby the others replaced the first syllable of roots ending in *kaŋ, *kaq, and *tac with *le-. Examples are as follows. Reflecting ††lekaŋ:

> Ilk *lekkang* 'separate' Kayan *lekang* 'gap' Mgg *lekang* 'separate' Ml *lekang* 'bursting, cracking under influence of heat'

Reflecting †lekaq 'split open':

> Mar *leka?* 'open' Tae' *lakka* 'split, burst' Muna *lengka* 'open' Sika *leka* 'split' Ml *lekah* 'split' NJv *plekah* 'crack, split' Arosi *roka* 'open, unfolded'

Reflecting *lepac: 'get free'

> Th *raput* 'get free, escape' Tag *alpas* 'free' Bar *lapa* 'get free' Bug *leppe?* 'free' Sal *lappasa* 'free' Mlg *lefas-ana* 'make s.t. free' Ml *lepas* 'free' TB *lopas* 'be free, disconnected' OJv *lepas* 'free'

The monosyllabic roots or sequences that resemble monosyllabic roots may themselves develop by contamination from similar sounding monosyllabic roots. An example of such a group is forms that end in reflexes of *luŋ, *luk, *kuk, and *kuŋ: all of the attestations have something to do with the notion of 'bending'. As discussed below, it is impossible in some cases to determine unequivocally whether these sequences were morphemes reconstructible for the protolanguage (PMP in the case of †luŋ, †luk, and †kuk, PAn in the case of *kuŋ) . *luŋ is attested first by disyllabization with addition of a prothetic vowel (cf. §A3.6.2, 4th¶):

> Tae' *elung* 'bent, curved' Bug *ellung* 'neck' Fordat *elun* 'bent, curved'

*luŋ is also attested by forms that consist of a petrified prefix added to it:

> *ka- added to *luŋ: Tag *kálung* 'held in the lap' Bar *kalu* 'bent stiff' Kel *kahung* 'deformed foot or hand' DPB *kalung* 'curved buffalo horns' (all probably independently developed)

Further, a form like NJv *mélung* 'bend, be bowed' attests to *luŋ. The first syllable was developed on the analogy of NJv *mélut* 'easily bent'. Similarly,*luk is attested by forms that were disyllabized in several different ways. The following forms show disyllabization by stretching the root or adding a prothetic vowel:

> Tag *lú?ok* Banjarese Ml *luhuk* 'bay' (§A3.6.2) and OJv *eluk* 'curve' and Nias *olu* 'popliteal space'

*luk is also attested by forms that consist of pretrified prefixes *ke-, *pe-, or *te- (as well as others) added to *luk:

> Mlg *heloka* 'crookedness, perversity' ND, Ml *peluk* 'embrace' OJv *peluk* 'bend, curve' Ml, OJv *teluk* 'bay'.

Although both *luŋ and *luk are attested over the range of the MP languages (a distribution that allows us to reconstruct them for PMP), it is not necessarily the case that forms ending in

/luŋ/ or /luk/ in the daughter languages reflecting *luŋ or *luk are in fact descendants of PMP forms. It is quite possible that forms ending in reflexes of *luŋ with this distribution were created in post-PMP times on analogy with forms ending in *luk (or *kuŋ). Similarly, forms ending in reflexes of *luk, with a distribution throughout the MP group, need not remount to PMP but may have been created more recently on analogy with forms ending in *luŋ or *kuk. The same thing may be said of forms ending in reflexes *kuk and *kuŋ having some connection with the meaning 'be bent'. All of these forms developed from something that existed in PMP, but at this point it is impossible to determine which of the morphemes attested are inherited directly from PMP and which developed later.

There are a number of other families of similar monosyllabic morphemes or sequences that, like the *luŋ, etc. family, above, have similarities of sound and meaning and derive from something in the protolanguage, but as is the case of the *luk, etc. family, forms ending in reflexes of the monosyllabic sequences of roots of these families cannot be unequivocally reconstructed for the protolanguage. The following list gives them (see the glossary for exemplification): *kaŋ, *kaq, *laq 'open, spread apart'; *tub, *tup, *kub, *kup, *keb 'close, cover'; *bun, buŋ, *duŋ 'cover over'; *puŋ, *pun, *puk, and possibly *buŋ and *buk 'pile up'; *tak, *tek 'cut'.

A3.9 Semantic characteristics of PAn roots that lead to similar independent developments in the daughter languages

The meaning of the root in PAn can account for the differing semantic outcomes that the reflexes have in the contemporary languages. The same unaffixed root may be reflected as a noun, an adjective, or a verb[120] in different languages and in some cases as all three in a single language. The kind of noun, adjective, or verb may also be different: the same root may refer to an instrument, to the product of an action, to the action itself, manner of action, or have other meanings as well in different languages or in the same language. On the basis of these different outcomes, we conclude that the PAn root had a range of meanings that these reflexes continue. For this reason, it is possible to relate forms in various languages with diverse meanings.

A3.9.1 Dynamic verbs

(a) Perhaps the most productive of these root types is that of dynamic verbs that can also be used nominally meaning 'the action of [doing so-and-so]'[121]

*kan 'eat, action of eating' (Tag *káʔin* 'eat' or 'action of eating', e.g. *káda káʔin ko nang manók* 'each time I eat chicken' [lit. 'each action of mine of eating chicken'])

(b) Another very productive root type is that of intransitive dynamic verbs which may refer to the action or event (as in A3.9.1(a) immediately above) or to whatever is produced by the action (or to s.t. that has the qualities of s.t. produced by the action):

---

[120] In the conservative languages that reflect the PAn verbal inflectional system, the verb forms in most cases occur with verbal inflectional affixation.

[121] In Tagalog, any dynamic verb may be used nominally in this meaning. There is no evidence that this was the case of PAn, for there are not many data that attest the same root used as a dynamic verb and as a noun referring to the action. However, this may be an artifact of the situation that few of our languages are as thoroughly documented as Tag.

*dabuk 'pulverize or s.t. that has been pulverized' (Cb *dábuk* 'pulverize' Fi *ravu* 'ashes' NJav *ḍawuk* 'grey-colored' [< meaning 'ashes']) *qetut 'to break wind' or 'flatus ventris' (St *ʔ-om-tut* 'to break wind' Pai *qetjutj* 'flatus') *iseq 'urinate' or 'urine' (Tag *íhiʔ* 'urine, urinate') *qulaɬ 'rain or rainfall' (St *æraɬ* 'to rain' Paz *udal* 'rainfall' Tag *ulán* 'to rain, rainfall')

In some cases, the thing produced may be a place:

*tebas 'fell' or 'area that has been cleared of trees' Pai *tjevas* 'cut, clear vegetation' Tag *tibaʔ* 'cut down (as a banana tree)' Mlg *tevy* 'clear land' NJv *teba* 'area in which certain animals make their home' TB *toba* 'name of a lake so called because it is located in the midest of cleared land' Fi *tova-tova* 'garden'

(c) If the root refers to a transitive dynamic action, as a noun it refers to the thing affected by of the action:[122]

*bitebit 'carry in fingers' or 'the thing carried' (Kav *bibit* 'pull by the ear' Tag *bitbit* 'carry s.t. with the fingers' NJav *bibit* 'seedling') *gita 'see' (Tag *kita* 'see' To *kite* 'appear (lit. be seen)'

(d) Some dynamic verbal roots may also refer to the being or instrument that performs the action:

*kamet 'take in the fingers' or 'thing that takes' (Tag *kamít* 'obtain' Cb *kamút* 'hand' Kel *gamet* 'hawk') *káɣuc 'scrape or thing that scrapes' (Cb *káɣus* 'scrape out s.t. coarse' Pai *karut* 'a rake') *qeɬeb 'close (door)' or 'door' (Paz *alep* 'close' Bon *ənə́b* 'door')

A3.9.2 Stative roots

(a) Roots that refer to a state or condition may also occur as verbal root that means 'bring s.t. into the state or condition'.[123]

*buka 'open, be opened' (At *bokaʔ* 'to split' Kav *buki* 'untie, undo' Tag *buká* 'to open, be opened' TB *buhá* 'opened' Fi (Bau) *fuke* 'uncover') *seqeɣet 'tie, make fast' or 'be fast' (Thao *ɬiθ* 'tight, constricted' Paz *xeʔet* 'tie together' Tag *higit* 'pull to make s.t. taut' Cb *hugút* 'tied tight')

(b) Another productive type is the root that refers to a state or condition or may describe the thing that is in that state:

*qila 'a mark' or 'have marks' (Mar *ila* 'mark on skin' Cb *ilá* 'identify' To *ʔila* 'freckled, with a mole, stain, or spot')

---

[122] This is reflected in the direct passive verbal form that has 0 affixation, exemplified in languages ranging from Northern Taiwan over the gamut of the An languages. E.g., colloquial Ml *pakai* 'wear s.t. or 'be worn':

Pakai sepatu saya [no break between *pakai* 'wear' and *sepatu* 'shoes']'Wear my shoes.' *Ini, sepatu saya,* ***pakai*** (= **dipakai** [passive]) 'Here, wear my shoes.'

[123] This in fact the same class of root as that of §A3.9.1(c), the only difference being that here I analyze these roots as being basically stative, whereas those of §A3.9.1(a) are analyzed as being basically verbs. To what extent this is a real distinction or is just a figment of the analysis can only be discovered on examining the systems of derivational affixation that developed in the daughter languages.

(c) Rather similar is the nominal root that refers to a thing that is characteristically in a state or may occur as a stative describing the state that s.t. is in:

> *bukul 'protrusion, protruding' (Kav *buqul* 'joint [not knee or elbow]' Ba *bungku* 'bump, hump' Tol *bukúl* 'full, bulging [as a basket or a snake]') *buŋkuk 'crooked' (Bug *bukku?* 'bent over' Ml *bungkuk* 'bent, hump-backed' ND *bungkok* 'crop, swelling in neck') *qudip 'alive' or 'life' (Ru *oḍípi* 'alive' Kav *izip* 'life') *tákut 'fear' or 'to fear' (Tag *takót* 'afraid' *tákot* 'one's fear' St *tikut* 'one's fear' Thao *tikot* 'afraid') *tuduɣ 'be asleep' or 'one's sleep' (Tag *túlog* Ml *tidur* 'to sleep, one's sleep')

(c1) A subclass of this type is the root that has the meaning of a noun that refers to a state or to a thing that is characteristically in that state:

> *quteɣ 'penile erection' or 'the erected penis' (Am *fitol* 'sexual arousal' Cb *utúɣ* 'penile erection' Mgg *uter* 'head of a drill, glans penis')

A3.9.3 Dropping of prefixes

In other cases, these nominal, verbal, or adjectival derivations developed from affixed forms, where the affixes had been lost. For example Ml *sekolah* 'school' can also be used as a verb and then means 'study at a certain place.' However, *sekolah* as a verb is a shortened form for the affixed form *bersekolah.* It so happens that in Ml some dialects have preserved the verbal affix *ber-* with this root and others have lost it (or the prefix is a variable). In this way, unaffixed roots in the daughter languages may show developments beyond those described in §§A3.9.1 and A3.9.2, above. Two patterns are widespread enough to merit discussion here.

(a) First is the case of verbal roots referring to motion. The instrumental passive affix roots could be added to such roots to form verbs referring to conveyance. Thus a verbal root referring to going s.w. may also come to mean 'bring s.t. s.w.'

> *katekat 'climb' or 'bring s.t. upward' (Am *katakat* 'lift up s.t. heavy with hands by o.s.' Cb *katkat* 'climb') *nakis 'go up' or 'bring upward' (Bun *ma-nakis* 'climb a slope' Ml *naik* 'go up' Kei *yaek* 'lift, raise')

(b) Second is the case of verbs that refer to a reflexive action (i.e., one that may devolve on the agent or on s.t. else). In languages that have widespread affixation, a derived verb refers to the reflexive action, whereas the root refers to a nonreflexive action (e.g., Tag *b-um-ágo* 'change s.t.' [< *bágo* 'new'] *magbágo* 'change o.s.' [= *-um-* + *pag-bágo*]). In languages that have lost the prefixes (often by weakening the antepenult) a root may be reflected with a reflexive or nonreflexive meaning.

> *suɣac 'wash off' St *s-om-owas* 'scrub' At *q-um-uwax* 'wash (hands, things)' Buli *uas* 'wash o.s.' *buɣiq 'wash' TB *buri* 'wash' Bugotu *vuri* 'wash o.s.'

Part B. Development of the Formosan Languages

B1. Introduction to the northwest Formosan languages

The northwest Formosan languages are the most important languages for the reconstruction of PAn, for they are the descendants of the languages spoken by the communities that remained in the area of the earliest settlement of Taiwan and accordingly did not make any of the innovations made by the ancestors of all other An languages. (Cf. the discussion in §A1.1.31.) They evince forms and meanings that elsewhere have been lost in the An languages. Of the languages in this region only Paz and St survived long enough to be documented to any depth whatsoever, and St, which is still healthy, has so far been treated in little detail. These are the two languages that provide the best evidence for PAn roots that remount to a PAn spoken at the earliest stages, at the first arrival from the mainland. The importance of identifying these roots is inestimable, for it is from these roots that cognates with Sino-Tibetan languages can best be established.

Thao and Atayalic are also important from this point of view. Although the ancestors of the Thao and Atayals did not remain with the ancestors of Paz and St, they split off from the remainder of the PAn communities not long after the earliest settlement on Taiwan. For this reason, they also give evidence of early PAn forms. Further documentation of both of these languages is imperative. For Thao, there is a short, but very reliable dictionary, prepared by R. Blust (2003). For Atayalic, there is a substantial dictionary of Squliq Atayal (Egerod 1980) and of Taroko Sediq (Pecoraro 1977) but very scanty data from more conservative dialects, such as Mayrinax, which can far better supply evidence for reconstructing the earliest stages of PAn than can the better documented but highly innovative Squliq and Taroko languages.

The rules in this and the following chapter provide the most decisive evidence for the earliest PAn phonology. Unfortunately, these two chapters also present a great number of unsolved problems and give hazy glimpses of lost processes that, for lack of data, cannot be fully understood.

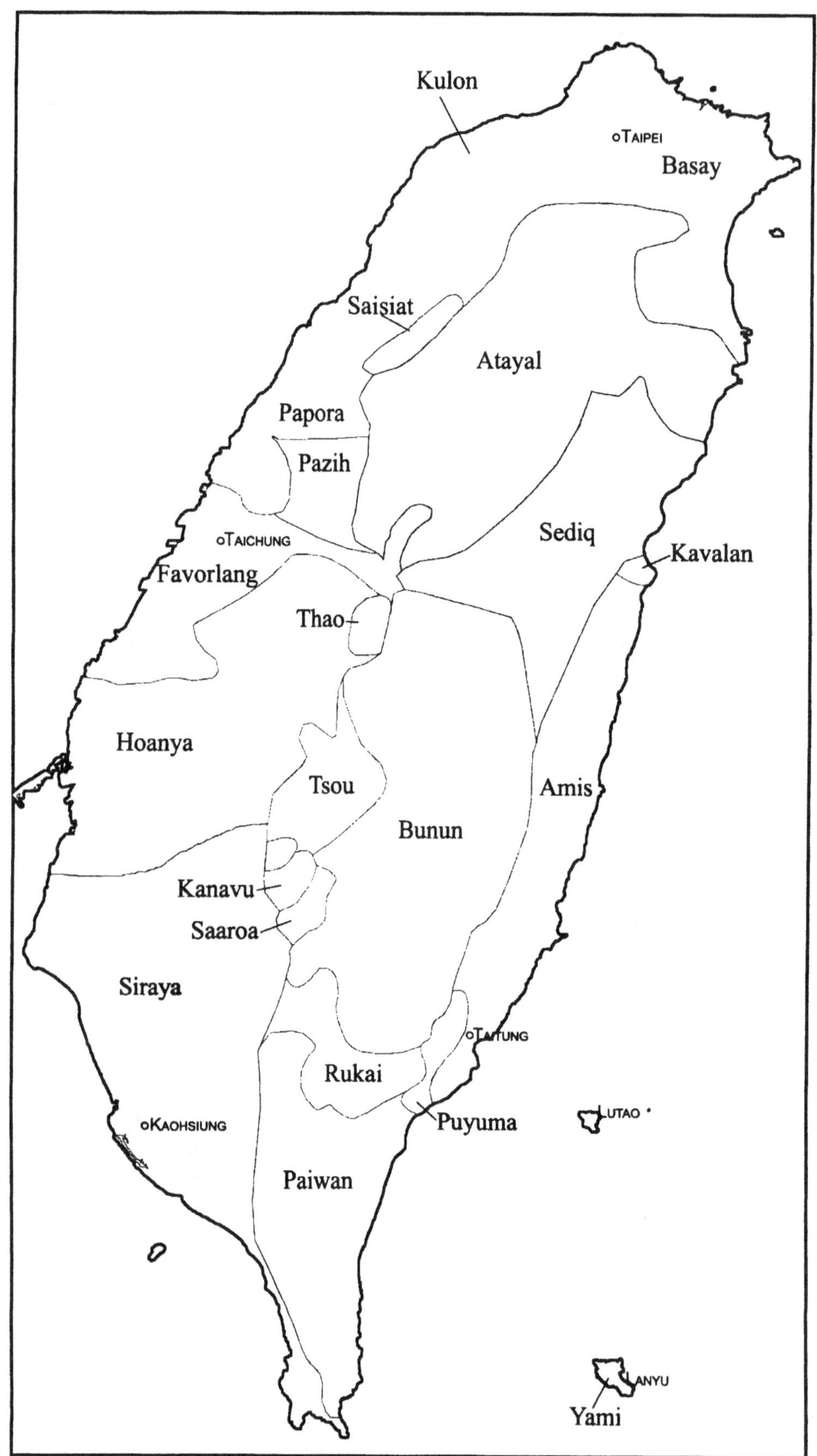

Map 3. The Formosan languages.

CHAPTER ONE, §1

Pazih

B11.0 Background and cultural factors that influenced the history of Pazih

Paz was spoken two hundred years ago on the central-western plains of Taiwan. In the first part of the nineteenth century, the Paz people removed to the Puli basin in the mountains to the east. Thanks to this movement, the language survived into the first part of the twentieth century. By the end of WWII the language was well on the way to extinction, but there was still time in the 1970s and 1980s for researchers to work with the last speakers, confirm texts and forms that had been taken down earlier, and gather enough information to lead to the compilation of a substantial dictionary (Li and Tsuchida 2001). As of 2006, the last speaker was said to be still alive and involved in adding to this dictionary. There were two dialects of Pazih, Paz and Kaxabu, that differed not very greatly from each other. Kaxabu has made two innovations in the phonology that have not been shared with Pazih. However, there has been considerable dialect mixture in the speech of the small number of informants Li and Tsuchida were able to work with, and this manifests itself in the fact that both dialects have forms that show the innovations and others that fail to show them (Li and Tsuchida 2001: 5).

The forms here quoted and analyzed derive exclusively from the dictionary. That work also gives a phonological history, which we have been able to draw on. Li and Tsuchida assume a PAn phonology that differs in many crucial respects from that assumed here, and thus the analysis presented in this chapter is not congruent with their analysis.[1]

The following chart represents the phonemes of Pazih:

CHART ONE. PHONEMES OF PAZIH

Consonants

voiceless	p	t	k	ʔ[2]
voiced	b	d	g	
spirants		z, s	x	h
liquid	w	l, r,y		
nasals	m	n	ng [ŋ]	

Vowels and Diphthongs

high	i		u
mid		e [ə]	
low		a	
diphthongs	uy, ay	iw	aw

No sequences of consonants occur except homorganic nasal plus stop. The occurrence of [ʔ] is predictable. /g/ does not occur in words directly inherited from PAn.

[1] Blust 1995b gives much of the same information as the dictionary. I cite the dictionary rather than Blust, as the dictionary is later and incorporates Blust's materials.

[2] [ʔ] is noncontrastive and therefore not a phoneme of Paz.

B11.1 Processes affecting the development of Paz from PAn

B11.1.1 Loss of syllables and contraction

B11.1.11 Loss or weakening of the leftmost syllable of the root

In the case of roots of three or more syllables, the root, with a few exceptions, was shortened by loss of the first syllable or elision of the penult. The antepenult was lost if it consisted of a vowel alone (including cases where *q- had been lost (§B11.3.14) or contained *e (including [ə] that developed).

*qalima > *rima* 'hand' *qaɬiŋu 'shadow' > *lingu* 'spirit, reflect' *qaɬuwaŋ 'ruminant' > *nuang* 'cow, buffalo' *qapucuk 'top' > *ti-puzu* 'top point' *qaselu > *suru* 'pestle' *qatipa > *sipa* 'turtle' *qusalipan > *haripan* 'millipede' *biɣengi > *xini-an* 'night' (< *beɣingi [§B11.1.3]) *sehapuy > *hapuy* 'fire' *seqeɣet > *xeʔet* 'tie together' (< *xet—§B11.1.2 [cf. *ma-xet* 'tight'])

In some cases, metathesis (§B11.1.3) took place before an antepenult consisting of *i- could be lost:

*iseɬaw > *sinaw* 'wash' (< *esinaw) (also *senaw*) *isepi > *sipi* 'dream' (< *esipi) *iseyup > *hium* 'blow'[3]

In two cases and possibly a third, a [ə] that developed in the antepenult was not lost but rather the penult was lost. Two of the following examples probably lost the penult by haplology:

*kiɬala 'perceive' > *kela* 'think' (< *kelala[4]) *liceqes > *deres* 'nit' (< *celeqes < *cileqes [/d-/ and the change of *i to /e/ are unexplained]) *paheɣaw > *puhaw* 'hoarse' (< *pehaw < *pehahaw [§B11.1.3])

Similar elision takes place in trisyllabic stems that develop vowel sequences. Trisyllabic stems that develop the sequences *ua *ia or *iu change these to /wa/ /ya/ and /yu/:[5]

*i 'name marker' + aku 'I' > *yaku* 'I'

Three proto-forms remained trisyllabics. Why these three forms remained trisyllabics is unknown, but it should be noted that their cognates in other Formosan languages remain trisyllabics and antepenultimate stress in PAn may have been the reason that the antepenult was not lost (§A3.5.3)

*qabaɣa > *abaxa* 'shoulder' *paqegu > *apuzu* 'gallbladder' (< *qapegu [§B11.1.3]) *tageɣaŋ > *takaxang* 'ribs'

Roots consisting of doubled monosyllabics, which in PAn had an epenthetic vowel between the two monosyllabic elements, kept the epenthetic vowel in most cases except if the syllable coda is /w/ or /y/—i.e., they did not lose syllables, as happened in many languages of Formosa and the Philippines. In some cases, however, the epenthetic vowel was lost in

---

[3] It is unknown if *ey > /i/ as in other An languages. If that is the case, the history of this form is as follows: *iseyup > *isiyup > *ihiyum > *hium*. An alternative hypothesis is that there was metathesis—i.e., *iseyup > *esiyup > *siyup > *hium.*

[4] This form also shows weakening (centralization) of the leftmost syllable.

[5] There are few examples of this rule in stems with a PAn etymology, but the rule is well exemplified in the morphophonemics of current Paz. Cf. Blust 1995b: 329.

reduplicated monosyllabic roots, and the resulting clusters underwent simplification. (Cf. the discussion in §A3.6.1 and the examples under §B11.1.13.)

B11.1.12 Loss of penult and contraction

The penult was lost if the antepenult had not been lost (§B11.1.11). If a q-onset was lost in the penult or final syllable, the vowel of the penult contracted with the vowel of the final syllable (B11.3.14). Further, stems of more than two syllables contracted sequences involving *u to /u/, except that *u before or after *a, contracted to /a/.

*bacuheq > *bazu* 'wash' (< *bacueq) *baŋeqeɣ > *tu-banger* 'putrid' (/-r/ not explained) *bintuqen > *bintul* 'star' (< *bintun [§B11.3.43, 3rd¶] < *bintuen) *daqaɬi > *dali* 'day' *qumah-qumah > *umamah* 'field' (< *umaumah < *qumaqumah)

B11.1.13 CC simplification

In some cases, roots consisting of a doubled monosyllabic element lost the epenthetic vowel (§B11.1.11, end, above). In that case, the first monosyllabic element subsequently lost its coda. This may happen with syllables having a nasal coda, even though Paz permits nasal clusters.

*bicebic > *biibis* 'besprinkle' (also *bibis*) *daŋedaŋ 'heat near fire' > *dadang* 'warm, broil' *cipecip > *hihip* 'suck' *cepecep > *zezep* 'suck' *pejepej 'press together' > *pepet* 'crowd each other, massage'

B11.1.2 Disyllabization of monosyllabic roots

The tendency to disyllabize monosyllabic roots, widespread throughout the An languages, also characterized pre-Pazih, but by the time of the Paz that is attested, this tendency was not operative. In fact, some of the old monosyllabic roots were retained as such, and many new ones developed. Nevertheless, there is evidence that some disyllabization of monosyllabic roots did obtain in Pazih, and there are examples of both disyllabization by lengthening the vowel nucleus and by petrifying prefixes (§A3.6.2). There are two examples of this process. *tun was a monosyllabic root meaning something like 'lead by pulling'. (Cf. the doubled form *tunetun in the glossary.) This root comes to mean 'weave' over a wide range of An languages (Mahdi 1987: 104). All of the reflexes of *tun in the meaning 'weave' manifest a lengthening of the vowel nucleus of the root *teun. Since we assume no vowel sequences in PAn, this disyllabization must have developed in later times and spread. An alternative explanation is that disyllabization occurred several times. The other example, *seqeɣet, developed into a monosyllabic root by syllable loss as described in §B11.1.11, above. This process left a root *ɣet, which subsequently became disyllabized by lengthening the root: *ɣeet or by adding a prefix that subsequently came to be interpreted as part of the root, *maɣet.

*teun > *tuʔun* 'weave' *seqeɣet 'firmly tied, tight' > *xeʔet* 'tie together firmly' also *ma-xet* 'tight'

The following list exemplifies roots attested with petrified prefixes:

*ba 'carry on back' > *i-ba* 'hold baby in arms' *(i-* 'locative prefix'[6]) *tuk > *i-tuk* 'on top' (*i-* locative prefix) *lem > *ka-rum* 'inside' (*ka-* locative prefix) *caw > *si-zaw* 'rinse' (*si-* instrumental passive prefix)

The following root exemplifies disyllabization by doubling:

*kuj 'lower shank' > *kudukut* 'heel'

A handful of monosyllabic roots remained monosyllabic in Paz:

*dem > *sem* 'dark' *kan > *kan* 'eat' *taw > *saw* 'person'

In at least one case, a disyllabic root became monosyllabic by eliding the penult. The rule seems to be that *u alone with no onset (other than [ʔ]) was elided in the penult before *w, but there is only one example:

*quway > *way* 'rattan' (< *uway)

B11.1.3 Metathesis

Metathesis happens occasionally in trisyllabic roots that have *i in the antepenult and *e in the penult. The *e of the penult was elided and a consonant cluster resulted. The open-syllable structure was reestablished by metathesizing the initial /i/ and the first consonant of the cluster, e.g., *isepi > *ispi > *sipi* 'dream'. This process is reflected over the entire range of the An languages (§A3.5.4).[7] Other examples of this process are as follows:

*biɣeni > *xini-an* 'night' (< *beɣini—with loss of the first syllable [§B11.1.11]) *iceɣab > *nukua-zixa* 'yesterday' *isenaw > *sinaw* 'wash'[8]

One example of metathesis in Paz is a form that also underwent metathesis in other Formosan languages:

*paqegu > *apuzu* 'gall bladder'

There are a few examples of purely Paz metathesis:

*biɣaq > *biarax* 'giant taro: *Alocasia macrorrhiza*' (< *bi-al-qaɣ < *b-al-iqaɣ < *b-al-iɣaq) *ciłaɣ 'ray' > *rizax* ' sun' (/r/ unexplained) *isu > *i-siw* (< i 'person marker' + *siw < *siu) *łagan > *langat* 'name' (< *ładang) *mula > *paxu-ruma* 'to plant' *nałaq > *langa* 'pus' *liceqes > *deres* 'nit' (< *celeqes < *cileqes [/d-/ unexplained]) *qidus > *dius* 'spoon, ladle' *tuduq > *tuʔut* 'leak (from roof)'

B11.1.4 Intercalated consonants

B11.1.41 The glottal stop

The occurrence of the glottal stop is predictable: all syllables must begin with a C, and if there is no C, then [ʔ] serves as the onset. Similarly, words must end in a

---

[6] The meaning of *iba* 'hold baby in arms' should lead one to infer that the prefix *i-* remounts to an instrumental passive prefix. If that is the case, the form is not inherited in Paz, for the instrumental passive prefix would have been reflected in Paz as /si/.

[7] An alternative explanation would be that elision took place after metathesis—that is, the initial *i and the penultimate *e metathesized, and only subsequently did the *e get lost—i.e, *isepi > *esipi > *sipi* 'dream'.

[8] The unmetathesized form *senaw* 'wash' also occurs. In this case, the antepenultimate *i- was lost. It is also possible that /i-/ was a prefix (cf. the discussion in the footnote to §A3.5.4, 5th¶).

consonant, and if there is no other C, then [ʔ] serves as the coda for the word. Thus, a noncontrastive glottal stop was intercalated between two vowel sequences.[9]

B11.1.42 *w, *y

No forms are found in the dictionary with /w/or /y/ between unlike vowels. This means that there is no contrast between a glide and its absence, and, in fact, a noncontrastive glottal stop may occur between unlike vowels (§B11.1.41, above).
An initial *w developed in the word for 'dog' *acu > *wazu*, as is the case in Pai, Am, and Kav. The form with *w-* was spread secondarily and probably arose by false cutting after a marker ending in *u.

B11.1.43 *h

We hypothesize that *h was added before a word initial sequence *uɣ.[10] The *ɣ then assimilated to the accreted /h/ (> /h/ [§B11.3.41, 2nd¶]):

*uɣat 'vein, sinew' > *huhas* 'vein, blood vessel

B11.2.0 Vowels and diphthongs

Paz has inherited the four vowels and the diphtongs of PAn. They are listed in §B11.0.

B11.2.1 *i

With exceptions due to syllable loss (§§B11.1.11, B11.1.12), *i remained /i/ in all environments.

*wiɣi > *ixi* 'left' *piliq > *piri* 'choose'

*i > /e/ in two cases. In the first case, it could be assumed that *i was weakened in the antepenult if it had not been entirely lost or metathesized (§B11.1.11):

*kiɬala 'perceive' > *kela* 'think' (elision of the penult)

In the second case, there is no explanation of the weakening of *i in the penult;

*ipen > *lepeng* 'tooth' (For /l/ < *ɬ-, cf. the fourth footnote to §A3.7.1; for the change of *-n > /-ng/, cf. §B11.3.43, 2nd¶.)

B11.2.2 *e

We begin by discussing disyllabic roots. The *e > /e/ in some environments but underwent assimilation in others. First, examples of the /e/ as a reflex:

*keɣet > *kexet* 'cut a piece off' *sipes > *hipet* 'cockroach' *sagek > *sazek* 'sniff, smell'

Second, *e > /u/ before *u and before *a:

---

[9] This statement requires qualification: (1) younger speakers failed to pronounce the glottal stop in many cases (Li and Tsuchida 2001: 3); (2) apparently the affix *-in-* did not have ʔ-onset when added to vowel-initial roots (but possibly they did have a ʔ-onset [Li and Tsuchida 2001: 3, top]); (3) further, the dictionary only transcribes a medial glottal stop between like vowels, and then only rarely. This leads me to believe that in fact, glottal stop did not occur between vowels in normal speech.
[10] This statement is a hypothesis rather than a rule, for there is only one example.

*bekac > *bukas* 'spring a trap' *ɬecuŋ > *luzung* 'mortar' *lepuc > *ruput* 'end, finish' *qaselu > *suru* 'pestle' *seban > *suban* 'carrying cloth for baby' *semay 'rice' > *sumay* 'cooked rice' *sepat > *supat* 'four' *tebus > *tubus* 'sugar cane' *telu > *tulu* 'three' *tebug > *subut* 'spring, water source'

There are several idiosyncratic developments of *e. There is no explanation, but the forms have good PAn etymologies. In some of these cases, Blust (1995b: 336) suggests that a merger of *e and *u was in the process of taking place in the speech of the last generation of Paz speakers, but it had not been carried through and thus resulted in cases where /u/ reflects *e and /e/ reflects *u.

In one case, *e > /u/ after *u. In most cases of *e after *u, the *e is maintained and *u > /e/ (§B11.2.3).

*buhet > *buhut* 'squirrel'

In two cases, *e > /u/ after *a:[11]

*kamet 'take in fingers' > *ka-kamut* 'fingers' *lem > *ka-rum* 'inside'

In one case, *e is assimilated to /a/:

*sema > *da-hama* 'tongue'

There are three other cases where *e > /a/. They are before /x/ and /h/, but it is not certain that the following /x/ or /h/ are the conditioning factors because there are countercases.[12]

*beɣay > *baxa* 'give' *tiŋeɣ > *singax* 'voice' *tageɣaŋ > *takaxang* 'ribs' *tumes > *sumah* 'body louse'

In the following case, *e is reflected with /a/. The form is clearly secondary, for the loss of *-k is also irregular:

*pugek > *puza* 'navel'

In trisyllabic roots, *e is lost by elision in many cases (§B11.1.12). It is reflected by a vowel only in some of the roots reconstructed as a reduplicated monosyllable with an epenthetic *e (§A3.6.1) and in the handful of roots that became disyllabic by virtue of losing a syllable other than the one containing *e (§B11.1.11).

First, in roots consisting of a reduplicated monosyllabic element with epenthetic *e: *e remains /e/ if the root vowel was *e. *e assimilates to the other root vowels. There are no attestations of doubled monosyllabic elements with *i that retain the epenthetic vowel.[13]

---

[11] In four cases *e was maintained after /a/ in the preceding syllable:

*daɣeq > *daxe* 'earth, soil' *ɣateb > *xasep* 'five' *sagek > *sazek* 'sniff, smell' *tapes > *tapes* 'winnow'

[12] *e did not develop into /a/ in the following two forms. But these forms may, in fact, not constitute countercases to a putative rule: note that the first case involves a root with *e in both syllables. Further, in the second case the *ɣ had been changed to /h/ (§B11.3.41) and the penult was lost by haplology (§B11.1.11). This may have happened before the *e could change to /a/ (if that indeed was the rule):

*keɣet > *kexet* 'cut off' *paheɣaw > *puhaw* 'hoarse' (< *pehaw < *pehahaw < *pehaɣaw [§B11.13])

On the other hand, there are two other cases in which *e > /a/ not before *ɣ or *h:

*qeɬeb > *m-alep* 'close (door)' *tapel > *mu-sapal* 'patch'

[13] In one case, the epenthetic vowel became /i/. There is no explanation. Cf. the discussion in §A3.6.1, middle.

*muɣemuɣ > *muximux* 'gargle'

*bakebak 'remove outer layer' > *bakabak* 'cloth made from hemp fiber' *bałebał 'k.o. reed' > *balabal* 'k.o. palm' *teketek > *teketek* 'chop' *kuj 'lower shank' > *kudukut* 'heel' (< *kujekuj)

Second, *e > /e/ in other trisyllabic roots where it had not gotten lost. In that case, *e has the same reflexes as in disyllabic roots:

*baŋeqeɣ 'putrid smell' > *tu-banger* 'rotten' *isenaw > *senaw* 'wash' *seqeɣet > *xeʔet* 'bind together' *tageɣaŋ > *takaxang* 'ribs'[14]

The *e assimilates to an *u of the following syllable, as is the case of disyllabic roots, as discussed in the 2nd ¶ of this section.

*paqegu > *apuzu* 'gallbladder' (< *qapegu)

B11.2.3 *a and *u

Except when lost in certain trisyllabic roots (§B11.1.11, above) *a remained /a/ in all environments:

*qabaɣa > *abaxa* 'shoulder' *amis-an > *amisan* 'north' *batu > *batu* 'stone' *daɣeq > *daxe* 'earth, soil' *ina > *ina* 'mother'

Except in the few cases where /u/ is elided (§B11.1.12), *u remains /u/.

*mugiŋ > *muzing* 'nose' *nunuh > *nunuh* 'breast' *qałingu 'shadow' > *lingu* 'spirit, reflect'

*u assimilates to /e/ in the following syllable, (with the exception mentioned §B11.2.2, 4th ¶):

*buɣes > *bexes* 'spray from mouth' *bukes > *bekes* 'hair' *luseq > *rese* 'tears'

*u also inexplicably changed to /e/ in the following form. The explanation offered by Blust (1995b: 336), discussed in §B11.2.2, 3rd ¶, above, most likely accounts for the /e/ in this form.

*jaɣum > *daxem* 'needle'

B11.2.4 Diphthongs

B11.2.41 *ay, *uy

*ay and *uy are retained unchanged.

*qatay > *asay* 'liver' *anay > *alay* 'termite' *łaŋuy > *languy* 'swim' *sehapuy > *hapuy* 'fire'

The following form is an unexplained exception:

*beɣay > *baxa* 'give'

B11.2.42 *aw, *iw

*aw and *iw are retained unchanged.

*babaw > *babaw* 'above' *laŋaw > *rangaw* 'fly' *taw > *saw* 'person' *baliw 'change, return to previous' > *bariw* 'buy' *laɣiw > *laxiw* 'flee, escape'

[14] In fact, this root contradicts the rule given in the 9th ¶ of this section, in that it failed to syncopate the penultimate *e (cf. the 6th ¶ of §B11.1.11, above).

The word for 'tree' has metathesized the *i and the *w (as happened also, but independently, in the languages of southern Taiwan and the Philippines):

*kasiw > *kahuy* 'tree' (< *kahwi < *kaswi)

The *i was absorbed into the preceding *ɬ in the following form and the *w developed syllabicity (> /u/) as in many Formosan languages:

*waɬiw 'honey bee' > *walu* 'bee, honey'

B11.3.0 Consonants

The following chart shows the Paz reflexes of the PAn consonants.

CHART TWO. DEVELOPMENT OF THE PAZIH CONSONANTS FROM PAN

PAn	Paz	PAn	Paz
p	*p*	m, n	*m, n*
t	*t, s*	ŋ	*ng*
k	*k*	h	*h*
q	*Ø*	c	*z*
b	*b*	s	*s*
d	*d*	l	*r*
j	*d*	ɬ	*l*
g	*k-, -z-, -t*	w	*w*
ɣ	x	y	*y*

B11.3.1 Voiceless consonants

In the Paz spoken by the last speakers, there was a tendency for stem final voiceless consonants to become voiced when a vowel initial suffix was added. However, the root-internal voiceless consonants did not become voiced.

B11.3.11 *p

*p remained /p/ in all positions.

*paŋa 'forking' > *panga* 'branch' *paqegu > *apuzu* 'gall' *piga > *piza* 'how much, many?' *sepat > *supat* 'four' *qaɬup > *alup* 'hunt'

In one case, a nasal was substituted for the final *-p. There is no explanation:

*iseyup > *hium* 'blow'

B11.3.12 *t

*t has two outcomes: a stop /t/ and /s/. /s/ developed when *t became an affricate *[c], as is the case of the other languages of northeast and southwest Taiwan (§A3.3.1, first footnote), and subsequently lost its affrication to become [s].

*t reflected as /t/:

*taɬam 'taste' > *talam* 'taste, try' *teketek > *teketek* 'chop' *tiyaɬ > *tial* 'belly' *batu > *batu* 'stone' *gita > *kita* 'see' *buhet > *buhut* 'squirrel'

*t reflected as /s/:

*talis > *saris* 'string, rope' *takaw > *sakaw* 'steal' *tebug > *subut* 'water source' *tumes > *sumah* 'body louse' *qatay > *asay* 'liver' *kutu > *kusu* 'head louse' *biɬit > *bilis* 'hold in hand' *sakut > *hakus* 'transport'

In the case of *táŋic > *angit* 'cry', initial *t- was lost when the first syllable of an infixed form *tumangic was lost by the phonological processes described in §B11.1.11 and the remainder was reanalyzed as consisting of a prefix *m-* plus a root *angit*—i.e., *tumaŋic lost the antepenult forming *mangic. This is attested in Paz as *mangit.* A root beginning in a vowel may form the active by prefixing *m-*. On analogy with this rule, the root of *mangit* is reanalyzed as *angit.*

Final *-t was lost in the following form. This may have been contaminated with the reflex of *ɬibu 'fenced in place', which is not attested in the dictionary but is quoted by Tsuchida (1976: 142) as *libu-patakan* 'bamboo protective fence for garden, etc.'

*libut 'surround' > *ribu* 'wall, fence, hedge'

B11.3.13 *k

*k remained /k/ in all positions:

*kasiw > *kahuy* 'wood, tree' *kutu > *kusu* 'head louse' *ciku > *ziku* 'elbow' *teketek > *teketek* 'chop up'

In one case, final *-k was inexplicably lost:

*pugek > *puza* 'navel' *qapucuk > *ti-puzu* 'top point'

B11.3.14 *q

*q was lost entirely. In roots of more than two syllables, when a medial *-q- was lost, the abutting vowels contracted, and when an initial *q- was lost, the entire leftmost syllable was lost (§B11.1.11):

*qatay > *asay* 'liver' *qusalipan > *halipan* 'millipede' *bituqen > *bintul* 'star' *daqaɬi 'daytime' > *dali* 'day' *daqis 'forehead' > *dais* 'face' *piliq > *piri* 'choose' *punuq 'head, main part' > *punu* 'head'

In one case, *-q is reflected with *-k, probably under the influence of a language in which *q was a stop. However, this language is unidentified. The currently spoken language nearest to Paz that has stop reflexes for *q and a cognate meaning 'house' is Bunun. Note that a synonym with the normal reflex of ∅ also is attested:

*ɣumaq > *xumak/ xuma* 'house'

B11.3.2 *h, *s, *c

*h and *s remained unchanged in Paz. *c became voiced (after *j had merged with *d) and subsequently lost its affrication (> /z/). Details are given in the subsections below.

B11.3.21 *h

*h was an unproductive phoneme in PAn. It remained unchanged in Paz except when lost by elision in trisyllabic roots (§B11.1.12). The following forms are all those attested in Paz that reflect *h:

*bayah > *bahah* 'embers' *buhet > *buhut* 'squirrel' *capuh > *sapuh* 'sweep' *ałih > *alih* 'near' *lahuj 'seaward' > *rahut* 'downstream' *nunuh > *nunuh* 'breast' *paheyaw > *puhaw* 'hoarse' *qumah 'cultivated field' > *umamah* 'field' (< *umah-umah) *sehapuy > *hapuy* 'fire' *ułah > *ulah* 'go first'

In trisyllabic roots, *h-onset of the final syllable was lost:

*bacuheq > *bazu* 'wash'(< *bacueq [§B11.1.12])

Final *-h was variably lost in the following root. There is no explanation:

*ułah, > *ula/ulah* 'go first'

B11.3.22 *s

*s most frequently > /s/ when not lost in trisyllabic roots that were elided (§B11.1.11). In nine cases, *s is reflected with /h/. The reflex /h/ is an innovation that started somewhere in central Formosa and spread, but the environment that gave rise to this innovation is unknown (cf. §A3.3.32). Examples of *s > /s/:

*sagek > *sazek* 'sniff' *seban > *suban* 'cloth for carrying baby' *busuk > *busuk* 'drunk' *bałas > *balas* 'male' *taqis > *sais* 'sew'

The following are the cases where *s > /h/:

*iseyup > *hium (<* *esiyup) 'blow' *kasiw > *kahuy* 'tree' *qusalipan > *haripan* 'millipede' (loss of leftmost syllable §B11.1.11) *łisebic > *ha-lipit* 'thin' (< *ha-lihpit) *sakut > *hakus* 'transport' *saweni > *u-huni* 'a short while ago' *sema > *da-hama* 'tongue' *sipec > *hipet* 'cockroach'*suni > *huni* 'sound *tumes > *sumah* 'clothes louse'

B11.3.23 *c

*c > /z/ initially and medially (probably first becoming [j] and then losing the affrication):

*ciku > *ziku* 'elbow' *cucu > *zuzu* 'breast' *acu > *wazu* 'dog' *cepecep > *zezep* 'suck'

In a root with final /-h/ *c is reflected with /s/:

*capuh > *sapuh* 'wipe'

In one case,*c is reflected with /h/. Perhaps this form developed initial /h-/under the influence of *hium* 'blow'

*cipecip > *hihip* 'suck'

In word-final position, *c lost its affrication but never became voiced—i.e., *-c > /-t/:

*balec > *pa-baret* 'answer' *hipec > *hipet* 'cockroach' *łisebic > *ha-lipit* 'thin'

In three cases, *-c is reflected as /-s/. These are verb forms and a possible explanation is that the *-c was reflected as /-z/ before suffixed forms.[15] This stem-final /-z/ was generalized to final position, and subsequently lost voicing, as did the voiced stops:

[15] There is evidence for this in the Paz vocabulary that has no PAn etymology. For example, there is a root-final /t/-/z/ alternation, which can be best explained if the /-t/ derives from an earlier *c that changed to *z, exemplified by bold characeters in the following example: *maabezebet* 'help each other (active)' *–paabezebezi* 'help each other (passive)' (Li and Tsuchida 2001: 4).

*bicebic > *biibis* 'spray water on' *bekac > *bukas* 'spring a trap' *kudic 'k.o. skin disease' > *kudis* 'scar, wound' (not inherited from PAn)

In one case, an initial *c was replaced by /d/. There is no explanation:

*liceqes > *deres* 'nit' (< *zeres < *celeqes < *cileqes)

B11.3.3 Voiced stops in Paz

The voiced consonants became voiceless at the end of a word.

B11.3.31 *b

*b remained /b/ in initial and medial positions. At the end of a word, it is devoiced (> /p/):

*babaw > *babaw* 'above' *buhut > *buhut* 'squirrel' *qabu > *abu* 'ashes' *debedeb > *zebezep* 'chest' *qeɬeb > *alep* 'close (door)'

In the case of the reflex of *ɬisebic, *b is assimilated to the preceding *s, as is the case of all An languages except Bunun: *ha-lipit* 'thin'.
In one case, Paz reflects *-b with /w/. This form has spread secondarily and is shared by Pai, Sar, and Thao. However, in none of these languages is /w/ the normal reflex of *-b:

*suwab > *suaw* 'yawn'

In one unexplained case, *-b is lost entirely:

*iceɣab 'yesterday' > *nakua-zixa* 'yesterday' (< *ciɣab [§B11.1.11, 2nd ¶])

B11.3.32 *d, *j

*d and *j merged and became /d/. In final position this *-d became devoiced, as happened to all voiced consonants in final position.[16]

*daŋedaŋ 'heat near fire' > *dadang* 'warm (body), broil' *daɬum > *dalum* 'water' *-da > *di-da* 'there' *jalan > *daran* 'road' *tuju 'point, indicate' > *tudu* 'point, instruct' *kuj 'lower shank' > *kudekut* 'heel' (< *kujekuj) *lahuj 'seawards' > *rahut* 'downstream'

In four cases, *d is reflected as /z/. There is evidence in the recordings of the spoken language that a change of /d/ > /z/ was ongoing in certain environments: many forms show variants with /d/ or alternatively /z/ (Li and Tsuchida 2001:5, top):

*damaɣ 'light, torch' > *zaman* 'torch'[17] *daquɣ 'down' > *pi-zaux* 'descend' *debedeb > *zebezep* 'chest'[18] *qudaŋ > *kuzung* 'shrimp, lobster' (not inherited)

[16] Blust (1995b: 325) states that the point of articulation of /t/ and /d/ differ and that this difference is maintained in word-final position. In other words, there is a contrast between /t/ and /d/ in word-final position, although both have voiceless allophones in that position. The dictionary does not mention this feature, and here we follow the dictionary, transcribing etymological root finals *-d and *-j with /-t/.
[17] The form *zaman* 'torch' is also attested in Pai, where it is clearly a borrowing from a dialect that normally changes *-ɣ > /n/ after a nasal on the left (as is the case of Puyuma). The Paz reflex, even though it coincides with the Pai form, is not connected with it. Its development is coincidental. However, we have no good explanation for the final /-n/ in the Paz reflex.
[18] The initial /z/ in this form may be explained by contamination with *zezep* 'suck', the reflex of *cepecep.

B11.3.33 *g

As onset of the penult or earlier, *g- > /k-/. As onset of the final syllable, *g spirantized, and subsequently its articulation moved forward in the mouth. That is, medially before the final syllable *-g- > /-z-/.[19] In final position, *g moved forward without spirantizing and merged with the reflexes of *-j and *-d—that is, *-g > /-t/.

*gáɣang > *kaxang* 'k.o. small fresh-water crab' *paqegu > *apuzu* 'gall' *sagek > *sazek* 'sniff' *tebug > *subut* 'spring, water source'

There is one case in which *g is reflected with /x/—i.e., *g moved back to merge with *ɣ. This form is also attested with a reflex of *ɣ in Favorlang, a now-extinct language that bordered Paz in its original home on the midwestern plains. Paz most likely borrowed this form from Favorlang or a neighboring source that had undergone the same development:

*dagam > *daxam* 'tame' (cf. Favorlang *darram* 'tame')

B11.3.4 Voiced continuants in Pazih

B11.3.41 *ɣ

*ɣ lost its voicing (> /x/).

*ɣinu > *xinu* 'winnowing tray' *ɣumaq > *xuma* 'house' *keɣet > *kexet* 'cut off' *laɣiw > *raxiw* 'flee, escape' *bucuɣ 'bow' > *buzux* 'arrow' *muɣemuɣ > *muximux* 'gargle'

When there was an *h or is currently an /h/ in the stem, the [x] that developed assimilated to /h/:

*baɣah > *bahah* 'embers' *paheɣaw > *puhaw* 'hoarse' (< *pehaw [§B11.1.11] < *pehahaw [§B11.1.3]) *uɣat > *huhas* 'vein, blood vessel' (for /h-/ cf. §B11.1.43)

There is one more case where *ɣ is reflected with /h/. It is unexplained:

*ɣawus > *haus* 'scoop up'

B11.3.42 *l and *ɬ

*l is reflected by /r/.[20]

*lahud 'seaward' > *rahut* 'downstream' *lebeŋ > *rebeng* 'bury (but not a human)' *piliq > *piri* 'choose' *qusalipan > *haripan* 'millipede' *telu > *turu* 'three' *gemel 'squeeze in hand' > *kemer* 'take a handful, grasp'

*ɬ is reflected as a lateral in all positions.

*ɬaŋuy > *languy* 'swim' *ɬecuŋ > *luzung* 'mortar' *baɬas > *balas* 'male' *qiɬas > *ilas* 'moon' *tuɬa > *tula* 'eel' *waɬiw > *walu* 'bee, honey' *qujaɬ > *udal* 'rain'

There are cases in which *ɬ merged with /n/. These are probably cases of dialect mixture—i.e., borrowings from the Kaxabu dialect, which reflects *ɬ with /n/. The following forms exemplify this:

---

[19] We say that spirantization preceded forward movement because medial *-g- did not merge with *-d- and *-j-, as would have been the case if it had moved forward before spirantization had taken place.

[20] Blust (1995bb: 328) describes /r/ as a "prealveolar to postdental flap". Cf. also the comment on the Kaxabu *l–*n merger in the section immediately following.

*qaɬuwaŋ > *nuang* 'buffalo, cow'[21] *luɬ > *ka-runu* 'roll up' *sebaɬ > *suban* 'carry baby with straps in front' *wanaɬ> *anan* 'right side'

In one unexplained case *ɬ is reflected with /r/:

*ciɬaɣ 'ray' > *rizax* 'sun' (< *zirax [§B11.1.3])[22]

B11.3.43 Nasals

*m, *n, *ŋ remained unchanged in all positions.

*mudiŋ 'face' > *muzing* 'nose' *qalima > *rima* 'hand' *qaɣem > *axem* 'pangolin' *nunuh > *nunuh* 'breast' *jalan > *daran* 'road' *laŋaw > *rangaw* 'fly' *ɬecuŋ > *luzung* 'mortar'

*n > /ng/ in roots that contained *ɬ (or contained an *ɬ that had developed by the nasalization process described in §A.3.7.1):

*naɬaq > *langa* 'pus' (< *ɬanaq) *qagan > *langat* 'name' (< *ɬanag < *ɬagan [§A3.7.1]) *ipen > *lepeng* 'tooth' (< *ɬipen)

In the Kaxabu dialect, *n and *l merged to become /n/. Dialect mixture has allowed this change to be reflected in the Paz dialect in some forms. In the word for 'star', a final /n/ is changed to /l/. This is by analogy: since many forms show variations between /l/ and /n/ (historically /l/), forms that historically have an /n/ may develop a variant with /l/:

*bituqen > *bintul* 'star' (< *bintun[23] < *bintuqen)

In a few cases, reconstructed with initial *n-, Paz reflects /z/ or /d/. We assume that the forms reflecting *n had undergone the process of nasalization (§A3.7.1), and the form with the initial /z/ or /d/ reflecting *d is the original root. (Cf. §B11.3.32 for /d/–/z/variation.)

*naquɣ (< *daqug) > *zaux* 'go down' *naɣa '*Pterocarpus* sp.' (< *daɣa) > *daxa* 'maple tree' *ɬagam[24] (< *dagam) > *dazam* 'tame'

The word for 'monkey' fails to reflect *-ŋ. There is probably an analogy of some sort to account for the final /h/ in this word, but we have not identified it.

*lutuŋ > *rutuh* 'monkey'

B11.3.44 *w and *y

*w remains /w/ initially. Medially, it does not contrast with its absence between front and back or back and front vowels.[25] There are no attestations of *w between like vowels.

---

[21] Tsuchida (1976: 139) suggests that the *ɬ loses its palatalization by assimilation to the /ng/ on the right. However, there are countercases where *ɬ > /l/ before a nasal on the right–e.g.,*ɬaŋuy > *languy* 'swim'.

[22] It is tempting to see the change to /r/ as a case of assimilation to the *ɣ on the right, but in fact, there are plenty of countercases: lexical items that evince /l/ followed by /x/, one of which has a PAn etymology: *baɬaɣ > *ba-balax* 'k.o. thorny vine: *Pisonia aculeata* Linn.' Blust (1995b: 334) quotes *lizax* 'sun', but it is not listed in the dictionary.

[23] Blust 1995b: 361 quotes *bintun*.

[24] This form, like some others, substitute the palatalized nasal /ɬ/ for the expected nasal (§A3.7.1). There is no explanation.

[25] *w between back and front vowels was preserved in one case, where the penult of the root was lost (§B11.1.2, end):

*quway > *way* 'rattan'

*wałis > *walis* 'fang' *wałiw > *walu* 'bee, honey'

There are two cases where *w is reflected by /b/. In both cases, *w stood before *i. There is no explanation:

*kawit > *kabit* 'hook' *wilih 'return' > *bilih* 'go back'

There are exceptions. The reflex of *wanał is clearly secondary, and there are other irregularities (cf. §B11.3.42, above). The *w-'s of *wanał and *wiɣi possibly were lost when they came to follow a prefix *ka- (frequently occurring with cognates in other languages), which was lost in Paz:

*wanał > *anan* 'right' (< *kawanał) *wiɣi > *ixi* 'left' (possibly from *kawiɣi)

The form *wada 'there is' is reflected as *hada* 'there is'. The probable explanation is that *wada itself is a complex form consisting of *wa- plus *da, where *da is the same morpheme as the reconstructed *da 'there (not distant)'. In that case *hada* etymologically consists of a prefix *sa- plus *da 'there'.
For final -w see §B11.2.42.
*y remained *y between two *a's. For final *-y, cf. §B11.2.41. *ey may have become /i/. (Cf. the first footnote to §B11.1.11.) There are no attestations of forms with *y in an environment other than between two *a's and in final position.

*qayam 'pet' > *ayam* 'bird' *daya 'inland' > *daya* 'east'

There is no contrast between *y and its absence between *i and *u or *a and between *u or *a and *i. (Cf. the parallel development of *w, discussed in the first paragraph of this section, above.)

CHAPTER ONE, §2

Saisiat

B12.0 Background and cultural factors that influenced the history of Saisiat

Saisiat (St) is spoken in two very close dialects: Tonghœʔ and Taai. There is one sound change that has made the two dialects sound rather different from one another: in Tonghœʔ *l > 0. This change has spread throughout the speech community (§B12.3.41). However, Li (1978) reported that he still found speakers of the Taai dialect where this change had not taken place. We quote the variants that have not lost reflexes of *l wherever they are attested. We refer to St as 'Saisiat', although in the speech of the most conservative Taai speakers, it is /ʃayʃilat/. ʃai means 'place', but the etymology of *ʃilat* is unknown. My sources for St citations are Tsuchida 1962, Li 1978, and brief work with native speakers in Taipei and in ʃai Walo, Tonghœʔ. My informants were Okay a Boa Titiyon (born 1973), Lalo Teheʃ Kaykaybaw (born 1967), and Parain a ʔŒmaw Kaybaybaw (born 1928). I should note that many of the forms with a lost /l/ were pronounced by informants with /h/ substituting for the the /l/. Where the published sources do not quote a St form that I elicited, I quote the elicited form, which may have /h/ for /l/.

Both Li (1978) and Tsuchida (1976) have published on the development of the PAn phonemes in St, and much of what is stated herein repeats what has been published. However, this treatment is fuller, and inasmuch as the PAn phonology assumed here is far from that assumed by Li and Tsuchida, the account of the how the St reflexes came into being here given differs substantially from either one of theirs.

The following chart shows the segmental phonemes of St. Four of the consonantal and one vowel phoneme have articulatory characteristics different from the representation of the transcription. The square brackets next to the transcription indicate their articulation. There are a few forms reported with /l/ in the Taai dialect that are now pronounced with /ɬ/. A summary of the PAn phonemes and their outcome in St is given in §B12.3.0.

CHART ONE. PHONEMES OF SAISIAT

Consonants

voiceless	p	t	ʃ, s [θ]	k	h, ʔ
voiced	b [β]		z [ð]		
liquid	w	l, ɬ	r, y		
nasal	m	n		ng [ŋ]	

Vowels and Diphthongs

high	i		u
mid	œ	e [ə]	
low	æ	a	
diphthong	uy, ay	iw	aw

B12.1. Changes that characterize St in general

B12.1.1 Disyllabization of trisyllabic roots

B12.1.11 Syllable loss

> *aqetih > *ma-ʔsih* 'ebb' (< *ma-aqtih) *baɣiyus > > *balyoʃ* 'typhoon' *beɣay > *mo-blay* 'give' *binesíq > *binʃiʔ* 'seed' *iqetáh > *kæ-ʔsæh* 'rice husk' *icebu < *kæ-hboʔ* 'urine' *isepi > *iʃpiʔ, ka-ʃpiʔ* 'dream' *laheyu > *lay-layoʔ* 'wither' *liceqes > *liʔʃiʃ* 'nit' (< *liqeces) *ɬisebic > *ɬipih-an* 'thin' *paqegu > *pæʔzoʔ* 'gall' *qeɬeb 'close' > *ʔæ-ʔɬeb* (< ʔa-ʔeɬeb) 'door'

Similarly, the sequence *ayi and *awu become /ay/ and /aw/ respectively when to the left of a final syllable:

> *kawiɣi > *kayliʔ* 'left (hand)' (< *kaili [§B12.3.43]) *kawil 'hook' > *kapa-kayl-an* 'hook' (< *kapa-kail-an [§B12.3.43])

Other penultimate vowels may also be elided:

> *bacuheq > *bæhiʔ* 'wash clothes' (<*baheʔ < *bahheq < *bahuheq) *bitík > *mo-btik* 'fillip' *jemaq > *rimʔæn* 'tomorrow' (< *jemaq-an) *jemaq + *kaha- > *kehæ-maʔ* 'eat breakfast' *siyuɬuq 'necklace' > *ʃiɬoʔ* 'hang (beads) around neck'

The following forms evince vowel loss in the leftmost syllable of the stem (and CC simplification in some cases):

> *icebu > *-hboʔ* 'urinate' kaɬusekus > *ka-kɬokœh* 'fingernail' *iseyup > *hiop* 'blow' (< *siyop < *esiyop) *pálisi > *piʃi-æn* 'taboo'[1] *qalima > *lima* 'hand' *sehapuy > *hapoy* 'fire' *tiqeɣáb > *selab* 'belch'

B12.1.12 Contraction

When a vowel sequence develops from the loss of *l or *q or from the addition of a prefix, contraction takes place between like vowels or sequences involving *e plus another vowel: if one of the vowels is *a, the *e is lost; if one of the vowels is *i, the *i is lost.

> *balec > *ʃo-bæh* 'revenge' *aqetíh > *ma-ʔsih* 'ebb' (< *ma-aʔtih < *ma-aʔetih) *tiqeɣab > *selab* 'belch'

---

[1] This form is from the Tonghœʔ dialect, in which *l is lost. There is no attestation from the Taai dialect that retains a reflex of *l.

B12.1.13 Trisyllabics maintained as trisyllabics

At least ten forms, reconstructed as trisyllabics in our data, do not reflect disyllabization in St. The conditions under which disyllabization takes place or fails to take place have not been discovered.

*balatúk > *balasok* 'woodpecker' *bítuqan > *bintœʔæn* 'star' *daleqám > *rælæʔæm* 'molar' *inaduq > *inadoʔ* 'long' *qabáɣa > *ʔæbalaʔ* 'shoulder' *qaɬiŋu 'shadow' > *ʔaɬingoʔ* 'reflection' *qaselu > *ʔæʃelœʔ* 'mortar' *qitelúɣ > *ʔœsizol* 'egg' (< *qetilúl < *qitelúl) *qusaɬap > *ʔoʃaɬap* '(fish) scales'

B12.1.2 Disyllabization of monosyllabic roots

There are a few examples of this process attested in St. The following form reflects a monosyllabic root disyllabized by petrification of a prefix:

*daŋ 'heat near fire' > *papa-rang* 'roast over fire'

The following form shows disyllabization by doubling:

*lem 'in dim light' > *lemlem* 'cloud'

The following form shows disyllabization by lengthening the vowel and inserting a /ʔ/ between the two moras:

*su > *ʃoʔo* 'you (sing)'

In the following example, the inserted glottal stop give evidence of a process of disyllabization by the addition of a prothetic *e-. *ʔerem is a disyllabicization of *rem < *jem, with automatic root initial glottal stop insertion. The *e that developed in the initial root syllable was subsequently elided with addition of a prefix:

*jem 'close eyes' > *mæʔrem* 'sleep' < *ma+*ʔerem

B12.1.3 Metathesis

Metathesis happens occasionally in trisyllabic roots that have *e in the penult.

*iseyup > *hiop* 'blow' (< *esiyop) *liceqes > *liʔʃiʃ* 'louse egg' *qiteluɣ > *ʔœsizol* 'egg' (< *qetilul < *qetiluɣ)

Roots that most commonly occur with affixes are not subject to this metathesis:

*icebu > *-hboʔ* (in *hœmboʔ* 'urinate' and *kæhboʔ* 'urine') (loss of the antepenult and elision of the medial vowel [§B12.1.11]) *isepi > *ka-ʃpi* 'dream'

The following form shows vocalic metathesis and an unexplained suffix -ɬ:

*bituka > *biskoɬ* 'stomach'

The following form shows metathesis unique to St:

*paqah > *ʔæpæh* 'thigh'

Names of flora and fauna are subject to metathesis (as well as other irregular processes). The following form shows an irregular infixation of /ang/ as well as metathesis:

*qusalipan > *ʔalongæhipan* 'centipede' (< *qaŋulasipan)

B12.1.4 Assimilation and dissimilation

Lack of attestations makes it impossible to give definitive rules of assimilation and dissimilation. However, it seems to be the case, on the basis of scattered examples, that /s/ and /ʃ/ assimilated to a spirant to the right. In the following examples, the *t that became a spirant (§B12.3.12) was assimilated to the /ʃ/ or the /h/ that developed from *-s or *-c at the end of the root:[2]

*taŋic > *-hangih* 'cry' (< *sangih) *talís > *ʃinaliʃ* 'cord' (< *saliʃ) *taqís > *ʃomæʔiʃ* 'sew' *tiŋás > *ʃingaʃ* 'particles in teeth after eating'

In the following example, *s > /s/ before /z/ or /l/ that developed from *g and *ɣ:

*sagek > *sazek* 'smell' *useɣ > *ngesel* 'nasal mucus'

*s also became /s/ before /s/ that developed from *c (§B12.3.23):[3]

*suɣac 'wash' > *sowas* 'scrub'

/l/ dissimilated from an /l/ to the right.

*qiteluɣ > *ʔœsizol* 'egg' (< *qetilul < *qetiluɣ [§B12.1.3])

In the Tonghœʔ dialect there was sporadic assimilation of /l/ or /ɬ/ to an /l/ that developed to the right or to the left. This change took place before /l/ was lost in Tonghœʔ. Taai does not reflect this change:

*diɣi > *mi-riri* 'stand' (Taai: *mirili*) *qaɬuj > *ʔæror* 'be carried by the current' (Taai: *ʔæɬor*)

There is a tendency for *a and *u to assimilate to the fronted reflexes of *a and *u to the right (§B12.2.3, end).

B12.1.5 Intercalation of /w/, /y/, and /ʔ/

B12.1.51 *w

There is no contrast between /oa/ and /owa/ or /ao/ and /awo/. The sources usually write *oa* and *ao* respectively (or *ua* and *au* for those sources that use *u* rather than *o* in the transcription) or the fronted reflexes in contexts where these develop (§B12.2.3). In some cases the sources write *wa* for /oa/. There are only two phonemic sequences /oa/ and /ao/. However, phonetically a [w]-glide developed after /o/ in pre-Saisiat, as is shown by the form *wali* 'come here!' (< *aɣi). The /w-/ can be explained as having developed from a prefix or preposed form that ended in /o/.

B12.1.52 *y

Between /i/ and another vowel, /y/ is noncontrastive. In this way /y/ is parallel to /w/.

*iseyup > *hiop* 'blow' (< *siyop < *esiyop [§B12.1.3])

Phonetically, a [y] developed between /i/ and another vowel, and this is reflected in the occurrence of /y/ when a preceding /i/ is lost by elision:

---

[2] Tsuchida (1976: 149) gives this rule under his citation of *tiŋas (his reconstruction: C_1iŋaS_{13}).

[3] Actually, he rule is that *s–*c > /s–s/. The *s and *c influenced each other.

*baɣiyus > *balyoʃ* 'typhoon'

B12.1.53 *ʔ

A glottal stop is automatically accreted to words ending in a final vowel. However, functors and pronouns do not undergo this process. In this way St is parallel to Amis (§B61.0). Further, in the Tonghœʔ dialect, where *-l was lost (§B12.3.41), no glottal stop is accreted to the final vowel that results from the loss of *-l.
Also forms inherited with an initial vowel automatically accreted a glottal stop. However, /ʔ/ became a contrastive phoneme when a sequence *ʔVC in the penult or antepenult was syncopated—that is, became /ʔC/. In short, a sequence /ʔC/ came to contrast with /C/. Intercalation of /ʔ/ occurs between a sequence of vowels that developed:

*jem 'close eyes' > *ejem + ma > *mæ-ʔrem* 'sleep' *su > *ʃoʔo* 'you' (< *suu) *uɬah > *minsa-ʔɬaʔ* 'first' (< *minsa-ʔuɬaʔ < *minsa-uɬaʔ) *wanaɬ + ka- > *kaʔnaɬ* 'right' (< *kaʔanaɬ < *kaanaɬ)

Intercalation did not take place between sequences /ai/ and /au/ that developed. These sequences are diphthongized.

*uɣát + *ka- > *ka-wlas* 'tendon, vein'

In the sequence /ia/, a glottal stop is sometimes intercalated and sometimes not. For example, in the reflex of *tiyaɬ 'belly' the noun, reflecting *tíyaɬ, does not intercalate /ʔ/, but the verb, reflecting *tiyáɬ, does:

*tiyaɬ > *tiaɬ* 'belly', *-siʔaɬ* 'eat'

B12.2.0 Vowels and diphthongs

St has inherited the four vowels of PAn and added two fronted vowels, as discussed below.

i		u
œ	ə	
æ	a	

The reflex of *u is written *o* in most sources, and we follow that practice here. In some sources, it is transcribed as *u*. ə is written *e*.

B12.2.1 *i

*i remains /i/ in all environments. (For elision of *i, cf. §B12.1.11.)

*bali > *bali* 'wind' *balíga > *balizaʔ* 'batten (in weaving)' *biliɬ 'behind, last' > *biliɬ* 'behind, follow' *bítuqan > *bintœʔæn* 'star'

B12.2.2 *e

*e remains a mid-central vowel in most environments.

*lebeŋ > *lebeng* 'bury'

However, *e > /i/ in a syllable with a spirant or a glottal stop coda (that is, a glottal stop coda that developed)—i.e., before /-ʔ/, /-h/, or /-ʃ/coda:[4]

*sipec > *hipih* 'roach' (< *hipeh) *bacuheq > *bæhiʔ* 'wash (clothes)' *daɣeq > *raliʔ* 'earth, soil' *liceqes > *liʔʃiʃ* 'louse egg' *biqel > *biʔiʔ* 'goiter'

This rule also applies when a nasal intervenes between the /ʔ/, /h/, or /ʃ/ and the *e:

*jemaq + *-an > *rimʔæn* 'tomorrow'

*e assimilates to /u/ on the right or the left if *e is not contracted

*ɬecuŋ > *lœhœng* 'mortar' *pugek > *pozok* 'navel' *qiteluɣ > *ʔœsizol* 'egg' (< [metathesis] *qisuzul < *qisezul)

*e in the penult of trisyllabics assimilates to *a in the final syllable.

*baɣeqaŋ > *rælæʔæm* 'molar' (/r-/ unexplained [§B12.3.31]) *quseɬap > *ʔoʃaɬap* 'scales (fish)'

In some cases, under unknown conditions, *e of the penult is contracted or elided. (Cf. §§B12.1.11 and B12.1.12.)

B12.2.3 *a and *u

*a and *u have two reflexes: fronted reflexes, [æ] and [œ] respectively, and nonfronted reflexes, [a] and [o] respectively. The fronted reflexes occur in stems where they abut on a laryngeal (/h/ or a /ʔ/ that developed from *q [§B12.3.14]) or in affixed forms of these stems. The nonfronted reflex occurs in all environments except abutting on /h/ and /ʔ/. *u and *a fail to front when their reflex abuts on an automatically inserted [ʔ], and most of the cases where *u and *a fail to front are cases where [ʔ] has automatically been inserted. First, examples of the forms that follow the rule:

*bíntuqan > *bintœʔæn* 'star' *capuh > *sapœh* 'sweep' *kasiw > *kæhœy* 'tree' (< *kasuy), *sema + *ka- > *kæ-hmaʔ* 'tongue' *qaɬuj 'be carried by current' > *ʔæɬor* 'wash away' *qulu > *ta-ʔœlœh* 'head' *útaq > *m-otæʔ* 'vomit'

There are cases, however, where /a/ and /u/ fail to front when abutting /ʔ/ < *q. These cases are indicated in the following examples by bolding. Most of these forms have other irregularities as well:

*qalad > ***ʔa**liz-ing* 'fence' *qaɬiŋu 'shadow' > ***ʔa**ɬingo* 'reflection' *qaɬipugu > *ka-ʔ**a**ɬipozaʔ-an* 'whorl' *qatáy 'liver' > *ma-ʔ**a**say* 'intestines' *qusalipan > ***ʔa**longæhipan* 'centipede' *uɬah > *minsa-ʔl**a**ʔ* 'go first'

In some cases, it is the morpheme boundary that has impeded fronting (although as *kæ-hmaʔ* < *sema 'tongue', cited above, shows, fronting may take place before a morpheme boundary):

*aqetih > *ma-ʔsih* 'ebb'

---

[4] The development of *e is analogous to the development of *a and *u, in that there is fronting before the laryngeals for all three phonemes, as Li (1978:140) points out. However, *e is also fronted before /ʃ/ that developed from *s.

There is a tendency to the assimilation of *a and *u to fronted reflexes of *a and *u to the right:[5]

*bagaq 'inform, report' > *bæzæʔ* 'listen to' *baɣah > *bælæh* 'embers' *búluq > *bœlœʔ* 'k.o. slender bambo' *daɣeqam > *rælæʔæm* 'molar'

There are as many cases where assimilation does not take place:

*tuɬuh > *soɬœh* 'roast directly on fire' *tutuh > *totœh* 'strike'

In the Tonghœʔ dialect, /a/ in the penult is backed to /o/ when abutting on an /l/ that was lost:

*galih > *koih* (Taai: *kalih*) 'dig' *ɣabuk > *hœbœh* 'dust' (< *labuk)

In *naɬaq, the /a/ of the final syllable has been changed to /i/, the same change as affected *e of final syllables before *q (§B12.2.2):

*naɬaq > *naniʔ* 'pus'

B12.2.4 Diphthongs

B12.2.41 *ay, *uy

*ay and *uy are retained unchanged (except for the fronting phenomenon adjacent to a laryngeal):

*beɣay 'give' > *blay* 'give' *qaqay > *ʔæʔæy* 'leg (human)' *matáy > *masay* 'die' *bábuy > *baboy* 'pig' *ɬaŋuy > *ɬangoy* 'swim' *sehapuy > *hapoy* 'fire'

B12.2.42 *aw, *iw

*aw and *iw are retained unchanged (except for the fronting phenomenon adjacent to a laryngeal):

*babaw > *babaw* 'above' *laŋaw > *langaw* 'fly' *baliw 'change, return to previous' > *baliw* 'buy'

The word for 'tree' has metathesized the *i and the *w (as happened in the Philippines, independently):

*kasiw > *kæhœy* 'tree' (< *kahwi < *kaswi)

B12.3.0 Consonants

The following chart shows the St reflexes of the PAn consonants.

[5] /æ/ also developed in the Tonghœʔ dialect before a following /i/: *baliw > *ʃibaliw* 'sell', but in the Tonghœʔ dialect, *ʃibæiw*.

CHART TWO. DEVELOPMENT OF THE SAISIAT CONSONANTS FROM PAN

PAn	St	PAn	St
p	*p*	ɣ, l	*l* (> ∅ in Tonghœ?)
t	*t, s, ʃ*	ɬ	*ɬ*
k	*k*	m, n, ŋ	*m, n, ng*
q	*ʔ*	h	*h*
b	*b*	c	*h*
d, j	*r*	s	*ʃ*
g	*k-, -z-, -z*	w, y	*w, y*

B12.3.1 Voiceless consonants

B12.3.11 *p

*p remained /p/ in all positions:

*paŋa 'forking' > *pangaʔ* 'branch' *páqegu > *pæʔzoʔ* 'gall' *piga > *pizaʔ* 'how much, many?' *capuh > *sapœh* 'wipe' *sépat > *ʃepat* 'four'

B12.3.12 *t

*t has two outcomes: a stop /t/ and an apico-dental or interdental spirant [θ]. This phoneme is transcribed /s/ here. *t became an affricate *c, as is the case of the other languages of northeast and southwest Taiwan (§A3.3.1), and subsequently lost its affrication and became [θ].

*t reflected as /t/:

*taɬam 'taste' > *talam* 'try' *taɬék > *taɬek* 'boil starches' *teketek > *tektek* 'chop' *tiyáɬ > *tiaɬ* 'belly'[6] *batu > *batoʔ* 'stone' *gíta > *komitaʔ* 'see' *ɬatad > *ɬatar* 'front yard, outside' *búhet > *ka-bhœt* 'squirrel'

*t reflected as /s/ ([θ]):

*taqí > *sæʔiʔ* 'feces' *tawa > *somawaʔ* 'laugh' *túsuɣ > *sœhœl* 'string beads, thread needle' *tuɬuh > *sœɬœh* 'roast over fire' *bataŋ 'main portion of tree' > *basang* 'body' *butuq 'genitals' > *bosœʔ* 'testicles, scrotum' *iqetah> *kæ-ʔsæh* 'rice husk' *binit > *biɬis* 'hold in hand' *kaɣát > *kalas* 'bite' *kúlit > *kolis* 'peel'

With stems ending in /ʃ/, initial *s (from *t-) > /ʃ/ (§B12.1.4):

*talís > *ʃinaliʃ* 'chord' *taqís > *ʃomæʔiʃ* 'sew' *tiŋás > *ʃingaʃ* 'particles in teeth after eating'

In one case, *t is reflected by /h/. This is a development from *s when there is a *c later in the stem—i.e., *t > *s > /h/ when /h/ occurs within the same stem to the right of the *t. Cf. the discussion of /h/ reflecting *c in §B12.3.23, below.

*táŋic > *hœmangih* 'cry'

[6] There is also a form *somiʔæɬ* 'eat', which may be connected, but the medial /ʔ/ is irregular if this form is cognate with *tiaɬ*. (Cf. the final paragraph of §B12.1.53.)

B12.3.13 *k

*k remained /k/ in all positions.

*kasiw > *kæhœy* 'tree' *kusekus 'scrape' > *koʃkoʃ* 'shave' *likuj > *likor* 'back' *ałak 'offspring' > *ałak* 'baby'

In one case, contamination between *puqu 'bone' and *bukul 'knot' gave rise to a reflex of /ʔ/ in place of /k/:

*bukul 'knot' > *bœʔœl* 'bone'

B12.3.14 *q

*q > /ʔ/, which is contrastive word medially (§B12.1.53, above).

*liceqes > *liʔʃiʃ* 'nit' (< *liqeces) *paqit > *pæʔis* 'bitter'

/ʔ/ from *q is contrastive root initially when the root is prefixed and finally when the root is suffixed if the affixational process causes elision (§B12.1.11):

*aqetih > *maʔsih* 'ebb' (< ma-aqtih) *iqetáh > *kæ-ʔsæh* 'rice husk' *jemaq > *rimʔæn* 'tomorrow'(< *jemaq-an)

In trisyllabic roots with *q- onset of the penult, the *q is lost without trace and the abutting vowels contracted:

*tiqeɣáb > *selab* 'belch'

Traces of *q abutting on *a or *u can be detected in that the /ʔ/ that develops from *q causes *a or *u to be fronted, whereas the automatically inserted /ʔ/ does not (§B12.2.3). For example, the /ʔœ/ in the first form, below, derives from PAn *qu, because the *u has been fronted, whereas the /w/ (which developed by loss of a mora from *u) in the second form derives from PAn *u because the *u has not been fronted:

*quway > *ʔœway* 'rattan' *uɣat + *ka- > *ka-wlas* 'tendon'

B12.3.2 *h, *s, *c

*h remained unchanged in St. *s tended to move back in the mouth becoming [ʃ], and as this happened, *c lost its affrication. Subsequently, the [s] that developed from *c became [h] (merged with reflexes of *h).[7] Details are given in the subsections below.

B12.3.21 *h

*h was an unproductive phoneme in PAn. It remained unchanged in St. The following forms are all those attested with *h in St:

*baɣah > *bælæh* 'embers' *bahałiɣ > *bałihæh* 'board' (< *bałihaɣ) *capuh 'wipe' > *sapœh* 'sweep' *aqetih > *ma-ʔsih* 'ebb' *ałih > *ʔał-ʔałih-an* 'near' *lahuj 'seaward' > *lœhœr* 'downhill' *quluh > *ta-olœh* 'head' *qumah 'cultivated field' > *ʔœmæh* 'mainland' *sehapuy > *hapoy* 'fire' *tułúh > *sołœh* 'roast' *tutuh 'strike' > *totoh* 'beat'

---

[7] St shares this innovation with Atayalic (§B2.3.2). These changes were probably completed before *t developed affrication (§B12.3.12). In any case, *t > [θ] in certain environments (§A3.3.1) and did not merge with inherited *s, nor with the [s] that developed from *c.

When introducing a penult that is elided (§B12.1.11), *h and *h < *s (§B12.3.22) were lost. *h was also lost when onset of the penultimate syllable of a trisyllabic root. The resulting vowel sequence was contracted (§B12.1.12):

kałusekus > *ka-kłokœh* 'fingernail' *laheyu > *lay-layoʔ* 'wither'

*h is assimilated to /ʔ/ preceding it in the same word:[8]

*iqetah > *kæ-ʔsæʔ* 'husk' *ułah 'begin' > *minʃaʔ-laʔ* 'first'

B12.3.22 *s

*s most frequently became /ʃ/. However, in nine cases *s is reflected with /h/. The reflex /h/ is an innovation that started somewhere in central Formosa and spread, but the environment that gave rise to this innovation is unknown (cf. §A3.3.32). Examples of *s > /ʃ/:

*simag 'oil' > *ʃimal* 'fat, grease' *binesíq > *binʃiq* 'seed for planting' *busuk > *boʃok* 'drunk' *baliyus > *balyoʃ* 'typhoon'

The following are the cases where *s > /h/:

*kasiw > *kæhœy* 'tree' *kałusekus > *kakłohœh* 'fingernail' *sema > *kæ-hmaʔ* 'tongue' *qusalipan > *ʔalongæhipan* 'millipede' (< *qalungasipan < *qangulasipan) *łisebic > *łihpih-an* 'thin' *iseyup > *hiop* 'blow' (< *esiyup) *sipec > *hipih* 'small cockroach' *tusuɣ 'string beads' > *sœhœl* 'thread needle, string beads' *tumes > *somæh* 'clothes louse'

In two cases, *s > /s/. These are possibly examples of assimilation (cf.B12.1.4, 2nd¶, above).

*sagek > *sazek* 'smell' *useɣ > *ngesel* 'nasal mucus'

B12.3.23 *c

*c > /h/ in the majority of cases:

*ciku > *hikoʔ* 'elbow' *cucu > *hœhœʔ* 'breast' *acu > *ʔæhœʔ* 'dog' *icebu > *kæ-hboʔ* 'urine' *sipec > *hipih* 'small cockroach'

In two cases, *c assimilated to a following *s (that is, became /ʃ/) or *h (that is, became /s/[9]). There is no explanation:

*liceqes > *liʔʃiʃ* 'nit' *capuh 'wipe' > *sapœh* 'sweep'

In one case, *c assimilated to /s/ that developed on the left:

*suɣac > *sowas* 'scrub' (cf. §B12.1.4, 3rd¶, footnote)

---

[8] The occurrence of /ʔ/ to the left in the root does not impede the retention of *h in *aqetih > *ma-ʔsih* 'ebb'. This root is also irregular in that the /a/ is not fronted, even though it abuts on /ʔ/ < *q (§B12.2.3).

[9] The assimilation took place when *c > [s]—that is, before the change to [h]: the assimilation was to [s], not to the /h/ that developed later.

B12.3.3 Voiced consonants, stops in PAn

B12.3.31 *b

*b remained /b/ in all environments. It is a bilabial fricative pronounced [β] except when preceded by /m/, in which case it is a stop [b].

*bábuy > *baboy* 'domesticated pig' *beɣay > *belay* 'give' *buhut > *ka-bhœot* 'squirrel' *tebuk 'hit hard' > *tombok* 'kill' (< *-om-* + *tebok*) *lebeŋ > *lebeng* 'bury' *ɬibúq 'fenced in place' > *ɬiboʔ* 'bird's nest, chicken coop' *qeɬeb > *ʔiɬeb* 'close'

In one case, *b- is reflected with /r/. The /r-/ possibly reflects an alternative prefix to the root *ɣeqaŋ.

*ba-ɣeqaŋ > *rælæʔæm* 'molar' (< *da-ɣeqaŋ)

In the case of the reflex of *ɬisebic, *b is assimilated to the preceding *s, as is the case of all An languages except Bun: *ɬihpi-han* 'thin'. (Cf. the comment on *sebic in the glossary.)

B12.3.32 *d, *j

*d and *j merged to /r/ in all positions. /r/ is a retroflex continuant, similar to English [r].

*daɬum > *raɬom* 'water' *daŋ 'heat near fire' > *papa-rang* 'roast over fire' *dílaq 'tongue' > *rilæʔ* 'lick' *dumá > *ʔa-romaʔ* 'other' *paɬid > *paɬir* 'wing' *jalan > *ralan* 'road, walk' *jem 'close eyes' > *mæʔrem* 'sleep' (< *ma+ *ʔerem) *qujaɬ > *ʔœraɬ* 'rain' *luhuj 'seaward' > *læhœr* 'downhill'

In two cases, *-d is reflected as /-z/ (an interdental voiced fricative [ð]). These forms are probably borrowed, but the source is unknown. The loss of the initial *s in the second case is also irregular:[10]

*qalad > *ʔalizing* 'fence' *sadem > *maʔazʔazem* 'think'

In one case *-d- is reflected as /-s-/. This is a borrowing. Note that the final nasal is also irregular:

*qudaŋ 'crustacean' > *ʔœson* 'shrimp'

B12.3.33 *g

As onset of the penult or earlier, *g- > /k-/. In the final syllable, *g > /z/ pronounced as an interdental voiced fricative [ð].

*gáɣang > *kalang* 'crab' *kuga 'how, do what?' > *kozaʔ* 'how much, how great' *paqegu > *pæʔzo* 'gall' *balug > *baloz* 'pigeon'

In one form, *g is reflected with another phoneme . There is no explanation.

*gumis > *romiʃ* 'beard'

---

[10] However, the change of *d to /z/ is reflected in one elicited variant of a form that is also attested with /r/:

*dilaq 'tongue' > *rilæʔ, riæʔ,* or *ziæʔ* 'lick'

B12.3.4 Voiced consonants and continuants

B12.3.41 *ɣ, *l

*ɣ and *l merged to /l/, pronounced [ɭ]—a retroflexed flap. The /l/ subsequently became lost in most current St speech (cf. §B12.0, above), and in the few forms in which it was maintained, it merged with /ɬ/. Here we quote an archaic type of St recorded by Li (1974) in Taai, which maintained the /l/ [ɭ] contrasting with /ɬ/.

*ɣateb > *laseb* 'five' *beɣay > *belay* 'give' *bagiyus > *balyoʃ* 'typhoon' *daɣeq > *rali?* 'earth, soil' *bucuɣ > *bœhœl* 'bow'*láŋaw > *langaw* 'fly' *luseq > *loʃi?* 'tears' *qaselu > *ʔæʃelo?* 'pestle' *telu > *tolo?* 'three' *bukul 'protruding bone' > *bœʔœl* 'bone'

Initially, the /l/ > /h/ in the Tonghœʔ dialect:

*lebeŋ > *lebeng* (Taai) *hebeng* (Tonghœʔ) 'bury' *likuj > *likor* (Taai) *hikor* (Tonghœʔ) *laheyu > *lay-layo?* (Taai) *hayayo?* (Tonghœʔ) *luseq > *loʃi?* (Taai) *hoʃi?* (Tonghœʔ)

The root final /l/ was lost and the preceding vowel lengthened except when /i/ in the final syllable originates from *e (§B12.2.2). Otherwise, /l/ was lost without a trace in Tonghœʔ.

*kawil > *ka-kaii* 'hook' *qawuɣ > *ʔæoo* 'k.o. bamboo' *simaɣ > *ʃimaa* 'grease'

Examples where the /l/ was lost without a trace:

*pálisi > *piʃi-an* 'taboo' *balec > *ʃo-bæh* 'revenge' *biqel > *biʔi?* 'goiter'

In the following example, *l > /z/. This may be motivated by dissimilation—i.e., *l–*ɣ > /z–l/, but it is the only example of its type.

*qiteluɣ > *ʔœsizol* (Tonghœʔ *ʔœsizoo*) 'egg' (< *qetilul < *qetiluɣ)

B12.3.42 Nasals and *ɬ

*m, *n, *ŋ remained unchanged in all positions. *ɬ is reflected as a palatal lateral [ɬ] in all positions. In the Tonghœʔ dialect, the palatalization is minimal.

*matá > *masa?* 'eye' *dumá > *ʔa-roma?* 'other' *daɬúm > *raɬom* 'water' *panaq > *pænæ?* 'shoot with bow and arrow' *bituqan > *bintœʔæn* 'star' *laŋaw > *langaw* 'fly' *lebeŋ > *lebeng* 'bury'

Two cases show irregular reflexes of *ŋ. They show other irregularities and are probably not directly inherited:

*taŋíla > *saɬiʔil* 'ear' *qudaŋ > *ʔœson* 'shrimp'

B12.3.43 *w and *y

*w is retained initially, between two *a's (§B12.1.51), and as the second element in diphthongs (§B12.2.42).

*lawac 'broad' < *lawæh* 'open' *tawa > *somawa* 'laugh' *waɬiw 'bee' > *waɬo*ʔ 'sugar'

However, *-w- is unaccountably lost in the following example:

*kawanaɬ > *kaʔnaɬ* 'right (hand)' (< *kaʔanaɬ < *kaanaɬ)

*w between *a and *i is lost. Note that *i lost syllabicity by syncopation (§B12.1.11)—i.e., became /y/:

*kawiɣi > *kayliʔ* 'left (hand)' *kawil 'hook' > *kapa-kayl-an* 'hook'

Otherwise, *w is lost. However, note that [w] between /o/ or /œ/ and /a/ is noncontrastive (§B12.1.51, above).

*quway > *ʔœay* 'rattan' (This form is transcribed *ʔœway* in some sources. The two transcriptions do not represent a contrast.)

*y is analogous to *w: *y is retained between two *a's, two *u's, or between *a and *u (§B12.1.52). (But note that *y is noncontrastive when between /i/ and another vowel [§B12.1.52].) *y is also retained as the second element in diphthongs (§B12.2.41).

*daya > *rayaʔ* 'inland' *laheyu > *laylayoʔ* 'wither' *qayam 'pet' > *ʔæyam* 'animal, meat' *yu > *mo-yo* 'you (plural)'

CHAPTER ONE, §3

Thao

B13.0 Background and cultural factors that influenced the history of Thao

The information we present here is based almost exclusively on the dictionary prepared by Robert Blust (Blust: 2003). There are other sources, but the information in those sources is covered by the dictionary. Thao (Th) is spoken in two villages in the area of Sun-Moon Lake in the center of Taiwan: Te-hua (Barawbaw) and Ta-p'ing-lin (Twapina) villages. These villages already had mixed Chinese-Thao populations in the 1930's, and all Thao have been exposed to Taiwanese since childhood. By 2003 there were only fifteen full speakers of Th in Te-hua and fewer in Ta-p'ing-lin, the youngest having been born in 1937. Local traditions state that the Thao people originated to the west and came to the shores of Sun-Moon Lake via lower elevations to the north, and this tradition probably rests on historical events. They most likely left their original homeland on the plains in 1662, when they were forced to flee after siding with the Dutch against Koxinga (Blust 2003: 6). The Thao have lived close to Bunun villages since arriving at Sun-Moon Lake and very likely have intermarried with them regularly. It is not surprising, then, that Th shows Bun influence. However, there is no close genetic relation with Bun. The older outside connections are from the extinct languages of the western and northwestern plains, and it is likely that the closest genetic connections of Th are to those languages.[1]

The following chart shows the inventory of segmental phonemes in Th. The letters in parentheses are the transcriptions employed in the dictionary.

CHART ONE. PHONEMES OF THAO

Consonants						Vowels and Diphthongs			
voiceless stop	p	t	k	q	ʔ	high	i		u
voiced stop	b	d				mid		e [ə]	
spirant	f	ð (z), θ (c), s, ʃ (sh)			h	low		a	
liquid	w	l, ɬ (lh), r, y				diphthong	uy, ay	iw	aw
nasal	m	n	ng [ŋ] (g)						

[1] Blust 1996 presents some of the evidence for this, the most important of which is shared phonological innovations and a small number of shared lexical innovations. It may well be that Th has its closest genetic connection with the now-extinct languages, but as Blust points out, it is also possible that these innovations spread secondarily. In any case, these innovations, whether spread secondarily or derived from a common protolanguage, are strong evidence that Th originated in the western and northwestern plains.

/t/ and /d/ have different points of articulation: /t/ is apico-postdental, whereas /d/ is apico-alveolar (Blust 1996: 273). /ð/ and /θ/ are interdental spirants. /ɬ/ is a voiceless lateral. Other details on the articulation of these phonemes are not available. The phonemes /b/, /d/, /l/, /h/, and /ng/ are not the normal reflexes of any PAn phonemes. They do occur in forms with a PAn etymology, but the forms that contain them are probably not directly inherited by Th. There is evidence that their occurrence in Th is under the influence of Bun: (1) the articulation of /b/ and /d/ as preglottalized voiced stops (Blust 2003: 30, §2.4.2.2) coincides with the articulation of /b/ and /d/ in Bun; (2) most of the forms with these phonemes have cognates in Bun and have precisely the same meanings (§B13.1.5). Stress is contrastive, but stress contrasts have a low functional low and developed in the recent history of Th. They do not reflect PAn stress contrasts.

B13.1 Processes affecting the development of Thao from PAn

B13.1.1 Loss of syllables and contraction

Both trisyllabic and disyllabic roots lost syllables by syncope in some cases. Trisyllabic roots could develop in three ways: (1) they could lose the antepenult, (2) they could lose the penult, or (3) they could remain trisyllabics. The rules have not been worked out as to the circumstances under which a trisyllabic root disyllabized or not, but if a root did disyllabize, whether the antepenult or the penult was lost was largely determined by the phonological make-up of the root. Disyllabic roots with *e in the penult in most cases lost the *e and developed an initial CC consisting of the original initial C of the root followed by the onset of the final syllable. (Cf. the examples in §B13.1.12, below.)

B13.1.11 Loss of antepenult

Syllables with *e in the antepenult or that developed an *e in the antepenult were lost:

*sehapuy > *apuy* 'fire', *seqeɣet > *ɬiθ* 'tight' (first, loss of the antepenult, then loss of the penult [§B13.1.12]) *iceɣab > *tiɬa* 'yesterday' < (*eciɣab [§B13.1.3, 3rd¶]) *iseɬaw > *ʃinaw* 'wash' (< *esinaw)

*i in the antepenult changed to [ə] and then was lost (unless it was metathesized as was the case of the *i in *iceɣab and *iseɬaw, cited above). In other words, an antepenult with *i was elided, but the syllable onset was not lost, as was the case with *e.

*palisi+an > *parʃian* 'taboo'[2] *tineun > *tnun* 'weave' *iqetah > *qθa* 'rice husk'

*a in the antepenult of some roots changed to [ə] and then was lost by elision. As is the case of *i, when *a in the antepenult is lost, the syllable onset is retained.

*aluga > *ruða* 'paddle' *bacuheq > *fɬuq* 'wash' *qaciɣah > *qtiɬa* 'salt' *qalima > *rima* 'hand'[3] *qaɬuwaŋ > *qnuan* 'deer, buffalo' *qatipa > *qθipa* 'land turtle'

A number of forms with *a or that developed /a/ in the antepenult retained it:

---

[2] *palisi-an behaved like a root, so that the *li of the antepenult was elided.

[3] *qalima 'hand' lost the antepenult onset as well as the vowel. It should be noted that this form shows loss of the first syllable in many Formosan languages, but not in the MP languages. This is clear evidence that the shorter form spread through the Formosan languages secondarily. The shape of the word for 'five' *lima, which was derived from *qalima 'hand', but in no language manifests the first syllable, probably influenced the shape of the reflex of *qalima.

*balatuk > *baraθuk* 'woodpecker' *ɣuqaɬay > *ayuði* 'male' (< *qaɣuɬay) *pacaqaɬ > *pataqað* 'carry with shoulder pole' *qabaɣa > *qaɬafa* 'shoulder' (< *qaɣaba) *qaɬiŋu > *ɬ-qaniðu* (< *qaŋiɬu) *qiteluɣ > *qariθuy* 'egg' (< *qelituɣ)

B13.1.12 Loss of penult

In trisyllabic roots, if the penult contained *e, it was almost always elided unless metathesis had taken place (§B13.1.3). This is the case of reduplicated monosyllabic roots that had developed a PAn epenthetic *e (§A3.6.1) as well as other trisyllabic roots. It is also the case of disyllabized roots with an affix that became petrified, forming a new trisyllabic root—that is, the new trisyllabic root subsequently lost the penult if it contained *e:

*daŋedaŋ > *sansan* 'warm by the fire' *quseɬap > *quʃðap* 'fish scales' *baqeɣu > *faqɬu* 'new' *qetaq + *ma- > *mataq* 'raw, uncooked' (< *maqetaq)

The *e of the penult was elided even in the case of trisyllabics that had lost the antepenult as well:

*iqetah > *qθa* 'rice hulls' *seqeɣet > *ɬiθ* 'tight'

Other vowels in the penult are sporadically elided. The conditions for the loss of the penults in these forms are not known. Most likely these forms are borrowed, for other Formosan languages manifest the same elisions.

*qamiti > *qamθi* 'a small shrub: *Solanum nigrum*' *siyuɬuq > *ʃiðuq* 'beads, necklace'

Disyllabic roots were also affected by syncope if they contained *e—i.e., the *e of the penult is lost, and the onset forms a cluster with the onset of the following syllable. This is a different development from that of the trisyllabic roots, for there the entire antepenult, including the syllable onset, was lost when the antepenult contained *e.

*beɣay > *ɬay* 'give'[4] *bekac > *fkat* 'unspring a trap' *betu > *fθu* 'blister' *seqeɣet > *ɬiθ* 'tight' *keɣet > *kɬit* 'cut, sever'

In one case *a in the penult of a disyllabic root was elided. There is no explanation:

*qapit > qpit 'pinch, press between'

If a sequence of like vowels arises, they are contracted. Similarly, *e is lost if a sequence of a vowel plus *e arises:

*qusuŋ > *qun* 'mushroom' (< *quuŋ) *bacuheq > *fɬuq* 'wash' (< *bcuq < *becuq < *becueq < *bacueq)

B13.1.121 Nonpermitted CCs that prevent *e elision from taking place

Clusters consisting of *t, or a /t/ that developed from *c or *s, immediately followed by *l or *b were disallowed in pre-Thao.[5] Syllables with*c or *s onset and *l or *b codas with an *e nucleus did not elide the vowel.[6]

---

[4] Although *beɣay was a disyllabic root, its reflex behaves like a trisyllabic root (in that the entire penult is lost, including the onset). This may be explained by analogy: the affixed form was treated like a trisyllabic root and the entire first syllable was lost (§B13.1.11)

[5] In current Th, /tf/ and/tr/ (which would reflect *tb/*cb and *tl/*cl) are allowed (Blust 2003: 22). We assume that the rule described here developed at a stage before those clusters were allowed.

*icebu > *tubu* 'urine' *qaselu > *qaʃuru* 'pestle' *tebus > *tufuʃ* 'sugar cane' *telu > *turu* 'three'

B13.1.13 CC simplification

In current Th, there is practically no restriction on consonant sequences that may occur root medially (Blust 2003: 21). There are almost no examples of CC simplification in forms inherited from PAn.[7] There are several cases in which it is possible that the coda of a doubled monosyllabic root was lost, but these cases may be either examples of initial syllable reduplication or cases where the forms are not inherited from PAn at all.

*taketak 'chop' > *tatak* 'fell' *cuɬ > *tutuð* 'stacked up' (< *cuɬcuɬ) *daɬ > *sasað* 'old' *put 'blow' > *fufut* 'k.o. flute'

B13.1.2 Monsyllabic roots

Except for the clitics, few monosyllabic roots are inherited as monosyllabics. In most cases, the monosyllabic roots are disyllabized with petrified prefixes or they occur doubled or with reduplicated first syllables. There are three PAn monosyllabic roots attested as such in the dictionary:

*baw > *faw* 'above' *kan > *kan* 'eat' *taw > *θaw* 'person'

There are several doubled or reduplicated monosyllabic roots. Here are two of them:

*kuj 'lower shank' > *kuskus* 'foot, leg' *daɬ > *sasað* 'old'

A few monosyllabic roots are reflected in Th with petrified affixes:

*gap 'feel, grope' > *ʃu-ðap* 'touch, fondle'

Monosyllabic roots developed in a few cases from earlier disyllabic roots when the penult with *e was lost by syncope. (Cf. the examples in §B13.1.12, above.)

B13.1.3 Metathesis

All but a handful of the roots or stems that remained or became trisyllabic in Th underwent metathesis:

*baqesin > *ɬqauʃin* 'sneeze' *ɣuqaɬay > *ayuði* 'male, husband' *qabaɣa < *qaɬafa* 'shoulder' *qaɬiŋu > *ɬ-qaniðu* 'shadow, reflection' *qiteluɣ > *qariθuy* 'egg' *qusalipan > *qarupiaθ* 'centipede' (< *qaruipaθ < *quraipaθ [for loss of *s, cf. §B13.3.22] < *qulasipaθ [change of /n/ > θ unexplained] < *qulasipan) *sulaɣ > *qɬuran* 'snake' (*qaluɣan < *qulaɣ-an [/q/ on analogy with *quleg 'worm', for which no Th reflex is attested]) *taŋila > *ɬarina* 'ear'

Some of the trisyllabics that disyllabized also show metathesis:

---

[6] The attestations all have *u as the nucleus of the final syllable, and the *e of the penult is assimilated to it. The rule is stated in terms that would cover all roots of this group regardless of nucleus. However, if this rule does not hold in the case of roots where the final syllable nucleus has a vowel other than *u, then the motivation for the failure of *e to elide is not C sequences that are disallowed, but rather the nature of the final syllable. (We have no attestations of forms that would reflect *(c,s)e(l,b)i(C) or *(c,s)e(l,b)a(C).) However, in many forms, *e is elided in the penult before *u in the final syllable if the onsets of the penult and the final syllable are other than those specified here.

[7] The only possible case of CC simplification is the loss of the entire antepenult in the case of trisyllabic roots with *e as nucleus.

*betihec > *buntuθ* 'lower leg' *liceqes > *riqniʃ* 'nit' *paqegu > *qaðpu* 'gall' (*< *qagpu < *qagepu < *qapegu)

Trisyllabic roots beginning in *ice- and *ise- tended to metathesize in many An languages (§A3.5.4). This metathesis is reflected in at least three Th forms:

*iceɣab > *tiɬa* 'yesterday' *iseɬaw > *ʃinaw* 'wash' *iseyup > *iup* 'blow' (< *hiup [§B13.3.22] < *siyup < *esiyup)

Metathesis also affected disyllabic roots. The rules determining the occurrence of metathesis have not been worked out. Suffice it to say, metathesis is a widespread phenomenon in Th. The first four of the following roots are metathesized in several Formosan languages, an indication that they spread from language to language. The remainder of these forms are metathesized only in Th:

*aɬay > *ayað* 'termite' *caqub 'cover' > *tafuq* 'roof' *ciɬaɣ > *tiɬað* 'sun' *daqu > *dauq* 'the soapberry tree: *Sapindus mukorossi*' *iɣaq > *quɬa* 'red' *kasiw > *kawi* 'wood, stick, tree' *lepac > *raput* 'get free, escape' *qilus > *qiur* 'clean oneself after defecating' *qusaw > *uqaw* 'thirst' *simaɣ > *ɬimaʃ* 'grease' *tilu > *ɬuri* 'deaf' *useɣ 'nasal mucus' > *n-uðuʃ* 'blood from nose' (< *nuʃuð [cf. §A.3.7.1 for nasalization of this root])

B13.1.4 Assimilation

/θ/, /s/, and *c undergo assimilation to the right in certain cases.

(1) assimilation of /θ/: The development *t > /θ/ (§B13.3.12) went by stages. First, *t > *ts (but did not merge with inherited *c). Second, *ts > /θ/. After the first stage of development (*t > *ts), the resulting *ts assimilated to an /r/ (< *l) or to an /ʃ/ on the right—that is, it became /ɬ/ before /r/ and /ʃ/ before /ʃ/:[8]

*tali > *ɬari* 'taro: *Colocasia esculenta*' *taŋila > *ɬarina* 'ear' *tilu > *ɬuri* 'deaf' (< *tuli) *taqis > *ʃaqiʃ* 'sew'[9]

(2) assimilation of /s/ (< *d, *j): /s/ > /ɬ/. After /s/ developed, it assimilated to /ɬ/ (< *ɣ) on the right—i.e., *s (< *d/*j) became /ɬ/ before /ɬ/:

*daɣa 'k.o. tree' > *ɬaɬa* 'Formosan maple' *diɣi > *ɬiɬi* 'stand' (<*siɬi) *jaɣum > *ɬaɬum* 'needle'

(3) assimilation of /s/ (< *d, *j): /s/ > /ʃ/ before /ʃ/ (< *s) on the right.

*daqis > *ʃaqiʃ* 'face'

(4) assimilation of *c: *c > /s/ before /s/ (< *d) on the right: [10]

---

[8] Note that this change took place after *t split into two phonemes *ts and *t. Only the forms that developed *ts underwent assimilation; forms that maintained /t/ did not:

*telu > *turu* 'three' *tapes > *tapiʃ* 'winnow'

[9] Tsuchida (1976: 149) mentions the rule for assimilating /θ/ to /ʃ/ on the right, as does Blust. (Cf. footnote 11, following the next footnote in this section.)

[10] This assimilation took place before *c lost its affrication to become /t/ (§B13.3.23), for /t/ < *t does not assimilate to an /s/ on the right:

*tuduq > *tusuq* 'leak, drip' *tujuq > *tusuq* 'point'

*cukud > *sukus* 'punting pole'[11]

(5) When *c came to abut on a spirant it became /ɬ/. This took place before *c > /t/ (§B13.3.23). Cf. footnote 10 to *sukus,* (4), above.

*bacuheq > *fɬuq* 'wash' (< *fcuq < *bcuq)

B13.1.5 Influence of Bunun

As mentioned above (§B13.0), Bun had a strong influence on Th. Forms with *b, *d, *l, and *h are prima facie taken to be loan words from Bun. A large portion of forms with these phonemes are identical to the Bun form; others are close, although not identical. For a minority of them, no Bun cognate is attested, but in view of the fact that the materials on Bun are, as of present, scanty, it is quite likely that in fact Bun cognates for the missing attestations do in fact exist, only they are not listed in the materials available. However, it should be noted that St also influenced Th at an earlier time than Bun but after *b and *d had become fricatives, so that some of these forms may in fact have been borrowed from St.[12]

PAn	Thao	Bunun
*bahi	*binanauʔað*	*binanauʔað* 'woman' (Idhokan)
*bahaɬiɣ	*bangqir* 'base of tree'	*banhil* (dialectally *banqil*) 'cypress'
*biɣebiɣ	*bipi* 'lips'	*bilbil* 'lips of vagina'
*biqel	*biqi*	*biqi* 'goiter'
*bulaw	*bulaw* 'golden'	*mabulav* 'yellow'
*tumes	*tumbuʃ*	*tumbus* 'clothes louse'
*daqu	*dauq*	*daqu* 'soapberry tree'
*kuden	*kudun*	*kudung* 'clay cooking pot'
*paŋudaɬ	*panadan*	*panadan* 'k.o. tree: *Cordia myxa*'
*qaɣaw	*qalaw*	*qalaw* 'snatch'
*hulec	*hulus*	*huluc* 'clothes'

B13.2.0 Vowels and diphthongs

Th has inherited the four vowels and diphthongs of PAn. They are listed in §B13.0.

B13.2.1 *i

*i remains /i/ in all environments with the exception of forms that elided the syllable with *i (§B13.1.11).

*binesiq > *finʃiq* 'seed rice' *wiɣi > *a-iɬi* 'left'

B13.2.2 *e

*e is lost in the penult and antepenult of trisyllabic and some disyllabic roots, as discussed in §§B13.1.11 and B13.1.12, above. Where *e is not lost, it has the following developments with some exceptions:

---

[11] Blust (2003: 79, §3.2.1) motivates this by a rule of sibilant assimilation—i.e., his rule is tantamount to ¶¶2, 3, and 4 in this section. Sibilant assimilation does not cover the rule in ¶1 in this section.

[12] The form *dauq* (in the list below) is in all likelihood a borrowing from St, as the St cognate shows the same metathesis.

(1) *e > u when followed by a labial or when in the penult followed by a syllable with /u/ (§B13.1.121):

*dakep > *sakup* 'catch' *qeleb > *quruf* 'knee' *qaɣem > *qaɬum* 'pangolin' *telu > *turu* 'three'

(2) *eq > /aq/:

*baɣeq > *banga* 'abscess' (Neither the /ng/ nor the loss of *q are explained.) *luseq > *ruʃaq* 'tears'

(3) Otherwise, *e > /i/—that is, *e > /i/ before nonlabial consonants:

*bukes > *fukiʃ* 'hair' *caleŋ > *tarin* 'pine' *ngipen > *nipin* 'tooth' *sagek 'sniff' > *ʃaðik* 'smell, odor' *teketek > *tiktik* 'chop'

There are a number of exceptions where *e > /u/ before a nonlabial. In three cases, the forms are clearly borrowings. The first two refer to cultural items, and the third is a form that shows irregularities in other Formosan languages, evidence that it spread secondarily. In the fourth case, the vowel of the final syllable may well have been influenced by another word similar in form and meaning:

*hulec > *hulus* 'clothing' *kuden > *kudun* 'clay cooking pot' *tumes > *tumbuʃ* 'clothes louse' *tukej > *tukus* 'prop, walking stick'

In other cases, *e > /u/, but there is no explanation. Most of these forms have other irregularities:

*betihec 'calf' > *buntuθ* 'lower leg' *lepac > *raput* 'get free' (< *rupat) *useɣ 'nasal mucus' > *nuðuʃ* 'blood from the nose' (< *nuʃuð [cf. §A.3.7.1 for nasalization of this root])

In one case, *e > /i/ before a labial. The St cognate of this form also manifests /i/ in the first syllable, and Th may have borrowed this form from there:

*jemaq > *simaq* 'tomorrow'

B13.2.3 *a and *u

Except when lost in certain trisyllabic roots (§B13.1.11, above), *a remained /a/ in all environments:

*daqaɬi 'daytime' > *saqaði* 'noon' *qabaɣa > *qaɬafa* 'shoulder' *ina > *ina* 'mother'

In one unexplained case, *a > /u/. The form is clearly of PAn origin, but no other language manifests /u/ in the first syllable:

*kaɣaw 'scratch, mite' > *kuɬaw* 'scratch (an itch)'

Except for the few cases where /u/ is elided (§B13.1.12), *u remains /u/:

*bucuɣ > *futuɬ* 'bow' *mugiŋ > *muðin* 'nose' *qaɬingu 'shadow' > *ɬ-qaniðu* 'shadow, reflection'

B13.2.4 Diphthongs

B13.2.41 *ay, *uy

*ay and *uy are retained unchanged:

*beɣay > *ɬay* 'give' *pagay > *paðay* 'rice plant' *babuy > *fafuy* 'pig' *sehapuy > *apuy* 'fire'

There is also a form *afu* 'cooked rice, meal' that is descended from *sehapuy, but it is not directly inherited in Th. The source is unknown: no language that is known to have affected Th reflects *p with [b], [f], or [v].

B13.2.42 *aw, *iw

*aw and *iw are retained unchanged.

*baw > *faw* 'above' *laŋaw >*ranaw* 'fly' *taw > *θaw* 'person' *baliw 'change, return to previous' > *fariw* 'buy'

The word for 'tree' has metathesized the *i and the *w (as happened independently in most of the Formosan and Philippine languages):

*kasiw > *kawi* 'tree'

B13.3.0 Consonants

The following chart shows the Th reflexes of the PAn consonants:

CHART TWO. DEVELOPMENT OF THE PAZIH CONSONANTS FROM PAN

PAn	Thao	**PAn**	Thao
p	*p*	h	*Ø*
t	*t, θ*	s	*ʃ*
k	*k*	c	*t*
q	*q*	m	*m*
b	*f*	n, ŋ	*n*
d	*s*	ɬ	*ð*
j	*s*	l	*r*
g	*k-, -ð-, -ð*	w	*w*
ɣ	*ɬ*	y	*y*

B13.3.1 Voiceless consonants

The voiceless consonants were the most stable in Th. *c lost its affrication (> /t/). Otherwise, the consonants underwent little change, except for the assimilations discussed in §B13.1.4.

B13.3.11 *p

*p remained /p/ in all positions.

*paŋa 'forking' > *pana* 'branch, bifurcation' *paqegu > *qaðpu* 'gall' *piga > *piða* 'how much, many?' *sepat > *ʃpat* 'four' *iseyup > *iup* 'blow'

In one or two cases /f/ is reflected instead of /p/. In the first case, the reconstruction is speculative (see the commentary in the glossary). In the second case, the resemblance may be fortuitous, for the form is onomatopoetic.

*lepag > *ma-rfað* 'fly' *put 'blow on' > *fufút* 'flute, whistle made of two blades of grass'

B13.3.12 *t

*t has two outcomes: a stop /t/ and /θ/. /θ/ developed when *t became an affricate *[ts], as is the case of the other languages of northeast and southwest Taiwan (§A3.3.1, first footnote). It subsequently lost its affrication to become [θ].

*t reflected as /t/:

*tałam 'taste' > *taðam* 'taste, try' *teketek > *tiktik* 'chop' *tiyał > *tiað* 'belly' *batu > *fatu* 'stone' *keɣet > *kłit* 'cut off'

*t reflected as /θ/:

*taketak 'chop, fell' > *θakθak* 'knock down' *takaw > *θakaw* 'steal' *kutu > *kuθu* 'head louse' *seqeɣet > *łiθ* 'tight' *uɣat > *ułaθ* 'vein, tendon'

After *t had become an affricate *[ts] in certain environments, *[ts] further assimilated to an /ł/ or to an /ʃ/ on the right. (Cf the examples in §B13.1.4.)

In one case, *t- underwent nasal substitution (§A3.7.1). Th is the only language that reflects nasal substitution in this form:

*tułuh 'roast' > *nuðu* 'glowing firewood'

B13.3.13 *k

*k remained /k/ in all positions:

*kasiw > *kawi* 'wood, tree' *kutu > *kuθu* 'head louse' *likuj > *rikus* 'back' *teketek > *tiktik* 'chop up'

In one case *k is reflected with /q/. This form may have been borrowed from a language that did not contrast /k/ and /q/ and pronounced the /k/ with post-velar allophones, such that they sounded to the Th speaker like /q/. Note that it is between two *u's:[13]

*tuku > *tuqu* 'prop, post'

B13.3.14 *q

*q remained /q/, a back velar voiceless stop in all positions, including the onset of a syncopated antepenult in trisyllabic roots (§B13.1.11):

*quway > *quay* 'rattan' *baqeɣuh > *faqłu* 'new' *pacaqał > *pataqað* 'carry over shoulder with a pole' *bagaq > *faðaq* 'inform, know' *punuq > *punuq* 'head, brain' *qaciɣah > *qtiła* 'salt'

There are a few cases where *q is lost. These are mostly forms that evince other irregularities, and it is likely that they are borrowings, although the source cannot be identified:

*baɣeq > *banga* 'abscess' *ɣuqałay > *ayuði* 'male' (< *qaɣułay) *pułetiq > *puði* 'white'

---

[13] *k normally remained /k/ between two *u's:

*cukud > *sukus* 'punting pole' *kukuh > *kuku* 'nail, claw'

There is also a reconstructed form *pukuh 'joint, node', which is connected with *puqu* 'joint in finger, bone'. In this case, there was contamination among several forms similar in sound and meaning and not a change of *k > /q/. The Th form reflects a form reconstructed for earliest PAn, *puqu, and is a retention rather than a development from *pukuh.

B13.3.2 *h, *s, *c

*h disappeared entirely, *s developed palatalization (> /ʃ/), and *c lost its affrication (> /t/).

B13.3.21 *h

*h was lost without a trace:

*lahuj 'seaward' > *raus* 'downriver' *baqeɣuh > *faqɬu* 'new' *tiheɬaw > *tilaw* 'clear'

B13.3.22 *s

*s most frequently became /ʃ/ when not lost in trisyllabic roots that were syncopated (§B13.1.11). In seven cases, *s is lost. In pre-Thao, *s in these forms became *h, which was subsequently lost (just as the *h inherited from PAn). The reflex *h is an innovation that started somewhere in central Formosa and spread, but the environment that gave rise to this innovation is unknown (cf. §A3.3.32).
Examples of *s > /ʃ/:

*sagek 'sniff' > *ʃaðik* 'smell, odor' *sepat > *ʃepat* 'four' *binesiq >*finʃiq* 'seed rice' *bukes > *fukiʃ* 'hair' *taqis > *ʃaqiʃ* 'sew'

The following are the cases where *s > ∅

*iseɣup >*iyup* 'blow' *kasiw > *kawi* 'tree' *qilus > *qiur* 'clean after defecating' *qusalipan > *qarupiaθ* 'centipede' (< *qaruipaθ < *quraipaθ < *qulasipaθ [change of /n/ > θ unexplained] < *qulasipan) *qusaw > *uqaw* 'thirst' *qusuŋ > *qun* 'mushroom' *sawak > *awak* 'waist'

There are two forms in which *s is reflected as /h/. These are forms, the cognates of which in the other Formosan languages (that preserve *s) do not reflect the change of *s to /h/:

*busat 'work, do' > *buhat* 'swidden'[14] *isu > *ihu* 'you (sing)'

B13.3.23 *c

*c > /t/ with some exceptions:

*ciɬaɣ 'ray' > *tiɬað* 'sun, ray' *acu > *atu* 'dog' *pacaqaɬ > *pataqað* 'carry over shoulder' *kacekac > *mu-katkat* 'undo'

*c > /s/ before /s/ (< *d) on the right. (Cf. the example in §B13.1.4(4).)
In three cases, *c > /θ/. They may be borrowed from St, although only the second example is attested in the scanty St data available. The third case is a form that spread secondarily in many of the Formosan languages:

*caliw 'give in exchange' > *θariw* 'buy, sell'[15] *capuh > *θapu* 'sweep' *qulec > *huluθ* 'clothing'

*c, in two words with an onomatopoetic meaning, got substituted for by other spirants, probably under the influence of other words with similar meanings:

---

[14] *Buhat* is probably not a reflex of *busat. The initial *b-* is an an anomaly.

[15] *ca- in *caliw was a prefix (*liw is also attested as a monosyllabic root—see the entry *liw in the glossary). It may be then that the /θa-/ of *θariw* remounts to a protoform *taliw. However, no other language attests a reflex of this.

*gacegac 'scratch' > *kaʃkaʃ* 'scratch up the soil' *kicekic > *kiɬkiɬ* 'grate, rasp'

There are two forms, with well-attested reflexes of PAn forms in many languages, that have idiosyncratic reflexes of *c in Th. There is no explanation:

*liceqes > *riqniʃ* 'nit' *ɬecuŋ > *runu* 'mortar'

B13.3.3 Voiced stops and *ɣ

The voiced stops became spirants. *b, *d, *j, and *ɣ also became voiceless. *d,*j, *g, and *ɣ moved frontward: *d and *j merged to become /s/ after inherited *s developed palatalization (§B13.3.22); *g became an interdental spirant /ð/, and *ɣ became a voiceless lateral /ɬ/.

B13.3.31 *b

*b > /f/ in all positions:

*babaw >*i-fafaw* 'above' *babuy > *fafuy* 'pig' *qaleb > *qaruf* 'knee'

In a number of cases, *b is reflected with /b/. In §B13.1.5 we suggest that these forms are in fact Bun borrowings, given that the majority of them have an attested cognate in Bun. In one form, medial *-b- is unaccountably lost. In another form, final *-b is unaccountably lost. In the second case, the *-b is also lost in cognates in the languages of northern Formosa—i.e., St, Paz, as well as the extinct language Favorlang, and probably also in Tsouic and Atayalic (although in the latter two, loss of word-final consonant is a regular process).

*libut > *riut* 'encircle, surround'[16] *iceɣab > *tiɬa* 'yesterday'

In one case, *-b is reflected with /w/, as is the case in the Paz cognate.[17]

*suwab > *maʃua-ʃuaw* 'yawn'

B13.3.32 *d, *j

*d and *j merged and became /s/:

*dakep > *sakup* 'catch' *qalad 'fence for a pen' > *qaras* 'fence, boundary' *tuduq > *tusuq* 'leak, drip' *jalan > *saran* 'path' *tujuq > *tusuq* 'point' *kuj 'lower shank' > *kuskus* 'foot, leg'

The word for 'two' has an initial /t/ instead of the expected /s/. This irregularity is shared with Amis, and it is possible that PAn in fact had a variant with initial *t instead of *d:

*dusa > *tuʃa* 'two'[18]

---

[16] The lack of an intevocalic /b/ has nothing to do with the environment. There is at least one other inherited root in Th reflecting the sequence *ibu where a reflex of *-b- is retained:

*ɬibu 'den, pen' > *ðifu* 'nest, lair'

[17] The extinct western languages Taokas, Papaora, and Siraya seem to have cognates of this form. They also have lost final *-b.

[18] Dissimilation cannot explain the /t-/. There is only one case of dissimilation, and that is discussed in the following footnote. Otherwise, Th has rules of assimilation: *d–*s > /ʃ–ʃ/ (§B13.1.4(3)). Perhaps the PAn form was *tusa, from *tus plus a linker *a. In that case, *dusa arose in postvocalic environments by a rule that voiceless consonants became voiced intervocalically, at least in atonic position. The notion that the /a/ of dusa is

*d and *j > /ɬ/ before *ɣ to the right in the same root. (Cf. the examples in §B13.1.4.)
In a handful of forms, *d > /d/. We hypothesize that these forms were borrowed from Bun. (Cf. the examples in §B13.1.5.)
In one case *-d is lost. A possible explanation is that this form is a borrowing from St *paɬir* 'wing' (where St [ɬ] is voiced and borrowed as [l] by Th) and the loss of the final C is connected with the occurrence of /l/ to the left.[19]

*paɬid > *pali* 'wing'

B13.3.33 *g

As onset of the penult or earlier, *g- > /k-/:

*gaɣaŋ > *kaɬan* 'crab' *gali > *kari* 'dig'

As onset or coda of the final syllable,[20] *g > /ð/. *g moved forward to fall together with the reflex of *ɬ (§B13.3.41)[21]—that is, it moved to interdental position together with the delateralized reflexes of *ɬ.

*kuga > *kuða* 'how?' *piga > *piða* 'how much, how many' *balug > *faɬuð* 'dove'

B13.3.34 *ɣ

*ɣ moved forward to become a palatalized lateral and subsequently[22] lost its voicing, becoming a voiceless lateral /ɬ/.

*ɣamit > *ɬamit* 'root' *seqeɣet > *ɬiθ* 'tight' *jaɣum > *ɬaɬum* 'needle' *bucuɣ > *futuɬ* 'bow'

After *ɣ became a palatalized lateral, but before it lost its voicing, the voiced lateral became /ð/ if there was an /r/ to the left (cf. the second footnote to §B13.3.32):

*lawaɣ > *rawað* 'flying squirrel' *linuɣ > *rinuð* 'earthquake'

An /n/ in the root also caused *ɣ > /ð/:

---

in its origin a linker comes from Sagart (2004: 417). He also suggests that *dusa was earlier, and *tusa developed analogically under the influence of *telu 'three'.

[19] Pre-Thao did not tolerate /r/ following /ɬ/ in the same root. The /r/ was dropped (as here). *qɬuran* 'snake' is not a countercase, for this form developed at a later stage when Th did allow an /r/ to follow /ɬ/. /ɬ/ following /r/ to the left was changed to /ð/ as in §B13.3.34, 2nd¶. Further, palatalized laterals developed from *t before /r/ (§B13.1.4).

[20] The only attestation that reflects final *-g is *faɬuð* 'dove' < *balug. This word may well not be directly inherited because it has an irregular reflex of *l.

[21] The merger of *ɬ and *g also occurred in Tsouic, but this took place quite independently. In Tsouic *g > *y (merging with the inherited *y), and then the *y hardened to become /ɬ/. Since *ɬ is reflected in Tsouic as voiceless [ɬ], this caused a merger of the reflexes of *g and *ɬ (§§B31.3.33 and B31.3.41). In the case of Th, *g moved forward but never merged with *y. *ɬ lost its lateralization and moved forward to become interdental [ð] and so merged with the reflexes of *g.

[22] Our hypothesis that devoicing of the reflex of *ɣ is subsequent to lateralization is supported by the evidence that *ɣ > /ð/ after /r/: *ɣ became [ð] in two stages: first, *ɣ became *[ɬ]; then if there was an [r] to the left, *[ɬ] > [ð]. The impetus for *[ɬ] < * ɣ to move forward to interdental position was provided by the need to avoid two voiced liquids in the alveolar-palatal region in the same root. If the *[ɬ] that had developed from *ɣ were already voiceless, there would have been no impetus for *[ɬ] to move forward.

*biɣiŋ 'edge' > *fa-fiðin* 'edge of a bed' *useɣ 'snot' > *nuðuʃ* 'blood from nose' (< *nuʃuð [cf. §A.3.7.1 for nasalization of this root])

In a few cases *ɣ is reflected with /l/. These forms are probably borrowed from Bun (although not all of them have cognates attested in Bun [cf. §B13.1.5]).[23]

*ɣawus > *lauʃ* 'scoop out' *qaɣaw > *qalaw* 'snatch, sieze' (Bun *qalaw* 'snatch') *waɣi 'day' > *qali* 'day, sky, weather' (Bun *vali* ' sun' [Th /q-/ may possibly reflect a prefix *qu—cf. the commentary to *waɣi.])

In one form, medial *ɣ is dropped and the vowels are contracted. This form has a PAn etymology, but it cannot be directly inherited. The source of the loan word is unknown. It should be noted that Bun and Pai also manifest irregular reflexes of this root:

*baɣaq > *faq* 'lungs'

There are three forms that have /y/ as a reflex of *ɣ. These forms manifest other irregularities, and they are most certainly borrowings, but the source is unknown.

*ɣuqaɬay 'male' > *ayuði* 'male, husband' (*yuaði < *yuqaɬi) *qiteluɣ > *qariθuy* 'egg' (< *qatiluɣ) *m-aɣi 'come here' > *n-ay* 'here'

B13.3.4 The liquids and nasals in Thao

B13.3.41 *l and *ɬ

*l is reflected by /r/.

*lahud 'seaward' > *rahut* 'downstream' *lebeŋ > *rebeng* 'bury (but not a human)' *ala > *ara* 'take' *telu > *turu* 'three' *gemel 'squeeze in hand' > *kemer* 'take a handful, grasp'

*ɬ became a voiced palatalized lateral and then moved forward to interdental position to become /ð/. In this way *ɬ merged with *g and *ɣ (cf. §B13.3.33, above):

*ɬam 'taste' > *ðamðam* 'tasty, chew' *paɬaw 'go' > *paðaw* 'walk' *cucuɬ > *tutuð* 'stacked up'

There are cases in which *ɬ > /n/. These are probably loan words from a language in which *ɬ > /n/, possibly Bun. (However, only three of them have attested Bun cognates.) The following forms exemplify this:

*iseɬaw > *ʃinaw* 'wash' *luɬ > *runrun* 'roll up' *ɬala > *ʃ-nara* 'ignite' *ɬatuq > *naθuq* 'k.o. tree' *paŋudaɬ > *panadan* 'k.o. tree' *qaɬuwaŋ > *qnuan* 'buffalo, deer'

In three cases, *ɬ is reflected by /l/—i.e., the palatal lateral lost its palatalization (as happened in Atayalic). These forms are probably loan words, possibly from St. (This is possible, even though *matilaw* has no cognate attested among the scanty data available from St.)[24]

---

[23] St also reflects *ɣ with /l/, but a St cognate for these forms is not attested among our scanty St data.

[24] The palatalization in current St is very light, almost absent, because inherited /l/ has gotten lost, but this was surely not the case at a time that Th could have borrowed from St. If these forms are St borrowings, the borrowing must have taken place after *ɬ had moved forward to interdental position (> [ð]), for otherwise they would have been borrowed with /ɬ/ and not with /l/.

*ɬawuŋ > *laun* 'shade, shadow' (St *ɬaong* 'shadow') *paɬid >*pali* 'wing' (St *paɬir*) *tiheɬaw > *ma-tilaw* 'clear'

In one case,*ɬ is reflected with /r/. This may be a case of dissimilation before a /ð/ (< *g) to the right. However, it is the only case, and the form shows another irregularity in its vowel reflex:

*qaɬipugu > *qaripaðu* 'whorl'

B13.3.42 Nasals

*m, *n remained unchanged in all positions.

*mudiŋ > *muzin* 'nose' *qalima > *rima* 'hand' *qaɣem > *qaɬum* 'pangolin' *naɬaq > *naðaq* 'pus' *jalan > *saran* 'road'

*ŋ merged with *n to become /n/:[25]

*laŋaw > *ranaw* 'fly' *taŋic > *θanit* 'weep' *caleŋ > *talin* 'pine'

B13.3.43 *w and *y

*w remains /w/ initially and medially. However, [w], between front and back or back and front vowels, does not contrast with its absence.

*waɬis 'fang' > *waðiʃ* 'wild boar' *kasiw > *kawi* 'tree, wood' *ɬiwaŋ > *ðiwan* 'thin (person)' *tawa > *θa-θawa* 'laugh'

There is one exception where *w was lost without explanation. The form is secondary. This innovation is shared with Knn, Sar (but not Tsou), St, and Paz.

*wiɣi > *a-iɬi* 'left'

In one unexplained case, *w has been replaced by *q. (Cf. the discussion of this attestation in §B13.3.34, 4th¶, above.)

*waɣi > *qali* 'day'

For final *-w, see §B13.2.42.
*y remained /y/ between two *a's.

*aɬay > *ayað* 'termite' *daya 'inland' > *saya* 'upriver'

There is no contrast between *y and its absence between *i and *u or *a and between *a and *i.
For *-y, cf. §B13.2.41. There are no attestations of forms with *y in an environment other than between two *a's and in final position.[26]

---

[25] No Th reflexes of words with initial *ŋ- in PAn are attested. However the prenasalized forms that reflect PAn *ŋ- in other languages (§A3.7.1) have cognates with /n-/ in Th:

*ipen > *nipin* 'tooth' (cf. St *nepen/ngepen* Tag *ngipin* 'tooth' [but Paz *lipen* < *ɬipen]) *useɣ 'nasal discharge' >*nuðuʃ* 'blood from nose' (cf. St *ngoʃel* Bun *ngusul* 'nasal discharge')

[26] However, *i 'name marker' added to vowel-initial pronouns > /y-/. (That is, the antepenult is lost §B13.1.11.)

*i+aku > *yaku* 'I, me' (< *iaku) *i + aken > *yakin* 'I, me' *i + amen > *yamin* 'we, us (excl)'

Chapter Two
Atayalic

B2.0 Background and cultural factors that influenced the history of Atayalic

The Atayalic languages, spoken in the northeast quarter of Taiwan, are composed of two closely related languages, Atayal (At) and Sediq (Sed), each of which is dialectally quite diverse. The languages and dialects, though historically close, differ greatly on the surface and for a large part are mutually unintelligible. The reason for this is that these languages have undergone great changes that have rendered the resulting forms unrecognizable or nearly so. These changes have had three causes: (1) addition of infixes after the penult of the root or of suffixes that have in many cases altered the form of the root in the process of affixation, (2) the existence of strong stress on the penult of the word, that has caused weakening in the unstressed syllables, (3) processes of normal phonetic change—loss of contrast in root-final consonants, spirantization of intervocalic voiced consonants, and other changes that came about as a result of the nature of the process of articulation in Atayalic. The process of suffixation or occasional infixation after the penult listed under (1) above is the product of what has been termed "male speech" (Li 1980b), whereby the inherited form was considered "female" and the affixed form "male". In most cases, only the male form has survived—i.e., the one that has developed furthest from the original PAn form. In some cases the attestation in any individual At or Sed dialect alone could scarcely lead to the sound laws that explain how the attested forms came into being. However, a study of forms in various Sed and At dialects, in most of these cases, leads to the reconstruction of an earlier proto-Atayalic ancestor of the attested forms, and this ancestor, though also changed from its PAn origin, has not developed so far that it cannot be compared to cognate forms in other languages.

A factor complicating the understanding of the development of PAn phonology in Atayalic is the large amount of borrowing that has gone on among the various Atayalic dialects, such that in those cases where a given PAn phoneme has different reflexes in various dialects, a given protophoneme may be reflected in several ways in any given dialect.

Fortunately for the purposes of this reconstruction, the groundwork for comparison of the Atayalic dialects was laid in Li 1981, in which forms from five dialects of At and three of Sed were compared for close to 350 items. In fact, this study makes a start toward formulating the sound laws that relate the attested forms to reconstructed PAn according to the phonology as it was understood at the time. In addition Li 1980 provides rules of morphophonemic alternation that make internal reconstruction possible and clarify the sound correspondences among the various dialects.

The At dialect that is considered the standard and that is the best attested, Squliq (Sq), is also the most strongly developed. Many of the attestations do not allow one to see a connection with the PAn ancestor.[1] For this reason, we take the dialect that is overall the most conservative, At Mayrinax (Mx), as the basic dialect for this study. Whereever we have the information we will quote the Mx attestation, and if the Mx attestation has undergone alterations such that it cannot be compared directly with the PAn form, forms in other At or Sed dialects are provided that enable us to discern the sound laws that led to the Mx form. If no Mx form is attested, forms in other At or Sed dialects are quoted, as many forms in other dialects as necessary to show how these forms are connected with the PAn etymon.
The Mx forms listed here have been checked with informants in Ciniɣabin, Mayrinax (Chin Shui), principally Mr. Baiso Yuke (born 1931), and in Cikitoo, where a divergent dialect, Kinhakol, is spoken, principally Mr. Tau Li Hayong (born 1918).

B2.01 Phonemics of Atayalic dialects

The following chart gives the phonemes of At:

CHART ONE. PHONEMES OF ATAYALIC

Consonants

voiceless	p	t	k	q	ʔ
voiced	b [β]	d		ɣ	
spirants		s, z		x	h
liquid	w	l,	r, y		
nasal	m	n		ng [ŋ]	

Vowels and Dipthongs

high	i		u
mid		ə	
low	e	a	o
diphthongs			uy
		aw, ay	

/ɣ/ is a voiced velar spirant in Mx and Kinhakul. It is a voiced velar stop [g] in some dialects.[2] /h/ has pharyngeal friction—i.e., it is pronounced [ɦ] in the speech of my Mx and Kinhakul informants. The sources state that /ʔ/ has pharyngealization in some dialects, but the two phonemes /h/ and /ʔ/ do not fall together in any dialect. According to the information that has been published, Sq and most of the At dialects have CC clusters only in reduplicated monosyllabic roots. However, the sources for Sed and At transcribe forms with consonant clusters. In fact, what is written as a cluster is in phonetically separated by [ə]. For example, a form written *mkbkaʔ* 'split' (Sq) in the sources is in fact pronounced as four syllables [məkəbəkaʔ]. A form written *gyar* 'flee' (Sq) is disyllabic: [giyar]. There is evidence that /ə/ is a phoneme: some stems have [ʔə] as the first syllable, e.g *ʔəzil* 'left (side) (Sq) < *ʔizil (attested in Kinhakul *ʔizil*) < *ʔiil (attested in Mx *ʔiil*). It is clear that a [ʔ] is automatically inserted initially before a V and finally after a V—i.e., [ʔ] is noncontrastive. If [ʔ] is noncontrastive, then in Sq the [ə] of [ʔəzil] must be contrastive. If /ə/ is contrastive in Sq,

---

[1] For example, it would be impossible to connect Squliq *byacing* 'moon' with PAn *bulaɬ without the attestations in other dialects, However, AtSkikun *byalting* demonstrates that the inherited root in Squliq is *bya-* and that the *-l* from *-ɬ was lost. Further the Palngawan form, *burating,* shows that *bya-* is from an earlier *bura-, so that we may reconstruct PAt *bural, which is directly connectable to PAn *bulaɬ.

[2] The sources all write *g* and state that this is a stop. In the area in which we did work with informants this sound was produced at the very back of the velum and was spirantized. I transcribe forms that we recorded with *ɣ* but quote the forms from the published sources as they are given—with *g*.

then it must be contrastive in all the Atayalic dialects. There are not many /ə/'s inherited from PAn. Most of the ə's that occur in the Atayalic dialects result from vowel weakening. Mx does not evince this phenomenon.
However, the glottal stop [ʔ] is contrastive intervocalically within the root. That is the only environment in which /ʔ/ is contrastive, for it is automatically inserted word initially before a vowel and word finally after a vowel. Between vowels in a sequence that developed when a consonant was lost or a suffix added /ʔ/ may be inserted, but it is not always inserted, for sequences of like-vowels occur in Mx. The following forms illustrate the insertion of /ʔ/ and the failure to insert it. No rule has been discovered that explains the two reflexes.

> *kaɣat > *kaat* 'bite' *kelem 'night, darkness' > *kuʔum* 'dark' *quwaŋ > *quwang* 'crack, fissure' *bulaɬ > *buwa-ting* 'moon'

A glide /w/ or /y/ is inserted between front and back vowels that came to abut—i.e., *i+a/u/* > *iya/iyu; *u+a/i* > *uwa/uwi; *a + i/u* > *ayi/awu.* In the synchronic phonology, vowel sequences consisting of a back followed by a front or a front followed by a back do not occur. In Sq /y/ is inserted everywhere in place of /w/. In the process of vowel weakening (§B2.1.1), the /y/ inserted between /i/ and another vowel is sometimes affricated (> /z/):

> *qaselu > *qsizuʔ* 'pestle' (< *qasiyuʔ < *qasiluʔ) (Sq) (cf. Mx *qasuuʔ,* Sed *səruʔ*)

However, /z/ did not develop in Sq *biyacing* 'moon' < *bulaɬ.

B2.1 Changes which characterize Atayalic in general

B2.1.1 Stress in the Atayalic dialects and its effects

Most of the Atayalic dialects developed strong stress on thepenultimate syllable of the word. This caused a reduction to a centralized vowel /ə/ of /a/ or /u/ in some or all of the other syllables in the word. Since most of the attestations have 'male speech' suffixes (B2.0), the stress in fact often falls on the final syllable of the root. /i/ of the antepenult is also subject to weakening or loss. The extent to which vowel weakening takes place is greater in some dialects than in others. Sq and the dialects most closely related to Sq are the most innovative in this: for example, in the case of *laŋaw > *ng-liʔ* 'fly' (Sq and Skikun), only one consonant of the root and the suffix (the male form) have been preserved. The other vowels, and in fact the entire root save for /ng/, have been lost. The rules for syllable reduction in the various dialects are too complicated to be within the scope of this study. Mx, however, is hardly affected by weakening—most of the Mx forms evince no weakening: *laŋaw > Mx *wangaw* 'fly'.

B2.1.2 CC simplification

Root final consonants are lost in most dialects when a consonant initial suffix is added. These suffixes are all from the 'male speech register', and since this register predominates, some Atayalic attestations do not reflect the root final consonant. [3]

> *biɣaq > *bga-yaw 'Alocasia'* (Sq) *lumut > *yumu-riq* 'moss' (Skikun) *batuk 'skull' > *batu-nux* 'head' *bulaɬ> *buwa-ting* 'moon'

---

[3] Skikun retains the root final consonant, however, and loses the initial C of the suffix in the following form: *bulaɬ > *buwal-ing* 'moon', cf. Mx *buwa-ting.*

Sometimes metathesis (§B2.1.4) preserved the root-final C:

*qaɬi-matek > *maktu-ruʔ* 'leech' (Palngawan)

When *ɣ came to abut on a C due to elision of the vowel following *ɣ, it became lost in most dialects. For example, the prefixes *paɣ-/maɣ-/naɣ- are reflected in Mx as *pa-/ma-/na-:*

**maɣ- + bahuq >mabahuq* 'wash (clothes) *biɣeŋi 'night' > *bingi* 'leave s.t. overnight and let it spoil'

In the following form the *ɣ was not lost, but rather became devoiced (as at the end of a word [§B2.3.34]) and metathesized:

*baɣiyus > *bayxu* 'storm' (< *baxyu < *baɣyu)

B2.1.3 Elision and vowel contraction

Trisyllabic roots with an *e disyllabize by losing the *e. The resulting CC cluster is usually simplified, but not always. The rules for when and how CC simplification takes place are not understood.[4]

*ɬisebic > *lihpiq* 'thin' (no CC simplification) *tahebu > *tboʔ* 'bottle gourd' (with CC simplification) *sehapuy > *hapuy* 'fire' *qetut > *tiɣi-qut-iʔ* 'break wind' (< *tqutiʔ [cf. Sq *tquc-iʔ*] < *tequtiʔ [§B2.1.4] < *qetut+iʔ)

Final syllables of disyllabic roots consisting of *el and *eɣ also get elided sporadically. This process probably happened in suffixed forms, and the allomorph of the suffixed form spread to root-final position:

*gatel > *ma-ka-kat* 'itch' *deŋeɣ > *pung* 'hear'

Antepentults with an *e nucleus were lost.. Antepenults other than those containing *e are lost sporadically. No rule has been found to determine when these antepenults are lost and when they are not lost:[5]

*bituka > *katuʔ* 'stomach' (Kinhakul) *daqaɬi > *qali-yan* 'noon'

When a vowel sequence develops, contraction may take place in most dialects. Contraction yields different results in different dialects, as the example of *baqeɣuh, immediately following, shows. The rules for when contraction takes place and when it fails to take place have not been established.

*baqeɣuh > *bah* 'new' (Sq) (< *bauh < *bauɣuh), *bugux/bagux* (SedTaroko < *bauɣuh) *bacuheq > *bahuq* 'wash' *bulehaɣ 'impaired vision' > *ma-buloq* 'blind' *kaɣat > *kat* (Sq) 'bite' (The Mx reflex is uncontracted: *kaat*)

---

[4] Roots beginning with *ice- or *ise- in PAn are not affected by this rule: *ice- and *ise- at the beginning of pre-Atayalic roots underwent metathesis in the penult and antepenult of (*ice > *ci- and *ise > *si-[§A3.5.4]).

[5] The most likely explanation is that the roots that lost the antepenult were suffixed with one of the 'male affixes', a factor that made the stress move further to the right from the antepenult of the root, as was the case of *qaliyan* 'noon':

*daqaɬi + -an > *deqaliyan > *qali-yan*

B2.1.4 Metathesis

Metathesis is widespread in the Atayalic languages. Roots containing *t plus another voiceless stop tend to metathesize when the syllables containing them and the vowels between them are not final in the word:

*qetut > *tquc-iʔ* 'break wind' (Sq) *bitúka > *katuʔ* 'stomach' (Kinhakul), *qaɬi-matek > *maktu-ruʔ* 'leech' (Palngawan)

There are cases of metathesis of syllables containing *q: either a q-onset and the vowel of the syllable or just the vowel is metathesized.

*daqaɬ > *qara-x* 'branch'*qaɣaw 'snatch' > *na-ɣaqaw* 'new land' *qepa 'hull' > *paqiʔ* 'chaff' *ma-qetaq > *mataq* 'raw' (<*mqataq < *məqataq < *maqatəq) *taɬeq 'soil in a paddy' > *cəlaq* 'mud, paddy' (< *teɬaq)

Metathesis is normally connected with vowel loss and is confined to dialects where this takes place. However, there are cases of metathesis with no vowel loss.

*bugeq 'foam' > *uba* 'water on top of rice' (< *bua cf. Sed *buwaʔ*)

There are cases of purposeful metathesis (for euphemism or to avoid pronouncing a taboo word).

*qaɬitu > *ʔaliyut-ux* 'evil spirit' *qaqiyut > *ciyuʔ* (Sq [antepenult lost]) 'copulate'

B2.2 Vowels and diphthongs

Except where weakening has taken place, Atayalic retains the inherited PAn *i, *a, and *u. *e merges with *i or *u.

B2.2.1 *i

*i remains /i/ in all environments:

*i 'name/person marker' > *i* 'particle prefixed to names of persons' *ina 'mother' > *ʔinaʔ* 'daughter-in-law' *biliɬ 'behind, last' > *s-bil* 'leave behind' *ciku > *hikuʔ* 'elbow' *gali > *k-um-ayiʔ* 'dig'

B2.2.2 *e

*e > /u/ in most dialects when in the final syllable:

*buhet > *bhut* 'squirrel' *caleŋ > *hawung* 'pine' (Sq) *daɣeq > *rawuq* 'earth, soil' *sipec > *ha-hipux* 'roach' *tapes > *tapus* 'winnow'

In some forms, *e > /i/ in the final syllable. There is no explanation, but note that in some dialects *e > /a/ in the same position:

*baŋeqeɣ > *saba-bangiʔ* 'smell bad' *biqel > *biʔix* 'goiter' *puteq > *mucih* 'secretion from the eye' (Sed *pucaq*) *tumes > *tumiq* 'clothes louse'(< *tumeq [an unexplained innovation])

There are exceptions before *-q. In several cases, *eq > *aq:

*puteq > *pucaʔ* (Sed) 'secretion from eye' *ma-qetaq > *mataq* 'raw' (<*mqataq < *məqataq < *maqatəq)

In the penult of disyllabic roots, *e is usually reflected with /e/ but sometimes with /u/. The conditions for one or the other outcome are not clear. Whether the first syllable has /e/ or /u/ is not correlated with reflexes of stress in other An languages.
*e > /u/ in the penult:

*beɣac > *buwax* 'hulled grain *kelem 'night' > *kuʔum* 'darkness' *ɬesuŋ > *luhung* 'mortar'

*e > /ə/ in the penult:

*beka 'split apart' > *ma-bəkaʔ* 'shattered" *qetut > *təquc-iʔ* (Sq)[6] 'break wind' *isepi > *səpi* 'dream' (< *sepi) *sema > *hənaʔ* 'tongue' *taɬeq 'soil in a paddy' > *cəlaq* 'paddy' (< *teɬaq)

In trisyllabic roots, *e was lost in syllables by elision, and the resulting CC was simplified (§B2.1.2).

*bacuheq > *ma-bahuq* 'wash' (< *bachuq < *bacehuq [§B2.14]) *baqeɣuh > *bah* 'new' (Sq) *saweni 'a while ago' > *sawni, soni* 'a while ago, today'

In some cases, as in the disyllabic roots above, penultimate *e is reflected with /u/:

*qaselu > *qasuu* 'mortar' (Skikun qsuyu)

In a few forms, /ə/ of other dialects is changed to /a/ in Mx by analogy, as follows: Mx retains inherited *a as /a/ in forms where other Atayalic dialects weaken *a to /ə/ (§B2.1.1). In some cases inherited *e is replaced in Mx by /a/ analogically to give the form the special Mx sound:

*isepi > *spi* 'dream' (Sq) but Mx *sapi-al*

B2.2.3 *a and *u

*a and *u remain /a/ and /u/ respectively when not weakened (§B2.1.1):

*baɣah 'embers' > *baɣah* 'charcoal' *busuk > *ma-busuk* 'drunk'

In the antepenult of a stem, *a > [ə]. The [ə] that develops remains /ə/ in some dialects. In Mx it becomes /u/:

*baliw 'change' > *bui-nah* (< *bəi-nah < *bəli-nah < *baliw-nah), *məbrinah* (Sed) 'return'

For /a/ in combination with /u/ or with /ə/, cf. §B2.2.42.

B2.2.4 Diphthongs

B2.2.41 *ay, *uy

*ay and *uy are retained unchanged when word final:

*pagay > *pagay* 'rice in husk' *ɬaŋuy > *lumanguy* 'swim'

When followed by a consonant-initial suffix from 'male speech', the /y/ of the diphthong was lost (§B2.1.2):

*qatay 'liver' > *qaca-haw* 'innards' *quway > *qwa-yux* 'rattan'

---

[6] In this paragraph I transcribe the penultimate /ə/ in Sq, although it is usually omitted in transcriptions.

B2.2.42 *aw, *iw

*aw is retained unchanged.

*babaw > *babaw* 'above' *laŋaw > *wangaw* 'fly'

When *aw comes to abut on a consonant, it is usually changed to /o/. Similarly, the sequences /aə/, /əa/ changed to /o/. Further, the sequence /uwa/, when unstressed and followed by a C, may change to /o/ variably.

*saweni > *sawni/soni* 'later' *taw + *ɣuqaɬay > *co-qoliq* 'man, person' (< *caw-quwalay < *caw-quɣaɬay [metathesis §B2.1.4]) *wasiyeɣ > *q-osiyaʔ* 'water' (/q-/ possibly derives from a prefix *qu-. Cf. commentary to *wasiyeɣ.)

There are only four Atayalic forms that reflect PAn *iw. *kasiw 'tree' has metathesized the *i and the *w (as happened in the Philippines and St, independently):

*kasiw > *kahuy* 'tree' (< *kahwi < *kaswi)

In the case of *waɬiw, the /i/ was absorbed into the palatalization of the *ɬ:

*waɬiw > *waluʔ* 'honey bee'

In the case of *baliw, the /w/ was lost before a C-initial suffix, analogous to loss of *y, discussed in §B2.2.41, preceding.

*baliw 'change' > *bui-nah* (< *bəi-nah *bəli-nah < *baliw-nah), *məbrinah* (Sed) 'return'

In the following case, the stem-final *w became lost before or after /i-/ (§B2.3.43, end):

*laɣiw > *m-aɣi-yay* 'flee'

B2.3.0 Consonants

CHART TWO. DEVELOPMENT OF THE ATAYALIC CONSONANTS FROM PAN

PAn	Atayalic	PAn	Atayalic
p	*p*	h	*h*
t	*t, c (s)*	c	*x, h*
k	m, n	s	*s*
q	*q, ʔ*	m, n	*m, n*
b	*b-*	ŋ	*ng*
d, j	*r*	ɬ	*l*
g	*k-*[7]	l	*l*
ɣ	*ɣ, r, ∅*	w, y	*w, y*

In final position, consonants are sporadically lost (replaced by noncontrastive [-ʔ]). The reason for this is the CC simplification that occurred in the creation of the male forms (§B2.1.2). The forms with the lost stem-final consonants were generalized. Since this was an analogical process, there is often variation whereby some dialects reflect the root-final -C and others do not, or occasionally the same dialect may reflect both variants:

*cep > *pasi-hub/h-um-uhuʔ* 'suck'

[7] There are several outcomes of *g as onset or coda of the final syllable.

B2.3.1 Voiceless stops

B2.3.11 *p

*p was stable in Atayalic:

*págay 'rice plant' > *payay* 'rice in husk' *dapaɬ > *rapal* 'sole' *capuh 'wipe' > *sapuh* 'sweep' *qaɬup > *qalup* 'hunt'

In a one case, *-p is reflected as /b/ in the At dialects that retain a distinction between -b/-p in final position. The explanation is unknown.

*isecep > *pasi-hub* 'suck'

Some Sed dialects have merged *-p and *-k (Li 1981:50). In some dialects of At and Sed, /-p/ varies with /-k/.[8]

*qaɬup > *maduk* 'hunt' (Sed) (< *madup < *qmalup)

In the following example, *-k has been substituted for by a *-p as a case of hypercorrection:

*bitik > *mcip* (Sq) 'fillip', *t-bcip* 'jump (of small insects)'

Some cases of *p are reflected with /m/. This is probably an internal Atayalic development, for some dialects retain a cognate with /-p-/:

*puteq > *mucih* 'eye secretion'[9] *sapaɣ > *sumamag* 'lay mats' (Sed: *smapag*) *nisebic > *halami-q* (Kinhakul) *lihpi-q* (Mx) 'thin' (Cf. the comment in the glossary to *sebic for the change of *b > *p.)

B2.3.111 Accretion of initial *p-*

Occasionally /p-/ is accreted to a root beginning with a vowel by an analogy involving the verbal conjugation. A prefix /m-/ forms verbs from roots beginning with a vowel and also from roots beginning with a /p-/ with the /p-/ lost. Thus, a verb beginning with /m-/ may be either to a root with an initial V or with an initial /p-/, and in some cases /p-/ has been added to a V-initial root by analogy (§A3.7.1, end).

*utaq > *putaq* 'vomit' (active voice: *mutaq*)

B2.3.12 *t

*t has two outcomes: a stop /t/ and an affricate /c/. *t became an affricate *c, as is the case of the other languages of northeast and southwest Taiwan (§A3.3.1, first footnote). In some of the dialects, /c/ further merged with /s/.
*t reflected as /t/:

*tuba > *tubaʔ* 'fish poison' *batu > *batu-nux* 'stone' *gíta > *kitaʔ* 'see' *ɬatad > *lataʔ* 'front yard, outside' *məlatat* 'go out' (Sed) *búhet > *bhut* 'squirrel'

*t reflected as /c/:

*taŋíla > *cangiyaʔ* 'ear' *kutu > *kucuʔ* 'louse' *qatáy 'liver' > *qaca-huw* 'innards' *taɬéq 'earth' > *cəlaq* also *səlaq* 'mud'

---

[8] This merger is an ongoing change (Li 1980: 380).

[9] Cb also reflects /m-/: *mútaʔ* 'eye sand'. It is possible, but not likely, that the development of a nasal in Cb is connected with the nasal in Atayalic. Other Philippine languages reflect initial *p- (Han *pútaq* 'gumminess').

In many cases, root-final *t is lost when a suffix has been added for men's speech.

*lumut > *dmu-riq* 'moss' (Sed)

In Sq, *t is always reflected as /c/ before /i/, either inherited or /i/ that developed in post-PAt times:

*telu > *cyu-gal* (Sq) (Mx *tuuʔ* 'three')

In some of the dialects, *-t is always reflected as /-c/:

*keɣet 'cut a piece off' > *kmərruc* (Sed) *kumut* (Mx) 'cut, kill'

In a few cases, initial *t is reflected with /l/ in some dialects. This is probably a nasalization of *t after it changed to /c/ or /s/ (depending on the dialect)—i.e., [s] or [c] is nasalized to [ɬ]. Then *ɬ > /l/ (§§A3.7.1, B2.3.41).

*tumes > *lumiq* 'body louse' *tusuɣ > *luhuɣ* 'skewer'

B2.3.13 *k

*k remained /k/ in all positions:

*keɣet 'cut a piece off' > *kumut* 'cut, kill' (Sed *kmərruc*)*aku > *s-akuʔ* 'I' *ciku > *hikuʔ* 'elbow' *buɣuk 'rotten' > *ma-buruk* 'rotten, decayed'

In a few cases, *k > /q/, but in almost all of these cases, one or more of the Atayalic dialects attests a reflex with /k/. This change is most frequent in Sed dialects.

*aɬak 'offspring' > *ʔulaq-iʔ* 'child' *kan > *qan-iq* 'eat' (Sed: *mə-kan* 'eat') *kasiw > *kahuy* 'tree' (Sq: *qho-niq*)

B2.3.14 *q

*q > /q/ in most Sed and in about half of the Atayal dialects. In some of the remaining dialects, *q is reflected by a pharyngeal affricated stop [ɦ] and in others, with glottal stop. We transcribe both of the first two as *q*. Where *q is reflected by [ʔ], the *q has been in effect lost, for [ʔ] is noncontrastive (§B2.1.01, above).

*qabu > *qabu-liʔ* 'ashes' *qaɣem > *qawum* 'pangolin' *daqis > *raqi-na-s* 'face' (where *-na-* is a male-speech infix) *taɬeq 'soil in a paddy' > *cəlaq* 'mud, paddy'

*q as onset of the penult in trisyllabic roots was lost if the root had not been disyllabized by loss of the first syllable.

*baqeɣuh > *bah* (Sq) *buguh* (Sed) 'new'

B2.3.2 *h, *s, *c

*h remained unchanged in Atayalic. *s tended to move back in the mouth becoming [ʃ], and as this happened, *c lost its affrication (> [s]). Subsequently, the [s] that developed from *c became [h] (merged with reflexes of *h). This is a development that Atayalic shares with St (§B12.3.2). Details are given in the subsections below.

B2.3.21 *h

*h was an unproductive phoneme in PAn. It remained unchanged in most Atayalic dialects. In many of the dialects, the reflex of *h is articulated with affrication in the pharynx [ɦ]. Some of the sources transcribe the [ɦ] with *x*—i.e., *h is reflected by [ɦ] and transcribed by *x*.[10] In many dialects (including Mx) /x/ is articulated with affrication in the velar region rather than in the pharynx. The /h/ pronounced with affrication in the pharynx [ɦ] contrasts with /x/—i.e., *h and *c do not fall together in those dialects:

*sehapuy > *hapuy* 'fire'[11] (loss of initial syllable [§B2.1.3]) *buhet > *buhut* 'squirrel' *baɣah 'embers' > *baɣah* 'charcoal'

*h-onset of the final syllable is lost in trisyllabic roots that were not disyllabized by loss of the first syllable:

*bacuheq > *bahuq* 'wash' (< *bahuheq) *ɣábihi 'night' > *ɣabi-yan* 'evening'

B2.3.22 *s

*s most frequently became /s/, pronounced with alveolar or even palatal closure [ʃ]. However, in eight cases *s is reflected with /h/. The reflex /h/ is an innovation that started somewhere in central or northern Formosa and spread, but the environment that gave rise to this innovation is unknown (cf. §A3.3.32). Examples of *s > /s/:

*simaɣ 'oil' > *simal* 'fat, grease' *busuk > *ma-busuk* 'drunk' *dusa > *rusa* 'two' *daqis > *raqi-na-s* 'forehead' *sagek > *s-um-auk* 'smell, sniff'

The following are the cases where *s > /h/:

*iseci 'flesh, contents' > *hihi-hihi* 'flesh, body, person' *kasiw > *kahuy* 'tree' *sema > *həma?* 'tongue' *qusuŋ > *quhung* 'mushroom' *ɬisebic > *lihpi-q* 'thin' *sipec > *ha-hipux* 'cockroach'

In three cases, *s > /q/ dialectally. These are possibly examples of dissimilation.

*suɣac > *q-um-uwax* 'wash' *tiŋas > *cingaq* 'food particles left in the teeth' *tumes > *sumiq* 'body louse' (Kinhakul)

In one case, *s- was lost (became noncontrastive [ʔ]):

*iseyup > *ʔ-um-iyup* 'blow'

In another case, *s was lost, possily because of /x/ to the left in the root:

*baɣiyus > *bayxu* 'storm'

B2.3.23 *c

*c > /x/ in a few cases. /x/ contrasts with /h/ in most Atayalic dialects.

*cucu > *xuxu?* 'breast' *beɣac 'hulled rice' > *buwax* 'hulled grain' *hipec > *ha-hipux* 'cockroach' *picaɬ > *minxal* 'once' *suɣac > *quwax* 'wash'

In most cases, *c > /h/ (falls together with the reflex of *h). The best explanation for the two reflexes of *c is that the change to /h/ was never completed in all the Atayalic dialects.

*cabuk 'belt' > *ha-habuk* 'cloth for holding child' *caleŋ > *hawung* 'pine' (Sq) *cep > *pasi-hub* 'suck' *ciku > *hiku?* 'elbow' *bacuheq > *bahuq* 'wash clothes' *bucuɣ >

[10] At least in the case of Taroko, transcribing [ɦ] with /x/ (as was done by Pecoraro 1971) is an error, for there is also a velar spirant /x/ that reflects *c and contrasts with /ɦ/, the reflex of *h.

[11] Pecoraro 1971 transcribes the Sed Taroko cognate mistakenly with *x*: *xapuy* 'cook'.

buh-in-uɣ 'bow' *iceɣab > *hira?* 'yesterday' (Sq) *iseci 'flesh, contents' > *hihi-hihi* 'flesh, body, person' *ɬesuŋ > *luhung* 'mortar' *kaɣuc > *k-m-aruh* 'scratch'

In a few cases, *c > /s/. There is no explanation:

*capuh 'wipe' > *sapuh* 'sweep'[12] *kicekic > *kə-kiskis* 'file' *iceɣab > *co-ɣisa?* 'yesterday' (<*cau-ɣisab [§B2.1.3] < *cau-esiɣab [§A3.5.4])

Final *c is replaced by noncontrastive glottal stop in one case. Some dialects manifest /-s/, and others manifest /-ʔ/ in this form. There is no explanation.

*ɬisebic > *hləpis* 'thin' (SedToda), *halami?* 'thin' (AtMatabalay)

In the following example, *c- was lost and replaced by /p-/ in the process of p-accretion (§B2.3.111, above):

*ciɬaɣ > *p-ilaw* 'light'

B2.3.3 Voiced stops and spirants

The voiced stops became voiceless at the end of words in all dialects except Mx.[13] They were completely lost in some dialects (replaced by [ʔ]).

B2.3.31 *b

*b remained /b/ initially and medially. It is a bilabial fricative pronounced [β] in most dialects:

*babaw > *babaw* 'above' *báɣah 'charcoal'> *baɣah* 'charcoal *buhut > *bhut* 'squirrel' *ɣabihi > *ɣabi-yan* 'night'

In the case of the reflex of *ɬisebic, *b is assimilated to the preceding *s, as is the case of all An languages except Bun: *lihpi-q* 'thin' (see commentary in glossary under *sebic).
A few dialects of At retain stem-final *-b as /-b/, but Mx is the only dialect that has preserved *-b as /-b/ word finally (§B2.3.3). There is only one attestation. The two other PAn forms with *-b that are attested for Atayalic have lost the final consonant (replaced *b with a noncontrastive [ʔ]). /-b/ is unstable in Mx and varies with /-ɣ/, as is the Sed case of /-p/ varying with /-k/ (§B2.3.11, above):

*suwab > *ma-suwab* 'yawn' (also *ma-suwaɣ* [Mx] *msuyap* [Sq] *qeɬeb > *q-um-lu?* 'close' *iceɣab > *co-ɣisa?* 'yesterday'

B2.3.32 *d, *j

*d and *j merged. *d,*j > /r/ in initial and medial positions. /r/ is a retroflex continuant, similar to English [r]. In most Sed dialects, initial *d-/j- > /d-/, but /-r-/ medially.

*dapaɬ > *rapal* 'sole' *daya > *k-raya, daya?* (Sed) 'inland' *dusa 'two > *rusa* 'two' *jalan > *raan* 'road, walk' *tujuq > *pana-turuq* 'point'

---

[12] We assume that the change of *c was in stages: *c > *s > /h/. Possibly the existence of *h to the right of the *c prevented the change of [s] > [h]. This is the only At reflex of a protoroot reconstructed with *h to the right of *c.

[13] The devoicing process occurs word finally (not stem finally). At the end of a stem before a suffix, an inherited voiced consonant retains its voicing.

In one case, medial *-d- was lost. After a prefix, roots with initial *d- normally reflect /-r-/ (-d- in Sed):

*pa-deŋ > *pawung-an* 'extinguish' *daɬ > *ra-ral* 'old' (Sq) also *smu-ral* (Sq) *smu-dal* (Sed) 'old thing'

Most reflexes of forms with inherited final *-d/*-j evince loss of *-d/*-j in At. However, in some forms, *-d is reflected in At with /-t/. Sed dialects evince *-t, but /-c/ (< *-t) after /i/.

*ɬátad > *lataʔ* 'outside' (Mx) *mə-latat* 'go outside' (Sed) *paɬid > *paliʔ* 'wing' (Mx) *palic* (Sed) *qaɬuj > *ma-alu-i-t* 'drift'

In one case, *-j- is lost. There is no explanation.

*qujaɬ > *qwal-ax* 'rain'

In the following form, *d- was lost and subsequently replaced by /p-/ by the analogy described in §B2.3.111, above. There is no explanation for the loss of *d-:

*deŋeɣ > *p-ung* 'hear'

B2.3.33 *g

As onset to the penult or earlier, *g- > /k-/.

*gali > *k-um-ayiʔ* 'dig' *gaɣaŋ > *ka-kaɣang* 'crab' *gumis > *kumis* 'body hair' *tageɣaŋ > *taklang* 'ribs'(Sed Taroko)

Medially, as onset to the final syllable, and finally, *g has several outcomes: (1) /ɣ/, (2) /r/ in Sq and in Sed dialects and /s/ in other Atayalic dialects, (3) /y/ in some dialects, (4) Ø. The same protoform may have two or more different outcomes in different dialects.

(1) medial *g > /ɣ/:[14]

*pagay > *paɣay* 'rice in husk' *qaɬipugu > *ʔalipuɣuʔ* 'hair whorl'

(2) medial and final *g > /s/ or /r/, depending on the dialect:

*piga > *piraʔ* (Mx) *pisaʔ* (Skikun) 'how many?' *b-al-iga 'weaver's sword' > *bagisaʔ* (Mx) *giraʔ* (Sq) (< *baliraʔ) *gilig > *mtk-kis* 'lie on side' (Skikun)

(3) medial *g > /y/:

*pagay > *payay* (Sed) 'rice in husk' *piga 'how many?' > *piyaʔ* 'several, how many' (Kinhakul)

(4) loss of medial and final *g:

*bagaq 'inform' > *baq* (Sq) 'know' *sagek > *s-um-auk* 'smell' *suwagi > *suwayiʔ* 'younger sibling'

There are some citations in which *g is reflected as /x/ or /h/ in the Sed dialects.

*ŋagan > *ngaxan* (Sed Taroko) *hangan* (Sed Toda) 'name' *mugiŋ > *muhing* 'nose' (Sed) *paqegu > *paxu-ng* (Sed) 'gall'

---

[14] There are no attested examples of *-g reflected by /-ɣ/.

B2.3.34 *ɣ

*ɣ has three outcomes, depending on the dialect: /ɣ/, /r/, or Ø. In Atayal dialects /ɣ/ is the most widespread reflex. However, many forms show a loss of *ɣ, and a handful reflect /r/, which predominates in the Sed attestations.

*ɣ > /ɣ/ ([g] in some dialects):

*ɣabihi > *ɣabi-an* 'evening' *ɣiq '*Imperata cylindrica*' > *ʔaɣiq* 'k.o. bush' *baɣah 'embers' > *baɣah* 'charcoal' *beɣay > *bəgay* (Sed Truwan) 'give' *biɣaq > *bga-yaw* (Sq) '*Alocasia*' *gaɣaŋ > *ka-kaɣang* 'crab' *jaɣum > *raɣum* 'needle' *laɣiw > *m-aɣi-yay* 'flee'

Final /-ɣ/ is devoiced (> /x/) sporadically:

*busuɣ > *buh-in-uɣ/buh-in-ux* 'bow'[15] *jeɣ > *macaq-rux* 'stand'

*ɣ > /r/:

*buɣuk 'rotten' > *buruk* 'rotten, decayed' *kaɣuc 'scratch' > *karuh* 'claw, hoe'

Loss of *ɣ:

*ɣabihi 'night' > *ʔabi* 'sleep' (Sq) *baqeɣu > *bah* (Sq) 'new', *beɣac < *buwax* 'hulled grain' *beɣay > *si-bai-q* 'give' *jaɣum > *rom* (Sq) 'needle' *kaɣat > *k-um-aat* 'bite' *keɣet 'cut' > *k-um-ut* 'cut, kill' *qabaɣa > *qbaʔ* (Sq) 'shoulder' *qaɣem > *qaum* 'pangolin' *wiɣi > *ii-l* 'left'

In some Sed dialects, the /-g/ that resulted from *-ɣ changed to /w/ in word-final position (but it is unchanged when preceding a suffix [Li 1980: 358]):

*sapaɣ > *samaw* 'spread out a mat' (but *smag-an*) (cf. §B2.3.11, 5th¶, for /m/ in place of /p/) *tusuɣ > *luhuw* 'thread a needle' (but *lhug-an)*

In one case, Mx also shows this Sed innovation:

*ciɬaɣ > *p-ilaw* 'light'

B2.3.4 Continuants

B2.3.41 *l and *ɬ

Medial *-l- is lost in Mx. Initial *l- > /w-/ in Mx. *l > /y/ in Sq and Skikun, and *l > /r/ in Sed and AtPalngawan. In Sed, when initial *l- comes to abut on a consonant due to loss of the following vowel, the *l is reflected with /d-/.

*laŋaw > *wangaw* (Mx) *rangaw* (Sed) 'fly' *biliɬ 'behind, last' > *s-bil* (Sq) (< *biyil) 'abandon, leave behind' *biqel > *biqir* (Sed) 'goiter' *caleŋ > *hawung* (Mx) *hayung* (Sq) *harung* (Sed) 'pine' *gali > *k-um-aiʔ* (Mx) *kmari* (Sed) 'dig' *jalan > *raan* 'road' *kelem 'night' > *kuʔum* 'dark' *lumut > *yumu-riq* (Skikun), *dmu-riq* (Sed) 'moss' *puluq > *mpuu* (Sq) (Chen 1980: 457 writes *mepuw*) 'ten' *telu > *tuu* (Mx) *cyu-gal* (Sq) *gatel > *kkwi* (Sq) (*t is assimilated to the preceding /k/: < *katuy < *katey) 'itch'

---

[15] Our informants, except for one, were quite definite that the final C of this form is /x/. One elderly informant pronounced this with a final /ɣ/.

The reflex of *-l in Mx is unknown. In two cases *-l is lost, as in medial position, and in one case it is reflected with /x/. It is possible that this final /-x/ is the remnant of a 'male speech' suffix:

*gatel > *maka-kat* 'itch' *kudamel > *kahma* 'thick' *biqel > *biʔix* 'goiter'

*ɬ in all positions is reflected in Mx as a voiceless palatal lateral [ɬ], written *l*. In some dialects, /l/ < *ɬ sporadically falls together with /n/. In Sed, at least in Taroko, the /l/ that develops from *ɬ falls together with /r/ (transcribed as *l* by Pecoraro 1971).

*ɬa > *la* 'already' ɬaŋuy > *l-um-anguy* 'swim' *paɬid > *paliʔ* 'wing' *qaɬup > *qalup* 'hunt' *taɬam > *t-um-alam* 'taste' *biliɬ 'behind, last' > *s-bil* 'abandon, leave behind' *daɬ > *ra-ral* (Sq) 'old'

In one case, *ɬ is reflected in Mx with /n/, as happened with cognates in Ru, Am, and Kav:

*wanaɬ > *ʔanan* 'right'

B2.3.42 Nasals

*m, *n, *ŋ remained unchanged in all positions:

*gumis 'down, body hair' > *kumis* 'body hair, animal hair' *sema > *həma* 'tongue' *mula > *muyaʔ* (Sq) 'to plant' *jaɣum > *raɣum* 'needle' *kelem 'night' > *kuʔum* 'dark' *nunuh > *nunuh* (SedTrunux) 'breast' *anu > *n-anu* 'what? *ipen > *ɣipun* 'tooth' *jalan > *raan* 'road' *ŋaŋa 'open mouthed' > *ngangah* 'stupid' *buŋa 'flower' > *bungaʔ* 'sweet potato' *laŋaw > *wangaw* 'fly' *caleŋ > *hawung* 'pine'

B2.3.43 Initial and medial *w and *y

Initial and medial *w and *y are reflected as glides, /w/ and /y/, respectively in Mx. A *w between back and front vowels is reflected by /y/ in Sq. Some Sed dialects sporadically lose *w.

*waɣi > *waɣiʔ* (Mx) *ʔariʔ* (Sed) 'day' *buwaq > *buwa-y* 'fruit' *suwab > *ma-suwaɣ* (Mx) *suyap* (Sq) 'yawn' *waɬiw > *walu* 'honey bee' *daya > *k-raya* 'inland' *qaqiyut > *ciyuʔ* 'copulate' (Sq)

The *w- is lost before or after *i:

*wiɣi > *ʔi-l* (Mx) *ʔiri-l* (Sed) 'left (side)' *laɣiw > *m-aɣi-yay* 'flee' (< *m-aɣiw-ay) *baliw-nah > *buwinah* 'return' (< *bulinah < *bəli-nah < *baliw-nah)

Chapter Three

Tsouic Reflexes of the PAn Phonemes

B3.0 Background and cultural factors that influenced the history of the Tsouic languages

The Tsouic languages comprise three languages, Tsou Saaroa [ɬaʔalua] (Sar), and Kanakanavu (Knn). Tsou, because of recent large changes in its phonology, looks very different from Sar and Knn, but all three turn out in fact to have undergone many developments in common on all levels of their syntax, morphology, and phonology and are closely related. Their history has been studied in detail (Tsuchida 1976 and also Li n.d.). The analysis here owes much to the groundbreaking work of these two studies, particularly Tsuchida 1976, in which some of the very difficult problems of finding correspondences have been solved. However, the PAn phonology assumed in that work is vastly divergent from the PAn phonology here assumed, and the account given here of how the Sar and Knn developed from PAn is very far from that given by Tsuchida 1976.
The best documented of these three languages is Tsou, but the changes in phonology that Tsouhas undergone are overwhelming and can best be described in terms of an earlier structure that resembles the current state of Sar and Knn, languages that are much more conservative in their phonology. Here we quote forms in these two languages and describe their development from PAn. We quote forms from Tsouonly insofar as they elucidate Sar or Knn forms or if they document the existence of a reflex of a given PAn protomorpheme in this group when there is no Sar or Knn attestation.

Both Sar and Knn are characterized by a fair amount of irregularity—that is, there are many forms of PAn provenience that do not follow sound laws that can be discovered. These forms are most likely dialect borrowings. This makes it apparent that these languages at anearlier time had a great deal of dialectal diversity, much more than now exists among the few remaining speakers of the languages. Ogawa (2006), which lists forms from Sar of three or four generations ago, shows a language of that time more diverse than the current language.

CHAPTER THREE, §1

Saaroa

B31.0 Saaroa

For Sar attestations the only published source available is Tsuchida 1976. The other forms listed here were gathered with the help of Paula Radetsky in Relece (Gaozhong village) on the main highway about 3 km to the north of the Han village of Baolai, Kao-Hsiung province. Paula also supplied me with a few forms that I failed to elicit. Our informant was Ereke (Inaranərəkə ɬaulacana), born July 24, 1924. Ereke is one of the last remaining speakers of Sar. Bunun speakers have been moving into the traditional Saaroa area since the 1930s. Tsuchida and Li report that Sar was still spoken in the village in the 1960s, but at this point only a handful of the people speak it habitually and only with the few other good speakers of Sar that remain. Otherwise Bunun and Mandarin are used in the village.

B31.01 Phonemics of Saaroa

CHART ONE. PHONEMES OF SAAROA

Consonants

stops	p	t	k	ʔ
spirants/ affricates	v [β]	s, c		
laterals		l, ɬ, r		
nasals	m	n	ng [ŋ]	

Vowels and Diphthongs

high	i		u
mid		ə	
low		a	

The canonical structure of the syllable in Sar is (C)V,—i.e., there are no C or V sequences within the syllable and no C codas. Sequences of two vowels are two separate syllables. Diphthongization does not occur.

/v/ is a voiced bilabial spirant [β]. /c/ is an apico-alveolar affricate. /l/is an alveolar tap with a slight retroflexion of the tongue [ɭ]. /r/ is a lateral with slight retroflexion and affrication against the alveolar region. /ɬ/ is a voiceless lateral with affrication between the blade of the tongue and the palate.

[ʔ] contrasts with its absence in initial and medial position. /ʔ/ developed from *q and *s (§§B31.3.14, B31.3.22).

Stress tends to fall as far left as possible but normally not on the inflectional prefixes *um-*, *uma-* and *ɬi-*. The stress contrasts that currently exist in Sar are recent developments and have nothing to do with the inherited PAn stress contrasts.

B31.1. Changes that characterize Saaroa in general

B31.1.1 Di- and trisyllabization

Tsouic reflects the general PAn tendency to disyllabize monosyllabic roots (§A3.6.2). Already by proto-Tsouic times, the PAn monosyllabic roots that had been inherited by Tsouic were disyllabized by adding a prothetic vowel or doubling the root.
Here are some Sar examples. First, disyllabization by adding a prothetic vowel:

> *ɣik > *uma-íriki* 'thresh by trampling' (< *ərik [§B31.2.2])

Second, disyllabization by doubling the root:

> *ceŋ 'stop up' > *əngə́əngə* 'stopper, plug' (< *əŋəŋ with echo vowel [§B31.21] and lost *c- [§B31.3.23]) *taw > *cú-cuʔu* 'man' (< *tawtaw)

Further, trisyllabic roots tended to be reduced to two syllables by a process of syncopation of the penult, similar to that found in most of the Formosan languages and the MP languages. However, the Sar process of disyllabization is independent of that in other An languages because it is constrained—confined only to penults with unstable consonants as onset: *q, *h, *s, *c, *w, and *y. (See §B31.1.3.)

B31.1.2 Process of trisyllabization

After the processes described in §B31.1.1 above took place, proto-Tsouic developed a canonical root of minimally three or more syllables—that is, a root may have three or four syllables (and possibly more), and disyllabic roots had to be made trisyllabic. The motivation for this development is unknown. The process of trisyllabization affected not only inherited disyllabic roots but also roots of three syllables that had been disyllabized in pre-Tsouic by contraction (§B31.1.3). Most often the disyllabic roots (inherited or developed in pre-Tsouic) became trisyllabic by developing echo vowels. Some disyllabic roots ending in a vowel were made trisyllabic by doubling the nucleus of the penultimate vowel (§B31.1.23).

B31.1.21 Echo Vowels and loss of final -C

C-final disyllabic roots (inherited from PAn or developed in pre-Tsouic) and monosyllabic roots (which invariably were disyllabized [§B31.1.1]) are reflected with an echo vowel, the same as the vowel of the preceding syllable. The exception is that the echo vowel after a syllable containing /a/ is /ə/.

> *ɬibuq > *ɬivuʔu* 'den of wild pigs' *seqeɣet > *má-ərəcə* 'tight' *taquweɬ> *caiɬi* (< *tawiɬ) 'year' *qabaŋ > *ʔávaŋə* 'boat'

Echo vowels occur also in the case of V-final stems. A glottal stop /ʔ/ is intercalated between the stem-final vowel and the echo vowel.[1]

> *kasiw > *kíuʔu* 'tree' *kútu > *kúcuʔu* 'louse' *ɬuká 'wound' > *ɬúkaʔa* 'a boil' *qatay > *ʔáciʔi* 'liver' *taw > *cú-cuʔu* 'man'

Echo vowels also developed in stems that ended in an *h ,*s, or in a *c in PAn that had been lost in Sar. A glottal stop was intercalated in the case of *h loss, but not with words that lost final *-s or *-c.[2]

---

[1] It is clear that the echo vowels developed after words accreted [-ʔ] codas (§B31.1.6).

*wałis 'fang' > *ałii* 'tooth' *buŋúh > *vúngu*ʔ*u* 'head' *balec > *umalia-váləə* 'answer' *łisebic > *má-łipii* 'thin' *taŋic > *tuma-tángii* 'weep'

In sporadic cases, the echo vowel that developed was /a/. In some of these cases, the final /-a/ is not an echo vowel, but derives from the suffix *-an. There are cases, however, where it is not apparent that there could have been a suffix *-an, for no meaning that can be reconstructed for *-an is commensurate with the root. In those cases, the /-a/ is an echo vowel. Those cases are probably remnants of dialectal variants:

*baɣah > *vára*ʔ*a* 'charcoal' *nunuh > *núunu*ʔ*a* 'breast' *łuka 'wound' > *łúka*ʔ*a* 'boil' *qusuŋ > *ʔúu*ʔ*uŋa* 'mushroom' *tiŋas 'particles in teeth after eating' > *łiu-tiŋaa* 'picked teeth' *tuduq > *túsua* 'leak from roof'

In PAn trisyllabic roots or in disyllabic roots that contain affixes (including reduplication) or before an enclitic or another form with which the root forms a compound, echo vowels do not develop if the stem ended in a vowel or in one of the consonants that were lost: *q, *s, *c, *h, w, or *y:

*punuq 'head' > *vunu*ʔ*u* 'brain', but *vunu-ku* 'my brain' *panaq > *ua-pana* 'shoot' *qałi-matéq > *ʔałimámaca* 'small paddy leech' *aqetih 'for water to recede' > *ʔúma*ʔ*aci* 'dam up water to catch fish' *tahepa > *cúma-capa* 'roast, burn' *tułu > *cumácułu* 'roast'

If a V-initial suffix is added to a form with an echo vowel, the echo vowel is lost by contraction (§B31.1.3) (or never developed):

*taquweł+an > *caiłi* 'year' *+a* > *caiła* 'year as a length of time'[3]

Note, however, echo vowels do develop in trisyllables and stems ending in consonants that were not normally lost in Sar:

*bałituk > *vałituku* 'money' *qułułaŋ > *ʔúłułaŋə* 'k.o. tree: *Cordia,* spp.' *sapaɣ > *uma-apárə* 'spread mats' *sipaɣ > *í-siparə* 'the opposite side (of the street, river)'

The following root lost its final consonant idiosyncratically[4] (*b was normally not lost). It developed an echo vowel but no [ʔ] coda:

*suwab > *maa-ua-uaə* 'yawn'

B31.1.22 Prothetic vowels

A few forms with /ə/ in the penult developed prothetic /ə/. These forms also developed echo vowels. No motivation has been discovered for the prothetic vowel:

*beɣac > *əvəraə* 'husked rice' *beteŋ > *ə́vəcəngə* 'millet' *delec > *ə́sələə* 'bow string' *tebus > *ə́təvə* 'sugar cane'

---

[2] The loss of *s and *c was subsequent to the development of [-ʔ]-word-final codas (§B31.1.6), for roots ending in an *s or *c that were lost do have the glottal stop before the echo vowel. However, roots that ended in *h evince a [ʔ] before the echol vowel—that is, the root-final [ʔ] developed after *-h had been lost.

[3] It is also possible that *caiła* developed directly from *tawiłan, rather than from *caiłi*, to which a suffix had been added.

[4] Note that Paz, Th, and Pai (dialectally) share this innovation. This form seems to have spread, but its distribution is surprising.

B31.1.23 Doubling the vowel nucleus of the penult

Disyllabic roots ending in a vowel, instead of adding an echo vowel may alternatively become trisyllabic by doubling the nucleus of the penult. There is no rule that determines whether an echo vowel is added to roots of this sort or whether the penult is doubled. The existence of this alternative process is probably due to dialect mixture. (This is the process of forming trisyllabic roots in Knn [§B32.1.22].)

*daqu > *caaʔu* 'soapberry tree' *icebu > *íivu* 'urine' *ɣuqaɬay 'male' > *raaɨi* 'the leader in an important ceremony'(loss of *q and contraction [< *ɣaɬi (§B31.1.3)]) *waɣi > *aari* 'day'

When the root was affixed, the doubling of the vowel did not take place:

*telu > *ú-tulu* 'three' (cf. the unaffixed alternant *túulu*)

B31.1.3 Vowel contraction

The consonants *q, *h, *s, *c, *w, and *y were unstable in Sar: they were either lost entirely or lost in certain cases. In PAn trisyllabic roots with one of these consonants as the onset of the penult or final syllable, they were lost, and the vowel sequence that resulted from the loss of these consonants was contracted if the sequence consisted of like vowels or consisted of /i/, /u/, or /a/ followed by /ə/. Sequences of like vowels contracted to single vowels, and /i/, /u/, or /a/ followed by /ə/ contracted to /i/, /u/, or /a/, respectively. In short, these trisyllabic stems in PAn became disyllabic in pre-Tsouic (only to be made three syllables again by the processes described above [§§B31.1.2ff.]). The following examples manifest loss of these consonants in penult onset:

*tuqelaɬ> *cúlaɨə* 'bone' *seqeɣet > *má-ʔərəcə* 'tight'[5] *tahebu 'vessel to hold or fetch water' > *távuʔu* 'gourd, calabash' *bahaɬiɣ > *váɨiri* 'board' *iseci > *máa-is-ana* 'contents' *icebu > *íivu* 'urine' *siyuɬuq > *ʔiɨuʔu* 'necklace, beads'

The following example shows the loss of these consonants in final-syllable onset position:

*ɣabihi 'evening' > *kuá-ravi* 'evening meal'

This rule also applies to roots that always occur with a given prefix. The contraction occured no matter what the vowel and whether the lost consonant was onset to the penult or the final syllable.

*qetáq + ma- > *má-taʔə* 'unripe' (< *maqetaq) *qaceŋ + ma- > *má-əngə* 'sneeze' (< *maaceŋ [§B31.3.14] < *maqaceŋ[6]) *qaciɬ + *ma- > *má-iɨi* 'salt'

Vowel sequences that developed by loss of intermediate consonants or by affixation of a vowel-final prefix or vowel-initial suffix to a root may or may not contract unless they involve a /ə/, in which case they always contract (cf. the first paragraph of this section). The difference in the outcomes is probably due to dialect mixture.
Here are four examples of suffixed forms in which contraction takes place:

---

[5] The /ʔ/ here reflects the root initial *s (§B31.3.22). The *q in the root is lost.

[6] Cf. Knn *ma-ʔasə́ng* 'sneeze' where the *c was not lost, but rather became /s/.

*beɣay > *ú-vera* 'give' (< *beɣan < *beɣian < *beɣay-an) *biɣeŋi > *vərəng-ana* 'night' (< *beɣeŋi-anan) *iseci > *máa-is-ana* 'contents' *paqit 'bitter' > + ma- > *má-paci* 'wine' (< *mapaiti < *mapaqiti)

The following forms show failure to contract. The first example is likely to have been a borrowing, for it also shows retention of *-s- (§B31.3.22):

*pálisi > *pálisia* 'taboo' (< *palisi + *-an) *qaɣicam 'plant with reedlike stem' > *áriamə* 'miscanthus stalks cut for use' *qałuj + *mu- > *mú-ałusu* 'be carried by current'

Otherwise, in cases other than those that meet the above-listed conditions, there is no syllable loss.[7]

B31.1.31 Diphthongization

Diphthongs arose from word-internal *au that developed if the pre-Sar stress was on the *a. If the stress was on the *ú, a diphthong did not develop—i.e., *áu > *aw and *aú > *au. These subsequently developed into /u/ and /au/ respectively (Tsuchida 1976: §4.5.32.2).

*qawúɣ > *auru* 'k.o. bamboo' vs. *qumáhqumah > *umuuma* 'planted field' (< *umáuma)

B31.1.4 CC simplification and vowel doubling

We assume that roots consisting of a doubled monosyllable had an epenthetic *e between them in PAn (§A3.6.1), forming a trisyllabic root. In pre-Tsouic this trisyllabic root was disyllabized (§B31.1.1, above). The resultant medial cluster was simplified, and the vowel of the first syllable was doubled (i.e., underwent compensatory lengthening).

*daŋedaŋ > *suma-saasangə* 'dry near fire' *demedem > *səəsəma* 'dark' *kicekic > *kuma-kiikisi* 'shave' *ŋuceŋuc > *si-ngunguu* 'snore'[8] (< *nguunguu [single vowel in the penult by the rule at the end of this section])

Compensatory lengthening did not take place if the root-initial C was one of the C's that had been lost—i.e., the loss of these C's took place prior to the simplification of clusters and compensatory lengthening:

*sapesap > *uma-apəəpə* 'grope' *ceŋeceŋ > *əngəngə* 'stopper, plug' (< *əŋəŋ)[9]

Roots consisting of a doubled disyllable underwent a similar process: the final vowel of the first repetition was dropped, the resulting CC was simplified, and the vowel preceding the lost consonant was doubled:

*łiki-łiki > *łiiłiki* 'armpit' (< *łikłiki) *bunga-bunga > *vuuvunga* 'flower' (< *buŋbuŋa) *qebel > *vuuvula* (< *beqbeqel < *beqel-beqel < *qebel [§B31.1.5]) 'smoke'

The addition of a derivative affix to roots of this type blocks compensatory lengthening—i.e., when affixes other than the inflectional affixes are added to these roots, one of the doubled vowels is lost:

---

[7] A form like *sikamə* 'mat' is not an exception. This underwent the widespread metathesis *ise > *esi > *si (§A3.5.4) in pre-Tsouic. Note that the /s/ reflex indicates that this form is not directly inherited (§B31.3.22):

*sikam > *sikam* 'mat' (< *esikam)

[8] Tsuchida (1976) reports two variant forms in which the epenthetic vowel between the two monosyllabic roots was retained and that do not evince CC simplification: *kumisi-kisi* 'shave' and *puri-ngusungusu* 'snore'

[9] The penult of this root was doubled (< /əə/) because both syllables developed echo vowels (§B31.1.21)—i.e., the first of the two ə's is an echo vowel.

pua + *łiiłiki* 'armpit' > *puałiłiki* 'put under the arms'

B31.1.5 Metathesis

Metathesis in Sar is a sporadic process. Some of the forms in Sar that evince metathesis show this process in other languages as well, and they may well have spread to Sar secondarily:

*ałay > *l-aiałə* 'termite' *sináwa 'breath' > *muru-nia-niaa* 'breathe' (<*nisawa) *taŋila 'ear' > *calínga* 'ear' *wanał> *ałanə* 'right side'

Others are metathesized only in Tsouic languages:

bitúka > *cívuka* 'belly' *baqeɣaŋ > *vángarə* 'molar' (< **baqeŋaɣ*) *cucu > *ʔususu* 'breast' (< *susuʔu [§B31.1.21]) *quway > *vuiʔi* 'rattan' (< *wuqay) *łeket > *ma-kəngəcə* 'sticky' (< *kełet [for /ng/ cf. §B31.3.41, end])

In two cases, sequences *ai and *ayi that developed with the loss of an intervening C are metathesized to *ia and *iay respectively, as evinced by the morphophemic alternation when the form is suffixed (cf. §B31.2.41, 3rd¶):

*kasiw > *kiuʔu* (< *kiuʔ < *kiaw < *kaiw) 'wood, tree' + *taa-a* > *taa-kia-a* 'place to keep wood' *taqi > *tiiʔi* 'feces' (< *tiay < *tayi) + *taa-a* > *taatiała* 'place to defecate' (< *taatiaya [§B31.3.43])

B31.1.6 Development of a noncontrastive glottal stop

In current Sar, /ʔ/ is a contrastive phoneme. However, in pre-Sar, the glottal stop was not contrastive. In some dialects in pre-Sar, a noncontrastive glottal stop developed word initially before vowels (and before vowels that developed with the loss of initial *s and *q) and word finally after vowels. Only subsequently did this glottal stop become contrastive, for this development did not affect all of the dialects. Present-day Sar, confined to only a handful of speakers, evinces a mixture: most forms deriving from PAn *q-, *s- or initial vowel reflect a word-initial glottal stop, but some do not. Similarly, most words reflect a word-final glottal stop, but a few do not.

Glottal stop in initial position and its absence:

*qabu > *ʔavuʔu* 'ashes' vs. *qayam 'pet' > *ałamə* 'bird'; *icebu > *ʔiivu* 'urine' (penultimate lengthening §B31.1.23) vs. *ina > *inaʔa* 'mother'; *siyułuq > *ʔiłuʔu* 'necklace' vs. *simaɣ 'grease' > *imarə* 'lard'; *uɣat > *ʔuracə* 'vein' and *qusuŋ > *ʔu-ʔuuŋ-a* 'mushroom' vs. *qujał> *usałə* 'rain'

Glottal stop reflected in pre-Sar final position and its absence:

*baɣaq > *varaʔə* 'lungs' vs. *dilaq 'tongue' > *súma-silaə* 'lick'; *luseq > *lə́əʔə* 'tears' vs. *daɣeq > *sarəə* 'earth'; *ŋucuq 'snout, beak' > *ngusuu* 'mouth'

Roots that ended in a vowel but did not develop an echo vowel (§B31.1.21, 5th¶) never reflect a pre-Sar final glottal stop. When Tsouic developed an open syllable canonical form (§B31.1.7), the glottal stop in word-final position was lost. For example, trisyllabic *icebu did not develop an echo vowel and has no final glottal stop. However, disyllabic *qabu did develop an echo vowel, for the rule is that disyllables added an echo vowel. Before an echo vowel, the glottal stop that ha developed in pre-Sar was not lost:

*icebu > *ʔiivu* 'urine' vs. *qabu > *ʔávuʔu* 'ashes'

B31.1.7 Development of canonical open syllables at the end of a word

Canonical open syllables came into being when echo vowels developed or word-final consonants were lost. Echo vowels developed with disyllabic forms, both those inherited and those developed in pre-Tsouic (§B31.1.1). Some forms of three or more syllables that were not disyllabized in pre-Tsouic or became trisyllabic by affixation also added echo vowels, but in most cases no echo vowel developed because the final C of the word was lost. It is not clear why some lost the -C and others developed echo vowels.[10] (Cf. the discussion of a similar phenomenon in Knn, §B32.1.21.)
First, forms of three or more syllables that lost the final -C:

*taquweɬ'year' + *-an > *caiɬa* 'year as a length of time'(< *tawiɬ [§B31.1.3] + *-an < *taquwiɬ [§B31.2.2] < *taquweɬ) *kaɬusekus > *ʔaɬuku* 'fingernail'

Second, words of three or more syllables that developed an echo vowel:

*baɬituk 'gold' > *váɬituku* 'money, gold' *qamisan 'cold wind' + -an > *ʔamisana* 'winter' *quɬuɬaŋ 'k.o. tree' *ʔuɬuɬangə* 'k.o. tree: *Cordia* sp.'

B31.2.0 Vowels and diphthongs

Except where assimilation and contraction took place, Sar retained the inherited PAn system.

B31.2.1 *i

*i remained /i/ in all environments.

*bitúka > *cívuka* 'stomach' *qaɬiŋu 'shadow' > *ʔáɬingu* 'image' *waɣi > *aari* 'day' *wiɣi > *iiri* 'left'

A sequence *iya that developed in the last two syllables of a word became *eya > /əɬa/.[11]

*ɣiq > *ərəɬa* 'sword grass' (*ərəɬa* [§B31.1.22] < *rəɬa < *rəya < *riya < *ɣiʔa [§B31.1.5] < *aɣiq [see the commentary to the entry for *ɣiq])

B31.2.2 *e

*e for the most part remained /ə/:

*beɣas > *əvəraə* 'hulled rice' *qaɣem > *ʔarəmə* 'pangolin' *seqeɣet > *má-ərəcə* 'tight' *luseq > *lə́əʔə* 'tears' *daɣeq > *sarəə* 'earth'

In a few cases, *e was assimilated to an /i/ or /u/ in a preceding or a following syllable or to a palatalized consonant *ɬ following. This change is sporadic, and the forms that evince it are probably borrowed. (Note that this is the normal reflex in Knn [§B32.2.2].) The common Sar change is for /u/ to assimilate to /e/ (§B31.2.3, end):

*buhet 'squirrel' > *tála-vucu* 'field mouse' *ɬesuŋ > *ɬúungu* 'mortar' *ubeŋ 'surrounding enclosure' > *ta-ʔuvunga* 'pigpen' *telu > *túulu* 'three' *biqel > *víʔili* 'goiter' *ɣik >

---

[10] At the end of the stem, *q, *s, *d, *h, *w, and *y are always lost. However, some stems ending in other consonants lost their final consonants as well and did not develop echo vowels, whereas other stems did not lose the stem-final C and developed an echo vowel.

[11] This is an ad hoc rule based on suggestions by Tsuchida (1976: 195, n. 75). A similar development accounts for the Knn cognate (§B32.2.1, end).

uma-íriki 'thresh by trampling' (< *ərik+ echo vowel) *taquweɬ> *cáiɬi* 'year' *weliq 'go back' + *pua-* > *pua-ili* 'return'

There are other unexplained cases in which *e > /u/:

*taɬeq > *cáɬuʔu* 'rice paddy' *taɬem > *cuma-caɬumu* 'bury' *qebel > *vúu-vula* 'smoke' (< R- + *bəqəl + *an)

In an irregular case, *eq > /a/ (< *ʔa):

*qaɬimateq > *ʔaɬimámaca* 'small leech of the paddy' (with loss of *-q and no echo vowel because of reduplication of the first syllable of the root [§B31.1.21, 5th¶])

B31.2.3 *a and *u

*a remained /a/ in all environments except when in a diphthong *aw or when vowel loss and contraction result in a diphthong /aw/ from the sequence *áu (see §B31.1.31). Other exceptions are cases of *a in the antepenult or earlier within a morpheme, where the *a was assimilated to an /ə/, /u/, or to the palatal onset of the following syllable. This second case of exceptions may be a rule, for there are no countercases.

*qaɬimatek > *ʔaɬimətəkə* 'leech'[12] *qaceŋ > *má-əŋə* 'sneeze' (< *ma-əəŋə with loss of one of the doubled vowels in an affixed form [§B31.1.24, 2nd¶]) *qumah 'field' > *úmuuma* 'field' (< *umah-umah) *qaɬitu > *ʔiɬicu* 'ghost, spirit' *qaɬuwaŋ 'ruminant' > *ta-iɬuangə* 'stag'

*u remained /u/ in all environmentswith one exception (see the following paragraph):

*daɬum > *saɬumu* 'water' *kútu > *kucuʔu* 'louse' *uɣat > *ʔúracə* 'vein, blood vessel'

Within a morpheme, *u assimilated to /ə/ before /ə/ in the following syllable:

*bukes > *vəkəə* 'hair' *luseq > *ləəʔə* 'tears' *tebus > *ətəvə* 'sugar cane' *tuqed > *t-aɬ-əsə* 'stump'

In the following form, *u unaccountably changed to // before *-q, and the *u of the preceding syllable assimilated to it:

*tuɬuq 'coconut milk' > *təɬə-a* 'resin, sap'

There are exceptions to the above rule, where *e assimilates to a preceding *u rather than that the *u assimilates to the *e (§B31.2.2, 2nd¶).

B31.2.4 Diphthongs

B31.2.41 *ay

*ay > /i/ in word-final position. Because of the development of echo vowels (§B31.1.21), *-ay is most commonly reflected with an echo vowel /iʔi/.

*qatay > *ʔaciʔi* 'liver' *quway > *vúiʔi* 'rattan' (< *wuqay)

If the root is affixed, the echo vowel does not develop (§B31.1.21, 5th¶):

*patay > *páa-paci* 'kill' *ngalay > *ngaliʔi* 'saliva' and *mau-ngá-ngali* 'spit'

In roots to which a vowel-initial suffix had been added, /i/ did not develop and *ay remained. The *y was then intervocalic and became /ɬ/ (§B31.3.43).

---

[12] The /a/ of the fourth syllable from the end was not assimilated because it is in a prefix.

*pa + *patay + *u > *paa-pacaɬ-u* (< *paa-pacay-u < *pa-pacay-aw) 'kill it'

There are a couple of exceptions. The first case is not inherited. In the second case, the stem final /i/ was generalized to position before a vowel-initial suffix and then lost (§B31.1.3, 1st¶).

*aɬay > *l-aiaɬə* 'termite' (< *ayaɬ) *beɣay > *ú-vera* 'give' (< *beɣan < *beɣian < *beɣay-an)

B31.2.42 *uy

*-uy >/uɬu/, where the final /u/ is an echo vowel (§B31.1.21):

*sehapuy > *ʔapuɬu* 'fire' *bábuy > *vavuɬu* 'wild pig'.

When there is a lateral to the left within the same phonological word, /ɬ/ was replaced by /l/.

*ɬaŋuy > *ɬangulu* 'swim' *taɣuq 'put' + *sehapuy 'fire' > *pi-taluʔapulu* 'set fire to s.t.'[13]

B31.2.43 *aw

*aw > /u/ in morpheme-internal or word-final position. When *aw is in the final syllable of a disyllabic stem, an echo vowel develops (§B31.1.21):

*taw > *cúcuʔu* 'person' (< *tawtaw [§B31.1.1])

But if the stem was affixed, no echo vowel developed:

*ibabaw > *ʔivavu* 'above' *kaɣaw 'mite, scratch' > *k-ará-aru* 'scratch'

There is one unexplained exception. This root developed an echo vowel /u/ instead of monophthongizing *aw, a development that characterizes Knn (§B32.1.21). It is probably a dialect borrowing:

*tiqáw 'goat fish' > *cíʔau* 'k.o. black riverine fish' (< *ciʔawu)

When a form with *-aw gets a vowel-initial suffix, the change to /u/ does not take place. *w is then intervocalic and like other intervocalic *w's becomes lost (§B31.3.43):

*iseɬaw > *ma-sinu* 'bathe' (<*sinaw) *tapaa-a* 'noun referring to location' + *sinaw > *tapaa-sina-a* 'bathing place' *kasiw > *kiuʔu* 'wood' (< *kiaw [§B31.2.44]) *kiaw +*taa-a* > *taakia-a* 'place to keep wood'

B31.2.44 *iw

There are only two forms reflecting *iw in Sar. In the first case, the *i was absorbed into a preceding palatal (ɬ). The *w became syllabic /u/and developed an echo vowel. In the

---

[13] The /l/ reflecting *ɣ in *talu-* derives from /r/, the normal reflex of *ɣ (§B31.3.34). /r/ followed by a lateral in the same word is changed to /l/ (cf. Tsuchida 1976: §§2.2.1.2.14 and 2.2.1.2)—i.e., *pitaruʔapuɬu > *pitaluʔapuɬu > *pitaluʔapulu*.

second case, metathesis took place when the *s was lost (§B31.1.5) and the resulting *aw > /u/ (§B31.2.43):[14]

*wałiw > *ału?u* 'honey bee' *kasiw > *kiu?u* (< *kiu? < *kiaw < *kaiw) 'wood, tree'

B31.3.0 Consonants

CHART TWO. THE SAAROA REFLEXES OF THE PAN PHONEMES

PAn	Saaroa	PAn	Saaroa
p	*p*	s, h	*Ø*
t	*t, c*	c	*s, Ø*
k	*k*	m	*m*
q, h	*Ø*	n	*n*
b	*v*	ŋ	*ŋ*
d	*s*	ɬ	*ɬ*
j	*s*	l	*Ø*
ɣ	*r*	w	*Ø*
g	*k-, -ɬ-*	y	*ɬ*

B31.3.1 Voiceless stops

B31.3.11 *p

*p was stable in Sar:

*pálisi > *pálisia* 'taboo' *pánaq > *ua-pana* 'shoot' *sapaɣ > *uma-apárə* 'lay mats' *sipaɣ > *ísiparə* 'the other side' *sapesap > *umaapə́-apə* 'grope'

B31.3.12 *t

*t has two outcomes: a stop /t/ and an affricate /c/. *t became an affricate *c, as is the case of the other languages of northeast and southwest Taiwan in certain environments (§A3.3.1).
*t reflected as /t/:

*tapic > *tápisi* 'skirtlike garmet' *túduɣ > *maa-ta-tusuru* 'sleep' *gíta > *kúma-kita* 'see' *witewit 'swinging to and fro' > *maria-itíiti* 'wave'

*t reflected as /c/:

*tałém > *cuma-cáłəmə* 'bury' *taŋíla 'ear' > *cálinga* 'earring' *kútu > *kúcu?u* 'louse' *qatáy > *?áci?i* 'liver' *láŋit > *lángic-a /langəc-a* 'sky'[15]

B31.3.13 *k

*k remained /k/ in all positions:

*kútu > *kúcu?u* 'head louse' *bitúka > *cívuka* 'belly' *qałimátek > *?ałimətəka* 'leech'

In four cases, *k- was lost. In the first case, it was replaced by /?/, and in the others, it was lost entirely:

[14] That this is the sequence of developments is supported by the morphophonemics as explained in §B31.2.43.
[15] The alternant with /ə/ is a borrowing from an unknown source. Knn also manifests /ə/ in the cognate (§B32.2.1).

*kaɬusekus > *ʔáɬuku* 'fingernail' *kaɣat > *um-arácə* 'bite' *kan > *um-an-u* 'eat!' *kedep > *mali-əsə́-əsəpə* 'blink'

B31.3.14 *q

*q > /ʔ/ in initial and medial position. In fact, *q- was lost, and a noncontrastive initial [ʔ-] developed in some pre-Sar dialects. This [ʔ] subsequently became contrastive (§B31.1.6).

*qabaŋ > *ʔavangə* 'boat' *qaɬitu > *ʔiɬicu* 'ghost' *qusuŋ > *ʔu-ʔuunga* 'mushroom' (R- + *qusuŋ +-an) *daqu > *cáaʔu* 'soapberry'

There are numerous exceptions to the above rule. In the first place, roots that are prefixed lost initial glottal stop. This is by the rule of §B31.1.3, whereby an unstable C (*q, *h, *s, *c. w, and *y) that was onset of the penult of trisyllables was lost:

*qaɬuj + mu- > *mú-aɬusu* 'be carried by current' *qetaq + ma- > *mátaʔə* 'raw' (< *maqetaq) *qaciɬ> *máiɬe* 'salt'

In a few cases, a glottal stop did not develop initially (§B31.1.6):

*qáɣicam 'plant with reedlike stem' > *ariamə* 'miscanthus stalks' *qujaɬ> *usaɬə* 'rain' *qumah > *umuuma* 'field'

There is a small piece of evidence that shows that when *-q- was lost before *i, a glide [y] developed that became /ɬ/. However, only one example is attested. Further, there are no parallels with *u or any other sequence *ai that developed, and the form has an unidentified suffix:

*taqis > *tuma-taɬís-ua* 'sew'

In final position, [ʔ] developed automatically after word-final vowel in pre-Tsouic (§B31.1.6), so that *-q was in effect lost: both forms with PAn root-final vowel and those with root-final *-q evince [ʔ] plus echo vowel (§B31.1.21) finally.
Forms that had final *-q reflected by /ʔ/ plus echo vowel:

*luseq > *lə́əʔə* 'tears' *ɬibuq 'den, pen' > *ɬívuʔu* 'wild pig's den' *punuq 'head' > *púnuʔu* 'brains'

Forms that had *-V reflected by final /ʔ/ plus echo vowel:

*ama > *amaʔa* 'father' *qabu > *ʔavuʔu* 'ashes'

In some cases, the final glottal stop did not develop (§B31.1.6):

*ŋucuq 'snout, beak' > *ngusuu* 'mouth' *daɣeq > *sarəə* 'earth' *dilaq 'tongue' > *súma-silaə* 'lick' *paheli 'spleen' > *palii* 'bile, gall bladder'

B31.3.2 *h, *s, *c

B31.3.21 *h

*h was lost without a trace in Tsouic.

*qumah 'field' > *umu-uma* 'field' *lahuj 'seaward' > *milaaláucu* 'go downhill'

B31.3.22 *s

*s was lost in most cases in Sar:

*qusalipan > *álalipa* (< *R- + *alipa) 'millipede' *dusa > *ú-sua* 'two' *wałis 'fang' > *ałii* 'tooth'

In some cases, initial *s- is replaced by /ʔ-/. Presumably this /ʔ/ developed when an automatic noncontrastive [ʔ-] developed in pre-Sar (§B31.1.6). The noncontrastive glottal stop developed only in some dialects, and because of dialect mixture, some initial *s's were replaced by /ʔ/ and some by Ø.

*simaɣ 'grease' > *imaɣə* 'lard' vs. *siyułuq > *ʔiłuʔu* 'necklace, beads'

There are at least nine forms with *s where the *s > /s/ in Sar. These are possibly cases where the change of *s > Ø was not carried through. Or they are cases of dialect mixture, which, in this instance, is tantamount to failure to carry through a sound change. In the other Tsouic languages, *s > /s/.

*ɣawus > *mali-rausu* 'spoon out solids from soup, etc.' *isekam 'weave mats' > *sikamə* 'mat' *pálisi + -an > *pálisi-a* 'taboo' *isiław 'wash' > *ma-sinu* 'bathe' *isełep > *malu-sapə* 'sleep' *qamisan > *ʔámisana* 'winter' (< *qamisan +an) *sipaɣ > *ísiparə* 'other side' *tasiq > *tuma tałís-ua* 'sew'

B31.3.23 *c

*c and *s apparently merged. *c, like *s, normally is lost:

*ceŋeceŋ > *əngə́əngə* 'stopper, plug' *icebu > *ʔivu* 'urine' *beɣac > *əvəraə* 'hulled rice'

There are at least eleven cases where *c is reflected by /s/. These are probably cases of dialect borrowing:

*cabung 'pay' > *sumasavungu* 'compensate for loss' *capił 'padding' > *maisaa-sápiłi* 'patch' *caweŋ > *saung-a* 'protective hat' *ciłaŋ 'shining' > *síłangə* 'bright' * ciwa > *ú-sia* 'nine' *cucu > *ʔú-susu* 'breast' *iseci > *máa-is-ana* 'contents' *kicekic 'file' > *kumakíi-kisi* 'shave' *ŋucuq 'snout, beak' > *ngúsuu* 'mouth' *suɣac > *tara-urasə* 'rinse off' *tapic > *tápisi* 'man's skirt'

B31.3.3 Voiced stops and spirants

The voiced stops underwent weakening, becoming affricates and spirants. *b > [β], *d and *j merged, becoming palatal affricates *[ɟ]. When *c became /s/ or Ø (§B31.3.23), articulatory space was available for the *[ɟ] to devoice and become *[c]. This *[c] subsequently lost its stop articulation entirely and became [s]—i.e., *d and *j > /s/. *g moved forward to merge with *y. Subsequently, this *y > [ɬ] (§B31.3.43). *ɣ moved forward to the space made available after *g had merged with *y and *j had become devoiced. The resulting sound was an [r] made with the blade of the tongue slightly raised toward the palate but not touching it—symbolized /r/.

B31.3.31 *b

*b became a bilabial voiced spirant [β], symbolized /v/:

*babaw > *ʔi-vavu* 'above' *qełeb > *páng-əłəvə* 'close'

In the case of the reflex of *łisebic, *b was assimilated to the preceding *s, as is the case of all An languages except Bunun. (Cf. the comment on *sebic in the glossary.)

*łisebic > má-*łipii* 'thin'

In an exceptional case, *-b was lost after the addition of an echo vowel (cf. §31.1.21):

*suwab > *ma-ua-uaə* 'yawn'

B31.3.32 *d, *j

*d and *j merged and became /s/:

*dapał> *sápałə* 'sole' *demedem > *sə́əsəm-a* 'dark' *dusa > *ú-sua* 'two' *cułud > *kiraaua-ułusu* 'move forward step by step' *dałih > *má-sałi* 'near' *qujał> *usałə* 'rain' *likuj > *líkusu* 'back'

The word for 'blood' has initial /c/ instead of the expected /s/. The form is most likely secondary. The source is probably Knn:

*daɣaq > *caraʔə* 'blood'

In one case, final *-j is reflected with /c/ instead of /s/. This is probably a Knn borrowing as well:

*lahuj 'seaward' > *milaa-laucu* 'go downhill'

In one case, *d- was replaced by *ł, which became /ł/. This is probably a nasalized form—i.e., < *łamaɣ (§A3.7.1).

*dámaɣ 'light, torch' > *łamaɣ 'fire, burn' > *łamarə* 'burn'

B31.3.33 *g

As onset to the penult or earlier, *g falls together with *k, as in many An languages:

*gali 'dig' > *kúmakali* 'dig up' *gíta 'see' > *kúma-kita* 'see'

Medial *-g- merged with *y. This became /ł/ as did *y (§B31.3.43):

*ŋagan > *ngáła* 'name' *łagam > *łałamə* 'tame'

The *y that developed from *g was lost before and after *i—i.e., abutting *i, *-g- was lost:[16]

*piga 'how many' > *u-piá-ini* 'how many'

B31.3.34 *ɣ

* ɣ became /r/ in all positions:

*ɣumaq 'house' > *pua-ruma* 'go into the house' *báqeɣuh > *váruʔu* 'new' *beɣác >*əvəraə* 'hulled rice' *símaɣ > *ímarə* 'lard'

B31.3.4 Continuants

B31.3.41 *l

*l was stable in Sar and is inherited without change in all positions:

*lawaɣ 'flying rodent' > *láarə* 'flying squirrel' *likuj > *líkusu* 'back' *luseq > *lə́əʔə* 'tears' *walu > *kú-alu* 'eight' *biqel > *víʔili* 'goiter'

The following form has spread secondarily, as indicated by the reflex /r/ < *l.

---

16 There is only one example, but the change is articulatorily well motivated. Further, there is evidence from forms that do not have a PAn etymology: the comparison of Sar *ais-a* 'between, middle' Knn *áisanə* 'boundary' with Maga Rukai *agísanə* 'boundary', where Rukai /g/ reflects an earlier *g, substantiates this rule, even though no extra-Formosan cognates are attested (Tsuchida 1976: 161, bottom).

*balug > *távaru* 'pigeon'

*ɬ in all positions is reflected as a voiceless palatal lateral /ɬ/.

*ɬa > *ɬa* 'and' *qaɬit > *aɬici* 'leather, bark' *bulaɬ> *vulaɬə* 'moon'

There are two exceptions. The first is doubtlessly a borrowing from a now-extinct dialect. The second developed very early. It has cognates with unexplained /n/ in all Formosan attestations:

*ɬeket > *ma-kəngəcə* 'sticky'[17] *iseɬaw 'wash' > *ma-sinu* 'bathe'

B31.3.42 Nasals

*m, *n, *ŋ remained unchanged in all positions.

*matáy > *máciʔi* 'die' *ama > *amaʔa* 'father' *qayam 'pet' > *áɬamə* 'bird' *nunuh > *nunuʔa* 'breast' *wanaɬ> *áɬanə* 'right side' (< *waɬan) *tinuen 'weave' > *tumatinəənə* 'weave, crochet' *ceŋeceŋ > *əngə́əngə* 'stop up'

*-n is lost in the following form. This form is perhaps a borrowing from a dialect like Knn where, under certain conditions, root-final C is lost (§B32.1.21, end). The accretion of /ʔ/ is by the rule of §B31.1.6. The *-n of the suffix is lost by the rule of §B31.1.7.

*jalan > *sálaʔa* 'road' (< *jalan +an)

B31.3.43 *w and *y

*w was lost in all positions. The loss of *w was subsequent to the development of noncontrastive glottal stop before vowels in word onset (§B31.1.6), so that forms that lost *w- did not develop syllable-initial [ʔ]. See §§B31.2.43, B31.2.44 for *-w in final position.

*walu > *kú-alu* 'eight' *wiɣi > *iiri* 'left' *sináwa 'breath' *maruania-niaa* 'breathe' *siwa > *ú-sia* ' nine'

There is one irregular reflex, *vuiʔi* 'rattan' < *quway. It is probably secondary, but a possible explanation is that *wu > /vu/. There are no other forms attested that developed from *wu. We assume the following development:

*quway > *wuqay (§B31.1.5) > *wuiʔ > *wuiʔi (§B31.2.41) > *vuiʔi* 'rattan'.

There are no attestations of an inherited initial *y- and only two attestations of a medial *-y- within disyllabic roots. In trisyllabic roots, *-y- was lost (§B31.1.3). Medial *-y- in disyllabic roots became /ɬ/. This account of the development of medial *-y- is supported by examples of reflexes in stem-final position before an echo vowel or before a vowel-initial suffix (§§B31.2.41, B31.2.42):

*qayam 'pet' > *áɬamə* 'bird' *babuy > *vavuɬu* 'wild pig' *pa + *patay + *aw > *paa-pacaɬ-u* (< *paapacay-u) 'kill it'

In one case, *-y- is reflected with /-i-/. This form is likely not directly inherited. Note that there is also metathesis and an unexplained initial /l/.[18]

*aɬay > *laiaɬə* 'termite' (< *layaɬ< *l-aɬay)

[17] Note the Knn cognate *mata-nəkə́cə* 'sticky'.

[18] The metathesis is shared by Atayalic, Tsouic, Th, Am, Pu, and Pai. These languages all manifest /-y-/ (or /-i-/ in their reflexes, the regular reflex in some, but not in others of these languages. Initial /l-/ is confined to the Tsouic languages and is no doubt a purely Tsouic innovation.

CHAPTER THREE, §2

Kanakanavu

B32.0 Kanakanavu

The data here were gathered in Min Sheng Ts'un (Takanua) and in Min Chuen Ts'un (Magacun) in San Min Hsiang , Kao-Hsiung, from four of the last remaining speakers of Knn. There are some published sources and manuscript sources that we consulted in adding to the data we elicited and in correcting our transcriptions (cf. the bibliography). Bunun speakers have been moving into the traditional Knn areas since the 1930s, and the ethnic Knn mostly went over to Bun. Bun together with Mandarin predominates. The few Knn speakers that remain are elderly and isolated, and they only speak Knn on the rare occasions when they come together, if then. Knn shares a good deal of its development with Sar, and the exposition here will follow that of Sar in §B31ff., above.

B32.01 Phonemics of Knn

Knn lacks /ɬ/ but otherwise has the same consonantal phonemes as Sar. In the vowel inventory, Knn has added three vowels that arose from the monophthongization of the diphthongs. In slow, careful speech, Knn also has three diphthongs (that became monophthongized in normal speech).

CHART ONE. PHONEMES OF KNN

Consonants

stops	p	t	k	ʔ
spirants/ affricates	v [β]	s, c		
laterals/ palatals		l, r, y		
nasals	m	n	ng [ŋ]	

Vowels and Diphthongs

high	i		u
mid	e	ə	o
low		a, ʌ	
diphthongs	aw	aĕ	ay

The canonical structure of the syllable in Knn is (C)V(N, w, y) where N may be any of the nasals. There are no C clusters and no C codas, except for /N,w,y/ and syncopated forms (§B32.1.5). Sequences of two vowels other than /aw/ /aĕ/ or /ay/ are two separate syllables. /aw/, /aĕ/, and /ay/ pronounced as a single syllable contrast with /au/, /aə/, and /ai/, pronounced as two syllables.

/v/ is a voiced bilabial spirant [β]. /c/ is an apico-alveolar affricate with blade closure in the palate before /i/ and otherwise only apical closure. /l/ is an alveolar tap with a slight retroflexion of the tongue [ɭ]. /r/ is an apical tap with greater retroflexion.

[ʔ] contrasts with its absence in initial and medial position. /ʔ/ developed from *q (§B32.3.14).
Stress is contrastive and correlates with other reflexes of the inherited PAn stress contrasts—i.e., Knn stress provides evidence for reconstructing PAn stress (§A3.5.2).[1] As is the case of contrastive stress in other languages, Knn has undergone stress shifts in some forms, so that Knn stress does not invariably reflect PAn stress patterns (cf. §§A3.5.2, A3.5.3).

B32.1. Changes that characterize Knn in general

B32.1.1 Di- and trisyllabization

Tsouic reflects the general PAn tendency to disyllabize monosyllabic roots (§A3.6.2). Already by proto-Tsouic times the PAn monosyllabic roots that had been inherited by Tsouic were disyllabized by adding a prothetic vowel or by stretching the root.
Here are some Knn examples of disyllabization, first by adding a prothetic vowel:

*ɣik > *uma-iríki* 'thresh by trampling' (< *ərik [§B32.2.2, middle])

Second, disyllabization by stretching the nucleus of the monosyllabic root:

*kan > *k-um-a-káən* 'eat' *pak 'make a flapping sound' > *paakə* 'wing' *pan > *páənə* 'bait'

Knn underwent little syllable elision due to stress. Elision is attested only in two situations: (1) elision of *ec, *ce, or *se in the penult of a root (§§B32.3.22, B32.3.23) and (2) in reduplicated monosyllabic roots into which an epenthetic vowel had been added in PAn (§A3.6.1). This epenthetic vowel was lost, and subsequently Knn developed echo vowels after each of the reduplicated syllables:

*kicekic > *mari-ngisi-ngisi* 'shave' (< *ngicngic < *kic +*N-) *ŋuceŋuc > *puru-ngusú-ngusu* 'snore' *tuketuk > *makía-tukutuku* 'pound' (< *tuktuk)

In current colloquial speech, elision occurs as discussed in §B32.1.5.

B32.1.2 Process of trisyllabization

After the processes described in §B32.1.1, above, took place, proto-Tsouic developed a canonical root of three or more syllables—that is, a root may have three or four syllables (and possibly more), and disyllabic roots had to be made trisyllabic. The motivation for this development is unknown. The process of trisyllabization affected not only inherited disyllabic roots but also roots of three syllables that had been disyllabized in pre-Tsouic by contraction (§B32.1.1). Most often the disyllabic roots (inherited or developed in pre-Tsouic) became trisyllabic by developing echo vowels. Disyllabic roots ending in a vowel were made trisyllabic by doubling the vowel nucleus of the penult (see examples in §B32.1.22).

[1] We mark stress for forms we elicited and for those forms in the sources where stress is marked. We found some forms only in sources that do not mark stress, and for those forms we give no stress indication.

B32.1.21 Echo vowels and loss of final -C

C-final roots and doubled monosyllabic roots are reflected with an echo vowel, the same as the vowel of the preceding syllable. The exception is that the echo vowel after a syllable containing /a/ is /ə/.[2]

> *bucuɣ > *vuúru* 'bow' *cekecek 'stuff, cram in' > *mia-cəkəcəkə* 'insert penis into vagina' *qabaŋ > *ʔaváŋə* 'boat' *seqeɣet > *ma-ə́rəcə* 'tight' *túbuq 'grow' > *cuvúʔu* 'shoot (bamboo, miscanthus, etc.)' *tuketuk 'strike' > *makia-tukutuku* 'pound' *wałis 'fang' > *anísi* 'tooth'

After *aw and *ay, the echo vowels are /u/ and /i/ respectively:

> *taw > *cáau* 'person' *enay 'sand' > *ənái* 'earth, soil'

Word-final *-n within the root is lost after unstressed *a, but retained after a stressed *á (Tsuchida 1976: 33). The same is true of *-w (in the diphthong *aw [Tsuchida 1976: §4.5.31.2]):[3]

> *jalán > *mu-caánə* 'leave' vs *muá-ca* 'be leaving' *iseław > *mari-sináw* 'wash utensils' vs *káɣaw > *kuma-kará-kara* 'scratch'

In a number of cases, echo vowels did not develop, and -C was lost. These were trisyllabic roots or roots that normally occur affixed. No rule can be found for determining whether echo vowels developed or -C was lost. The two processes are probably a case of dialect mixture. (Cf. the discussion of a similar phenomenon in Sar, §B31.1.7.)

> *biceqak 'split' > *mari-viʔa* 'crack, tear off' *daluc 'slip' > *macalu* 'smooth, slippery' *iceɣab 'yesterday' > *mia-əra* 'yesterday' *nú-ura* 'tomorrow' (< *nu-əra [§B32.2.2]) *łisebic > *ma-nípi* 'thin' *táŋic > *tumá-tangi* 'cry'

The suffix *-an is reflected as *-anə* with echo vowel (alternatively, *-an* with echo vowel elided [§B32.1.5]), or as *-a* (with final *-n lost). Whether *-anə/an* or *-a* is chosen, is not governed by a phonological rule but depends on the stem:

> *taɣuq 'put down' + *-an > *tarúʔanə* 'field hut' vs. *báqeɣuh+*-an > *vaʔúru-a* 'new' *ubeŋ 'enclosure' > *ta-ʔəvə́ŋ-a* 'pigpen' *tasał 'stay' + *an > *tanása* 'house' (< *tanas [§B32.1.4] + -an) *tanása* 'house' + *-an > *tanásan* 'village'

If a V-initial suffix is added to a form with an echo vowel, the echo vowel is lost by contraction (§B32.1.3) (or never developed):z

> *taquweł'year' > *caini- +anan* > *cainána* 'year' (an alternative account: *taquweł-anan >*tawił-anan > *cainána*)

The final -C of a root is dropped when it has been prefixed or is a member of a compound. The final -C's of both members of the compound are dropped in the following form:

> *delec 'cord' + *bucúɣ 'bow' > *cə́ə-vuúru* 'bowstring'

---

[2] Note, however, that in recent times there has been a tendency to lose vowels within the morpheme after nasals (§B32.1.5), so that the echo vowels after a nasal are lost in normal speech. Thus *ʔavángə* 'boat', cited above, is normally pronounced *ʔaváng*.

[3] The analogous rule for *-ay does not hold: *áłay > *ngáai* 'saliva'.

This is also the case of an inherited monosyllabic root that always occurs prefixed:

*bit 'carry s.t. hanging down' > *umari-vi* 'hold a baby in the arms'

B32.1.22 Doubling of the vowel of the penult

Disyllabic roots ending in a vowel or in a final C that was lost (*-q, *-h) were made trisyllabic by doubling the vowel of the penult.[4]

*daqu > *caáʔu* 'soapberry tree' *icebu > *m-íivu* 'urinate' *kútu > *kúucu* 'louse' *lima > *íima* 'five' *ɬibu 'fenced in place' > *níivu* 'nest of wild pig' *baɣah > *váara* 'embers'

When these V-final roots are affixed, vowel doubling does not take place.[5]

*lima + u- > *u-líma* 'five' (cf. *íima*, above) *kútu + -ini > *kucú-ini* 'his louse' (cf. *kúucu*, above) *taw > *cáau* 'person' + *ka-an > *ka-cáu-a* 'group of people'

One of two doubled vowels in root-final position is lost:

*jalán > *muá-ca* 'be leaving' (< *muá-caa < *muá-caan [§B32.1.21]) *tawa > *maá-caca* 'laugh' (< *maa-taa-taa < *maa-tawa-tawa)

B32.1.3 Vowel contraction

In trisyllabic roots, when the onset of a penult with *e is lost or when the penult is *yu, there is contraction of the penultimate *e or *u with the vowel of the antepenult. The following examples manifest loss of the penult-onset C and contraction. The vowel that results from contraction is doubled if the root ends in a vowel. It has an echo vowel if the root has a -C coda:

*tahebu 'vessel to hold or fetch water' > *táavu* 'gourd, calabash' *iseci > *a-ʔisi* 'exist' (the penult is not doubled because of the prefix [§B32.1.22, above]) *icebu > *m-íivu* 'urinate' *siyuɬuq > *sinuʔu* 'necklace'

This rule also applies to the following case, where the prefix has become petrified (as if the root were three syllables beginning with /ma/):

*qetáq + ma- > *matáʔə* 'raw' (< *maqetaq)

The following examples show the loss of *h in final-syllable onset and subsequent contraction:

*ɣabihi 'evening' > *koó-ravi* 'eat supper' *pacuheq > *əpacə* 'wash' (< *əpacə[6])

Echo vowels are normally contracted (or never developed) before a vowel-initial suffix (§B32.1.21). Root-final vowels are not contracted. However, in the following forms, a vowel before a vowel-initial suffix was lost. This is not normal in Knn, and the forms are probably dialectal borrowings (cf. Sar *vərəngana* 'night' (§B31.1.3, end):

---

[4] Note that *q is usually reflected with /ʔ/ [§B32.3.14], but sometimes is lost. When a root-final *-q is reflected by /-ʔ/, trisyllabization is affected by an echo vowel, as in other C-final roots [§B32.1.21]:

*weliq 'do again' + *pua- > *puá-iʔi* 'come back' (*pua-weliq > *pua-iliʔ > *pua-iiʔ > *pua-iiʔi [addition of echo vowel] > puá-iʔi [vowel shortening after addition of prefix])

[5] This rule affects a wider range of forms than just the V-final disyllabic roots. An example is *pua-iʔi* 'return'. Cf. the explanation in the immediately preceding footnote.

[6] The prothetic /ə/and loss of *-q are unexplained. The form is probably a borrowing.

*biɣeŋí > *vərə́ng-ana* 'night' (< *beɣengi-anan) *qaɬipugu > *ʔanipula* 'hair whorl' (< *ʔaɬipugu-an) *kaɬuskus > *ʔanuka* 'fingernail' (< *ʔkaɬuku-an [with loss of *s (§B32.3.22)][7])

B32.1.4 Metathesis

Metathesis in Knn is a sporadic process. Some of the forms in Knn that evince metathesis have cognates in other languages that also show this process, and they may well have spread to Knn secondarily. These same forms are metathesized in Sar as well (§B31.1.5):

*aɬay > *l-aían* 'termite' *laŋaw > *taa-ngaláw* 'gnat' *sináwa 'breath' > *ngisaa* 'breath' (<*nisawa) *taŋíla 'ear' > *caínga* 'ear ornament'

Others are metathesized only in Tsouic languages:[8]

bitúka > *cívuka* 'belly' *qaɬuj > *ma-acun* 'be carried by current' *tasaɬ 'stay' > *tanás-a* 'house'

B32.1.5 Elision

Syllables shaped /Nə/ (where N = nasal consonant) tend to lose the /ə/ in normal speech. In this way disyllabic roots have again entered the language.

*enem > *ə́nəmə/ənəm* 'six' *jalan > *caanə/caán* 'road' *quɬuɬaŋ > *ʔənə́nang/ə́nnang* 'k.o. tree'

Further, echo vowels also are optionally lost after nasals:

*daɬúm > *canúmu/canúm* 'water' *qáɬuj > *ma-acúnu/ma-acún* 'be carried by current'

There are other examples of elision of vowels in the speech of our youngest informant, but these are for the most part not registered in the literature:

vánituku 'money' > *vántuku*, *usúpatə* 'four' > *usúpat*, etc.

There is also loss of /se/ and /ce/ discussed below, §§B32.3.22, B32.3.23. Further, in normal speech, clitics may cause elision in the morphs that precede (Sung 1969: *passim*). The form *máa-rang-cu* 'has become old' probably arose by elision from *mamarúrangə-cu* 'has become old'.

B32.1.6 Monophthongization

The diphthongs in normal speech become monophthongs: /ay/ > /e/, /aě/ > /ʌ/, /aw/ > /o/. Further, sequences /au/, /ua/, /ai/, /ia/, and /aə/ may become monophthongs: they are doubled if the resulting form is not trisyllabic:

*taŋíla > *caínga/ceénga* 'earring' (< *taliŋa) *-ɣuqáɬay > *sasa-ruánay/sasaróne* 'man' *saweni 'later on' > *sauni/sooni* 'today' pua + *weliq > *puá-iʔi/pó-iʔi* 'come back' (the monophthongized prefix is a single vowel because the word in which it occurs has three syllables) *qaleb > *aěvə/ʌ́və* 'knee'

---

[7] Replacement of *k- by initial /ʔ/ is unexplained. Cf. Sar *ʔaɬuku* 'fingernail' (§B31.3.13).

[8] The form *ʔipakuʔay* 'how?' probably arose by metathesis (< *ʔipa-kuʔag < *ʔipa-kuga? < ipa-kuga). The form is probably a borrowing because of the inserted /ʔ/ (§B32.1.7).

B32.1.7 Glottal stop insertion

In a small number of cases, a glottal stop was inserted after a vowel-final prefix and before a vowel-initial root or before a root that had lost an initial C. There is no explanation for the sporadic glottal stop in these cases:

> *ubəŋ 'enclosure' > *ta-ʔəvəŋ-a* 'pigpen' *cuŋu > *ʔuʔúngu* 'horn' *likuj 'back' > *tara-ʔiku-ʔikúcu* 'look back'

In one case, an initial and a final glottal stop are accreted:

> *kuga 'how' > *ʔipa-kuʔay* 'how?' (< *ʔipa-kuʔag < *ʔipa-kugaʔ < *ipa-kuga[9])

B32.2.0 Vowels and diphthongs

Except where assimilation has taken place, Knn retains the inherited PAn system.

B32.2.1 *i

*i remains /i/ in all environments.

> *bitúka > *civúka* 'stomach' *qaɬiŋu 'shadow' > *ʔaníngu* 'image, shadow' *waɣi > *pa-ari* 'dry in sun' *wiɣi > *iíri* 'left'

*i, within a root, > /ə/ before *e in the following syllable:

> *biɣeŋi > *vərəŋana* 'night' *iceɣab > *mia-əra* 'yesterday' (< *mia-əəra [§B32.1.22, 2nd ¶]) *liqeɣ > *əʔə́rə* 'neck' *tiqeɣab > *cuma-cərávə* 'hiccough, belch'

This assimilation does not occur in the case of some (but not all) forms beginning with *ise- and *ice-. *e after *is- and *ic- is often elided (§§B32.3.22, B32.3.23). This elision took place before the assimilation of *i to *e, with the result that roots that underwent elision reflect /i/ rather than /ə/. There is no explanation as to why assimilation occurs before elision in some cases and after elision in others.

> *iseci > *ʔa-isi* 'exist' *icebu 'urine' > *m-iivu* 'urinate' *ɬisebic > *ma-nipi* 'thin' *biceqak 'split' > *mari-viʔa* 'crack'

In one case *e of the final syllable assimilates to the *i of the preceding syllable. It is a form that spread through almost all the languages of Taiwan:

> *biqel > *viʔli* 'goiter'

In the following form, *i > /ə/ before /a/ in the final syllable. There is no explanation.[10]

> *laŋit > *kak-ángec-a* 'heavens' (< *ka+*ka+laŋit+an [with contraction of *aa after the *l was lost])

A sequence [iʔa] that developed > /ə/ (Tsuchida 1976: 195, n.75).[11] There are two forms that attest this rule:

---

[9] We take the prefix *ipa-* to derive from PAn *si 'instrumental passive' + *pa-. The /ʔ/ is therefore an accretion.

[10] Sar also attests this development as an alternant (footnote to §B31.3.12).

[11] The forms that illustrate this rule may in fact be secondary, for the rule is unmotivated. However, no source is attested. The development of *ɣiq in Sar follows a similar path (§B31.2.1, end).

*ɣiq 'saw grass' > *rəəʔə* '*Miscanthus* grass used for thatching' (*rəəʔə* [doubling of the vowel of the penult: §B32.1.22] < *rəʔə < *riʔa < *ɣiʔa [§B32.1.4] < *aɣiq [see commentary under *ɣiq]) *dilaq 'tongue' > *cuma-cəʔə* 'lick' (< *ciʔa < *ciʔal [§B32.1.4] < *cilaʔ)

B32.2.2 *e

*e for the most part remains /ə/:

*qebel > *əə́və* 'smoke' *maa-əvə* 'smoky' *enem > *nəəmə* 'six' *seqeɣet > *ma-ʔə́rəcə* 'tight'

In most cases, *e is assimilated to an /u/ in a preceding or a following syllable. There are exceptions where /u/ is assimilated to /e/ (§B32.2.3, end):

*báqeɣuh > *vaʔúru-a* 'new' *búhet > *vuútu* 'squirrel' *qitelúɣ > *icúuru* 'egg' *tuqeláɬ> *cuʔúan* 'bone' *qetúɣ > *muru-ucuru* 'have an erection' *qetút > *ʔutútu* 'break wind' *télu > *u-túlu* 'three'[12]

*e also assimilated to /i/ in the following syllable:

*ɣik > *uma-iríki* 'thresh by trampling' (< *eɣik) *weliq 'do again, go back' > *puá-iʔi* (< *pua-iiʔi [§B32.1.22, 2nd footnote] < *pua-iiʔ < *pua-iliʔ)

/ə /, like /u/ (§B32.2.3), optionally assimilates to a preceding /c/—i.e., /cə/ > /ci/:

* delec > *cə́ə-vuúru/cíə-vuúru* 'bowstring'

In three cases, *e assimilates to *a in the same word. There is no explanation. These forms may be borrowings:

*keɬaŋ 'remember' > *apa-kanang-ənə* 'allow to recognize' *qaɬimatéq >*nimácaʔə* 'paddy leech' *taɬeq 'soil in paddy' + *-an > *cana-a* 'wet field'

B32.2.3 *a and *u

*a remains /a/ in all environments.

*qayam 'pet' > *ʔalamə* 'meat' waɬis 'fang' > *anísi* 'tooth' *ina > *cí-ina* 'mother'

There are exceptions to this rule: in some forms, *a within a morpheme, is optionally assimilated to a /ə/ on the right. These are sporadic examples, and they usually are variants of forms with /a/:

*pan > *páənə/pə́ənə* 'bait' *qaɬimátek-an > *ʔanimatə́ka/ʔanimətə́ka* 'river leech' *qaɬimateq > *nimácaʔə/nimə́caʔə* 'leech of paddies' *tiqeɣab > *cuməcərəvə* 'belch'

In one case *a is assimilated to a following *ɬ. This is probably a dialectal borrowing. Cf. Sar *ta-iɬuangə* 'stag', where assimilation of *a > /i/ before *ɬ is likely to be regular (§B31.2.3).

*qaɬuwaŋ 'ruminant' > *inuang* 'doe'

*u remains /u/ in all environments:

---

[12] Tsuchida 1976: §4.4.4 suggests that *ə > /u/ by assimilation to a stressed /ú/ in an adjacent syllable, but at least *utúlu* 'three' and most of the other forms among these examples are countercases in that the /u/ in the adjacent syllable is not stressed.

*púnuq 'head' > *punúʔu* 'brain'

There are exceptions to the above rule, where *u assimilates to a preceding or following *e rather than that the *e assimilates to the *u (§B32.2.2). The two different forms of assimilation are probably due to dialect mixture. Cf. the similar development in Sar (§§B31.2.2, B31.2.3).[13]

*becuɣ > *mavəcərə́-kə* 'sated' *bukés > *vəkə́sə* 'hair on head' *luséq > *əsə́ʔə* 'tears' *ubeŋ 'surrounding enclosure' > *ta-ʔəvə́nga* 'pigpen' *ɣebun 'lay eggs' > *ma-ərə́vənə* 'brood' *tebús > *təvə́sə* 'sugar cane' *teɬúq 'coconut milk' > *tənə́ʔə* 'resin, sap' *tuqed > *t-an-ə́ʔəcə* 'stump of tree'

In a couple of cases all the /u/'s in the root vary with /ə/. There is no explanation:

*quɬuɬang > *ʔə́nnang/ʔunúnang* 'k.o. tree' *qudip > *ʔuma-ʔuciʔucípi/ʔumaʔəciʔəcipi* 'alive'[14]

/u /, like /ə/ (§B32.2.2), optionally assimilates to a preceding /c/ (that is, > /i/):

*qitelúɣ > *iciúru/icúuru* 'egg' *tusuɣ 'string beads' > *cuma-ciúru/cuma-cuúru* 'thread a needle'

B32.2.4 Diphthongs

B32.2.41 *ay and *aw

*ay and *aw are reflected as /ay/ and /aw/, respectively. They are most commonly followed by an echo vowel (§B32.1.21, 2nd¶)—that is, they are manifested as /ai/ and /au/ respectively, but if the root is affixed, the echo vowel does not develop:

*enay 'sand' > *ənái* 'earth, soil' *mata-ənáy* 'come down to the ground' *taw > *cáau* 'person' (/a/ doubled §B32.1.22) *iseɬaw > *mari-sináw* 'wash (utensils)'

If a suffix beginning with vowel is added to roots ending in *-ay and *-aw, the *y is in intervocalic position and becomes /l/ (§B32.3.44). The *w is in intervocalic position and is lost (§B32.3.44):

*patáy > *mia-pacáy* 'kill' *miapacay+ -a* 'imperative' > *miapacála* 'kill!' *alalakáw* 'rise (sun, moon)' + *ta-a* 'location' > *ta-alalaká-a* 'east (place where the sun, moon rises)'[15]

B32.2.42 *uy

*-uy > /ulu/, where the final /u/ is an echo vowel. For the lateralization of *y, see §B32.3.44, footnote.

*bábuy > *vavúlu* 'wild pig' *ɬaŋuy > *nangúlu* 'swim' *sehapuy > *apúlu* 'fire'

---

[13] Note that the development in Knn is independent from that in Sar. Not all the same cognates show /ə/ < *u and /u/ < *e in the two languages. Tsuchida 1976: §4.4.3 suggests that *u > /ə/ by assimilation to a stressed /ə́/ in an adjacent syllable, but there are three counter cases in the examples given here, where *u assimilates to an unstressed /ə/ in the preceding syllable.

[14] One informant gave us *ʔumaʔaciʔacípi*. There is no explanation.

[15] Examples are taken from Tsuchida 1976, §§2.1.1.3.3, 2.1.1.3.4. Cf. the back formation *nganai* 'name', derived from *nganal* (< *ŋalan by metathesis), as in *nganal aku* 'my name'.

B32.2.43 *iw

There are only two forms reflecting *iw in Knn. In the first case, the *i was absorbed into a preceding palatal *ɬ (> /n/). The *w became syllabic /u/. In the second case, the /s/ was lost. The resulting *i in a sequence lost its syllabicity and became lateralized by the rule of §B32.3.44.

*waɬiw > *aánu* 'honey bee' *kásiw > *káalu* 'wood, tree' (< *kayu < *kaiw) (doubling of the vowel by the rule of §B32.1.22)

B32.3.0 Consonants

The Knn consonantal phonemes and their PAn origins is summarized as follows:

CHART TWO. DEVELOPMENT OF THE KNN CONSONANTS FROM PAN

PAn	Knn	PAn	Knn
p	*p*	g	*k-, -l-, -l*
t	*t, c*	ɣ	*r*
k	*k*	l	*Ø, l*
q	*ʔ*	ɬ	*n*
h	*Ø*	m	*m*
s	*s*	n	*n*
c	*c*	ŋ	*ng* [ŋ]
b	*v* [β]	w	*Ø*
d, j	*c*	y	*l*

B32.3.1 Voiceless stops

B32.3.11 *p

*p was stable in Knn:

*pánaq > *panáʔə* 'shoot' *sapaɣ > *suma-sapárə* 'lay mats' *sipaɣ > *mua-sipárə* 'ford a stream' *sapesap > *mati-sapə́sapə* 'grope'

B32.3.12 *t

*t has two outcomes: a stop /t/ and an affricate /c/. *t became an affricate *c, as is the case of the other languages of northeast and southwest Taiwan in certain environments (§A3.3.1, first footnote).
*t reflected as /t/:

*talís > *talísi* 'cord' *túduq 'leak, drip' > *tucúʔu* 'leak through roof' *qaɬimátek > *ʔanimatə́ka* 'leech' *witewit 'swinging to and fro' > *mari-itíiti* 'wave'

*t reflected as /c/:

*túqelaɬ> *cuʔuán/cuʔúanə* 'bone ' *taŋíla 'ear' > *caínga* 'earring' *kútu > *kúucu* 'louse' *uɣat >*urácə* 'vein, sinew'

B32.3.13 *k

*k remained /k/ in all positions:

*kútu > *kúucu* 'head louse' *bitúka > *civúka* 'belly' *łekét > *mata-nəkə́cə* 'sticky' *tuketuk 'strike, peck' > *makía-tukutuku* 'pound'

B32.3.14 *q

*q > /ʔ/ in all positions:

*qámis 'north' > *ʔamís-anə* 'cold time, place' *qełeb > *pi-ʔə́nəvə* 'close (door)' *liqeɣ > *əʔə́rə* 'neck' *tuqeláł> *cuʔuán* 'bone' *pánaq > *panáʔə* 'shoot'

There are a small number of exceptions. These are most likely borrowings from a dialect in which *q was lost.

*qusuŋ > *uúngu* 'mushroom' *ɣuqáłay 'male' > *sa-ruanáy* 'male (animal) qetáq > *matáʔə* 'raw' *seqeɣet > *ma-ə́rəcə* 'tight' (alternatively, *maʔə́rəcə*) *tiqeɣáb > *cuma-cərávə* 'belch' *jemaq 'tomorrow' > *mua-cəməcəmə* 'leave early in the morning' *łibúq 'surrounded area' > *niívu* 'den of wild pigs' *ŋucuq 'snout, beak' > *ngu-r-usu* 'lips, snout'

B32.3.2 *h, *s, *c

B32.3.21 *h

*h lost without a trace in Tsouic:

*qumah > *ʔumá-ʔuma* 'cultivated field' *lahuj 'seaward' > *mua-láucu* 'go downhill'

B32.3.22 *s

*s > /s/:

*sapesap > *mati-sapə́sap* 'grope' *dusa > *cúusa* 'two' *wałis 'fang' > *anísi* 'tooth'

*se (and *ce [§B32.3.23]) in the penult and in the antepenult was lost other than in reduplicated monosyllabic roots

*iseci > *a-ʔísi* 'exist' *seqeɣet > *ma-ʔə́rəcə* 'tight' *sehapuy > *apúlu* 'fire'

In a number of sporadic cases, *s was lost, as in other Formosan languages (but not necessarily in cognate lexical items [cf. the discussion in §A3.3.32]):

*dusa > *kara-cua* 'for two people to drink together'[16] *gusam 'thrush' > *masu-kuámə* 'painful' *kásiw > *káalu* 'wood, tree' (< *kayu < *kaiw) *łisebic > *ma-nípi* 'thin' *qusalipan > *ʔalalipáng* 'milliped' *qusuŋ > *uúngu* 'mushroom' *suni 'soft noise' > *mari-uni-uni* 'whistle' *tiŋas > *tíinga* 'food particles in teeth' *tusuɣ 'string beads' > *cuma-ciúru/cuma-cuúru* 'thread a needle'

In one case, *s is reflected with /c/. There is no explanation. The form is not directly inherited:

*isepi > *siʔəcəpə/səʔəcə́pə* 'sleep'

---

[16] Note that PAn *dusa is reflected with and without /s/ in Knn—cf. *cúusa* 'two'.

B32.3.23 *c

*ce and *ec in the penult get lost other than in reduplicated monosyllabic roots (as does *se [§B32.3.22]).

*balec > 'answer, revenge' > *malí-vali* 'answer, talk back' (< *-baleci)' *icebú > *m-iívu* 'urinate' *iceɣab > *mia-əra* 'yesteday' (< *əcəra [§B32.2.1] and shortening of the doubled vowel after the prefix [§B32.1.22])

Otherwise, *c has three reflexes. Except for the above case, no environments have been discovered to account for the three different reflexes of *c. The differences are probably due to dialect mixture.

*c > Ø:

*bucúɣ > *vuúru* 'bow' *caləŋ > *alə́ŋə* 'pine' *cuŋu > *ʔuʔúngu* 'horn' *caqaɬ> *pusu-aʔánə* 'carry on the shoulder' *qacíɬ> *ma-ʔaíni* 'salty'

*c > /s/:

*ciɬaŋ > *sinángə* 'light, ray' *ŋucenuc > *puru-ngusúngusu* 'snore' *qaceŋ > *ma-asəng* 'sneeze' *iseci 'contents' > *ʔa-isi* 'exist' *kicekic > *mari-ngisí-ngisi* 'shave' *ŋucuq > *ngu-r-usu* 'lips, snout' *qáɣicam 'plant with reedlike stem' > *ʔarisang* 'pigeon pea'

*c > /c/:

*becuɣ > *ma-vəcərə́-kə* 'sated' *ciɬaɣ 'ray of light' > *niku-cingar-a* 'window' *cucu 'breast' > *mari-ucuucu* 'suck' (with unexplained prothetic /u/[17]) *ica > *u-cá-ni* 'one' *pacuheq > *əpəcə* 'wash clothes'

B32.3.3 Voiced stops and spirants

Knn shared the development of the voiced consonants with Sar (§B31.3.3ff.), but Sar developed *d and *j further.

B32.3.31 *b

* b became a bilabial voiced spirant [β], symbolized /v/:

*bábuy > *vavulu* 'wild pig' *qabu > *ʔaávu* 'ashes' *qaleb > *aə́və* 'knee'

In the case of the reflex of *ɬisebic, *b is assimilated to the preceding *s, as is the case of all An languages except Bun. (Cf. the comment in the glossary under *sebic.)

*ɬisebic > *ma-nípi* 'thin'

In an exceptional case, *-b was devoiced:

*suwab > *masu-suapə* 'yawn'

B32.3.32 *d, *j

*d and *j merged and became /c/:

*daŋedaŋ 'heat near fire to cook, etc.' > *cumacangcáng* 'dry clothes near fire' *daɣeq > *caráʔə* 'blood' *dusa > *u-cúusa* 'two' *takid > *maa-takíci* 'stick' *qudip >

[17] This form is probably related to Sar *ʔususu* 'breast', which we hypothesize arose by a metathesis of *susuʔu (§B31.1.5).

ʔumaʔuciʔucipi 'be alive' *daɬih > *ará-cani* 'near' *qujáɬ> *ʔucánə* 'rain' *lahuj 'seaward' > *mua-láucu* 'go downhill' *likuj-an > *ku-kúca* 'back'

In one case, final *-d was replaced by /ʔ/—i.e., the *d was lost, and [ʔ] plus an echo vowel developed. The form is probably a borrowing, but the source is unknown.

*tímid 'jaw, chin' > *cimíʔi* 'cheek, face'

In one case, *d is assimilated to a preceding /r/ < *ɣ:

*ɣudaŋ 'be grown' > *mama-rúrangə* 'become old'

In one case, *d was replaced by *ɬ:

*dámaɣ 'light, torch' > *namar-ənə* 'burn'[18]

B32.3.33 *g

As onset of the penult or earlier syllable and of monosyllabic roots, *g falls together with *k, as in many An languages.

*gusam 'thrush' > *masu-kuámə* 'painful' *tageɣaŋ 'chest' > *takəranga* 'breast bone'

*g onset or coda of the final syllable merged with *y and subsequently became /l/. (Cf. the analogous development in Sar [§B31.3.33].)

*ŋagan > *nganal-aku* 'my name' (< *ŋalan-aku < *ŋayan-aku) *págay 'rice in field' > *palái* 'glutinous rice' *bálug 'dove' > *ta-valulu* 'k.o. large bird'

Abutting *i, *-g- was lost—that is, *ig/*gi > *iy/*yi > /i/:

*piga 'how many' > *u-pía* 'how much is it?'

B32.3.34 *ɣ

* ɣ became /r/ in all positions:

*ɣiq > *rə́əʔə* 'sword grass' *báqeɣuh > *vaʔúrua* 'new' *beɣác >*və́əra* 'hulled rice' *diɣi > *muá-ciri* 'stand' *qápuɣ > *ʔapúru* 'lime'

In two cases, *ɣ was lost, but the Knn forms may not reflect the reconstructed form directly:

*kaɣát 'bite' > *kaacə* 'rake' *beɣay > *mó-vua* 'give'

B32.3.4 Continuants

B32.3.41 *l

*l is unstable in Knn and is almost (but not completely) lost in certain environments—i.e., the following rules have exceptions:[19]

(1) *l > Ø abutting on *e (inherited) or /ə/ that developed.

*qaleb > *ʔaə́və* 'knee' *qebel > *əə́və* 'smoke' *luseq > *əsə́ʔə* 'tears'

[18] This development is shared by Sar *ɬamarə*, Ts *hmo-i* 'burn', and Pai *ɬama* 'burnt'.

[19] Tsuchida (1976: 298–99) suggests that loss of *l was determined by the occurrence of /n/ to the right in the same word. The problem with that rule is that there are many exceptions where *l was not lost and further many cases of *l loss in forms that do not have /n/ to the right in the same word.

There are four exceptions. The first example is not directly inherited. In the second, the /l/ was preserved because /tuu/ cannot occur at the end of a word (§B32.1.22, end). The other two exceptions are unexplained:

> *caleŋ > *aláŋə* 'pine' *telu> *u-túlu* 'three' *matítulu* 'take three in the hand' vs. *ma-túu-nu* 'thirty' and *maria-túu-nu* 'pull three times' *balec > 'answer, revenge' > *malí-vali* 'answer, talk back' (< *-baleci)' *biqel > *viʔíli* 'goiter'

(2) *l > Ø abutting on /i/. In this case, there are at least four exceptions:

> *likuj > *ku-kúc-a* 'back' (< R- + *kuc+a [with elision of *i-] < ikuc+an) *taŋíla 'ear' > *caínga* 'earring' *kulít > *kuíci* 'peelings' *palisi > *p-u-aisí-a*[20] 'taboo' *lima > *iíma* 'five' but *u-líma* 'five'; other exceptions: *qusalipan > *ʔalilipáng* 'milliped' *paheli > *páali* 'bile, gall bladder' *talis > *talísi* 'cord'

*l > Ø between like vowels:

> *jalan > *caánə* 'road' *laŋit > *kak-ángec-a* 'heavens' (< *ka+*ka+laŋit+an [with contraction of *aa after the *l was lost]) *ŋalay > *ngáai* 'spittle' *biliɬ'behind, last' > *pari-vii-viíni* 'follow' *pulut > *puucu* 'k.o. tree with sticky sap'

There are a few exceptions. In the first example, the metathesis took place after the rule for the loss of /l/. The other cases are unexplained:

> *laŋaw > *taa-ngaláw* 'gnat' *ala 'take' > *m-aala* 'take' *ɬala > *ngáala* 'flame' *búluq > *vulúʔu* 'k.o. slender bamboo' *quluh 'head' > *musu-ʔulu* 'do ahead of others'

In one case, *l is dropped in an environment in which it is normally not dropped. The word is probably a borrowing:[21]

> *bulaɬ> *vuánə* 'moon'

Otherwise—i.e., not abutting on /i/ or /ə/ and between two unlike vowels, *l > /l/:

> *lahuj 'seaward' > *mua-láucu* 'go downward' *balug 'pigeon' > *ta-válulu* 'k.o. large bird'

The changes of *y > /l/ and *-g- to /-l-/ (§§B32.3.44, below, B32.3.33, above) are posterior to the loss of *l: the /l/ that develops from *-g- and *y is not lost:

> *págay 'rice in field' > *palái* 'glutinous rice' *kasiw > *káalu* 'tree' (< *kayu < *kahyu < *kasyu)

B32.3.42 *ɬ

> *ɬ> /n/ in all positions:
>
> *ɬaŋuy > *maka-nangúlu* 'swim' *qaɬup > *ʔum-anupu* 'hunt (with dogs)' *qujaɬ > *ʔucánə* 'rain'

*ɬ or an *ɬ that developed is sporadically reflected with /ng/:

---

[20] There is no explanation for the /u/ in this form. No other reflex of *palisi has anything like it, nor is there an /u/ inserted in a similar environment in any other form I know in any language.

[21] Cf. the commentary to *bulaɬ in the glossary.

*łala > *ngáala* 'flame' *ciłaɣ 'ray' > *niku-cingar-a* 'window' *qáłit 'skin, bark, pelt' > *ʔangiici* 'leather' *sináwa > *ngisáa* 'breath'

B32.3.43 Nasals

*m, *n, *ŋ remained unchanged in all positions (except for the loss of final *-n in certain environments[§B32.1.21, 3rd¶]):

*matáy > *mi-matáy* 'die' *qamis 'north' > *ʔamís-anə* 'cold time, place' *qayam 'pet' > *ʔalámə* 'meat' *enem > *ənəm* 'six' *wanał+an > *ananán* 'right side' *ŋucəŋuc > *puru-ngusúngusu* 'snore' *qałiŋu 'shadow' > *ʔaníngu* 'image, shadow' *cinaŋ 'shining' > *sinángə* 'light, beam'

In a few cases, a final nasal is reflected with /ng/. There is no explanation. These forms are likely to be secondary:

*qaɣicam 'k.o. fern' > *ʔaricang* 'pigeon pea' *qusalipan > *ʔalalipáng* 'large millipede'

In one case, *n is dissimilated sporadically to /r/ after /ng/ on the left:[22]

*teŋen 'right' > *utucəngərə* 'sleep on the right side of the bed'

B32.3.44 *w and *y

*w was lost initially and medially. (For *aw and *iw, cf. §B32.2.41, B32.2.43.)

*walu > *aálu* 'eight' *wiɣi > *iíri* 'left' *sináwa' > *ngisáa* 'breath' *siwa > *u-sía* 'nine'

There are no attestations of an inherited *y-. Medial and final *y became /l/ (cf. §B32.2.42).[23]

*qayam 'pet' > *alámə* 'pet' *daya 'inland' > *muá-cala* 'go upward' *iseyup > *pulu-alupu* 'blow with breath'

In one case, *-y- is reflected with /i/. This form is likely not directly inherited. Note that there is also metathesis and an unexplained initial /l/.[24]

*ałay > *laíanə* 'termite' (< *layał< *l-ałay)

[22] This is a rule given by Li (n.d.) under the headword *cəngən. There are countercases where /n/ does not dissimilate after a nasal on the left, e.g. *anan* 'right side' (< *wanał)

[23] The process whereby [y] > [l] involved the development in pre-Knn of lateralization, which resulted in a palatalized lateral. The same development affected pre-Sar. In Knn, this palatalized lateral lost its palatalization (> [l]). In Sar, it merged with the reflex of *ł (§B31.3.43).

[24] Cf. the note to the Sar cognate §B31.3.43.

CHAPTER FOUR
Rukai

B4.0 Background and cultural factors that influenced the history of Rukai

Rukai (Ru) is the name given to five diverse dialects or closely related languages: Tanan, situated in Pinan, Taitung Hsien, Budai, situated in Pintung Hsien, and three dialects or languages Maga, Tona, and Mantauran, situated in Maolin, Kao-Hsiung Hsien. In this study, Budai is the dialect whose development is treated in detail, for that was the dialect with the fullest available data. Wherever a Budai source is attested, that is what is quoted. The other languages or dialects are quoted only insofar as they attest the occurrence in Ru of a form not attested by Budai or as they shed light on the Budai form attested and clarify the developments. The material here presented is almost entirely based on secondary sources: Li 1977 and Ching-hwa Kao 1985. For backup and clarification I have drawn on Tsuchida 1976 and Zeitoun 2006. Li 1977 presents the basic rules for the development of PAn to Budai, and thus solved many of the problems presented by the data. However, that work assumes a PAn phonology rather different from that presented here, and we present a different account of how the Ru forms came into being from PAn from that presented by Li.

In the summer of 2006, while stuck by inclement weather for a day in the town of Liò Kuēy, Kao-Hsiung Hsien, I met a good speaker of Budai, whose name I unfortunately lost, with whom I worked for several hours and was able to confirm the published descriptions of the Budai segmental phonemes (Li 1977: 5). In one respect, my findings differed from those of Li: /r/ was realized by my consultant as a voiced velar fricative [ɣ] rather than a tongue-tip trill.[1]

CHART ONE. PHONEMES OF RUKAI

Consonants

voiceless	p	c	t	k
voiced	b	d	ḍ	g
fricative	v	ð, s, θ		
liquid	w	ɬ [l], y	ḷ	r [ɣ]
nasal	m	n		ng [ŋ]

Vowels and Diphthongs

high	i		u
mid		ə	
low		a	
diphthong	uy, ay	iw	aw

The vowels occur lengthened. Lengthening is transcribed by doubled vowels. /u/ is transcribed here as *o*. /ə/ is transcribed *ə*. Stress is contrastive in Budai, but developed in

[1] Not having had access to the community, I have no idea as to what extent [ɣ] is found in the community, how it is distributed, or whether it is an idiosyncratic pronunciation of my consultant.

post-PAn times: PAn stress contrasts have been lost. However, syncopation in disyllabic roots in Maga reflects PAn stress: PAn stress on the final syllable is reflected in Maga by elision of the penult, and stress on the penult of disyllables is reflected by retention of the penult in Maga.

B4.1. Changes that characterize Rukai in general

B4.1.1 Disyllabization of trisyllabic roots

PAn unstressed *e in the penult or antepenult of trisyllabic roots is lost except in the case of doubled monosyllabic roots.[2] The *s preceding the lost *e is also lost. If there is an *e in the antepenult as well as the penult, only one *e is lost.

*paqegu > *pago* 'gall' *sehapuy > *apóy* 'fire' *seqeɣét > *ǝ̆ɤǝ́cǝ* 'tight' * beɣáy > *báay* 'give' (*a is lengthened by the rule of §B4.1.21.)

In some cases (but not all) a consonant was lost after the *e was lost. There was compensatory lengthening of the vowel in the syllable that preceded the consonant that had been lost:

*liceqes > *a-ḽisǝǝsǝ* 'louse egg' (< *a-lisqǝs) *baqeɣu > *baav-anǝ* 'new' (< *baqɣu) *tuqeláɬ > *cooḽaɬǝ* 'bone' (< *tuqlaɬ)

When the *e was stressed, it was not lost, nor was the preceding *s lost:

*qasélu > *asóḽo* 'pestle'

*i is lost in the antepenult of trisyllabic roots.

*iqetah > *ǝ́ca* 'rice hull' (but Maga *icaa*) *isekan > *kaangǝ* 'fish' (with loss of penultimate *ǝ and compensatory lengthening of the vowel [§B4.1.21]: *isekan > *ǝkanǝ > *kaangǝ* [change of *n >/ng/ not explained]) *ikasu > *koso* 'you (sing)' *icebu > *óbo* 'bladder' *iseyup > *iipi* 'blow' (< *iip < *iyup < *seyup) (*eyu > /i/ [§§B4.2.2])

In cases in which metathesis of the penultimate and the antepenultimate vowels took place (§A3.5.4), the change occurred before the loss of *i in this position. (In other words, *i moved from the antepenultimate position to the penult, where it was not lost.)

*isepi > *sipi* 'dream' (< *esipi) *seɬaw > *oa-sinaw* 'wash' (< *esinaw)

Penultimate or earlier unstressed *u and *i lost their syllabicity when loss of a consonant or glide caused them to abut on a following unlike vowel other than *e:

*kuwaw 'large bird' > *kwaw* 'hawk' *uɣat > *wácǝ* 'artery, vein' *suwab > *ma-swa-swabǝ* 'yawn' *liyús > *ḽyós* 'turn'

Similarly, a word-final sequence *au or *ai that develops with the loss of an intervening consonant diphthongizes:

*bahi > *aba-bay* 'girl'

---

[2] In most cases where the sources give the stress, it is on the epenthetic /ǝ/ between the two doubled monosyllabic forms. The /ǝ/ of the penult in these forms was not lost, probably because it is stressed. However, we do not know for sure that the stress is on the /ǝ/ in all cases because stress placement is not completely predictable, and the sources do not always give the stress.

The following trisyllabic root lost its antepenult when a suffixed form became petrified:

*palisi > *ḷisy-an* 'taboo'[3]

B4.1.2 Disyllabization of monosyllabic roots

Ru attests disyllabization of monosyllabic roots by the various pan-Austronesian processes: doubling, by addition of a prothetic /ə
/, by stretching the nucleus, and by petrification of an affixed form (§A3.6.2). They may also disyllabize by addition of an echo vowel (§B4.1.3—a phenomenon confined to Ru and the Tsouic languages). An example of disyllabization by addition of an echo vowel:

*ɣik > *iki* 'thresh by trampling'

By doubling:

*daŋedaŋ 'heat near fire' > *ḍangə̀ḍangə* 'hot, roast'

The following forms show disyllabization by adding [ə] to the vowel nucleus:

*pan > *paənə* 'bait' *tan 'set a trap' > *taənə* 'trap'

The following root remained monosyllabic but occurs only with affixes:

*gac > *wa-gac* 'scratch'

B4.1.21 Lengthening of vowels when a monosyllabic root developed

When sound changes led to the development of a monosyllabic root (before the development of echo vowels [§B4.1.3]), the nucleus was lengthened (doubled):

*beɣay > *baay* 'give' *aqetih 'for water to recede' > *o-cii* 'dam up stream to catch fish' (Mag) (< *tih < *qetih) *isekan > *kaangə* 'fish'

B4.1.22 Reduplication in Rukai to avoid monosyllabic roots

Monosyllabic roots that developed by vowel loss or contraction sometimes reduplicated in order to achieve a disyllabic form. The process of adding echo vowels took place subsequent to this reduplication. This development took place with forms that did not otherwise have affixation:

*buhet > *bo-booto* 'squirrel' (< R + *boot + echo vowel)

B4.1.3 Development of echo vowels

Morphemes ending in a -C in proto-Ru developed an echo vowel—i.e., morphemes ending in a -C in PAn except for *-h and *-q, which were lost in proto-Ru, developed an echo vowel, producing a proto-Ru syllable structure of (C)V(y,w). The syllable structure of current Budai is (C)(y,w)V(y,w) or C(y,w)V_1V_1 (y,w). The w-/y- glides developed from *u and *i, as discussed in §B4.1.1, end, and the double vowel, by the loss of *ɣ or *h between two like vowels (§B4.3.41, middle). The echo vowel is /i/ after /i/, /o/ after /o/ and /ə/ after /a/ or /ə/. Here are some examples of echo vowels:

*liceqes > *a-ḷisəəsə* 'nit' *qalad > *aḷaḍə* 'fence' *baqeɣuh +-an > *baavanə* 'new'

---

[3] The source for the citation is Kao 1985, who does not write echo vowels. No doubt this form is pronounced /ḷisyanə/.

B4.1.4 Simplification of consonant clusters

No consonant clusters are reconstructed for PAn (§A.3.6.1) and none developed in pre-Ru. However, in some dialects, stems consisting of doubled monosyllabic roots lost the medial epenthetic vowel (A.3.6.1, end) producing consonant clusters. These were simplified. There is one example in the attestations of PAn roots in Budai that shows both a reflex of a simplified cluster and an variant reflex that inherits the monosyllabic root with an epenthetic vowel. Both variants were probably borrowed because of the /ḷ/ in place of /ɬ/ in the prefix, and the /k-/ (< PAn *q [§B4.3.14]) in the prefix of the second form:

*buŋebuŋ 'cover to protect' + *qaɬi > *aḷi-vovongo/kaḷi-vongovongo* 'umbrella'

B4.2.0 Vowels and diphthongs

Ru has inherited the four vowels and diphthongs of PAn, listed in §B4.0. The reflex of *u is written *o* in most sources on Budai, but in some it is transcribed as *u*. /ə/ is written *e*, but we transcribe it as *ə*.

B4.2.1 *i

*i remains /i/ in most environments:

*alima > *aḷíma* 'hand' *agi > *ági* 'younger sibling' *ica > *íθa* 'one'

*i assimilated to *e in the following syllable if it had not been lost by syncopation or if metathesis (§B4.1.1, middle) had not taken place.[4]

*liqeɣ 'neck > *ḷə́ə* 'neck' *pilek > *s-kərpə* 'eyelid'

Before *c or *s, /i/ was lost in the antepenult if metathesis had not taken place (§B4.1.1, middle)

B4.2.2 *e

*e remains a mid-central vowel in most environments:

*tenék > *cə́nəkə* 'thorn' *dayeq > *dáə* 'earth'

*e is assimilated to /o/ before or after *u with the exceptions noted in §B4.2.3, middle.

*becuɣ > *ma-bocoko* 'sated' *buhet > *bo-booto* 'squirrel' *icebu 'urine' > *óbo* 'bladder' *qaselu > *asóḷo* 'pestle' *ɬecunx > *ɬoongo* 'mortar' *tebus > *cobóso* 'sugar cane' *telu > *tóḷo* 'three' *teɬúq > *tóɬo* 'coconut milk'

*e is assimilated to /i/ in the following syllable (if metathesis had not taken place beforehand [§B4.1.1, middle]), and by the same token, *ey > i:

*beli 'buy' > *sapangi-biḷi-an* 'price' *iseyup > *iipi* 'blow' (*ísipi < *ísip < *ísiup)

*e is lost by contraction or elision in many cases (§B4.1.1).

---

[4] An exception is *liceqes > *aḷisə́əsə* 'nit' in Budai, where the sequence /aḷi-/ was retained unchanged, as this is nearly homophonous with the reflex /aɬi/ of the prefix *qaɬi-. Other dialects do not retain the /i/: e.g. Tona *aəsə́əsə*.

B4.2.3 *a and *u

*a remained /a/ in most environments:

*aselu > *asó̜lo* 'pestle' *aɣak 'lead by hand' > *arak* 'guide' *bitúka > *bicóka* 'stomach'

*u remained [u], written *o*, in most cases:

*buɣuk > *book* 'rotten' *dusa > *ḍosa* 'two' *kulabaw > *koḷábaw* 'rat' *paqegu > *págo* 'gall'

In two isolated cases,*u assimilated to a following *e. There are two other cases in which *u > /ə/, although there was no other *e in the word. These forms have probably spread secondarily. Indeed, the Tsouic languages evince similar developments in the cognates to these forms.

*luseq > *ḷə́sə* 'tears' *pugek > *pəəke* 'navel') *lum > *ḷəmə* 'ripe' *suni 'soft noise' > *sənay* 'sing'

Occasionally *u and *a are lost by elision:

*seyap > *waa-sipi* 'count' (*waasip < *waasiap < *siap [§B4.2.2] + waa-) *iseyup > *iipi* 'blow' (< *íiup < *ísiup) 'blow' *siyuɬuq > *siɬo* 'beads'

A sequence *ua that develops by loss of an intervening C or by the addition of an affix beginning with *a- to a stem ending in *u- becomes *uwa. Subsequently the *u is elided in stems of four syllables or more roots or it is maintained in trisyllabic stems. The *w > /v/, like the *w inherited from PAn (§B4.3.44).

*ɣuqaɬay > *sa-ovaɬay* 'male' (< *uwaɬay < *uaɬay) *baqeɣuh >*baav-anə* 'new' (< *baaw-an < *baew-an <*baeu-an) *taɣuq-anan > *taovananə* 'field hut'

B4.2.4 Diphthongs

The diphthongs are retained unchanged:

*qenay > *ə́nay* 'sand' *quway > *ováy* 'rattan' *bábuy > *báboy* 'wild pig' *ɬaŋúy > *ɬangoy* 'swim' *kulabaw > *koḷábaw* 'rat' *láŋaw > *aḷaḷángaw* 'fly' *baliw 'change, return to previous' > *mwa-báḷiw* 'return home'

The reflex of *waɬiw 'bee' developed as in other Formosan languages: *i of the final syllable was absorbed by the /ɬ/, the reflex of the preceding *ɬ, and the final *-w was given syllabic value:

*waɬiw > *vaɬo* 'bee'

B4.3.0 Consonants

The following chart shows the Ru reflexes of the PAn consonants.

CHART TWO. DEVELOPMENT OF THE RUKAI CONSONANTS FROM PAN

PAn	Ru	PAn	Ru
p	*p*	j	*d*
t	*t, c*	g	*g*
k	*k*	ɣ	*r, ∅*
q	*∅*	l	*ñ*
h	*∅*	ɬ	*ɬ*
c	*θ, s, ∅*	m, n	*m, n*
s	*s*	ŋ	*ng*
b	*b*	w	*v*
d	*ḍ*	y	*ð*

B4.3.1 Voiceless consonants

B4.3.11 *p

*p remained /p/ in all positions:

*páqegu > *pago* 'gall' *piga > *pia* 'how much, many?' sépat > *səpátə* 'four' *cepecep > *θəpə́θəpə* 'suck'

B4.3.12 *t

*t has two outcomes: a stop /t/ and an apico-alveolar affricate /c/, as is the case of the other languages of northeast and southwest Taiwan (§A3.3.1).
*t reflected as /t/:

*tan 'set a trap' > *taən* 'trap' *qaɬimátek > *ɬimatə́kə* 'leech' ɬatad > *ɬátaḍə* 'front yard' *keɣet > *kəətə* 'cut'

*t reflected as /c/:

*tenek > *cə́nəkə* 'thorn' *butuq 'genitals' > *bóco* 'scrotum' *bitúka > *bicóka* 'stomach' *kaɣát > *kaacə* 'bite'

In one exceptional case, *t is reflected with /θ/. This is a form that has the affricate reflex in other northeast and southwest Taiwan languages. It is a borrowing, but the source is unknown:

*qatay > *aθay* 'liver'

In a couple of cases where other northwest and southeast Formosan languages reflect an affricated or spirantal reflex of *t, the Ru cognate reflects an stop in one or another dialect (but not necessarily in all Ru dialects), and vice versa (§A3.3.1):

*talis > *taísi* (Tona) *tési* (Maga) *cálisi* (Bd) 'hemp, cord' *tiŋas > *mu-tngásə* (Maga) *mwa-cíngasə* (Bd) 'remove food particles from teeth'

There is also a case where one of the Ru dialects evinces an affricate where the northwest and southeast Formosan languages reflect a stop:

*tebus > *cobóso* (Bd) *tbúsu* (Maga) 'sugar cane'

B4.3.13 *k

*k remained /k/ in all positions:

*kaɣát > *kaacə* 'bite' *bitúka > *bicóka* 'stomach' *beɣek > *bəəkə* 'domesticated pig'

B4.3.14 *q

*q > Ø:

*qabú > *abó* 'ashes' *taqis > *cáisi* 'sew' *liceqes > *aḷisəəsə* 'nit' *liqeɣ > *ḷəə* 'neck' *luséq > *ḷə́sə* 'tears'

In a few cases, *q is reflected with /k/. These are probably borrowings from a dialect in which *q is reflected with [q]—where [k] is the Ru sound closest to [q]:

*púluq > *póḷoko* (cf. Pai *poloq*) 'ten' *taqi > *cáki* (cf. Pai *tsaqi*)'feces'

B4.3.2 *h, *s, *c

*h was lost without a trace, *s remained unchanged in Ruk, and *c had a number of outcomes. Details are given in the subsections below.

B4.3.21 *h

*h left no trace in Ruk:

*bahaɬiɣ > *baaɬi* 'cypress, board' *capuh 'wipe' > *swapə* 'broom' *aqetih 'for water to recede' > *o-cii* 'dam up creek *lahuj 'seaward' > *ḷaodo* 'below' *quluh > *a-oḷo* 'head' *qumah > *omá-oma* 'cultivated field' *sehapuy > *apóy* 'fire' *tuɬúh > *oa-cúɬo* 'roast'

B4.3.22 *s

*s > /s/ with very few exceptions:

*simaɣ 'oil' > *simaa* 'fat' *su > *so* 'you (sing.)' *isepi > *sipi* 'dream' (< *esipi) *luséq > *ḷə́sə* 'tears'

When unstressed *se occurs in the penult or antepenult, the sequence is lost (§B4.1.1):

*iseyup > *iipi* 'dream' *isekan > *kaangə* 'fish' *sehapuy > *apóy* 'fire' *seqeɣet > *əɽə́cə* 'tight'

B4.3.23 *c

*c had four different reflexes, and the conditions for the different outcomes are not determinable. The different reflexes are most likely due to dialect mixture that took place before proto-Ru, for the four outcomes are reflected consistently in the Ru dialects for the most part (but not entirely). The four outcomes cannot be attributed to PAn (do not reflect four different PAn phonemes) because these different reflexes correlate with only one reflex in other An languages. (Cf. the comment on the reflexes of *ɣ, §B4.3.41, below.) The four different reflexes probably developed as follows: first, *c > /θ/. Second, this /θ/ changed to [s], but the change was not carried to completion, leaving some forms with original *c reflecting /θ/ and some, [s_1] (which continued to contrast with /s/ < *s). This [s_1] < *c subsequently > Ø, but again the change was not carried to completion. The [s_1] that did not change merged with /s/ < *s.
In five cases, *c > /θ/:

*beɣac > *bəraθə* 'hulled rice' (but Maga *bəə́sə)* *cabuŋ > *θávongo* 'compensate' *cepecep > *θəpə́θəpə* 'suck' *cucu > *θóθo* 'breast' *ica > *iθa* 'one' (but also Budai *isa*)

In some cases, *c > Ø:

*balec > *twa-baḷə* 'answer' *bucuɣ > *bóo* (Maga *bsoo*) 'bow' *caleŋ > *aḷəngə* (Maga *srə́ngə)* 'pine' *icebu 'urine' > *óbo* 'bladder' (< *cubu [§§B4.1.1] < *icubu [§B4.2.2]) < *icebu (Maga *sbo*) *iceɣab > *kw-ia* 'yesterday' *ɬecuŋ > *ɬóongo* 'mortar' *ŋucuq 'snout' > *ngongó-an* 'nose' (< *ŋuŋu < *ŋuq)

In some cases, *c > /s/ (in other words, fell together with *s):

*calemcem > *ma-saḷəməsəmə* 'dusk' capuh > *swapə* 'sweep' *cigi > *sgii* 'winnow' *ica > *isa* 'one' *liceqes > *a-ḷisə́əsə* 'louse egg' *qaceŋ > *b-asəngə* 'sneeze'

In two cases *c is retained as /c/. These forms were probably borrowed in pre-Ru from a neighboring language (e.g., Amis):

*becuɣ > *ma-bocoko* 'sated' *gac > *wa-gacə, gacə́-gacə* 'scratch'

B4.3.3 Voiced consonants, stops in PAn

B4.3.31 *b

*b remained /b/ in all environments:

*bábuy > *báboy* 'wild pig' *beɣay > *báay* 'give' *buhet > *bo-bóto* 'squirrel' *ɬibúq 'fenced in place' > *ɬibóo* 'pen' *qeɬeb > *wa-əɬəbə* 'close'

In the case of the reflex of *-sebic, *b is assimilated to the preceding *s, as is the case of all An languages except Bun (see the commentary in the glossary under *-sebic).

*-sebic > *ma-d-ɬipsi* 'thin' (Maga)

In a few cases, *b is reflected as /v/ (the normal reflex in the Mantauran dialect). The forms that reflect /v/ are probably borrowings (if not from a Ru dialect, then from a neighboring language that reflected *b with a voiced labial spirant):

*ɬabek 'surf' > *ɬavek* 'sea' *balug > *ta-vago* 'pigeon' *bagaq 'inform' > *vaga* 'word, language' *bali > *vaḷig* 'wind' (the /g/ is unexplained) *cabuŋ > *θávongo* 'compensate'

B4.3.32 *d

*d > /ḍ/:

*daŋedaŋ 'heat near fire' > *ḍangəḍangə* 'roast' *dumá >*-ḍomá-nə* 'other' *qudip > *oḍípi* 'alive' *ɬátad > *ɬataḍə* 'front yard, outside'

In four cases, *d is reflected with /d/. These forms are probably borrowings, presumably from a dialect in which the proto-Ru *d–*ḍ contrast was lost (e.g., Mantauran):

*daɣeq > *daə* 'earth' *daɬi > *me-d-dali* 'near' (Maga) (/l/ also irregular) *daqu > *daw* 'soapberry tree' *diɣi > *idii* 'stand' (The prothetic /i-/ is also unexplained) *paɬid > *paridi* 'wing' (The /r/ is also unexplained.)

B4.3.33 *j

*j > /d/ in initial and medial position. In final position, *-j falls together with *-d—i.e., > /-ḍ/.

*jalan > *kadaa-daḷán-anə* 'road, path' *qujał > *ódałə* 'rain' *qałuj 'be carried by the current' > *mw-ałoḍo* 'be washed away'

B4.3.34 *g

*g remained /g/ in initial and medial positions:[5]

*gac > *wa-gac* 'scratch' *gemegem > *wa-gəməgəmə* 'hold in fist' *págay > *págay* 'rice plant' *-igan > *kw-igaanə* 'when? (past)'

In one case, *-g- is lost. There is no explanation. It is likely a borrowing. Note that in neighboring Tsouic, *-g- is normally lost in after *i:

*piga > *pía* 'how many?' (Cf. Knn *o-pia* 'how much is it?')

B4.3.4 Voiced consonants, continuants in PAn

B4.3.41 *ɣ

*ɣ has two reflexes, and it is impossible to find an environment that determines when one or the other reflex occurs. The different reflexes are most likely due to dialect mixture that took place before proto-Ru, for the two outcomes are reflected consistently in the Ru dialects for the most part (but not entirely). The two outcomes cannot be attributed to PAn (do not reflect two different PAn phonemes) because these different reflexes correlate with only one reflex in other An languages (cf. the comment to §B4.3.23, above).
For the most part, *ɣ was lost in all the Ru dialects except Tona and Mantauran (Li 1977, §2.1.5). *ɣ > /ʔ/ in Tona and Mantauran. Here are a few of the numerous examples:

*ɣuqałay > *sa-ovάłay* 'man, male' *saʔwałay* (Tona) *ʔaołai* (Mantauran) *beɣay > *wa-baay* 'give' *wa-baʔay* (Tona) *o-vaʔay* (Mantauran) *qapuɣ 'lime' > *wa-apóo* 'chew' (Tona *wa-apoʔo*) *baqeɣuh > *báav-anə* 'new' *beɣek > *bəəkə* 'domesticated pig' *bahałiɣ > *vaałi* 'board, Chinese cypress' *biɣebiɣ > *biibí-anə* 'lips'

When final *ɣ was lost, the preceding vowel was lengthened. The sequence of events was as follows: *-ɣ > *ʔ. (It remained /ʔ/ in Tona and Mantauran.) An echo vowel developed after *-ʔ (§B4.1.3). Subsequently *-ʔ was lost, except in Tona and Mantauran.[6]

*bałáɣ 'k.o. thorny vine' > *błáa* '*Smilax china*' *bucúɣ > *bóo* 'bow' *qapuɣ 'lime' *wa-apóo* 'chew' *sapáɣ 'spread mat'> *sápaa* 'mat' *simaɣ > *simaa* 'fat'

There is no lengthening of the final vowel in two cases (but the echo vowel is manifested in Tona [see the footnote to this section]):

*lawáɣ > *ḷavá* 'flying squirrel' *łamuɣ > *łámo* 'dew'

---

[5] No attestation has been found of a reflex of PAn final *-g that is directly inherited by Budai from PAn.

[6] The cognates of these forms, where they are attested, manifest echo vowels: *qapuɣ 'lime' > Tona *wa-apoʔo* 'chew' *bucúɣ > Tona *bosoʔo* 'bow' *liqeɣ > Tona *əʔə́* 'neck' *sapáɣ 'spread mat'> Tona *sapaʔa* 'mat' *simaɣ > *simáʔa* 'fat' *lawáɣ > Tona *aváʔa* 'flying squirrel' *łamuɣ > Tona *łamoʔo* 'dew'

*ɣ is also reflected as /r/ in a small number of cases. These are probably secondary in origin—that is, they spread through the Ru dialects in early times after the change of *ɣ to *ʔ. The situation is parallel to that which obtains in Pai (cf. Paiwan §B72.3.41), but not the same forms reflect /r/ from *ɣ in Ru as in Pai.

> *ɣudaŋ 'be grown' > *ma-roḍang* 'old (person)' *aɣak > *arakə* 'guide' *beɣac > *beraθə* 'hulled rice' *gaɣut > *garoco* 'comb' *seqeɣet > *ərə́cə* 'tight' *wiɣi > *viri* 'left' *damaɣ 'light' > *ḍámarə* 'moon'

*ɣ is reflected as /k/ in one case and /g/ in another. These are unexplained and probably are of secondary spread:

> *becuɣ > *ma-bocoko* 'sated' (cf. Sar *ma-vacoko* and Knn *ma-vəcərəkə* 'sated') *ɣiq 'sword grass' > *igi 'Miscanthus* stalks used for thatching' (proclitic /i/ also unexplained)

B4.3.42 *l

*l remains /ḷ/, a retroflexed lateral [ɭ], in all positions. In the Maga dialect, *l > /r/ (falls together with the /r/-reflex of *ɣ), and in Tona it disappears.

> *lima >*ḷima* 'five' *walu > *wáḷo* 'eight' *calemcem > *masaḷəməsə́mə* 'dusk' *kudemel > *ma-kóḍəməḷə* 'thick'

In a few cases, *l is reflected as ∅ or as /r/. These are borrowings from Tona or Maga.

> *tali > *tái* 'taro'

B4.3.43 The nasals and *ɬ

*m, *n, *ŋ remained unchanged in all positions.

> *matá > *máca* 'eye' *lima > *ḷima* 'five' *enem > *ə́nəmə* 'six' *tenek > *cə́nəkə* 'thorn' *kan > *kanə* 'eat' *ŋalay > *ngáḷay* 'saliva' *taŋíla > *caḷinga* 'ear' *ɬecuŋ > *ɬóongo* 'mortar'

*ɬ is reflected as a front unretroflexed lateral [l] in all positions.[7] Palatalization is minimal.

> *ɬecuŋ > *ɬóongo* 'mortar' *kiɬalá 'perceive' > *kiɬaḷa* 'hear' *tuqelaɬ > *cooḷaɬə* 'bone'

In two cases, *ɬ is reflected as /n/. Secondary spread from other languages is the likely explanation in these cases, for cognates in other languages that reflect *ɬ with a palatalized consonant also manifest /n/ in these forms. (Cf. the commentary to *iseɬaw and *baɬaw in the glossary.)

> *baɬaw 'wash' > *ma-banaw* 'bathe' (cf. Pai*vanaw* 'take a bath') *iseɬaw 'wash' > *oa-sinaw* 'wash clothing' (cf. Knn *mari-sinə́w* 'wash utensils')

In the following two cases, there was apparently a rule of assimilation to an /n/ preceding in the same word, but this was probably the rule of another (unknown) language—i.e., the forms were borrowed: not all Ru dialects make this change.

> *naɬaq > *nána* 'pus' *wanaɬ > *vánanə* Bd (variant) *vánaɬə* Tana *vanáɬə* 'right side'

---

[7] It is written as *ɬ*, here to distinguish it from the *ḷ*, a retroflexed lateral [ɭ].

B4.3.44 *w and *y

*w > /v/ initially and medially. (For *w and *y as second members of diphthongs, cf. §B4.2.4.)

*qúway > *ováy* 'rattan' *wiɣi > *viri* 'left'

The sequence *we > /o/

*weliq 'go back, do back' > *s-oḷi* 'return'

In some cases, the change of *e > /i/ in a syllable preceding a syllable with /i/ (§B4.2.2) took place before *we > /o/, and therefore the sequence /we/ is reflected as /vi/:

*weliq > *sivi-vrii* 'return' (< *sivi-viri) (Maga)

In the Budai dialect, *w was lost after *a before *i (Li 1977: 12) :

*jaqewis > *adáiɬi* 'far' (Tona *maʔa-dáviɬi)* *taquweɬ > *cáiɬi* 'year' (Mag *cvéɬe*)

*y > /ð/ medially.

*káwayan > *kavaðanə* 'k.o. bamboo'

After *i, however, *y remained, and the /i/ was lost by elision:

liyus 'go around'> *ḽyos* 'turn'

The sequence *ey > /i/ (§B4.2.2, end):

*iseyup > *íipi* 'blow'

Chapter Five

Bunun

B5.0 Introduction

Bunun is spoken in the highlands of central and eastern Taiwan. The language has several hundred thousand speakers and is still healthy, although at the present time in a number of villages the young people are growing up speaking Mandarin or Taiwanese. Li (1988) distinguishes five dialects, two of which are in the north and close, two of which are in the center and close, and one that is found in the south. These three groups differ sharply from each other both in vocabulary and phonology (and probably also in grammar). There are several sources for data presented here: (1) Nihira 1988, (2) Li 1988, (3) Duris 1987–88 and (4) an unpublished list of vocabulary in eight dialects consisting of around one thousand items prepared by S. Tsuchida (1997).[1] I visited the central Bunun area for a week in 1997 and spent time checking out forms from these sources with speakers.[2]

The following table shows the segmental phonemes of the northern dialects of Bun , Takitudu, and Takibakha.

CHART ONE. PHONEMES OF BUNUN

Consonants

voiceless	p	t	c	k	q, ʔ
voiced	b	d			
spirants	v	ð, s			h
liquids	w	l	y		
nasal	m	n		ng [ŋ]	

Vowels

high	i		u
low		a	

The central and southern dialects lack /c/: earlier *c > /s/—i.e, in those dialects PAn *c and *s have merged. Further, the southern dialect, Ishbukun, has changed [q] > [x]. Also, /l/ in Ishbukun is a voiceless lateral [ɬ]. In the southern dialects, all words ending in a vowel get an accreted /-ʔ/. This is not the case in the northern and central dialects: there is a contrast between /-ʔ/ and its absence. In this study, only forms from one dialect are quoted. If a northern form is attested, that is what is quoted. If no northern form is available, a central form is quoted. If neither northern nor central forms are attested, we quote Ishbukun, the southern dialect.

---

[1] Professor Tsuchida very kindly provided me this list in 1997, when I was preparing to visit the Bunun area. I do not know the period of time when these forms were collected. The file containing these forms is listed in the bibliography as Tsuchida 1997.

[2] I found that Tsuchida's and Li's materials to be most accurately transcribed, and in this study, I follow their transcriptions when they are at variance with other sources.

There are only three vowels and no diphthongs in the analysis of Li (1988). However, one source, Nihira (1988), quotes [o] and [e] as variants for forms with /au/ and /ai/, an indication that these two sequences have diphthongized in some varieties or dialects.[3]

B5.1 Changes that characterize the Bunun reflexes in general

PAn roots have been reformed into disyllabic roots with very few exceptions: (1) roots of three or more syllables have for the most part contracted; (2) monosyllables have been disyllabized by stretching out the vowel nucleus, in some cases by inserting a glottal stop and in others by simply lengthening the vowel in one of two alternative ways: either by a sequence of like vowels or by a sequence of a vowel plus /u/ (the reflex of *e). Further, metathesis is widespread, particularly in roots that contain /q/ and /s/, but other examples of metathesis are also attested.

B5.1.1 Syllable loss

Trisyllabic roots disyllabize by elision of the penult (loss of vowels of the penult) other than *i:[4]

> *baɣequh > *baqlu* 'new' *baqesiŋ > *qasbing* 'sneeze' (with metathesis [§B5.1.3]) *binesiq 'seed rice' > *binsiq* 'seed' *aqetih 'for water to dry up' > *mat-aqtiʔ* 'dam up to fish' (< *mat-aqeti > *mat-eqati) *ɣabihi 'evening' > *labi-an* 'night' *isekan > *iskaan* 'fish' *liceqes > *icqus* (with unexplained loss of *l-, §B5.3.61) 'nit' *ɣuqaɬay > *ba-nanað* 'male' (< *ba-lanað [with the loss of *q discussed in §B5.3.21, end] < *ba-lqanað < *ba-laqunað < *ba-luqanað) *qaɬuwaŋ 'bovine' > *qanwang* 'animals like deer or buffalo' *qasulipan > *qapis* 'centipede'[5] < *qalpis (loss of *l [§B5.3.61]) < *qalupis < *qasulip (with the *-an lost through its reanalysis as an affix) *tineun (from earlier -in- + *teun < *tun) > *ma-tinʔun* 'weave' (with intercalation of /ʔ/ and subsequent elision [§B5.3.22]) *tuqelaɬ > *tuqnað* 'bone'

In affixed forms that were reanalyzed as roots, the same process of loss of medial vowel took place:

> *keɣaŋ 'hot and dried up' > *ma-klang* 'hot, sunny' *tened > *si-tnuʔ-in* 'sink' *saqit > *manu-cqit* 'sharp' *qetaq > *ma-tʔaq* 'raw'

*e in the antepenult was elided:

> *seqeɣet > *ma-squt* 'tight' (northern: *ma-cqut* < *masqlet) *sehapuy > *sapuð* 'fire'

If a trisyllabic root developed in pre-Bun so that it occurred only suffixed, the antepenult of the root was lost, rather than that the penult of the root was elided:

> *basequ + -un > *saq-un* 'having a bad smell' (< *saquun < *basaquun [§B5.2.3(2)]) *daqaɬi + -an > *qani-an* 'daytime' (< *daqani-an)

This penultimate vowel loss in trisyllabic roots is sometimes blocked by a process whereby the last two syllables of the root were reanalyzed as the root and a new affix replaced the first syllable:

---

[3] Further, Nihira often writes *o* in place of *u*, e.g., *qoma* instead of *quma* in our sources. In those cases, *o* is most likely a subphonemic variant (but possibly phonemic, as the distribution of [o] is independent of environment).

[4] However, an *i is lost in *labi-an* 'evening' < *ɣabíhi 'evening' by the rule of §B5.2.0, middle. I have also assumed *i-elision in *sisðup* 'slurp' < *sisiɣup [§B5.3.44]).

[5] In most dialects this root is reduplicated, as names of insects often are: *qaqapis*.

*beɣekec 'bundle' > *ma-luquc* 'tie up' *pacaqaɬ > *an-caqan* 'carry over shoulder' (where *pacaqan was analyzed as containing a root *caqan)

Nasal insertion before first consonant of the penult also apparently blocks vowel loss:

*bituqan > *bintuqan* 'star'

*i is normally not lost in medial syllables:

*qaɬitu > *qanituʔ* 'spirit, ghost'

B5.1.2 Monosyllabic roots

Monosyllabic roots may become disyllabized by lengthening the vowel to two moras with or without insertion of a /ʔ/ between them (§B5.1.4).

*baq 'down' > *baaq* 'riverside of house, down the mountain' *kan > *kaun* 'eat' (also *m-aʔun* < *kmaʔun) *ɣiq > *liiq* 'saw grass: *Imperata cylindrica'* *e > *uu* 'yes' *enem > *nuum* 'six' (< *nem [§B5.1.21]) *taw 'person' > *taʔu* 'another person'

In the case of *isekan 'fish', which consists of a root *kan plus the prefix *ise-, Bun treats the final syllable as a monosyllabic root—i.e., *iskaan* 'fish', with lengthened /a/.

B5.1.21

The numerals *ica 'one' and *enem 'six' lose the first syllable and subsequently lengthen the nucleus when not proclitic. The loss of the inherited penult began in proclitic position. Subsequently the shortened form was generalized:

*ica > *caa* 'one' *enem > *nuum* 'six'

B5.1.3 Metathesis

A few roots show metathesis. No rules can be discovered to indicate the environments in which metathesis is favored.

*baqesiŋ > *qasbing* 'sneeze' 'understand' *juɣami > *dumali* 'straw' *qusalipan > *qapis* 'centipede' (< qapis-an < *qasipan < *qaslipan < *qasulipan) *quncg 'pith, flesh' > *nuqus* 'marrow' *taŋila > *tainga* 'ear' (Ishbukun: *tangia*)

Sequences of *ʔC that developed (§B5.1.4) automatically metathesized:

*ma- +*qetaq > *matʔaq* 'raw' (< *maʔtaq < *maʔetaq, with loss of *q [§B5.3.2])

In one case, metathesis seems to have been stimulated by the need for euphemism: *qaqiyut 'have sexual intercourse' > *pa-quit* 'have sexual intercourse' (< *pa-qaquit)

B5.1.4 The status of /ʔ/

First, we should address the final [-ʔ]. In the Ishbukun dialect, all word-final vowels are automatically closed with [ʔ]—i.e., final glottal stop is noncontrastive in that dialect. The northern and central dialects did not develop an automatic word-final [ʔ], but many forms that historically were closed with V came to be closed with [ʔ], so that in the northern and central dialects, /ʔ/ is contrastive in final (as well as medial) position.[6] For a discussion of whether the contrast in the northern and central dialects between /ʔ/ and its absence

---

[6] Further, in the Takitudu dialect, one of the northern dialects, words ending in -V developed [-h] after the -V. This is the conclusion I draw from Tsuchida's statement (1976: 184), "All [Takitudu] words end in a consonant when pronounced in isolation, The final *h* and *ʔ* are replaced by zero when they come to be medial by suffixation or in phrases when followed by a particle."

developed secondarily or reflects a PAn contrast, see Wolff 2009. We conclude that the contrast does not remount to PAn and assume that the forms of the northern and central dialects with accreted final /-ʔ/ developed the final /ʔ/ under the influence of Ishbukun dialects or possibly by borrowing from one of the neighboring languages in which [ʔ] is automatically accreted to roots ending in a vowel.[7] Further, forms ending in *-h (which came to end in a vowel in pre-Bunun [§B5.3.22]) never get an accreted /ʔ/ in the northern and central dialects (but do so automatically in Ishbukun).[8]
Second, in medial position, /ʔ/ is contrastive in all dialects. [ʔ] arose when loss of a medial C gave rise to vowel sequences or when a monosyllabic root was disyllabized (cf. §B5.1.2). One of the vowels of a sequence *VʔV* may have been elided (§B5.1.1), giving rise to CCs where /ʔ/ was the one of the consonants:

> *enem 'six' + a- > *aʔnum* (< *aenem) 'six people' *ɣiq > *liʔiq* 'sword grass' *bulehaɣ > *buʔal* 'cataract' (< *buaɣ < *bulhaɣ) *gali > *ma-kaʔi* 'dig' *qetaq + *ma- > *matʔaq* 'raw' (< *maʔetaq, with loss of *q [§B5.3.21] and metathesis) *tineun > *tinʔun* 'weave'

The rule whereby /ʔ/ is inserted between vowels is facultative: in some cases, no glottal stop is accreted, and the resulting form has VV. If the two abutting vowels were alike, they were contracted unless they were the nucleus of a root. (Cf. the examples in §B5.2.0, 3rd¶.)

B5.1.5 The status of /h/

/h/ occurs in the northern and central dialects in initial and medial but not in final position.[9] Ishbukun cognates of northern and central forms with /h/ normally have nothing—i.e., noncontrastive [ʔ] in root-initial and Ø in medial position:

northern and central dialects	Ishbukun	
i-hapav	*i-ʔapav*	'shallow'
huluc	*ʔulus*	'clothing'
banhil	*baniɬ*	'cypress'

[7] Am, At, and St all automatically accrete a noncontrastive [ʔ] to close a root-final V. It is not likely that the Bun /-ʔ/ developed by spreading a [-ʔ] that had developed between the stem-final vowel and the initial vowel of a suffix to the unsuffixed form. The reason this is unlikely is that when vowel-initial suffixes are added to forms with final /-ʔ/, the glottal stop is lost (Tsuchida 1976: 184).

[8] Zorc (1982: 121) suggested that there was a correlation between [h] in Takitudu (= lack of final /-ʔ/ in the other northern and central dialects of Bun [cf. the footnote immediately following]) and the occurrence of final /-h/ in Am, Paz, St, or At. He saw this correlation as evidence for a laryngeal in PAn. However, as explained in this section, there is no correlation. To be sure, we may say, on the basis of the limited data available, that if a form has /-h/ in Am, etc. the cognate in northern and central Bun dialects will have final vowel and [-h] in Takitudu. But the reverse is not true: if Am, etc. have a final vowel, the cognates in the northern and central Bun dialects may or may not have final vowel and in Takitudu may or may not have [-h]. In short, final vowels in the northern and central dialects and [-h] in Takitudu may correspond to forms in Am, etc. with /-h/ or they may correspond to forms in Am etc. with Ø. PAn *-h is reconstructed if the cognates in Am, Paz, St, or At have /-h/. If the Am, etc. cognates have Ø [ʔ], a final vowel is reconstructed for PAn. In short, Bun final vowel (= Takitudu [-h]) may reflect a PAn *-h or it may reflect a PAn final vowel. For this reason, Bun does not provide evidence for reconstructing PAn *-h. On whether northern dialects attest a contrastive /-h/, cf. the following footnote.

[9] Some of the northern dialects developed [-h] after a word-final V (cf. the immediately preceding footnote). In these dialects the contrast is between [-Vh] and [-Vʔ]. Whether the [-h] in these dialects is phonological or is subphonemic cannot be discussed in detail here. The [-h] is taken to be a subphonemic phenomenon—that is, we treat the material from the northern dialects ending in [-Vh] as phonemically /-V/ (for in any case phonetic final vowel does not occur). Further, the [-h] occurs only in absolute word-final position. Once the word is suffixed or followed by an enclitic, the vowel is voiced throughout—i.e., [-h] does not develop.

/h/, in the northern and central dialects, has the regular reflex of *l- as its main source (§B5.3.61). Otherwise /h/ occurs in forms that have a PAn etymology but are not directly inherited from PAn. In three cases, /h/ is in a loan word that had *h in PAn: *banhil* 'cypress', *ma-tapha* 'dry on fire', and *puhut* 'squirrel' (< *bahaɬiɣ, *tahepa, and *buhet [§B5.3.22]). In several cases, /h/ is in a loan word that derives from a PAn form with *s (§B5.3.31): *ma-hacaq* 'sharpen' (< *sacaq). In two cases, /h/ is in a loan word that drives from a PAn form with *q: *haul* 'river' and *hutan* 'sweet potato' (< *qaluɣ and *qutaɬ [§B5.3.21]) Further, there is *huluc* 'clothing', which derives from a form that probably had initial *q-,*qulec. In one case, /h/ is in a loan word that derives from PAn. In this form, /h/ reflects *ɣ: *bahaq* 'lungs' (< *baɣaq [§B5.3.44]).

B5.2.0 Vowels and diphthongs

Most Bun dialects have just three vowels: Bun has lost *e (merged it with *u or *a). Some dialects have developed /e/ and /o/, but almost all inherited forms manifest /i/ and /u/ for *i or *u. Also Bun has no diphthongs in inherited forms: PAn diphthongs with *y are for the most part reflected with /-Vð/, and PAn diphthongs with *w are for the most part reflected with /-Vv/ (§§B5.3.62, B5.3.63).

Bun developed vowel sequences of unlike vowels with the loss of medial consonants:

*telu > *tau* 'three' *gali 'dig' > *ma-kai* 'dig' (also *ma-kaʔi*)[10]

If a sequence of like vowels was inherited or developed through consonant loss, the two vowels are contracted:

*ɣabihi 'evening' > *labi-an* 'night' *qaɬipugu > *qanipu* 'whorl'

However, if the two vowels are the nucleus of a root, they are not contracted (or perhaps they were contracted and then disyllabized to avoid a monosyllabic root [§B5.1.2]):

*jalan > *daan* 'road'

B5.2.1 *i > /i/

*i > /i/ in all positions:

*cíku > *ciku* 'elbow' *binesiq > *binsiq* 'seed for planting' *aqetih 'for water to recede, leaving dry land' > *mata-qtiʔ* 'dam up for fishing'

The sequence *ii is contracted to /i/ (§B5.2.0, above).

In one unexplained case *i > /u/ before a syllable containing /u/. (However there are many examples of *i being reflected as /i/ in this position as well.) Many languages have irregular reflexes of this root.

*linuɣ < *hunul* 'earthquake'

B5.2.2 *a > /a/

*a > /a/ in all positions:

*acu > *acuʔ* 'dog' *wanaɬ > *vanan* 'right' *walu > *wauʔ* 'eight'

In one case, *a is reflected as /i/. There is no explanation. There are also cases of unexplained /i/ < *e (§B5.2.3, below).

---

[10] The protoform *gali may, in fact, not be the source for Bun *kai* 'dig'. *Kai* may be a disyllabization of the root *kay 'dig', a root also attested in *ma-kaðkað* 'dig'.

*damaɣ 'light, torch' > *dimaɬ* 'light' (Ishbukun)

B5.2.3 *e >/u/, /a/

The most general case is that *e > /u/:

*enem > *nuum* 'six' (< *nem) *ɬecuŋ > *nucung* 'mortar' *tuqed > *tuquʔ* 'stump' *seqeɣet 'tied tight' > *ma-squt* 'tight (clothing)'

/e/ in the medial syllable of a trisyllabic root is lost by elision, as discussed above in §B5.1.1. *e > /a/ in two environments. (1) before *q:

*daɣeq > *dalaq* 'earth' *iseq > *isax* 'urine' (Ishbukun [< *iseq]) *luseq > *usaq* 'tear' *pa-cuheq > *mapa-cʔaq* 'wash' (with intercalation of [ʔ] and elision of medial *u [§B5.3.22])

(2) after a syllable with nucleus /a/:

*balec > *mim-baac* 'do back, get revenge' *baseq-un > *saq-un* 'stinking' *caleŋ 'pine tree, pitch' > *caang* 'torch, pine' *sagek > *saak* 'sniff' *paqegu > *paqav* 'gall' (< *paqeu) *qaleb > *qaaʔ* 'knee'

There are several forms, however, that manifest /u/ from *e in a syllable following a syllable with /a/-nucleus. There is no explanation, and it is impossible to say whether the forms cited in (2) of this section above reflect the normal development or whether the following forms do:

*kamet 'take in fingers > *ma-kamut* 'pinch' *qadeŋ > *halung* 'mole' *qaɣem > *qalum* 'pangolin' *qateb 'four enclosing walls' > *qatuʔ* 'pitfall trap' *sated 'deliver' > *ma-satuʔ* 'see off' *tapes > *ma-tapus* 'winnow' *waɣed > *valu* 'k.o. vine'

In one case, *e is reflected with /a/. There is no explanation:

*telu > *tauʔ* 'three'

*e is also reflected as /a/ in another form where the reflex is not determined by the environment. In this case the final syllable may have been reanalyzed as a suffix *-an:

*bituqan > *bintuqan* 'star'

The reflex of *delec 'bow string' is quoted with /o/ in our source (Nihira): *isdoos* 'bow string'. We do not have a citation for this form for a dialect that does not contrast [u] and [o]. Apparently, this form occurs in one of the dialects that do not contrast [c] and [s].
*e > /i/ before final *-ɬ:[11]

*taquweɬ 'year' > *ka-tavin* 'last year'

In a few cases, which are unexplained, *e is reflected by /i/:

*biqel > *biqi* 'goiter' *deɣemun > *dilmun* 'wild pig's nest'

One of the forms with unexplained /i/ from *e also abuts on an unexplained /s/ < *t:

*tebus > *sibus* 'sugar cane'

---

[11] I have found only one exemplification of this rule. The reconstruction of /e/ in the final syllable of *taquweɬ is based on reflexes in the MP languages. All the An languages of Taiwan reflect *i in the final syllable, which we assume to be a matter of assimilation to the final palatal. This rule did not affect many of the MP languages (cf. *taquweɬ in the glossary).

B5.2.4 *u > /u/

*u is faithfully reflected by /u/ in all positions:

*acu > *acuʔ* 'dog' *ɣumaq > *lumaq* 'house' *kutu > *kutu* 'louse' *cukecuk 'insert' > *man-cukcuk* 'stab, insert'

B5.2.5 Diphthongs

Bun reflects no diphthongs in inherited words. PAn diphthongs with *y are reflected as vowel plus /ð/ (if at the end of a word) and those with *w, with vowel plus /v/ (cf. §§B5.3.62, B5.3.63 for examples). In inherited monosyllabic roots, diphthongs are reflected as vowel sequences (with or without intercalated [ʔ]):

*taw 'person' > *taʔu* 'another person'

B5.3.0 Consonants

Bun reflects the PAn consonants in all positions as shown by the following chart:

CHART TWO. DEVELOPMENT OF THE BUNUN CONSONANTS FROM PAN

PAn	Bunun	PAn	Bunun
p	*p*	g	*k- -Ø-, -Ø*
t	*t*	ɣ	*l*
k	*k*	m	*m*
q	*q* (*x* [Ishbukun])	n	*n*
h	*Ø*	ŋ	*ng*
s	*s*	l	*h-, -Ø-, -Ø*
c	*c* (*s* [central and southern dialects])	ɬ	*n*
b	*b*	w	*v*
d, j	*d*	y	*ð*

B5.3.01 Clusters

Medial consonant clusters—i.e., roots containing CVCCV(C), are frequent in Bun as a result of loss of the medial vowel in trisyllabic roots (§B5.1.1).

B5.3.1 Voiceless stops

*p > /p/ in all positions:

*pagay > *paað* 'rice' *pitu > *pituʔ* 'seven' *puceg > *pusuʔ* 'navel' *dapaɬ > *dapan* 'footprint' *ipen > *nipun* 'tooth' *gapegap > *kapkap* 'grope' *cepecep > *ma-cupcup* 'suck' *kacepal > *ma-kacpal* 'thick'

*t > /t/ in all positions:

*taŋic > *tangic* 'cry' *taw 'person' > *taʔu* 'another person' *telu > *tau* 'three' *tiŋas > *tingas* 'food in teeth' *tuqas 'old' > *tuqas* 'elder brother/sister' *batu > *batu* 'stone' *pitu > *pituʔ* 'seven' *baɣat 'athwart > *balat* 'blow sideways' *saqit > *manu-sqit* 'sharp'

In one case, medial *t is prenasalized (as is the case of reflexes of this root in many other languages):

*bituqen > *bintuqan* 'star'

In three cases of *t abutting on /i/, *t is reflected as /s/. There is no explanation, and the citations manifest other unexplained irregularities as well (/i/ from *e [§B5.2.3, end] and reflection of *-q- with /ʔ/):

*tebus > *sibus* 'sugar cane' *paqit 'bitter' > *mapaʔis* 'sour, bitter' *ɣamit > *lamis* 'root'.

*k > /k/ in all positions:

*kaɣat > *kalat* 'bite' *ciku > *ciku* 'elbow' *aɣak 'walk in procession' > *alak* 'bring'

In the sequence *-ɣek- in the middle of a root, the *k > /q/—that is, becomes assimilated to *ɣ (prior to the change of *ɣ to /l/ [§B5.3.44]):

*beɣekec 'bundle' > *ma-luquc* 'tie up' (< *ma-ɣeqec, with the first syllable reinterpreted as a prefix)

B5.3.2 *q and *h

B5.3.21 *q

*q had two outcomes. In the northern and central dialects, *q > /q/, a back velar stop, and in the south, *q became /x/, a velar fricative.

*qabu > *qabu* 'ashes' *qumah > *quma* 'field' *daqis > *daqis* 'forehead' *jaqewis > *daqvis-an* 'far' *daɣeq 'earth' > *dalaq* 'soil, world'

In two lexical items, *q is reflected as /h/. There is a great deal of dialect mixture, but the occurrence of /h/ in place of /q/ cannot be readily explained as a borrowing from a southern dialect, where *q is reflected as [x]. The southern dialects evince /ʔ/ for these items. (Cf. §B5.1.5 for the correspondence /h/ in the northern and central dialects and [ʔ] in Ishbukun.)

*qutaɬ 'small plant'> *hutan* 'sweet potatoes' (Ishbukun: *ʔutan*) *qaluɣ 'deep water' > *haul* 'river' (Ishbukun, Paycian: *ʔaul*)

In two items, medial or final *q is reflected as /ʔ/. Possibly the change is due to the existence of *q in both syllables of the root in the first case. The second case has an irregular final consonant (§B5.3.1) and is probably not directly inherited.

*ma-qetaq 'raw' > *ma-tʔaq 'raw'* (< *ma-ʔtaq <*ma-qtaq) *paqit 'bitter' > *mapaʔis* 'sour'

*q is lost in two roots that had or developed three or more syllables. In most cases of roots of two or more syllables containing *q, Bun manifests apocope and retention of *q, but in these two cases, *q is lost, with no explanation. Further, the vowel sequences that develop with the loss of *q are contracted:

*ɣuqaɬay 'male' > *ba-nanað* 'male' (< *ba-lanað < *ba-laqunað < *ba-luqanað) *taquweɬ 'year' > *ka-tavin* 'last year'[12]

*q is lost in one other form. There is no explanation. This form is attested in only one of the central dialects, Idhokan, and in Ishbukun.

*qapuɣ > *ʔapul* 'lime'

B5.3.22 *h

*h is lost in all positions, but there are traces: medially, loss of *h may result in the development of /ʔ/ (cf. §B5.1.4):

---

[12] The *q of *taquweɬ is lost in Bun and in most of the languages from northern Luzon through Taiwan. South of that area through Oceania, *q is clearly reflected in this form in languages that reflect *q.

*pacuheq > *ma-pacʔaq* 'wash' (< *ma-pacuʔeq < *ma-pacueq)

In final position, *-h invariably results in final vowel in the northern and central dialects (but automatic [-ʔ] in Ishbukun).

Three forms with a PAn *h unaccountably manifest /h/. The first is attested only a central dialect, and the second, only in the northern and central dialects and not in the south. Also the third form has a final /-ʔ/, even though it is not attested for a southern dialect, where it is assumed /-ʔ/ originated. *Banhil* is probably borrowed from Am; *puhut* is also borrowed, as indicated by initial /p-/; but there is no explanation for *matapha*ʔ:

*bahaɬiɣ > *banhil* 'buttress projection in tree trunk' *buhet > *puhut* 'squirrel' *tahepa 'smoke fish' > *ma-tapha*ʔ 'dry on fire'

B5.3.3 *s and *c

B5.3.31 *s

*s is retained as /s/ in all positions, with a small number of unexplained exceptions:

*sagek 'sniff, kiss' > *saak* 'smell' *símaɣ 'oil' > *simal* 'fat (meat)' *dusa > *dusa*ʔ 'two' *luseq > *usaq* 'tears' *isekan > *iskaan* 'fish' *tuqas 'old' > *tuqas* 'elder sibling'

In the northern and central dialects, *s > /c/ in two situations: (1) after an /n/ that developed:

*seyap 'count' > *qan-ciap* 'think' (< *qan-siap)

(2) *s also became /c/ when it came to abut on /q/ or /p/:[13]

*saqit + manu- > *manu-cqit* 'sharp' *seqeɣet > *ma-cqut* 'tight' *kasepal > *kacpal* 'thick

In four cases, *s was lost. There is no explanation, as /s/ is manifested as the reflex for *s in all dialects. Except for the first example, these forms also appear with Ø or /h/ in other Formosan language and have spread secondarily (§A3.3.3ff.). There is no explanation for the first case.

*bukes > *qul-buuk* 'hair on head' (< *busek) *qusuŋ > *quung* 'mushroom' *iseyup > *ma-ʔiup* 'blow' *sema > *ma-ma* 'tongue'

In two cases *s is reflected with /h/ in the northern dialects and Ø [ʔ] in Ishbukun (but it remains /s/ in the central dialects). The change of *s > h may have been motivated by dissimilation from the /c/ onset of the following syllable in the first case.

*sacaq >*ma-hacaq* 'sharpen' (central: *ma-sasaq* Ishbukun *ma-ʔasaq*) *sapaw 'be on the surface' *i-hapav* 'shallow' *tun-hapav* 'swim'

B5.3.32 *c

*c > /c/ in all positions in the northern dialects. In the central and southern dialects *c > /s/—that is, merges with the reflex of /s/:

*ciku > *ciku* 'elbow' *cucu > *cucu* 'breasts' *puceg > *pucuq* 'navel' *taŋic > *tangic* 'cry'

---

[13] However, *sq did not become /cq/ in the following form. We assume that the variant of the central dialects (in which *c and *s merge) spread to the northern dialects:

*ti + *seqeɣet > *tisqut* 'belt'

The hypothesis that this rule also applies to *sp is based on the one example *kacpal* 'thick'. Further, there is no articulatory explanation as to why *sp and *sq should change to /cp/ and /cq/, but *s in *sk remain unchanged in *iskaan* 'fish'. Possibly, the /s/ did not change to /c/ because /is/ still had the status of prefix.

In a few cases, *c is reflected by /s/ in all dialects. These may be explained as borrowings by the north from the southern dialects in which *c is regularly reflected as /s/:

*cuk > *cuk* 'insert' and *paka-suk-un* 'weaver's sword' *ica > *tasʔa* 'one' (< *taʔ-esa [with prothetic [e-] in disyllabization (§B5.1.2) < *ca, which developed from *ica by apocope of /i/ when in proclitic position]) *beɣac 'husked rice' > *blas* 'boiled rice' *delec > *is-doos* 'bow string'[14]

B5.3.4 Voiced stops

B5.3.41 *b

*b is most widely reflected with /b/ in initial and medial position.

*baw 'above' > *i-baʔav* 'far up in the mountains' *balug 'k.o. pigeon' > *babalu* 'green dove' *busek > *mis-busuk* 'drunk' *qabu > *qabu* 'ashes'

In one case, *b is reflected with /d/. The /d-/ possibly reflects an alternative prefix to the root *ɣeqaŋ. The final /-m/ is also unexplained (cf. *baɣeqaŋ in the glossary):

*baɣeqaŋ > *dalqam* 'molar'

In final position, there are two examples where *-b > ʔ. In southern dialects, the *-b is reflected as /-b/:

*qateb 'four enclosing walls (as in trap) > *qatuʔ* 'fall trap' (southern: *xatub*) *isuwab > *su-suaʔ* 'yawn' (< *su-suwab < *suwab) (Ishbukun: *sisuab*)

There is one form that looks connected to a PAn root *kub 'cover over', but the form is found only in southern dialects, and the first part is not explained:

*kub > *matu-kub* 'cover'

In a few forms, *b is reflected with /v/. In one case, the same PAn root is also reflected with /b/. The forms with /v/ are taken to be borrowings from an unknown source:

*baq 'mouth' > *vaqvaq* 'jaw' (< *baqebaq) *bibi > *vivi* 'duck' *binesiq 'seedling' > *visiq* 'seed to plant' (as well as *binsiq* 'seed of millet' and *bisiq* 'seed grain') *baliw > *hu-vaiv* 'exchange' (but also *baliv* 'buy' [with unexplained /l/ (§B5.3.61)]) *suwab > *si-suav* 'yawn' (Ishbukun)

In several forms, *b is reflected with /p/. The forms with /p/ are taken to be borrowings from an unknown source. There is no other explanation for them.

*buɣebuɣ 'broken into small pieces' > *pulpul* 'shattered' *buhet > *puhut* 'squirrel' *buwaq 'fruit' > *puaq* 'flower' (also *buaq* 'name of k.o. flower')[15]

In the case of *binauʔað* 'woman' < *bahi + R- + -in- [i.e., *binabahi 'woman'], the medial *b was apparently replaced by *u by an unexplained analogical process.[16]

B5.3.42 *d, *j

PAn *d and *j fell together. In initial and medial position, *d and *j > /d/:

---

[14]This citation comes from the dictionary (Nihira 1988: 111), where it is transcribed with /o/ with no explanation (although the introduction states specifically that there is no phoneme /o/ in Bun).

[15] In the case of *pacʔaq* 'wash' (< *pa+cuehq), most other languages reflect *bacuheq. We do not assume this form to be another example of /p/ reflecting *b. Rather in this case, I have taken the root to be *cuheq and assume that the Bun form reflects a different prefix from other languages.

[16] *binabahi > *binauahi > *binauhai > *binauað > *binauʔað.*

*dałum > *danum* 'water' *deɣemun > *dilmun* 'nest of wild pig' *duɣi > *duliʔ* 'thorn' *dusa > *dusaʔ* 'two' *jalan > *daan* 'road, walk' *tuduɣ > *ma-tudul* 'sleepy'

In final position, d and *j become /ʔ/:

likud > *hikuʔ* 'back' *qałuj 'carried by the current' > *qanuʔ* 'be adrift' *téned > *su-tunuʔ-in* 'sink'

B5.3.43 *g

Initial in monosyllabic roots and as onset of the penult or earlier, *g falls together with *k:

*gaɣaŋ > *kalang* 'crab' *gapegap 'feel, grope' > *kapkap* 'grope in water'

As onset of the final syllable, *g > Ø:

*piga > *pia* 'how many?' *sagek 'sniff, kiss' > *saak* 'smell'

There are only three PAn forms with final *-g with reflexes in Bun. In one case, *-g is reflected by /-q/, in another, *-g is reflected by /-s/, and in a third case, *-g is lost. In the last case, the occurrence of /l/ shows that the form is not directly inherited from PAn (§B5.3.61).

*puceg > *pucuq* 'navel' *quneg > *nuqus* 'marrow, grease' *balug 'k.o. pigeon' > *babalu* 'green dove'

B5.3.44 *ɣ

*ɣ > /l/ in all positions:

*ɣabíhi 'evening' > *labi-an* 'night' *ɣiq > *liiq* '*Imperata cylindrica*' *ɣumaq > *lumaq* 'house' *aɣak 'walk in procession' > *alak* 'bring with' *deɣemun > *dilmun* 'pig's nest' *bulehaɣ > *buʔal* 'cataract' *bucuɣ > *bucul* 'bow'

In one case, where the reflex of *ɣ abuts on /s/, *ɣ is reflected as /ð/:

*siɣup > *sisðup* 'slurp (noodles)' (< *si-sɣup <*si-siɣup)

When the following syllable begins with /n/, the /l/ that developed from *ɣ is assimilated and becomes /n/:

*ɣuqałay > *ba-nanað* 'male' (< *ba-lanay < *ba-luanay)

In one unexplained case, *ɣ is reflected with /h/ in the northern and central dialects and by Ø in Ishbukun. There are other irregularities in this reflex as well. The form is not directly inherited in Bun:

*baɣaq > *bahaq* (Ishbukun: *baak*) 'lungs'

B5.3.5 Nasals

*m, *n, *ŋ > /m/, /n/, and /ng/, respectively, in all positions.

*mata > *mataʔ* 'eyes' *lima 'five' > *himaʔ* 'five' *enem 'six' > *nuum* 'six' *jalan > *daan* 'road' *ŋagan > *ngaan* 'name' *taŋic > *tangic* 'cry' *łecuŋ > *nucung* 'mortar'

*-m- > /mb/ between two /u/'s:

*tumes > *tumbus* 'body louse'

Irregular reflexes of the nasals are in forms that are not directly inherited from PAn:

*paŋudał 'pandanus' > *panadan* 'k.o. tree: *Cordia mixta*' *baqeɣaŋ > *dalqam* 'molar'

Bun reflects the process of nasalization of root-initial phoneme (§A3.71). The following form occurs with initial vowel or with a reflex of initial *ŋ in other An languages. In Bun it has an initial /n-/:

*ŋipen/ípen > *nipun* 'tooth'

There are other forms that have initial /ng/ in Bun for which some languages reflect initial vowels:

*ŋuseɣ > *ngusul* 'nasal mucus' *ŋagan > *ngaan* 'name'

B5.3.6 Liquids

B5.3.61 *l and *ɬ

*l > /h/ in initial position in the northern and central dialects and was lost in Ishbukun. Medially and finally, *l is lost entirely.

*likud > *hikuʔ* 'back' *lutuŋ > *hutung* 'ape' *bulaɬ > *buan* 'moon' *jalan > *daan* 'road' *biqel > *biqi* 'goiter' *taŋila > *tainga* and *tangia* (Ishbukun) 'ear'

In a few forms, the /h/ that developed initially was lost sporadically in all dialects:

*qalima 'hand' > *ima* 'hand' (but *lima 'five' > *himaʔ* 'five') *liceqes > *icqus* 'nit' *luseq > *usaq* 'tears'

In two cases, /ʔ/ developed variably between two vowels that became adjacent after the loss of *l (§B5.1.4):

*tali > *taʔi* 'taro' (as well as *taiʔ)* *jalan > *daʔan* 'walk' (as well as *daan)*

*l is reflected by /l/ in several forms, none of which seem to be inherited directly from PAn, even though the forms are of PAn origin:

*baliw 'change, return'> *baliv* 'buy' *balug 'k.o. pigeon' > *babalu* 'green dove' *bulaw 'reddish color' > *ma-bulav* 'yellow' *galaŋ > *kalang* 'wedge' *kasepal 'thick' > *ma-kacpal* 'thick' *lem$_{1,2}$ 'inside, dim light' > *luʔum* 'keep to oneself, cloud' (also *luluman* 'jail' *luhuman* 'cloudy') *liwa 'left' > *mu-livaʔ* 'wrong' *qulec 'covering for body' > *huluc* 'clothes' *putul 'cut off' < *ma-putul* 'short'

In one case, *l may have become *y, which is reflected with /ð/:[17]

*tuqelaɬ > *tuqnað* 'bone' (< *tuqðan < *tuqeyan)

*ɬ > n in all positions:

*ɬuka 'wound' > *nukaʔ* 'eruption, boil' *daɬum > *danum* 'water' *qaɬitu 'evil spirit' > *qanituʔ* 'ghost' *qaɬipugu > *qanipu* 'whorl'

There are five exceptions (as opposed to a large number of regular reflexes). There is no explanation of any of these. In one form, *ɬ is reflected with /ð/ (< *y):

*tuɬa > *tuðaʔ* 'eel'

The other irregularities are one of a kind: *ɬ > /l/, *ɬ > /ngq/, *ɬ > /ql/, *ɬ > /ng/:

---

[17]This assumes metathesis and that *l >/y/ in some unknown language that was the source for this form. Another possible explanation for *tuqnað* 'bone' is that *-að* is a suffix and the *l got lost, as is normal—i.e., *tuqelaɬ + *ay > *tuqlan + *-ay > *tuqan + ay > *tuqnað*. The problem with this is that a suffix *-ay has not been identified in the scanty information on Bun morphology available.

*capiɬ 'padding' > *sapil* 'sandals' *ciɬaɣ 'ray of light' > *ma-cingqal* 'bright' *suɬuc > *huqlus* 'pull out' (borrowed from an unknown source) *tasaɬ 'stay at a place' > *asang* 'village' (with irregular loss of *t as well)

B5.3.62 *w

In all positions, *w > /v/, including in PAn diphthongs:

*walu > *vauʔ* 'eight' *waɣi > *vali* 'sun' *qanuwaŋ 'k.o. bovine' > *qanvang* 'deer and other bovines' *caliw 'give in exchange' > *ma-caiv* 'give' *isiɬaw > *ma-sinav* 'wash' *lawaɣ > *haval* 'flying squirrel' *ka-liwa 'left' > *mu-livaʔ* 'wrong' (/l/ not explained) *siwa > *sivaʔ* 'nine' *taqweɬ 'year' > *ka-tavin* 'last year' (loss of *q unexplained)

However, intervocalically, *-w- was lost in the sequences *uwa and *awu with one unexplained exception:

*buwaq > *puaq* 'fruit *qawuɣ > *qaul* 'k.o. bamboo' *quway > *quað* 'rattan'

The exception is the following form, where *awu > /avu/:

*ɬawuŋ > *navung* 'shade'

In the case of *waɬiw 'honey bee', the *i was absorbed into *ɬ and the final *-w became syllabic, as is the case of all Formosan languages that attest a reflex of this form:

*waɬiw > *vanu* 'honey bee' (< *waɬu).

In monosyllabic roots with a diphthong with *w, the root was reformed into one with two syllables. In some cases, the vowel preceding the diphthong was doubled, and *w > v. In others, the *w > u and was made a separate syllable (with or without an intercalated /ʔ/):

*baw 'above' > *i-baʔav* 'far up in the mountains' *daw > *dau* 'reportative particle' *taw 'person' > *taʔu* 'another person'

*bangaw 'biting insect' has a reflex *bango* 'green bottle fly' (quoted by Nihira), a dialectal form. It is unknown if a cognate is found in a dialect that does not have /o/ and what it would be.

B5.3.63 *y

*y > /ð/ (a voiced interdental spirant) in all positions, including in diphthongs:

*i-aku > *ðaku* 'I (nominative)' *bayu 'pound with a pestle' > *baðu* 'pound rice' *daya 'inland' > *daðaʔ* 'above' *qayam 'pet' > *qaðam* 'bird' *matay > *matað* 'die' *pagay > *paað* 'rice' *qatay > *qatað* 'liver' *sehapuy > *sapuð* 'fire'

However, the sequence *iya > ia, and *iyu > iu

*tiyaɬ > *tian* 'belly' *qaqiyut > *pa-quit* 'have sexual intercourse' (< *pa-qaqiut) *iseyup > *ma-ʔiup* 'blow' (*ey > /i/, see immediately below)

In one case, a sequence *iu seems to have developed into *iyu:

*laheyu > *is-laiðu* (< *is-laiyu < *is-lahiu) 'wither'

In one form, *iyu > ivu, although other cases provide evidence that *iyu > /iu/. The explanation probably lies in dialectal mixture, but the evidence has not turned up to date:

*baɣiyus 'storm' > *balivus* 'heavy rain'

The following form was borrowed from an unknown source and did not develop [y] at the end of a word:

*ałay > *anai* 'termite' (also *aʔali* [northern dialect])

The sequence *ey becomes /i/:

*seyap > *qan-ciap* 'count'

The form *bábuy became *babuʔ* 'pig'.[18] There is no explanation why the *y of *uy should have become /-ʔ/ (like final *-b, *-d, and *-j) instead of the expected /-ð/.

[18] The extinct languages of the western plains, Babuza, Papora, and Hoanya, reflect *babu* 'pig' with a normal reflex of /u/ < PAn *uy. However, there is no evidence that Bun was ever located anywhere near where these languages were spoken, and it is unlikely that these languages are the source of the aberrant Bun form.

CHAPTER SIX, §1

Amis

B61.0 Background and cultural factors that influenced the history of Amis

Amis (Am) is spoken on the east coast of Taiwan, in an area stretching from Taitung north along the plains as far as Hualien. There are four dialects of Amis. They evince a certain amount of diversity, probably enough so that the dialects are not mutually intelligible. The language is still healthy and is being used by the children in some rural areas, but like all of the Formosan languages, it is giving way to Taiwanese or Mandarin Chinese. The data here presented are based primarily on Fey (1986), who reports on "standard Amis", the dialect spoken in the central area, and secondarily on Duris (1969–70), who covers dialects throughout the Amis area. A few items are cited from Tsuchida 1976 or Chen 1980. The following chart shows the segmental phonemes of Am. Am also has the sound [ʔ], which is probably not a phoneme, and the phoneme /x/, which is marginal. /x/ does not occur in forms inherited from PAn. [ʔ] is added automatically in three positions: (1) to all word-final vowels except in the case of markers, enclitic particles, and pronouns;[1] (2) [ʔ] is also automatically added between unlike vowels;[2] (3) [ʔ] also occurs as onset to /e/ at the beginning of a root. This /e/ was elided phonetically but is still present in the phonology (§B61.2.2, 2nd ¶). Stress falls on the final syllable in the Am dialects.

CHART ONE. PHONEMES OF AMIS

Consonants

voiceless stops	p	c	t	k	
fricatives	f	ɬ	s	x	ɦ
liquids and semivowels	w	y, l	r		h
nasals	m		n	ng [ŋ]	

Vowels

high	i		o [u]
mid		e [ə]	
low		a	

There are also the four diphthongs /aw/, /ay/, /oy/, and /iw/. The transcription of the consonants here adopted represents the pronunciation more closely than the orthography

[1] This distribution of glottal stop is remarkably similar to that of St (§B12.1.53), but the development of [ʔ] in Am is doubtlessly independent of that in St.

[2] Our sources are unclear on this point. Fey (1986) transcribes some words with *owa* and some with *oa*, some with *iya* and some with *ia*. I have not had extended access to speakers, but I assume on the basis of the very limited descriptions that these distinctive orthographies represent phonemic contrasts. Further, I assume that the form without the glide is broken by noncontrastive glottal stop. The introduction to Fey's dictionary makes me suspect that in some cases the noncontrastive glottal stop is transcribed with an apostrophe. (Cf. the footnote immediately following.)

sanctioned for writing Am (and employed by Fey, but not the other sources). The following list gives the equivalents: /ɦ/, /ɬ/, and /ŋ/ are written apostrophe, *d*, and *g*, respectively, in the sanctioned orthography. They are a pharyngeal voiceless fricative, a voiceless lateral fricative, and a voiced velar nasal, respectively.
The vowels are transcribed as indicated in the chart above and follow the sanctioned orthography employed by Fey. Note that the one back vowel is transcribed *o* here and in the sanctioned orthography. Glottal stop is not transcribed here nor does Fey do so in most cases.[3] /e/ occurs word initially in Am, but is not written. Initial /e/ is written with an apostrophe, which represents the phonetic glottal stop that occurs before the /e/, and in actual pronunciation /e/ is elided (cf. the statement under (3) above the chart of the Am phonemes). CC does not contrast with CeC: some clusters are pronounced with no intervening vowel; others may have an epenthetic /e/ (Fey 1986: 21).[4] The sanctioned orthography writes /e/ only in word-final syllables, and we follow this practice.
There is no contrast between /i/ preceded or followed by a back vowel and /i/ plus a glide (/y/) preceded or followed by a back vowel. In cases where such sequences developed in the penult and the final syllable,[5] /y/ was automatically inserted:

*taqi > *tayiɦ* 'feces' (< *taɦi [§B61.1.3])

B61.1 Changes that characterize Am in general

Am is remarkably conservative in comparison with other languages. Am underwent few changes in its phonology in developing from PAn.

B61.1.1 Loss of a syllable by syncopation

PAn roots may lose one or two syllables in their development to Am: (1) by the loss of the antepenult, (2) by the loss of the penult, or (3) if the root had initial *i, it may lose both the penult and antepenult (cf. the reflexes of *iqetah and *iqebed listed in §B61.1.11, below).

B61.1.11 Loss of the antepenult

Loss of the antepenult was never an active process in Am. Some of the forms that manifest antepenult loss are probably borrowings from neighboring languages, and in fact some of the forms that have lost the antepenult show other irregularities in their reflexes.

---

[3] The dictionary does not allow me to make an unambiguous statement on this point. It states (Fey 1986: 20), "Amis has heavy and light glottal stops, but uses only one symbol for these in spite of a few minimal pairs (e.g. *'es'es*)." I take this to mean the following: there are two forms [ʔesʔes] 'whittle' and [ɦesɦes] 'whistle', both written the same way. In short the glottal stop is sometimes transcribed with an apostrophe in the dictionary, just as is /ɦ/, which is always transcribed with an apostrophe. There are some cases where the dictionary writes apostrophe, but historically no /ɦ/is expected. Without access to speakers, I cannot determine if these are cases of /ɦ/or /ʔ/. For lack of better information, I take them here to contain /ʔ/. The forms in question are *'cak* 'ripe' *'nem* 'six' and *ca'ag* 'branch, which I assume to be phonemically /ecak/, /enem/, and /caang/ respectively, for the expected reflex of reconstructed PAn etyma would be [ʔcak], [ʔnəm], and [caʔaŋ]. They may contain /ɦ/ instead of [ʔ], but the occurrence of [ɦ]would be difficult to explain.

[4] There is no definitive information as to which clusters are subject to epenthetic schwa insertion. Evidently, sequences transcribed CC may be [CəC] or [CC] and the difference is not phonological (Fey 1986: 21).

[5] Earlier in the word, sequences *ai and *oi become diphthongs /ay/ and /oy/.

However, loss of *i in the antepenult seems to be a regular sound law.[6] At least four forms evince loss of an antepenultimate *i. Only one form evinces loss *a in the antepenult:

> *qaciɣah > *cilah* 'salt'[7] *iqebed > *fifer* 'to fly' *iqetah > *fitah* 'rice husk or bran' *siyuɬuq > *oɬofi* 'beads' *tineun > *tnoon* 'weave'

In the following example, the *i of the antepenult moved to the penult by metathesis with *e and therefore was not lost. The *e that came to be in the antepenult was subsequently lost (cf. the discussion of this process in the An languages in general in §A3.5.4).

> *iseyup > *fiiyof* 'blow'

In the following example, the *i of the antepenult is a preposition referring to time and therefore was not lost.

> *saweni > *i-soni* 'a little while ago' (< *i-saoni)

B61.1.12 Loss of the penult

*e > /e/ in the penult. Note, however, that penultimate /e/ is elided in all but careful speech and in any case does not contrast with its absence—i.e, trisyllabic roots with a penultimate /e/ are pronounced alternatively in two or three syllables, and disyllabic roots with /e/ in the penult are pronounced alternatively in one or two syllables, with an exception discussed below in this section. *u in the penult of trisyllabic roots is also elided.

> *buhuwaŋ > *fohang* 'hole' (< *buhwaŋ)

In the following case, *h was lost (§B61.3.21), and the subsequent vowel sequence *ue was contracted to *e:

> *bacuheq > *facafi* 'wash' (< *baceq < *bacueq)

In two cases, a trisyllabic root underwent unexplained loss of *a in the penult:

> *bahaɬiɣ > *fahɬil* 'cypress' *tiqadaw > *tifiraw* 'stretch the body to see'

A penultimate *i was elided. It is a change that affects Bun[8] and all the MP languages as well and probably spread to Am very early. The origin is unknown:

> *qaɣicam 'k.o. reed' > *fialcam* 'dry stalks usable for kindling'

/e/ does not elide in a few cases. They are all cases of /e/ before /l/, but this is probably not a rule, for there are forms with sequences *el where /e/ is elided:[9]

---

[6] There are four forms that retain /i/ in the antepenult, as do their cognates in other languages. The first two cases may have retained the antepenult because it was in an affix (cf. the final paragraph of this section). In the case *fitoka*, there is no explanation. For *fitafiol*, cf. the footnote to §61.3.42.

> *tiqadaw > *tiŋraw* 'stretch the body to see better' *tinaqi > *tinafii* 'intestines' *bituka > *fitoka* 'stomach' *qiteluɣ > *f-itafiol* 'egg'

[7] Variations *cirah* and *cinah* are also attested. This is an indication that this form is not inherited from PAn.

[8] Cf. Southern Bunun *xaslam* '*Miscanthus* stalks'. This may be the source of the Am form, but this is not totally certain because the Bun form shows metathesis, and the Am form does not.

[9] /e/ is elided before /l/ in the penult of the following two disyllabic roots—i.e., they are pronounced as monosyllabics in normal speech:

> *celem > *clem* 'sink' *pilek 'eyelash' > *plek* 'blink' *sa-plek* 'eyelash' (< pelek [change of /i/ > /e/ unexplained])

*qatimela > *fiatimela* 'flea' *qaselu > *fiasolo* 'pestle' *telu > *tolo* 'three' (cf. §B61.2.2, middle, for change of *e > /o/)

In the following example, *e in the penult fails to elide because *i in the antepenult was lost (§B61.1.11).

*tineun > *tnoon* 'weave'

B61.1.13 Epenthetic vowels in doubled monosyllabic roots

There are three roots consisting of doubled monosyllabic elements that have an epenthetic vowel /a/ between the doubled syllables. See §A3.6.1 for a discussion of this phenomenon.

*katekat 'put, go up' > *katakat* 'lift s.t. heavy with the hands by oneself' *watewat > *watawat* 'flutter' *wiŋewiŋ 'shake from side to side' > *wingawing* 'wag the tail'

B61.1.2 Disyllabization of monosyllabic roots

Amis, like most of the An languages (and unlike Pai and Pu), disyllabizes monosyllabic roots inherited from PAn (§A3.6.2) except in the case of enclitics.[10] Four of the processes of disyllabization evinced in the history of the An languages are attested by Am: (1) lengthening the vowel nucleus (including disyllabizing diphthongs and intercalating laryngeals), (2) addition of a prothetic vowel, (3) doubling the monosyllabic root, and (4) petrifaction of an affix—reanalyzing a root plus affix as a new root. The following list exemplifies these processes.

Lengthening of the vowel nucleus:

*kan > *kaen* 'eat' *taw > *tawo* 'another person' *ɬib 'overhanging rock shelter > *ɬihif* 'cave, den'

Addition of a prothetic vowel:

*cak > *ecak* [ʔcak] (written *'cak*) 'ripe'

Doubling of the monosyllabic root:

*ba > *fafa* 'carry on back' *cek 'pack tight' > *cekcek* 'press, crowd together, press grain down'

Petrification of affix:

*kuj 'back' > *ikor* 'after behind' (< *i 'locative' + *kuj) *ket 'stick' > *siket* 'attach' (< *si- [< *ise- [§A3.5.4])

B61.1.3 Metathesis

Metathesis is evinced by a handful of forms. For two of these, cognates in several other languages show the same metathesis, an indication that the forms have spread from language to language secondarily, even though they clearly have a PAn origin. In the case

---

[10] However, monosyllabic roots have developed in contemporary Am by the processes of penult elision of disyllabic roots in colloquial speech, discussed immediately above in §B61.1.1.

of *daqu the same metathesis is evinced by Thao.

*aɬay > *a-ayaɬ* 'termite' *balug > *fanol* 'k.o. pigeon' *kasiw 'wood, tree > *kasoy* 'firewood' *daqu > *raofi* 'soapberry tree'

The other cases of metathesis are purely Am phenomena. No phonological motivation can be found. Possibly taboo is the grounds for the metathesis of *taqi 'feces':

*seyap > *asip* 'count' (< *siyap [§B61.2.2, end]) *caŋa > *caʔang* 'branch'[11] *qusaw > *ma-sofiaw* 'thirsty' *mula 'plant crop' > *pa-loma* 'plant (grown for its flowers or fruits)' *taqi > *tayifi* 'feces' *tiŋeɣ 'voice' > *tngil* [teŋil] 'hear' *tusud > *toros* 'knee' (dialectal) *quleg 'worm' > *fioner* 'snake'

B61.2 Vowels and diphthongs

Am has inherited the four vowels and diphtongs of PAn, listed in §B61.0. *e is written /e/ and pronounced [ə].

B61.2.1 *i

*i remains /i/ in most positions:

*piliq > *pilifi* 'choose' *ɣabihi 'evening' > *lafii* 'midnight' *saweni > *i-soni* 'a short while ago'

*i is lost in the antepenult in four forms (§B61.1.11).

B61.2.2 *e

*e remains a mid-central vowel in most cases:

*ɣamec 'crush, crumble' > *lamec* 'mix with hands'

However, in the penult, /e/ does not contrast with its absence—that is, CC and CeC do not contrast, and intial /e/ occurs phonologically but not phonetically.[12]

*enem > *enem* [ʔnəm] 'six' *keɣet > *klet* 'cut'

/e/ also occurs in the first syllable of a doubled monosyllabic root:

*cepecep > *cepcep* 'suck'

*e > /a/ before *q or before /fi/ that developed:[13]

*bacuheq > *facafi* 'wash' *luseq > *losafi* 'tears' *ɬiteq 'sticky sap' > *ɬitafi* 'lump of clay for making pots' *qaɬimateq > *ɬaɬintafi* 'leech' *seqeɣet > *safilet* 'tighten' *qiteluɣ > *f-itafiol* 'egg' (The origin of /fi/ is discussed in §B61.3.42, 2nd footnote.)

---

[11] The sources do not make it clear whether this form is pronounced [cafiaŋ] or [caʔaŋ] Cf. the third footnote to §B61.0, above. In this case, it is likely that a noncontrastive glottal stop developed between the two *a's that came to abut after metathesis had taken place.

[12] *enem 'six' is only one of two PAn forms reconstructed with initital *e. *enem is reflected with an ʔ-accretion and syncopation of the *e: [ʔnəm]. Phonemically, this is /enem/. However, Fey (1986: 38) cites *'nem,* and my interpretation of the transcription involves the assumption of a pronunciation [ʔnəm], phonologically /enem/. Cf. the third footnote to §B61.0, above.

[13] There is a form that suggests *e > /a/ before a glottal stop as well. Duris (1969-70: 63) cites aʔnem 'six persons' (< *ʔeʔenem, a reduplicated root, where the glottal stop was preserved when coming to abut on a C).

*e is assimilated to /o/ in the following syllable if *e is not elided (§B61.1.1ff.):

*qaselu > *ɦasolo* 'pestle' *telu > *tolo* 'three' *tineun > *tnoon* 'weave'

There are other forms in which *e > /o/, but the circumstances that determined the change to /o/ are not known. The Am reflex may in fact not be cognate with the reflexes of the protoroot in other languages, for these forms manifest other irregularities.

*lebeŋ 'bury' > *ɬfong* 'immerse' *lebleb 'hidden by being covered' > *loflof* 'inside of house'

*e is reflected as /i/ after /i/ in the following form, as in other Formosan languages. The form spread secondarily:[14]

*iseq > *isiɦ* 'urine'

The sequence *ey > /i/:

*seyap > *asip* 'count' (< *siyap [§B61.1.3])

The sequence *we > /wo/ or /o/ after a consonant:

*caweŋ > *sawong* 'protective hat' *weliq > *c-oli* 'return'

*we also became /o/ after a vowel in the following form, a dialectal variation, as in other variants of the root, the *e was lost by elision (§B61.1.13):

*saweni > *ano-saoni* 'after a while'

B61.2.3 *a and *u

*a remained /a/ in all environments:

*qabaɣa > *ɦafala* 'shoulder' *qacawa > *ɦacawa* 'in-law' *bituka > *fitoka* 'stomach'

In a form that also has an irregular reflex of *ɣ, and *a is reflected as /i/. There is no explanation.

*jaɣum > *rinom* 'needle'

*u remains /o/ in all environments except in the single case of penult elision listed in §B61.1.12, above.

*bubu > *fofo* 'fish trap in rivers' *cucu > *coco* 'breast'

B61.2.4 Diphthongs

The diphthongs are retained unchanged except for monosyllabic roots, described in §B61.1.12, above, where the *w and *y are made syllabic:

*pagay > *panay* 'rice (harvested grain)' *quway > *ɦoway* 'rattan' *bábuy > *fafoy* 'pig' *ɬaŋuy > *ɬangoy* 'swim' *lawlaw 'light' > *lawlaw* 'lamp' *láŋaw > *la-langaw* 'fly' *laɣiw 'flee' > *laliw* 'escape'

The form *kasiw reflects a metathesis of the final diphthong, as does its cognate in the Philippine languages and in the languages of northern Taiwan:

*kasiw 'wood, tree' > *kasoy* 'firewood'

---

[14] Chen (1980: 378) reports *iseʔ*.

One form manifests an irregular reflex /i/ of *ay. No explanation has been found:

*beɣay > *pa-fli* 'give'

B61.3 Consonants

The following chart shows the Am reflexes of the PAn consonants:

CHART TWO. DEVELOPMENT OF THE AMIS CONSONANTS FROM PAN

PAn	Am	PAn	Am
p	*p*	g	*k-,- n-, -n*
t	*t*	ɣ	*l [ḷ]*
k	*k*	l	*l [ḷ]*
q	*ĥ*	ɬ	*ɬ*
h	*h*	m	*m*
s	*s*	n	*n*
c	*c*	ŋ	*ng*
b	*f*	w	*w*
d, j	*r*	y	*y*

B61.3.1 Voiceless consonants

B61.3.11 *p

*p remained /p/ in all positions:

*piga > *pina* 'how much, many?' *pacepac 'beat to remove' > *pacpac* 'thresh' *sepat > *sepat* 'four' *cepecep > *cepcep* 'suck'

In a handful of unexplained cases, *p is reflected with /f/. These forms are likely to be cognate with reflexes of the same PAn root in other languages, but no good explanation has turned out for the /f/ and other irregularities in some of these forms as well:

*kapit 'held by pinching' > *kafit* 'attached to' (probably influenced by *kabit 'carried by hanging') *palit 'exchange' > *falic* 'change' *pucuq > *f-al-ocoĥ* 'heart' *iseyup > *ĥiyof* 'blow'

B61.3.12 *t

*t remains /t/ in almost all cases:

*telu > *tolo* 'three' *tiyaɬ > *tiyaɬ* 'belly' *tuɬuh > *toɬoh* 'roast' *mata > *mata* 'eye' *bituka > *fitoka* 'stomach' *sepat > *sepat* 'four' *uɣat > *olat* 'vein, tendon'

In one case, *t is reflected with /c/. The form has been contaminated by a word of similar meaning:

*tukej 'support, prop' > *coker* 'prop up' (cf. *cokor* 'cane' [< *cukud])

In one case, *t has been replaced by /n/ in the process of nasalization (§A3.7.1):

*tabaw 'float up' > *mo-navaw* 'float up'

B61.3.13 *c

With a few exceptions, *c > /c/:

*cek 'pack tight' > *cekcek* 'press, crowd together, press grain down' *cucu > *coco* 'breast' *bacuheq > *facaq* 'wash' *bakec 'belt, sash' > *fakec* 'wind (sash , rope, etc.) around'

A few roots with *c manifest reflexes with /s/ in Am. Some of these forms can be explained as being contaminated by other forms with similar meanings or not being inherited from PAn:

*bacebac > *fasfas* 'sprinkle' (probably an analogically created form on the basis *basaq 'wet' and *bicebic 'sprinkle') *qiceqic 'scrape' > *ħisħis* 'shave' (cf. *kiskis* 'scrape') *kecekec > *mikeskes* 'scratch' (cf. *kiskis* 'scrape')

A couple of these forms are borrowings from neighboring languages or learned borrowings:

qaɬisipec > *ɬaɬipis* 'roach' (< Pu *ɬaɬipis*)[15] *ŋucuq 'snout, beak' > *ngosoħ* 'nose' (possibly < At *ngusu* 'nose') *caweŋ > *saong* 'sun hat' *qiduc > *iros* 'spoon' *tugic > *toris* 'scratch a line' (Cf. Pai *turis* 'scratch a line', which also has the characteristics of secondary spread.)

There are two forms in which the /s/ reflex has no explanation:

*betac > *ftas* 'burst open so that insides come out' *cupaq > *sopaħ* 'spit'

In one case *c is reflected with /ɬ/. I assume that the process of nasalization (§A3.7.1) has affected this root:

*cahebay 'hang' > *ɬahpay* 'hang out clothes'

*c > /ɬ/ by assimilation to /ɬ/ on the left:[16]

*ɬecuŋ > *ɬoɬang* 'mortar'

B61.3.14 *k

*k remained /k/ in all positions:

*kaɣat > *kalat* 'bite' *paheku > *paku* 'k.o. edible fern' *cakecak > *cakcak* 'chop up into pieces'

B61.3.15 *q

*q > /ħ/ in most cases:

*qabu > *ħafo* 'ashes' *tuqas > *toħas* 'old' *liqeɣ > *liħel* 'neck' *piliq > *piliħ* 'choose'

There are two cases in which *q was lost. In the first case, loss of the final *-q is unexplained. The forms could possibly be borrowings from Ru, which has lost *-q. In the second case, Ru influence is not likely because the putative Ru source is doubled, whereas the Am form is not.

---

[15] The Pu form means 'water beetle', but we may assume that the original meaning was 'cockroach' and it was in this meaning that Am borrowed it. It is a borrowing from Pu because the Pu reflex follows Pu sound laws (cf. §B71.2.2).

[16] There is only one example involving *c-onset of the final syllable. There is a counterexample, but there *c is the coda:

*suɬuc > *soɬoc/hoɬoc* 'pull out'

*weliq > *c-oli* 'return' (RuBd *sioli* 'return') *qumah > *omah* 'cultivated field' (RuBd *oma-oma* 'field')

B61.3.2 *h, *s

Am is one of the few languages that retains both of these phonemes as /h/ and /s/ respectively in most environments.

B61.3.21 *h

*h is reflected as /h/ in all environments, with two exceptions, when it is lost.

*bahi 'female' > *fa-fahi* 'wife' *paheku > *pahko* 'k.o. edible fern' *baqeɣuh > *fafiloh* 'new'

*h is lost in trisyllabic roots when onset of the final syllable. Here are two

*bacuheq > *facafi* 'wash' *ɣabihi 'night' > *lafii* 'midnight'

As onset of the penult in trisyllabic roots *h is not lost:

*buhuwaŋ > *fohang* 'hole' *cahebay 'hang' > *łahbay* 'hang up wash' *cahełaɣ 'shine' > *cahłal* 'come out between showers (sun)'

B61.3.22 *s

*s > /s/, and in ten cases, /h/. First, the regular reflex /s/:

*sapesap 'grope' > *sapsap* 'feel with the hands' *sema > *sma* 'tongue' *luseq > *losefi* 'tears' *kusekus > *koskos* 'scrape'

In nine cases, root-initial *s- is reflected with /h-/, and in one case, medial *-s- is reflected with /-h-/. These forms are clearly secondary, although no origin for the /h/ can be established. Note that *h also irregularly reflects *s in languages of northern Taiwan (§A.3.3.32), but only in the cognates of five of the forms discussed here, and not in the cognates of the other five. Those cognates manifest /s/. Note also that four of these ten have variants with /s/.[17] Some of these forms evince other irregularities in the phonology:

*busat 'lift' > *fohat* 'open, uncover' *sacek 'plant with dibble stick' > *hcek* 'stake, post' *saweni > *i-honi* 'a while ago' (also *i-soni*) *sebic > *ko-hpic* 'thin' *semay '*Oryza sativa*' > *hmay* 'cooked rice' *siɣup 'slurp, sip' > *hlip* 'suck with straw' *sagek > *hanek* 'smell' (also *sanek*) *sukaq 'loosen, open' > *hokafi* 'loosen (belt)' *sułuc > *hołoc* 'pull out (of enclosure)' (also *sołoc*) *suni > *honi* 'noise, sound' (also *soni*)

In one case, /s/ is reflected with /c/. In this case, there is contamination with a word of similar meaning:

*liyus 'turn' > *liyoc* 'twist, turn the direction of s.t.' (cf. *pilec* 'twist and break')

B61.3.3 Voiced consonant stops in Am

There is a tendency to weaken the voiced consonants. *b, *d, *j become fricatives. *ɣ moved forward to fall together with *l.

---

[17] In fact a fair number of forms listed in Fey 1986, most of which do not have a PAn etymology, have variants with /s/ alternating with /h/ in initial position.

B61.3.31 *b

*b > [v] in pre-Amis and became voiceless in the central dialect, but remained /v/ dialectally.[18]

*babuy > *fafoy* 'pig' *becuɣ > *fcol* 'sated' *buhet > *fohet* 'squirrel' *qubał > *ɦofał* 'grey hair' *qełeb > *ɦiłef* 'close, shut'

B61.3.32 *d *j

*d and *j for the most part fell together and became /r/:

*duma > *roma* 'other' *tuduq >*toroɦ* 'drip' *cukud > *cokor* 'walking cane' *jaɣum > *rinum* 'needle' *qujał > *ɦorał* 'rain' *kuj > *i-kor* 'back'

*d and *j > /l/ normally when there was another *l in the root or /l/ developed (from *ɣ [§B61.3.41]):

*daɣaq > *lalaɦ* 'blood' *damaɣ 'light, torch' > *lamal* 'fire'[19] *sadiɣi > *salili* 'house post' *jalan > *lalan* 'path' *jiɣuc > *liloc* 'bathe' *qałuj > *ɦalol* 'be carried by current'

In one case, however, the assimilation to /l/ does not happen. Rather *l assimilates to the /r/ that developed from *d. The form is not directly inherited, but the origin is unknown:

*laduŋ 'sheltered place' > *rarong* 'temporary hut'

/l/ also reflects *d/*j in two loan words of unknown origin:

*uda 'young' > *molaɦ* 'immature' (also *moraɦ)* *tajem > *talem* 'sharp'

In five cases, *d is reflected by /ł/. There is no explanation.[20]

*bedebed 'spool, wind' > *fełfeł* 'bind' *demedem 'have feelings' > *łemłem* 'endure illness' *liduŋ 'protect, hide' > *liłong* 'shelter' *deŋ > *pa-łeng* 'extinguish' *culed 'go inside' > *soleł* 'insert' (/s/ unexplained)

In one case, *l is assimilated to /n/ in the same root.[21] The /n/ onset of the final syllable is also irregular. Note that a regular reflex also occurs:

*dałum > *nanom* 'water' (also *rałom* 'carry water from source')

---

[18] Fey (1986) transcribes *f* for all dialects, but Duris (1969–70: 2) writes *v* and indicates that the phoneme is voiced.

[19] In Am and Kav, the reflex of *damaɣ means 'fire, burn'. The meaning 'burn' was originally carried by the nasalized derivative of *damaɣ, *łamaɣ, (§A3.7.1), and its spread to the reflex of *damaɣ is an innovation shared by Am and Kav.

[20] With the exception of the form *soleł* (< *culed), which also has an unexplained /s/ instead of the normal /c/-reflex from *c-, these examples are all monosyllabic roots with the a vowel nucleus *u or *e. This fact indicates that the root structure might have had a role in developing the /ł/-reflex of *d. However *lalong* 'shelter' < *laduŋ also contains the root *duŋ and has a normal reflex of *d. Further, monosyllabic roots with an /a/ nucleus have the normal reflex of *d:

*dabedab 'set fire to' > *rafraf* 'be enflamed *daŋedaŋ 'heat near fire' > *rangrang* 'hold near fire to heat'

[21] Tsuchida (1976: 140) suggests that the reflex /n/ < *d is an assimilation—i.e., *dałum > *dañum > *nañum > *nanom* (§B61.3.43,end). This is probably correct, but there is only one attestation of the rule.

The form *tusa* 'two' does not reflect *dusa, but is probably the descendent of a PAn variant of *dusa to be reconstructed as *tusa.[22]

B61.3.33 *g

*g became voiceless when it was onset to a monosyllabic root or to the penult or earlier and merged with *k-, as in many An languages.

*gamay > *kamay* 'hand' *gap 'feel, grope' > *kapkap* 'reach out and grope', *ha-kap* 'touch lightly' *gisegis > *kiskis* 'scrape'

In medial and final position, *g became nasalized and moved forward, merging with *n:

*pagay 'rice plant' > *panay* 'rice with hull' *piga > *pina* 'how many?' *tebug 'spring' > *tfon* 'well'

After a preceding *ŋ, however, *g nasalized but did not move forward—i.e., > /ng/:

*qagan > *ngangan* 'name' (< *ŋagan [§A3.7.1])

There are two exceptions, where *g is reflected with /r/. The first of these forms has doubtlessly spread secondarily, and the second probably did so, too, although the source is unknown:

*tugic 'incise' > *toris* 'line' *wagay 'separate two things' > *waray* 'separate two quarreling parties'

B61.3.4 Continuants

B61.3.41 *ɣ

*ɣ > /l/ in all environments:

*ɣumaq > *lomaq* 'house' *gaɣaŋ > *kalang* 'k.o. crab' *wiɣi > *ka-wili* 'left (side)' *liqeɣ > *liñel* 'neck' *suɣ > *sulsul* 'pass threads through'

There is a handful of forms that evince other reflexes of *ɣ. They are all unique and show other irregularities as well. Their origin is unknown. In the first case, *ɣ is reflected with Ø, in the second, with /n/, and in the third and fourth, with /r/.

*qaluɣ > 'deep spot in river' > *ñalo* 'small river' *jaɣum > *rinom* 'needle' *ɣecep > *rcep* 'soak in' *iɣiŋ 'slanted' > *ñiring* 'have head bent to one side'

B61.3.42 *l and *ɬ

*l remained /l/, a retroflexed lateral flap [ḷ] in all positions.[23]

*laɣiw > *laliw* 'escape' *lilit 'wind around' > *lilit* 'wind cloth around head' *lukut > *lokot* 'k.o. fern *ala > *ala* 'take' *kalekal 'dig' > *kalkal* 'search inside'

There is a handful of exceptions that have no explanation. The following case is probably a dialect borrowing. There are dialects that have variants that sound like an /r/ to speakers of

---

[22] It is possible that the /a/ of *tusa* is a petrified linker and that the root *tus-* reflects the original PAn form. The forms reflecting *dusa remount to an allomorph with *d that developed in postvocalic position. Thao also reflects *tusa (§B13.3.32).

[23] I deduce this from Duris's comment to the effect that *l* is pronounced like the *r* in Japanese (Duris 1969–70: 2): "L correspond au R japonais, ni l ni r."

other dialects (or perhaps the /l/ and /r/ have fallen together—but the sources transcribe an /l/–/r/ distinction for all dialects). The standard dialect seems to have borrowed the /r/ variant of the following form:

*quleg 'worm' > *ħoner* 'snake' (< *ħoren [§B61.1.3])

In the first of the following forms, *l seems to have been lost by a regular sound change, but the reflex of *l in the second is unexplained. The forms are clearly related to cognates in other languages derived from the same proto-form:

*qiteluɣ > *f-itaħol* 'egg'[24] *lebeŋ > *ɬfong* 'immerse'

The following form has spread secondarily throughout the languages of Taiwan and the Philippines:

*bulaw 'copper colored' + *-an > *foɬawan* 'copper, brass'

*ɬ is reflected as a voiceless palatal lateral [ɬ] in all positions.

*ɬaŋuy > *ɬangoy* 'swim' *qaɬiŋu > *ħaɬingo* 'shadow *tuɬa > *tuɬa* 'eel' *tiyaɬ > *tiyaɬ* 'belly'

In one case, *ɬ is reflected with /l/ instead of /ɬ/. This may be by assimilation:

*qaɬuj > *ħalol* 'be carried off by current' (< *qalur < *qaɬur)

In several cases, *ɬ is reflected with /n/. Most of these cases are doubtlessly forms that have spread secondarily:

*baɬaw 'wash' > *fanaw* 'wash' (cf. Ru *ma-banaw* 'take a bath') *iseɬaw 'wash' > *nanaw* 'wash' (cf. Knn *mari-sináw* 'wash utensils') *qaɬitu > *ħanito* 'evil spirit' (cf. Bu *qanitu* 'ghost') *taɬam > *tanam* 'taste' (cf. Bun *tanam* 'taste')

In the following case, it is unknown how the form originated:

*kaɬusekus > *kanoos* 'claw, finger- or toenail' (loss of *sek unexplained)

We hypothesize that when there is a nasal in the root, the reflex of *ɬ assimilates and becomes /n/. There are only three examples to substantiate the hypothesis:

*daɬum > *nanom* 'water' *ɬagam > *ma-nanam* 'tamed'[25] *wanaɬ > *ka-wanan* 'right (side)'

B61.3.43 Nasals

*m, *n, *ŋ remained unchanged in all positions:

*mata > *mata* 'eye' *lima > *lima* 'five' *enem > *enem* 'six' *ni > *ni* 'genitive marker' *tineun > *tnoon* 'weave' *kan > *kaen* 'eat' *ŋalay > *ngalay* 'saliva' *taŋila > *tangila* 'ear' *daŋedaŋ > *rangrang* 'hold near fire to dry'

---

[24] Most likely the *l was lost in CC simplification. The development of *fitaħol* was possibly as follows: *bV- + qiteluɣ > *blitequɣ (apocope of vowel of prefix and metathesis of *l and *q) > *biltequɣ (metathesis of *i and *l) > *bitequɣ (*l lost in a cluster with *t) > *fitaħol* (*e > /a/ by the rule of B61.2.2, 4th¶).

[25] The existence of a Pu cognate with /n/ reflecting *ɬ (Pu *nadam* 'tamed') makes it more likely that this form did not develop in Am but was borrowed.

B61.3.44 *w and *y

*w > /w/ as syllable onset except where lost by syllable elision (§B61.1.1, above). (For *w and *y as second members of diphthongs, cf. §B61.2.4.)

*wałis 'fang' > *wałis* 'tooth' *qawuɣ '*Bambusa* sp.' > *ƒiawol* 'bamboo' *siwa > *siwa* 'nine' *tawa > *tawa* 'laugh'

The sequence *we > /wo/ and /o/, depending on the environment (§B61.2.2, end). *y > /y/ medially.

*baɣiyus > *faliyos* 'typhoon' *qayam 'animal raised for food' > *ƒiayam* 'bird, chicken' *tiyał > *tiyał* 'belly

The sequence *ey > /i/ (§B61.2.2, end).

CHAPTER SIX, §2

Kavalan

B62.0 Background and cultural factors that influenced the history of Kavalan

Kavalan (Kav) is spoken on the east coast of Taiwan in several villages in Hualien, within the larger area in which Am (Sakizaya dialect) is spoken. The language is still actively spoken but is not being learned by the younger generation. There is no information as to the age of the youngest speakers, but the sources make it clear that at present there are some middle-aged speakers who use the language in daily life. The homeland of Kav was located considerably north of the current location. The current Kav villages were established by migration from the homeland in 1840, and in the original homeland the language has died out. There is a small amount of literature on Kav, the most important being the dictionary by Li and Tsuchida (2006). We rely almost entirely on this dictionary for our citations here. Where there are differences in transcription between the earlier sources and the dictionary, we follow the transcription of the dictionary, as the compilers of the dictionary took into account the earlier materials and corrected them where necessary.

Kav shows few innovations in common with Am aside from lexical innovations, which are borrowed from Am. In phonology, Kav shares only the change of *g > /n/, a change that probably spread from Am to Kav (cf. the discussion in §A3.3.2, 3rd¶), and the merger of *d and *j, which is shared by the majority of Formosan languages.

The following chart shows the Kav phonemes. The phonemes in parentheses are not found in inherited forms. We follow the orthography of the dictionary here and give the phonetic value of the phonemes written /b/ and /e/ in square brackets in the chart. The phoneme /ɣ/ is written *R* in the dictionary and /ʔ/ is transcribed with an apostrophe. We write *ɣ* and *ʔ* respectively. /z/ is retroflexed and is merging with /r/ in one of the two Kav dialects now spoken—that is, some speakers pronounce forms with /z/ variably with /r/ (Li and Tsuchida 2006: 11). /r/ itself is characterized as a flap initially and medially and as retroflexed finally.

CHART ONE. PHONEMES OF KAVALAN

Consonants

stops	p	t, (d)	k, (g)	q , ʔ
spirants	b [β]	z, s, l[1]	ɣ	(h)
nasals	m	n	ŋ	
liquids	w	r	y	

Vowels

high	i		u
mid		e [ə]	
low		a	
diphthongs	iw	aw, ay	uy

[1] /l/ is described as a "lateral fricative". Its allophones are [d], [ð], and [ɬ], depending on the position in the word (Li and Tsuchida 2006: 3).

Stress is predictable and falls on the final syllable of the word. Consonants may be single or geminate, and geminate consonants may occur initially and medially. In final position, the only attested geminates are /-nn/ and /-ŋŋ/. If a root ends in a double consonant, the double consonants are manifested before a suffix. In word-final position, the two consonants are simplified: e.g., *kall-* 'dig' is attested as *kmal* (active) *kalli* 'imperative' The contrast between geminate and single consonants is neutralized in clusters at the beginning of a word. Only geminate consonants occur as the second element of initial clusters. By convention in the orthography, only single consonants are written in this position, a practice we follow here, as well. In other words, there is no contrast between [$C_1C_2C_2$-] and [C_1C_2-] in word-initial position. Phonetically, what occurs is [$C_1C_2C_2$-], but the orthography as well as our transcription is C_1C_2-.

B62.1 Changes that characterize Kav in general

Stress and metathesis as well as loss of contrasts has made Kav one of the less conservative languages in its phonology. It shares little in its phonological development with other extant Formosan languages, but probably did share innovations with the now extinct languages, Basay and Trobiawan, which were spoken in the northeast corner of Taiwan, near where Kav was spoken before 1840.

B62.1.1 Loss of a syllable by syncope

PAn roots may lose one or two syllables in their development to Kav: (1) by the loss of the penult, (2) by loss of the antepenult, or (3) by loss of the penult and the antepenult or (4) by loss of the final syllable.

B62.1.11 Loss of the penult

*e > Ø in the penult in almost all cases, in disyllabic as well as in trisyllabic roots. The following examples show loss of *e in disyllabic roots:

*beɣac > *bɣas* 'hulled rice' *depa > *zpi* 'fathom' *lepaw 'hut' > *rpaw* 'house'

There are exceptions in disyllabic roots. After a [ʔ] that developed initially (§B62.1.5), *ʔe > /i/:

*łecuŋ > *insung* 'mortar' (< *ʔensuŋ < *ełcuŋ [§B62.1.3]) *qełeb >*ineb* 'close' *qebel > *q-iɣeb* 'smoke' (< *ʔeɣeb < *ʔebeɣ < *ʔebel)

The *i in the penult followed by *y- onset in the final syllable was elided as well:

*peniyu > *penu* 'sea turtle' (< *penyu)

The following root remains disyllabic because it reflects a petrified instrumental passive prefix *ise-. There was metathesis of the vowel of the prefix and the vowel of the root, and the antepenult was lost by apocope:

*kepit + *ise- > *qipit* 'hold under a ' (< *ekipit < *ikepit < *isekepit)

For the other exceptions, there is no good explanation:

*becuɣ > *bisuɣ* 'sated' *beɣek 'pig' > *burek* 'young of cow, pig' *telu > *turu* 'three'

There are no exceptions for the loss of *e in the penult of trisyllabic roots:

*baɣeqaŋ > *ɣzim* 'molar' (< *zɣim < *dɣim [§B62.1.13] < *deɣiim [§§B62.2.3] < *deɣaʔam [§B62.3.14] < *deɣaqam < *daɣeqam < *baɣeqam[2]) *iseguŋ > *unung* 'nose'

In the following case, however, metathesis took place before syncope of penultimate *e:

*qaselu > *saɣu* 'pestle' (< *qesalu [§B62.1.12])

In many cases, the loss of *e in the penult leads to the development of clusters, which most frequently underwent assimilation (§B62.1.4):

*baŋesis > *bangsis* 'fragrant' *baqesiŋ > *bassing* 'sneeze' *saɣejał 'ladder' > *sazzan* 'bridge' *tuqelał > *tiɣɣan* 'bone'

In cases of trisyllabic roots where the penult and the final syllable contracted after the loss of the *h-onset of the final syllable, the resulting form was disyllabic. If the nucleus of the initial syllable of the resulting root was *e, it was lost by the rule given in the first paragraph of this section above:

*betihec > *btis* 'calf' (< *betis < *beties [§B62.1.13])

In one case the *a of the penult that developed after elision of the antepenult was lost. there is no explanation:

*aqetih > *ʔtell* (< *ʔti < *qti < *aqti)

Sporadically, *u of the penult in trisyllabic forms is lost (that is, in trisyllabic roots or in affixed disyllabic forms):

*bacuheq > *qi-basi* 'wash' (< *qi-baceq) *bułi > *mu-nbi* 'hide'

B62.1.12 Loss of the antepenult

In the case of trisyllabic roots with *a or *i as the nucleus of the penult and most often those with *u as the nucleus of the penult, the antepenult is lost.

*aluga > *p-runa* 'paddle' *biceqak > *siaq* 'split apart slightly' (< *beciqak [B62.1.3]) *dalukap 'sole' > *ɣuqap* 'palm, sole' *juɣami > *ɣami* 'straw' *leqacem > *-asim* (*kam-asim* 'sour orange' *kama* 'orange') *qalima > *rima* 'hand' *qaniŋu > *ningu* 'shadow, reflection'

In one case, penultimate *i changed to /e/ (as is the case in all the cognates in languages outside of the Tsouic group) and became lost. The coda of the first syllable was also lost in CC simplification, although CC simplification otherwise did not take place (§B62.1.4). The form probably spread secondarily.

*qaɣicam 'plant with reedlike stem' > *isam* 'stalk of cogon grass: *Imperata cylindrica*' (< *qasam (§B62.2.3) < *qaɣsam < *qaɣecam)

There are three cases of trisyllabic roots in which the initial consonant of the root is retained. The first two of these forms are not directly inherited, and the third may also be a borrowing:

*palisi > *prisin* 'taboo' (the irregular /n/ also occurs in the Am cognate) *guɣita > *qlita* 'octopus' (/l/ is not the regular reflex of *ɣ) *kałuskus > *qnukus* 'fingernail'

---

[2] See the commentary to the entry *baɣeqaŋ in the glossary for an explanation of the irregular initial and final of this root.

B62.1.13 Contraction of vowels

The sequence *ie that developed by loss of medial *h or *q is contracted to /i/. There is only one example:

*betihec > *btis* 'calf'

In another case, where the sequence arose by loss of *q, *ie contracts to /u/. There is no explanation for the two outcomes.

*tiqeɣab 'belch' > *tuab* 'cough'

Like vowels contract:

*buluq > *bul* 'k.o. thin bamboo' (< *buul < *buqul [§B62.1.3]) *ɣabihi > *ɣabi* 'evening' *baɣeqaŋ > *ɣzim* 'molar' (< *zɣim < *dɣim [§B62.1.13] < *deɣiim [§§B62.2.3] < *deɣaʔam [§B62.3.14] < *deɣaqam < *daɣeqam < *baɣeqam[2])

B62.1.2 Disyllabization of monosyllabic roots

Kav, like most of the An languages (and unlike Pa and Pu), disyllabized monosyllabic roots inherited from PAn (§A3.6.2) except in the case of enclitics.[3] Disyllabization was effected by (1) doubling or reduplicating the monosyllabic root, (2) petrifying a prefix, (3) doubling the coda, or (4) adding a prothetic vowel.

(1) Examples of reduplication and doubling:

*ba > *baba* 'carry on back' *bit 'carry in fingers' > *bibit* 'pull on ears'

(2) Examples of disyllabization by petrifaction of an affix:

*lin > *ta-rin* 'move' *pun > *sa-pun* 'gather' (*sa- is a variant of the instrumental passive prefix*si-/*ise-) *teb > *q-teb* 'cut off' (< *ka-teb)[4]

(3) When the coda is doubled, the root is bimoraic but probably not disyllabic:

*baŋ 'excavated, hollowed out' > *bangng* 'irrigation canal' *kan > *qann* 'eat' *pan > *pann* 'bait'

(4) Examples of disyllabization by adding a prothetic vowel:

*daɬ > *ʔzan* 'old' (< *ʔedan < *edan)

In a few cases Kav has retained a monosyllabic root. These are forms that always occur affixed:

*ɣik > *m-ɣik* 'thresh by trampling' *tup > *t-m-ub* 'cover' (/-b/ arose by contamination. Cf. the commentary to *tup in glossary.)

B62.1.21 Epenthetic vowels in doubled monosyllabic roots

There is one case where Kav retains the epenthetic vowel that developed in penultimate position in doubled monosyllabic roots (§A3.6.1, 2nd¶). Normally, the *e that developed between the two elements in doubled monosyllabic roots was lost (§B62.1.11), but in the following case an *i developed as the epenthetic vowel:

---

[3] However, monosyllabic roots have developed in contemporary Kav by the processes of penult elision of disyllabic roots, discussed in §B62.1.11.

[4] In this case, the root was again reduced to a monosyllable when the penult was weakened (cf. the footnote to *btu* 'stone' given in §B62.2.3, end).

*tuketuk 'summit, top' > *tkituk* 'top of mountain'

B62.1.3 Metathesis

A large number of roots evince metathesis directly or evince this process indirectly through the effects that it had. First, in trisyllabic roots where the first two syllables were *(C)ise and *(C)ice, metathesis takes place as in many of the Formosan languages (§A3.5.4):

*biceqak > *m-siaq* 'split (< *besiak < *beciqak) *iseyup > *m-siup* 'blow' (< *esiyup) *kepit + *ise- > *qipit* 'hold under arm' (< *ekipit < *ikepit < *isekepit) *qiteluɣ > *tiɣuɣ* 'egg'

Other cases of metathesis involved *ɣ, *l, or a glottal stop that developed (§§B62.1.5):

*baɣeqaŋ > *ɣzim* 'molar' (< *zɣim < *dɣim [§B62.1.13] < *deɣiim [§§B62.2.3] < *deɣaʔam [§B62.3.14] < *deɣaqam < *daɣeqam < *baɣeqam[2]) *balug > *banur* 'pigeon' (< *barun) *buluq > *bul* 'k.o. thin bamboo' (< *buqul) *damaɣ 'light, torch' > *ɣamaz* 'fire' (*zamaɣ* also attested) *daqaɬi > *ʔlan* 'day' (*qlan < *qnal < *qnai < *qaɬi) *jaɣum > *razum* 'needle' *jalan > *razan* 'road' *jiɣuc > *m-ruzis* 'bathe' (< *ɣujic) *ludaq 'spit' > *m-ɣzuaq* 'belch' *mula > *m-ruma* 'to plant' *qaciɬ > *assim* 'salt' (< *aʔsim < *ʔasim) *qebel > *q-iɣeb* 'smoke' *qusalipan > *ɣusipan* 'centipede' (< *qalusipan) *tiŋadaq > *tiazang* 'look upward' *tuduɣ 'sleep' > *m-turuz* 'doze' *tiheɬaw > *tngiraw* 'clear (water)' (< *tiŋraw [§B62.1.4, end] < *tiqɬaw) *wagay 'separate' > *massaɣiway* 'divorce' (< *massi-ɣaway < *massi-waɣay [< Am *waray* 'separate quarreling parties'])

Metathesis left a trace in the the effects of a glottal stop that developed from initial vowel (§§B62.1.4, B62.1.5):

*ica > *issa* 'one' (<*iʔsa < *ʔisa)

Metathesis also took place in some forms that had or developed nasal onsets on one of their syllables:

*buɬi > *mu-nbi* 'hidden' (< *mu-bni) *ɣinu 'winnow' > *niniɣ* 'filter' (< *niniɣu < *niɣu) *ɣuqaɬay > *ɣunanay* 'male' (< *ɣuannay < *ɣuaʔnay < *ɣuaqnay) *qagan > *nangan* 'name' (< *ŋanan < *ŋagan [§A3.7.1]) *ɬecuŋ > *insung* 'mortar' (< *ʔensung [§B62.2.2] < *ʔencuŋ) *ɬisebic > *impis* 'thin (< *nipis < *ɬispic < *ɬisbic)

B62.1.4 Assimilation

In trisyllabic roots, there is rightward assimilation when CCs develop after penultimate vowel loss through syncopation (§B62.1.1ff.):

*jakejak > *zazzek* 'step on' (/e/ of the final syllable is unexplained) *saɣejaɬ 'ladder' > *sazzan* 'bridge' *tacetac > *tattas* 'rent, ripped'

I assume a *ɣ infix, where the reflex of *ɣ was assimilated to the following consonant in the following form:

*batu > *battu* 'throw' (< *baɣtu)

This rule precedes the loss of *q (§B62.3.14), for the *q is assimilated to the following consonant. First *q > *ʔ; then *ʔ is assimilated to the following C:

*baqesiŋ > *bassing* 'sneeze' (< *baʔsiŋ < *baqsiŋ) *qetaq > *matti* 'raw' (< *maʔtaʔ < *ma-qetaq) *tuqelaɬ > *tiɣɣan* 'bone'

Clusters consisiting of *qC that developed in disyllabic roots from metathesis also assimilate the *q to the following C (via *ʔ):

*qaciɬ > *assim* 'salt' (< *aʔsim < *aqsim (§B62.1.3)

Clusters consisting of a nasal followed by a consonant are not assimilated, however:

*baŋesis > *bangsis* 'fragrant'

The rule does not hold in the case of trisyllabic roots that lose the antepenult (§B62.1.12): first the antepenult is lost, and then if the vowel of the penult is *e, it is lost. Assimilation does not take place in disyllabic roots when *e of the penult is lost:

*baɣeqaŋ > *ɣzim* 'molar' (< *zɣim < *dɣim [§B62.1.13] < *deɣiim [§§B62.2.3] < *deɣaʔam [§B62.3.14] < *deɣaqam < *daɣeqam < *baɣeqam[2]) *betihec > *btis* 'calf' (< *betis < *beties [§B62.1.13])

Roots of three syllables or more that had penultimate syllables consisting of *se lost the *s without a trace (§B62.3.2, 4th¶).
In one case, in a cluster containing *ɣ, assimilation did not take place, and further *ɣ is lost. There is no explanation:

*qaɣicam 'plant with reedlike stem' > *isam* 'stalk of cogon grass: *Imperata cylindrica*' (< *qasam [§B62.2.3]) < *qaɣsam < *qaɣecam)

The word for 'star' had an idiosyncratic development. It must be borrowed, but the source is unknown. The first two syllables were treated like an independent word, and there was juncture before the suffix *-an*:

*bituq-an > *buqti-an > *buʔtel-an > *burtellan* 'star' (The assimilation of *ʔ to /r/ is idiosyncratic and unexplained. The change of *-i > /el/ is paralleled by the examples of §B62.2.1. The doubling of the /l/ is due to the /ʔ/ in the preceding syllable.)

The following form manifests dissimilation of *h from the following consonants similar to the case of *q in the word for 'star', described immediately preceding (that is, *q > /r/). The *ɬ also changes to /ŋ/, rather than to its normal development /n/ (§B62.3.44).

*tiheɬaw > *tngiraw* 'clear (water)' (< *tiŋraw < *tiqɬaw)

B62.1.5 Insertion of glottal stop in pre-Kav

There is evidence in the reflexes of *a (§B62.2.3) that dialectally in pre-Kav a glottal stop was inserted as onset to word-initial syllables with a beginning vowel and as coda to word-final syllables that had no other coda.

*aku > *iku* 'I' (< *ʔiku < *ʔaku) *buka 'open' > *buki* 'untie' (< *bukaʔ) *depa > *zpi* 'fathom' (< *zpaʔ) (also *mu-zpa* 'to measure by span' *pula 'brown' > *puri* 'green'

Further evidence of an earlier glottal onset in word-initial position is furnished by cases of metathesis:

*ica > *issa* 'one' (< *iʔsa < *ʔisa)

However, glottal stop insertion was a dialectal feature and did not affect the majority of the forms that are attested in current Kav, nor is it a feature of current Kav. However, words that earlier had initial vowel where the vowel got lost by syncope are an exception: disyllabic roots that earlier had initial vowel in the penult developed an initial /ʔ/and lost the vowel. If the onset of the final syllable was a liquid, the /ʔ/ may assimilate to the following liquid forming a double initial consonant:

*enem > *ʔnem* or *nnem* 'six' *iseci > *ʔsi* 'meat' *semay > *ʔmay* or *mmay* 'cooked rice' (loss of initial *s unexplained)

This rule also holds for disyllabic roots (or roots that developed into disyllabic roots) beginning in a *q that was lost:

*daqaɬi > *ʔlan* or *llan* 'day' (*qlan < *qnal [§B62.2.1] < *qnai < *qaɬi) *qetut > *ʔtut* 'break wind' *aqetih > *ʔtell* (< *ʔti < *qti [§B62.1.11, end]) < *aqti)

It should be noted that the /ʔ/ occurs preconsonantally only in word-initial position. Medially—i.e., after a prefix, it assimilates to the following consonant:

*aqetih > *ʔtell-i* 'decrease the water'(imperative) *ma-ttel* 'dry' (adjective)

However, a root-initial glottal stop (before a vowel) is variably retained after a vowel-final prefix. That is, the /ʔ/ may be dropped in rapid-speech forms:

ibu 'ashes' (< *ʔibu < *qabu) + *qa-an* (noun forming affix referring to location) > *qaʔibuan/qaybuan* 'kitchen, ash-tray'

B62.2 Vowels and diphthongs

Kav has inherited the four vowels and the diphthongs of PAn, listed in §B62.0. *e is written /e/ and pronounced [ə].

B62.2.1 *i

When not syncopated, *i > /i/:

*bali > *bari* 'wind' *iluɣ > *iɣuɣ* 'stream' *ɬisebic > *impis* 'thin'

In six cases, final *-i or *-i that developed after loss of final *q or *h became /-el/ after C, /-l/ after a vowel, and /ll/ after *q.[5] This rule is operative only in roots with *q-, *t-, *l-, or *ɬ-onset of the final syllable. These are well-attested forms of basic vocabulary, the rule is nearly exceptionless,[6] and the change can be motivated.[7] Tsuchida 2006 also deals with the

---

[5] We assume that *q assimilated to the following *l to account for suffixed derivatives of the root *tal* that show a geminate /ll/: *qattallan* 'toilet (lit. place for feces)' (< *kaʔtaʔlan < *kataʔlan < *kataqlan < *kataqian—*ql > *ʔl [§B62.3.14] > /ll/ [§B62.1.4, end]). (I assume also that the prefix *ka- developed a [ʔ] coda, as evidenced by the geminated /t/.)

[6] There are three exceptions, only the first of which is unexplained. In the second case, metathesis took place before the change was in effect, and the third case is a form that is a learned borrowing throughout the An area:

*bali > *bari* 'wind' *buɬi 'hidden' > *mu-nbi* 'hide, put away' *lali > *tu-rani* 'nose flute'

[7] This change involved all consonants articulated with the tip and the blade of the tongue, attested before *i in root-final syllable (except the reflex of *n, which probably had a retroflexed articulation [as opposed to the reflex of *ɬ]). The change occurred after the loss of *q, which caused a *y-transition to develop, but before *ɬ merged with *n.

Kav reflexes of *i. There he attributes the /l/ reflex to influence from the extinct Basay language, which was spoken adjacent to the Kavalan area, just to the north, and reflects *i with /c/ in certain environments.[8] However, as stated here, this rule holds water for Kav. In other words, both Kav and Basay made this innovation, but it is not known whether the change took place in Basay and spread to Kav, or vice versa. It could also be a change that remounts to proto-Kavalan–Basay.

*daqaɬi > *llan* 'day' (*qlan < *qnal < *qnai < *qaɬi) *aqetih > *ʔell* 'ebb' *taqi > *tal* 'feces' (< *tall (§B62.0, end) < *taʔl) *tinaqi > *tnal* 'intestines' *gali > *kall-i* 'dig, excavate (imperative)' (< *kalel-i) *piliq > *pamill-i* 'choose (imperative)' (< *p-am-ilel-i)

There is also one case of medial *y that is reflected with /l/:[9]

*qayam > *alam* 'bird'

B62.2.2 *e

*e was lost in the penult by syncope in most roots and words, with some exceptions. There were also some other environments in which *e was syncopated. (Cf. the discussion in §B62.1.11 for examples.) *e > /i/ when it is adjacent to *ʔ (< *q or a glottal stop that developed in syllable-initial position [§B62.1.5]):

*bacuheq > *qi-basi* 'wash' (< *ki-baceq [§B62.1.11, end) *luseq > *ɣusi* 'tears' *puteq > *puti* 'secretion from eye' *ɬecuŋ > *insung* 'mortar' (< *ʔensuŋ < *eɬcuŋ (§B62.1.3]) *qebel > *q-iɣeb* 'smoke' (< *ʔeɣeb < *ʔebeɣ < *ʔebel) *qeɬeb > *ineb* 'close'

Otherwise (in final syllables or in doubled monosyllabic roots), *e > /e/:

*bedebed > *berber* 'wind' *buɣes > *buɣes* 'spurt water from mouth'

There are a few exceptions. In the following examples, *e is reflected with /u/. The first two are borrowings and show other irregularities. *tebuc also has an unexplained loss of the initial *t-. The other forms are basic vocabulary, and there is no good explanation for them.

*buhet 'squirrel' > *buɣut* 'flying squirrel' (/ɣ/ irregular as well [< Am *fohet* 'squirrel']) *qulec > *qulus* 'clothing' (/q/ is irregular as well [< Squliq At *lukus* 'clothing']) *cepecep > *s-um-upsup* 'suck' *iseguŋ > *unung* 'nose' *tebuc > *ubus* 'redeem' *telu > *turu* 'three'

In the following examples, *e is reflected with /i/ even though it was not adjacent to [ʔ]. The word for 'nettle' is clearly a borrowing, and 'sour' is probably contaminated by *assim* 'salty'.

---

8 Basay cognates of these forms, where they are attested, reflect Basay /c/, which was probably an affricate or a palatalized stop, articulated with the front part of the tongue. This /c/ reflex resulted from an earlier palatalization of the preceding consonants, which had developed before *-i. This is a hypothesis: in fact, we do not know the precise sequence of events in Basay, nor the precise phonetic nature of this phoneme in Basay. Nor have I been able to determine if the development to /c/ in Basay occurred in exactly the analogous environments to the development of /l/, etc. from /i/ in Kav.

9 There is no explanation of where this form comes from. /l/ is not the normal reflex of intervocalic *y (§62.3.45). This is not likely to be a borrowing from Basay, for **acam* 'bird' is not attested in Basay. The word for 'bird' was elicited in the Basay list and recorded as *manuk*. Of course there could have been a form **acam*, which went out of use. In any case, it was not elicited, and if *acam had been a normal Basay form, it would have been recorded. Kav *alam* could possibly be a borrowing from Ishbukun Bunun, where the reflex is *ʔaðam* 'bird' (although admittedly, Ishbukun is not spoken in an area adjacent to Kav).

In the case of *ɣisis* 'nit', *e was changed to /i/ before the *ʔ (< *q) was lost. There is no explanation for the /i/ in *bisuɣ* 'sated'.

*becuɣ > *bisuɣ* 'sated' *leqacem > *kam-asim* 'sour orange' (*kama* 'orange') *liceqes < *ɣisis* 'nit' (< *lisiʔis) *lateŋ > *prating* 'stinging nettle'

B62.2.3 *a

*a > /a/ except in two environments: (1) when syncopated in the antepenult (§B62.1.12) and (2) when adjacent to *ʔ (which subsequently became lost—that is, *ʔ < *q or that developed before a syllable-initial vowel), in which case *a > /i/. This rule mirrors the rule of the first paragraph of §B62.2.2, immediately preceding. First, examples where *a > a:

*saɣejaɬ 'ladder' > *sazzan* 'bridge' *tawa > *tawa* 'laugh'

Examples of *a > /i/ adjacent to *ʔ (< *q or from syllable-initial vowel):

*aku > *iku* 'I' (< *ʔaku) *qabu > *ibu* 'ashes' *ma-qetaq > *matti* 'raw'

This rule does not hold if the *a in the final syllable follows an /i/ in the penult:

*siwaq > *smi-siwa* 'make a thin cut'

We assume that there was glottal stop insertion in word-final position variably to account for the /i/ reflex in the following forms. The glottal stop must have been variable (or dialectal) to account for the fact that *-a in final position only sometimes changes to /i/:

*buka 'open' > *buki* 'untie' (< *bukaʔ) *depa > *zpi* 'fathom' (< *zpaʔ < *depaʔ) (also *mu-zpa* 'to measure by span') *pula 'brown' > *puri* 'green'

In one case, *a in the penult of a disyllabic root is lost. This possibly developed in a suffixed form in which case the *a would have appeared in the antepenult and become weakened by the rule of §B62.1.12.[10] In that case, subsequently the weakened allomorph of the root was generalized:[11]

*batu > *btu* 'stone'

B62.2.4 *u

Except when syncopated in the antepenult (§B62.1.12), *u > /u/ with a few exceptions:

*lutuŋ > *ɣutung* 'monkey' *qusalipan > *ɣusipan* 'centipede' (< *lusipan < *qalusipan)

In four cases, *u is reflected with /i/. There is no explanation other than that these are borrowed from an unknown source. It should be noted that the reflex of *cucu also shows /i/ in the penult in the extinct Basay language.

*cucu > *sisu* 'breast' *cudu > *sizu* 'spoon' *qudip > *izip* 'life' *tuqelaɬ > *tiɣɣan* 'bone'

In two cases, where the reflex is doubled or reduplicated, a final syllable consisting of /u/ is lost:

---

[10] The initial consonant of the root was retained exceptionally (§B62.1.12). This can be explained by a hypothesis to the effect that too much of the root would have been lost if the initial consonant had not been retained.

[11] An alternative hypothesis is that this is a rapid-speech form that became generalized. Support is offered by the form *mti* 'raw', the short form of *matti* 'raw', which also loses the /a/ of the penult.

*ɣinu 'winnow' > *niniɣ* 'filter' (< *niniɣu < *niɣu [§B62.1.3]) *layehu > *m-rayray* 'withered' *tuɬuh 'roast, burn s.t.' > *tutun* 'burn'

B62.2.5 Diphthongs

The diphthongs remained unchanged.

*aw > /aw/:

*buɣaw > *buɣaw* 'chase, drive' *laŋaw > *rangaw* 'a fly'

*iw > /iw/:

*laɣiw 'flee' > *ɣaɣiw* 'run' *ciciw 'chick' > *sisiw* 'young of birds and small animals'

In the case of *waɬiw, the *i is absorbed by the *ɬ and the final *w is vocalized, as is the case of cognates in many languages:

*waɬiw > *wanu* 'honeybee, honey'

*ay > /ay/:

*patay > *patay* 'dead *quway > *uway* 'rattan''

*uy > /uy/:

*babuy 'wild pig' > *babuy* 'pig' *ɬaŋuy > *m-nanguy* 'swim'

B62.3 Consonants

The following chart shows the Kav reflexes of the PAn consonants:

CHART TWO. DEVELOPMENT OF THE KAVALAN CONSONANTS FROM PAN

PAn	Kav	PAn	Kav
p	*p*	g	*k-,- n-, -n*
t	*t*	ɣ	*ɣ*
k	*k, q*	l	*r, ɣ*
q	*∅*	ɬ	*n*
h	*∅*	m, n	*m, n*
c,s	*s*	ŋ	*ng*
b	*b*	w	*w*
d, j	*z*	y	*y*

B62.3.1 Voiceless consonants

B62.3.11 *p

*p remained /p/ in all positions:

*pakepak > *p-m-aqpaq* 'flap wings' *pagay > *panay* 'rice plant' *depa 'a fathom' > *mu-zpa* 'measure by the span' *gapegap > *kapkap* 'feel grope'

In one case, *p is reflected with *b. The final /-d/ in this form is irregular as well, and the word must be a borrowing from an unknown source:

*puceg > *bused* 'navel'

B62.3.12 *t

*t remains /t/ in almost all cases:

*taqis > *tais* 'sew' *kutu > *qutu* 'louse' *mata > *mata* 'eye' *sakut > *saqut* 'transport'

In one case, an initial *t is reflected by /n/. This may well be the petrification of a nasalized form (§A3.7.1):

*tukub > *nukub* 'cover'

In the following case, the initial syllable of the Kav reflex does not correspond to the initial syllable of the cognates. There is no explanation:

*tebuc > *ubus* 'redeem'

The following example has many irregularities and may not be connected with the PAn form, but if it is, it is borrowed from an unknown source:

*ɬatad > *nasan* 'area outside of house'

B62.3.13 *k

*k split into two phonemes: /k/ and /q/, where /k/ is stopped further front than /q/. In general, /k/ is reflected before or after /i/ and /e/, and /q/, otherwise. However, there are exceptions to this distribution such that /k/ and /q/ contrast.

(1) Adjacent to *i or /i/ that developed from *a, *k > /k/:

*kilat > *kilat* 'bright' but *qmilat* 'glitter' (< *kumilat) *tik > *tiktik* 'tatoo' *aku > *iku* 'I'

However *k > *q after *a, even though /i/ follows:

*daki > *zaqi* 'grime on skin' *dakis > *zaqis* 'climb'

The following are exceptions. They reflect /q/ adjacent to /i/:

*bitik 'spring, jerk' > *btiq* 'go off with a jerk' *kita > *qita* 'see' (This is probably a generalization of the allomorph that occurred before the infix *-um-: *mqita* 'see' [< *qumita]' *pikepik 'slap lightly' > *piqpiq* 'clap hands, flap wings' (Possibly there is contamination with *paqpaq* 'flap wings'.)

(2) Adjacent to *e that was not syncopated—i.e., before or after *e in final syllables, *k > /k/:

*sagek 'sniff, smell' > *m-sanek* 'smell bad' *pekepek 'beat' > *pekpek* 'hit with a stick' *tikep > *tkep* 'deadfall trap'

However, a preceding /u/ causes the reflex to be /q/:

*bukes > *buqes* 'hair on head' *tukej > *tuqed* 'prop, support'

There are cases of *k before /e/ that are affected by contamination with words of similar meaning:

*keb 'cover' > *qebqeb* 'k.o. bamboo lattice work to cover chickens' (contaminated by *qubqub* 'cage')

(3) Adjacent to /a/, *k > /q/:

*dalukap 'sole' > *ɣuqap* 'palm, sole' *biceqak > *m-siaq* 'split'

There are a few exceptions that evince /k/ instead of /q/ adjacent to /a/. Most of them have other irregularities as well:

*dakat > *ɣakat* 'step, step over' *kalekal 'dig' > *karkar* 'weed with hoe' *cakecak 'chop' > *s-em-aksak* 'chop wood with axe' *taketak 'chop, fell' > *taktak* 'chop into small pieces' (semantic contamination with *saksak* 'chop with axe') *upak 'bark' > *tumpak* (< *ta-+*um+*upak[12]) 'peel, pare'

(4) Adjacent to /u/, *k > /q/:

*kutu > *qutu* 'louse' *bukul 'knob-shaped protrusion' > *buqul* 'joint, knot in wood' *busuk > *busuq* 'drunk'

If the *k was after *i, the reflex is /k/, even though it is followed by /u/:

*ciku > *siku* 'elbow' *likuj 'back' > *m-rikuz* 'do too late'

There are some exceptions that evince /k/ instead of /q/ adjacent to /u/:

*kuwaw 'k.o. large bird' > *kwaw* 'k.o. hawk' *tukub > *nukub* 'cover' *tuketuk > *tkituk* 'top, summit'

B62.3.14 *q

*q > *ʔ, which disappeared in most cases:

*biceqak > m-siak 'split' *daqis 'forehead' > *zais* 'face' *ɣiq 'sword grass' > *ɣiɣi* 'saw' *kuq 'bend' > *pi-ku* 'bend low'

*q left traces adjacent to *e and *a in that these phonemes became /i/ (§§B62.2.2, B62.2.3):

*qabu > *ibu* 'ashes' *luseq > rusi 'tears'

/ʔ/ also remained word initially in disyllabic roots with a penult consisting of *e or with monosyllabic roots that disyllabized by addition of a prothetic *e (§B62.1.2(4)). The *e that was inherited or had developed was lost:

*daɬ > *ʔzan* 'old' (< *ʔedan < *edan)

*q also left traces when it was the onset of the penult in metathesized disyllabic roots or in trisyllabic roots that were disyllabized by the loss of the penult (§B62.1.11). The *q > *ʔ, which was subsequently assimilated to the onset of following syllable (§B62.1.4):

*baqesiŋ > *bassing* 'sneeze' *qaciɬ > *assim* 'salt' (< *aʔsim < *aqsim [§B62.1.3]) *qetaq > *matti* 'raw' (< *maʔtaʔ < *ma-qetaq) *tuqelaɬ > *tiɣɣan* 'bone'

In the following form, the *ʔ was lost and did not assimilate to the onset of the final syllable. There is no explanation:[13]

*qaselu > *saɣu* 'pestle' (< *saʔelu < *saqelu)

The following form developed a *ʔn cluster because of metathesis:

*ɣuqaɬay > *ɣunanay* 'male' (< *ɣuannay < *ɣuaʔnay < *ɣuaqnay)

---

[12] Cf. §B62.1.11, end, for loss of *u in the penult.

[13] It might be that *ʔ was lost after *a before *ɣ, but not after other vowels or before other consonants. That would account for the single medial consonant in *saɣu* 'pestle' but doubled medial consonants in *tiɣɣan* 'bone' and in *ɣunanay* 'male' (< *ɣuannay < *ɣuaʔnay) However, there is no confirmatory evidence. A more likely hypothesis is that simplification of doubled consonants is a variable rule, and *saɣu* is from earlier *saɣɣu. Confirmation is offered by the variant *mti* 'raw', which occurs as well as *matti* 'raw'.

In a few forms, *-q is reflected with /-q/. These forms could be borrowings from another language, where *-q is reflected with /-q/ or occasionally /-k/:[14]

*baɣaq > *balaq* 'lungs' (Cf. At Squliq *balak* 'lungs') *buwaq > *buiq* 'bloom'[15] *ludaq > *m-ɣzuaq* 'belch' (cf. Pai *ludjaq* 'spit')

In the following form, /-q/ is accreted on the root, although the PAn etymon is reconstructed with *-h:

*betuh 'blister, explode' > *btuq* 'explode' (Squliq At *bsuh* 'callus')

In two cases,*-q is reflected with /-ɣ/. The source of the /-ɣ/ is unknown. The second example may unconnected with the PAn etymon:

*butuq 'genitals' > *butuɣ* 'testicles' *peɬuq > *puniɣ* 'full' (possibly, < *puniʔ < *puneq)

B62.3.2 *h, *s, *c

*h was lost without a trace. *s and *c merged to become /s/ in most cases:

*caleŋ-en > *saɣngen* 'pine' *ciciw 'chick' > *sisiw* 'young of small animals or birds' *cucu > *sisu* 'breast' *ica > *issa* 'one' (< *iʔsa < *ʔisa <*isa) *paca > *pasa* 'go toward' *ɣamec 'crush and mix in hands' > *ɣames* 'mix with both hands'

Note, however, that *c assimilated to the following C in clusters (§B62.1.4).
The following form replaced *c- with *q on the analogy of a root with similar meaning beginning in /qa-/:

*caɣup > *qaɣup* 'scoop up with cupped hands' (cf. *qaɣus* 'scoop up sand and the like')

Reflexes of *s:

*sebaɬ > *sban* 'carrying cloth for child' *baŋesis > *bangsis* 'fragrant' *tusud > *tusuz* 'knee' *taqis > *tais* 'sew'

In roots of three or more syllables, *s-onset of the penult before *e is lost:

*iseci 'contents, flesh' > *ʔsi* 'meat' (loss of *i unexplained)[16] *ɬisebic > *impis* 'slender' (< *nipis < *ɬispis) *qiseɬep > *ma-inep* 'sleep' *iseguŋ > *unung* 'nose' (initial /u/ unexplained) *kaɬusekus > *qnuqus* 'fingernail'

In the following forms, metathesis prevented the loss of *s:

*iseyup > *siup* 'blow' (< *esiyup) *qaselu > *saɣu* 'pestle' (< *saqeɣu)

The following disyllabic root lost the *s onset of the penult. There is no explanation. The form may be a borrowed or possibly it had an unidentified prefix, lost after the loss of *s.

*semay > *ʔmay* 'cooked rice' (< *emay)

---

[14] Possible sources could be Atayal, Bunun, or Paiwan, where *-q is reflected as a postvelar stop, but cognates are not always attested in all three of these languages. However, cognates of all of these forms are attested in Paiwan, which currently is located at a great distance from Kav. There could be another source as well if the borrowing took place before *q changed from a postvelar stop in that other source.

[15] This may be from Bunun, where *puaq* means 'bloom' and *buaq* refers to a specific flower. Everywhere else, reflexes of *buwaq mean 'fruit' (or 'k.o. fruit').

[16] Cf. the discussion of the loss of *a in *btu* 'stone' (< *batu) in the footnote to §B62.2.3.

The following form retained the *s-onset of the penult on analogy with other forms with similar meaning:

*kusekus > *qusqus* 'scrape, scratch' (cf. *qisqis* 'scrape' < *kicekic)

B62.3.3 Voiced stops in Kav

There is a tendency to weaken the voiced consonants. *b, *d, *j become fricatives. *ɣ remained unchanged or > /r/.

B62.3.31 *b

*b > /b/, pronounced []:

*babaw > *babaw* 'above' *betihec > *btis* 'calf' *qabu > *ibu* 'ashes' *iceɣab > *siɣab* 'yesterday' *qateb > *iteb* 'deadfall trap'

The only exception is in the antepenult of a trisyllabic root that had been lost by apocope (§B62.1.12).

B62.3.32 *d *j

*d and *j for the most part merged and became /z/:

*dasedas > *zaszas* 'chest' *duma > *zuma* 'other' *qudip 'alive' > *izip* 'life' *laduŋ > *razung* 'shade' *jalan > *razan* 'road, path' (< *lajan [§B62.1.3]) *qujał > *uzan* 'rain' *kuj > *kukuz* 'lower part of leg'

There are several exceptions in the reflexes of *d and one exception in the reflex of *j. In a few cases *d is reflected with /ɣ/. In others, *d and *j are reflected with /l/. There is no explanation:

*bedec > *bles* 'belly'[17] *dakat > *ɣakat* 'step' *daluc > *m-lalus* 'slide off' *dilaq > *rilam* 'tongue' (metathesis and unexplained /-m/) *qadep 'front, facing side' > *ngaɣep* 'horizontally placed'(< *ŋadep [§A3.7.1]) *tidem > *tlem* 'dark' (loss of /i/ unexplained) *tukej > *tuqel* 'prop, support'

There are other unexplained irregularities. In the case of the following form, the unexplained initial may have been contaminated with *banaw* 'wash':

*danaw > *banaw* 'lake, pond'

In one case, the reflex shows nasalization:

*dem 'dark' > *mra-nem* 'cloudy' (also *mɣi-zemzem* 'dim', which reflects *d directly)

Irregularities in other forms may have come about through contamination, but the source is unknown:

*diɣi > *qiɣi* 'stand' *tuduq > *tulel* 'leak, drip'[18]

---

[17] Note that this form evinces /l/ rather than /ɣ/, even though the *l was adjacent to *e. There is no explanation.

[18] A possible explanation for *tulel* is that it developed *i in the final syllable (cf. §B62.2.4, 2nd¶ for other cases of *u > /i/), and subsequently *-i > /el/ (§62.2.1, 2nd¶). But nevertheless, the /l/ (< *d) remains unexplained, as in the examples of the second paragraph of this section.

B62.3.33 *g

*g became voiceless when initial in monosyllabic roots or onset of the penult or earlier and merged with *k-, as in many An languages—i.e., *g- became /k-/ and /q-/.

*gaɣut 'comb' > *qaɣut* 'harrow' *gap 'feel, grope' > *kapkap* 'grope, touch to find' *gisegis > *qisqis* 'scrape off'[19]

There are two forms that manifest irregular initial consonants where cognates in other languages reflect *g-. These have possibly been reformed by contamination, or possibly they contain petrified lost prefixes:

*gaɣaŋ > *waɣaŋ* 'crab' *gumis > *umis* 'body hair'

As onset or coda of the root-final syllable, *g became nasalized[20] and moved forward, merging with *n:

*pagay > *panay* 'rice plant' *sagek 'sniff, smell' > *sanek* 'smell bad' *balug > *banur* 'pigeon' (< *barun)

There are several exceptions where *g has reflexes other than /n/. The first of these forms has doubtlessly spread from Am, as it has undergone the same semantic shift as well as the same phonological innovation (or possibly the form has spread from Kav into Am). The second also has widespread irregular cognates and seems to have spread through the An area secondarily. The other two are probably also borrowings, the first, from Atayalic and the second, from an unknown source:

*wagay 'separate > *massaɣiway* 'divorce' (< *massiɣaway < *massi-waɣay) *tugic 'incise' > *turis* 'lines' *bunag > *buqan* 'sand' (cf. At *bunaqi* 'sand') *puseg > *bused* 'navel'

B62.3.4 Continuants

B62.3.41 *ɣ

*ɣ is reflected in two ways: (1) with /ɣ/ and (2) with /r/. There are no environments that determine the occurrence of one or the other reflex, and basic vocabulary is included in both sets of reflexes. There are two possible explanations: (1) dialect mixture (i.e., *ɣ > /r/ in some dialects), (2) a change of /ɣ/ > /r/ that was not carried to completion. I have found no evidence to support one or the other of these two possibilities. The most widely attested reflex is /ɣ/ (in forty-five out of fifty-four citations that attest one or the other of these reflexes):

*ɣabihi > *ɣabi* 'evening' (also *mrabin* 'spend the night')*qaɣem > *iɣem* 'pangolin' *bucuɣ > *busuɣ* 'bow'

At least nine roots have reflexes of *ɣ with /r/:

---

[19] Note that *kapkap* and *qisqis* are irregular in that they manifest /k/, where /q/ is the regular reflex, and /q/ where /k/ is the regular reflex, respectively. The irregular reflexes are due to the influence of other forms of similar meaning.

[20] We assume that *g was articulated further forward than *ŋ, so that when it became nasalized, it was positioned to fall together with *n, rather than with *ŋ.

*beɣek 'pig' > *burek* 'young of cow or pig' *ɣapuc 'tie' > *rapus* 'come loose (knot)' *jaɣum > *razum* 'needle' *jiɣuc > *m-ruzis* 'bathe' *lawaɣ > *rawar* 'flying squirrel' *paheɣaw > *m-paraw* 'hoarse' *timuɣ > *timur* 'south wind' *tuduɣ 'sleep' > *m-turuz* 'doze' *wiɣi > *ka-wiri* 'left (side)'

Three of the roots reconstructed with *ɣ have reflexes with /l/. The first may be borrowed from Atayalic because of the /-q/ (§B62.3.14). The second may be a borrowing from Am. The source of the last form is unknown.

*baɣaq > *balaq* 'lungs' *sabaɣat > *sbalat* 'strong east/southeast wind' *guɣita > *qlita* 'octopus'

In one case, *-ɣ is reflected with /-k/. The origin of the /-k/ is unexplained:

*qapuɣ > *apuk* 'lime'

In one case, *ɣ is reflected with /z/. This is possibly a borrowing from an MP language as no other extant Formosan language shows a reflex of this root.

*łuɣ > *nuzu* 'coconut'

When *ɣ was the first element in a CC that developed by syncope of the penult, it was assimilated to the following C (§B62.1.4). *ɣ was also lost in the following form, and the preceding *i > /u/. There is no explanation:[21]

*tiqeɣab 'belch' > *tuab* 'cough'

B62.3.42 *l

*l, like *ɣ, has two reflexes: /r/ and /ɣ/. Neither of the two reflexes is heavily preponderant: we have identified thirty-four attestations that reflect *l with /r/ and twenty-two that reflect *l with /ɣ/. There is some difference in the distribution of the two reflexes: only /ɣ/ develops when *l came to be in a CC that arose from vowel syncope (§B62.1.11).[22] Further, only /ɣ/ develops when there is another /ɣ/ in the word (whether from *l or from *ɣ). These two factors of distribution leave other environments where the /l/ and /ɣ/ reflexes both occur in inherited forms of roots with *l. As in the case of the reflexes of *ɣ, there are two possible explanations: (1) dialect mixture (i.e., *l > /ɣ/ in some dialects of pre-Kavalan and /r/ in others), (2) *l > /ɣ/ > /r/, where the final step was not carried to completion.

First, examples of *l > /r/:

*likuj 'back' > *ku-rikuz* 'follow' *bali > *bari* 'wind' *bulał > *buran* 'moon' *telu > *turu* 'three' *lawaɣ > *rawar* 'flying squirrel' *kalekal 'dig' > *karkar* 'weed with hoe'

Second, examples of *l > /ɣ/:

*layaɣ > *ɣayaɣ* 'sail' *lebeŋ 'grave, bury' < *ɣbeng* 'deep below, bottom' *liceqes > *ɣisis* 'nit' *luseq > *ɣusi* 'tears' *baliga > *bɣina* 'batten of a loom' *iluɣ > *iɣuɣ* 'small stream'

---

[21] In this case the *ɣ was the second element in a CC, in which environment it may have been lost as a matter of a regular change. However, there are no other examples to support this hypothesis. Further, the change of *i to /u/ is unexplained.

[22] The one exception is *lepaw, which is reflected as *rpaw* 'house'.

There are also cases in which *l is reflected with /l/. In two cases, the *l remained /l/ because it abutted on an /l/ that developed from *i (§B62.2.1):

*galih > *kall-i* 'dig (imperative)' *piliq > *p-am-ill-i* 'choose (imperative)'

Other cases are probably borrowings. In some of the cases, the source can be identified with a high degree of certainty:

*bilaŋ > *bilang* 'count' (< Tag) *buluq > *bul* 'k.o. thin bamboo' *daluc 'slippery' > *m-lalus* 'slide off' *dilaq > *rilam* 'tongue' (< RuBd) *kilat > *kilat* 'bright, glitttering' *qilus > *klis* 'wipe after defecating' *qulec > *qulus* 'clothing' (< Squliq At *lukus* 'clothing') *tilem > *tlem* 'dark'[23]

In five cases, *l is reflected with nasals. There is no explanation:

*caluɣ 'watercourse' > *sanuɣ* 'large river' *lali > *tu-rani* 'nose flute' *lem > *mri-nemnem* 'sink' *liyus 'go around something' > *nius* 'whirlwind' *ŋalay > *ngangay* 'saliva'[24]

B62.3.43 *ɬ

*ɬ is reflected as /n/ in all positions.[25]

*ɬaŋuy > *nanguy* 'swim' *qaɬiŋu > *ningu* 'shadow *tuɬa 'eel' > *b-tuna* 'k.o. snake' *bulaɬ > *bulan* 'moon'

In three cases *ɬ is reflected with /l/ instead of /n/. These are probably loans from Am or Atayalic:[26]

*ɬiteq 'sticky sap' > *lita* 'clay' *ɬawaŋ > *lawang* 'gate' *taɬam > *talam* 'taste' (cf. At *talam* 'taste')

In one case *-ɬ is reflected as /-m/. This was possibly contaminated with the word for 'sour', *kamasim*, which contains the root *kama* 'orange plus *asim* 'sour' (< *leqasem).

*qaciɬ > *assim* 'salt'

In a second case, *ɬ is reflected with /ngɣ/. The initial is also irregular and the word is undoubtedly borrowed, but the source is unknown.

*waɬis > *bangɣis* 'fang'

B62.3.44 Nasals

*m, *n, *ŋ remained unchanged in all positions:

*mata > *mata* 'eye' *lima > *rima* 'five' *enem > *nnem* 'six' *nunuh 'breast' > *nunu* 'suck milk, nurse' *tineun > *t-um-nun* 'weave' *kan > *qann* 'eat' *ŋalay > *ngangay* 'saliva' *ɬaŋuy > *nanguy* 'swim' *qumaŋ > *umang* 'hermit crab'

---

[23] This form may possibly be derived from *tidem 'cloudy' (but not likely). The /l/ is not the regular reflex of *d (§B62.3.32).

[24] In this case, /ŋ/ possibly arose by assimilation to /ŋ/ on the left, but there is no confirmatory evidence.

[25] The sequence /ny/, which arose by elision in trisyllables (§B62.1.11), also changed to /n/:

*peniyu > *pnu* 'sea turtle'

[26] Li and Tsuchida (2006: 145) suggest Am as the source of *lita* 'clay'.

B62.3.45 *w and *y

*w remained /w/initially and medially. For *-w finally in diphthongs, see §B62.2.5.

*wanał > *ka-wanan* 'right (side)' *kawit > *pa-kawit* 'hook' *sawak > *sawak* 'waist'

When abutting on *u, /w/ is lost:

*ɣawus > *ɣaus* 'scoop up' *suwab > *kar-suab* 'yawn'

An exception is *quway, which retains the /w/ after /u/:

*quway > *uway* 'rattan'

*y > /y/ medially except after *i. There are no attestations of reflexes of *y-. For *-y finally in diphthongs, see §B62.2.5.

*daya 'inland' > *zaya* 'west' *ɣaya > *ɣaya* 'great, large'

The form *wiya* 'leave' is probably connected with *bayaq leave, but it is a borrowing in Kav because of the irregular vowel, the /y/ after /i/, and the initial /w/. *qayam 'bird' is reflected as *alam* 'bird', and there is no explanation (cf. §B62.2.1, end, footnote).

CHAPTER SEVEN, §1
Puyuma

B71.0 Background and cultural factors that influenced the history of Puyuma

Puyuma (Pu) is spoken in southeast Taiwan in some of the villages close to Taitung. There is a certain amount of dialectal diversity, but not to the extent of the diversity of the Atayalic or Rukai languages, where the dialects are mutually unintelligible. The Pu dialects are said to be intelligible among themselves. According to Cauquelin (1991: 11), there are two dialects: that spoken in Nanwang and that spoken in Katipul—i.e., the dialect spoken in the six northern villages and the dialect spoken in the six southern villages. Of the northern dialects, Nanwang was investigated by Cauquelin 1991, and Puyuma (=Nanwang),[1] Pinaski, and Ulibulibuk (in some of the literature called Mulibulibuk) were investigated by Ting 1978. Of the southern dialects, Tamalakaw was investigated by Tsuchida 1983, and Kasabakan, Likavung, and Katipul were investigated by Ting 1978. The language is now no longer being spoken by children anywhere, but it was still widely learned by children as recently as forty years ago, and there are good speakers under fifty. The data here presented is based primarily on Tsuchida 1983 and Cauquelin 1991 and secondarily on Ting 1978. Forms are quoted from Tsuchida 1983 (Tamalakaw dialect) whenever they are attested. When they are not available, forms are quoted from other dialects (as reported by Cauquelin 1991 or Ting 1978) and marked as being attested in those dialects.

Pu made many lexical and some phonological innovations together with Pai. Pu and Pai have much in common in their morphology and syntax, as well, but it remains to be investigated which of these common features are inherited from PAn and which have been innovated.

The following chart shows the segmental phonemes of Pu, as described by Tsuchida 1983. The cognate reflexes in Nanwang, as described by Cauquelin, are given in parentheses in those cases where they differ from the Tamalakaw phonemes. Stress falls predictably on the word-final syllable in Nanwang and Tamalakaw (and probably in the other dialects as well). The transcription here follows Tsuchida as modified (see the table following the next), and forms attested in other sources are transcribed for consistency's sake according to the modified Tsuchida transcription as here adopted. The symbol *ṭ* represents a retroflexed [ṭ].

---

[1] The same village is called both Nanwang and Puyuma in the literature, but the designations refer to different areas in the same village (apparently overlapping to some extent). In the few cases where Cauqelin and Ting report different reflexes in the Puyuma and Nanwang dialects, the difference doubtlessly has to do with variation within the same dialect, possibly even within the speaker. I use the term "Nanwang" to refer to this dialect, whether reported by Ting as "Puyuma" or whether reported as "Nanwang", except when Ting and Cauqelin report different variants of the same form.

CHART ONE. PHONEMES OF PUYUMA

	Consonants						Vowels			
voiceless	p	t	ṭ	k	ɦ (ʔ)		high	i		u
voiced	b	d	z (ḍ)				mid		e [ə]	
continuants	v, w	ɬ (l), s	ḷ (ḷ)	r	h (g)		low		a	

There are also the three diphthongs /aw/, /ay/, and /uy/. There are differences among the Pu dialects in the articulation of some of the consonantal phonemes. First, /ɦ/ is a pharyngeal fricative in Tamalakaw (and also in Pinaski, Ulibulibuk, Kasabakan, and Likavung), but in the Katipul and Nanwang dialects, it is a glottal stop [ʔ]. Second, Tamalakaw /z/ corresponds to a voiced and retroflexed apical stop [ḍ] in Nanwang. In Tamalakaw, /z/ is described as a voiced retroflexed sibilant with a dental variant.[2] Ting transcribes it as *d* or *ð*, depending on the dialects. /r/ is a voiced apico-alveolar trill. /ɬ/ is a voiced apico-dental lateral, palatalized in some dialects (Ting 1978: 328) but not in Nanwang, and /ḷ/ is a voiced retroflexed lateral [ḷ]. The sources have all transcribed /r/, /ɬ/, and /ḷ/ in different ways. The following chart indicates the transcription in our main sources and the transcription here adopted:

Cauquelin	Tsuchida	Ting	Wolff
l	l	l	ɬ
ḷ[3]	r	L	ḷ
r	R	r	r

Consonant clusters that developed tended to be pronounced with an epenthetic /e/. There is no contrast between /CeC/ and /CC/, and the sources do not always agree with each other in their transcription: sometimes the transcription is *CeC* and sometimes *CC*: *ɦaspa* 'astringent' (Tsuchida 1983: 18) *asepa* (Cauquelin 1991: 60). (Cf. §B71.1.1, below.) Similarly, a glide was automatically inserted between front and back vowels: there is no contrast in inherited forms between *ia, ua, au, ai, ui, iu* and *iya, uwa, awu, ayi, uwi,* and *iyu*, respectively.[4] The sources are not consistent with each other as to whether to write /y/ and /w/ in those cases: *tiyal* 'belly' is transcribed *tiyal* (Tsuchida: 1983: 50) and *tial* (Cauquelin: 1991: 211, Ting: 1978: #547).

---

[2] The articulatory description is taken from Quack (1985: 10).

[3] In fact the ḷ in the printed version looks a bit more like ɬ. However, a retroflexed ḷ is what is meant.

[4] However, in current Pu, when a vowel sequence develops, a glottal stop is automatically inserted between the two vowels. In Nanwang the /ʔ/ that developed automatically between vowels does not contrast with the /ʔ/ that developed from *q (corresponding to /ɦ/ in Tamalakaw). The glottal stop that developed in Katipul, however, does contrast with the reflex of *q (Quack 85: 10). In words borrowed from Chinese, for example, a glottal stop is automatically inserted between the abutting vowels. Further, when a vowel-initial suffix is added to a stem ending in a vowel, a glottal stop is automatically inserted between the abutting vowels: e.g., *palisi* + *-i* > *palisii* [palisiʔi] 'pray'. For this reason, I prefer to transcribe Pu forms with the semivowel glide that historically developed automatically abutting front and back vowels. However, there are no roots with a PAn etymology that have *iʔa, uʔa, aʔi, uʔi,* or *iʔu*.

B71.1 Changes that characterize Pu in general

Pu, like Pai, is conservative in its phonology, but less so than Pai because stress causes a great deal more syncopation in Pu than in it does in Pai. However, in comparison with other languages, Pu like Pai underwent few changes in its phonology in developing from PAn.

B71.1.1 Disyllabization of trisyllabic roots: loss of the penult and loss of the antepenult

There is a tendency to lose an unstressed *e and occasionally, other unstressed vowels in trisyllabic roots or trisyllabic stems that developed with the addition of affixes. Some of these changes are made by other languages, and some are peculiar to Pu.
Loss of the penult:

B71.1.11 Loss of penult

In trisyllabic roots a central penultimate vowel consisting of [ə] does not contrast with its absence—i.e., a VCCV that developed from VCeCV (by syncopation of the penultimate *e) may still be pronounced as three syllables (cf. the comment in the introduction §B71.0). E.g. *qacepa 'astringent' may be reflected as [ɦaspa] or [ɦasəpa]. Similarly, stems with Cuw and Ciy in the penult do not contrast with disyllabic roots having a medial sequence Cw and Cy, respectively, and stems with wuC and yiC in the penult do not contrast with disyllabic stems with a medial sequence wC and yC, respectively. E.g. aydan 'when' may be pronounced [aydan] as two syllables or [ayidan] as three.
In one case, loss of the *e in the penult when a prefix was added led to loss of the root-initial consonant in CC simplification:

*ki + *deŋeɣ > *kinger* 'hear' (< *kidŋeɣ)

B71.1.12 Contraction of vowels

After *s and *h were lost (§B71.3.2), if a vowel sequence developed, it was contracted: *e abutting *i or *a is lost, *u abutting *e is lost.[5]

*sehapuy > *apuy* 'fire' *iseci 'contents, flesh' > *isi* 'meat, muscle' *iseyup > *iyup-* 'blow' *binesiq < *viniq* 'seed for planting' *bacuheq > *vaseɦ-* 'wash' *qaɬisipec > *ɬaɬipes* 'roach' (< *ɬaɬipes [*qa- is replaced analogically by reduplication < *qaɬipes])

In at least one case, *cahebay, there was syncopation of the penult prior to the loss of the *h.[6]

*cahebay > *sapay* 'hang' (< *cahpay < *cahbay)

This sequence of events may also have been followed by two of the forms cited immediately above[7] (as is the case of cognates in other Formosan languages), but there is no evidence in Pu.

---

[5] However, in the following form, the loss of the *s between *i and *e resulted in *e:

*qiseɬep > *a-ɬupeɦ* 'sleep' (< *a-ɬepeq < *a-qeɬep < *a-qieɬep)

[6] We assume this sequence of events to account for the reflex *p in place of *b: when the penult was lost (*cahebay > *cahbay), the *b became voiceless *p by assimilation to the preceding *h (> *cahpay). Only then was *h lost, producing the attested *sapay* 'hang'.

[7] That is, *iseci > *isci> *isi* and *binesiq > *binsiq > *vini*.

*u in the penult of trisyllabic forms is weakened (cf. the example in §B71.2.3, 3rd¶). This rule accounts for the loss of *u in the following case where the stem had become trisyllabic by the addition of a prefix (= reduplication of the first CV of the root) after the *s was lost:

> *qusaw > *ĥa-ĥaw* 'thirsty' (Nanwang)[8] (< *qaqwaw < *qaquwaw < *qa-qusaw) *qudaŋ > *ĥa-ĥzang* 'shrimp' (< *ĥa-ĥuzang < *qaqudaŋ)

Further, when *h is lost between like vowels, the like vowels are contracted:

> *ɣabihi *'evening'* > *ma-ravi* 'supper'

B71.1.13 Loss of *q onset of the penult in trisyllables

The *q onset of the punult in trisyllables was lost. The resulting vowel sequence was contracted (*aa, *ae, *ee[9] > /a/, *ie > /e/, *ua > /wa/):

> *buqaya 'crocodile' > *vwaya* 'shark' *seqeɣet > *aret* 'narrow and tight' (with loss of the *e that resulted from the contraction) *jaqewis > *dawi-ɬ* 'far' *ma- + *qetaq > *maĥat* 'raw' (< *mataĥ < *maetaĥ < *maˀetaĥ) *tiqeɣab > *ţerav* 'belch'

In prefixed forms, the antepenult of the root was lost and the *q onset of the penult retained:

> *daqaɬi 'daytime' > *kar-ĥaɬi-an* 'noon'

*q-onset of the penult in PAn was not lost if metathesis had taken place (§B71.1.3)—i.e., metathesis took place before the loss of *q-onset of the penult:

> *iqetah > *ĥeţa* 'husk and bran' (< *qietah) *leqacem > *ĥarsem* 'sour' (< *qalecem) *paqegu > *ĥapdu* 'gall' (< *qapegu)[10]

B71.1.14 Loss of penultimate vowels other than *e

There is one case of loss of *i in the penult of a trisyllabic root. This is an exceptional development. The *i is not lost in other trisyllabics with *i in the penult, e.g. *ţalinga* 'ear' < *tangíla. The form probably has been borrowed:

> *qaɬitu 'evil spirit' > *ĥaɬtu* 'owl'

There is also a case where *a of the penult was lost:

> *tibawác > *ţivuwas* 'destruction, end (final point)'

B71.1.15 Antepenultimate weakening or loss

The antepenultimate vowel is in some cases weakened to /e/ (which may subsequently be lost). In other cases, it is not weakened (listed in §B71.1.17, below). The rule determining the loss/weakening of the antepenult or its retention may possibly be linked to stress patterns (§A3.5.3). The antepenult was lost in many forms in many An languages, but not all the same languages lose or weaken the antepenult in the same roots. Thus the

---

[8] In the Tamalakaw dialect, no reduplication took place, but rather the monosyllabic root with a diphthong that resulted from the loss of a medial consonant was disyllabized by the rule of §B71.1.2(3): *ĥawu* 'thirsty'.

[9] I assume *ee > /a/ on the basis of only one attestation. However, it is an articulatorily motivated change. When a *q was lost, it normally had changed to [ˀ] prior to disappearing. When *e had come to abut on [ˀ], it changed to [a]—i.e., *eqe > *eˀe > *aˀe > *ae > /a/. (I do not assume that *eq > *aq: there are counterexamples.)

[10] But in the case of *mataĥ* (< *maqetaq), described in this section above, metathesis took place after loss of *q.

ultimate answer to the question of the conditions under which the antepenult is weakened or lost may lie in the history of development at a later stage. It is a change that may have happened independently or it may have been spread by language contact. The following list gives examples of antepenultimate weakening or loss:

*baɣeqaŋ > *vereñang* 'molar' *bu- + *qiteluɣ > *ve-ṭinun* 'egg' (<*bu-tinun < *butiluɣ (§B71.1.3) < *bu-iteluɣ) *cakay 'climb up on to s.t.' > *sekay-an* 'ladder' *kudemel > *kezemel* 'thick' *qalima > *lima* 'hand' *qiseɬep > *a-ɬupeñ* 'sleep' (> *a-ɬepeñ < *a-ɬepeq < *a-qeɬep < *a-qieɬep[11]) (Nanwang: *a-ɬepeʔ*) *tineun > *tenun* 'weave' (< *teneun) *siyuɬuq > *uɬu* 'beads' (< *iuɬuq) *taseyup > *-tiyup* (< *ta-iyup [§B71.2.2, middle]) stem of *pa-tiyup* 'play on flute'

Similarly, the antepenultimate vowel of a disyllabic root with a petrified suffix was weakened or lost:

*acu + -an > *suwan* 'dog' (< *asuwan)

An antepenultimate [i] before /y/ and [u] before /w/ was automatically lost:[12]

*buqaya > *vwaya* 'crocodile' *suwagi > *wadi* 'younger sibling' (< *uwadi) *pa- + ta-iseyup + -an > *patyupan* (< *patiyupan) 'bamboo flute'

In one case, the prefix *qaɬi- lost the first syllable. This innovation is reflected in all the languages in which a reflex of this root is attested except for Sar and Knn:

*qaɬimatek > *ɬimatek* 'leech'

B71.1.16 Special behavior of doubled monosyllables

Note that the leftmost vowel of doubled monosyllabic roots is never weakened:

*pakepak > *pakpak* 'wings' *cipecip > *sipsip* 'suck' *buɬebuɬ > *vuɬvuɬ* 'fontanelle'

As is the case of Pai, some Pu forms retain the penultimate epenthetic vowel of the reduplicated monosyllabic root (cf. §B72.1.15).

*sapesap > *apuap* 'grope'

B71.1.17 Retention of the antepenult in trsyllables

Trisyllabic roots in other cases retain the antepenult unchanged. The rules governing retention are unknown:

*bituqen < *vituñen* 'star' *cahebay > *sapay* 'hang' (< *cahpay < *cahbay) *leqasem > *ñarsem* 'sour' (< *raqesem) *puɬetiq > *vuɬti* 'white *qacepa > *ñaspa* 'astringent' *qaɬegaw > *kadaw* 'sun' *qapegu > *qapdu* 'gall' (< *paqegu) *taŋila > *ṭalinga* 'ear' *tinaqi > *ṭinañi* 'intestines'

B71.1.18 A trisyllabic root in which *-iyu develops loses syllabicity on the *u (*iyu > /iw/):

*baɣiyus > *variw* 'storm'-

---

[11] An alternative explanation is that /a/ is not a prefix but rather the reflex of *i in the antepenult. However, in other cases *i does not change to /a/ in the antepenult (§B71.1.15). A prefix shaped /a/ is also assumed for *a-ʔayip* 'count' from *seyap.

[12] There is no contrast between Ciy and Cy or Cuw and Cw in the syllables to the left of the penult.

B71.1.2 Disyllabization of monosyllabic roots

Pu, like Pai, evinces the tendency to disyllabize monosyllabic roots only to a minor extent, although this tendency characterizes the history of the majority of the An languages, and that certainly began in PAn times (§A3.6.2).

(1) Doubling is the most productive process of disyllabization:

*kuj 'back' > *kuzkuz* 'carry on the back' *teb 'cut off' > *tevtev* 'chop' *biɣ > *virvir* 'lips'

(2) There is one example of a monosyllabic root that disyllabized by the addition of a prothetic vowel, homophonous with the root vowel:

*ɣik > *irik* 'thresh with with the feet'[14]

(3) Some of the dialects tolerate monosyllabic roots, e.g., Nanwang *luq* 'tears' (< *luseq) *kuy* 'leg' < *kuj. Tamalakaw (and other dialects as well) do not tolerate monosyllabic roots. *luseq and *kuj are reflected as *uleq* 'tears' (< *suleq with metathesis) and *kuwi* 'leg' respectively. In the Tamalakaw dialect, a monosyllabic root containing a diphthong disyllabized the diphthong.

*taw > *ṭau* 'person' *kuj 'lower shank' > *kuwi* 'leg' (< *kuy) *qusaw >*ɦawu* 'thirsty' (< *ɦaw < *qaqaw (§B71.1.13) < *qaqusaw)

When an affix was added to a disyllabic root whose vocalic content was a back and front vowel and the medial root consonant had been lost, the vowel sequence that developed after the loss of the medial consonant became tautosyllabic—i.e., [yi] > /y/:

*bahi + *R-an > *va-vay-an* 'woman' (< *ba-bai-an)

A few PAn monosyllabic roots remained monosyllabic in Tamalakaw. They always occur affixed or compounded with other roots. In some cases, the affix became petrified:

*but >*u-vut* 'pull out with ease, one by one' (< *um-but) *kan > *kan* 'eat' *lum 'ripe'> *ma-lum* 'dry' *put > *ma-put* 'blow' *dem > *zem-kerem* 'twilight, evening' (Nanwang)

Clitic monosyllabic roots remained monosyllabic.

*su > *u* 'you (genitive sing.)' *ɬa > *ɬa* 'already, by now'

---

[13] A countercase *penu* 'sea turtle' (< *peniyu) is a borrowing.

[14] This innovation is shared by Knn and Sar, where it is a regular development (whereas in Pu it is the unique example of a prothetic vowel of any sort, let alone one that harmonizes with the root nucleus. It seems to have spread to Pu from Knn or Sar. Although now these languages are separated from Pu by a large area of Bun speech, it is known that Bun has moved into formerly Knn and Sar territory, so that these languages may in fact have bordered on Pu at an earlier time.

B71.1.3 Metathesis

Many cases of metathesis in Pu are the result of secondary spread from another language. The evidence for this is that in some of the cases the same metathesis is found in the reflexes in several languages, and the occurrence of metathesis is independent of language boundaries: dialects of the same language may evince cases where metathesis did not occur.

*ałay > *ayan* 'termite' *liceqes > *łiĥsa* 'nit' (< *liceqa) *ma- + *qetaq > *maĥat* 'raw' (< *mataĥ < *maetaĥ < *maʔetaĥ) *paqegu > *ĥapdu* 'gall' *taŋila > *ţalinga* 'ear' (Nanwang *ţangila*) *wanał > *tara-wałan* 'right side' (also *taĥ-wanał* 'south' [Chen])

A sequence *iCe was metathesized to *eCi and with subsequent loss of *e in the following form. This kind of metathesis is widespread in the An languages (§A3.5.4), but it is the only example of this kind in Pu. The cognates in St and Kav also reflect this metathesis but it is probably an independent development in those languages:

*bu- + *qiteluɣ > *ve-ţinun* 'egg' (< *bu-tinun < *bu-tiluɣ < *bu-iteluɣ)

Other cases of metathesis are a purely Pu phenomenon, but metathesis is not widespread. Some of the cases of metathesis do not occur in all dialects. Loss of *s or *ɣ (§§B71.3.2, B71.3.41) gave impetus to metathesis in some cases:

*kasiw > *kawi* 'tree' *luseq > *uleĥ* 'tears' (< **lueĥ* [Nanwang: *luĥ*]) *maɣuqałay 'male' > maaĥinay-an 'man' (< *ma-iĥanay) *seyap > *a-aip* 'count' (Nanwang) (< *a-iap) *tusud > *tuzu* 'knee'

No motivation can be found for the following cases of metathesis:

*atac > *asat* 'high' (Nanwang) (Tamalakaw: *aţas*) *dilaq 'tongue' > *lidaĥ* 'lick' *laŋaw > *nga-ngalaw* 'a fly'[15] *laŋit > *lingaţ* 'heaven' (Nanwang *langiţ*) *naquɣ > *pa-ĥanun* 'go down' (< *pa-qanuɣ) *paN- + *piliq > *palimiĥ* 'choose' (< *pamiliĥ) *qaceŋ > *esang* 'cough' *qałuj > *mua-łaĥud* 'be adrift' (<*-łaquj)[16] *qiɣaq > *zem-iyar* 'red'

B71.2 Vowels and diphthongs

Pu has inherited the four vowels and diphtongs of PAn, listed in §B71.0. *e is written /e/ and pronounced [ə].

B71.2.1 *i

*i remains /i/ almost everywhere except in the unstressed positions described in §B71.1.1ff.

*ini > *ini* 'this' *qałimatek > *łimatek* 'leech' *ɣabihi 'evening' > *ma-ravi* 'supper' *palisi > *p-en-alisi* 'taboo'

---

[15] Maga Rukai and Knn also show this metathesis, and it is possible that this form has spread from one of these to Pu or from Pu to these languages (cf. the immediately preceding footnote).

[16] Knn also evinces this metathesis, and Pu may have borrowed the Knn form or vice versa (cf. the two immediately preceding footnotes). The semantic change that the Knn reflex underwent may well be prior to the spread of this form.

In one form, Pu reflects *i with /u/. The /u/ is unexplained and puzzling:

*biqel > *vuñel* 'goiter'

B71.2.2 *e

Except for the syncopation and contraction listed in §B71.1.1ff., above, *e remains a mid-central vowel in most environments.

*enem > *enem* 'six' *getil > *hetil* 'pinch off' *tikel > *tikel* 'bend' *luseq > *uleq* 'tears' *quleg > *ñuled* 'worm' *telu > *telu* 'three'

*e is reflected as /i/ after /i/ in the following two forms. There is no explanation, but it should be noted that other Formosan languages share this innovation. The forms spread secondarily or were influenced by cognates in other languages:

*iseq > *isiq* 'urine' *qaɬisipec 'roach' > *ɬaɬipis* 'kind of water beetle' (< *qaɬipis)

The sequence *ey > /i/:

*seyap > *a-aip* 'count' (< *a- iap)

In some forms, *e is assimilated to /u/ in an adjacent syllable. Note that a similar phenomenon is evinced in Pai and Ru although not always in the cognates of these forms or confined to them. From this, we may conclude that influence from other languages is the explanation:
*betúh > *vuṭu* 'blister, callus' *ɬecuŋ > *ɬusung* 'mortar' *tuked > *tukuz* 'support, prop' (Nanwang)
*e is also reflected by /u/ in other contexts. In most of those cases a cognate with /e/ occurs in one of the dialects. The change of *e to /u/ is unexplained in those cases:[17]

*qiseɬep > *a-ɬupeñ* 'sleep' (> *a-ɬepeñ < *a-ɬepeq < *a-qeɬep < *a-qieɬep) (Nanwang: *a-ɬepeʔ*)

In one case, *-es > /a/. There is only one example. The other protoforms with *-es are not directly inherited by Pu.

*liceqes > *ɬiñsa* 'nit' (< *liceqa [§B71.1.3])

B71.2.3 *a and *u

*a remained /a/ in all environments. No exceptions are attested:

*aɬak > *aɬak* 'child, offspring'

*u remained /u/ in all environments except in the cases of contraction listed in §B71.1.1ff., above.

*bubu > *vuvu* 'grandparent' *cucu > *susu* 'breast'

*u in the penult of trisyllabic forms is weakened to /e/ or lost (§B71.1.12). In the following case, an *u in the root-final syllable changed to /e/. This may possibly be the result of vowel

---

[17] There are numerous cognate forms where one or several dialects manifest /e/ and other dialects manifest /u/. Many of the cases are roots with a PAn etymology. However, there are only a few attestations of forms in Tamalakaw that reflect PAn *e with /u/.

weakening when the *u came to stand in the penult in a suffixed form, developing an allomorph with /e/. This allomorph then spread throughout the paradigm:

*siɣup > *irep* 'sip' (Possibly, *iɣup-aw > *irep-aw* and subsequent generalization of *irep*)

In a trisyllable that retained the antepenult, a sequence *ua in the penult and final syllable changed to /va/:

*qacu + -an > *asvan* 'smoke' (< *qacuan)

The same rule accounts for the development of /v/ in the following form:

*caw > *savsav-i* 'wash' (*caw > *sau (§B71.1.2(3)) + doubling > *sausaui > *sausavi)

Subsequenty, the first occurrence of the monosyllabic root was made to harmonize with the second:

*sausavi > *savsavi* 'wash'

B71.2.4 Diphthongs

The diphthongs *ay, *uy, and *aw are retained unchanged with the exception of monosyllabic roots, described in §B71.1.2(3), above, where the *w and *y are made syllabic.

*qatay > *ɦaṭay* 'liver' *sehapuy > *apuy* 'fire' *takaw > *ṭakaw* 'steal'

There are only two forms attested in Pu that reflect the diphthong *iw. In the first case, there is metathesis after the loss of *s (§§B71.1.3, B71.3.2):

*kasiw > *kawi* 'tree'

The reflex of *waɬiw 'bee' developed as in other Formosan languages: *i of the final syllable is absorbed by the /ɬ/, the reflex of the preceding *ɬ, and the *w is given syllabic value:

*waɬiw > *waɬu* 'honey, honeybee'

B71.3.0 Consonants

The following chart shows the Pu reflexes of the PAn consonants:

CHART TWO. DEVELOPMENT OF THE PUYUMMA CONSONANTS FROM PAN

PAn	**Pu**	**PAn**	**Pu**
p	*p*	g	*h-,- d-, -d*
t	*t, ṭ*	ɣ	*r*
c	*s*	l	*l [ḷ]*
k	*k*	ɬ	*ɬ*
q	*ɦ*	m	*m*
h	*ø*	n	*n*
s	*ø*	ŋ	*ng*
b	*v [β]*	w	*w*
d, j	*d, z*	y	*y*

B71.3.1 Voiceless consonants

B71.3.11 *p

*p remained /p/ in all positions.

*piga > *pida* 'how much, many?' *paqegu > *ɦapdu* 'gall' *sepat > *pat* 'four' *cipecip > *sipsip-* 'suck'

In one case, *p is reflected with /v/. There is no explanation, but the Pu form is probably connected with the reflexes of the reconstructed protoform in other languages:

*puɬetiq > *vuɬʈiɦ* 'white'

B71.3.12 *t

*t has two outcomes: an apico-dental stop /t/ and an apico-alveolar retroflexed stop /ʈ/ [ʈ], where the retroflexed reflex has the same distribution as the affricated reflex in other languages of northeast and southwest Taiwan (§A3.3.1, first footnote).

*t reflected as /t/:

*telu > *telu* 'three' *timid > *timiz* 'chin *tuqed > *tuɦez* 'stump' *tuketuk 'strike, peck' > *tuktuk* 'rap, tap' *qaɬimatek > *ɬimatek* 'leech' *utaq > *utaɦ-an* 'vomit' *gaɣut > *harut* 'comb' *sepat > *pat* 'four'

*t reflected as /ʈ/:

*taketak 'chop off, fell' > *ʈakʈak* 'partly come off' *taqi > *ʈaɦi* 'feces' *kutu > *kuʈu* 'head louse' *uɣat 'nerve, sinew' > *uraʈ* 'blood vessel'

In one case, *t is reflected as /s/. This form was probably borrowed from Pai before the change of *c > /s/ (§B71.3.13, below):

*katu 'send' > *kasu* 'bring' (cf. Pai *katsu* 'carry, bring')

B71.3.13 *c

After *s was lost (§B71.3.2, below), *c > /s/. There are no exceptions:

*cucu > *susu* 'breast' *bacuheq > *vaseɦ-* 'wash' *iseci 'flesh, contents' > *isi* 'meat, muscle' *balec > *vales* 'revenge, retaliate'

B71.3.14 *k

*k remained /k/ in all positions. There are no exceptions:

*kaɣat > *karaʈ* 'bite' *kudemel > *kezemel* 'thick' *bituka > *viʈuka* 'stomach (as food)' *ciku > *siku* 'elbow' *pakepak > *pakpak* 'wing'

B71.3.15 *q

*q > /ɦ/. In Nanwang, *q > /ʔ/. As mentioned in the third footnote to §B71.0, a glottal stop is automatically inserted in vowel sequences that develop in current Pu (but not in vowel sequences that developed in the past when *s and *h were lost between vowels). Further, a glottal stop developed automatically before word-initial vowel. Thus, in Nanwang, the reflex of *q does not contrast with its absence in syllable onset. It is only contrastive in coda position. However, in Tamalakaw and most of the Pu dialects, the reflex of *q /ɦ/ remained contrastive in all positions.

*qabu > *ɦavu* 'ashes' *taqis > *tsaɦi-* 'sew' *daɣeq > *dareɦ* 'earth'

In several cases, *q is lost. This is most likely due to the influence of the Nanwang dialect, where *q > [ʔ] and became noncontrastive when syllable onset—i.e., these forms were borrowed by the Tamalakaw dialect from Nanwang.

*qapuɣ > *apur* 'lime' (Nanwang) *qiɣaq > *zem-iyar* 'red'

*q is also lost in the onset of the penult in trisyllabic roots, with contraction of the resulting abutting vowels (§B71.1.13).
There are also other cases in which *-q was lost. For these, there is no explanation other than that, in the Nanwang dialect, *q > [ʔ], which in many environments was noncontrastive and is said to be weakly pronounced (even where it is contrastive) and often dropped (Teng 2006: 18). These then came about by the generalization of rapid-speech forms:

*butuq 'genitals' > *buʈu* 'testicles' (Nanwang) *siyuɬuq > *uɬu* 'beads' *puteq > *puʈe* 'secretion from the eyes' (Nanwang)

In two cases *q is reflected with /k/. These forms are probably borrowings from Pai, where the reflex of *q is a back velar voiceless stop.

*qaɬegaw > *kadaw* 'sun' *qaɬit > *kaɬiʈ* 'fur, pelt, leather'

B71.3.2 *s and *h

*s and *h left little trace in Pu. In trisyllabic stems, with the loss of medial *h or *s, contraction of the abutting vowels took place, depending on the vowels (see the examples in §B71.1.12). Here are some more examples:

*bahaɬiɣ > *vanin* 'board' *sehapuy > *apuy* 'fire' *ba-bahi-an > *va-vay-an* 'woman' *sapesap > *apuap* 'grope'

Other examples of *h-loss:

*buhet > *vut* 'squirrel' *quluh > *ɦulu* 'head' *qumah > *ɦuma* 'cultivated field' *lahuj > 'seaward' > *lawuz* 'east'

Other examples of *s loss:

*setek > *etek* 'chop down' *simaɣ > *imar* 'grease, fat' *siwa > *iwa* 'nine' *sulag > *unan* 'snake' *gusam 'thrush' > *ma-huwam* 'suffering from thrush' *qamis > *qami* 'north' *qilus > *ɦilu* 'wipe after defecating' *tebus > *tevu* 'sugar cane'

In a few cases, *s is reflected with *s. Some of these are forms that have spread secondarily and most of them show other irregularities as well:

*iseq >*isiɦ* 'urine' *liyus 'go around s.t.'> *u-liyus* 'turn around' *palisi > *p-en-alisi* 'taboo' *siɣup > *sirep* 'sip'

Another case is an example of a root that has probably been influenced by forms with a similar meaning:

*kusekus > *kuskus-* 'scrape off' (influenced by *ki-kiskis* 'shave' < *kicekic)

B71.3.3 Voiced consonants, stops in PAn

B71.3.31 *b

*b > /v/ [β] –i.e., a bilabial voiced fricative. In Nanwang *b remains a stop.

*baɣah > *vara* 'embers *beɣay > *va-verai* 'give' *buhet > *vut* 'squirrel' *ɬibu 'fenced in place' > *ɬivu* 'den of wild pigs' *qeɬeb > *qeɬev* 'close, shut'

B71.3.32 *d *j

*d and *j merged. These two protophonemes have two reflexes /z/ and /d/. In Nanwang these two phonemes are reflected with /ḍ/ and /d/. The two reflexes are not correlated with the protophonemes: /z/ reflects both *d and *j, and so does /d/. This is an innovation that Pu shares with Pai (§B72.3.32). There is consistency among the Pai dialects and Pu dialects with very few exceptions: for the most part, forms that reflect *d and *j with /z/ in Puyuma (or /ḍ/ in Nanwang) not only have /z/ in the other Pu dialects but also have /z/ in Pai (if Pai forms are attested), and forms that have /d/ in Pu have cognates with /d/ in all the Pu dialects and also have /dj/ in Pai (if they are attested).[18]
First /z/ as a reflex:

*daya 'inland' > *zaya* 'west' *dekel > *zekel* 'choke' *kudemel > *kezemel* 'thick' *tujuq > *tuzuñ* 'point' *sated > *atez-an* 'escort home' *tuked > *tuñez* 'stump' *lahuj 'seaward' > *lawuz* 'east' *tukej > *tukuz* 'support'

Second /d/ as a reflex:

*danaw > *danaw* 'pond' *dilaq 'tongue' > *lidaq* 'lick' *jaɣum > *dawum* 'needle' *qujaɬ > *qudaɬ* 'rain' *qaɬuj > *mua-ɬañud* 'be adrift'[19]

In one case, *-j > *-y in Tamalakaw. There is no explanation. The reflex in Nanwang is regular:

*kuj 'lower shank' > *kuwi* 'leg and foot' (< *kuy) (Nanwang *kukuz*)

In the following example, *d was lost before *e in the penult of a root that had been prefixed: the penult was syncopated (§B71.1.11), and the resulting CC was simplified:

*ki- + *deŋeɣ > *kinger* 'hear' (< *ki-dnger < *kidenger)

The following form has an irregular reflex of the initial and the final consonant. There is no explanation, but the form is clearly cognate with reflexes of *daqaɬ in other languages:

*daqaɬ > *sañaz* 'branch'

B71.3.33 *g

*g > /h/ as onset to monosyllabic roots or to the penult or earlier. In Nanwang this is articulated as [g].

---

[18] This is not entirely true. There is a handful of discrepancies within the dialects: e.g.,Tamalakaw *zaya* 'inland' is reflected as *daya* in the Puyuma dialect. Between Pai and Pu there is also remarkable consistency. The cases where the reflexes do not correspond are the reflexes of *daqu > Pu *daqu* Pai *zaqu* '*Sapindus mukorossi*', which is of secondary spread, and three forms that show /ḍ/ in Paiwan, not the normal reflex of *j and *d in any case: *dusa > Pu *za-zuwa* Pai *ḍusa* 'two' *kudemel > Pu *kezemel* Pai *kuḍemel* 'thick'. There are two other forms that do not correspond in Pai and Pu but give no indication of secondary spread: *jeket > Pu *paa-zeketַ* Pai *pa-djekets* 'paste' and *tujuq 'point' > Pu *tuzu* 'point' Pai *tsudjuq* 'finger'.

[19] All our attestations of final *-d in Pu are reflected as /-z/. (In Pai both /-z/ and /-dj/ reflect *-d: e.g., *waɣed > *vaudj* 'vine' [no attested cognate in Pu]).

*gaɣaŋ > *harang* ‘crab’ *gatel > *haṭel* ‘itch’ *getil > *hetil* ‘pinch and break off’ *guci > *husi* ‘gums’ *tageɣaŋ > *tahrang* ‘chest, breast’

There are two exceptions. These forms are probably borrowings. In the first case, a reflex with /k-/ is found in all the Formosan languages that attest a reflex, those that normally reflect *g- with /k-/ as well as those that kept the reflex of *g- a separate phoneme from *k-:

*galih > *kali* ‘dig’ *giliŋ ‘roll over s.t.’ > *ta-kili-kiling* ‘wheel’

As onset or coda of the final syllable, *g > /d/:

*kuga > *kemuda-kuda* ‘how?’ *ŋagan > *ngadan* ‘name’ *piga > *pida* ‘how many?’ *quleg > *ħuled* ‘worm’

There are exceptions. The explanation might be as follows: there are few attestations reflecting *g as onset or coda of the final syllable. Except for the two examples given here, they reflect /d/. However, these two examples show /z/, and that might be because *g fell together with *d and *j as onset or coda of the final syllable. In other words, *g, just like *d and *j, evinces two reflexes, /d/ and /z/—i.e., the merger of *g with *d and *j had taken place before the merged phonemes split into /d/ and /z/:

*gilig ‘side’ > *ta-hiliz* ‘lean’ (Nanwang) *ɬagam ‘tame’ > *ɬazam* ‘know’ (Nanwang)

The following form may be a borrowing from Am *tfon* ‘well’. In Am, *-g is normally reflected as /-n/. (Note that Pu shares the semantic innovation of Am.)

*tebug ‘spring’ > *tevun* ‘well’

B71.3.4 Voiced consonants, continuants in PAn

B71.3.41 *ɣ

*ɣ > /r/ in most environments:

*ɣeken > *reken* ‘coiled cloth for putting (hot) things on’ *ɣik > *irik* ‘thresh by stomping’ *ɣumaq > *rumaħ* ‘house’ *kaɣat > *karat* ‘bite’ *keɣet > *keret* ‘cut’ *iɣiŋ > *iring* ‘slant’ *ikuɣ > *ikur* ‘tail’ *simaɣ > *imar* ‘grease, fat’

Root-final *-ɣ > /-n/ when there had been an *n or *l in the same word:

*bahaniɣ >*vanin* ‘board’ *damaɣ ‘light’ > *pa-daman-an* ‘dawn’ *naquɣ > *pa-ħanun* (< *pa-naħun [§B71.1.3]) *qiteluɣ > *veṭinun* ‘egg’ *sulaɣ > *unan* ‘snake’

There are two cases in which *ɣu- > /i/. They are both in trisyllabic stems, and the /i/ is in the penult or antepenult. This may be a rule, but the second example has an irregular reflex of *ɬ as well.

*ma-ɣudaŋ > *ma-idang* ‘old person’ *maɣuqaɬay > *maaħinay-an* ‘male, man’ (< *maiħiaɬay)

There are two examples where *ɣ does not obey the above rules. They are very likely to be borrowings:

*jaɣum > *dawum* ‘needle’ (also *daʔum*. cf. Pai *djaum* ‘needle’) *timuɣ ‘rainy wind’ > *timul* ‘south’ (Nanwang) (cf. Am *timol* ‘south’)

B71.3.42 *l and *ɬ

*l remains /l/, a retroflexed lateral [ḷ] in all positions.

*lima > *lima* 'five' *dalukap > *dalukap* 'sole of foot' *gatel > *haṭel* 'itch'

When *l is followed by *ɣ within the root, *ɣ is changed to /n/ (§B71.3.41) and *l is assimilated to the /n/ that developed:

*qiteluɣ > *veṭinun* 'egg' *sulaɣ > *unan* 'snake'

There are many exceptions. Some of the forms are clearly borrowings from another language. Others probably spread from one dialect to another. Since the three phonemes /l/, /ɬ/, and /r/ are close in their articulations but not articulated in exactly the same way in all of the dialects, it is highly possible that one of these phonemes could be substituted for the other in the process of dialect borrowing.[20] For example *kulabaw 'rat' is reflected in Pinaski with the expected /l/ *kulavaw*, but in Puyuma it is reported as *kuɬabaw* (Ting 1978: No. 390a) and in Nanwang *kurabaw.*

The following examples show *l reflected as /ɬ/. Of these,*bakal and *bulawan are known to have been spread throughout the An languages by borrowing, and *ɬawɬaw* has clearly been borrowed from Am:

*bakal 'iron tool' >*vakaɬ* 'k.o. knife' *bulaw-an 'gold-colored metal' > *vuɬawan* 'brass, copper' *lateŋ > *ɬingaten* 'nettle tree' *lawlaw 'light' > *ɬawɬaw* 'lamp' (Nanwang) (cf. Am *lawlaw* 'lamp') *lemek > *a-ɬemek* 'soft, flexible' *liceqes > *ɬiɦsa* 'nit'[21] *likuj > *ɬi-ɬikud* 'back'

The following examples show *l reflected as /r/. The word for 'goiter' manifests other irregularities as well:

*biqel > *vuɦer* 'goiter' *jalan > *daran* 'road' (Nanwang, but Tamalakaw *dalan*) *dem-kelem > *zem-kerem* 'evening' (Nanwang) *leqacem > *ɦarsem* 'sour'

In two cases, Kasabakan manifests /d/ [ð] < *l. The origin is most certainly secondary spread, but the source is unknown:

*bulawan > *vudawan* 'copper' *qiliɣ 'downstream' > *ɦidir* 'mountainside'

*ɬ is reflected as a front unretroflexed lateral /ɬ/:

*ɬa > *ɬa* 'already' *aɬak > *aɬak* 'child, offspring' *qaɬimatek > *ɬimatek* '(paddy) leech' *qujaɬ > *qudaɬ* 'rain'

In several cases, *ɬ is reflected as /n/. First, *ɬ is dissimilated to /n/ after /l/ on the left:

*bulaɬ > *vulan* 'moon, month' *luluɬ > *lulun* 'roll up (as a mat)' *qaluɬ > *ng-alun* 'wave'

In one case, contamination with a word of similar meaning is the likely explanation:

---

[20] In fact only examples of /l/ replacement by /ɬ/ or /r/ are attested. There are no examples of /r/ or /ɬ/ that were replaced.

[21] The Pai cognate also manifests /ɬ/ in place of /l/ (§B72.3.42): *ɬiseqes* 'nit'. This was likely an analogical change on the model of the reflex of the animal prefix *qaɬi-. This innovation was probably made only once and the form spread secondarily.

dałum > *danum* 'water'[22] (cf. *danaw* 'pond' < *danaw 'lake, pond')

For other cases, the likely explanation is secondary spread of cognates that reflect /n/ in other languages—that is, they were directly or indirectly borrowed from languages that merge *ɬ and *n (§A3.3.4).

*łagam 'tame' > *nadam* 'tame' (cf. Am *mananam* 'tamed') (also *łazam* 'know' [Nanwang]) *bahałiɣ > *vanin* 'board' *maɣuqałay > *maaĥinay-an* 'man, male'

B71.3.43 Nasals

*m, *n, *ŋ remained unchanged in all positions.

*matá > *maṭa* 'eye' *lima > *lima* 'five' *enem > *enem* 'six' *punuq 'head, main part' > *punuĥ* 'brains' *kawayan > *kawayan* 'k.o. bamboo' *naquɣ > *pa-ĥanun* 'go down' *ŋaŋa > *pi-nganga* 'open the mouth' *taŋíla > *ṭalinga* 'ear' *łecuŋ > *łusung* 'mortar'

The sequence *ny, which developed by syncopation, is reflected by /n/ in one case. The form is probably borrowed from a language that reflects *ɬ with /n/:[23]

*peniyu < *penu* 'turtle' (< *penyu)

B71.3.44 *w and *y

*w > /w/ initially and medially. (For *w and *y as second members of diphthongs, cf. §B71.2.4.)

*walu > *walu* 'eight' *wiɣi > *tara-wiri* 'left side' *buwaq > *vuwaĥ* 'fruit' *kawayan > *kawayan* 'k.o. bamboo' *siwa > *iwa* 'nine'

If a stem ending in a diphthong /aw/ is affixed, the /w/ is pronounced as a bilabial glide:

*qaɣaw >*ĥaraw* 'snatch'+ *-i* > *ĥarawi* 'snatch it!'

*y > /y/ medially.

*daya 'inland' > *zaya* 'west' *iseyup > *iyup-* 'blow' *kawayan > *kawayan* 'k.o. bamboo' *tiyał > *tiyał* 'belly'

If a stem ending in a diphthong /ay/ or /uy/ is affixed, the /y/ is pronounced as a palatal glide:

*bahi + R-an > *vavayan* 'married woman' (Nanwang) *babuy + *paɣ-an > *parvavuyan* 'know how to hunt' (Nanwang)

The sequence *ey > /i/ (§B71.2.2), and if a vowel followed, a palatal glide developed:

*seyap > a-ʔayip 'count' (< *a-iyap [§B71.1.3])

---

[22] Tsuchida (1976: 140) suggests that the reflex /n/ in this form is due to assimilation to a nasal on the right. However, there are countercases: e.g., *tałam > *tałam* 'taste'.

[23] I assume two steps in the change: *ɬ > *ny > /n/. In the languages that made this change, *ny < *niy was depalatalized just as occurred with the *ny that developed from *ɬ (cf. the development in Kav [§B62.3.43, 1st footnote]).

Chapter Seven, §2

Paiwan

B72.0 Background and cultural factors that influenced the history of Paiwan

Paiwan (Pai) is located in Pingtung and Taitung counties in southern Taiwan. There is a certain amount of dialectal diversity, but not to the extent of the diversity of the Atayalic or Rukai languages, where the dialects are mutually unintelligible. The Paiwan dialects are said to be intelligible among themselves. The language is now no longer being spoken by children, but it was still widely learned by children as recently as thirty years ago, and there are good speakers under forty. The data here presented is based primarily on Ferrell 1982 and secondarily on Ho 1978. Ferrell presents the Kuɬaɬao dialect, spoken in the village of Tjuabar and listed by Ho as the 'Tjuabar' dialect. The following chart shows the segmental phonemes of Pai. [ʔ] and [h] are marginal phonemes and do not occur in forms with cognates in other An languages. /ɬ/ is a voiced palatalized lateral. Stress is predictable in all Pai dialects and falls on the penult.

Chart One. Phonemes of Paiwan

Consonants

voiceless	p	ts [c]	t	tj [č]	k	q	ʔ
voiced	b	d	ḍ	dj [ǰ]	g		
continuants	v, w	r[1], s	l [ḷ]	ɬ, y			h
nasal	m	n			ŋ		

Vowels

high	i		u
mid		e [ə]	
low		a	

There are also the four diphthongs /aw/, /ay/, /uy/, and /iw/.

B72.1 Changes that characterize Pai in general

Pai is remarkably conservative: compared to other languages the phonology underwent few changes in developing from PAn.

B72.1.1 Weakening of the antepenult and vowel contraction

Weakening of the antepenult is a minor process in Pai and takes place only under specific circumstances. In most cases, trisyllabic roots are retained as trisyllables.

[1] The Stimul dialect merges /l/ and /r/. In the Butanglu dialect, /r/ is a uvular trill [ʁ].

B72.1.11 Loss of *i in the antepenult

*i is lost in the antepenult of trisyllabic roots with some exceptions. This rule also affected Rukai and Amis (§§B41.1.1, B61.1.11), but it is unknown whether this is a shared innovation among the three languages or if it took place independently in each of them.

> *biɣeŋi > *vengi-n* 'night' *iseci > 'contents, flesh' > *seti* 'meat' *isekam 'weave a mat' > *sekam* 'mat' *iseɬaw > *senaw* 'wash' *isepi > *sepi* 'dream'

If the loss of the *i resulted in a CC, an epenthetic /e/ was inserted:

> *tineun > *tjenun* 'weave'

*i in the antepenult did not weaken in five exceptional cases: in two, the stress was on the antepenultimate *i. Two other forms reflect a prefix *qaɬi-, and the vowel is preserved to keep the prefix intact. For *bitúka, there is no explanation:

> *bitúka > *vitsuka* 'stomach' *bítuqan > *vitjuqan* 'star' *líceqes > *ɬi-seqes* 'louse egg' *ɬíkubu 'spring upwards' > *ɬikuvu* 'springboard, high jump' *qaɬimatek > *ɬi-matjek* 'leech'

In a few cases, metathesis of the penultimate vowel and the antepenultimate *i took place (as happened in many of the An languages [§A3.5.4]). This change took place before the loss of *i in this position (in other words, *i moved out of the antepenultimate position where it could be lost). An antepenult consisting of *e alone was lost.

> *qiteluɣ > *qetsilu* 'egg' *iceɣab > *-tiaw* 'the day before or after' (< *ciɣab < *eciɣab)

B72.1.12 Vowel contraction

When a medial C was lost, the vowels on either side of the C contracted as follows: V_1V_1 > /V_1/, u+a/a+u > /a/, u+e > /e/, e+u > /u/, a+e/e+a > /a/:

> *baɣeqaŋ > *vaqang* 'molar' *baqeɣuh > *vaqu-an* 'new' *juɣami > *djami-a* 'straw' *qabaɣa > *qava-n* 'shoulder' *bacuheq > *vateq* 'wash' *bahaɬiɣ > *vaɬi* 'board' *sinawa > *nasi* 'breath' (< *sina [§B72.1.3] < *sinaa) *sehapuy > sapuy 'fire'

This process also affected disyllabic roots. However, *u+*e is contracted to /u/:

> *baɣaq > *va* 'lungs' *buhet > *vutj* 'squirrel' *buɣuk > *ma-vuk* 'rotten' *gaɣaŋ > *gang* 'crab' *kaɣat > *kats* 'bite' *qaɣum > *qam* 'pangolin'

In the following two cases, *ɣe or ɣu > /u/ and failed to contract. There is no explanation: these forms have probably spread secondarily.

> *jaɣum > *djaum* 'needle' *waɣed > *vaudj* 'creeper'

B72.1.13 Contraction of *-an

In adding a suffix *-an to a vowel-final trisyllabic stem, *an contracted with the stem-final vowel

> *biɣeŋi > *vengi-n* 'night' *qabaɣa > *qava-n* 'shoulder'[2]

---

[2] This rule does not apply to disyllabic stems. Cf. *seqaɬi > *qaɬi-an* 'spindle and whorl for weaving'. *seqaɬi apparently lost the antepenult (¶4, immediately following) before the rules of contraction took effect, and became disyllabic, as opposed to *biɣeni and *qabaɣa.

B72.1.14 Other cases of syllable loss

There are a few other cases of syllable loss: the first syllables of a few trisyllabic roots were lost, and the roots *qaɬegaw and *saɣejaɬ underwent loss of the penult.[3] These forms were probably borrowed or influenced by cognates in other languages. The source cannot be identified:

*qalima > *lima* 'hand' *qaɬegaw > *qadaw* 'day, sun' *qaɬuwaŋ > *ɬuang* 'water buffalo' *saɣejaɬ > *tadaɬ* 'ladder' (< *saɣjaɬ [/t/ unexplained]) *seqaɬi > *qaɬi-an* 'spindle and whorl for weaving'

The following form probably also spread secondarily. The medial *q and *e were lost:

*qetaq + *ma- > *matjaq* (< *maqtaq)

B72.1.15 Epenthetic vowels in doubled monosyllabic roots

Doubled monosyllabic roots are reconstructed with an epenthetic *e between the two monosylles (§A3.6.1). These are reflected for the most part in Pai, as in the Philippine languages, with a lost epenthetic vowel. However, in a handful of cases, an epenthetic vowel has been retained. The reason for maintaining the epenthetic vowel may have to do with the stress pattern of the doubled root.[4] The epenthetic vowel is /i/ between two *i's and otherwise /a/, but in some cases /e/ is reflected without explanation. The following forms show the epenthetic vowel in Pa:

*buɬebuɬ > *valuɬavuɬ-an* 'down, small feathers' *gisegis "scrape off" > *gisagis* 'rub against' *kaɬusekus > *kaɬusekus-an* 'fingernail' *witwit > *vitjivitj* 'dart back and forth'

B72.1.2 Disyllabization of monosyllabic roots

Pai, like Pu, evinces the tendency to disyllabize monosyllabic roots only to a minor extent, although this tendency characterizes the history of the majority of the An languages, and that certainly began in PAn times (§A3.6.2). The only productive process of disyllabization is that of doubling the monosyllabic root:

*biɣ > *virvir* 'lips' *kud 'grate, rasp' > *kuḍkuḍ* 'small hoe for weeding' *kuj 'lower shank' > *kuzkuz-an* 'heel' *lam 'impetuous' > *lamlam* 'precipitous'

A monosyllabic root that was inherited with a diphthong or that developed a diphthong by loss of a consonant and contraction (§B72.1.12, above) disyllabized the diphthong:[5]

---

[3] I conclude that the *e in this form was lost and that the resulting CC was simplified to /d/—i.e., the loss of the *e and simplification of the CC took place before *© was lost (§B72.3.41) because /d/ does not reflect *j otherwise (§B72.3.3.2). Cf. §B72.3.34, end.

[4] In the Philippine languages, forms that retain the epenthetic vowel of the reduplicated monosyllabic roots invariably have stress on this vowel. However, there are few of these forms attested either in the Philippine languages or in Pai, and there is no correlation, mainly because few cognates have been found between forms that retain the epenthetic vowels in Pai and those that do so in the Philippine languages. In most cases of these forms, either a Pai or a Philippine cognate is lacking. In the few cases where cognates are attested, the Philippine forms mostly show no epenthetic vowel, whereas Pai does, or Pai shows no epenthetic vowel where the Philippines languages show one. There is only one case of correlation *witewit > Pai *vijivitj* 'dart back and forth', Bikol *witíwit* 'mechanical swing ride at carnival'. (But Tag *witwit* 'shake the little finger' has lost the epenthetic vowel. In PAn, nouns and verbs frm the same root may have had different stress patters. Bikol reflects a noun and Tag reflects a verb from this root.)

[5] But when an affix is added the diphthong is not disyllabized—the *w and *y do not take on syllabicity.

*taw > *tsau-tsau* 'person' *beɣay > *vai* 'give'

Pai inherits some PAn monosyllabic roots unchanged and in fact developed additional monosyllabic roots when loss of intervocalic consonants led to vowel contraction (§B72.1.12, above).

*kan > *kan* 'eat' *lum > *ma-lum* 'ripe' *łeŋ > *łeng* 'look, stare' *pan > *pan* 'bait'

B72.1.3 Metathesis

Metathesis is an isolated process that took place early, probably well before proto-Paiwanic. Some of the forms that manifest metathesis have cognates in other languages that show similar or the same metathesis:

*ałay 'termite'> *ayał* 'termite nest' *taŋila > *tsalinga* 'ear' *wanał > *ka-navał* 'right (side)'

Some of these cases of metathesis are purely a Pai phenomenon.

*pakepak > *kapkap* 'wing' *linuɣ > *luni* 'earthquake' *qałiŋu > *qaiłung-an* 'shadow' *qugiŋ > *qidung* 'charcoal' *sinawa > *nasi* 'breath' (< *nisa < *sina < *sinaa)

B72.2 Vowels and diphthongs

Pai has inherited the four vowels and diphthongs of PAn, listed in §B72.0. *e is written /e/ and pronounced [ə].

B72.2.1 *i

*i remains /i/ everywhere:

*piliq > *p-n-iliq* 'choose' *palisi > *palisi* 'taboo' *saweni > *sawni* 'a short while'

In the antepenult before *c or *s, *i was lost if metathesis had not taken place (see the examples of §B72.1.11).

B72.2.2 *e

Except for the syncopation and contraction listed in §§B72.1.11, B72.1.12, above, *e remains a mid-central vowel in most environments.

*enem > *enem* 'six', *luseq > *luseq* 'tears' *pełuq > *pełuq* 'full'

*eɣ > /u/. In most cases, this /u/ is contracted with the vowel that follows after the loss of *ɣ (§B72.1.12), but in final position it remained /u/:

*beɣay > *vai* 'give' *liqeɣ > *liqu* 'neck'

The following form spread secondarily:*e is irregularly reflected as /i/ after /i/:

*iseq > *isiq* 'urine'

The sequence *ey > /i/:

*seyaq 'shame' > *siaq* 'shyness' *seyup 'blow' > *s-em-iup* 'suck in air'

---

*taw 'person' + *kina-R-an > kinatsava-tsavan 'body' (*w > v [§B72.3.44]), *waɣi 'sun' > *v-n-ay-vay* 'dry in the sun'

In the following form, *e is assimilated to /u/ in the following syllable (as is the case in many languages). There is no explanation:

*cequɬ > *tuquɬ* 'carry on the head'

B72.2.3 *a and *u

*a remained /a/ in all environments:

*qaselu > *qaselu* 'pestle' *balatuk > *valatsuk* 'woodpecker' *bituka > *vicuka* 'stomach'

In one case, *a is replaced by /e/, probably under the influence of an undetermined form of similar meaning:

*dakep > *djekep* 'catch (animal)'

*u remains /u/ in all environments except in the cases of contraction listed in §B72.1.12, above.

*bubu > *vuvu* 'grandparent' *cucu > *tutu* 'breast'

B72.2.4 Diphthongs

The diphthongs are retained unchanged with the exception of monosyllabic roots, described in §B72.1.2, above, where the *w and *y are made syllabic:[6]

*pagay > *paday* 'rice plant' *quway > *quay* 'rattan' *babuy > *vavuy* 'wild pig' *ɬaŋuy > *ɬanguy* 'swim' *laŋaw > *la-langaw* 'fly' *kasiw > *kasiw* 'tree'

B72.3 Consonants

CHART TWO. DEVELOPMENT OF THE PAIWAN CONSONANTS FROM PAN

PAn	Pa	PAn	Pa
p	*p*	g	*g-, -d-, -d*
t	*tj [č], ts [c]*	ɣ	*Ø*
c	*t*	l	*l*
k	*k*	ɬ	*ɬ*
q	*q*	m	*m*
h	*Ø*	n	*n*
s	*s*	ŋ	*ng*
b	*v*	w	*w*
d, j	*dj [j], z*	y	*y*

B72.3.1 Voiceless consonants

B72.3.11 *p

*p remained /p/ in all positions:

*piga > *pida* 'how much, many?' *paqegu > *qapedu* 'gall' *sepat > *sepatj* 'four' *cepecep > *teptep* 'suck'

---

[6] The reflex of *waɬiw 'bee' developed as in other Formosan languages: *i of the final syllable is absorbed by the /ɬ/, the reflex of the preceding *ɬ, and the *w is given syllabic value: *waɬiw > *aɬu* 'honey'

In three cases, *p is reflected with /b/.[7] The cognates of these forms in other languages all show irregularities. These forms have developed by contamination with forms of similar meaning (cf. the comments under the appropriate entries in the glossary).

*piɣas > *bias* 'roe of fish, shellfish' *pukuh 'knot, node' > *buqu* 'protruberance' *putaq > *butsaq/putsaq* 'foam, bubble'

B72.3.12 *t

*t has two outcomes: a palatal stop /tj/ [č] and an apico-alveolar affricate /ts/ [c], as is the case of the other languages of northeast and southwest Taiwan (§A3.3.1, 1st footnote). In pre-Paiwan, *t developed palatalization (> [č] /tj/). This provided impetus for *c to lose its affrication—i.e., *c became [t] /t/.[8] Once *c had changed to /t/, there was space available for a new [c] to develop. Thus, when the split of *t (§A3.3.1) spread to Pai the *tj [č] split into two phonemes /tj/ and /ts/.[9]

*t reflected as /tj/:

*telu > *tjelu* 'three' *timid > *tjimiz* 'lower mandible, jaw' *tukej > *tjukez* 'prop' *qetut > *qetjutj* 'break wind' *utaq > *mutjaq* 'vomit' *sepat > *sepatj* 'four'

*t reflected as /ts/:

*taqi > *tsaqi* 'feces' *tebug > *tsevud* 'spring water' *tiqaw 'k.o. fish' > *tsiqaw* 'fish' *bituka > *bitsuka* 'stomach' *katu 'send' > *katsu* 'carry, bring' *uɣat 'nerve, sinew' > *uats* 'blood vessel'

In one case, *t is reflected with /s/. There is no explanation:[10]

*tepec 'squeeze to get s.t. out' > *sepet* 'wring out'

B72.3.13 *c

*c > /t/, by the changes explained in §B72. 3.12, above:

*cucu > *tutu* 'breast', *bacuheq > *vateq* 'wash' *capaw > *tapaw* 'hut in fields' *iseci 'flesh, contents' > *seti* 'meat' *delec > *zelet* 'bow string'

Medial or final *c > s if there is a *c or *s elsewhere in the root:

*liceqes > *łiseqes* 'louse egg' *siŋuc 'snuffle mucus up into nose' > *singus* 'sniff' *qiceqic > *ki-qisaqis* 'rub up against'

In a few other cases, *c is reflected as /s/. These are doubtless borrowings from a language in which *c > /s/:[11]

---

[7] These are the only forms with /b/ that have a PAn etymology.

[8] Or rather perhaps the case is that as *c lost its affrication, this pushed *t to develop palatalization.

[9] I conceive of the spread of this change as a process whereby cognates with [ts] are borrowed from a neighboring language, replacing the original forms that had had [t] with the cognate having [ts].

[10] Dissimilation is not likely to be the explanation for there are counterexamples.

[11] It is probably no coincidence that except for the name marker *ci, these are stems that contained both *t and *c, but there are cases of stems containing *c and *t that reflect *c with /t/, as is normal:

*tecek "stick with' > *tsetek* 'have an injection'

*ci > *si* 'personal name marker' *talec 'taro' > *tjales* 'begonia' *tec 'cut off ' > *etses* 'break off head of grain for planting' (also evinces irregular addition of prothetic vowel to a monosyllabic root) *tugic > *tsuris* 'scratch a line'

In the following case, *c > /tj/. There no explanation:

*ta9ic 'cry' > *tsaŋitj* 'wail'

B72.3.14 *k

*k remained /k/ in all positions:

*katu 'send' > *katu* 'carry, bring' *kudemel > *kuḍemel* 'thick' *bitúka > *bicuka* 'stomach' *ałak > *ałak* 'child, offspring' *nacuk > *pi-natuk* 'boil'

In three cases, *k is reflected by *q. The first example is probably not inherited from PAn. The *q in the other two cases probably arose by contamination with forms of similar meaning that had /q/.

*bałituk > *vałitjuq* 'money, shiny metal' *takeb 'be covered with s.t.' > *tsaqev* 'lid' (cf. *taquv* 'mushroom cap') *pukuh 'knot, node' > *puqu* 'protruberance'

B72.3.15 *q

*q > /q/:

*qabu > *qab*u 'ashes' *taqis > *tsaqis* 'sew' *liqeɣ > *liqu* 'neck' *luseq > *luseq* 'tears'

In four cases, *-q was lost without explanation:

*baɣaq > *va* 'lungs' *łibuq > *łivu* 'pen' *púnuq 'head' > *qulipa-punu* 'crown of head' *qetaq 'raw' > *matjaq* 'unripe' (< *ma-qetaq)

B72.3.2 *h, *s

*h was lost almost without a trace, *s remained unchanged. Details are given in the subscctions bclow.

B72.3.21 *h

*h left little trace in Pai. With the loss of medial *h in trisyllabic roots, contraction of the abutting vowels took place, depending on the vowels (§B72.1.12):

*bahałiɣ > *vałi* 'board' *sehapuy > *sapuy* 'fire' *quluh > *qulu* 'head' *qumah > *quma* 'cultivate a field' *tułúh > *tsułu* 'roast'

An *h between two unlike vowels in a disyllabic root was lost, but the vowels did not contract nor do they form a diphthong:

*lahuj > *lauz* 'seaward' *ba-bahi-an > *va-vai-an* 'woman'[12]

B72.3.22 *s

*s > /s/ with very few exceptions

---

[12] In this case, I ascribe the failure of the /ai/ to diphthongize (> /ay/) to the fact that the *h left a trace in the prosody. Cf. *vnay-vay* 'dry in the sun' < *waɣi, where the *ɣ was lost without a trace, and diphthongization took place (§B72.1.2, footnote). This is speculative, for there are no additional parallel examples, and alternative explanations are also possible.

*sapegiq 'stinging (pain)' > *sapediq* 'tender footed' *sema > *sema* 'tongue' *su > *su* 'you (sing.) *isepi > *sepi* 'dream' *luseq > *luseq* 'tears' *kusekus > *kuskus* 'scrape, shave'

*s of the penult onset is assimilated to *c onset of the following syllable in the first of the following two examples, but in the second it is not. There is no explanation:

*sacaq > *tataq* 'sharpen' *iseci 'contents, flesh' > *seti* 'meat'

B72.3.3 Voiced stop consonants

There is a tendency to weaken the voiced consonants. *b, *d, *j become fricatives or affricated stops, and *ɣ disappears entirely.

B72.3.31 *b

*b > /v/ with some exceptions:

*babuy > *vavuy* 'wild pig' *beɣay > *vai* 'give' *buhet > *vutj* 'squirrel' *ɬibu 'fenced in place' > *ɬivu* 'pen' *qeɬeb > *qeɬev* 'close, shut'

In the case of the reflex of *-sebic, *b is assimilated to the preceding *s, as is the case of all An languages except Bunun (see the commentary in the glossary under *-sebic).

*-sebic > *ɬu-sepit* 'thin'

In a few cases, *b is reflected as /b/. These are probably borrowings from a dialect or language (unidentified) in which *b is preserved as *b:

*biqel > *biqel* 'goiter' *buhuwaŋ > *buang* 'hole' *buɣes > *bures* 'spew water from the mouth' *tebuk > *tsebuk* 'hit with a thump' *tabetab > *ma-tsabtsab* 'be slapped repeatedly'

In two cases, *-b is reflected as /-w/. Dialectal mixture is probably the explanation:

*iceɣab > *-tiaw* 'day before or after' *suwab > *me-suaw* 'yawn' (Paiwan dialect: *em-suav*)

In one exceptional case, *b is reflected as /g/. There is no explanation:

*butebut 'pluck out' > *gutsguts* 'weed a rice paddy'

B72.3.32 *d *j

*d and *j for the most part fell together. These two protophonemes have two reflexes /z/ and /dj/, but the two reflexes are not correlated with the protophonemes: /z/ reflects both *d and *j, and so does /dj/.[13] This is an innovation that Pai shares with Pu (§B71.3.32). With very few exceptions, there is consistency among the Pai dialects and Pu dialects: for the most part, forms that reflect *d and *j with /z/ in Pai have cognates with /z/ in Pu (if Pu forms are attested), and forms that have /dj/ in Pai have cognates in Pu with /d/ (if they are attested). Cf. the first footnote to §B71.3.32 for exceptions.
First /z/ as a reflex:

*daŋedaŋ 'heat near fire' > *zangzang* 'hot (body, weather)' *daɬum > *zaɬum* 'water' *duma > *zuma* 'other' *damaɣ 'light, torch' > *zama-n* 'torch' (< *zamaɣ-an) *djama*

---

[13] It is notable that the majority of Pai reflexes of initial and medial *j show /dj/ and not /z/. There are only two forms (out of ten) that evince /z/ and one is probably secondary: *jaɣiŋaw 'k.o. herb' > *zangaw* '*Piper betle*' *kejem > *tji-kezem* 'have eyes closed'

'morning' *qudang > *quzang* 'shrimp' *tuduq 'leak, drip' > *tjuzuq* 'leak, drop of water' *tuqed > *tjuqez* 'stump' *jaɣiyaŋaw 'an herb: sweet flag' > zangaw '*Piper betle*' *kejem > *tji-kezem* 'have eyes closed' *likuj > *likuz* 'back'

Second /dj/ as a reflex:

*danaw > *djanaw* 'lake' *dilaq 'tongue' > *djilaq* 'lick' *ludaq > *ludjaq* 'spit, spittle' *waɣed > *vaudj* 'vine' *jaɣum > *djaum* 'needle' *damaɣ 'light, torch' > *djama* 'morning' *qujaɬ > *qudjaɬ* 'rain' *tujuq > *tsudjuq* 'finger' *qaɬuj > *si-qaɬudj* 'be carried by current'

A few words reflect *d with /ḍ/. In no dialect of Pai is /ḍ/ the normal reflex of any PAn phoneme, but /ḍ/ is a phoneme of normal frequency, and it is found in basic vocabulary derived from PAn. The occurrence of /ḍ/ in reflexes of PAn roots is sporadic among the dialects. That is, /ḍ/ crops up as a reflex of *d in one or another dialect and in some cases in several dialects. A likely explanation is as follows: the merger of *j and *d was not completed in all dialects. [ḍ] was the reflex of PAn *d in pre-Paiwanic, and this [ḍ] merged with *j for the most part, but in a few exceptional cases failed to do so. Subsequently, these cases of unmerged /ḍ/ spread to one or another of the Pai dialects, but the dialect that originally had retained *[ḍ] has not been documented or it has subsequently lost some of its earlier forms with /ḍ/, for there is no documented dialect that manifests all of the forms that reflect PAn *d with /ḍ/. /ḍ/ appears in some of these forms in the various dialects. The following forms are attested with /ḍ/. Most of them evince other irregularities as well:

*daqaɬ > *ḍaqa* 'branch' (loss of *ɬ is unexplained) *dikiq > *ḍikitj* 'small' (final /tj/ unexplained) *dusa > *ḍusa* 'two' (also attested dialectally with the regular reflex: *djusa*) *kud 'grate' > *kuḍkuḍ* 'small hoe for weeding' *kudemel > *kuḍemel* 'thick' *dekuŋ > *ḍ-em-ukung* 'bend' (/u/ in the penult irregular) *qaluɬ > *ḍaluɬ* 'wave' (origin of /ḍ/ unknown) *paŋudaɬ > *panguḍaɬ* 'pandanus'

B72.3.33 *g

*g remained /g/ in initial position in monosyllabic roots and as onset of the penult or earlier:

*gatel > *gatsel* 'itchy' *gemegem > *gemgem* 'fist' *gisegis 'scrape off' > *gisagis* 'rub against (like an eraser)'

There is one exception. Cognates of this form reflect initial /k-/ in all the Formosan languages, including those that normally reflect *k- with /g-/. This form has spread by borrowing:

*galih > *k-m-ali* 'dig'

As onset or coda of the root-final syllable, *g > /d/:

*kuga 'how?' > *ma-kuda* 'what happened to?' *ŋagan > *ngadan* 'name' *piga > *pida* 'how many?' *sabig > *sabid* 'absolutely identical' *tebug 'spring' > *tsevud* 'spring water'

However in the following form, which also shows other irregularities, *g is reflected with /-r-/, as it is in neighboring languages:

*tugic > *tsuris* 'draw a line'

B72.3.4 Voiced consonants, continuants in PAn

B72.3.41 *ɣ

Normally, *ɣ is lost:

*ɣumaq > *umaq* 'house' *gaɣaŋ > *gang* 'crab' *diɣi > *mi-zi* 'stand erect' *duɣi > *djui* 'thorn' *layaɣ 'sail' > *la-laya* 'banner' *liqeɣ > *liqu* 'neck' *tusuɣ > *tsusu* 'string beads'

In a fair number of cases, *ɣ is reflected with /r/. This is parallel to the situation in Ru where *ɣ also is alternatively reflected with Ø or with /r/. In some dialects, *ɣ is reflected with [ɣ] rather than [r]. Reflection with /r/ (or /ɣ/) as opposed to Ø is not correlated with these two developments in Ru. Forms that have Ø in Pai may have a cognate with /r/ in Ru, and forms with /r / in Pai may have a cognate with Ø in Ru. The following list gives the Pai reflexes of *ɣ attested with /r/ or /ɣ/ dialectally:

*aɣi 'come here!' > *ari* 'let's go!' *biɣ > *virvir* 'lips' *buɣes > *bures* 'spew water from the mouth' *gaɣut > *garuts* 'comb' *guɣita > *guritsa* 'octopus' *ɣawut 'sharpen' > *r-m-auts* 'split wood' *keɣet 'cut a piece off' > *keretj* 'reap with a small knife' *kaɣut 'scratch with an edge, scrape' > *karuts* 'rake' *kuɣap > *kurap* 'skin ailment' *uɣat > *ɣuats/ruats* 'vein, sinew' (dialectal, with metathesis) *wiɣi > *ka-viri* 'left'

In one case, in a form not directly inherited, a cluster •ɣj developed. This became *g and is reflected as /d/:

*saɣejaɬ > *tadaɬ* 'ladder' (< *saɣjaɬ [/t/ unexplained])

B72.3.42 *l and *ɬ

*l remains /l/, a retroflexed lateral [ḷ], in all positions:

*lima > *lima* 'five' *lukut > *lukuts* 'k.o. epiphyte' *alap > *alap* 'take' *sulig > *ma-sulid* 'sleep together' *kudemel > *ma-kuḍemel* 'thick'

In one case, *l is reflected as /r/, which can be explained as assimilation to an /r/ to the right. There is only one case and no countercase. Another explanation is that this form is a borrowing from one of the Pai dialects that reflect *l as /r/.

*suluɣ 'drop, lower slowly' > *surur* 'a taut, stretched line'

In one case, *l is reflected with /ɬ/, as is the case of its cognate in Pu. This was likely an analogical change on the model of the reflex of the animal prefix *qaɬi-. This innovation was probably made only once, and the form spread secondarily:

*liceqes > *ɬiseqes* 'louse egg'

*ɬ is reflected as a front unretroflexed voiced palatal lateral [ɬ] in all positions:

*ɬabek 'surf' > *ɬavek* 'sea, ocean' *aɬak > *aɬak* 'child, offspring' *qaɬimatek > *ɬimatjek* '(mountain) leech' *tuqelaɬ > *tsuqelaɬ* 'bone'

In two cases, *ɬ is reflected as /n/. Secondary spread from other languages is the likely explanation in these cases, for cognates in other languages that reflect *ɬ with a palatalized consonant also manifest /n/ in these forms. (Cf. the commentary to *iseɬaw and *baɬaw in the glossary.)

*baław 'wash' > *vanaw* 'take a bath' (cf. Ru *ma-banaw* 'take a bath') *iseław 'wash' > *semenaw* 'wash' (Cf. Knn *mari-sináw* 'wash utensils')

B72.3.43 Nasals

*m, *n, *ŋ remained unchanged in all positions:

*mata > *matsa* 'eye' *lima > *lima* 'five' *enem > *enem* 'six' *ni > *ni* 'genitive marker' *tineun > *tj-m-enun* 'weave' *kan > *k-m-an* 'eat' *ŋilu 'teeth on edge' > *ngilu* 'pain' *taŋila > *tsalinga* 'ear' *qeteŋ > *qetseng* 'barrier, fence'

B72.3.44 *w and *y

*w > /v/ initially and medially, with a few exceptions. (For *w and *y as second members of diphthongs, cf. §B72.2.4.)

*walu > *valu* 'eight' *witewit 'swing to and fro' > *vitjivitj* 'dart back and forth' *kawayan > *kavayan* 'thorny bamboo' *siwa > *siva* 'nine' *taquweł > *tsavił* 'year'

*w > Ø between /u/ and /a/ or between/u/ and /i/:

*ławuŋ > *łaung* 'shade' *quway > *quay* 'rattan' *tuwiq > *tjuiq* 'bird sp.'

In a few other unexplained cases, *w was lost:

*wałis 'fang' > *ałis* 'tooth' *wałiw 'honey bee' > *ału* 'sugar' *sinawa > *nasi* 'breath' (< nisaa < *nisawa)

In one unexplained case, *w is retained as /w/:

*lawa 'broad' > *me-lawa* 'wide'

*y > /y/ medially between two *a's:

*daya 'inland' > *i-zaya* 'upland, upriver' *káwayan > *kavayan* 'k.o. bamboo'

After *i, *y is lost:

*liyus 'go around'> *lius* 'go around s.t.' *tiyał > *tsiał* 'belly'

The sequence *ey > /i/ (§B72.2.2):

*seyaq 'shame' > *siaq* 'shyness'

There are no Pai attestations of *y in other environments.

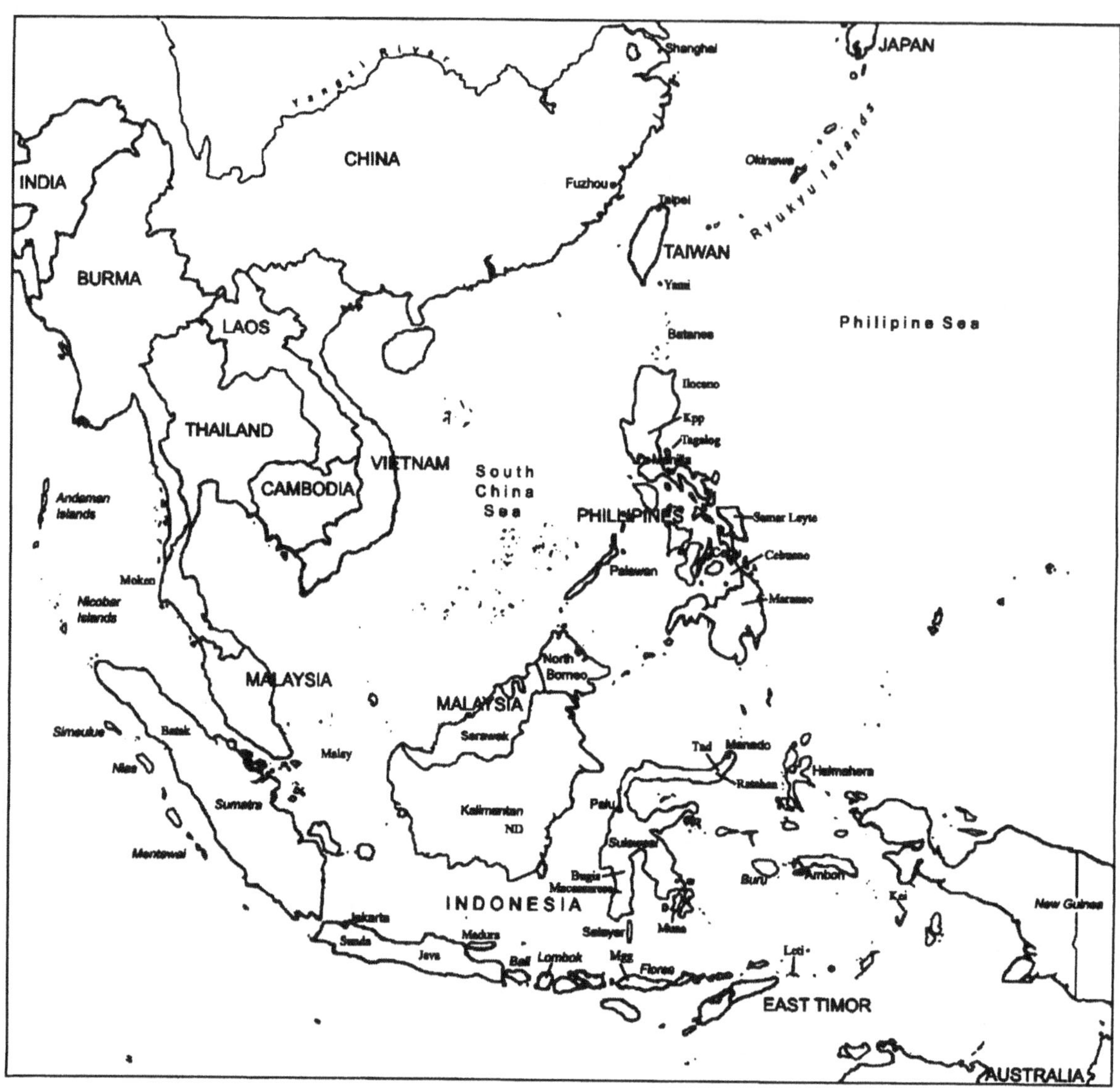

Map 4. Location of the Malayo-Polynesian languages not Oceanic.

PARTS C - G. DEVELOPMENT OF THE MALAYO-POLYNESIAN LANGUAGES

The Austronesian languages spoken outside of Taiwan (except for the Kra-Dai languages)[1] descend from a one of the Formosan languages that was brought to the Northern Philippines a millennium or more after the arrival of the Austronesians in Formosa (§A1.1). After a portion of the community departed from Taiwan, their language, called 'Proto-Malayo-Polynesian' (PMP), split from the rest of the An languages and underwent numerous innovations (§A1.1.32). In the course of four millennia, as the MP communities spread out to settle in the vast areas occupied by Austronesian speakers today, their languages diversified greatly. The innovations in the lexicon and phonology of the MP languages will be described in Parts C-G, below.
The following chart shows the correspondences between PAn and PMP consonants. The PAn vowels and diphthongs were inherited unchanged in PMP. The consonants underwent some changes, but certainly did not undergo sharp changes: as can be seen in the chart, PMP had changed only *ɬ, *s, and *h in the space of more than a millennium after the earliest PAn. In the course of the next four millennia or so, the daughter languages for the most part made considerable changes, as will be seen in the succeeding chapters, but some of them were remarkably conservative in retaining the PMP phonology. This conservatism of PMP allows us to describe the developments of the MP languages in terms of development from PAn without obscuring the picture, and makes possible a comparison with developments of the Formosan languages

CHART ONE: THE DEVELOPMENT OF PMP PHONEMES FROM PAN

PAn	**PMP**	**PAn**	**PMP**
*p	†p	*l	†l
*t	†t	*ɬ	†ñ, †l, †n
*k	†k	*m, *n	†m, †n
*q	†q	*ŋ	†ng [ŋ]
*b	†b	*c	†c
*d	†d	*s	†h
*j	†j	*h	Ø[2]
*g	†g	*w	†w
*ɣ	†ɣ	*y	†y

[1] The Kra-Dai languages may also descend from the Formosan languages. Cf. the comment in the last footnote to §A1.1.31.

[2] Although *h was lost in PMP, medial *h left traces in the form of hiatus, that contrasted with a glide transition—i.e., *h was lost but vowel sequences developed (§A3.3.31).

C. The Philippine languages

The 'Philippine languages' is a designation given to the languages spoken in the Philippines and adjacent areas (the northern arm of Sulawesi, North Borneo, and also Yami spoken on Orchard Island, politically part of Taiwan, but in a subgroup with the languages spoken on the Batanes Islands in the northern Philippines). Chamorro (treated here in §C2. ff.) is considered by many scholars to be among the Philippine languages. The Philippine languages are of particular interest to the reconstruction of PAn because the Philippines were the earliest settled area outside of Formosa, and the rest of the An languages are thought to have been brought to their current locations from the Philippines. (Cf. the discussion of §§A1.1.3ff.) They are also of interest for the reconstruction of PAn because they happen to be conservative in their phonology to a large extent, and in some cases very conservative in their morphology and syntax. The Philippine languages do not form a subgroup although they have made many innovations in common, not shared by the other MP languages. These were innovations that spread secondarily: they are found on the lexical, phonological, and morphological levels, possibly also on the syntactic level (although this has not been investigated to any great extent). Some of these changes have not spread to all languages of the area but have left islands of retention from PMP.[3] On the phonological level, there are three important innovations from PMP: (1) the mergers of *d, *j together with *g as onset or coda of the root-final syllable;[4] (2) the change of *q to /ʔ/ and its loss in word-initial position, which left two islands of retention in Kalamian of northern Palawan and Tboli in southern Mindanao, where *q merged with /k/; and (3) the change of *ɣ to /g/ which spread to an area from the Tagalog regions in Luzon (and affected also a few of the languages of northern and central Luzon) to northern Sulawesi and northern Kalimantan.

[3] In other words, I assert here that there is no such thing as 'Proto-Philippine' as opposed to PMP. Indeed it is possible to establish subgroups among the Philippine languages, but the first-order Philippine subgroups are coordinate with other MP subgroups that can be established.

[4] An island of retention is found in a single almost unknown Negrito language of Panay, Inati, for a dialect of which (Sogodnun spoken by only a handful of people) a palatal reflex is reported in the word for 'rain' *udyan* (Pennoyer 1986: 26). Further, Chamorro, §C2ff. which probably originated in the Philippines, retains a contrast in the reflexes of *j and *d. The Chamorros left the Philippines before the merger had spread to their community in the Philippines. Finally, languages of northern Luzon do not merge the reflexes of a *g onset in the root-final syllable with *d and *j.

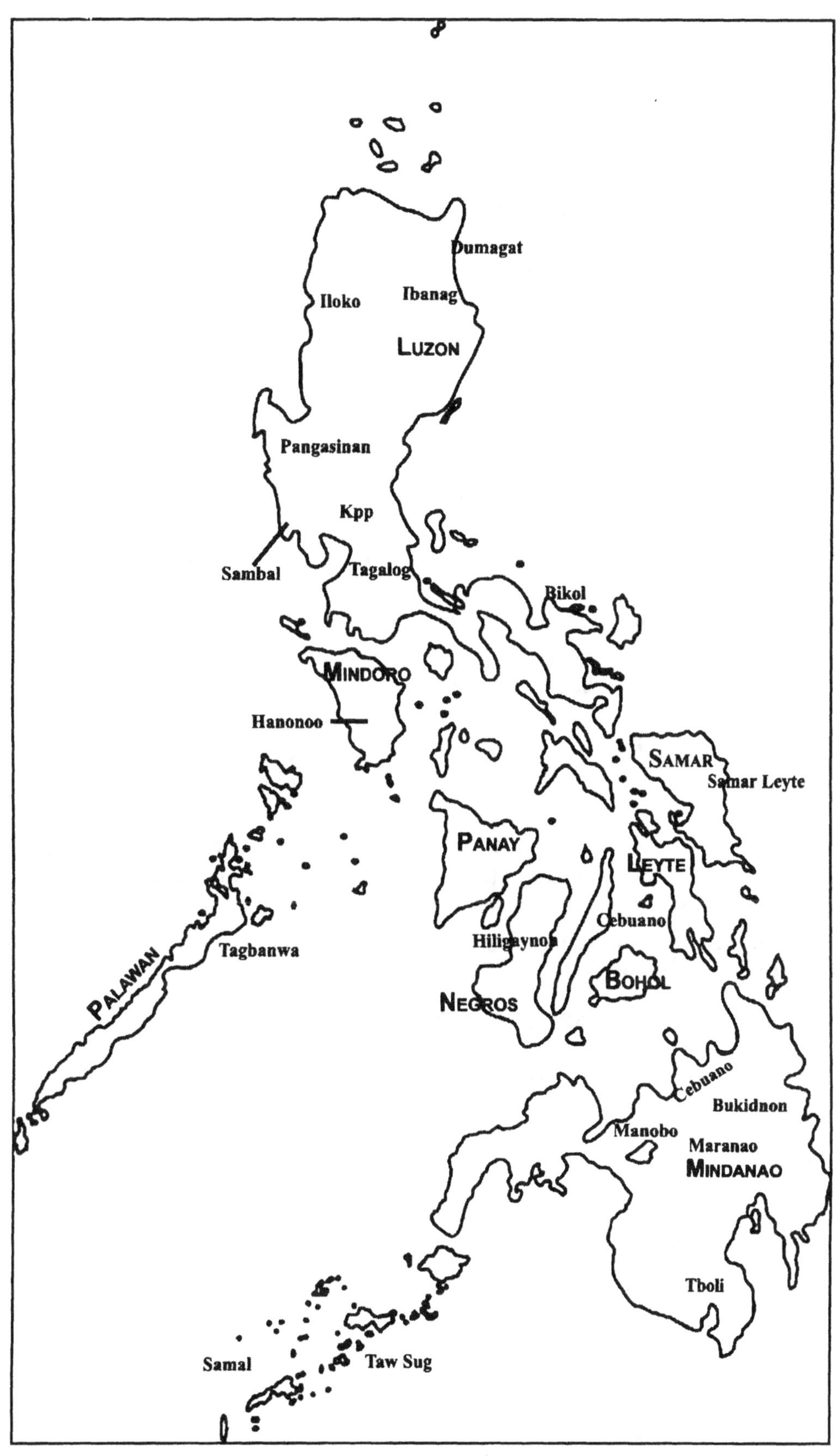

Map 5. The Philippines.

CHAPTER ONE
Tagalog

C1.0 Tagalog and the Philippine languages

Tagalog (Tag) is the official language of the Philippines and is spoken widely as a second language throughout the Philippines. It is the native language of the Manila metropolitan region and the surrounding provinces and has spread to many areas of the Philippines where Tagalogs have migrated. It is spoken as a second language by most of the younger population of the Philippines. Tag is one of the "Philippine languages" (cf. the introduction immediately preceding). On the basis of comparison with other Philippine languages, we may conclude that Tagalog originated far to the south of its current location. The irretular reflexes of *l (§C1.3.42), for example, is one of the indications of this fact. Even though Tag is more innovative in its phonology and morphology than some of the other languages of the Philippines, we treat it here exhaustively rather than one of the more conservative languages because (1) it was one of the languages on which Dempwolff (1938) based his first reconstruction; (2) it has a great importance as the national language of the Philippines; (3) it is extensively documented in dictionaries, the earliest of which was published in 1613 (San Buenaventura1613). In addition to the innovations listed above, common to the Philippine languages, Tag has merged the medial reflexes of *j, *d, and *g (which first became /r/) with the reflexes of *l. This innovation is shared by a large number of languages located on the western half of an imaginary line running from the Tag provinces on Luzon, southward to Mindanao. Further, Tag has merged *e and *i (or *u, depending on the environment). Finally, the northern Tag dialects have lost /ʔ/ except in phrase-final position, a change that is spreading through the entire Tag area. Where in certain instances these innovations obscure the Philippine reflection of protoforms, we quote forms from other Philippine languages that did not make the innovation.
The following chart lists the phonemes of Tag. There are palatalized consonants /ʃ/ and /c/, not listed in this chart, that have developed in historical times and are not found in words with a PMP (or PAn) etymology.

CHART ONE. PHONEMES OF TAGALOG

Consonants

voiceless stops	p	t	k	ʔ
voiced stops	b	d	g	
spirants		s		h
nasals	m	n	ng [ŋ]	
liquids	w	l, r	y	

Vowels

high	i		u
mid	e		o
low		a	
diphthongs	iw	aw, ay	oy

The vowels may be short or long, except in absolute final[5] position, in which case there is no length contrast. With a very few exceptions vowels in closed syllables are short.[6] Primary stress in Tag falls in the long vowel furthest to the right in the phonological word (the word plus enclitics), and if there is no long vowel in a word, stress falls on the end. Here we mark the long vowels with an acute accent, and if the word does not contain a long vowel we mark the final syllable with an acute accent. In the following examples, the stressed syllable is written in bold italics:

*magkákátúl**ú**yan* 'will get married' ***má**nanagat* 'a fisherman' *wa**lá?*** 'not there'

It should be noted that Tag has enclitics that form a phonological word with the morphological word that precedes them. This means that the placement of word stress may be on an enclitic:

*Walá na **ngá** e* 'It's all gone.' *Babasahin **kó*** 'My reading matter.'

There are complexities in the orthography of the word-final syllable. We make three points. First, /i/ and /u/ are automatically lowered to [e] and [o], respectively, in final syllables. Second, in final syllables, [i] does not contrast with [e] and [u] does not contrast with [o]. Third, when not word final, /ay/ and /aw/ variably became /é/ and /ó/ respectively—that is, when not final, they may be pronounced long /e/ and long /o/ or /ay/ and /aw/. The upshot of this is that /e/ and /o/ have two origins: (1) < *i and *u, (2) < *ay and *aw, in which case they vary with /e/ and /o/, respectively (but /e/ and /o/ < *i and *u do not vary with /ay/ and /aw/).[7] Here we follow standard orthography in transcribing forms with /e/ and /o/: we write *ay* and *aw* for /e/ and /o/ that derive historically from *ay and *aw (and vary with /ay/ and /aw/), and we write *e* and *o* for /e/ and /o/ when these phonemes developed from *i and *u.

C1.1 Changes that characterize Tag in general

Tag, like most of the Philippine languages, has undergone metathesis and a large amount of disyllabization by syncope of trisyllabic forms and lengthening of monosyllabic roots. That, together with the change of the segmental protophonemes, has rendered a portion of the Tag vocabulary different enough from the original PAn form to make cognates unrecognizable as such. However, in many cases, the change from the PAn form is not very great and cognates with forms from the more conservative of the Formosan languages or other MP languages are readily apparent.

---

[5] We say 'absolute final' (rather than root final or word final) because the final vowel of a root may be long or short if an enclitic follows it and forms a phonological word with it:

wala? 'not there' + *na* 'by now' > *walá na* 'no longer there' (Cf. the discussion at the end of this section.)

[6] Only one form inherited from PMP has a long vowel in a closed syllable. It became closed by virtue of having a nasal intercalated as the coda of the penult (§A3.7.2):

*pícan > *mínsan* 'once'

Otherwise closed syllables are always short. In forms with closed syllables, the stress automatically falls on the end. Therefore, we normally do not quote the stress in Tag forms with closed penults, although in this chapter we do do so when the discussion involves stress of the Tag reflex.

[7] This variable rule, although of wide application in the current language, only affects one word with a PMP etymology.

C1.1.1 Loss of a syllable by syncope

PAn trisyllabic roots may lose a syllable in their development to Tag by the loss of the penult or by the loss of the antepenult.

C1.1.11 *e > ∅ in the penult of trisyllabic roots. Similarly, *u before *w and *i before *y are lost in the penult of trisyllabic roots. These rules are almost without exception:

*saɣejał > *hagdán* 'stairs, ladder' *seqeɣet > *higít* 'tight, tied tight' *iseguŋ > *ilóng* 'nose' *baɣiyus > *bagyó* 'typhoon' *qałuwaŋ 'large ruminant' > *anwáng* 'carabao'

In a few forms, metathesis of the *e in the penult and an *i in the antepenult took place before the loss of *e:

*isełáw > *hináw* 'wash hands' (< *siław < *esiław)[8]

C1.1.12 Other penultimate vowels in roots of three syllables or more are lost if the stress was or had come to be on the end syllable (§A3.5.3).

*beɣunáy > *bignáy* 'a tree: *Antidesma bunius*' *paŋudáł > *pandán* 'pandanus' *pacaqán > *pasán* 'carry on the shoulder' (Cb *pasʔan* 'carry on the shoulder') *qamití > *antí* 'a shrub: *Solanum nigrum*'

However, the antepenult was lost in the following form, perhaps because it was felt to be a prefix:

*palisi 'taboo' > *lihí* 'crave s.t. in pregnancy'

If the root had a liquid onset in the penult or final syllable, syncope does not take place in most cases:[9]

*bałituk > *balitók* 'gold ore' *dusa + R- > *dalawá* 'two'[10] *qałiméqec 'invisible' > *alimís* 'secret' *inúm 'drink' + -en > *inumín* 'drink it' *talikuj > *talikód* 'turn the back' *tiŋadaq > *tingaláʔ* 'look upwards'

C1.1.13 All the MP languages are affected by a loss of *e in the antepenult in some words.

*sehapuy > *apóy* 'fire' *iseław > *hináw* 'wash hands' (< *siław < *esiław)

However, a consonant followed by *e in the antepenult was not lost in the Philippine languages if it was metathesized in post-MP. The C was lost in Tag but not in other Philippine languages in CC simplification and is indirectly reflected by compensatory lengthening (§C1.1.16).

---

[8] Tag /i/ may reflect *i or *e (i.e., Tag provides no evidence for metathesis). However, Cb /i/ must derive from *i and not from *e. Therefore, Cb *hináw* derives from *siław and not *seław and gives the evidence that metathesis took place.

[9] However, syncope of the penult does take place in some forms, especially in forms consisting of a disyllabic root plus affix:

*beli + *en > *bilhin* 'buy it' (< *bilihin) *palatík 'spear gun' > *paltík* 'home-made gun'

[10] This form varies with *dalwa*. In the case of the variant *dalawa*, the *u of the penult changed to /a/ because unstressed vowels in the penult between liquids are neutralized. Cf. *palayók* 'pot for cooking staple' < Ml *periok* [pəriyuk] 'pot', where the penult was borrowed as /a/.

*leqacem > *ma-ásim* 'sour' (< *alsem [cf. Cb *aslum* 'sour'] < *qalecem [§C1.1.3])
*seqaɬi 'string warp threads in loom' > *hánay* 'row, line' (< *haʔnay < *seqeɬai [cf. Cb *hanʔay* 'string warp threads in loom'])

C1.1.14 In a few trisyllabic roots, the antepenult was lost. The first two of these forms are secondary. In the third case, the cognates may possibly have petrified prefixes, and the Tag reflex has petrified the prefix *maN-* with this root:

*mantálaq 'morning, evening star' > *tálaq* 'planet, bright star' *qacuwal 'pry up' > *suʔál* 'push with lever' (< *acuwal [§C1.1.42]) *ti-qadaw > PMP †ti-daw 'look at, stretching the neck' > *pan-dáw* 'inspect traps'

In pre-Tagalog in trisyllables that had not been disyllabized, the contrast of the vowels in the antepenult was neutralized. In the following form we assume that the antepenult was weakened to *e before the penult was lost by the rule of §C1.1.11:

*ɣetac 'break through' + *ba- > *bigtas* 'unstitched' (< *beɣtac < *beɣetac < *baɣetac)

C1.1.15 Contraction of vowels

When loss of a C between two vowels led to a vowel sequence, contraction between the two vowels takes place under two circumstances: (1) like vowels contract and become long; (2) *e merges with an abutting vowel:

*bahaɬiɣ 'butress root' > *pánig* 'board' (/p/ by contamination) *sicuheq 'wash' > *hísoʔ* 'brush teeth' *bulehaɣ 'cataract' > *bulág* 'blind' *paheɣaw > *págaw* 'hoarseness'

C1.1.16 Simplification of consonant clusters

Consonant sequences that developed by syncope of the medial syllable in trisyllabic roots were simplified if they contained laryngeals that were lost: *ʔ (from PAn *q or from hiatus) and *h (from PAn *s). (Cf. the examples in §C1.1.44ff., below.) The clusters *ls, *ld, *lŋ, and *gd that developed in trisyllabic roots by syncope of the medial syllable also were simplified. As is the case of the laryngeals (§C1.1.441), if the lost consonants had been codas of the penult, the preceding vowel was lengthened. If they had been the onset of the final syllable, there was no compensatory lengthening. These changes are shared by other central Philippine languages (but not by all of them):

*caleŋaɣ > *sángag* 'cook without oil' (< *salŋaɣ) *leqacem > *ma-ásim* 'sour' (< *alsem [cf. Cb *aslum* 'sour'] < *qalecem [§C1.1.3]) *qaɬegaw > *áraw* 'sun, day' (< *aldaw [cf. Bik *aldaw* 'sun, day']) *qulun 'rest head' + *-an 'locative' > *únan* 'pillow' (< *ulnan < *qulunán) *siɣejaq > *higáʔ* 'lie down' (< *higdaʔ [cf. Cb *higdaʔ* 'lie down'])

C1.1.2 Disyllabization of monosyllabic roots

Tag, like most of the An languages, disyllabized monosyllabic roots inherited from PAn (§A3.6.2), except in the case of enclitics.[11] Disyllabization was effected (1) by doubling or reduplicating the monosyllabic root, (2) by petrifying a prefix, (3) by lengthening the nucleus, or (4) by adding a prothetic vowel, the reflex of *e.
(1) Examples of reduplication or doubling:

---

[11] Not all of the Philippine languages disyllabize monosyllabic roots. For example, the form *puc, discussed under (4) of this section, is reflected in Mar as *pus* 'stub, butt, unconsumed part of firewood'.

*biɣ 'lips' > *bibíg* 'mouth' (cf. Ilk *birbir* 'rimming') *bit > *bitbit* 'carry in fingers'

(2) Examples of disyllabization by adding a petrified affix:

*but + *ise- > *íbot* 'pull out plants, nails, and the like'

(3) When the nucleus was lengthened, *e [ə] developed after the vowel of the root, and a glottal stop developed between the vowel and *e. Further, the root vowel was often (but not always[12]) lengthened.[13] This development is common to most of the languages of the Philippines. In Tag the *e > /i/ or when adjacent to /u/, *e > /u/ (/o/ finally) (§C1.2.2). Otherwise, it became /i/:

*kan > *káʔin* 'eat' (< *kaʔen) *ɣik > *giʔík* 'thresh' *luk 'concave' > *lúʔok* 'bay'

In some cases /h/ was intercalated between the two vowels that had developed in disyllabization:

*buc > *búhos* 'pour out'

Monosyllabic roots containing diphthongs or glides disyllabized by stretching the diphthong or glide:

*taw 'man' > táwo 'man' (dialectal)[14] *łuɣ > *niyóg* 'coconut'

(4) Examples of disyllabization by adding a prothetic vowel:

*puc 'ended' > *upós* 'consumed' (< *epus)

C1.1.21 Epenthetic vowels in doubled monosyllabic roots

Doubled monosyllabic roots developed an epenthetic vowel in PAn between the two monosyllabic elements. In Tag, almost all of these epenthetic vowels were lost by syncope, although traces remain in the treatment of *ł in a few monosyllabic roots (cf. the examples below in §C1.3.432). In some of the Philippine languages, a stress developed on the epenthetic vowel, and this is reflected in a long vowel in the penult. This vowel usually harmonizes[15] with the root vowel:

*watewat 'flutter > *watáwat* 'flag' *bicebic 'sprinkle' > *b-al-isbis-an* 'roof gutters' (Cf. Cb *bisíbis* and *bisbis* 'sprinkle')

C1.1.3 Metathesis

Many of the Philippine languages evince a large amount of metathesis. In Tag, however, metathesis is not a process that has lead to major reformation of inherited forms. Aside from the metathesis that affects all of the MP languages (§A3.5.4), in many of the Philippine languages, metathesis affects sequences of laryngeals or continuants (liquids and /s/). Tag shows only a few examples of these cases of metatheses:

---

[12] In a few forms, disyllabized from monosyllabic roots, the penult was apparently shortened and the stress shifted to the end, as, for example, in *giʔík* 'thresh' < *ɣik. The Cb cognate is variable in vowel length: both *gíʔuk and giʔúk* occur. There is no explanation for the stress pattern.

[13] In suffixed forms the root penult—i.e, the original root vowel, may be shortened. For example, the root 'eat' *káʔin* (< *kan) has a nominal derivative *kánin* 'cooked rice' < *kaʔnin < *kaʔinín. Cf. §C1.1.12 for the loss of the penult in this form. For the lengthening of /a/ after the loss of *ʔ, see §C1.1.441).

[14] Manila Tag has changed this to *táʔo* by an analogical process described in §C1.1.42.

[15] An example where the epenthetic vowel was stressed but reflects *e rather than harmonizing is SL *hapúhap* 'look for by groping' < *sapésap.

*baɣaŋáw > *bangyaw* 'botfly' (< *bayngaw < *bayangaw [§C1.3.41, 2nd¶]) *łiki-łikí > *kili-kilí* 'armpit' (< *liki-likí) *qusalipan > *alupíhan* 'centipede' *seqeɣet > *higít* (< *seɣeʔet < *seɣeqet) *tiqeɣab 'belch' > *tigáb* 'gasp' (< *tiɣeʔab < *tiɣeqab) *tiheław > *tináw* 'clear' (< *tineʔaw)[16] *tusuq > *tu-tuʔo* 'true' (< *tuqus + *R-)

In Cb, for example, this metathesis is widespread (the examples quoted are all from Cb):

*baqeɣu > *bagʔu* 'new' (< *baʔgu* [attested dialectally]) *qałegaw > *adlaw* 'day' (< *aldaw) *kałuskus 'fingernail' > *kalukhu* 'scrape (< *kaluhkuh) *leqacem > *aslum* 'sour' (< *alsem < *qalesem)

A few forms show idiosyncratic metathesis (unless otherwise indicated the examples are from Tag):

*atac > *ma-taʔás* 'high' (< *taac) *basequ > *bahóʔ* 'smelly (< *baseuq) *jaqewis > *dáyo* 'stranger' (< *daʔyu < *jaqiwes < *jasiweq[17]) *kudemel > *ma-dakmel* 'thick' (SL) (< ma-kademel [/a/ < *u in the antepenult) *liseqec > *lisáʔ* 'nit' (*leceq < *leseceq[18] < *liseceq) *ŋucuq 'snout, beak' > *ungós* 'upper lip' *qaselu > *hálo* 'pestle' (< *haʔlu < *haʔelu <*saqelu)

In a few disyllabic roots, an unstressed penultimate vowel was metathesized to initial (preconsonantal position). These forms show other irregularities and are borrowed:

*ɣetac 'break through, open' > *agtás* 'cut short path' *geteŋ > *igtíng* 'tautness' (< *gitíng) *lepac > *alpás* 'freed from what is restraining' (also *lipás* 'past, gone by') *łibú 'pen' > *ulbóʔ* 'pigpen'

In one case, /d/ > /r/ before a vowel-initial prefix (§C1.3.32). Subsequently, the /r/ was generalized throughout the paradigm and after that, metathesized with a preceding /l/:

*buleg > *buról* 'hill' (< *bulur < *bulod [cf. Cb *búlod* 'low hill'])

C1.1.4 Insertion of laryngeals

Vowel-initial syllables developed a laryngeal in most of the Philippine languages. This is /ʔ/ in most cases in Tag.

*atac > *ma-taʔás* 'high' (< *taas by metathesis [§C1.1.3]) *balu > *báʔo* 'widow, widower' (< *bau [§C1.3.42, 2nd¶])

In word-initial position [ʔ] is lost, both the automatic [ʔ] that developed before vowels and the [ʔ-] that developed from *q-.

16 We reconstructed *tiheław and not *tiłehaw on the basis of a dialectal Cb *tiʔnaw* 'clear' (urban Cb shows metathesis *tinʔaw*). For this reason we assume that Tag *tináw* reflects metathesis.

17 I am assuming this metathesis for two reasons: (1) this form accounts for the other reflex: *ma-láyoʔ* 'far' (*jaqewis > *jasiweq > *daiweq > *dayuʔ > *-láyoʔ* [after a vowel final prefix]); (2) the reflexes in the other MP languages also can be explained as developments from *jasiweq.

18 We assume a weakening of the antepenult *i to *e in pre-Tagalog and subsequent contraction of the two *e's that developed. Cb reflects *liceqes with *lusáʔ*, which shows that the antepenult was weakened to *e. We assume that Tag and Cb innovated *liceqes the same way.

C1.1.41 /ʔ/ reflecting *h-

In some cases, the presence of a glottal stop indicates that the PAn form had an *h between two vowels. When this *h was lost, a vowel sequence developed in which a [ʔ] was intercalated to avoid hiatus:

*buhet 'squirrel' > *búʔot* 'rabbit' (< *buut < *buet)

In some cases, the glottal stop in a Philippine languages is the only indication of the occurrence of *h in the PAn etymon. In the northern Tag dialects this /ʔ/ was lost when abutting on a C. Cf. §C1.1.44 for a discussion of glottal-stop loss:

*baɣehat > *bigát* 'heaviness' (< *begʔat < *beʔgat < *beʔeɣat < *beeɣat < *beheɣat[19] cf. Cb *bugʔat* 'heavy') *buheni > *búni* 'k.o. skin infection' (Cb *bunʔi* 'k.o. skin infection' < *bunehi [metathesis]) *betehus > *buthuʔ* 'appear' (Cb) (< *butesuʔ < *buteʔus < *buteus) *ɣabihí > *gabʔi* 'night' (Tag southern dialect) (< *ɣabihi)

A glottal stop did not invariably develop when hiatus had come into being. When the hiatus was between the antepenult and the penult, the two vowels contracted if the penult was short. See the examples of §C1.3.21. Here is another example:

*ta- + emic > *tamís* 'sweetness' (Stress moved to the end probably because *tamis* is an adjective.)

C1.1.42 Insertion of glottal stop in the middle or at the end of a word

In northern Tag dialects the contrast between /awu/ and /aʔu/and /ayi/ and/ aʔi/ was lost. Subsequently, in these dialects, a glottal stop developed to replace /w/ and /y/ glides after /a/ followed by /i/ or /u/. However, because of dialect mixture the contrast was reinstated in those dialects that had lost it. Thus, there is variation between glottal stop and a glide in forms that have these sequences:

*bahi + R- > *babaye/babaʔe* 'woman' *ɣuwaŋ 'hole' > *guʔáng/guwáng* 'hollow' *taw > *táwu/táʔo* 'person'

Glottal stop codas developed sporadically in loan words ending in a vowel. Some of these derive from PAn or PMP, but the presence of a glottal stop coda in Tag indicates that the form is not directly inherited:

*balaŋa > *balangaʔ* 'k.o. wide-mouthed clay pot' *buɣesu > *pani-bughoʔ* 'be jealous' *buŋuh > *bungóʔ* 'skull' *kiwa > *kaliwáʔ* 'left' *paheli > *palíʔ* 'spleen' *paniki > *paníkiʔ* 'fruit bat' *tambuɣi > *tambúliʔ* 'horn made of a conch shell'

Further, a final glottal stop also developed in vocatives and negatives before a pause and was in many cases spread throughout the paradigm:

*kaka > *kakáʔ* 'eldest brother or sister' *wada 'there is' > *waláʔ* 'there is not'

---

[19] The *e of the antepenult developed early at a stage in which the contrast between the vowels in the antepenult was neutralized but before the antepenult became /a/ as discussed in §C1.2.2.

C1.1.43 Insertion of /h/

An /h/ develops preceding a vowel initial suffix[20] and in a small number of other items that developed vowel sequences.

*baqeɣuh 'new' > *bágo; bágo* 'new' + *-in* > *bagúhin* 'renew' *uɫah 'first ahead of others' > *úna* 'first' *úna*+ *-an* > *unáhan* 'do s.t. before he/she does it' *beli > *bilí* 'buy' *bilí* + *-in* > *bilhín* 'buy it' (< *bilihin)

An /h/ developed in the following forms when *l was lost (§C1.3.42):

*baláy > *báhay* 'house' (< *báay [with stress shifted to the first of two consecutive vowels] < *baáy) *quleg > *úhod* 'worm' (also *úʔod*) *caleɣ > *sahíg* 'flooring'

An intervocalic /h/ developed when a phonetic final [-h][21] and a /ʔ/ metathesized:

*taqu 'know, be familiar' > *pagká-tahoʔ* 'understanding' (< *pagkátaʔu [pagkátaʔuh])

C1.1.44 Loss of laryngeals

In the northern Tag dialects (and spreading throughout the Tag dialects currently) /ʔ/ is lost except intervocalically and in absolute final position (§C1.3.14). This rule holds for the [ʔ] that developed in syllable-onset position (§C1.1.4, above) and for the [ʔ] that developed from *q (§C1.3.14). There are four developments caused by the loss of the laryngeals:

C1.1.441 A [ʔ] onset is lost without trace, but loss of a [ʔ] coda caused compensatory lengthening of the preceding vowel:[22]

*baqeɣuh > *bágo* 'new' (< *baʔgo [cf. Bik *baʔgu* 'new']) *ciqeŋit >*síngit* 'chink, slit, tight corner' *qaselu > *hálo* 'pestle' (< *haʔlu < *saqlu < *saqelu)

An exception is the following form, which shortened the penult (moving the stress to the final syllable) for onomatopoetic reasons:

*baqesin > *bahín* 'sneeze' (< *baʔhin < *baʔehin)

C1.1.442 Post-consonantal [ʔ] that was lost does not cause compensatory lengthening:

*baɣeqaŋ > *bagáng* 'molar' (< *bagʔang [cf. Cb *bagʔang* 'molar']) *bulehaɣ 'cataract, having impaired vision' > *bulág* 'blind' (< *bulʔaɣ < *buleʔaɣ < *buleaɣ)

C1.1.443 *s (> PMP †h) was lost in trisyllabic roots with a short-vowel penult, when it was the onset of the penult or the final syllable. First, the penult was lost, and then the resulting

---

[20] The intercalation of /h/ before affixes has very few exceptions because final vowels in a phonological word became devoiced automatically—i.e., a non-contrastive [h] coda developed.

[21] Final [-h] is non-contrastive in Tag. A vowel in final position automatically devoices—i.e., automatically adds an [-h].

[22] There are exceptions, where preconsonantal *ʔ (that is, a *ʔ-coda preceding a syllable with C onset) did not cause compensatory lengthening. There is no good explanation. Metathesis of the *ʔ to post-consonantal position is a possible explanation (for there was no compensatory lengthening when post-consonantal /ʔ/ was lost). Metathesis is not a likely explanation in the case of *bahín* 'sneeze' (we assume the accent shifted because of sound symbolism), but metathesis is likely in the case of *tigáb* 'belch':

*baqesin > *bahín* 'sneeze' (< *baʔhin [cf. Cb *baʔhun* 'sneeze']) *tiqeɣab 'belch' > *tigáb* 'gasp' (cf. Han *tigʔab* 'belch')

*hC cluster (< *sC) was simplified with compensatory lengthening in the cases where the *s had been the onset of the penult (i.e., loss of an *h-coda like the loss of a *ʔ-coda caused compensatory lengthening):

*isepún > *ípon* 'gather' (< *ihpun < *ispun) *qiseɬép > *panag-ínip* 'dream'

However, in the following forms compensatory lengthening does not take place. There is no explanation:[23]

*iseguŋ > *ilóng* 'nose' *kasepal > *kapál* 'thick'

C1.1.444 If *s onset of a final syllable was lost but without compensatory lengthening of the penult:

*bakesaw > *bakáw* 'tree of tidal swamp: *Rhizophora* spp.' (< *bakhaw < *baksaw [cf. Cb *bakhaw* '*Rhizophora*']) *busekag > *bukád* 'open up (flower)' (< *bukhag [cf. Cb *bukhad* 'spread out s.t. rolled up'] < *bukesag)

Note that rule for laryngeal loss applies to trisyllabic roots. Stems consisting of a disyllabic root plus a prefix are not affected by this rule. The penultimate vowel is lost (§C1.1.1), but the reflex of the *s-onset of the final syllable is not lost:

*pa- + nakis > *panhik* 'go up' (< *pa-nahik < *pa-nasik [§C1.1.3])

Metathesis caused a retention of a reflex of *s in the following forms, for a reflex of initial *s (i.e. *s onset of the antepenult) is retained (§C1.3.222):

*qaselu > *hálo* 'pestle' (< *haʔlu [cf. Cb *halʔu* 'pestle'] < *saqelu) *quseɬap > *hunʔap* 'fish scales' (WBM) (< *huʔnap < *huʔeɬap < *suqeɬap) *udesi > *hulí* 'last' (< *hudi < *udhi [cf. SL *urhi* 'last'])

In the following case, the reflex of the *s-onset is retained in a root that was trisyllabic in PAn. This probably was borrowed from a language that did not lose laryngeals:

*binesiq > *binhiʔ* 'seed'

There is one exception, where the *s-onset of the penult was lost in PMP before the rule of compensatory lengthening was in effect.

*ɬisebic > *nipís* 'thin'

C1.1.5 Vowel length

The Philippine languages north of Mindanao and on the east coast of Mindanao retain the PAn root stress patterns to a large extent: in Tag and other central Philippine languages, these patterns are reflected as vowel length. However, these patterns have been disturbed through analogy, for morphology requires accent shift in some cases: nominalization involves shift of stress (a root with a long penult becomes shortened, and a root with a short penult becomes lengthened); statives shorten the penult if it is long. The original stress pattern has also been disturbed when compensatory lengthening occurs under certain circumstances (§§C.1.1.15, C.1.1.16, C1.1.44ff.). Finally, sporadic addition of a

[23] If we assume that metathesis had taken place between the *s and the *g, that would explain the short penult in this form (cf. the following paragraph), but there is no supporting evidence to show that the shortness of the penult unequivocally proves that metathesis had taken place.

mora when a C is lost or in disyllabization (§C1.1.2) has led to lengthening of vowels in some cases:

*taw > *táwo/táʔo* 'person' *baláy > *báhay* 'house' (< *báay)

C1.2 Vowels and diphthongs

Tag has merged *e with /i/ but has retained the other vowels and the diphthongs. In historical times *i split to /i/ and /e/and *u split into /u/ and /o/. Cf. the comment at the end of §C1.0.

C1.2.1 *i, *u

When not syncopated, *i > /i/:

*sadiɣi > *halígi* 'post' *udesi > *hulí* 'last'

In a few cases, the /i/ in final position is lowered to /e/. There are dialects in which /i/ in final syllables is always lowered to [e] or even [ɛ]. These forms were borrowed from one of those dialects.[24]

*ba-bahi > *babáʔe* 'woman' *taqi > *táʔe* 'feces'

When not syncopated, *u > /u/. In word-final syllables /u/ is automatically lowered to /o/.[25] There is no contrast between /u/ and /o/ in final syllables.

*bitúka 'stomach' > *bitúka* 'intestines' *buɣuk > *bugók* 'rotten' *bukij 'mountain' > *búkid* 'cultivated field' *acu > *áso* 'dog' *qaluɬ > *álon* 'long wave, swell'

C1.2.2 *e

*e was lost in the penult by syncope in trisyllabic roots. Otherwise, *e > /i/ with some exceptions:

*beɣekec > *bigkis* 'bundle' *cepecep > *sipsip* 'suck' *qaɬiméqec > *alimís* 'furtive, secret' (< ʔalimiʔís) *qatep > *atíp* 'roof'

*e is assimilated to /u/ when adjacent to syllables with *u and lowered to /o/ in final syllables:

*bukes > *buhok* 'hair' *bekut 'bent' > *bukót* 'hunch-backed'

*e > /a/ before *q and *s—i.e., *eq >/aʔ/ and *es > /a/:

*bugeq > *bulá?* 'foam' *buɣes > *buga* 'spew water out, spit chewed herbs on wound'

However, *eq in position following a syllable with *i becomes /iʔ/:

*iseq > *íhi?* 'urine'

Syncopation of *e in the penult took place before *e changed to /a/ before *q. In the following form the penult was elided before it could change to /a/:

---

[24] The pronunciation /i/ or /e/ in final syllables is variable in some cases:

*laki + R- > *laláki/laláke* 'male'

[25] Lowering occurs only in word-final syllables. In stem final position before a suffix /u/, is not lowered:

kudkód 'grate' + *-an* > *kudkurán* 'grater' *inóm* 'drink' + *-in* > *inumín* 'drink it'

*qalimeqec > *alimís* 'invisible' (< *ʔalimʔes < *ʔalimeʔés)

In at least one case, a penult with *e before *q was not elided until after *eq > *aʔ. After *aʔ had developed, there was metathesis, and then the *e that had moved to the penult was elided. There is no explanation for why the *aʔ had time to develop before elision of the penultimate *e:

*deɣeqec 'move vigorously' > *dagʔás, dagás* 'with haste' (< *daɣeʔec < *deɣaʔec)

In the following form, the *e contracted with a preceding *u after the *h between *u and *e was lost (§C.1.1.15) and before *eq could become /aʔ/:

*sícuheq 'wash' > *hísoʔ* 'cleaning of teeth by rubbing'

In the antepenult of trisyllabic roots, *e > /a/:[26]

*dusa + R- > *dalawá* 'two' (< *daduwá < *duduhá [§C1.3.223]) *enem + R- > *eenem > *ánim* 'six' (< *aʔnim [§C1.1.1] < *aʔenem < *eʔenem [cf. SL *éʔenem* 'six']) *sepat + R- > *ápat* 'four' (< *aʔpat< *aʔepat< *eʔepat) *telu + R- > *tatló* 'three' (< *tetelu)

In stems with a petrified prefix, *qaɬi-, the*i remains /i/—i.e., it does not change to /a/:

*qaɬibaŋbaŋ > *alibangbang* 'k.o. butterfly'

The sequence *we > /u/ (/o/ in final syllables) initially and adjacent to *u:

*weliq 'do again, do back' > *uwiʔ* 'return home', *ulíʔ* 'again' *taquweɬ > *taʔón* 'year'

After *a, the sequence *we > /wa/:[27]

*qawec > *awás* 'diminished'

An exception is the following form, which probably was borrowed into Tag after the change of *we > /u/ had been completed:

*caweŋ > *sawing* 'protective hat'

C1.2.3 *a

*a > /a/ in all positions:

*qacawa 'in-law' > *asáwa* 'spouse' *qaɬiŋu > *aníno* 'shadow'

C1.2.4 Diphthongs

The diphtongs remained unchanged.[28]

---

[26] There was neutralization of vowel contrasts in the antepenult of trisyllabic roots. All vowels are reflected with /a/ in Tag. In other Philippine languages, neutralization takes place, and the vowels of the antepenult are all reflected with the reflex that *e has in other environments:

*qudip + *-en 'raise (an animal, person)' > *alípin* 'slave' (Cf. Cb *ulípun* 'slave' < *elipen)

There is also neutralization of the unstressed penult of trisyllabic stems that are not syncopated. Cf. the citation of *dusá > *dalawá* 'two' in this section.

[27] This hypothesis is born out by only one example, and until another example turns up, it cannot be substantiated

[28] Note the variable rule that /aw/ > /ó/ and /ay/ > /é/ word medially (§C1.0, end). However, /ó/ does not occur in forms inherited from PAn or PMP, and /é/, only in one:

*taŋíla > *ténga* 'ear' (discussed in this section)

*aw > /aw/:

*buɣaw > *búgaw* 'chase, drive' *laŋaw > *lángaw* 'a fly'

In the following form, *-aw is reflected as /-o/. It is not directly inherited:

*qaɬimáŋaw > *alimángo* 'large swamp crab' (Cb *alimángu* 'crab of swamps')

*iw > /iw/:

*ciciw > *sísiw* 'chick'

In the case of *kasiw 'tree', there was metathesis of the *w and *i, and *w gained sonority, while *i lost sonority (as happened in other languages of the Philippines and Formosa):

*kasiw > *káhoy* 'tree, wood' (< *kahyu < *kahiw)

*ay > /ay/:

*patay > *patáy* 'kill' *quway > *úway* 'rattan'

When *ay came to be in the penult, it changed to /é/ variably :

*taŋíla > *ténga* 'ear' (< *táynga < *taínga < *talínga [§C1.1.3])

*uy > /oy/:

*babuy 'wild pig' > *báboy* 'pig' *ɬaŋuy > *langóy* 'swim'

C1.3 Consonants

CHART TWO. TAGALOG REFLEXES OF THE PAN CONSONANTS

PAn	Tag	PAn	Tag
p	*p*	g	*k-, -l-, -d*
t	*t*	ɣ	*g*
k	*k*	l	*l*
q	*ʔ*	ɬ	*n*
h	*Ø*	m	*m*
s	*h*	n	*n*
c	*s*	ŋ	*ng* [ŋ]
b	*b*	w	*w*
d, j	*d, -l-, -d*	y	*y*

C1.3.1 Voiceless consonants

C1.3.11 *p

*p remained /p/ in all positions:

*pakepak > *pakpak* 'wing, clap' *pagay > *pálay* 'rice plant' *depa 'a fathom' > *dipá* 'fathom, spread arms' *gapegap > *kapkap* 'feel around, grope'

In one case, *p is reflected by /b/ in a word that was contaminated by another form of similar meaning. This innovation was shared by Paiwan and all the MP languages:

*pukuh > *bukó* 'node in cane-like plants' (contaminated in PMP or earlier by *bukul 'knob shaped. Cf. *búkol* 'boil, tumor', Cb *bungkul* 'bulging bones in joints')

The process of nasalization (§A3.7.1) has led to the reflection of *p as /m/ in a small number of cases:

*pícał > *mínsan* ‘once’ (For the n-intercalation cf. §A3.7.2.)

C1.3.12 *t

*t remains /t/ in almost all cases:

*taqis > *tahiʔ* ‘sew’ *kutu > *kútu* ‘louse’ *mata > *matá* ‘eye’ *kaɣat > *kagát* ‘bite’

In one case, an initial *t is reflected by /n/, the petrifaction of a nasalized form (§A3.7.1):

*takaw> *nákaw* ‘steal’

In one case, a *-t is replaced by /-d/ as the result of contamination with a word of similar meaning:

*penet ‘plugged up’ > *pínid* ‘close, cover over’ (Cf. Bon *pedped* ‘press together’ < *pejepej.)

C1.3.13 *k

*k remains /k/ in all environments:

*kaɣat > *kagát* ‘bite’ *aku > *akó* ‘I’ *aɣak > *ágak* ‘lead by the hand’ *ɣik > *giʔík* ‘thresh by trampling’

In one case, *k is replaced by /ʔ/ by contamination:

*bukul ‘knob-shaped protrusion’ > *buʔól* ‘ankle’

In one case, final *-k was replaced by glottal stop, probably for taboo reasons:

*nunuk ‘k.o. banyan tree’ > *núnoʔ* ‘k.o. dangerous supernatural being’ (cf. Akl *nunúk* ‘a *Ficus* tree believed to be inhabited by supernatural beings’)

C1.3.14 *q

*q > [ʔ] in all the Philippine languages except in two speech islands (Kalamian Tagbanwa and Tboli), where *q merged with *k. In Tag, this [ʔ] was lost in initial position, but is retained as /ʔ/ in medial and final positions:

*qabú > *abó* ‘ashes’ (cf. Kalamian *kabu* ‘ashes’) *qepa > *ipá* ‘chaff’ (cf. Kalamian *kepa* ‘chaff’) *qujał > *ulán* ‘rain’ (cf. Kalamian *kuran* ‘rain’) *liqeɣ > *liʔíg* ‘neck’ *baq ‘put down’ + *R- > *babáʔ* ‘go down’

When the /ʔ/ that developed in medial position was in a syllable that was syncopated, the /ʔ/ was dialectally lost, as explained in §§C1.1.441 and C1.1.442:

*baqeɣu > *bágo* ‘new’ (< *baʔgo < *baʔeɣu)

Intervocalic /ʔ/ is lost by the dialectal process described in §C1.1.42:

*bituqen > *bituwín* ‘star’

In one case, a final /ʔ/ (< *-q) is lost. There is no explanation:

*bilaq > *bíla* ‘split bamboo’ (< * bilaʔ)

C1.3.2 *h, *s, *c

C1.3.21 *h

*h is lost in all environments, but it left traces in some intervocalic positions. First, *h-onset of the final syllable of all roots was lost and caused a vowel sequence to develop, into which a glottal stop was intercalated (§C1.1.41). This glottal stop was lost in trisyllabic roots in the northern Tag dialects (§§C1.1.441, C1.1.442).

*layehu > *layʔu* 'withered' (Cb) (*layeʔu < *layeu) *bulehaɣ 'cataract' > *bulág* 'blind' *buhet 'squirrel' > *búʔot* 'rabbit'

Second, in trisyllabic roots where *h was onset to the penult, the *h-onset was lost, but a glottal stop did not develop to break the hiatus after the *h had been lost. Rather the vowel sequence that had developed contracted. In Tag, the vowel that resulted from contraction was long (cf. §C1.1.41).

*buheni > *búni* 'skin infestation' *caheɫáɣ 'shine (of sun)' > *sanág* 'bright' (Cb)[29] *paheɣaw > *págaw* 'hoarse' (< *paeɣaw) *tahepa > *tápa* 'dry meat'

C1.3.22 *s

In disyllabic or monosyllabic roots, *s > /h/ in initial and medial positions. In final position, *-s > became *-h. Subsequently the *-h was lost.[30]

*busat > *búhat* 'make, do; lift' *sagek 'sniff, smell' > *halík* 'kiss (by sniffing)' *bukes > *buhók* 'hair' (metathesis prior to loss of *-h) *tebus > *tubó* 'sugar cane' *iseyup > *híhip* 'blow' (< *R- + *híp < *síp < *síup [loss of antepenult] < *esiyup [§C1.1.13])

In doubled monosyllabic roots, however, final *-s is reflected as /-h/ in many of the Philippine languages:

*dasedas > *rahdah* 'chest' (Itbayaten) *kusekus 'scrape' > *kukhu* 'scrape' (Cb) (< *kuhkuh)

In trisyllabic roots ,*s > /h/ under some conditions and is lost under others, described in the following subsections.

C1.3.221 *s > /h/ initially and medially.
(a) in initial position:

*sabáɣat > *habágat* 'west or southwest wind'

(b) in medial position:

*aɣúsuq > *agúhoʔ* 'the Australian pine: *Casuarina equisetifolia*'

C1.3.222 Initial *s- also becomes /h-/ in trisyllabic roots that became disyllabized by syncope of the penult:

[29] In this Cb word, the penult was probably shortened by the rule that unaffixed statives have short-vowel penults.
[30] This rule applied to all of the Philippine languages, and in most of them, describes the current phonology. In some of the Philippine languages, /h/ was lost. Akl and perhaps some other languages developed a contrast between /-h/ and /Ø/, but this contrast does not reflect the retention of the PAn contrast between *-s and *-Ø or *-h.

*saɣejáɬ > *hagdan* 'ladder' *lag- + *isinawa > *ma-ginháwa* 'comfortable' (Cb *ginháwa* 'breath') (*isinawa + *lag-[31] > *lag-sinawa > *lag-hináwa > *ginháwa* [loss of leftmost syllables in quadrisyllabic stems and metathesis: *ghin- > *-ginh-]

Clusters with *s that developed when the penult syncopated simplified, losing the *s. (Cf. the examples in §C1.1.443 for loss of medial -s- and exceptions.)

C1.3.223 In trisyllabic roots when the penult was short but not syncopated, initial *s was lost in PMP:

*sehapúy > *apóy* 'fire'

Medial *s, which had become *h, was lost in pre-Tagalog in trisyllabic stems with a short penult:

*dusa + R- > *dalawa* 'two' (< *duduwá < *duduhá [cf. Cb *duruhá* 'two']) *ika- + *su > *ikáw* 'you (sing.)' (< *ikahú)

In Kpp, *s was lost entirely. Forms borrowed in Tag from Kpp reflect Ø instead of /h/:

*sipec > *ípis* 'cockroach'

C1.3.23 *c

*c > /s/ in all positions:

*caŋa > *sangá* 'branch' *cekecek > *siksík* 'stuffed full' *cíku > *síku* 'elbow' *cuɬud > *sunód* 'following, next' *ácu > *áso* 'dog' *qacíɬ > *asín* 'salty' *dicedic 'make thin cut' > *disdis* 'to lance' *suɣac > *húgas* 'wash (utensils)'

C1.3.3 Voiced consonants stops in Tag

*b remained unchanged. *d and *j merged, becoming /d/ initially and finally and /l/ medially. Initially, *g > /k/ when onset to a monosyllabic root or onset of the penult or earlier. As the onset or coda of the final syllable, it merged with *d and *j.

C1.3.31 *b

*b remained unchanged:

*babaw > *bábaw* 'shallow' *bitebit > *bitbit* 'carry s.t. in fingers' *qabu >*abó* 'ashes' *iba > *ibá* 'other, different' *dabedab > *dabdab* 'set on fire' *debedeb > *dibdib* 'chest'

The only exceptions are borrowings or forms that have been contaminated with other forms of similar meaning.

*bahaɬiɣ 'board, buttress root' > *pánig* 'panel' (influenced by reflex of *pánig, attested in other Philippine languages, but not attested in Tag [cf. Cb *pánig* 'flat object']) *kaban > *káwan* 'herd, flock' (< Ml)

Reflexes of *sebic 'thin' show reflexes of *pic as in all languages apart from Bunun:

*ɬisebic > *nipís* 'thin'

C1.3.32 *d,*j

*d and *j merged and became /d/ initially and finally and /l/ medially.[32]

[31] The etymology of *lag- is unknown. It probably formed a compound with the reflex of *nisawa.

*daŋedaŋ > *dangdang* 'place near fire to heat' *daw 'look at' + R- > *dálaw* 'visit' (< *dadaw) *udesi > *hulí* 'last' *kudekud > *kudkod* 'grate' *jeket 'stick' > *dikit* 'pasted' *qujał > *ulán* 'rain' *qałuj > *ánod* 'be carried by current'

When the *d that had developed from *d and *j came to abut on a consonant because of syncope, it did not change to /l/, but remained /d/.

*saɣejał > *hagdan* 'ladder'

In Tag, the /d/ that resulted from *d and *j changed to /r/ when it came to be preceded by a vowel in prefixation or metathesis. However, this change was variably undone by analogy: /d/ initial in a root > /r/ after a vowel-final prefix, but the /r/ is variably changed back to /d/:

*dateŋ > *datíng* 'come' *datíng* + R- > *dárating/dádating* 'will come'

But an initial *d that became intervocalic by metathesis or by a petrified prefix invariably changed to /r/. In that case, it does not vary with /d/:

*jeket > *pa-rikít* 'ignite'

In some cases, initial *d is reflected with /l/ that developed by analogy. The stem that occurred after a vowel-final prefix was extended to the unprefixed root:

*dalem > *lálim* 'depth' *ma-lálim* 'deep' *dapit 'near' > *lápit* 'nearness' *dátaɣ 'flat area' > *látag* 's.t. spread out flat'

*nd that developed in PMP is reflected both by /r/ or /nd/. There is no explanation for the two reflexes:

*pundul > *puról* 'blunt' (cf. Tausug *mapundul* 'blunt') *paŋudał > *pandan* 'pandanus' *sejam > *hirám* 'borrow' *sejen 'press down as in bowel movement' > *hirín* 'chocked up with emotion' *tujuq 'point' > *túroʔ* 'teach' *ludaq > *luráʔ* 'spit' (< *lundaq [cf. SL (northern dialect) *ludáʔ*[33]])

In borrowings from Ml, *d is reflected with /r/:

*uda 'young' > *múraʔ* 'unripe' (Cf. Ml *muda* 'young, unripe'.)

C1.3.33 *g

*g became voiceless as onset of the penult or earlier or in monosyllabic roots and merged with *k-, as in many An languages:

*galih 'dig' > *káli* 'dig out root crops' *gap > *kapkap* 'grope in s.t. to find' *getil > *kitíl* 'pinched of (stems of flowers, etc.)'

A number of forms reflect /g/ initially from *g-. These are borrowing from Kpp, which has had a strong influence on Tag and reflects initial *g- with /g-/:

*gilid > *gílid* 'edge' *geteŋ > *igting* 'tightness', *ba-gting* 'taut' *giliŋ > *gíling* 'grind by rolling over, mill' *gumis 'body hair' > *gumí* 'beard' *gusam 'thrush' > *guhám* 'mange, severe rash'

---

[32] In other words medial *d, *j merged with /l/ in Tag and in the western Visayan languages, but not in the other central Philippine languages. In those languages, *d and *j became /r/ medially.

[33] SL reflects *nd that developed in PMP both with /d/ and /nd/.

As onset of the final syllable, *g moved forward to become *d, merging with *d, *j. Subsequently, the *d that developed became /l/, as did the reflexes of *d and *j (§C1.3.32, above):

*bugaq > *bulá?* 'foam' *sagek 'sniff' > *halík* 'kiss' *isegun > *ilóng* 'nose'

When the /d/ that had developed came to abut on a consonant because of syncope, it did not change to /l/ but remained /d/, as was the case of /d/ < *d, *j:

*paqegu > *apdó* 'gall' (< *apegu < *qapegu)

Similarly, when the *d that developed abutted on a nasal, it was retained as *d but then subsequently changed to /r/ as was the case of other sequences *nd that had developed (§C1.3.32, end):

*qałegaw > *áraw* 'day, sun' (< *qandaw < *qanedaw)

In final position, *g also became /d/, merging with *d and *j:

*puceg > *púsod* 'navel' *quleg > *úhod* 'worm'

C1.3.4 Continuants

C1.3.41 *ɣ

*ɣ > /g/ in all positions:

*ɣabihi > *gabí* 'night' *ɣik > *gi?ík* 'thresh by stomping' *baqeɣu > *bágo* 'new' *qaɣaw > *ágaw* 'snatch' *qapuɣ > *ápog* 'lime' *deŋeɣ > *diníg* 'hear'

In loan words from Kpp, *ɣ is reflected with /y/:

*baɣaŋaw > *bangyaw* 'botfly' (< *bayngaw < *bayangaw) *daɣámi > *dayámi* 'straw' *juɣu 'corner > *dúyo* 'opposite end from where one is' *jaɣum > *ka-ráyom* 'needle' *calaɣ > *saláy* 'nest' *taɣum > *táyom* 'indigo'

A number of forms show irregular reflexes of *ɣ. In one case, the form has been contaminated and spread through a number of languages:

*ɣeken > *dikín* 'coil put under burdens placed on head' (cf. Bkl *gukún* 'carrying coil')

Other cases of irregular reflexes of *ɣ are loan words:

*beɣek 'domesticated pig' > *bi?ík* 'baby pig' *culuɣ 'shoot of creeper' > *súlol* 'offspring' *línuɣ > *lindol* 'earthquake' *pakeɣ > *páko?* 'nail' *qatuɣ 'stack up, arrange' > *hátol* 'judgment in court' (< Ml) *tambuɣi > *tambúli?* 'horn made of a conch' *teŋeɣ > *tangal* 'tree of mangrove swamp'

C1.3.42 *l

The regular reflex of *l is /l/:

*qáluł > *álon* 'long rolling wave, swell' *beli > *bilí* 'buy' *laŋit > *lángit* 'sky' *qaselu > *hálo* 'pestle' *buqul 'protruding bone' > *bu?ól* 'ankle'

However, Tag has borrowed at least seventeen basic forms from a language or dialect that lost /l/ in intervocalic and final position. This language has not been identified.[34] When an *l was lost was between two like vowels, a laryngeal was intercalated (§C1.1.4). When an *l was lost was between unlike vowels either a laryngeal was intercalated or a glide developed (cf. the discussion in §C1.1.42).

*balay > *báhay* 'house' *balu > *báʔo* 'widow, widower' *baluɬ 'bundle'> *báʔon* 'provisions' *beŋel > *bingí* 'deaf' *buliɣ > *buwíg* 'bunch, cluster of fruit or coconuts' *buluq > *búhoʔ* 'k.o. bamboo' *bulaɬ > *buwán* 'moon' *caleɣ > *sahíg* 'floor' *caleŋ 'pine' > *sáhing* 'damar resin' *celcel > *sisí* 'regret' *gatel > *katí* 'itchy' *jalan > *dáʔan* 'road, street' *puluq > *sam-póʔ* 'ten' *quleg > *úhod* 'worm' *taŋila > *ténga* 'ear' (< *taynga < *talinga) *weliq > *uwíʔ* 'return home' (also *ulíʔ* 'do again')

C1.3.43 *ɬ

*ɬ becomes /n/ and /l/, as described in §A3.3.4:

C1.3.431 *ɬ > /l/ as onset to the penultimate or earlier syllable with a short vowel:

*ɬecúŋ > *lusóng* 'mortar' *ɬimác > *limás* 'bail out water' *baɬitúk > *balitók* 'gold ore' *qaɬibaŋebáŋ > *alibangbáng* 'k.o. butterfly' *qaɬiɣuwan > *ligwan* 'bee' *qaɬimátek > *alimátik* 'leech'

In doubled monosyllables, where in the first root *ɬ > /l/, the *ɬ of the repeated root also becomes /l/ (but cf. the final three paragraphs of §C1.3.432, immediately following):

*buɬebúɬ > *bulbol* 'body hair' *ɬiki-ɬikí > *kili-kilí* 'armpit' (< *liki-likí [§C1.1.3]) *ɬaweɬaw > *lawlaw* 'splash around in the water with the hands or feet'

C1.3.432 *ɬ > /n/ otherwise—i.e., as onset and coda of the final syllable (including monosyllabic roots[35]) or as onset of the penult or earlier syllable with a long vowel:

*qaɬíŋu > *aníno* 'shadow' *qáɬuj > *ánod* 'be carried by current' *aɬák > *anák* 'son, daughter' *qacíɬ > *ma-asín* 'salty' *qáluɬ > *álon* 'long rolling wave, swell' *ɬuɣ > *niyóg* 'coconut'

In the following example, the *l that developed from *ɬ formed a cluster by syncope of the medial syllable. Subsequently, the cluster was simplified by dropping the *l:

*qaɬegaw > *áraw* 'day, sun' (< *aldaw)

In doubled monosyllabic roots, syncope of the epenthetic vowel in the penult was variable, and in some cases, syncope took place before *ɬ > /l/. In those cases, *ɬ > /n/:

*ɬikeɬik > *niknik* 'gnat, fly' (< *ɬikɬik)

In some cases of a doubled monosyllabic root, the doubling took place after the change of *ɬ > /n/:

---

[34] In fact, many of the languages originating in Mindanao and the central Philippines have unstable *l's*—that is, lose the *l or replace it with a glide, and in many of them, this change affected some, but not all of the forms that had inherited or developed an [l]. Much of the basic research that would supply clues for the origin and spread of this areal feature has not been done.

[35] But when the monosyllabic root was doubled with an epenthetic vowel between the monosyllabic elements, the stress was on the final syllable and the *ɬ > /l/ (cf. examples in this section).

*ɬam 'taste' > *malinamnam* 'tasty' (*ɬam > *nam, which was subsequently doubled)

There is one example of initial *ɬ- before a short penult in a disyllabic root that does not change to /l/. Note, however, that in an affixed form of the root, the *ɬ does change to /l/. This root may in fact have had two different prefixes *ɬi- and *ni-

*ɬisebic> *ma-nipís* 'thin (not thick)' Cf. *alipís* 'thin slice')

C1.3.44 *m, *n, *ŋ

*m, *n, *ŋ remained unchanged in all positions:

*mata > *matá* 'eye' *lima > *limá* 'five' *enem > *ánim* 'six' *naɬaq > *nána?* 'puss' *tenek > *tiník* 'thorn' *qulun 'rest head' + -an > *únan* 'pillow' (< *ulunán) *ŋaŋa > *ngangá* 'open mouth wide' *ŋucuq > *ngúso?* 'snout' *ɬaŋuy > *langóy* 'swim' *baɣeqaŋ > *bagáng* 'molar'

However, *ŋ is dissimilated to /n/ when to the left of /g/, but not abutting on it:

*deŋeɣ > *diníg* 'hear' (cf. *pakinggan* 'listen to it' < *paki-deŋeɣ-án with loss of the antepenult and syncope of the penult, where *ŋ > /ng/) *taŋíɣi > *tanígi* 'Spanish mackeral' *tiŋeɣ > *tiníg* 'voice'

*ŋ is assimilated to /n/ when it was to the right of a syllable with /n/-onset:

*qaɬíŋu > *aníno* 'shadow'

Nasals that come to abut on a C are assimilated:

*dateŋ > *datíng* 'come' + *-an* > *datnán* 'come to it' *sametik > *hantik* 'k.o. ant' *teŋaq 'half' > *gi-tna?* 'half-way'

This assimilation is did not invariably take place in the case of doubled monosyllabic roots:

*baŋebaŋ 'excavated' > *bambang* 'ditch' *daŋedaŋ > *dandang* 'place near fire'

With no assimilation:

*diŋediŋ > *dingding* 'inside wall'

C1.3.45 *w and *y

*w is reflected by /w/ in all positions, except that the sequence *we has a special outcome (§C1.2.2, end). (Cf. §C1.2.4 for diphthongs with *w.)

*qacawa 'in-law' > *asáwa* 'spouse' *liwa > *ka-líwa?* 'left' *lawi > *lawí* 'tail feathers' *cawuq > *sáwo?* 'anchor' *qúway > *úway* 'rattan' *walu > *waló* 'eight' *watawat 'flutter' > *watáwat* 'flag'

In the case of *ciwa, however, /w/ is lost. There is no explanation. This is an innovation shared by most languages in the Philippines:

*ciwa > *siyam* 'nine'

*y > /y/ in medial position. For diphthongs with *y see §C1.2.4. No reflexes of *y are attested in initial position.

*baɣiyus > *bagyó* 'hurricane' *buqáya > *buʔáya* 'crocodile' *dúyan 'shake' > *dúyan* 'cradle' *heyaq > *hiyá?* 'shame' *lampuyaŋ > *lampuyáng* 'k.o. wild ginger'

CHAPTER TWO

Chamorro[1]

C2.0 Background and cultural factors that influenced the history of Chamorro

Chamorro (Chmr) is spoken on the Mariana Islands, located in the Pacific around 1,300 miles to the east of the Philippines. The ancestors of the Chmr speakers came to this area 3,000 years ago or more, bringing with them knowledge of rice cultivation as well as seafaring skills. There is little in the phonological history of Chmr that enables us to determine where the people originated. The language clearly made the Malayo-Polynesian innovations (§A1.1.32), and this excludes Formosa as a place of origin. Most likely the Chamorros originated in the Philippines, as a route starting from the Philippines is the shortest and easiest route to the Marianas, but Sulawesi cannot be ruled out.[2]

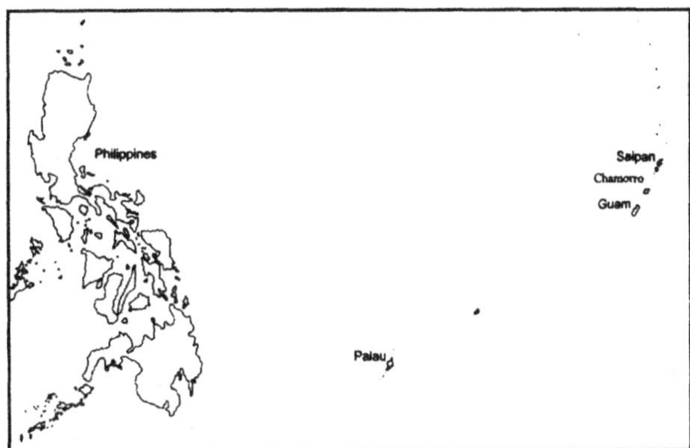

Map 6. Location of Chamorro and Palau vis-a-vis the Philippines[3]

Chmr underwent strong influence from three sources: first, there is a clear layer of Oceanic influence, in the lexicon, in the grammatical structure, and in the phonology (cf. §C2.3.3).. Second is the Hispanic influence, which is overwhelming. In the wars of Spanish conquest and under the harsh rule that followed, the population was depleted to one-tenth of the estimated original population over the course of four generations. This lost population was replaced by immigrants, almost all men and very largely from the Philippines, who came

---

[1] This historical phonology of Chmr was worked out in detail in Blust 2000, which informs much of what is said here. The principal difference between my treatment and Blust's, aside from our very different reconstructions of the protoforms in a number of cases, is that I reconstruct contrastive stress for the proto-language and motivate different patterns of disyllabization by stress differences. Otherwise our treatments differ only on minor points.

[2] Blust (2000:105–6) suggests that Sulawesi be ruled out as a Chmr homeland because the word *pakyo* 'typhoon' is inherited from PAn, and typhoons do not occur (and surely did not occur) in Sulawesi.

[3] Map 9, p. 625, shows the location of Chamorro (Marianas) vis-à-vis the Oceanic languages.

there as soldiers, deserting ship crews, exiles, and others seeking employment. This population of immigrants, which arrived gradually throughout the 250 years of Spanish rule, married into the Chmr community. They were numerous enough that by the end of the Spanish occupation in 1899, there remained no family that did not consist of descendents of immigrants who had intermarried with Chamorros. Although the wives and children of the immigrants were good speakers of Chmr, the immigrants were not. The Chmr that they picked up was heavily interlarded with the lexicon and grammar of the Spanish lingua franca that was current among the crews of the ships and soldiery. Much of this Hispanic overlay came to be adopted into the speech of the native-born Chmr speakers and replaced original Chmr forms. As a result, the Chmr dictionary shows an astounding 50 or 60% vocabulary of Hispanic origin and a substantial number of grammatical features that originate in a lingua franca Spanish. The third influence was from the Philippine languages. This is mainly in the realm of vocabulary items, mostly names for foods, plants, and equipment that the Filipinos brought into the Chmr communities that they joined, but there are words from other domains as well. They have not been studied in detail, and little is known of their origin or the extent of Philippine influence.

The strong foreign influence on Chmr has made much of the history of the language unknowable. Although Chmr is among the better documented An languages, it is possible to determine the An or MP etymology of only some 300 roots, as compared to five or six hundred roots among the other well-documented languages. The others have been lost, mainly under the overwhelming Hispanic influence. In addition, all dialectal diversity has been wiped out. Shortly after the Spanish conquest, the entire population was forcibly resettled on Guam, and the other islands were entirely depopulated. It was only after a space of two generations that the authorities permitted settlement outside of Guam. As a result, the dialectal diversity that must have existed in precontact times was wiped out, and the current language manifests an amalgam. Thus there is a fairly hefty amount of variation in the current language and irregularities in the reflection of reconstructed forms that can be attributed to what must have been dialectal diversity at an earlier time.[4]

The following chart shows the inventory of segmental phonemes in Chmr. The letters in parentheses represent phonemes that do not occur in inherited forms:

CHART ONE. PHONEMES OF CHAMORRO

Consonants

voiceless	p	t	ch	k	ʔ
voiced	(b)	(d)		g	
spirants	f	s			h
liquid	w	l, r	y		
nasals	m	n	ñ	ng [ŋ]	

Vowels and Diphthongs

high	i		u
mid	e		o
low	æ	a	
diphthong	(uy)	ay	aw

/ch/ is apico-palatal stop with slight affrication. We transcribe *ch* rather than *c*, because that is the normal Chmr orthography of this sound. /ʔ/ is transcribed here as such, but in the Chmr orthography, with an apostrophe. /æ/ and /a/ are both normally written *a*. The diphthongs in the orthography are represented as vowel sequences *ui, ai,* and *ao*. These are transcribed here as /uy/, /ay/, and /aw/, respectively. Otherwise, the transcription presented here is that of the

[4] Blust 2000 solves many of the problems that the history Chmr presents.

orthography used in the Chmr community.[5] Stress is minimally contrastive: for the most part stress falls on the penult of the word except when the word ends in a diphthong, in which case the stress is on the diphthong. There are numerous exceptions. The current stress in Chmr has nothing to do with the stress that existed in PAn. However, Chmr manifests traces of PAn stress in the retention or loss of penultimate syllables in trisyllabic roots or in affixed roots that have become trisyllabic stems or words (§C2.1.12).

C2.1 Processes affecting the development of Chmr from PAn

C2.1.1 Loss of syllables and contraction

There were three ways in which trisyllabic roots developed further: (1) they could lose the antepenult, (2) they could lose the penult, or (3) they could remain trisyllabics. However, most trisyllabic roots were affected by syncope. The rules have not been worked out as to the circumstances under which a trisyllabic root disyllabized or not, but if a root did disyllabize, whether the antepenult or the penult was lost was largely determined by the phonological make-up of the root (cf. §§C2.1.11 and C2.1.12).
Further, disyllabic roots with *e in the penult in most cases, lost the *e and developed an initial CC consisting of the original initial C of the root followed by the onset of the final syllable. (Cf. the examples in §C2.1.12, below.)

C2.1.11 Weakening or loss of antepenult

In trisyllabic forms that were inherited or developed by affixation, when the penult was stressed, the antepenult was weakened or lost:

*qúlun-an > *alunan* 'pillow' (< *ulúnan[6])

The following forms evince loss of the antepenult:

*qaɫimáŋaw > *akmangaw* ' mangrove crab' *tiŋádaq > *ngæha?* 'look up'

C2.1.12 Loss of penult

In trisyllabic roots with *e in the penult or with *i before *y or *u before *w in the penult, the *e and *i or *u was lost:

*paheɣaw > *a-fægaw* 'hoarse' *baɣiyus > *pakyo* 'storm' *qaɫegaw > *atdaw* 'sun'

When disyllabic roots with final stress in PAn (that is, originally with short penults) became trisyllabic by the addition of an affix, the penultimate vowel was lost:

*suɣác + *pa- > *fa-ʔgas* 's.t. to wash with' (< *fa-ʔugas [§C2.1.53] < *fa-ugas) *daluc 'slip' > *ma-hlos* 'smooth' *cakay + -an > *sahyan* 'vehicle' (< *sahi-an) *sapaɣ 'mat' + *-i > *gwafi* 'lay a mat on' (< *apɣi [cf. §C2.1.52 for /gw-/, §C2.3.35 for loss of *ɣ])

---

[5] Blust (2000: 87) points out that /w/ and /y/ in syllable onset are invariably preceded by [g] and [d], respectively. The orthography transcribes a /w/ in syllable onset as *gw*, a practice followed here as well (as this simplifies the exposition of the developments that took place in several cases). However the [d-] onset of the /y/ is ignored by the orthography and ignored here as well.

[6] The same rule holds for Chmr as for the An languages in general: in derived or inflected forms the accent stays on the penult if the root has penultimate stress, and the accent stays on the final syllable if the root had final stress, except in cases where stress shift comprises part of the derivative morpheme (§A3.5, 2nd¶).

However, when the disyllabic root had penultimate stress (a long vowel in the penult) the penultimate vowel was not lost:

*qápuɣ > *afok* 'lime' + -i > *afuki* 'put lime on' *págay 'rice' + paN-an > *famaʔayan* 'rice field' (< *pamagáyan)

The same rule holds for trisyllabic roots. In the following example, there was a doublet with a retained penult and one in which the penult had been lost. We assume that the two different reflexes represent alternative stress patterns. In this case, there is evidence of alternative stress patterns from other languages as well (cf. the citations in the glossary):

*qaɬítu, *qáɬitu 'spirit' > *aniti* 'spirit of the ancestors', *anti* 'soul, spirit'

C2.1.13 Vowel contraction

Vowel contraction took place in pre-Chmr when *s was lost, resulting in a vowel sequence:

*ɬisebic > *ka-nifes* 'thin' (< *niefec < *ɬiepic)

When *i or *u came to abut on *e in trisyllabic roots after a medial consonant was lost, the resulting sequence contracted to /i/ and /u/ respectively. The sequence *iseyu contracted to /i/:

*buɣesu > *ugoʔ* 'jealous' *iseq > *m-eʔ-m-eʔ* 'urine'(< *miq-miq [doubling] < *mieq [loss of antepenult (§C2.1.11)] < *umiseq) *iseyup > *gwa-if-e* 'blow' (< *sa-ip-i [the prefix *sa- is hypothetical and the lowering of the final *i is unexplained]) *kanuhec > *nosnos* 'squid, cuttlefish' (with loss of the initial syllable [§C2.1.11])

C2.1.2 Monsyllabic roots

Chmr disyllabized inherited monosyllabic roots, save those that were pretonic. They disyllabized by the addition of prefixes that became petrified:

*but 'uproot' + *ɣa- > *gapot* 'pull by hair'

They also may have disyllabized by doubling or reduplicating:

*baq 'down' > *papaʔ* 'put down' *ɬam 'taste' > *ñamñam* 'chew, eat' *quc 'chew (on sugar cane or the like) > *uʔos* 'peel with teeth, tear off with the teeth as in eating sugar cane' *taw > *tawtaw* 'man'

Monosyllabic roots that developed by vowel contraction (§C2.1.13, above) also were doubled:

*iseq + *-um- > *umiseq > *meq > *meʔ-meʔ* 'urine' *kanuhec > *nosnos* 'squid, cuttlefish' (with loss of the initial syllable [§C2.1.11])

There is at least one case where a monosyllabic root disyllabized by adding prothetic /e/. This root further reduplicated and added /g/ between the two /u/'s that had developed from *e (§C2.1.52):

*tec < *gutos* 'break off (string, etc.)' (< *ugutus < *uutus < *utus < *etes)

Some of the monosyllabic roots remained monosyllabic, but they are bound to affixes—that is, they never occur unaffixed.

*cak 'ripe cooked' + ma- > *masa* 'ripe, cooked'

C2.1.3 Metathesis

There was a widespread tendency for syllables with /i/ followed by /u/ in the same word to metathesize. (/u/ developed from *u and from *e [§C2.2.2].) We have the following examples of words derived from the protolanguage:

*bituqen > *puti?un* 'star' *biɣeŋi > *puengi* 'night' (< *beɣiŋi [loss of *ɣ not explained])
*inum > *gimen* 'drink' (*gimun < [second metathesis] < *gumin [intercalation of /g/(§C2.1.52)] < *umin [first metathesis])

The metathesis of forms beginning with *ise- also is covered by this rule, but in fact this metathesis is widely shared among Formosan and MP languages (§A3.5.4) and occurred earlier than the others here listed..

*iseguŋ > *gwi?eng* 'nose' (< *wigung < *uwiguŋ < *eiguŋ < *esiguŋ) *isepi > *gwifi* 'dream' (< *uwipi < *uipi < *eipi < *esipi)

There is one case of *i followed by *a that metathesized *i and *a:

*sukay > *gwahi* 'dig up' (< *gwaki < *waki < *huaki < *hukay)

The word for 'ear' evinces the metathesis found in the other MP languages and in many Formosan languages:

*taŋila > *talænga* 'ear' (/æ/ unexplained)

The following words evince an idiosyncratic metathesis:

*besuɣ + *ka- > *haspok* 'satiated' *tuɣun > *tunok* 'go down'

There was a strong tendency to metathesize syllables with /?/ in forms of three or more syllables. The rules have not been worked out. They are dependent on the accentual patterns of the forms involved:

C2.1.31

$CV_1?V_2CV- > ?V_1CCV-$ (with loss of the V_2 in the penult):

*leqacem > *ma-?aksom* 'sour' (< *ma-?alsem < *ma-?alesem < *male?acem)

C2.1.32

?VCV> CV?V

*seqeɣet 'tight' > *gu?ot* 'retain by force' (< *?ugut < *uqugut) *taqu-en 'know' > *tagu?on* 'obedient, trustworthy, reliable' (< *ta?ugon < *taquwen)

C2.1.33

VCV?V > V?CVV

ugu? 'jealous' + -i > *u?guyi* 'be jealous of'

C2.1.34

$V_1?V_2C > V_2?C$ (with the loss of the V_1 of the antepenult) *u 'future marker' + *un- 'second person singular' > *uʔn-* 'second person future'[7] (< *uʔun- [§C2.1.53]) < *uun-)

C2.1.4 Assimilation and dissimilation

Voiced consonants become devoiced in syllable-coda position. In the following example, *ɬ > *l in PMP. The *l came to be in coda position after the penult was syncopated (§C2.1.12), changed to [d] in the coda and subsequently devoiced (§C2.3.41):

*qaɬegaw > *atdaw* 'sun' (< *algaw < *qalegaw)

/h/ (< *k [C2.3.13] or < *d [§C2.3.32]) assimilated to a /k/ to the left in the same word or when abutting on a /k/ to the right (that is, /h/ > /k/):

*deŋeɣ 'hear' + *iʔ- (unidentified prefix) > *eʔ-kungok* 'listen' (< *eʔ-hungok < *eʔ-deŋeɣ)

In internal syllables that developed with a /k/ as coda, the internal coda assimilated to the initial consonant of the following syllable (cf. the examples §C2.3.132).
/t/ both inherited from *t and developing from *l (§C2.3.41) is sporadically dissimilated to /k/ when coming to abut on a following consonant:

*leqacem > *ma-ʔaksom* 'sour' (< *ma-ʔalsem < *ma-ʔalesem < *maqalecem [§C2.1.3])
*qaɬimaŋaw > *akmangaw* 'mangrove crab' (< *qatmaŋaw < *qalmaŋaw < *qalimaŋaw)

*u assimilates to an /i/ in the immediately preceding syllable within the same phonological word (§C2.2.2, 2nd¶):

*ɣumaq > *gumaʔ* 'house' *gi gimaʔ* 'in the house'

C2.1.5 Intercalation of consonants

C2.1.51 Intercalation of /w/

*w developed between /a/ and /u/ or /u/ and another vowel (both when the /u/ < *u and when /u/ < *e). Subsequently, /g/ developed before the /w/ (cf. §C2.1.52, following):

*dusa > *hugwa* 'two' (< *duwa < *dua) *iseguŋ > *gwiʔeng* 'nose' (< *wigung < *uwiguŋ < *eiguŋ < *esiguŋ [§C2.1.3, 2nd¶]) *sehapuy > *gwafi* (*wapuy < *uwapuy < *uapuy)
*isepi > *gwifi* 'dream' (< *uwipi < *uipi < *eipi < *esipi)

A sequence [gwu] that may develop by this rule is simplified to /gu/ (or /go/ when closed by a coda):

*qacu + *-en > *asgon* 'smoky' (*< asugwun < *asuwun < *asuen)

C2.1.52 Accretion of /g/

/g/ developed before any /u-/ or /w-/ onset:[8]

*buwaq 'fruit' > *pugwaʔ* 'betel nut' *dusa > *hugwa* 'two' (< *duwa < *dua) *qacawa > *asagwa* 'wife' *lahud 'seaward' > *lagu* 'north' *uɣat > gugat 'vein sinew' (< *ugugat < *uugat) *walu > *gwalo* 'eight'

---

[7] Costenoble 1940: 296. Other grammars do not list this form, and Costenoble does not exemplify this prefix together with a verb stem.
[8] Blust (2000: 98–99) provides parallels from the history of other languages that show change of a [w]-glide to [gw] to be a natural articulatory development. I find these persuasive.

The /u/ that had developed from *e also underwent the accretion of /g/:

*jaqewis > *chagoʔ* 'far' *enem > *gunum* 'six' *tec < *gutos* 'break off (string, etc.)' (< *utus < *etes) *luseq > *lagoʔ* 'tears' (< *lagwuq < *lawuq (change of *u to /a/ unexplained)

Roots that had initial *a- or *i- or developed *a- or *i- (after the loss of *s) develop an initial /gw-/. Presumably this process came into being by analogy: roots with initial *a-/*i- developed *wa-/*wi- by extending the alternant that occurred after a marker ending in *-u. This initial *wa- or *wi- then developed initial /g-/ (> /gwa-/ or /gwi-/).[9]

*aku > *gwahu* 'I' *ini 'this' > *gwini* 'here'

The loss of *s preceded the development of [g]-accretion, so that roots with initial *sV- also accrete /g/:

*sapaɣ 'spread out (mat)' > *gwafak* 'mat' *isekan > *gwihan* 'fish' *suŋuc 'pull out of enclosure' > *gunos* 'wean'

*q- onset at the beginning of a word blocked development of /g/:

*qujaɬ > *uchan* 'rain' *quleg > *ulo* 'worm'

In the following case, form with *q onset in PAn underwent metathesis of the kind described in §C2.1.32 (where the *s onset of the penult was moved to the front), so that it accreted /g-/ in initial position:

*quseɬap > *goʔnaf* '(fish) scales' (< *guʔunap < *uʔunap < *huʔunap [§C2.3.21])

In four cases, *gw that developed was simplified to /g/. Perhaps this was a dialectal development:

*i > *gi* 'preposition referring to place' *luwaq > *lugaq* 'spit out' (< *lugwaq) *qaɣusuq > *gagu* 'tree: *Casuarina equisetifolia*' (< *gwagu < *awu) *suwab > *ma-gap* (< *magwap) 'yawn'

In the following case, metathesis took place, /g/ developed before *u, metathesis took place a second time, and *u- > *i (by assimilation [§C2.1.4, end]), which lowered to /e/ in the closed syllable:

*inum > *gimen* 'drink' (*gimun < [second metathesis] < *gumin [intercalation of /g/] < *umin [first metathesis])

C2.1.53 Intercalation of laryngeals

A glottal stop was inserted between two vowels that came to abut, except in those environments in which /g/-insertion took place (§C2.1.52). Therefore, when *s between two

---

[9] Blust (2000:100) hypothesizes that the accretion of initial [w] is a normal articulatory development. However, he can find no explanation for it, nor can I. Since there are parallel developments of [w]-accretion elsewhere in individual lexical items in a number of languages (e.g. *ácu 'dog' is reflected with initial /w-/ in several Formosan languages), I hypothesize that the development was analogical. Blust (2000:99) discounts this possibility because the morpheme that could give rise to such an analogy has not been identified. There are at least five examples of inherited forms where [w]-accretion fails to take place:

*ala 'take' > *ala* 'basket' *asiq 'pity' > *asiʔ-i* 'forgive *ini > *ini* 'this' (as well as *gwini*) *ipil > *ifet* 'a tree: *Intsea bijuga*' *iting 'cluster' > *iteng* 'break off (fruit)'

vowels was lost or a vowel-final prefix was added to a vowel-initial stem, a glottal stop was inserted.

*suɣac 'wash' + *pa- > *fa-ʔgas* 'something to wash with' (< *paʔugas < *pa-uɣac) *uɬah + pa- > *foʔna* 'be first' (< *fuʔana [§C2.1.34] < *faʔuna < *pauɬah)

In more recent developments, /h/ was inserted between vowel sequences. E.g., forms of Hispanic provenience with /ia/ often have variants with /iha/. Examples of an inherited form with intercalated /h/ are the following:

*qusáw + *ma- > *ma-ʔo* or *ma-ʔho* 'thirsty' (< *ma-quáw/*ma-quháw) *ulaw 'dazed' + *mama- > *mamahlaw* 'ashamed' < *mamahulaw < *mamaulaw)

There are some roots with an inserted /ʔ/ or /h/ that have no explanation. This sporadic insertion of a laryngeal is found in words that have no An or MP etymology and also is found in a few that are clearly related to reconstructed An or MP roots.

*layaɣ > *læʔyak* 'sail' (also *læyak*) *pacaŋ 'one of a pair' > *faʔsæhng-e* 'separate, set aside' *baŋun 'rise' > *pæhngon* 'arouse, wake s.o. up'

C2.2.0 Vowels and diphthongs

Chmr added three vowel phonemes to the original four and lost one by merging *e and *u. *i and *u developed lower allophones that became contrastive and *a developed a fronted allophone that became contrastive—i.e., *i > /i/, /e/; *u > /u/, /o/; *a > /a/, /æ/. *e merged with *u before the split occurred and thus shows two reflexes /u/ and /o/. These splits did not affect all of the dialects that existed in precontact times, and there is variation, such that there are forms that fail to evince the lowering of *i and *u or the fronting of *a.

C2.2.1 *i

*i (like *u [§C2.2.2] lowered in closed syllables (> /e/) and finally after a closed syllable. Otherwise, *i normally remained /i/:

*aqetih 'water recede' > *maʔte* 'low tide' *-*pitu > *fitu* 'seven' *talis > *tali* 'rope' *paqit > *faʔet* 'bitter' *cikecik 'search through' > *sesse* 'delouse' (< *seksek < siksik)

The local passive affix *-i exemplifies this process of lowering:

*basequ 'smell' + doubling + -*i > *pawpagw-e* 'apply perfume to' *peɣec-i > *foks-e* 'squeeze out' *qatep 'roof' + *i > *afte* 'put a roof on'

The following example shows an unstressed sequence [iy] developing into [əy] and subsequently /uy/:

*tiyáɬ > *tuyan* 'belly'[10]

There are some unexplained exceptions. *i > /u/ in one case, and *i > /æ/ in another:

*dílaq > *hulaʔ* 'tongue' *taŋila > *talænga* 'ear'

---

[10] Costinoble (1940: 121) quotes *tiyan* 'belly'. The development of /u/ was probably dialectal. Blust (2000:93) suggests that /u/ replaced earlier /i/ by an analogical process in *tuyan* 'belly' and *hulaʔ* 'tongue'

C2.2.2 *e, *u

*e fell together with *u—i.e, *e, *u > *u in pre-Chmr. Subsequently, *u developed lower allophones in closed[11] syllables and finally after a closed syllable (analogous to the development of *i [§C2.2.1]). These allophones became contrastive—i.e., [u] >/u/ and [o] > /o/. /o/ occurs in closed syllables.

> *baqeɣuh[12] > _paʔgo_ 'new'*deŋeɣ > _hungok_ 'hear' *ɬecuŋ > _lusong_ 'mortar' *qalep > _alof_ 'beckon' *ɬabek > _napu_ 'rough surf' *ɬepuq > _ñufoʔ_ 'scorpion fish' *qabu > _apu_ 'ashes' *juɣuq > _chugoʔ_ 'sap, juice'

In trisyllabic roots with *e in the penult, *e was lost (after it had become *u, as always):

> *quseɬap > _goʔnaf_ '(fish) scales' (< *guʔunap < *uʔunap < *huʔunap [§C2.3.21])

*u, including the *u that developed from *e, assimilated to an *i in the preceding syllable. The *i that developed lowered to /e/ if it was in a closed syllable:[13]

> *inum > _gimen_ 'drink' (< *gimun [cf. the citation in C2.1.3 for the history of the development of this form]) *ipen > _nifen_ 'tooth' *iseguŋ > _guiʔeng_ 'nose' *liduŋ > _liheng_ 'shelter' *qaɬitu 'spirit' > _aniti_ 'ancestor spirits' (now 'devil') *uɬah > _foʔna_ 'be first' (< *fuʔana < *fa-una) but _foʔna_ + _-in-_ > _fineʔna_ 'first' *qaɬiŋu > _æninge-n_ 'shadow'

In two cases, *-u > /aw/. There is no explanation (in the second example there is also an unexplained loss of *ɣ):

> *bayu > _fayaw_ 'pestle' *linuɣ > _linaw_ 'earthquake'

In one case, *e is reflected as /e/ (lowered from *i in a closed syllable). The likely explanation is contamination with *jaqit 'sew, attach':

> *jeket > _chetton_ 'adhere'[14]

In one case, *u in an open penult was lowered. There is no explanation but note that affixed forms of the same root are not lowered. Perhaps the lowering is due to dialect mixture:

> *túqas 'old' > _toʔa_ 'mature'

C2.2.3 *a

*a remained /a/ but was fronted to /æ/ in stressed position sporadically. The rule for fronting is unknown. Except for two cases, /æ/ occurs in the penult in inherited words (but there are many cases of fronting in other positions in words not inherited from PAn). The two exceptions are as follows:

---

[11] That is, in closed syllables in current Chmr. *-s ,*-h, *-k and *-q were lost at an earlier stage and roots ending in PAn *-us/*-es, *-uh/*-eh, and *-uk/*-ek develop in the same way as vowel final roots:

> *ɬabek > _napu_ 'rough surface' *nunuk > _nunu_ 'banyan'

[12] This root ended in a vowel in PMP—i.e. the *u was not in a closed syllable. (Cf. the immediately preceding footnote.)

[13] _gumaʔ_ 'house' (<*ɣumaq) has a variant in _gimaʔ._ This variant arose from the phrase _gi gimaʔ_ 'in, at, to the house' where the /u/ assimilated to the preceding /i/, and _gimaʔ_ subsequently spread to positions not after /i/.

[14] The form _chetton_ could derive from *jaqit-en: *jaqiten 'contiguous' > *jaʔiten > *jiʔaten (metathesis) > *jiʔten (syncope) > _chetton._ It is not likely that _chetton_ derives from *jeketen 'adhering'. This would have produced *_chutton_. The form _chetton_ took on the meaning of putative *_chutton_, which then disappeared.

*qaɬiŋu > *æninge-n* 'shadow' *qudaŋ > *uhæng* 'shrimp'

There are more cases of forms containing /a/ in the stressed penult that do not front than there are of cases in which fronting does take place. Here are examples of fronted and of unfronted reflexes of *a in the penult:

*tajeɣ 'stand' > *tæchu* 'be upright' *tiŋadaq > *ngæhaʔ* 'look upwards' *tacik > *tasi* 'sea' *taŋic > *tanges* 'weep'

C2.2.4 Diphthong

C2.2.41 *ay, *aw

*ay and *aw are retained unchanged in most cases:

*beɣecay > *foksay* 'paddle' *matay > *matay* 'die' *qaɬimaŋaw > *akmangaw* 'mangrove crab' *taw > *tawtaw* 'person'

There are a few exceptions. There is no explanation for them:

*pagay > *faʔi* 'rice in the field' *cakay 'climb up on to' > *aʔ-sahe* 'summit' *qusáw > *ma-ʔo* 'thirsty' (< *ma-qáw < *ma-quáw) *lakaw > *lahu* 'walk'

C2.2.42 *uy, *iw

There are very few examples of these diphthongs. On the basis of the following cases it appears that these diphthongs became /u/:

*laɣiw > *fa-lagu* 'flee' *kasiw > *hayu* 'tree' *ɬaŋuy > *ñangu* 'swim'

There is at least one counter-example. Perhaps the different outcome is due to dialectal mixture:

*sehapuy > *gwafi* 'fire'

C2.3.0 Consonants

CHART TWO. CHAMORRO REFLEXES OF THE PAN CONSONANTS

PAn	Chmr	PAn	Chmr
p	*f*	j	*ch*
t	*t*	g	*Ø*
k	*h*	ɣ	*g*
q	*ʔ*	l	*l*
h	*Ø*	ɬ	*ñ, n, l*
s	*Ø*	m, n	*m, n*
c	*s*	ŋ	*ng*
b	*p*	w	*w*
d	*h*	y	*y*

C2.3.1 Voiceless consonants

The voiceless consonants remained voiceless, but except for *t they changed considerably. In internal syllables that developed with a /k/ as coda, the internal coda assimilated to the initial consonant of the following syllable (cf. the examples §C2.3.13).

C2.3.11 *p

*p became /f/ in all positions:

*paqit 'bitter' > *fæʔet* 'salty' *qapuɣ > *afok* 'lime' *qalep > *alof* 'beckon'

C2.3.12 *t

*t was stable and remained /t/ in all positions:

talis > *tali* 'rope' *kutu > *hutu* 'louse' *laŋit > *langet* 'sky, heaven'

C2.3.13 *k

*k > /h/ in initial and medial positions and was lost in word-final position:

*kasiw >*hayu* 'wood, tree' *kutu > *hutu* 'head louse' *mekemek 'broken into bits' > *mohmo* 'chewed food' *teken 'stick to lean on' > *tohn-e* 'lean on a stick' *cak 'ripe' > *ma-sa* 'ripe, cooked'

There are some exceptions where /k/ remained /k/. These words are probably not inherited. They mostly show other irregularities:

*kamaliɣ > *kamalen* 'barn for storing' *manuk 'bird' > *mannok* 'chicken' *pakepak > *pakpak* 'clap hands' *taketak > *taktak* 'chop up'

When *k came to abut on a following voiceless consonant, it was assimilated to it:

*bakebak > *pappa* 'strip off bark' *bekebek 'pulverize' > *poppo* 'powder, decayed matter' *cikecik 'search through' > *sesse* 'delouse' *jeket+en > *chetton* 'adhere' (< *jekten) *beka 'split open' > *pokkaʔ* 'shatter, crack open' (< *beʔkaʔ [with /-ʔ/ added to each syllable on analogy with other words meaning 'break open, split,' and the like])

When *k is followed by *k in the same word, they both revert[15] to /k/ When a cluster *Ck developed by loss of a vowel or affixation, the cluster became /kk/:

*ka- + kasiw 'wood' > *kákayu* 'stem' *kutu 'louse' + *paɣ- > *fakkutu* 'delouse' (< *paɣ-kutu)

If *k was followed by *d in the same word, the *k > /k/ and *d > *h—i.e., *k–*d > /k–h/ (§C2.3.32),[16] This rule is an extension of the rule of the immediately preceding paragraph, whereby *h became /k/ to the right of a /k/:

*daya + ká- > *ká-kaya* 'go inland' (< *ka-haya < *ka-daya)

If *k was preceded by *d in the same word, the *d > /h/, and *k > /k/—i.e., *d–*k > /h–k/. This rule came into effect after the rule of the preceding two paragraphs ceased to operate (for /h/ did not become /k/):

*jaket > *hakot* 'seize' (< *daket [by contamination with *dakep 'seize'])

---

[15] The *k's changed to [h] and then changed back to /k/. This is proven by the fact that /h/ < *d (as illustrated in the immediately following paragraph also becomes /k/.

[16] This rule is based on a single example. However, it is likely in view of the fact that *kVkV > /kVkV/.

C2.3.14 *q

*q > [ʔ] in all positions. However, since word-initial vowel developed [ʔ], the [ʔ] that had developed from *q in word-initial position was noncontrastive.[17] In medial and final position however the glottal stop is contrastive—/ʔ/:

*baqeɣu 'new' > *paʔgo* 'now, today' *bitúqen > *putiʔon* 'star' *buwaq 'fruit' > *pugwaʔ* 'betel nut' *daqáɬi > *haʔani* 'day' *qujaɬ > *uchan* 'rain'

In trisyllabic stems *q- onset of unstressed syllables is lost:

*básequ > *paw* 'smell' *tiqeɣáb > *tugap* 'belch' *túqas + *ma- > *matua* 'highest class in traditional Chmr society' (cf. *toʔa* 'mature', where /ʔ/ is retained in a disyllable)

In the following form, the medial *q was lost because the root occurs as a prefix—i.e., it forms a word together with the word that follows it (and therefore follows the rule given in the preceding paragraph):

*jaqet > *chæt-* 'slightly, un-, dis-' *chæt-bunita* 'not very pretty' *chæt-malagu* 'not a good runner' *chæt-aʔani* 'dreary day'

The following form is probably a euphemism, the result of a deliberate phonemic substitution. It is not likely that the medial /k/ has a common origin with the medial /k/ in the cognate roots in some of the Philippine and Formosan languages (because*k > /h/ [§C2.3.13, above]).

*taqi > *takeʔ* 'feces'

C2.3.21 *h, *s

*h and *s disappeared entirely without a trace. Comparison with Tag (§C1.3.22) shows that *s > *h and then was lost:

*baqeɣuh 'new' > *paʔgo* 'now, today' *dusa > *hugwa* 'two' (< *duwa < *dua) *lahuj > *lagu* 'north' (< *lau) *quseɬap > *goʔnaf* '(fish) scales' (< *guʔunap < *uʔunap < *huʔunap) *suɣac 'wash' + *pa- > *fa-ʔgas* 's.t. to wash with' (< *pa-uɣac < *pa-suɣac) *talis > *tali* 'rope'

C2.3.22 *c

*c > /s/ in all positions:

*cucu > *soso* 'breast, suckle' *qacawa > 'in-law' > *asægwa* 'spouse' *suɣac 'wash' > *faʔgas* 's.t. to wash with'

In one case *c is reflected with /h/. This may be a borrowing from an Oceanic language:

*cay > *hay* 'who?'

C2.3.3 Voiced stops and *ɣ

*b ,*d, *j became voiceless. This is an areal development: most of the Oceanic languages also devoiced these phonemes. It is very likely that this development happened in

---

[17] As Blust points out (2000:99). *q- onset before a vowel blocks [g-] accretion (§C2.1.52). In short, *q- onset leaves traces. At the time that [g-] accretion took place *q had not fallen together with the automatic vowel-initial [ʔ].

Chmr through contact with Oceanic languages. *g was lost, and *ɣ moved forward to become a voiced stop /g/. /g/ subsequently became devoiced when it closed a syllable.

C2.3.31 *b

*b > /p/ in all positions:

*baqeɣuh 'new' > *paʔgo* 'today' *baq 'put down' > *pa-paq* 'down, below' *qabu > *apu* 'ashes' *suwab > *ma-gap* 'yawn'

In a number of cases, *b is reflected with /b/. These are forms that have been borrowed. In some cases, the source is probably one of the Philippine languages, but not in all cases. The final example here evinces the peculiar Chmr innovation *g > /ʔ/ (§C2.3.34). The source of forms with /b/ that are not from the Philippines is unknown.

*qaɬi-baŋbaŋ > *a-babang* 'butterfuly *babuy > *bæbuy* 'pig' *balut > *balut-an* 'wrap up' *bahaɬiɣ > *banek* 'buttress root' *baŋesis > *bangi* 'fragrant' *bugeq > *buʔoʔ* 'foam'

One form evinces /f/ < *b. There are other irregularities in the form as well. It is probably a borrowing, but the source is unknown:

*bayu > *fayáw* 'pestle'

The form *ɬisebic 'thin' lost the penult and devoiced the *b, as in all languages but Bunun. (Cf. the comment to *sebic in the glossary.)

*ɬisebic > *ka-nifis* 'thin' (< *ɬispic)

In one case *b- is lost without explanation. This form also manifests /-ʔ/, as do the cognates in many of the Philippine languages.

*buɣesu > *uguʔ* '(sexually) jealous'

C2.3.32 *d

*d > /h/ in initial and medial position. There is no reflex in Chmr of a form reconstructed with final *-d. Presumably, *d > [s] before *c underwent changes and this [s] > /h/. (Subsequently *c > /s/.)

*daqaɬi > *haʔani* 'day' *demedem > *homhom* 'dark, obscure' *tuduq > *tuhoʔ* 'drip'

There is a handful of exceptions. They show other irregularities that make it clear the forms are not directly inherited (if they are connected at all):

*cuduŋ 'push forwards' >*suʔon* 'push, stoke fire' *caduŋ 'sheath' > *saʔæng* 'put out of the way'

When /h/ (< *d) is preceded by /k/ in the same word, the /h/ > /k/:

*daya + ká- > *ká-kaya* 'go inland' (< *ka-haya < *ka-daya)

When a cluster *Ch developed by loss of a vowel or affixation, the *h (< *d) became /k/:[18]

*deŋeɣ 'hear' + *iʔ- (unidentified prefix) > *eʔ-kungok* 'listen' (< *eʔ-hungok < *eʔ-deŋeɣ)

[18] The /h/ < *d became /k/ as did the /h/ < *k (§C2.3.13).

C2.3.33 *j

*j > /ch/ in initial and medial position:

*jalan > *chalan* 'way, road' *qujaɬ > *uchan* 'rain'

In final position *-j probably was lost. There is, however, only one example:

*lahuj 'seaward' > *lagu* 'north'

When *j came to be in a cluster because of vowel loss, *j > /s/. (Probably the [c] that had developed was simplified to [s].)

*juɣuq 'sap' > *chugoʔ* 'sap, juice' *ma-sgoʔ* 'juicy' *tajem + *-i > *tasm-e* 'sharpen'

The following form shows /h/ as a reflex of *j-. This irregularity is explained by contamination with *dakep 'seize' (no reflex attested).

*jakut > *hakot* 'seize' (< *daket [by contamination])

The following form shows an irregular reflex of *j- and other irregularities as well. It is probably a loan word:

*jalikan > *alihan* 'trivet' (also *halihan, haliʔan*)

C2.3.34 *g

The reflex of *g- in initial position is unclear. There is one form that manifests /g-/, if it is connected, and there are two that manifest /h-/ (indicating that *g- merged with *k-, as in many languages):

*gem 'hold' > hugom 'embrace'[19] *galih 'dig' > *hali* 'harvest root crops' *gatel > *ká-kætot* 'itchy' (< *hætot + *ha-) 'itchy' [§C2.3.13])

As onset and coda of the final syllable, *g > /ʔ/.[20]

*igan > *ng-iʔan* 'when' *iseguŋ > *gwiʔeng* 'nose' (< *wigung < *uwiguŋ < *eiguŋ)
*pagay > *faʔi* 'rice in the field' *quleg > *quloʔ* 'worm'

When coming to abut on a C, *g > /d/:

*qaɬegaw > *atdaw* 'sun' (< *aldaw < *qalegaw)

C2.3.35 *ɣ

*ɣ moved forward to become a voiced stop /g/:

*ɣabut 'uproot' > *gapot* 'pull by the hair' *qabaɣa > *apaga* 'shoulder' *laɣiw + *pa- > *falagu* 'flee'

When *ɣ came to close a syllable (that is, was at the end of a word or was internal preceding a vowel that was elided), it became [g] and then lost voicing like all syllable-final consonants—that is, *-ɣ > /-k/:

---

[19] The origin of the first syllable is unknown. It may be that this form only coincidentally resembles *gem. Costenoble quotes a form *kuʔum* 'hold', which probably remounts to *gem (although there is no other example in Chmr of disyllabization by stretching the nucleus).

[20] The steps whereby [d] became [ʔ] are unclear. The example of *atdaw* 'sun' in the following paragraph indicates that *g became *d before becoming /ʔ/. The inherited *d became /h/ (§C2.3.32), so that *g could move forward to become *d. But why this *d should have change to /ʔ/ is unknown.

*baɣehat 'heavy' > *mækkat* 'difficult, heavy' (< maɣʔat < maɣeat[21]) *baɣiyus > *pakyo* 'storm' *peɣec + -i > *foks-e* 'press out' *qapuɣ > *afok* 'lime'

*ɣ also became /k/ when it came to follow a voiceless consonant:

*caleɣ + i > *satk-e* 'flooring' (< *satg-i < *salg-i)

However, when *ɣ was root final and came to precede a consonant suffixation or compounding, it was lost:

*sapaɣ 'mat' + *-i > *gwafi* 'lay a mat on' (< *apɣi) *tajeɣ 'stand' + *n 'compound-forming morph'+ *bulu 'animal hair' > *tæcho-n-pulu* 'for animal hair to stand on end'

A possible rule is the following: when *ɣ came to abut on *j, the sequence *ɣj > /ñ/.

*saɣejaɬ > *l-añan* 'ladder'[22]

A number of forms remounting to PAn or to a later protolanguage that are reconstructed with *ɣ have irregular reflexes. They are not directly inherited:

*baqeɣaŋ > *ákakam/akaham* 'molar' *naɣa > *nana* 'a tree: *Pterocarpus indica*' *kamaliɣ > *kámalen* 'storage barn' *linuɣ > *linaw* 'earthquake'

C2.3.4 The liquids and nasals

C2.3.41 *l and *ɬ

*l > /l/ in initial and medial positions. When *-l came to close a syllable (either at the end of a word or when a closed syllable developed from vowel syncope) it became /-t/.[23]

*lahud 'seaward' > *lagu* 'north' *jalan >*chalan* 'way' *caleɣ > *satk-e* (< *calg-i < *caleg-i) *celecel > *sotsot* 'contrite' *ɬemec 'disappear' > *ma-tmos* 'drowned' (< *ma-lmec < *ma-lemec)

The /-t/ that developed from *l was sporadically dissimilated to /k/ before an abutting consonant (§C2.1.4):

*leqacem > *ma-ʔaksom* 'sour' (< *ma-atsem < *ma-ʔalsem < *ma-ʔalesem < *ma-qalecem) *qaɬimaŋaw 'mangrove crab' > *akmangaw* 'mangrove crab', *atmangaw* 'spotted sea crab' (< *qalmangaw < *qalimangaw)

*ɬ developed to /ñ/, /n/, and /l/, as in the other MP languages, depending on the stress pattern of the PAn root (§A3.3.4)— i.e., > /ñ/ initially before stressed syllable, /l-/ before unstressed syllable in the penult or earlier, and otherwise /n/. Medial *ɬ sporadically became /ñ/ in roots with penultimate stress. Evidently, /ñ/ depalatalized in some of the dialects that existed in pre-Hispanic times, for the reflex /n/ in place of expected /ñ/ occurs in some attestations, and there are doublets with both /ñ/ and /n/ in some cases.

---

[21] Evidently, the first syllable was replaced by the adjectival prefix *ma- in pre-Chmr.

[22] There is only one example, and the initial /l/ is also not explained.

[23] Evidently *-l > [d], and this [d] became devoiced when it closed a syllable. The evidence for this is not only that it is the natural articulatory route for a change of [l] to [t], but also the fact that when an [-l] coda abuts on a voiced consonant, it becomes [-d], e.g. *caluɣ > *saddok* 'river' (< *caldug [the origin of the extra *d is unknown]).

In initial position:

*ɬam 'taste' > *ñamñam* 'chew, eat' *ɬámuk > *ñamu* 'mosquito' *ɬaŋú 'woozy' > *la-langu* 'unconscious, faint' *ɬecúŋ > *lusong* 'mortar'

In medial position:

*quseɬáp > *goˀnaf* 'fish scales' *láɬa > *laña* 'oil'

In final position:

*bulaɬ > *pulan* 'moon'

The [l] that developed from *ɬ became /t/ (or /k/ [§C2.3.41]) when coming to abut on a consonant because of syncope, just as is the case of /l/ < *l:

*qaɬegaw > *atdaw* 'sun' (< *algaw < *qalegaw) *qaɬimaŋaw 'mango crab' > *akmangaw* 'mangrove crab' *atmangaw* 'spotted sea crab' (< *qalmangaw < *qalimangaw)

Two forms with initial *ɬ and end stress are reflected with /ñ/ and variably with /n/:[24]

*ɬaŋúy > *ñangu/nangu* 'swim' *ɬepúq > *ñufoˀ/nufoˀ* 'lion fish'

*tuqelaɬ 'bone' is reflected with final /-ng/, as is the case in many MP languages:

*tuqelaɬ > *toˀlang* 'bone'

C2.3.42 Nasals

*m, *n, *ŋ remained unchanged in all positions:

*maɣi > *magi* 'hither' *kima > *hima* 'clam' *dalem > *halom* 'inside' *nunuk > *nunu* 'banyan' *dasuwen > *hagon* 'leaf' *ŋac > *nga-ngas* 'chew' *deŋeɣ > *hungok* 'hear' *iseguŋ > *gwiˀeng* 'nose'

C2.3.43 *w and *y

When it was syllable onset, *w developed a [g]-onset (§C2.1.52). (Final *-w is discussed in §§C2.2.41, C2.2.42.)

*wada > *gwæha* 'there is' *lawac 'broad' > *lagwas* 'long and slender'

Syllable-onset *y remained /y/. (Final *-y is discussed in §§C2.2.41, C2.2.42.)

*daya 'inland' > *haya* 'inland' *qayuyu > *ayuyu* 'coconut crab'

---

[24]No definitive explanation is available. These forms may have spread secondarily. More likely, they developed a variant with stress on the penult.

CHAPTER THREE

Ratahan

C3.0 Introduction

Ratahan (Rat) is one of the five Sangiric languages, which form a subgroup (Sneddon 1984: §1.4.0). Sangiric languages are spoken in two separate places in northern Sulawesi among the Minahasan languages. Other Sangiric languages are spoken on the islands to the north between Sulawesi and the Philippines. Rat is called *Toratán* by its speakers (lit. 'people of the plains', although now the villages in which the language is still alive are located in the higher elevations). It is spoken in an enclave about 150 kilometers south of Manado, Kecamatan Ratahan, Northern Sulawesi, in an area bounded by Tondano to the north, Tontemboan to the northwest and west, and Tonsawang to the south. Ratahan and Minahasan farmers tend interspersed fields in some areas. Their language of communication is Manado Ml, which is spoken as a first or second language by nearly all the population of northeast Sulawesi. Rat is well on the way to extinction, being replaced by Manado Ml. In the larger towns and in all but three villages, Pangu, Wioi, and Wongkai, the language is for all intents and purposes dead. In the three villages in which Rat is still alive, there were very few good speakers under fifty in the 1990's, and with a small number of exceptions, nobody under 60 used the language habitually with anyone. To my knowledge, no children have learned the language or used it in the home or with their playmates for the past forty to fifty years. The Rat material is based on fieldwork I conducted together with Nikolaus Himmelmann in the villages of Pangu and Wongkai during the summers of 1996–8. This work was published as a grammatical sketch (Himmelmann and Wolff 1999). Written sources for Rat included the dictionary by Kolinug (1990) and the historical study by Sneddon (1984).

CHART ONE. PHONEMES OF RATAHAN

Consonants

voiceless stops	p	t	c	k	?
voiced consonants	β, b	d	(j)	(g)	
spirants		s		h	H
nasals	m	n		ng [ŋ]	
glides and laterals	(w), y	l, r			

Vowels

high	i		u
mid	e		o
low		a	
diphthongs	ay, ey	oy	aw, ow

The phonemes /j/ and /g/ do not occur in inherited forms. The phonemes /b/ and /d/ are marginal in inherited forms. In pre-Ratahan they were the allophones of /β/ and /r/, respectively, that occurred after nasals. In recent times, a contrast developed. /β/ is a bilabial fricative, devoiced in word-final position [ɸ]. The dictionary usually transcribes /β/ as *w*.[1] An alternative spelling *b* is given in some cases for forms that we transcribed as β.[2] Rat diphthongs at the end of a word contrast with vowel sequences—i.e., /ai/ contrasts with /ay/, /ei/ with /ey/, etc. Words with a final diphthong are stressed on the syllable preceding the diphthong (e.g. *rángow* 'dense, tight'), whereas words with a vowel sequence at the end are stressed on the first of the two vowels at the end (e.g. *rangóu* 'hole'). The diphthongs /aw/ and /ay/ may alternatively be pronounced as /ow/ and /ey/, respectively. However, the reverse is not true: There are forms with /ow/ and/ey/ that do not have variants with /aw/ and /ay/. /w/ occurs only as the second element of a diphthong. /ᴴ/ occurs only in word-initial position in inherited words and is of variable articulation ranging from [h] to ∅ (cf. §C3.3.41). Rat retains little trace of the original PAn stress system, but it has developed stress contrasts since MP times.

C3.1 Changes that characterize Rat in general

Rat has a tendency to form disyllabic roots (§A3.6.2). First, under the influence of stress, roots of more than two syllables were reduced to two syllables by the process of syncope or other types of syllable loss, with the exception of some of the stems of four syllables, which were reduced to three syllables. Second, roots that became monosyllabic because of sound changes and roots that were inherited as monosyllables from PAn were disyllabized by processes that are widespread throughout the Austronesian area (§A3.6.2).

C3.1.1 Disyllabization of trisyllables

C3.1.11 In trisyllables, a penult with *e nucleus was elided if the onset of the penult or of the final syllable was *s, •ɣ, or *h.

> *baɣehat > *βaa* 'weight' *basequ > *βau* 'smell' *beɣekec > *βikis* 'tie together, bundle' *binesiq > *βine* 'seed for rice' *udesi 'last' > *sam-uri* 'behind, later' (< *sa+ *-um- +*udesi)

Reduplicated monosyllables, which are reconstructed with penultimate epenthetic *e, elide the *e in Rat:

> *paɣatepat 'tree of mangrove swamp' > *paapaʔ* 'k.o. tree' (< *paatpat < *paɣatpat)

Similarly, penultimate *u and *i preceding a *w and *y glide are elided:

> *dasuwen 'leaf' > *raung-e* 'betel' (< *dauun [§C3.2.36]) *peniyu > *tom-ponú* 'turtle' (< *tom-penyu [§C3.3.43, footnote]) *taquweɬ > *taun* 'year'

An exception is discussed in §C3.1.13, below.

C3.1.12 The antepenult was weakened or lost if there is no lost consonant in the penult or the final syllable, under several conditions, listed as follows:

C3.1.12a If the penult nucleus was *e:

[1] /β/ is transcribed as *w* in Himmelmann and Wolff 1999, as well. We cannot do so here because of the need to give an unequivocal transcription of the sequences /aw/ and /ow/, which contrast with /aβ/ and /oβ/, respectively.

[2] None of our recordings showed [b] for [β]. We were not able to examine further with elicitation from the elderly fluent speakers available to us, whether a variant with /b/ in fact exists for these forms.

*leqacem 'sour' > *lising* 'vinegar' (< *lecem (/-ng/ unexplained) < *leqecem < *laqecem [§C3.1.4]) *paqegu > *puru* 'gall' (< *qapegu) *qiteluɣ > *tuʔu* 'egg' (§C3.3.42, end, for loss of *l, §C3.1.5 for insertion of [ʔ]) *sapedec 'sharp in taste' > *pirís* 'find s.t. to be sharp, hot in taste' (< *sepedec)

or if the penult consisted of *qi or *i:

*laqeya > *lia* 'ginger' (< *leqia < *laqia [§C3.2.36]) *qisuwab > *koyaβ* 'yawn' (< ka-uyab < *uiab < *suqiab)

C3.1.12b If the root had four syllables, the first syllable is lost:

*qaɬimátek > *lamatik* 'leech'(The /a/ of the antepenult is unexplained) *qaɬipulec > *limpurus* 'whirlwind' (with sporadic nasal accretion [§C3.1.6, below] and /-r-/ by analogical contamination with a reflex of *qaɬipugu 'whorl'[3]) *ma-ɣuqaɬay 'male' > *muaney* 'male' *qusalipan > *lipan* 'centipede' (with loss of the antepenult, as well [§C3.1.12d, below])

C3.1.12c If the antepenult consisted of *i (or *qi or *si), the antepenult was lost in words that did not lose a C in the penult or in final syllables:[4]

*iseci 'flesh, contents' > *si* 'meat' (< *seci [cf.§C3.1.16, below, for the loss of *se-.])

If the penult had a vowel onset, *i > /y/:

*ama-ŋ + *i- (name marker) > *yama-ng* 'father' *yaʔ* 'I' (< *i + *aku)

In the case of *ikau* 'you' (< *i + *kasu), the *i- person marker was restored.
In one case of a form with an antepenult consisting of *si-, the penult was elided variably in PAn, and Rat inherited the variant that elided the penult but retained the antepenult (cf. the commentary in the glossary to *siyuɬuq):

*siyuɬuq > *ino* 'necklace of beads'

C3.1.12d The antepenult was also weakened or lost if it had an *a or *e nucleus. This change took place before the loss of the penult under the rule of C3.1.11 above.

*baɣeqaŋ > *bunga* 'molar' (< *beŋaɣ < *beɣeŋaq < *beɣeqaŋ) *baqeɣu > *βuu* 'new' (< *beqeɣu) *cahebay > *sumpay* 'hang' (< *ceepay) *kasepal > *kupal* 'thick' *leqacem > *lising* 'sour' (< *leqecem < *laqecem) *qaɣicam > ^{H}*isam* 'k.o. creeping fern' (< *qaɣecam)[5] *qacawa 'in-law' > *saβa* 'spouse' *sabaɣat 'monsoon wind' > *βaeʔ* 'wind' *seqeɣet 'tight' > *eheʔ* 'near' *taseyup > *cup* 'blow' (< *tiup < *teseyup)

This rule does not apply to the following words, where the loss of *q-, *h-, *s-, or *w- onset of the final syllable (§§C3.3.14, C3.3.2, and C3.3.61) caused the vowels of the penult and final syllables to abut and contract. This took place before the antepenult was weakened:

---

[3]A reflex of this form has apparently not survived in Rat, but it existed in pre-Ratahan, for the form *limpurung* 'a round winnowing basket' must be connected with *qaɬipugu.

[4]Thus, the instrumental-conveyance passive prefix reflecting *si-/ ise- was lost. E.g., *katakuʔ* 'be afraid of it' (< *ikatakut [cf. Tg *ikatákut* 'be afraid on account of it'])

[5]The penult of this root was changed to *e in MP languages, as well as in Bunun and Amis (i.e., in pre-MP times). There is no explanation.

*betihec > *βitis* 'calf' *jaqewis > *ma-raw* 'far' (< *rau < *jaweq < *jawiseq) *pasaqał > *pasán* 'carry over the shoulder'[6]

In the following case metathesis took place after this rule was in effect, allowing /a/ to reappear in the antepenult in this form:

*liceqes > *lasia* 'nit' (< *lisaa [§C3.2.34] < *licaqa)

C3.1.13 Two trisyllables with *a in the antepenult failed to weaken the antepenult. There is no explanation. These forms may have been borrowed, but the source is unknown:

*banuwa 'place where there is s.t.' > *βanúa* 'village' *jalikan 'trivet' > *ralikan* 'cooking hearth'

Further, trisyllables (inherited as such or developed) with *i or *u in the antepenult and a vowel other than *e in the penult remained trisyllabic:

*binuaŋ > *binuang* 'k.o. tree' *ma-ɣuqałay > *muaney* 'male' *tinaqi > *tinai* 'intestines' *tiŋadaq > *tingara* 'look upwards' *agi + *tu- > *tuari* 'younger sibling'

C3.1.14 Metathesis led to disyllabization of trisyllables when the antepenult came to consist of *e:

*iceɣab > *ka-neaβ* 'yesterday' (< *łiɣab [metathesis of *i and *e in PAn [§A3.5.4] and nasalization of *c, which took place in PAn [§A3.7.1])

C3.1.15 In the case of doubled monosyllables, the first of the two monosyllables with *a nucleus replaced the vowel with *e ([ə]) in proto-Sangiric, variably if the monosyllable had a nasal coda (Sneddon 1984:8) (cf. §C3.1.12d).

*palaqpaq > *kalupa* 'midrib' (< *-al- + *pepa [replacement of *p by /k/ unexplained]) *paŋepaŋ 'cliff' > *pumpang* 'river bank'

C3.1.16 Loss of syllables in disyllabic roots

Penults consisting of *e that had not been deleted by the rules given in §§C3.1.11 and C3.1.12a were elided. That is, if the onset of the penult with *e had been lost, *e was elided:

*enem > *num* 'six' *iseci 'content, flesh' > *si* 'flesh' (< *seci [§C3.1.12c]) *luseq > *lo* 'tears' (< *elo [§C3.2.2] < *eluq < *seluq [§C3.1.4])[7] *semay > *may* 'rice' (< *emay) *sepat > *pa?* 'four'

In unexplained cases, the penult was lost in a disyllable with a vowel-onset other than *e:

*quway > *oi* 'rattan' (< *way [§C3.3.61]) *sapaɣ 'spead out (mat)' > *umpá* 'underlayer, sheet'[8] *sated > *ntur* 'deliver' (with sporadic nasal accretion [§C3.1.6]) *ubuc + ka- > *kaβus* 'used up' (< *ka + bus[9])

[6]Stress on the final syllable reflects two vowels that contracted (Wolff and Himmelman 1999: 15).

[7] This account is suggested by Sneddon 1984:13.

[8] Why *sapaɣ developed /u/ in the penult and *sated does not is unclear. Possibly, *umpá* derives from *sumapaɣ, but elision of *a in the penult is unparalleled, and it is unclear why it should have taken place.

[9]I assume that *ubuc > *buc to account for the /a/ in the penult of *kaβus*. If *u had not been lost, the rules of contraction would have caused the penult to become /o/ (§C3.1.21b). Another possible explanation is that the rule of contraction is dialectal and that this is a dialectal borrowing.

In rapid speech, the final /u/ of clitics gets lost. In one case, the final /u/ of the rapid speech form of a clitic has been generalized—that is, the *-u is lost entirely:

> *kunu 'quotative' > *kun* '[so-and-so] said'

The reflex of *liqeɣ 'neck' lost the penult when it was the second member of a compound:

> *kasiw + *liqeɣ > *kau-he* 'neck' (< *ɣeq < *liɣeq [metathesis])

C3.1.2 Vowel contraction

When intervocalic consonants were lost, the abutting vowels usually contracted.

C3.1.21 Sequences that developed involving *u

C3.1.21a *ue > /o/ in one case, but *we > /u/ (§C.2.36):

> *qusełap > *onop* 'fish scales'

C3.1.21b *ua, *au in affixed roots > /o/. Cf. the analogous development of *aw and *wa (§§C3.2.53, 3rd¶, C3.3.61):

> *culuq 'torch' + R-an > *sasolon* 'lamp' (< *sasuluan [the penult of the root assimilated to the final [§C3.2.2, 5th¶]) *qisuwab + ka- > *koyaβ* 'yawn' (< *kauyab < *ka-suiab < *kasuqiwab) *taqu + R-an > *taton* 'know' (< *tatauan) *ułah 'be first' + *pa- > *pona* 'ahead'

If the sequence was not affixed, contraction did not take place:

> *basequ > *βau* 'smell'

*u + *aw > /ow/:

> *buɣaw > *βow* 'chase away' (< *buaw)

C3.1.21c *eu > /u/, just as *e was changed to /u/ before labials (§C3.2.32):

> *cequł 'carry on the head' > *sun* 'carry on the head' (< *seun)

C3.1.21d *ee > *e and subsequently, > /u/, or if final in the root, /uu/. *ee came into being when *a in the antepenult was weakened (§C3.1.12d):

> *baqeɣu > *βuu* 'new' (< *beqeɣu) *baɣeqaŋ > *βunga* 'molar' (< *βuang < *βuɣang < *βeqeɣang) *kasepal > *kupál* 'thick' (< *kesepal)

C3.1.22 Other sequences involving *a:

C3.1.22a *ae > /a/:

> *mic > *emic (§C3.1.3) + *ma- > *mamis* 'sweet' *qetaq + *tama- > *tamata* 'raw' *tasep > *tap* 'winnow'

C3.1.22b *ia/*iya > /e/, in clitics:

> *iya > *e* in *ise* 'he, she' (> *iya + *i- 'name marker' + *s- 'nominative')

The first person independent pronoun, *yaʔ* (< *iaku [< *i- person marker + *aku] was formed after the rule of contraction took place.

C3.1.22c *wa, and *aw became /o/ when not in the final syllable and when not followed by a consonant. (Cf. §C3.1.21b, above, for *ua and *au. See §C3.3.61 for *wa.)

*kawałan > *koanen*' right' *kawiɣi > *koí* 'left' *qisuwab > *k-oyaβ* 'yawn' (< *ka-suwiqab) *wai > *oi* 'mango' (< *oy [§C3.1.3])

C3.1.23 Sequences involving *i or *y:
A sequence *ey or *ei > /i/ (§C3.2.36):

*laqeya 'ginger' > *lia* 'ginger '(< *leya) *taseyup > *cup* 'blow' (< *tiup < *teyup) 'blow'[10] *seyaq 'shame' > *ma-hia-n* 'jealous'[11]

*iye > /e/:

*wasiyeɣ 'water' > *mang-ae?* 'to water' (/-ʔ/ is unexplained.)

C3.1.24 In trisyllables or words that occurred as part of compounds, *uqu > /u/ and *aqa > /a/—i.e., the medial *q was lost and the two vowels contracted:

*punuq > *pun [X]* 'an [X] (tree)' (< *puun < *puqun [metathesis]) *pasaqał > *pasan* 'carry over the shoulder'

C3.1.3 Disyllabization of monosyllabic roots

Rat does not evince a strong tendency to disyllabize monosyllabic roots. Many inherited monosyllabic roots remained monosyllabic, not only those that occurred typically as clitics but others as well, and in fact some disyllabic roots became monosyllabic by losing syllables with *e (§C3.1.16). In pre-Ratahan, however, the tendency to disyllabize monosyllabic roots did obtain, and the processes were the same as those found in other An languages (§A3.6.2). Here are some examples of PAn monosyllabic roots that remained monosyllabic:

*but > *βu?* 'yank out' *gem > *kum* or *ngkum* (with nasal accretion [§C3.1.6]) 'hold in hands' (also *kungkum* 'fist') *lem 'shade, in dim light' > *lum* 'overcast' *tan > *tan* 'set trap' (also *tain*)

A few monosyllables are disyllabized by the addition of a prothetic /u/, probably a petrifaction of the prefix *um-:[12]

*baw 'above' > *uβow* 'above' *buł > *uβun* 'fontanel' *cuk > *usuk* 'stab' *dem > *undúm* 'be remembered' (with nasal accretion [§C3.1.6])[13]

Some monosyllabic roots that were inherited or developed stretched the vowel nucleus. The historical process was probably metrically determined—i.e., the vowel nucleus was lengthened according to the metrical environment.[14] Subsequently in some cases, the longer alternant became generalized to all phonological environments:

---

[10]For the loss of the *a of the initial PAn syllable in *lia* and *cup*, see §C3.1.12d, above.

[11]It is not absolutely certain that this form is directly inherited. The meaning is not the same as that of cognates and the occurrence of /h/ is unexplained. /h/ may have developed as a transitional feature, but few parallels are attested.

[12] This is not absolutely certain. A prothetic *e would have resulted in /u/ in these forms, and it is perfectly possible that they were disyllabized by the addition of a prothetic *e, which would have become /u/ (§§C3.2.32–C3.2.33).

[13] I suggest that the /n/ is the product of nasal accretion rather than a remnant of the coda of the prefix *um-. The evidence is that the other monosyllabic roots with a prothetic /u/ do not have a nasal coda after the /u/.

[14]An example is the form *ia?* alternatively *ya?* 'I, me'. The longer variant *ia?* occurs in stressed position, e.g., when it functions as the predicate. The shorter variant occurs in clitic position.

*ɣiq > *ee* 'saw grass: *Imperata cylindrica*' (Cf. §C3.2.1 for the lowering of *i to /e/.) *tan > *tain* 'set a trap' (also *tan*) *way > *oi* 'mango' (< *oy) *i 'name marker' + *aku > *yaʔ* and *iaʔ* 'I, me'

A handful of forms disyllabized by doubling the root:

*ba 'carry on the back' > *βaβa* 'carry a child in a cloth, carrying cloth' *baw > *βaβow* 'shallow' *biɣ > *βiβi* 'lips'

C3.1.4 Metathesis

Rat reflects the cases of metathesis that occurred in late PAn and in PMP times (§A1.1.32, 3rd¶). Here we discuss metathesis peculiar to Rat. A small number of roots reflect vocalic metathesis:

*baɣeqaŋ > *bunga* 'molar'(< *beŋaɣ < *beɣaŋ < *beɣeqaŋ) *binesiq 'seed' > *βine* 'seeds for rice' (< *beniq < *benisiq)[15] *qisuwab 'yawn' > *k-oyaβ* 'yawn' (< *ka- + *suwiqab) *liceqes 'nit' > *lasia* 'nit' (<*lisaa) *leqacem > *lising* 'sour' (< *lecem < *leqecem < *laqecem) *luseq > *lo* 'tears' (< *elo [§C3.2.2] < *eluq < *seluq)

One form shows consonantal metathesis:

*peɣec 'squeeze out' > *hepes* 'pinch, clinch' (< *ɣepec)

C3.1.5 Intercalation of glottal stops

When two vowels came to abut, a glottal stop was optionally inserted between them. For example, *iteluɣ 'egg' is reflected as *tuʔu* and also as *tuu* (with loss of *i in antepenult [§C3.1.12c] and irregular loss of intervocalic *l [§C3.3.42]).[16] This may account for the following cases in which a glottal stop is accreted at the end of a root—i.e., these forms developed a glottal stop before another form beginning in a vowel, and the forms with the accreted glottal stop was generalized:

*daki > *rakiʔ* 'grime' *tabeq > *taβaʔ* 'fat from pig'

A glottal stop is also accreted at the end of roots referring to terms of relationships or titles that are used as terms of address. The process whereby glottal stops are sporadically added to terms of address stems from the use of the term as vocative. This process is widespread throughout the Philippine languages.

*kaka > *kakaʔ* 'elder sibling' *sipaɣ 'sibling-in-law' > *ipaʔ* 'sister-in-law

C3.1.6 Prenasalization stop consonants

As in many western An languages, nasals are sporadically accreted at the end of open penults in the root:

*sated > *ntur* 'deliver' (< *anted with unexplained loss of *a [§C3.1.16]) *qaɫipulec > *limpurus* 'whirlwind' (discussed in §C3.1.12b)

[15] We assume metathesis because the penult of *βine* can only derive from earlier *e and not *i (§C3.2.1). The *i of *binesiq can only have changed to *e by metathesis, for *i in the antepenult was otherwise stable.

[16] Niemann in the mid-nineteenth century quotes *tuhu* 'egg', a form that had undergone metathesis (< *teɣu), where *ɣ is reflected by /h/.

Nasals were also sporadically accreted initially before voiced consonants. In some cases, the initial nasal derives from a nasal before a medial consonant in a form in which the first syllable was elided. But other cases cannot be explained in that way, and the origin of the nasal is unexplained:

> *bulu 'body hair, feathers' > *mbulu* 'body hair, feathers'[17] *dapedap > *ndap* 'k.o. tree: *Erythinia*' *dem 'think, remember' > *undúm* 'remember' *gem > *ngkum* 'hold in hands' (cf. *kungkum* 'fist')

In one case /-ng/ is accreted to the end of a word (probably by analogic extension of a form that occurs in compounds or phrases).[18]

> *buŋa 'flower' > *βungang* 'flower'

Nasals may also be accreted to names and terms of address, as is common in languages of the region:

> *ama 'father' > *yamang* 'father' (with the prefix *i-* used before names, titles, and personal pronouns).

C3.2 Vowels and diphthongs

Ratahan has added two vowels to the PAn four-vowel system, (*i, *a, *e, and *u) and lost the central vowel *e—that is, Ratahan has a five-vowel system: /i, e, a, o, u/. *i split into /i/ and /e/, *u into /u/ and /o/, and *e usually split into /i/ and /u/ according to the environment. *a remained /a/ in most environments, but in some, became /e/, as detailed below. The diphthongs continued as diphthongs with changes to be outlined below.

C3.2.1 *i

*i > /i/:

> *inum > *inum* 'drink' *kami > *kami* 'we (excl.)' *tiŋadaq > *tingara* 'look upwards'

Before a final *-q, which was subsequently lost, *i > /e/—i.e., -iq > /e/:

> *binesiq 'seed' > *βine* 'seeds for rice' (< *beniq < *benisiq [§C3.1.4]) *ɣiq > *ee* 'k.o. saw grass: *Imperata cylindrica'* *weliq 'go back' > *mang-ule* 'return home' *piliq > *pile* 'choose'

*i was lowered to assimilate to an /e/ or /o/ that developed in an adjacent syllable:

> *ibeɣ 'salivate' > *eβe* 'saliva'[19] *sipec > *epes* 'roach' *biluk > *βelok* 'veer' *bitebit 'carry in the fingers' > *βeβeʔ* 'carry s.t. light in the hand'

Note that the /i/ of *βine* 'seeds for rice', cited in the paragraph above, was not lowered. This is because /i/ that developed from *e did not assimilate to the vowel of the final syllable—i.e., the rule of assimilation was no longer in effect when *e changed to /i/.

---

[17]Sneddon (1984) reconstructs *bembulu for the Proto-Sangirese. This is an example of medial nasal accretion and loss of the antepenultimate syllable (§C3.1.12d). A similar explanation may well account for the nasal of *ndum*, for cognates *dumdum* and *handum* are manifested by Cb and other languages of the Philippines.

[18]The Minahasan languages share this innovation, and this form may well be a borrowing from them. (Cf. §C4.1.7.)

[19]For the developments of /e/ and /o/ in the final syllable, see §C3.2.35.

*i is sporadically lowered to /e/ in doubled forms. Cf. the /e/ in the final syllable in the example for *bitebit in this section in the paragraph immediately preceding. There is another attestation of a lowered *i:

*łiki-łiki 'underarm'> *kele* 'arm between elbow and shoulder' (< *kili-kili)

/i/ in the antepenult was often lost as part of the process of elision of vowels of antepenult or earlier (§§C3.1.12a, C3.1.12c).

C3.2.2 *u

*u remained /u/ in most cases:

*buɣuk > *βuuk* 'rotten' *kałusekus > *kanuku* 'nail, claw' *maɣuqałay > *muane* 'male'

*-uq > /-o/ (analogous to the development of *-iq to /-e/ (§C3.2.1). Also the *-u that had developed a final glottal stop (§C3.1.5) was lowered to /-o/:[20]

*puluq 'ten's' > *ma-pulo* 'ten' *pucuq > *puso* 'heart' *apu 'grandparent, ancestor' > *apoʔ* 'dead chieftain' (< *apuʔ [cf. §C3.1.5, end, for the accretion of /-ʔ/])

However, if the final syllable is stressed, the lowering did not take place:[21]

*pekuq 'curved, rounded' > *pukú* 'bend'

In one case, the *-q > /ʔ/ was not lost, nor was *u lowered. The reconstruction of this form with *-q is dubious:

*caluq > *saluʔ* 'catch, intercept'

*u was lowered to assimilate to /e/ or /o/ that developed in the following syllable (cf. the analogous development of *i, §C3.2.1, above):

*culuq 'torch' +R-an > *sasolón* 'lamp' (< *sasulon < *sasuluan < *sasuluqan)

A sequence of *ue that developed became /o/ (§C.3.1.21a). A sequence *eu became /u/ (§C3.1.21c).
There are a few cases in which *u > /o/ without explanation. Some of the forms are clearly secondary:

*daqu 'a tree: *Dracontomelum edule'* > *rao* 'k.o. tree' *ɣumaq 'house' > *^{H}oma* 'sheathe for sword' *łuwaŋ 'opening' > *loang* 'loose, too wide' *luwati > + R- > *loloati* 'worm' *muɣemuɣ + *qumałi- > *mai-momo* 'gargle') *qałutaŋ > *nonang* 'k.o. tree' *tukup 'cover over' > *tongkop* 'cover'

In at least two cases, the same inherited root reflects both /u/ *and* /o/:

*qubał 'grey hair' > *uβan* 'grey hair' and *oβanen* 'having grey hair' *suluɣ 'drop' > *uu* and also *uo* 'lower rope'

---

[20]The final /-ʔ/ that developed from *-t (§C3.3.12) did not cause a preceding /u/ or /i/ to lower—i.e., the rule of lowering was no longer in effect when final *-t > /ʔ/:

*bekut > *βungkuʔ* 'bent' *paqit > *paiʔ* 'bitter'

[21]Disyllabic roots with *e in the penult normally developed stress on the final syllable. The *e subsequently changed to /u/. In other words, *u in the final syllable was stressed after a penult with *e nucleus and therefore not lowered before *-q coda.

C3.2.3 *e

C3.2.31 *e > i in most environments:

*ceŋet > *singi* 'acrid in smell' *ɣamec 'crush, crumble' > ^{H}*amis* 'knead' *gatel > *katil* 'itch' *łecuŋ > *lisung* 'mortar'

C3.2.32 *e > u before labials and in monosyllables, both those that were inherited as such and those that developed to monosyllables:[22]:

*depa > *rupá* fathom' *qatep > *atup* 'roof, thatch' *qitem > *itum* 'black' *sated > *ntur* 'deliver'

C3.2.33 *e assimilated to an /i/ or /u/ in the following syllable:

*kepit 'pinched together' > *kipíʔ* 'carry under the arm' *bekut > *βungkuʔ* 'bent' *pekuq 'curved, rounded' > *pukú* 'bend'

In one case, the resulting /u/ was lowered to /o/. Possibly the /o/ in the antepenult of this word (the prefix) caused the *u of the penult to lower:

*peniyu 'sea turtle' > *tom-ponú* 'turtle'

In several unexplained cases, *e > /u/. These forms probably arose from dialect mixture—i.e., there were dialects of Rat (no longer attested) that changed *e to /u/ in more environments than the ones specified here:

*baɣeqaŋ > *βunga* 'molar'(< *beŋaɣ < *beɣaŋ < *beɣeqaŋ) *beɣek 'pig' > *βio* 'wild pig' (< *beɣoʔ [C3.2.2, 2nd ¶] < *beɣuʔ [C3.3.13]) *celet > *suleʔ* 'insert between' *ɣetac > ^{H}*utas* 'break off'[23] *leŋa > *lunga* 'sesame'

C3.2.34 *eq, -es > /a/:

*liceqes > *lasia* 'nit' (< *lacia [metathesis] > *licaa < *licaqa) *tałeq > *tana* 'earth' *tumes > *tuma* 'clothes louse'

C3.2.35 There was a tendency for the *i and *u that developed from *e to be lowered to /e/ and /o/ respectively when they were adjacent to *ɣ or *c if the root did not contain *a or *u.

*beɣay > *βeey* 'give' *ibeɣ 'salivate' > *eβe* 'saliva' *sipec > *epes* 'roach' *peɣec 'squeeze out' > *hepes* 'pinch, clinch' *cekecek 'stuff, fill chock full' > *sesék* 'tight' *seqeɣet 'tight' > *eheʔ* 'near' *cepecep 'suck' > *sosopan* 'pipe'

There are counterexamples, where lowering does not take place. These are all forms that have /i/ in the syllable that was not adjacent to *ɣ or *c. Either lowering did not take place or the rule of §C3.2.33, above caused the lowered vowel to raise. Why some words show lowered vowels in the penult and final syllable and others show /i/ in the penult and final syllable is unexplained. Possibly, the lowering was a change that was never carried to completion. The evidence for that has not turned up, and may be unrecoverable in view of the

[22]The rule does not hold for inherited monosyllabic roots unless they were also monosyllabic in Rat. Thus, the following reflex has /e/ (from earlier *i) and not /u/ or /o/. The occurrence of /e/ instead of /i/ is explained in §C3.2.35.

*cekecek 'fill chock full' > *sesék* 'tight'

[23]The directly inherited form ^{H}*itas* 'break off' also occurs.

fact that the number of good speakers with intact phonology is declining precipitously. These are the counterexamples:

*deŋeɣ > *ringi* 'hear' *teɣi > *tii* 'k.o. small sea fish' *tiŋeɣ > *tingi* 'voice'

The *i that developed from *e in the following examples also lowered. There is no explanation:

*beŋel > *βengel* 'deaf' *celet > *sule?* 'insert between' *kamet 'take in fingers' > *kame?* 'beckon'

C3.2.36 The sequences *we/*ew and *ye/*ey changed to /u/ and /i/ respectively:

*dasuwen 'leaf' > *raung-e* 'betel' *taquweɬ > *taun* 'year' *weliq 'return' > *mang-ule* 'return home' *seyap + *ta- > *cap* 'count' (< *tiap < *teyap < *teiap < *taiap < *tasiap) *seyaq 'shame' > *ma-hian* 'jealous' (< *ma-iya-an [/h/ developed in transition; stress on penult is unexplained.]) *seyup + *ta- > *cup* 'blow' (< *tiup < *teyup < *teiup < *taiup < *tasiup) *wasiyeɣ 'water' > *mang-ae?* 'have water' (< *waiiɣ [The final /-ʔ/ is unexplained.])

C3.2.4 *a

In general, *a > /a/:

*aɬak > *anak* 'child, offspring'

*a > e in the final syllable when there is an *a in the penult and the final syllable closed with an alveolar or *g:[24]

*qagan > *aren* 'name' *palag > *paler* 'palm' *bayad > *βar* 'pay' (< *βaer [§C3.1.22a])

This rule does not apply if the /a/ of the final syllable is stressed:

*pacaqaɬ 'carry over shoulder' > *pasán* 'carry over shoulder'[25]

When the reflex of *a abuts on a reflex of *e (but not /ey/) contraction takes place producing /a/ (§C3.1.22a), and when the reflex of *a abuts on /u/ it usually becomes /o/ (§C3.1.21b). In one case, *a > /u/ possibly by dissimilation in the penult in a word that inherited four *a's:

*damaɣ 'light, torch' + *ka- + R- > *kararuma* 'morning star'

Reflexes of *a in forms which are clitic have idiosyncratic developments:

*kamu 'you (pl) > *kumú* 'you (plural)' *kita 'we (incl.) > *kite* 'we (incl.)'[26]

*a is frequently lost as part of process of vowel loss in the antepenult or earlier (§C3.1.12d). *a is reflected with /o/ in the final syllable of the following example. There is no explanation. The /o/ of the first syllable results from the contraction of *ue (< *use):

*quseɬap > *onop* 'fish scales' C3.2.5 Diphthongs

---

[24] This is widely exemplified because reflexes of the suffix shaped *-an, which is of wide occurrence, all occur in allomorphs shaped /-en/ in roots with /a/ in the penult:

*kan 'eat' + *R- + *-an > *kakanen* 'place to eat'

[25] The final accent may either be inherited or developed in recent times, but in any case the change of *a to /e/ most likely happened after the loss of the medial syllable and the development of stress, and for this reason we conclude that stress blocked the change of *a to /e/.

[26] In fact, final *a > /e/ in pronouns, and this is a change that all Sangiric languages evince (Sneddon 1984:9)

C3.2.51 *ay

*ay > /ey/ when final except in monosyllabic roots:

*bahi + *R-*-in- > *βaβiney* 'female' (< *bey + *R-*-in-) *balay 'large open hall' > *βaley* 'house' *matay 'die' > *matey* 'dead' *maɣuqałay > *muaney* 'male'

In monosyllabic roots *ay remains /ay/:

*cay > *say* 'who?'

When not final in the root, *ay > /e/:

*taytay 'narrow passage' > *tetey* 'bridge'

When preceded by /w/ *ay > /oy/ (§C3.6.1)

*quway > *oi* 'rattan (with elision of the first syllable [§C3.1.16] and subsequent disyllabization [§C3.1.3]) *way > *oi* 'mango'

In one disyllabic root, *ay is reflected with /ay/. It is not inherited. In a second, the word lost the penult (§C3.1.16) and was treated like a monosyllabic root:

*punay > *punay* 'dove' *semay > *may* 'rice'

C3.2.52 *uy and*iw

*uy > /i/:

*babuy > *βaβi* 'pig' *tuluy 'continue' > *tuli* 'drop in somewhere'

*iw in two cases becomes /iu/ (that is, [iu] or [yu]). In the first case, *s was lost and sonority shifted from the *i to the *w, as was the case in many of the An languages. The second case was influenced semantically and in its shape by *liu* 'go around (< *liyus):

*kásiw > *kayu* 'wood, tree' *caliw 'give in exchange' > *saliu* 'overtake'

In another case, *iw is reflected by /oy/. This is probably a borrowed form, although in fact there are no counterexamples.[27] (Cf. the Tdn cognate, *waluy*, which also evinces a sequence, /uy/, that is irregular [§C4.2.52] and shows the same semantic development.)

*baliw 'return, go back' > *βaloy* 'become changed'

C3.2.53 *aw

*aw > /ow/

*babaw 'clean weeds' > *βaβow* 'clean weeds' *nakaw 'steal' > *takow* 'steal' (with analogical replacement of *n by /t/)

In monosyllables *aw > /aw/:

*qałegaw > *law* 'sun'[28]

When followed by a coda or in non-final position *aw > /o/:

---

[27] If *uy > /i/, it is unlikely that *iw should have become /oy/.

[28] The data are not decisive on this point. The problem is that /ow/ is a variant sequence in all forms that contain /aw/ (but not not vice-versa [cf. §C3.0, end]). The dictionary sometimes transcribes *ou* in forms that we recorded with /aw/. (In others, the dictionary transcribes *au*.) Where our only source is the dictionary, then we follow the dictionary even in those cases where the dictionary only reports *ou* but in all likelihood variants with /aw/ do exist.

*taqu +R-an > *taton* (< ta-taw-an

In one case, *-aw > /o/ in final position. A possible explanation is that the sequence *aow, which would have resulted from the proto-form, was automatically simplified to /ao/:

*kaɣaw > *kao* 'scratch' (< *kaow)

In three cases, *aw is reflected with /aw/. These forms are borrowed from an unknown source:

*ciwa > *siaw* 'nine' *tuŋaw 'flea' > *tungaw*'k.o. mite' *tiheɬaw > *tinaw* 'clear'

In one unexplained case *-aw > *-u:

*talaw > *talu* 'coward'[29]

C3.3 Consonants

CHART TWO. REFLEXES OF THE PAN CONSONANTS IN RATAHAN

PAn	Rat	PAn	Rat
p	*p*	g	*k-, -r-, -r*
t	*t*	ɣ	*Ø*
k	*k*	l	*l*
q	*Ø*	ɬ	*n, l*
s, h	*Ø*	m	*m*
c	*s*	n	*n*
b	*β*	ŋ	*ng* [*ŋ*]
d, j	*r*	w, y	*β, y*

C3.3.1 Voiceless consonants

The voiceless stops (except *q) are preserved initially and medially. Finally, *p and *k are preserved, but final *-t is changed to glottal stop, /-ʔ/.

Rat allows no consonant clusters other than homorganic nasals followed by a stop. In doubled monosyllabic roots, the final C of the first monosyllable was lost if it was not a nasal:

*cepecep 'suck' > *sa-sosop-an* 'tobacco pipe' *paɣatepat 'k.o. mangrove' > *paapaʔ* 'k.o. tree' *cikecik 'search through' > *sisik* 'look for lice'*bukebuk 'wood-borer' > *βuβuk* 'eaten by a wood-borer' *muɣemuɣ > *mai-momo* 'gargle' *dicedic 'make a thin cut' > *riris* 'rag, scissors'

C3.3.11 *p

*p remained /p/ in all positions, except where affected by CC simplification (§C3.3.1):

*pálag 'palm of hand' > *paler* 'palm, sole' *qápuɣ > *apu* 'lime' *qatep > *atup* 'thatch, roof'

Some reflexes of *-p- manifest sporadic prenasalization (§C3.1.6):

[29]This form may have been contaminated with a reflex of the form *talu 'be defeated', which is not attested in the data we have for Rat.

*cahebay > *sumpáy* 'hang over rack, line' *qaɬipulec > *limpurus* 'waterspout, whirlwind' (contaminated by *qaɬipugu 'hair whorl') *sapaɣ 'mat' > *umpá* 'underlayer, sheet'

C3.3.12 *t

Unless it was simplified in CC's (§C3.3.1), *t remained /t/ initially and medially. Finally *t > /ʔ/:

*qatay > *atey* 'liver' *sepat > *paʔ* 'four' *takut > *takuʔ* 'afraid'

In a couple of cases, *-t > Ø. The explanation probably lies in the fact that in connected speech the /ʔ/ that occurred in word-final position was lost before a following stop-initial word, and the alternant without the final /-ʔ/ was generalized:

*ɣakit > ^{H}*aki* 'raft' *ceŋet 'acrid smell' > *singi* 'bad smell'

C3.3.13 *k

In most cases, *k remained /k/:

*kásiw 'tree, wood' > *kayu* 'wood, tree' *jeket 'set fire to' > *rikiʔ* 'set fire to' *aɬak 'child' > *anak* 'child, offspring'

In the reflex of *aku 'I', *k > /ʔ/, probably as the generalization of a rapid-speech form:

*aku > *yaʔ* 'I' (with a petrified prefix *i-*)

In at least two cases,*-k was lost. There is no explanation. In the first example, the /o/ of the final syllable developed because *-k changed to *-ʔ (§C3.2.2, 2nd¶), which was subsequently lost:

*beɣek 'pig' > *βio* 'wild pig' *nacuk 'boil' > *nasu* 'cook staple'[30]

C3.3.14 *q

*q is lost in all positions:

*qatay > *atey* 'liver' *paqit > *paiʔ* 'bitter' *luwaq 'vomit' > *lua* 'spit out'

Final *-q left a trace in that *-q caused preceding *i and *u to lower to /e/ and /o/ respectively (§§C3.2.1, C3.2.2).

C3.3.15 *c

*c > /s/ in all environments, except in clusters, where it was lost (§C3.3.1):

*cai > *say* 'who' *qacawa 'in-law' > *sawa* 'spouse' *becuɣ > *βisu* 'full, sated' *betíec > *βitis* 'calf'

In one case, *c is lost without explanation. Note that the same PAn root also has a reflex that evinces /s/, but with a changed meaning:

*puceg 'navel' > *puir* 'navel' also *pusir* 'whorl of hair'

---

[30] The existence of a variant of this root without *-k may go back to late PAn times. Paiwan attests a variant without a reflex of *-k: *ɬatu* 'boil meat'. (Paiwan also attest *natuk* 'boil' with a reflex of final *-k and an unexplained initial /n/ instead of the normal /ɬ/.)

In one case, *c seems to have dissimilated to /t/ before a *c on the right. This is not a general rule, and in fact there is a variant *sisik* (with a reflex that was not dissimilated):

*cikecik > *tisik* 'look for lice'

C3.3.2 *h, *s

*h and *s were lost without a trace:

*sagek 'sniff' > *arik* 'kiss' *binesiq 'seed rice' > *βine* 'rice in husk' *dusa > *ruá* 'two' *luseq > *lo* 'tears' *cebus 'splash liquid on' > *suβu* 'foam, froth; extinguish fire' *tapes > *tap* 'winnow' (< *taep < *tasep)

Examples of -h loss:

*bahi + *R-*-in > *βaβiney* 'female' *betihec > *βitis* 'calf' *capuh > *sapu* 'sweep' *tuɬuh > *tunu* 'roast'

C3.3.3 Voiced stops

The voiced stops were weakened, becoming continuants: *b > /β/; *d and *j fell together and became /r/. *g as onset or coda of the final syllable merged with *d and *j—i.e., became /r/. When it was onset to the penult or earlier, *g- > /k-/, as in many languages. In discourse, when the initial continuants /β/ and /r/ are preceded by a nasal, they are automatically replaced by /b/ and /d/ respectively, or possibly, a nasal protected the /b/ and /d/ from becoming continuants.

C3.3.31 *b

*b weakened to /β/ in initial and medial positions except when protected by a nasal. In final position /β/ has a voiceless allophone [ɸ].

*baq 'go, put down' > *βa* 'direction downward' *beɣekec > *βikis* 'bundle *qabu > *aβu* 'ashes' *ibeɣ > *eβe* 'saliva' *iceɣab > *ka-neaβ* 'yesterday' (< *ɬiɣab metathesis of *i and *e in PAn [§A3.5.4] and nasalization of *c that took place in PAn [§A3.7.1]) *qisuwab > *koyaβ* 'yawn' (< *ka-uiab <*ka-suiqab [metathesis])

When protected, *b remained /b/:

*tambak 'earth piled up for dam, grave' > *tambak* 'add soil to make even' *timbaw 'be at the top' > *timbow* 'rise to the surface'

A few borrowed words with /b/ are pronounced [b] and have established a contrast between /β/ and /b/:

*balu > *balu* 'widow' *binuwaŋ > *binuang* 'k.o. tree'

Niemann, writing in the nineteenth century, transcribed /β/ as *w*. We write *w* here when the source of the form is Niemann (i.e., the word is unknown to current speakers). Further, Kolinog (1990) occasionally transcribes /w/, where /β/ is expected, probably in error:

*cebus 'splash' > *suwu* 'foam, froth' (inform: *suβú*) *lebeŋ 'bury' > *liwing* 'grave' *buteliɣ 'cyst' > *nu-wuti-wuti* 'be in bunches (fruit)'

C3.3.32 *d, *j

*d and *j merged, becoming /r/ in all positions except when protected by a nasal. In initial position:

*deŋan 'together' > *pu-ringan* 'accompany' *dilaq 'tongue' > *rila* 'tongue' *jalan > *ralen* 'way'

In medial position:

*tuduq 'leak, drip' > *turo* 'leak' *tujuq 'point' > *pan-turo* 'show'

In final position:

*likud > *likur* 'back' *qaɬuj > *yandur* 'carry by current' (with initial /i-/ accreted by analogy from the form with the instrumental passive prefix and sporadic insertion of /d/ between the nasal and the following vowel)

*d >/d/ when protected by *n (just as *b > b after a nasal). There are no attested reflexes of *j after a nasal.

*demedem 'dark, cloudy' > *rundum* 'dark, cloudy' *dap > *ndap* 'a tree: *Erythrina*'

The following form shows a change of *j > /l/. It is a unique example.[31]

*jaqet 'bad' > *lalaiʔ* (also *ndalaiʔ* and *ralaiʔ* 'bad' (< *jajaqet [reduplication])

In one case, *d onset was assimilated to an *l onset on the left (i.e., in the preceding syllable):

*laduŋ > *ma-lalung-an* 'sheltered area'

In another case, it was the *l on the left that was assimilated to the *d on the right (*liduŋ > *rirung* 'protect' [§C3.3.42]). These two different ways of assimilation are probably the result of dialect mixture.

C3.3.33 *g

As onset of the penult or earlier or of monosyllabic roots, *g- > /k-/:

*gatel 'itch' > *katil* 'itch' *gem > *ngkum* 'hold in hands'

As onset or coda of the final syllable, *g > /r/ (i.e., merges with *d and *j):

*isegung 'nose' > *irun* 'nose' *ɬagam 'tame' > *naram* 'usual' *pálag 'palm of hand' > *paler* 'palm, sole'

In the following example, *g onset of the penult was lost in a trisyllabic root. The explanation probably has to do with the fact that Rat did not allow sequences of /l/ onset followed by an /r/ onset.[32] We assume that the *r that developed from *g was assimilated to the /l/ on the left and that subsequently the penult was elided by haplology:

*qaɬegaw > *law* 'sun' (< *lelaw < *leraw < *legaw [with loss of antepenult (§C3.1.12d)])

*g was also lost in the following root The loss of *-g- is unexplained:

*qugiŋ '> *b-oeng* 'charcoal' (< *ba-qugiŋ, with contraction [§C3.1.21b] and vowel harmony [§C3.2.1])

In one unexplained case, *-g > /-ʔ/:

---

[31] The expected form would have had two /r/'s. There are several words inherited from PAn which are reflected with /r-/ onset of the penult and of the final syllable, e.g. *daŋedaŋ > *rarang* 'heat near fire'

[32] The data are inconsistent as to the treatment of [l] that developed before an [r] onset of the following syllable (§§C3.3.32, end and C3.3.42). In any case, the sequence is disallowed.

*belag > *βila?* 'spread out (mat, books)'[33]

C3.3.4 Voiced continuants

C3.3.41 *ɣ

In initial position, *ɣ was lost in some forms,[34] is reflected as /h/ in a few, and is reflected as /ᴴ/ in others. The reason for the three reflexes is that *ɣ was changing during the last few decades that Rat was still alive and healthy. It may be that these phonemes are in fact variables in the speech of the last few speakers. In the earliest records of Rat, reflexes with initial *ɣ are recorded as having *h*. Nowadays, /h/ is pronounced with strong affrication [x]. [ᴴ] is very weakly pronounced and prevents contraction with a preceding vowel from taking place. Forms with an initial vowel may optionally be pronounced with a weak glottal stop, but forms with initial /ᴴ/ never get a glottal stop initially. The dictionary transcribes the three reflexes differently, but transcribed many forms with /h/ that our informants, current speakers, pronounced with /ᴴ/. I follow the transcriptions of the recordings of our informants. Forms with initial PAn *ɣ were all transcribed by Niemann with initial /h/.
Examples of *ɣ > /h/:

*ɣudaŋ > *hudang* 'old' *ɣucuk > *husuk* 'ribs' *peɣec > *hepes* 'pinch, choke, massage' (§C3.1.4)

Examples of *ɣ > /ᴴ/:

*ɣakut 'tie together' > *ᴴaku?* 'tie fast' *ɣetac > *ᴴitas* 'break off'

Examples of *ɣ > ∅:

*ɣiq > *ee* 'saw grass'

In medial and final position, *ɣ is lost entirely except for two words. In both cases, there probably was syllable loss, causing *ɣ to be initial. Subsequent disyllabization by addition of a prothetic vowel in one case and compounding in the second, resulted in a form in which /h/, the reflex of *ɣ, was no longer word initial. *e > /e/ by the rule of §C3.2.35 in these examples:

*seqeɣet 'tight' > *ehe?* 'near' (< *he? < *ɣet < *qeɣet) *liqeɣ > *kau-he* 'neck' (< *kau* + *-he* < *ɣeq < *liɣeq [metathesis])

In several cases, *ɣ is reflected with /r/. These forms are mostly borrowed from Manado Ml:

*buteliɣ 'cyst' > *βutir* 'seed' *caŋeɣ > *sare* 'lean against' (< *sadeɣ < *sandeɣ < *saneɣ) *quɣut > *uru* 'massage deeply' *suɣac > *uras* 'wash'

C3.3.42 *l

*l > /l/ with very few exceptions:

*laŋit > *laŋi?* 'sky' *jalan > *ralen* 'road, way' *gatel > *katil* 'itch'

---

[33]There is also a form *βilar* 'board', which is connected. It is probably the directly inherited form, for it evinces the regular reflexes.

[34] With the exception of one case, for all of the forms that our informants pronounced with initial ∅ < *ɣ, Sneddon lists initial /ᴴ/.

*l assimilates to an /r/ onset of the following syllable:

*liduŋ > *rirung* 'protect, cover over'

In another case, it was the *d on the right that was assimilated to the *l on the left (*laduŋ > *ma-lalung-an* 'protected area' [§C3.3.32]). These two different ways of assimilation are probably the result of dialect mixture.
In at least five cases, *l > Ø. This must be the result of dialect mixture.[35] The environment is not an explanation because there are counterexamples where reflexes of *l are retained.

*buliɣ 'ear, bunch, stalkful' > *βui* 'stalkful of bananas' *qiteluɣ > *tuu* and *tuʔu* 'egg' (with the insertion of /ʔ/ between a sequence of two vowels of the same quality [§C3.1.5]) *alap > *aaʔ* 'take' (/ʔ/ unexplained) (also *alap*) *suluɣ 'drop' > *uu* or *uo* 'lower ropes' *caleɣ 'flooring' > *sai* 'floor'

C3.3.43 *ɬ

*ɬ underwent the changes found throughout the MP languages (§§A1.1.32, 4th¶, A3.3.4). In addition, PMP †ñ < *ɬ underwent depalatalization, as it did in many of the MP languages.[36] As onset to an unstressed penult or earlier syllable, *ɬ- becomes /l-/. Otherwise, *ɬ > /n/. This rule can be restated as given in the following paragraphs:

C3.3.431 *ɬ > /n/ medially before the final syllable and at the end of a root

*aɬák > *anak* 'child' *láɬa > *lana* 'oil' *qasiɬ > *asin* 'salt'

C3.3.432 *ɬ > n before a vowel that was stressed in PAn, including in monosyllabic roots:

*ɬam 'taste' > *mau-nanam* 'tasty' (< ɬamɬam, with the /n/ developed from the doubling of a monosyllabic root [§C3.1.3]) *ɬuɣ 'coconut' > *niu* (with insertion of /i/ as part of process of disyllabization) *ɬípic 'thin' (< *ɬisebic) > *nipis* 'thin' *kaɬuskus > *kanuku* 'nail, claw'.

C3.3.433 *ɬ > /l/ in other positions—that is, before a short (unaccented) vowel of the penultimate or earlier syllable:

*qáɬegaw > *law* 'sun' *ɬesúng > *lisung* 'mortar' *qaɬimátek > *limatik* 'leech'

C3.3.5 *m, *n, *ŋ

*m, *n, *ŋ > /m/, /n/ and /ng/, respectively (except that in clusters the nasal was assimilated to the articulation of the following consonant):

*inum > *inum* 'drink' *manuk 'bird' > *manuk* 'chicken, bird' *enem > *num* 'six' *kami > *kami* 'we (excl.)' *qagan > *aren* 'name' *ŋaŋa > *nganga* 'open mouth' *daŋ + R- > *rarang* 'cook, heat'

---

[35] A similar phenomenon characterizes some of the languages of the central and southeast Philippines. Cf. the discussion of this phenomenon in Tagalog (§C1.3.42.)

[36] The sequence /ny/, which arose by elision in trisyllables (§3.1.11), also changed to /n/:

*peniyu > *tom-ponú* 'turtle'

There are a few unexplained exceptions. In three forms, /ng/ reflects *-m or *-n:[37]

*leqacem 'sour' > *lising* 'vinegar, sour toddy' (< *le?ecem (§C3.1.12a) < *laqecem [§C3.1.4])[38] *dawusen 'leaf' > *raung-e* 'betel' *papan 'board' > *papang* 'board, plank'

In the following case, the replacement of *-n by /ng/ probably has to do with the generalization of the allomorph before a word beginning with /k/:

*punuq > *po?ong* 'base of tree'(also *pung* in the phrase *pung kayu* 'tree', and *pun* in the phrase *pun akel* 'sugar palm tree') The lowering of the *u and the reflection of *q with /?/ indicates that *po?ong* is not a direct inheritance.[39]

In one case, a final *-ŋ is reflected with /n/. There is no explanation:

*iseguŋ > *irun* 'nose'

In the following case *-n- is reflected as /-ng-/. It may be a rule that an *n onset assimilated to a *g coda. It is the only example of a syllable with this onset and coda. Note that assimilation did not take in a syllable with *n- onset and *ɣ coda:

*qunég > *ungir* 'pith' *linuɣ > *linu* 'earthquake'

C3.3.61 *w

*w > /β/ as syllable onset before *a with two exceptions:

*walu > *βalu* 'eight' *cawa 'python' > *saβa* 'snake' *qacawa 'in-law' > *saβa* 'spouse' *sawak > *aβak* 'body'

The first exception is when the sequence *wa is followed by a vowel or /y/ (i.e., the sequence *way). In that case, *wa > /o/ (*way becomes /oy/):

*way > *oi* 'mango' (< *oy and disyllabization [§C3.1.3]) *quway > *oi* 'rattan' (for loss of the penult, cf. §C3.1.16)

The second exception is that after a prefix ending in *a-, *w combines with the *a to form /o/. This is the same rule as that governing contraction of *a and *u (§C3.1.21b)

*wanaɬ + ka- > *koanen* 'right' (< *koanan) *wiɣi + *ka- > *koi* 'left' (< *koii* [attested by Niemann as *kohii* with /h/ transition])

The following form spread into Rat secondarily and does not follow the sound law:

*bulaw+ -an > *βulaun* 'gold'

For final *-w, cf. §§C3.2.52, C3.2.53.

C3.3.62 *y

*y is attested only medially between two *a's and between *a and *u and became /y/. Between *i and *a or *u, *y does not contrast with its absence.

---

[37] Manado Ml neutralizes word final nasals—all are pronounced [ŋ]. It is possible that the final nasals in these words developed under Ml influence. Also there is a dialect of Ttb that has neutralized the final nasals in most cognates (Sneddon 1978: note 37).

[38] We assume that the change of *-m to /-ŋ / took place after the operation of the rule of §C3.2.32, whereby *e > /u/ before labials.

[39] This form may also be explained as the disyllabization of a monosyllabic root (§C3.1.3) with intercalation of [?] between two like vowels (§C3.1.5) and sporadic lowering of the vowel.

*daya 'inland' > *raya* 'term used in telling a person to go northwards' *bayaq 'leave' > *βaya* 'permit, set free' *kasiw > *kayu* 'wood' *liyus 'go around' > *liu* 'go through, around'

However, if the root ends in a consonant that was not lost, *y was lost between *a's because of the effect of the change of the *a in a closed final syllable to /e/ (§C3.2.4):

*bayad 'pay' > *βar* 'pay' (< *βaer)

Initial /y/ in inherited forms derives from an antepenultimate *i- that lost syllabicity (§C3.1.12c). Otherwise, a reflex of initial *y is not attested:

*ama + *i- > *yama-ng* 'father' (< *i-ama)

*y contracts with *e when it is adjacent to it (§C3.2.36). For final *y, cf. §§C3.2.51, C3.2.52.

CHAPTER FOUR

Tondano

C4.0 Introduction

Tondano (Tdn)is one of the five Minahasan languages of northern Sulawesi, Indonesia. Tdn is also called 'Tolour'. Both designations mean 'people of the sea'. The other four Minahassan languages are Tonsea (Tse), Tombolu (Tblu,) Tontemboan (Ttb), and Tonsawang. The Minahasan languages can be determined to form a subgroup by virtue of the innovations that they have made in common. They are considered to be among the 'Philippine Languages', and indeed many of the innovations made by languages of the Philippines have been made by Tdn and the other Minahasan languages, but it is not certain that in fact, these innovations remount to a proto-Philippine language. Rather they were most probably made after PMP times and spread through the Philippine and Minahasan languages. The term 'Minahasa' was invented by Dutch linguists to refer to these five speech communities, which have much in common culturally as well as linguistically, and distinguish them from other speech communities of northern Sulawesi with which some of them are in contact: the communities of the Samal and Sangiric language speakers. The Minahasan languages are bound to the west by the Gorontalic languages, which also are considered to group with the languages of the Philippines.

The Minahasan languages as a whole are not well documented. The dictionaries that exist, with the exception of the dictionary for Ttb (Schwarz 1908), are limited word lists, and for two of them, Tonsawang and Tblu, practically nothing has been published except texts, and they are limited. Sneddon 1978, based on fieldwork, is the best source for these two languages. All the Minahasan languages are endangered. The languages are still spoken by young people in rural areas, but the majority of the population, most especially the elite, has been switching to the Manado dialect of Malay. This process began more than a century ago, and has been proceeding with ever-increasing speed since.

The Minahasan languages have influenced one another to a great degree, and forms have moved through the area, probably replacing cognates that had been inherited from PMP. Many of these forms evince irregularities of sound correspondences that were the normal development in only one small sub-portion of the total area covered by the Minahasan languages. As a result, Tdn manifests a sizeable number of reflexes of PMP and PAn that do not follow the sound laws.

My principal source for information on Tdn is F.S Watuseke, a native speaker of Tdn, who complied a manuscript dictionary (Watuseke 1974) and who has made Tdn and other Minahasan languages the object of a life-long study. I have also compared his forms with those quoted by Sneddon 1978. The forms quoted in this study are from the dialect spoken in the town of Tondano, with the exception of a few which occur in Kakas, but not Tondano. These few have been marked 'Kakas'. All of the Tondano forms have been substantiated by

Mr. Watuseke. A second source of data was Sneddon 1978. This source has been useful first, in supplying citations from other Minahasan languages for those protoforms where no Tdn citation is available and second, for presenting the data that allows us to explain some of the forms with irregular correspondences. I have checked Ttb forms quoted in this chapter and in the glossary with Schwarz 1908.

The following chart shows the phonemes of Tdn. /ɣ/ is a marginal phoneme. It is of relatively infrequent occurrence, but it appears in words of PAn or PMP provenience. This phoneme is found in the other Minahasan languages (pronounced [g] there) in cognate forms and seems to have come into Proto-Minahasan through contact with an unidentified language that had [ɣ] or [g] as the reflex of PAn *ɣ and *g.[1]

CHART ONE. PHONEMES OF TONDANO

Consonants

voiceless stops	p	t	k	ʔ
voiced stops		d		
spirants		s	ɣ	
nasals	m	n	ng [ŋ]	
glides and laterals	w, y	l, r		

Vowels and Diphthongs

high	i		u
mid	ɛ	e	o
low		a	
diphthongs	ɛi		ou

C4.1 Changes that characterize Tdn in general

Tdn has a tendency to form disyllabic roots (§A3.6.2). First, under the influence of stress, roots of more than two syllables were reduced to two syllables by the process of syncope or other types of syllable loss, with the exception of some of the stems of four syllables, which were reduced to three syllables. Second, roots that became monosyllabic because of sound changes or roots that were inherited as monosyllables from PAn were disyllabized by processes that are widespread throughout the Austronesian area (§A3.6.2).

C4.1.1 Disyllabization of trisyllables

C4.1.11 An *e nucleus in the penult is elided if it had *h, *ɣ, *q, or *s onset of the penult or of the final syllable. The following examples show elision of the penult:

> *baŋeqeɣ > *wangɛ* 'smell bad' *baɣeqáŋ 'molar' > *waʔang* 'tooth' *beɣekec > *waʔkes* 'tie up, bind' *binesiq 'seed' > *wɛnɛʔ* 'rice in husk' (with vowel harmony [§C4.2.1]) *deɣeqec 'move vigorously' > *reɣec* 'for wind to blow' *básequ > *wou* 'smell' (< *baqu) *isepi > *ipi* 'dream' *pakehu > *paku* 'k.o. fern' *qaselu > *alu* 'pestle' *saɣejáɬ > *aran* 'ladder' *tahebu 'vessel to fetch water' > *tabuʔ* 'fishpond' *tahepá > *tapa* 'smoke fish or meat' *udesi > *m-uri* 'behind, back, rear'

Elision of the penult also occurred in roots containing a prefix that had been petrified (i.e., the root occurred only with the prefix):

> *ubuc + *ka- > *kawus* 'finished' (< *ka-ubus)

The following form shows elision of a penult with *i before a final syllable with *e:

> *jaqewis > *rouʔ* 'far' (< *jauq < *jaweq < *jawiseq)

[1] The Gorontolic languages reflect *ɣ with [g] (or a development from that), but they do not reflect *g that way.

In the following form, a penult with *a was elided, something that normally did not take place. Perhaps this was because the word originally had four syllables. Subsequently, the initial syllable was lost:

*qaɬimatéq > *lintaʔ* 'leech' (< *limtaq [cf.§C4.2.3 for the change of *e to /a/]) < *qalimteq)

C4.1.12 In a large number of cases (but not in all[2]), the antepenult is weakened in trisyllables. There is no explanation for why weakening should have taken place in some trisyllables, but not in others. Since some of these forms with weakened antepenult are basic vocabulary, there is no reason to believe that they are not inherited. The conclusion is either (1) that Tdn results from mixture of two dialects that treated the antepenult differently or (2) antepenultimate weakening is a variable (lack of field data makes it impossible to say which of these two possibilities is the correct one):[3]

*aqetih 'for water to recede' > *eti* 'dry up" *bahi + R- in- > *wewɛnɛ* 'female' (< *babɛnɛ < *babinay) *báqeɣu > *weru* 'new' (< *beqeɣu) *caheɬáɣ > *senaʔ* 'shining like a star' (< *ceheɬaɣ) *biɣeŋi > *wengi* 'night' *binuwáŋ > *wenoang* 'k.o. tree' *daɣa + R- > *reraa* 'maiden' *láqeya > *lia* 'ginger' (< *leqiya < *leqeya) *paqepaq + *-al- > *pelaʔpaʔ* 'stem of palm frond' *palisi > *peliʔi* 'taboo' *paqegu > *peru* 'gall' (< *qepegu < *qapegu) *pasaqáɬ > *pesaʔan* 'carry over shoulder' *tuktuk 'beak' > *toʔtok* 'beak' *tumetoʔtok* 'woodpecker' (< *tumutuktuk)[4] *weliq 'do again' + *ca- > *suliʔ* 'repay' (< *sa-uliʔ)

Similarly, in the following form, the penult was elided, but the antepenult was weakened prior to elision:

*qaɬegaw > *edo* 'day' (< *enggaw < *eɬegaw)

In one case, the antepenultimate vowel was weakened to /a/. This is an innovation shared by the languages south of the Philippines and took place in pre-Tondano.

*qiteluɣ > *atelu* 'egg'

C4.1.13 Initial *i is lost in trisyllables:

*isuɣej > *soroʔ* 'move over' (< *iseɣuj) *iceŋet 'sharp, biting' > *senget* 'stinging ant' *ikasu > *ko* 'you (sg) ' *iqetah > *eta* 'rice husks'

C4.1.14 Otherwise, with some exceptions, trisyllables are retained as trisyllables with no loss or weakening:

*betíhec > *wetiʔis* 'calf' *buqaya 'crocodile' > *wuaya* 'daring' *ɣabihi 'night' > *ka-awiʔi-n* 'yesterday, last night' *minaŋa > *minanga* 'branch of river' *sadiɣi > *arii* 'post' *taŋila > *talinga* 'ear'

---

[2] For examples of forms in which the antepenult was not weakened, cf. §C4.1.14, below.

[3] Weakening of the antepenult may in fact be a variable in the speech community. There is at least one case in my data that shows variation between a weakened antepenult and an antepenult with the full inherited vowel. Comparison of current Tondano with the earliest records shows that the process of antepenultimate weakening in some cases took place recently:

*dadaɣa > *reraa/raraha* (Niemann 1869–70) 'maiden'*ɬiki-ɬiki > *kikilɛʔ/ kekilɛʔ* 'underarm' (metathesis and haplology)

[4] The /u/ of the infix *-um-* was not weakened in this case, as it was a recognized morpheme, but the *u of the reduplicated syllable was.

The following form obeys none of the above rules. It was affected by sound symbolism:

*baqesiŋ > *wa?an* 'sneeze'

C4.1.2 Consonant cluster simplification

CC's that developed were simplified: *l was lost, nasals assimilated to the following C, and otherwise the first C > /?/. Thus, the final consonants of the first syllable of reduplicated monosyllables became /?/ after the epenthetic *e had elided:[5]

*baqebaq > *wa?mba?* 'mouth' (Kakas) *bitebit 'carry in fingers' > *wi?wit* 'pull on a string, line' *buɣebuɣ 'broken into small pieces and scattered' > *wu?wur* 'strew, scatter, sow' *cikecik 'search through thoroughly (as for lice)' > *si?sik* 'small beetle which bores in wood and crops'[6]

No glottal stop developed in the following case of a reduplicated monosyllable. The other Minahasan languages also reflect an open first syllable. It is possible that in Proto-Minahasan the monosyllabic root was disyllabized not by doubling, but by reduplication—that is, the prefixation of the first consonant and vowel of the root:

*bukebuk > *wuwuk* 'wood-borer' (possibly from *bubuk)

Examples with *-l and final nasals:

*celecel > *sesel* 'regret' *pun 'gather' > *pumpun* 'fill with solids'

An example of CC simplification in a trisyllabic root that disyllabized:

*beɣekec 'bundle > *wa?kes* 'tie up, bind'

*qC was simplified to C in the following examples. They are not directly inherited and also show an irregular reflex of *ɣ (§C4.3.41(1)):

*baqeɣuh > *weru* 'new' (< *beqɣu < *beqeɣu) *deɣeqec 'move vigorously' > *reɣes* 'for wind to blow' (< *deqɣec < *deqeɣec)

*Cq > /?/:

*baɣeqaŋ 'molar' > *wa?ang* 'tooth'

There are exceptions. Forms with *ɣ-coda in a doubled monosyllable failed to develop a medial glottal stop, possibly because the penult was made to conform to the final syllable, where the coda was normally lost:

*cuɣecuɣ > *susu* 'follow from behind' *qali-muɣemuɣ > *li-mumu* 'rinse out mouth'

In one case of a doubled monosyllabic root, the nasal coda became /i/ and the preceding *e became /ɛ/. The onset of the second syllable was protected from spirantizing, as if it had been a nasal stop preceded by a nasal (§C4.3.32). This is a borrowing from a dialect of Ttb in which this change is regular:

*demedem > *rɛidem* 'dark'

---

[5] Some of the Minahasa languages did not simplify CC's. Here are two examples:

*gacegac 'scratch' > *ka?kas* 'scratch' (Tse *kaskas* 'scratch') *kepekep 'clasp' > *ke?kep* 'cover, enclose' (Tse, Tblu *kepkep* 'cover, embrace')

[6] In the case of *si?sik*, a variant *sisik* is also attested. Why the /?/ should have been lost is unexplained.

A cluster *ɣC that developed in the following case lost the *ʔ or never developed it. This is a form that is not directly inherited from PAn. The vowels are also irregular:

*deɣemun 'nest, lair' > *rumun* 'brood (hen)'

C4.1.3 Disyllabization of monosyllabic roots

A few forms in Tdn reflect disyllabization of monosyllabic roots by stretching the vowel nucleus or by adding a prothetic /e/. If stretching a nucleus resulted in the development of a vowel sequence, a glottal stop was intercalated between the two vowels (§C4.15):

*ica > *esa* 'one' (< *ca, a generalization of the form that developed in proclitic position)
*mic > *emis* 'sweet' *pan > *paʔan* 'bait' *tan > *taʔan* 'snare animals'

In one case, no glottal stop developed. This form, possibly because it occurs widely in derivations, remained monosyllabic longer than others and only disyllabized after the rule of glottal-stop insertion ceased to operate:[7]

*kan 'eat' > *kaan* 'food'

Many roots disyllabize by reduplication:

*gac > *kaʔkas* 'scratch' *ɬam > *nanam* 'taste' *pun > *pumpun* 'gather'

Monosyllabic roots with a diphthong disyllabize by adding /i/ after *ay and /u/ after *aw:

*cay > *sɛi* 'who?' (< *sayi) *taw > *tou* 'person' (< *tawu)

When the monosyllabic roots are in compounds, they do not disyllabize:

*taw + *lahuj > *tolour* 'Tondano (lit. the sea people)'

There are examples of disyllabization by petrifaction of an affixed monosyllable:

*cuɬ + *um- > *unsun* 'stack up'

C4.1.4 Metathesis

Tdn reflects some of the metathesis that took place in PMP or earlier:

*bukes > *wuʔuk* 'hair' (< *busek) *ɣinu > *iu* 'winnowing tray' (< *niu* [also attested] with analogic recutting of *en* 'marker' + *iu* < *niɣu) *ɬiki-ɬiki > *kikilɛʔ/ kekilɛʔ* 'underarm' (< *kili-kili by haplology) *paqegu > *peru* 'gall' (< *qepegu < *qapegu) *taŋila > *talinga* 'ear' *tapes > *taʔap* 'winnow' (< *tasep) *tilu > *tuli* 'deaf' *tusuq 'true' > *tuʔu* 'indeed, truly' (< *tuqus)

There are other cases of metathesis that are specific to Tdn or to Tdn and nearby languages:

*debedeb > *weʔwer* 'chest' *deɣeqec 'move vigorously' > *reɣes* 'for wind to blow' (< *deqɣec < *deqeɣec) *liqeɣ > *lɛɛʔ* 'neck' (< *leɣiq) *taquweɬ > *taʔun* 'year' (< *taqwun < *taqewun)

---

[7] The evidence for this is that the cognate reflexes in the other Minahasan languages are still monosyllabic. In Tonsawang there is variation between *kan* and *kaan* 'eat'. However, in the case of the disyllabization of other roots, the other Minahasan languages evince glottal stop intercalation when the vowel nucleus was streteched to two moras, just as Tdn does. The following two examples are reflected in most, if not all, the Minahasan languages:

*pan > *paʔan* 'bait' *tan > *taʔan* 'snare' (not attested in Tonsawang)

C4.1.5 Intercalation of glottal stops

At an early stage of pre-Tondano, /ʔ/ was inserted in root-internal vowel sequences of like vowels, both those that developed from loss of *s or *h (§C4.3.2) and those that developed by stretching monosyllabic roots:

*bitíhec > *wetiʔis* 'calf of leg, shank' *bukes 'hair' > *wuʔuk* (with loss of *s) (< *buuk < *busek) *pan > *paʔan* 'bait' *tapes > *taʔap* 'winnow' (< *tasep)

The process of glottal stop intercalation came to an end before the loss of *ɣ.[8] That is, vowel sequences that developed from the loss of *ɣ are not separated by a glottal stop:

*baɣah > *waa* 'live coals' *keɣet 'cut off' > *kɛɛt* 'tap sugar palm' *sadiɣi > *arii* 'house post'

With a few forms, /-ʔ/ is added after a final vowel. This is a sporadic development found with forms that occur frequently as vocatives in many of the An languages either as a regular or as a sporadic process.

*ama > *amaʔ* 'father' *apu > *opoʔ* 'grandparent, ancestor' *kaka > *kakaʔ* 'elder sibling'

Other instances of glottal stop addition in word-final position are irregular. In most of these cases, the glottal stop was added under the influence of another language (probably Ml[9]), as some of the cognates also evince final -ʔ:

*tabuh 'scoop water' > *tabuʔ* 'fish pond' *teka 'come, arrive'> *tekaʔ* 'for a bird to alight' *keɬa > *tenaʔ* 'hit mark' *pa > *pɛʔ* 'still' *buka > *wukaʔ* 'open'[10]

Tdn also evinces glottal stop insertion before the onset of the final syllable in four inherited forms. Possibly, the glottal-stop was inserted by sound symbolism:

*bataŋ 'main part of tree' > *waʔtang* 'k.o. rattan' *beŋel > *weʔngel* 'stupid' *ɬemec 'disappear' > *leʔmes* 'sufficate, choke' *pacek 'wedge' > *paʔsek* 'pole'

C4.1.6 Prenasalization of medial stop consonants

Like the other Hesperonesian languages, Tdn evinces sporadic prenasalization of medial stops in disyllabic roots (§A3.7.2). The process of prenasalization is not as frequent in Tdn as in the languages further west, and in fact there was a tendency to simplify nasal clusters.[11] Here are some examples of prenasalized medial stops in Tdn that are not prenasalized in languages in which this process is more frequent than in Tdn:

*geteŋ > *kenteng* 'taut' (cf. Ml *gentang* 'cloth made taut to cover, as a drum') *babaq > *waʔmbaʔ* 'mouth' (cf. OJv *babah* 'opening, door')

---

[8] The loss of *ɣ took place after the earliest records of Tdn in the nineteenth century. Niemann (1869–70) records /h/ in some of the forms that reflect *ɣ. Other Minahasan languages evince a reflex of *ɣ (/ʔ/, /h/, or compensatory lengthening).

[9] That is, the influence is recent, and the source of influence in this case is standard Ml as spoken in Sulawesi. In some of these cases, the other Minahasan languages do not evince final glottal stop accretion.

[10] A possible explanation for the accretion of a glottal stop in this word is contamination with words meaning 'open, split' ending in /ʔ/.

[11] Simplification of word-medial nasal clusters is widespread in Tonsawang.

There are a few examples of forms that had nasal clusters in pre-Tondano that were simplified by losing the nasal:

*cumbu > *subu* 'wick' *qaɬegaw > *edo* 'day' (< *endaw < *eŋgaw < *qeɬegaw)

C4.1.7 Forms that resemble reflexes of PAn forms but show irregularities

There are a fair number of forms that closely resemble cognates in other languages that have been inherited from the protolanguage, but they show irregularities that cannot be explained. Some of these are discussed in the sections below. Others have reformed their final syllable on the basis of analogies that have not been identified. Finally, a number of forms are clearly cultural borrowings—that is, they refer to articles or to flora or fauna and clearly have spread from language to language. Still they should be taken into account because they are widely discussed or resemble inherited forms in other languages.

C4.1.71 Forms evincing an irregular end:

*buŋa > *wungang* 'flower' *buŋkuk > *wengkur* 'crooked' *caŋkut 'cought on hook' > *sangkong* 'hang on hook' *cuŋecuŋ > *suʔsuk* 'go against wind' *ketiŋ 'tendon at wrist or foot' > *kεnter* 'Achilles' heel' *kúden > *kurεʔ* 'pot' *maga > *pera* 'dry' *paɬid 'wing' > *pepalen* 'door (the part that opens and closes)' *piliq > *pεlεng* 'choose' *tebiŋ > *tebir* 'edge, side'

C4.1.72 Cultural borrowings:

*butun > *witung* 'k.o. tree' *kalacaɣ 'plaited bamboo strips' > *kelasεi* 'fish trap of plaited bamboo' *kulu > *kurur* 'breadfruit' *wacay 'axe' > *uwasεi* 'iron'

One form referring to a body part is clearly connected with a reconstructed root, but has three unexplainable irregularities. The other Minahasan languages and also Sangirese languages show the same reflex:

*balikat 'shoulder blade' > *paluka* 'shoulder'

C4.2 Vowels and diphthongs

C4.2.1 *i

When not elided (§C4.1.13), *i > /i/ except in cases of vowel harmony:

*kicekic > *kiʔkis* 'grate, file' *sadiɣi > *arii* 'house post'

*i is lowered to /ε/ when there is an /ε/ or /o/ in the preceding or following syllable (just as *u is assimilated to an /o/ in the preceding or following syllable [§C4.2.2]):

*ibeɣ 'salivate' > *εwε* 'saliva' *línaw 'calm' > *lεno* 'clear, pure (of water)'

*i before /ʔ/ (< *q or intercalated [§C4.1.5]) was lowered to /ε/ in two cases. This is an exception, not the rule, for there are examples of *iʔ, where *i did not lower—i.e., *iq > /iʔ/:

*binesíq > *wεnεʔ* 'seed' (< *biniq [where the penult is lowered by vowel harmony] < *binsiq) *ɣik > *lεʔεk* 'thresh' (< *liik [§C4.1.3] [/l/ unexplained]) *diqediq > *riʔriʔ* 'small bubbles in boiling' *puɬetiq > *putiʔ* 'white'

*-i became /εʔ/ by semantic contamination in the following case:

*ɬiki-ɬiki > *kikilεʔ*/ *kekilεʔ* 'underarm' (< *kili-kili by haplology) (Cf. *kilεʔ* 'tickle')

C4.2.2 *u

When not elided, *u is retained as /u/, with some exceptions:

*kutu > *kutu* 'head louse' *luseq > *luɛʔ* 'tears' *pitu > *pitu* 'seven'

*u is lowered to /o/ before /ɛ/ or /o/ in the following syllable:[12]

*bulaw 'reddish color' > *wolo* 'albino' *tuŋaw > *tongo* 'mite' *tuketuk 'beak' > *toʔtok* 'beak' *tumetoʔtok* 'woodpecker' *tunetun 'lead on a rope' > *tonton* 'lower, let down e.g. on rope' (Sneddon)

With three exceptions, *u > /o/ when coming to abut on an /a/ after *-ɣ- *-s- or *-w- were lost:

*binuwaŋ 'k.o. tree' > *wɛnoang* 'k.o. tree' (with assimilation of *i to /ɛ/ [§C4.2.1])
*baŋkuwaŋ > *wangkoang* 'k.o. pandanus' *suɣac > *oas* 'wash' *uɣat > *oat* 'vein'

*u was not lowered before /a/ in the following forms. There is no explanation for the failure of /a/ to lower:

*banuwa > *wanua* 'village' *luwaq > *luaʔ* 'vomit' *tu- + *agi > *tuari* 'younger sibling'

Two forms referring to flora evince /o/ in other environments. Three other examples also show /o/ instead of /u/. They all evince other irregularities:

*daqu > *daʔo* 'a fruit tree: *Dracontomelon edule*' *qaɬiŋu > *lelɛno* 'shadow, reflection'
*quɬúɬaŋ > *kanonang* 'k.o. tree' *túlak > *todo* 'push' *tukup > *songkou* 'cover over'

Further, reflexes of *tunetun 'lead on a rope' and *tuketuk 'beak', cited in this section five paragraphs above, and *pekuq 'bent' manifest an unexplained lowering of *u:

*pekuq > *pekoʔ* 'bent' (also *pekuʔ* 'snapped, bent to point of snapping')

C4.2.3 *e

When not elided, *e is retained as /e/, with some exceptions:

*enem > *enem* 'six' *qatep > *atep* 'roof' *qiteluɣ > *atelu* 'egg'

*e followed by a ʔ-coda at the end of a syllable or word > /a/:[13]

*beɣekec > *waʔkes* 'tie up into a bundle' (< *beʔkes < *beɣkes) *qaɬimateq > *lintaʔ* 'leech'

In disyllabic roots (or roots that disyllabized),*e abutting on /ʔ/ is assimilated to an /a/ and to an /u/ in an adjacent syllable. (Cf. §§C4.1.5, C4.3.14 for the development of /ʔ/ from *q and from consonants that were lost.)

*bukés > *wuʔuk* 'hair' *cequɬ > *suʔun* 'carry on head' *paqet > *paʔat* 'to chisel' *tabeq > *tawaʔ* 'fat (on animal body)' *taɬeq > *tanaʔ* 'land, soil, ground' *tapés 'chaff' > *taʔap* 'winnow' (< *tasep) *teɣac > *taʔas* 'k.o. wood' *tuqed > *tuʔur* 'stump'

---

[12] *luɛʔ* 'tears' is an unexplained exception.

[13] The following case is a counterexample. In this case, *e did not change to /a/ because it was the nucleus of a doubled monosyllabic root:

*kepekep 'clasp' > *keʔkep* 'cover'

The following form is an exception to this rule:[14]

*luseq > *luɛʔ* 'tears'

*e abutting on a /ʔ/ assimilated to an /i/ in the preceding syllable:

*betíhec > *wetiʔis* 'calf of leg, shank' (< *betiʔes)

If *e was preceded by *i without an intervening /ʔ/ (or other consonant), the sequence *ie was changed to /ɛ/. In the following two examples, *e was changed to /ɛ/ after the instrumental passive prefix *i-, and the allomorph with /ɛ/ was generalized:

*sejam > *eram* 'lease, rent' + *i-* > *ɛram* 'borrow' (< *i-eram) *seqeɣet > *ɛrɛt* (< *i-eɣet < *iseɣet < *ise-seqeɣet)

Similarly, *edo* 'day' (< *qaɬegaw) was changed to /ɛdo/ after the proclitic animate marker, *si*, which normally occurs before the word for 'sun'. Currently, the normal reflex /edo/ only has the meaning 'day', and the reflex meaning 'sun' is invariably /ɛdo/.

*qaɬegaw > *edo*; *si* + *edo* > *si ɛdo* 'the sun'

When followed by *ɣ, *e > /ɛ/:

*baŋeqeɣ > *wangɛ* 'smelling bad' *beɣay > *wɛɛ* 'give' *ibeɣ > *ɛwɛ* 'saliva' *keɣet 'cut a piece off' > *kɛɛt* 'tap sugar palm' *liqeɣ > *lɛɛʔ* (< *leɣiq)

There are forms with *eɣ that do not follow these rules. Some of them are clearly secondary, as they show irregular reflexes of *ɣ. The final example has the shape of the Manado Ml cognate, and it is a borrowing. However, the origin of the form is unknown (standard Ml: *tengar*).

*baqeɣu > *weru* 'new' *deɣeqec 'move vigorously' > *reɣes* 'for the wind to blow' *teŋeɣ > *tiing* 'k.o. mangrove' (Manado Ml *tiing* 'k.o. mangrove')

The sequences *ew and *cy changed to /u/ and /i/ respectively:

*taquweɬ > *taʔun* 'year' (< *taquun) *weliq + *ca- > *suliʔ* 'repay' (< *sa-uliq [C4.1.12][15]) *laqeya > *lia* 'ginger (< *leia < *leqiya < *leqeya) *seyap > *iap* 'count'

*e following a syllable with /ɛ/ nucleus became /ɛ/—i.e., *ɛe > /ɛɛ/:

*keɣet 'cut a piece off' > *kɛɛt* 'tap sugar palm' *seqeɣet > *ɛrɛt* (< *i-eɣet < *iseɣet < *ise-seqeɣet)

In the following form, *e is reflected by /a/, probably under the influnce of Manado Ml:

*kebel > *kawal* 'invulnerable'

C4.2.4 *a

When not elided, *a is reflected by /a/, with some exceptions:

*alap > *alap* 'take' *ina > *ina* 'mother' *jalan > *lalan* 'road, way'

---

[14] Presumably, *luseq developed to *luʔɛʔ, and there are no counterexamples to a rule that the ʔ-onset to a syllable with ʔ-coda is lost. However, the vowels of this word are also irregular.

[15] The loss of the /a/ of the prefix was early, before the change of *a discussed in §C4.2.4, below.

When followed by a syllable with initial /u-/, *a moved back to /o/. A phonetic /w/ arises between the *a and the *u—i.e., *au > *awu. *aw in turn became /o/ (as is the case of diphthong *aw):

*lahuj 'seaward' > *lour* 'lake' *jaqewis > *rouʔ* far' (< *jauq < *jasuq < *jaqus < *jaquis)
*taw > *tou* 'person' (< *tawu)

*a moved back to /o/ before /ʔu/ variably:

*taquweɬ > *toʔun* 'year' (also *taʔun*)

*a was not lowered before /w/ in Tdn, but in Ttb, it was. The following form is borrowed from Ttb (Sneddon 1978: 185, note 20):

*sawak > *ouak* 'body'

The loss of medial *ɣ (§C4.3.41) took place after the backing of *a before /u/. Therefore, an /a/ abutting on /u/ from an earlier *aɣu did not move back:

*taɣum > *taum* 'indigo'

In two forms, *a is reflected as /o/. There is no explanation. The first form is found in other Minahasan languages and is secondary in Tdn. The second form also has an irregular reflex of *ɣ and an intercalated glottal stop, which, like the cognate in Cb (cf. glossary under *ɣamec), probably arose by contamination with a word of similar meaning:

*apu > *opoʔ* 'grandparent, ancestor' *ɣamec > *roʔmec* 'knead'

In affixational processes, when an prefix ending in /a/ was added to a stem beginning in *i or *u, a diphthong formed which then monophthongized as did the diphthongs in final syllables (§§C4.2.51, C4.2.53):

*iɣaq + ma- > *m-ɛa* 'red' (< *ma-iɣaq) *iyak + *ka- > *kɛak* 'shriek' (< *kaiyak)

*a is reflected as /ɛ/ in a few forms. In the first case, there is no explanation for the change:

*lemaq > *lemɛʔ* 'not strong' *pakan > *mɛkan* 'feed' (< um- + pakan)

In the case of *pɛʔ* 'still, yet' (< *pa), possibly an unidentified marker *i* or *y* was added to this form (cf. §C4.2.51, immediately following). (/ʔ/ is also unexplained.) The second case is unexplained. However, it should be noted that verb prefixes that derive from forms with *a nucleus are several cases reflected with /‰/ nucleus (Watuseke 1985: 33–35).

C4.2.5 Diphthongs

C4.2.51 *ay

*ay > /ɛ/, and when stretched to two syllables (§C4.1.3), *ayi > /ɛi/:

*beɣay > *wɛɛ* 'give' *cay > *sɛi* 'who?' (< *sayi) *qatay > *atɛ* 'liver'

Loan words with *ay are borrowed with /ɛi/:

*ɣuqaɬay > *waranɛi* 'name of heroic person' *talicay > *talisɛi* 'a seashore tree: *Terminalia*' *wacay 'axe' > *uwasɛi* 'iron'

C4.2.52 *uy and*iw

*uy > /i/:

*sehapuy > *api* 'fire'

The reflex of *iw is unknown. There are only three attestations reflecting *iw, and each is different from the other. In the case of *kasiw, after the loss of *s, sonority shifted to the final *-w and was lost in the *i, as is the happened independently in many languages:

*kasiw > *kayu* 'wood, tree'

In the other two examples there are different outcomes, and it is unknown which is inherited and which is borrowed:

*baliw 'return, go back' > *waluy* 'change' *ciciw < *sisi* 'chick'

C4.2.53 *aw

*aw > /o/. When disyllabized (§C4.1.3), *aw > /ou/ (< *awu):

*qałegaw > *edo* 'day' *talaw > *talo* 'fearful' *taw > *tou* 'person' (< *tawu)

In two cases, *aw is reflected with /ou/. These forms spread to Tdn from another Minahasan language, but the source is unknown:

*ciwa > *siou* 'nine' (< *siaw) *lepaw > *lekou* 'field hut'

C4.3 Consonants

CHART TWO. DEVELOPMENT OF THE TONDANO CONSONANTS FROM PAN

PAn	Td	PAn	Td
p	*p*	g	*k-, -r-, -r*
t	*t*	ɣ	*Ø*
k	*k*	l	*l*
q	*Ø, -ʔ-, -ʔ*	ł	*n, l*
s, h	*Ø*	m	*m*
c	*s*	n	*n*
b	*w*	ŋ	*ng* [ŋ]
d, j	*r*	w, y	*w, y*

C4.3.1 Voiceless consonants

C4.3.11 *p

*p remained /p/ in all positions, except where affected by CC simplification (§C4.1.2):

*alap 'take' > *alap* 'take' *qápuɣ 'lime' > *apu* 'lime' *pálag 'palm of hand' > *palar* 'palm, sole'

Some reflexes of *-p- manifest sporadic prenasalization (§C4.1.6):

*qapit 'pinch together' > *ampit* 'together with' *qipit 'pinch together' > *impit* 'carry under arm'

In one case, clearly a secondary form, *p has been replaced by /k/. The form has other irregularities, as well (§C4.2.53, end):

*lepaw > *lekou* 'field hut'

C4.3.12 *t

Unless it was simplified in CC's (§C4.1.2), *t remains /t/ in almost all cases:

*telu > *telu* 'three' *sated > *ater* 'transport, convey' *pat > *epat* 'four'

In the following form, the final *-t became /ʔ/ before a suffix and the suffixed form became generalized:[16]

*kulit + *-na* '3rd person possessive' < *kuliʔ-na* 'skin, bark'

There are three forms that show various irregular reflexes of *t, for which there is no definitive explanation. The first example may have been taken from Manado Ml, which loses final consonants. The last two examples have been contaminated by forms of similar meaning. The reconstruction of *tumpul is problematic, as attestations in many languages evince contamination:

*quɣut > *uru* 'massage' *tepak > *sepɛʔ* 'slap' *tumpul > *sumpul* 'dull'

C4.3.13 *k

Unless it was simplified in CC's (§C4.1.2), *k remains /k/ in almost all cases:

*kásiw > *kayu* 'wood, tree' *lekep 'do completely' > *lekep* 'complete' *taketak > *taʔtak* 'chop down' *-metik > *lala-mentik* 'k.o. large black ant'

The following form with an irregular reflex of *k and /ʔ/ accretion was borrowed by all the Minahasan languages, possibly from standard Ml:

*keɬa > *tenaʔ* 'hit mark'

In one case, *k is reflected with /ɣ/. This form may have been contaminated, but the source is unknown, and the provenience of /ɣ/ is a mystery. See the comment at the end of §C4.0:

*keɬaŋ > *ɣenang* 'remember'

C4.3.14 *q

*q is reflected as /ʔ/ medially in disyllabic roots and finally in all roots. Initially, *q is lost.

*qámis > *ami-an* 'north, northwind' *páqa > *paʔa* 'thigh' *tuqas > *tuʔa* 'old' *luwaq > *luaʔ* 'vomit' *táɣaq > *taaʔ* 'chop'

In trisyllabic roots ,*q is lost, for the most part. It has been changed to /ʔ/ in only four trisyllablic forms. The explanation for retention or loss of [ʔ] may have to do with stress on the final syllable in pre-Tondano. *q is retained as /ʔ/ immediately before a stressed final syllable. *tináqi 'intestines' seems to be an exception in that /ʔ/ (< *q) is not lost even though it does not come before a stressed final syllable. However *tinaʔi* is, in fact, not an exception, for it was probably influenced by *taʔi* 'feces' (< *táqi). In the first example, the fact that a CC developed, may have lead to the preservation of /ʔ/:

[16] Tdn normally affixes a possessive suffix to words referring to body parts or other closely associated things. In other words, this word practically never occurs without a suffix, a feature that lead to the generalization of the allomorph with final /ʔ/ that occurs in CC's (§C4.1.2). Cf. Ttb *kulit* 'skin' *kuliʔna* 'his skin'.

*baɣeqáŋ 'molar' > *waʔang* 'tooth' *pacaqáɬ > *pesaʔan* 'carry over the shoulder' *taquwéɬ > *taʔun* 'year' *tináqi > *tinaʔi* 'intestines'

In the following forms, a glottal stop that had developed in other environments was lost:

*báŋeqeɣ > *wangɛ* 'smell bad' *básequ > *wou* 'smell' (< *baqu) *buqaya 'crocodile' > *wuaya* 'daring' *leqacém > *esem* 'sour' *láqeya > *lia* 'ginger' (< *leqiya <*leqeya) *páqegu > *peru* 'gall' (< *qepegu < *qapegú)

The loss of *ʔ < *q took place before the intercalation of /ʔ/ between vowels when a medial consonant was lost or in the process of disyllabization (§C4.1.5).
In two cases, final *-q is lost. In the first case, the *q was probably lost when a suffix was added (where the *q would have been lost before an unstressed vowel—i.e., *báyaq + *-an > *bayáqan > *wayaan* 'release it'. The second is probably a borrowing. It also evinces an irregular /r/ < *ɣ (§C4.3.41):

*bayaq 'leave' > *waya* 'permit allow, release' *ɣebaq > *rewa* 'fallen in'

C4.3.15 *c

Except when coming to be in a CC (§C4.1.2), *c > /s/ in all environments:

*capuh > *sapu* 'brush, sweep' *becuɣ > *wesu* 'full, satisfied' *pacaqaɬ > *pesaʔan* 'carry over the shoulder' *bitíhec > *wetiʔis* 'calf of leg, shank' *kicekic > *kiʔkis* 'file, grate'

C4.3.2 *h, *s

*h and *s were lost, but medially they left a trace in hiatus between two vowels, into which /ʔ/ is intercalated (§C4.1.5).
First, examples of -h loss in final position (as is the case of all MP languages):

*paqah > *paʔa* 'thigh' *capuh > *sapu* 'sweep

When intervocalic *h was lost, the hiatus with [ʔ] intercalation developed in only in a few forms. In others, there was no [ʔ] intercalation. The difference in the two outcomes may have to do with stress patterns, but more likely there was variation in pre-Tondano. (Cf. the discussion of loss of intervocalic *ʔ < *q in §C4.3.14.) Here are all the attestations of reflexes of intervocalic *h:

*betihec > *wetiʔis* 'calf' *caheɬaɣ > *senaʔ* 'shining like a star' *lahuj 'seaward' > *lour* 'lake' *ɣabihi 'night' > *ka-awiʔi-n* 'last night' *pakehu > *paku* 'k.o. fern' *tahebu 'vessel to hold water' > *tabuʔ* 'fishpond' *tahepa > *tapa* 'smoke meat'

Where the *h was onset of the penult in a trisyllabic root and the antepenult was lost, *h left no trace:

*sehapuy > *api* 'fire'

Except for three cases, *s disappeared without a trace:

*sadiɣi > *arii* 'post' *suɣac > *oas* 'wash' *binesiq 'seed rice' > *wɛnɛ* 'rice in husk' *dusa > *rua* 'two' *luseq > *luɛʔ* 'tears' *tasaɬ 'remain' > *taang* 'endure long' *cebus 'splash liquid on' > *sewu* 'extinguish fire with water'

In the following three cases, an intervocalic *s or an *s that came to be in intervocalic position left hiatus when it was lost, and a glottal stop was intercalated into the hiatus (§C4.1.5):

*bukés > *wuʔuk* 'hair' (< *busek) *pálisi > *peliʔi* 'taboo' (< *palisí) *tápes > *taʔap* 'winnow' (< *tasép)

C4.3.3 Voiced stops

The voiced stops were weakened, becoming continuants: *b > /w/; *d and *j fell together and became /r/. *g as onset or coda of the final syllable merged with *d and *j—i.e., became /r/. When it is onset to the penult or earlier, *g- > /k-/, as in many languages. In discourse, when the initial continuants /w/ and /r/ are preceded by a nasal, they are automatically replaced by /b/ and /d/ respectively. This is of high frequency because a syntactic marker shaped /en/ (/em/ before labials) occurs in most sentences.

In disyllabic clitics, intervocalic voiced consonants and continuants were lost:

*da + *ci- 'person marker' > *sεa* 'they' (< *sεda < *si-eda [C4.2.3, 6th¶] < si-da) *kami > *kεi* 'we (exclusive)' (< *kai) *kayu > *kou* 'you (pl)' (< *kau)

C4.3.31 *b

*b weakened to /w/ in initial and medial positions except when protected by a nasal:

*baqebaq > *waʔmbaʔ* 'mouth' *beɣekec > *waʔkes* 'tie up' *qabu > *awu* 'ashes' *ibeɣ > *εwε* 'saliva' *lebeŋ 'bury' > *leweng* 'press the leg in the mud' *debedeb > *weʔwer* 'chest' (< *bedebed)

In the following case, *b was protected by a nasal, which was lost after the change of *b > /w/ had taken place:

*cumbu > *subu* 'wick'

There are only two attestations of *-b that remount to the protolanguage. In one case, it is reflected as /-b/, as it is in other Minahasan languages:

*lebeleb 'hidden by being covered' > *leʔleb* 'step in mud'

In the other case, *-b is reflected as /-w/. I take this to be the normal reflex, and the example above to be a borrowing. The reason for this is that there are other examples of forms that do not, as far as is known, remount to the protolanguage, in which Tdn /-w/ corresponds to /-b/ in other Minahasan languages:

*keb + doubling > *keʔkew* 'cover' (Tse: *kebkeb* 'cover')

In the case of *pukuh 'knob, node', Tdn, like all the MP languages, voiced the intial C (> PMP †buku > *wuku* 'knuckle')

C4.3.32 *d, *j

*d and *j merged becoming /r/ in all positions except when protected by a nasal:[17]

[17] The only example of a prenasalized medial *d that remounts to PAn is *rεidem* 'dark' (< *demedem), but this form is borrowed from Ttb. After the marker *en*, an initial /r-/ automatically changes to /d-/.

*dayeq > *raaʔ* 'blood' *dadaya > *reraa* 'maiden' *udesi > *m-uri* 'behind, back rear' *sated > *ater* 'transport, convey' *jayámi > *raami* 'dry rice stalk' *jayum > *roum* 'needle' *qujał > *uran* 'rain' (Kakas) *sayejał > *aran* 'ladder' *lahuj 'seawards' > *lour* 'lake'

*d and *j assimilated to an /l/ on the right:

*dalig 'buttress root' > *lalir* 'slab of wood used as cutting board' *dilaq > *lilaq* 'tongue, speak' *jalan > *lalan* 'road, way'

In one case, *d is reflected with the marginal phoneme /ɣ/. Sound symbolism is the probable explanation:

*cedu > *seɣu* 'hiccough'

There are two cases in which *d- is reflected with /d-/. These forms are probably loan words:

*dataɣ > *data* 'flat area' *daqu > *daʔo* 'a fruit tree: *Dracontomelum edule*'

C4.3.33 *g

As onset of the penult or earlier or of monosyllabic roots, *g- > /k-/:

*gac > *kaʔkas* 'scratch' *geteŋ > *kenteng* 'taut'

As onset or coda of the final syllable, *g > /r/ (i.e., merges with *d and *j):

*łagam > *naram* 'tame' *pálag 'palm of hand' > *palar* 'palm, sole'

When protected by a nasal *g is reflected by /d/. In the following example, a preceding nasal caused *g to become /d/, and subsequently, the nasal cluster was simplified:

*qałegaw > *edo* 'day' (< *endaw < *eŋgaw < *qełegaw)

In two cases, *g is reflected with the marginal phoneme /ɣ/. There is no explanation:

*gusam > *ɣoam* 'thrush' *gaɣut > *ɣarot* 'scratch a line' (/r/ and /o/ also irregular [§C4.3.41])

C4.3.4 Voiced continuants

C4.3.41 *ɣ

*ɣ has two reflexes: (1) it is lost; (2) *ɣ > /r/. Both reflexes have developed in basic vocabulary. However, many of the forms that evince /r/ < *ɣ also show other irregularities, and we assume that (1) is the normal reflex. /r/ probably developed in dialects. Many of the forms with /r/ and other irregularities evince /r/ and the same irregularities in the other Minahasan languages. They are forms that have spread through the Minahasan languages. Some of the forms with /r/ are borrowings from Ml or other languages. First, examples of loss of *ɣ:

*ɣabun > *awun* 'smoke, mist' *aɣi > *ai* 'come!' *wiɣi > *ka-wii* 'left' *qiteluɣ > *atelu* 'egg'

When *ɣ came to abut on a C through syncopation of a medial syllable it became /ʔ/ (§C4.1.2) and affected the quality of a preceding *e (§C4.2.3, 2nd¶):

*beɣekec > *waʔkes* 'tie up into a bundle' (< *beʔkes < *beɣkes)

*ɣ also left traces in environments where it was lost but affected the quality of the vowel that preceded (§C4.2.3, 8th¶):

*baŋeqeɣ > *wangε* 'smelling bad' *beɣay > *wεε* 'give' *ibeɣ > *εwε* 'saliva' *keɣet 'cut a piece off' > *kεεt* 'tap sugar palm' *liqeɣ > *lεεʔ* (< *leɣiq)

The following forms evince /r/ < *ɣ:

*baqeɣu > *weru* 'new' *baɣat 'thwart' > *warat* 'at an angle, slanting' *báɣu 'a bush: *Hibiscus tiliaceus*' > *weru* 'name of tree' (/e/ unexplained) *buɣuk > *wuruk* 'bad, rotten' *buɣebuɣ 'broken into small pieces and scattered' > *wuʔwur* 'strew, scatter, sow' *dápuɣ 'place for cooking fire' > *ramporan* 'trivet' *gaɣut 'comb' > *karut* 'scrape out' *guɣita > *kurita* 'octopus' *ɣakut 'tie together > *rakut* 'tie to' *ɣamec 'crush and mix in' > *roʔmes* 'knead' (/o/ unexplained) *ɣebaq > *rewa* 'fallen in' *ɣetac 'break through, break open' > *retas* 'break (of rope)' *ɣúcuk > *rusuk* 'rib' *ɣuqałay 'male' < *waranεi* 'name of heroic man' *isuɣej > *soroʔ* 'move over' (/o/ and /ʔ/ irregular) *pataɣ > *patar* 'plain' *piɣas > *peraʔ* 'fish roe' (/e/ and /ʔ/ also irregular) *taŋiɣi 'Spanish mackeral' > *tangiri* 'a mythical fish'

Some of the forms with /r/ < *ɣ have Malay cognates with the same meaning and are probably borrowings from Malay:

*ɣákit 'planks or logs tied side by side' > *rakit* 'raft' (Ml *rakit* 'raft') *uɣut > *uru* 'massage deeply' (Manado Ml *uru* 'massage')

In three cases, *ɣ is reflected by the marginal phoneme /ɣ/ (cf. §C4.0, end):

*deɣeqec 'move vigorously' > *reɣes* 'for wind to blow' *qaɣa > *aɣa* 'k.o. tree' *sipaɣ 'other side' > *ipaɣ* 'brother-/sister-in-law'

In one case, *-ɣ is reflected with /-ʔ/. This is probably a borrowing from Ttb, where *ɣ is reflected as /ʔ/:

*basuɣ 'mix' > *wauʔ* 'mix staple with liquid'

C4.3.42 *l

*l > /l/ with very few exceptions:

*laŋit > *langit* 'sky' *puluq > *puluʔ* 'ten's' *telu > *telu* 'three' *celecel > *sesel* 'regret'

*l assimilates to an /r/ onset that developed in the following syllable:

*ludaq > *ruraʔ* 'spit'

In the following case, *l assimilated to an /r/ < *d to the left. This is a counterexample to the rule of §C4.3.32, above, whereby *d assimilated to an /l/ on the right. It is probably not directly inherited: [18]

*dalem 'deep' > *rarem* 'inside'

[18] Note that other Minahasan languages have *lalem* 'deep' as well as *rarem* 'inside', where *lalem* is clearly the inherited form and *rarem,* secondary.

In two unexplained cases, *l is reflected with /d/. The first example is probably borrowed from Tse. The second example has so many other irregularities that it may in fact not descend from the protolanguage at all.

*galih 'dig' > *kadi* 'ditch' *tulak > *todo* 'push'

C4.3.43 *ɬ

*ɬ underwent the changes found throughout the MP languages (§§A1.1.32, 4th¶, A3.3.4). In addition, PMP †ñ < *ɬ underwent depalatalization, as it did in many of the MP languages. As onset to an unstressed penult or earlier syllable, *ɬ- becomes /l-/. Otherwise, *ɬ > /n/. Examples of *ɬ > /l/:

*ɬiki-ɬikí > *kekilɛʔ* 'underarm' (< *kili-kili < *liki-liki) *ɬimác > *limas* 'bail out' *qaɬimateq > *lintaq* 'leech'

Examples of *ɬ > /n/:

*ɬam > *nanam* 'taste' *taɬeq > *tanaʔ* 'earth' *saɣejaɬ > *aran* 'ladder'

In two cases, medial *ɬ > /y/. This may be a regular reflex, for in both cases the penult was stressed in PMP, and there are no counterexamples—i.e., following a stressed syllable, *ɬ onset of the final syllable became /y/:

*áɬam > *ayam* 'plait' *qáɬuj > *ayur* 'be carried by the current'

In final position, *ɬ is in two cases reflected with /ng/, as is the case of the reflexes of *n sporadically (§C4.3.5)—i.e., *-ɬ > *-n > /ng/. These forms were borrowed from Manado Ml or from a Minahasan dialect in which /-ng/ replaced an earlier *-n (Sneddon 1978: note 37):

*cucuɬ > *susung* 'stack up' *tasaɬ 'remain' > *taang* 'endure long' (Cf. Manado Ml *tahang* 'endure'. Note also that no glottal stop developed [§C4.1.5].)

C4.3.5 *m, *n, *ŋ

The nasals are reflected with little change. In a few forms, a final *m or *n is reflected as /ng/. This seems to be the influence of Manado Ml, in which final nasals are neutralized:

*binuwaŋ > *wenoang* 'k.o. tree' (Manado Ml *binuang)* *butun > *witung* 'k.o. tree' (Manado Ml *bitung*) *kaban > *kawang* 'herd, flock' (Manado Ml *kawang*) *lilin > *liling* 'candle' (Manado Ml *liling* 'candle')

In the following forms no Manado Ml cognate is attested. In all probability, these forms were borrowed from a Minahasan dialect in which /-ng/ replaced an earlier *-n (Sneddon 1978: note 37):

*ipen > *ipeng* 'tooth' (Kakas) *pejem > *pereng* 'shut eyes' *qayam 'raised animal' > *paʔyang* 'play' (< *paqayam) *sayun 'shake' > *wayong* 'swing back and forth' (/w/ unexplained)

Assimilation takes place in the case of nasals that come to abut on consonants:

*qaɬimatéq > *lintaʔ* 'leech' (< *alimateq) *cuɬ + *um- > *unsun* 'stack up'

C4.3.51 *m

*m is reflected as /m/ everywhere:

*matay > *matɛ* 'dead' *lima > *lima* 'five' *enem > *enem* 'six'

C4.3.52 *n

*n is reflected as /n/ in most environments:

*naɬáq > *nanaʔ* 'pus' *ina > *ina* 'mother' *talun 'fallow lands' > *talun* 'forest'

C3.3.53 *ŋ

*ŋ > /ng/ in all positions.

*ŋaŋa > *nganga* 'open mouthed' *tiŋas > *tinga* 'food caught in teeth' *tutuŋ > *tutung* 'set afire'

When coming to abut on a voiced consonant, *ŋ was lost:[19]

*daŋedaŋ > *rarang* 'warm by fire' (< *daŋdaŋ)

C4.3.61 *w

Initially *w- remains /w-/:

*walu > *walu* 'eight' *wiɣi + *ka- > *ka-wii* 'left'

There is no contrast between /w/ and its absence between /a/ and /u/ or /o/. Thus *w can be said to have been lost between *a and *u:

*ɬuwaŋ 'opening' > *loang* 'wide and spacious' *buwaq > *wuaʔ-na* 'fruit'

Otherwise, *w > /w/:

*qawec 'diminish' > *awes* 'increase'

For *w at the end of a word, cf. §§C4.2.52, C4.2.53.

C4.3.62 *y

There is no contrast between /y/ and its absence between *i and *a. Therefore, we may say that *y is lost between *i and *a:

*tiyaɬ > *tian* 'belly'

Otherwise, *y > /y/:

*bayaq 'go away' > *waya* 'permit' *buqaya 'crocodile' > *wuaya* 'daring' *sayun 'shake' > *wayong* 'swing back and forth'

For *y at the end of a word, cf. §§C4.2.51, C4.2.52.

---

[19] There happens to be no other attestation in Tdn of an -*ŋ* coda followed by a consonant. In other Minahasan languages, this sequence becomes /ŋC/:

*teŋ + doubling > *tengteng* 'stare' (Tse)

CHAPTER FIVE
Pamona

C5.0 Background and cultural factors that influenced the development of Pamona

Central Sulawesi is an area with a large number of languages spoken by small speech communities. However, Pamona, called "Bare'e" by the Dutch scholars N. Adriani and A. Kruyt is an unusually widespread language, spoken over a wide area in Central Sulawesi. It is spoken in an area stretching from Poso southward to Tentena and eastward to Ampana. The name "Bare'e" comes from the word for 'not, there is not'. The word for 'there is not' is the way the various languages are popularly designated in Central Sulawesi. This is not necessarily a precise way to designate a language or a speech community, for many languages share the same word for 'not', and in the case of Pamona, only some dialects use *bare'e*. The eastern dialects use *taʔa* 'not, there is not'. Pamona shows a great deal of variation, which most likely has resulted from the spread of this language to groups speaking other now-lost languages. Further, the literature describes word taboo and shamanic speech, all of which increase the extent of borrowing from neighboring languages. Finally, until the twentieth century, slave-taking from neighboring tribes was widespread. Slaves were widely used for child-rearing, and as a result Pamona-speaking children were exposed to forms from neighboring languages. For this reason Pamona manifests cases of multiple reflexes for PAn forms or for PAn phonemes or phonemes in specific environments. There is a large amount of descriptive information on the languages and cultures of Central Sulawesi, written in the first two decades of the twentieth centuries by Albert Kruyt and N. Adriani, which has been helpful in understanding the bewildering material that is presented by our principal source (Adriani: 1928).

CHART ONE. PHONEMES OF PAMONA

Consonants

voiceless	p	t		k	ʔ
voiced	b	d		g	
spirants		s			h
liquid	w	l, r	y		
nasals	m	n	ny [ñ]	ng [ŋ]	

Vowels and Diphthongs

high	i		u
mid	e		o
low		a	

Stress normally falls on the penult, but in some trisyllabic roots that end in an echo vowel (§C5.1.4), the stress is on the antepenult.

C5.1 Processes affecting the development of Pamona from PAn

C5.1.1 Syncope in roots of three or more syllables

C5.1.11 PAn trisyllabic roots were in certain cases affected by syncope. An antepenult or earlier syllable consisting of *a in pre-Pamona—that is, PAn *a, *sa, or *qa, normally was lost:

> *eqatíh 'for water to recede' > *oti* 'dried up (river bed, etc.)' (< *aqeti) *qajeláy 'a grain: *Coix lacryma-jobi'* > *jole* 'job's tears' *sapegíq > *poi* 'smarting pain'

However, in the following cases the antepenult with *a, *sa, or *qa was not lost. There is no explanation:

> *páqegu > *apoju* 'gall' (< *qapegu) *qabaɣa > *awaa* 'shoulder' *qalima 'hand' > *alima* 'take' (dialectal *olima*) *qaɬitu 'evil spirit' > *anitu* 'spirit of the temple'

An antepenult consisting of *wa > /u/:

> *wasiyeɣ > *ue* 'water' (*uia < *waiya < *waiyeɣ [§C5.2.2])

There are three stems consisting of four syllables, and they behave differently from each other. One underwent syncoptation of the penult; one lost the first syllable; and one retained all four syllables. There is no explanation for the differences in development. These forms likely are secondary. Other languages of central and south Sulawesi show similar reflexes of these forms:

> *qaɬimáŋaw > *alimango* 'k.o. large shellfish' *qaɬimatéq > *alinta* 'leech' (< *qaɬimetáq) *qusalípan > *alipa* 'milliped'

C5.1.12 If the trisyllabic root contained *e, the *e was lost:

> *basequ 'smell' > *wau* 'smell' *baqeɣaŋ 'molar' > *bagangi* 'jaw' (with echo vowel §C5.1.4]) *isepi > *ipi* 'dream' *isepun > *impu* 'gather' (with /m/ intercalation [§C5.1.51]) *betihec 'calf' > *witi* 'foot, leg' (/i/ of final syllable by contamation with *winti* 'kick with calf in a game') *sehapuy > *apu* 'fire'

Similarly, *i before *y and *u before *w was lost:

> *nisawa 'breath' > *nawa-nawa* 'heart, thoughts' *gi-nawa* 'feel a certain way' (< *niyawa [loss of *y unexplained]) *qaɬiɣuwan 'bee' > *nyawa* 'k.o. wasp' (< *ɬyaɣuwan < *ɬiqaɣuwan)

In one case *e was not lost. The environment of the *e is unique to this form, and it is probably the normal development of *e in this environment.

> *liceqes 'nit' > *lioso* 'nit' (< *liqeces)

C5.1.13 In most other cases, trisyllabic roots are reflected with three syllables:

> *binaŋa > *winanga* 'mouth of river' *kalacaɣ > *kalase* 'splint of woven bamboo'
> *paqacan > *pasaʔa* 'carry over shoulder' *talicay > *talise* 'a tree: *Terminalia*' *taŋila > *talinga* 'ear'

C5.1.14 There are numerous exceptions, however, where roots of three or more syllables without *e weaken the left-most syllable or syncopate it. There are contradictory rules. Some of these probably can be explained by the accentuation or that the weakening and syncopation occurred at different times. However, these rules have not been worked out. In other cases, the forms with the weakened syllable are not directly inherited. First, is the weakening of *i in the antepenult. In some cases, the syllable with *i was lost entirely:

*sinawa > _nawa-nawa_ 'thoughts' *qiteluɣ > _toyu_ 'egg'

In other cases, the *i was weakened to /e/:

*binuwaŋ > _wenua_ 'k.o. tall tree: _Octomeles moluccana_' (dialectal: _winua_) *biɣengi > _wengi_ 'night' *bitaquɣ > _betaʔu_ 'a tree: _Calophyllum inophyllum_' *bituqen > _betuʔu_ 'star'

In two cases, *i is weakened to /o/ (< [ə]):

*tineun > _tonu_ 'weave' (< *teneun) *qałipulec > _lompiu_ 'whirlwind' (< *limpuyu)

In one case, *a of the penult is lost, as in most MP languages:

*tiqadaw > _tiro_ 'look downwards'

There are several cases in which *a of the antepenult was weakened to [ə] rather than becoming lost. In most of the cases, the [ə] became /o/ (cf. the citations in §C5.2.41). Finally, there are cases where the *a of the antepenult became /e/:

*lalatu 'spark' > _lelatu_ 'k.o. stinging ant' *qałegaw > _eo_ 'sun, day' *saɣejał > _eja_ 'ladder, steps'

C5.1.15 Vowel contraction

When /e/ came to abut on another vowel with the loss of an intervening consonant, contraction took place.

*beɣay 'give' > _wai_ 'give' *bacuheq > _wusoʔ-i_ 'wash' (< *buceheq < *becuheq) *baqeɣu 'new' > _woʔu_ 'again' (< *boqu < *boqɣu) *qatimela > _antila_ 'flea' (< *antiela [§C5.1.3])

Two *i's that came to abut because of loss of the intervening C contracted:

*ɣabihi 'evening' > _owi_ 'earlier, beforehand' *diɣi 'stand' > _ka-ridi-ridi_ 'growing straight upward' (ka- + *di, reduplicated and then doubled again) *palisi 'taboo'> _mom-pali_ 'obey taboos'

The word for 'left' did not contract the two consecutive /i/'s that developed. On the other hand, the word for 'right' contracted the two /a/'s that came to abut. The explanation is probably that different dialects treated vowels sequences differently and these forms are the result of dialect mixture.

*ka-wiɣi > _kaii_ 'left (hand) *ka-wałan 'right' > _kana_ 'right'

Normally two /a/'s and two /u/'s that came to abut did not contract:

*aɣusuq > _oguu_ 'the Australian pine: _Casusarina equisetifolia_' *qabaɣa > _awaa_ 'shoulder'

The sequence *iya contracted to /e/ like the diphthong /ay/ (but dialectally remained /ia/:

*ɣambiya 'sago palm' > _rombe_ 'k.o. palm' (dialectally _rombia)_ *wasiyeɣ > _ue_ 'water' (*uia < *waiya < *waiyeɣ [§C5.2.2, 2nd¶])

C5.1.2 Monsyllabic roots

As in the other An languages, the PAn monosyllabic roots were disyllabized for the most part (cf. §A3.6.2). The common processes of disyllabization were as follows:

C5.1.21 Doubling of the root:

*cuɬ 'stack up' > suncu 'things stacked up' (< cuɬcuɬ) *gac 'scratch' > *kangkas-i* 'scratch' (< *kaskas [with medial nasalization [§C5.1.51])

C5.1.22 Disyllabization by addition of prothetic [ə] (/o/):

*cek 'pack tight'> *oso* 'close upon one another, close together' *kab 'open, uncover' > *oka* 'broken open' *mic > *m-omi* 'sweet' *pan > *opa* 'bait' (< *epan) *peŋ > *ompo* 's.t. blocked off'

C5.1.23 Reanalyzing an affixed form as a single root—i.e., petrifying the affix:

*bun 'cover with sand' > *i-wu* 'cover over an opening in the ground' (< *is- 'instrumental passive' + *bun) *deŋ 'extinguish' > *para* 'finished' (< *pa- causitive' + *deŋ) *ɬam > *nami* 'taste' (< *ɬam + *-i local passive)

C5.1.24 Stretching the nucleus: this process is widely attested in other central Sulawesi languages, but the only attestation I have discovered in Pamona is clearly not inherited because of the intercalated glottal stop (§C5.1.52):

*kan + -in- > *kinaʔa* 'food'

C5.1.3 Metathesis

We assume metathesis to have taken place in some cases to explain the reflexes. Some of these cases of metathesis are widespread and took place before the MP languages split off or took place in all of the MP languages:

*nakis 'go up' > *nai* 'for water to rise' (< *nasik) *mpo-ne* 'climb' (< *pa-nasik) *paqegu > *apoju* 'gall' *punuq 'head, chief part of s.t.' > *puʔu* 'trunk' *taŋila > *talinga* 'ear'

Other cases are peculiar to Pamona or to languages of Sulawesi:

*bacuheq > *wusoʔ-i* 'wash' (< *buceheq < *becuheq [§C5.2.41]) *balatik 'make taut to spring back' > *watika* 'spring lance' (< *batikal) *basequ > *wau* 'smell' (< *baqesu) *calaɣ 'nest' > *sea* 'nest' (< *sae) *ciwa 'nine' > *sio* 'nine' (< *ciaw) *deɣeqec 'move vigorously' > *da-dasa* 'hasten' (< *deceq < *deɣeceq) *eqatih 'for water to recede' > *oti* (< *aqeti[1]) 'dried up (river bed, etc.)' *kutu > *tuku* 'louse' *-metik 'k.o. ant' > *onti* 'ant' *liceqes > *lioso* 'nit' (< *ɬiqeces) *qaɬimateq > *alinta* 'leech' (> *qaɬimetaq) *qatimela > *antila* 'flea' (< *amtiela)

C5.1.4 Development of open syllables

Pamona allows for no consonant syllable codas except for nasal consonants homorganic with a consonant-onset in a following syllable of the same word. That is, all word-final consonants and all syllable final consonants that had developed with syncope were lost except for nonfinal nasals. In the case of doubled monosyllabic roots ending in a

---

[1]Metathesis is hypothesized to have taken place to account for the loss of *a. *a is normally lost in trisyllabic roots beginning in *a (§C5.1.11), whereas there are no examples of *a lost in medial syllable of trisyllabic roots.

consonant, the medial cluster is sometimes (but not always[2]) replaced by a nasal cluster (cf. §C5.1.51):

*baqebaq 'mouth' > *wambaq* 'mouth of river' *diŋediŋ > *rindi* 'wall'

A fairly large number of forms have retained the final consonant and have added an echo vowel (usually /-i/). Most of these forms give evidence of being loan words, and it is probably the case that all forms with the echo vowel are in fact borrowings from a neighboring language, although in some cases there is nothing else in their semantic character or in the phonological make-up to give an indication of secondary origin. Here are some examples:

*baqeɣaŋ 'molar' > *bágangi* 'jaw' (with /g/ reflecting *ɣ, as is found in many languages of the area) *dapdap 'Erythina spp.'> *dodapi* 'a tree: *Erythina* spp.' (Dialectal reflexes *roda* and *lalapi* also occur) *isekan 'fish' > *ikane* 'viand' *paciɣ 'sand' > *pásigi* 'reef, sandbank' (with /g/ reflecting *ɣ) *sabaɣat 'strong monsoon' > *barati* 'southwest wind' (with /r/ reflecting *ɣ)

In some cases, the echo vowel is likely to have been a suffix form reinterpreted as part of the root and the C preceding the echo vowel is the inherited root-final C:

*ɬam > *nami* 'taste' (< ɬam + -i) *balut 'wrap' > *waluta* (< *balut + -an) 'bag of bark cloth for rice' *taɬem > *tónomi* 'plant' (see §C5.2.42 for the vowels)

C5.1.51 intercalation of nasals

Pamona also manifests the tendency to develop nasal coda to penultimate syllables before a final syllable with C-onsets, similar to that found in other western MP languages, is also found in Pamona (cf. §A3.7.2).

*ɬecuŋ 'mortar' > *noncu* 'mortar' *gac > *kangkaci* 'scratch' (< *kakas-i < *kaskas-i)

Not all the forms that commonly developed an intercalated nasal in other MP languages necessarily evince one in Pamona:

*taŋkay 'stem' > *takay* 'counter for stem-like things'

C5.1.52 Intercalation of laryngeals

Pamona did not undergo intercalation of [h] or [ʔ]. However, neighboring languages did do so, and forms from these languages are borrowed with intevocalic laryngeals. Two example of forms with a PAn etymology that developed intervocalic laryngeals when a medial C was lost are the following:

*um- + *aɣi > *m-aʔi* 'come here' *tasaɬ > *taʔa/taha* 'remain, stay'

When a vowel initial root is doubled, the second morph of the doubled root develops /ʔ/ onset. In pre-Pamona vowel initial roots automatically developed [ʔ]-onset. This [ʔ] was lost

[2]The following forms exemplify cases where the medial cluster was simplified with no nasaliation:

*biɣebiɣ 'lips' >*wiwi* 'lip, edge' *buqebuq 'pour water'> *bubu* 'poured out' *daŋedaŋ 'heat by fire' > *ma-roro* 'roast' *dapedap > *roda* '*Erythina*' *puqepuq 'pluck' > *pupu* 'pluck'

in word-initial position in current Pamona, but in medial position, [ʔ] was not lost:[3] (§C5.3.11):

*e > *oʔo* 'yes' (doubling of monosyllabic root [§C5.1.21])

C5.2.0 Vowels and diphthongs

Pamona has added one vowel to the four-vowel system of PAn (*i, *e, *a, *u). Pamona has /i, e, a, o, u/. In general *i, *a, and *u are inherited in Pamona unchanged. *e comes from PAn *ay and from some cases of *e, and *o comes from PAn *aw and from some cases of *e. Details and exceptions are given in the following sections. The diphthongs are treated separately.

C5.2.1 *i

*i > /i/ in all positions with a few exceptions.

*piliq > *pili* 'choose' *inum > *inu* 'drink' *binaŋa > *winanga* 'mouth of river' *tiŋadaq > *tingara* 'look upwards' *liceqes 'nit' > *lioso* 'nit'

In some cases, *i in the antepenult is weakened to /e/ (cf. the examples in §C5.1.14). There are also cases of *i lowered to /e/ in the penult. There is no explanation for them. Some of the forms with lowering of *i evince other irregularities, an indication that these forms are not directly inherited:

*liqeɣ > *leʔe* 'neck' *ɣiq > *lee*[4] 'a grass: *Imperata cylindrica*' *pařiki 'fruit bat' > *paneki* 'flying fox' *qitem > *ma-eta* 'black'

In the case of the following form, *i is lowered to /e/ probably by contamination with a reflex of *cakay 'climb' (although this is not attested for Pamona). In any case, this form is not directly inherited, as the initial /d/ is not the regular reflex of initial *d-:

*dakis > *dake* 'go up, climb'

In some cases, *i is lost when vowels abutting contract (§C5.1.15).

C5.2.2 *e

*e is lost by syncope or contraction, as discussed in §§C5.1.1ff. In nonfinal syllables, the most general case is that *e > /o/. Examples in the penult:

*becuɣ > *bosu* 'sated' *betak > *bota* 'split' *teken > *toko* 'stick, staff'

In final syllables, *e is normally reflected by /a/:

*dateŋ 'come' > *rata* 'having arrived' *jaqet > *jaʔa* 'bad' *kuden > *kura* 'clay pot' *qiseřep > *ina* 'sleep' *qutek > *uta* 'brains' *tuqed 'stump' > *tuʔa* 'trunk, stump'

However, if the penult has /o/, the /a/ < *e of the final syllable is assimilated to the /o/ (cf. §C5.2.42):

*keŋekeŋ 'cramp, stiff, tight' > *koko* 'make oneself small, draw oneself in tightly' (< *koka) *celecel > *soso* 'regret'

---

[3] Cf. the development of /ʔ/ < *q: /ʔ/ is found only as onset of the final syllable of the root. Otherwise, it is lost (§C5.3.11).

[4]The form /lee/ is clearly cognate with other reflexes of *ɣiq '*Imperata*', but it is not directly inherited in Pamona.

There are a few other cases when *e of the final syllable is reflected as /o/, but these are exceptions, and all but one are borrowings.

*balec 'answer' > *balo* 'spin one's top against the opponent's' *pacek > *paso* 'wedge' *caleɣ 'flooring' > *salo-dopi* 'wooden floor' (shamanic texts) *qageŋ 'charcoal'> *ayo* 'tree used for charcoal'

In six examples, *e > a in the penultimate syllable. These are cases of dialect mixture:

*bekac 'trace'> *waka* 'place where s.t. was before' *belaq 'cleft' > *bala* 'split' *deɣeqec 'move vigorously' > *da-dasa* 'run away in haste' (< *deceq < *deɣeceq) *lepac > *lapa* 'get free' *peɣaq > *paa* 'squeeze, wring out' *petik 'pluck' > *pati* 's.t. broken off (fruit, branch)'

C5.2.21 *e > /e/

In the case of words ending in *-eg, the *e becomes *a, as in §C5.2.2, 2nd¶, above, after which the rule of §C5.2.43 applies, whereby *a > /e/ before *-g.[5]

*puceg > *puse* 'navel' *quleg 'worm' > *ule* 'snake, worm' *quneg > *une* 'pith, inside part of s.t.'

*ey > /e/:

*seyaq > *ea* 'shame'

*e also becomes /e/ in the following forms. There is no explanation.

*bedebed 'spool, wind' > *wewe* 'wind around itself'[6] *liqeɣ > *leʔe* 'neck'

*e also changes to /e/ before velar consonants *k, *g, *ɣ, and *ŋ in the penult in some cases. These forms result from dialect mixture:

*beka > *beka* 'split' *beŋa 'be agape' > *benga* 'wrench open with the hand' (cf. *bonga* 'wide open') *beɣac > *wea* 'husked rice' *biɣeŋi > *wengi* 'night' (< *beɣeŋi [§C5.1.14] [cf. *wongi* 'dark' with the regular reflex]) *cekel > *sengko* 'curved, bent' *iceŋet > *sengu* 'stinger of bee or wasp' *qaɬegaw > *eo* 'sun'

There are as many cases of /o/ developing from *e before a velar as there are cases of /e/. At least some of the forms with /o/ are directly inherited:

*beŋel > *wongo* 'deaf (in set expressions)' *deŋan 'accompany' > *rongo* 'wife' *leŋa > *longa* 'sesame' *paqegu > *apoju* 'gall' *sapegiq >*poi* 'smarting pain' *teŋaq > *tongo* 'middle'

In the following case, *e > /a/. There is no explanation:

*peɣaq > *paa* 'squeeze, wring out'

---

[5]The only exceptions are *buleg 'single hill' > *buyu* 'mountain' and *caleg 'flooring' > *salo*, which occurs only in shamanic speech. *Buyu*, with irregular reflex /u/ (§C5.2.22), and *salo*, from shamanic texts, are not inherited forms.

[6] Possibly there was contamination with an unknown form. This same root also seems to reflect *-g in other languages (cf. the commentary in the glossary).

C5.2.22 *e > /u/

In several cases, *e is reflected with /u/. In three of them, the occurrence of /u/ in an adjacent syllable may have something to do with the change of *e to /u/, but this is certainly not the normal sound change, as there are more than a dozen countercases in words that are clearly inherited:

*bituqen 'star' > *betuʔu* 'star' *buleg 'single hill' > *buyu* 'mountain' *cequɬ 'carry on head' > *suʔu* 'carry on head' *iceŋet 'sharp, stinger' > *sengu* 'stinger of bee or wasp' *tikeɣ > *tiu* 'reed used for weaving'

In the following case, the sequence *uyu, that developed from *ule (§C5.3.51), was in unstressed position and became /iu/:

*qaɬipulec > *lompiu* 'whirlwind' (< *limpuyu [for /o/ cf. §C5.1.14])

C5.2.3 *u

*u is reflected as /u/ with very few exceptions:

*dapuɣ > *rapu* 'cooking place' *duɣi > *rui* 'thorn' *kutaɬa > *kutana* 'ask' *punuq 'head as main part of s.t.' > *puʔu* 'trunk of tree' *puqepuq > *pupu* 'pluck'

A sequence *ɣuwa > /wa/:

*ɣuqaɬay 'male' > *wani* 'sing praises' *qaɬiɣuwan 'bee' > *nyawa* 'k.o. small wasp'

In a few forms, *u is reflected by /o/. These forms are not directly inherited, and many of them show other irregularities:

*bunag > *bone* 'sand' (possibly contaminated with a reflex of *qenay, which is not attested) *kuɣapu 'grouper' > *pogapu* 'k.o. sea fish' (cf. Cb *pugápu* 'grouper') *pasuq 'wild mango > *pao* 'k.o. small mango' *suni 'soft noise' > *oni* 'noise, sound' *cucuq > *suso* 'snail' *tahebu 'vessel to hold water' > *tabo* 'half coconut or gourd used as cup' *taɣum 'indigo' > *táomi* 'indigo' (with echo vowel [§C5.1.4, 2nd¶]) *tucuk > *tosu* 'prick, pierce'

In two cases, *u is reflected with /e/. There is no explanation:

*bunut 'coconut husk' > *benu* 'husk of coconut or betel-nut' *buqebuq > *webu* 'sprinkle on'

C5.2.4 *a

*a is most generally reflected as /a/:

*qayam 'pet' > *aja* 'dog' *taŋila > *talinga* 'ear' *aɬak > *ana* 'child, offspring' *dasedas > *dada* 'chest' *tuqas > *tuʔa* 'old'

C5.2.41 *a in the antepenult

*a in the antepenult was sporadically weakened. This weakening was a dialectal phenomenon and there are many cases where weakening did not take place, presumably because of dialect mixture. If the antepenult was shaped *a, *sa, or *qa, it was most generally lost (§C5.1.11).

*a of the antepenult in some cases is reflected as /o/(< [e]):

*aɣuqus > *oguu* 'the Australian pine: *Causarina*' *baɣequ 'new' > *woʔu* 'again' *ɣabihi 'night' > *owi* 'past, earlier time' *kałusekus > *konuku* 'finger- or toenail' (< *kałuskus) *paŋudał > *póndani* 'pandanus' *sametik 'k.o. stinging ant' > *onti* 'ant'

In one case, metathesis took place after the *e that had developed changed to /o/:

*bacuheq > *wusoʔ-i* 'wash' (< *bucoheq < *bocuheq < *becuheq)

This change of *a to /o/ is also manifested in words not inherited from PAn, but cognates have /a/ in the antepenult in other languages:

*kamaliɣ 'shed' > *komali* 'smithy' *lampuyang 'k.o. ginger plant' > *lompiu* 'k.o. edible weed' *anasaw 'sugar palm: *Arenga* sp.' > *konaw* 'sugar palm'

Monosyllabic roots with *a nucleus that were disyllabized by doubling (§C5.1.21) weakened the /a/ of the first of the doubled syllables:

*bałebał 'k.o. reed' > *bomba* 'reed for baskets, tie roof lathes' *dapedap > *roda* 'k.o. tree: *Erythina* spp.' *palaqpaq (*-al- + *paqpaq) 'frond' > *palopa* 'palm branch'

However, in a fair number of forms, the antepenult with *a was not weakened. These forms are dialectal borrowings, or there may possibly be an explanation for them in the accentual pattern (cf. the citations in §§C5.1.11, C5.1.13).

C5.2.42 Other cases of *a > /o/

*a is reflected as /o/ before or after an /o/ (that developed from *e [§C5.2.2, 1st¶]):[7]

*deŋan 'together' > *rongo* 'wife' (cf. *rángan-i* 'accompany' of dialectal origin) *depa 'fathom' > *ropo* 'fathom' *keła 'hit mark' > *kono* 'hit mark' *cakep > *soko* 'seize, catch' *pecaq > *poso* 'broken into pieces' *tałem 'plant' > *tónom-i* 'plant' *tebac 'cut vegetation' > *towo* 'fell, cut down' *teŋaq 'middle' > *tongo* 'middle' *sepat 'four' > *opo* 'four'

There are more countercases, where /a/ did not assimilate to an /o/ in the same root, than where the rule applies:

*balec > *balo* 'spin one's top against the opponent's *benaŋ 'thread' > *wona* 'fine fibres in sago palm meal' *betak > *bota* 'split' *gatel > *kato* 'itchy' *iqetah > *ota* 'chaff' *leŋa > *longa* 'sesame' *pacek > *paso* 'wedge' *qageŋ 'charcoal' > *ayo* 'charcoal producing tree' *paqegu > *apoju* 'gall' (< *qapegu) *caleɣ > *salo-* 'floor' *teka 'come, arrive' > *toka* 'be present, available'

There are other forms where *a is reflected as /o/. In the first case, the form is attested in many languages of central Sulawesi, and it is clearly a borrowing. The other cases are also probably borrowings:

[7] This change of *a > /o/ before a following /o/ took place after the change of /a/ > /o/ in the first syllable of doubled monosyllabic roots, a rule cited in §C5.2.41, immediately above. Therefore, the examples cited there have /a/ in final syllable after an /o/ in the penult. However, there must have been dialects that made this change after the rule of §C5.2.41, and borrowings from those dialects reflect /o/ in both syllables:

*daŋedaŋ > *ma-roro* 'roast by fire' *qałibaŋbaŋ > *aliwombo* 'butterfly' *tacetac > *tótosi* 'cut through with one blow' *kan > *kon-i* 'eat' *calay 'preserve by drying' > *sole* 'roast, bake, fry' *dataɣ 'flat area' > *rato* 'flat area' *lakaq > *yongko* 'step' *tambak 'earth piled up for dam' > *tomba* 'puddle, pool'

C5.2.43 *a > /e/

*a before a final *-g is reflected as /e/.

*bunag > *bone* 'sand' *palag 'palm' > *pale* 'hand, arm, forepaw'

In the following forms, *a before *ɣ and *-c has changed to /e/. Normally *-aɣ and *-ac > /a/:

*calaɣ 'nest' > *sea* 'nest' (< *sae) *kalacaɣ 'material of plaited bamboo' > *kalase* 'splint of plaited bamboo' *łimac > *lime* 'bail' *salac > *pang-ale* 'forest'

The form *ina 'mother' is reflected as *ine* 'mother' and *ina* 'mother'. We hypothesize that *ine* is from *inay, a term of address—i.e., Pamona may form terms of address by adding /-y/ to the final vowel, as do many of the western An languages.

C5.2.5 Diphthongs

C5.2.51 *ay

*ay > /e/ in most cases.

*beɣecay > *wose* 'paddle, oar' *matay > *mate* 'die'

The sequence /ai/ that developed in stems that became monosyllabic > /ai/:

*nakis 'go up' > *nai* 'for water to rise' (< *nasik) (Cf. the development to /e/ when the stem was disyllabic: *mpo-ne* 'climb' (< *-pa-nasik))

A sequence /ayi/, that develops, became /ai/:

*beɣay > *wai* 'give' (< *beayi)

In two cases, *ay > /i/. These are probably loan words:

*abay 'accompany' > *abi* 'friend' *ɣuqałay 'male' > *wani* 'give praises'

C5.2.52 *-aw

*-aw > /o/:

*babaw 'above' > *wawo* 'upper areas' *qałimaŋaw 'mangrove crab' > *alimango* 'k.o. large shellfish'

There are a few exceptions, probably borrowings:

*liŋaw > *lingu* 'bewildered' *linaw > *lindu* 'calm water' (also *lindo* 'calm, unroiled')

Where /aw/ occurred in a stem that had become monosyllabic, it was disyllabized in two ways. The first is the inherited development (> /au/) and is parallel to the development of *ai, §C5.2.51, above. The second (> ou/) is a borrowing, as it also evinces other irregularities and is attested only in poetic styles:

*taw > *tau* 'man' *caweŋ 'protective hat' > *sou* 'hut, shelter' (< *caung)

C5.2.53 *-uy, *-iw, *we

*-uy > /u/:

*babuy > *wawu* 'pig' *łaŋuy > *nangu* 'swim' *sehapuy > *apu* 'fire'

*-iw > /i/:

*baliw 'one of two, one of a pair' > *bali* 'reverse side, opposite part' *laɣiw 'flee' > *lai* 'depart from a place'

The word for 'tree' shows that after the *s was lost, the *i became a glide and the *w a vowel, as happened widely among the MP languages. Subsequently the /y/ that developed became /j/:

*kasiw > *kaju* 'tree' (< *kayu < *kahiw) also *kayu* 'tree' (shamanic style)

The sequence *we and *ew > /u/

*taquweł 'year' > *taʔu* 'time it takes a plant to grow from seed to seed producer', *dasuwen 'leaf' > *nau* 'counter for things that come in sheets or leaf-like shapes' *caweŋ 'protective hat' > *sou* 'hut temporary shelter' *jaqewis > *jasiweq > *jasweq > *jauq > *n-jaʔu* 'far'[8]

C5.3.0 Consonants

CHART TWO. DEVELOPMENT OF THE PAMONA CONSONANTS FROM PAN

PAn	Pamona	PAn	Pamona
p	*p*	j	*j*
t	*t*	g	*Ø*
k	*k*	ɣ	*Ø*
q	*Ø, -ʔ-*	ł	*ñ, n, l*
h	*Ø*	m, n	*m, n*
s	*Ø*	ŋ	*ng [ŋ]*
c	*s*	l	*l, -y-*
b	w	w	*w*
d	*r*	y	*j*

The consonants, aside from the nasals, are reflected only in syllable onset—i.e., final C's other than nasals are lost.

C5.3.1 Voiceless stops

The voiceless stops remain unchanged for the most part.

*p > /p/:

*panaq 'shoot with bow and arrow' > *pana* 'bow' *pitu 'seven' > *pitu* 'seven' *sehapuy 'fire' > *apu* 'fire' *lampin 'wrapper, diaper' > *lampi* 'cloth to cover'

*t > /t/:

*tacik 'sea' > *tasi* 'sea' *qetut > *otu* 'break wind'

*k > /k/:

[8] This account does not take care of a double metathesis, which data from other MP languages indicate must have occurred—i.e., *jaqewis > †jahewiq in PMP. Therefore, Pamona must have re-metathesized the reflex to *jaqewih, which became *jaquih, as indicated here.

*kasiw > *kaju* 'wood' *kima > *kima* 'large clam' *paheku > *paku* 'edible fern' *lakaq > *yongko* 'step'

In a couple of cases, -k- is lost. The forms are not directly inherited:

*lakaw 'walk'> *me-lao* 'go out to get something' *tikeɣ > *tiu* 'a reed used for weaving'

C5.3.11 *q

*q became glottal stop when onset of the final syllable of the root:

*baqeɣu > *woʔu* 'again' (< *boqu < *boqɣu) *bituqen > *betuʔu* 'star' *bitaqug > *betaʔu* 'k.o. tree: *Calophyllum inophyllum'* *paqit > *paʔi* 'bitter' *paqa > *paʔa* 'thigh' *pacaqaɬ > *pasaʔa* 'carry over shoulder' *taquwen 'year' > *taʔu* 'season it takes a plant to grow from seed to producing seeds' (< *taqun < *taqwen) *tuqas > *tuʔa* 'old' *qucequc > *uʔu* 'suck out s.t. of which the residue is discarded (sugar cane)'

When it was the onset of the penult or earlier, *q disappeared without a trace:

*buqaya 'crocodile' > *wuaja* 'cry of astonishment, anger' *liseqec > *lioso* 'nit' (< *liqeces) *ma-qetaq > *mata* 'raw' *qaselu > *i-ayu* 'rice pestle'

The following form, which manifests /ʔ/, is an exception. It is a borrowing and shows other irregularities as well:

*laqeya 'ginger' > *luʔa* 'k.o. large betel nut'

C5.3.2 *h, *s

*h and *s disappeared entirely without a trace:

*cahebay > *sampe* 'be draped over' *paheku > *paku* 'edible fern' *dusa 'two' > *rua* 'two' *qaselu 'pestle' > *i-ayu* 'pestle for stomping rice' *sated > *ata 'deliver'*

C5.3.3 *c

*c > /s/ in initial and medial position:

*acu > *asu* 'dog' *beɣecay > *wose* 'paddle, oar' *cikcik 'search thoroughly' > *sisi* 'look for lice with the fingers' *cucu > *susu* 'breasts'

After /n/, /s/ has the pronunciation [c] reflected by a spelling 'tj' in the sources. [c] is a subphonemic difference reflected in the orthography. [c] does not contrast with [s]:

*ɬecung > *noncu* 'mortar' *cucun 'stacked up' > *suncu* 'things piled up on each other' (both examples with intercalated nasal [§C5.1.51])

In one case *c is reflected with /j/. There is no explanation:

*ŋucuq > *nguju* 'snout'

C5.3.4 Voiced stops and *ɣ

*b and *d are weakened except when protected by a nasal. *j remains /j/. *ɣ and medial *-g- disappear entirely.

C5.3.41 *b

*b has two reflexes: /b/ and /w/. The two reflexes result from dialect mixture.[9] Here we hypothesize that the inherited reflex is /w/, except when protected by a preceding nasal, in which case *b > /b/. Here are some examples:

*batu 'stone' > *watu* 'stone' *beɣecay 'oar' > *wose* 'paddle, oar' *bubu 'fish trap' > *wuwu* 'fish trap' *qabu 'ashes' > *awu* 'ashes' *qubi 'a yam: *Dioscorea alata'* > *uwi* 'yam, taro' *tebac 'cut vegetation' > *towo* 'fell, cut down' *tuba > *tuwa* 'fish poison: *Derris elliptica''* *qaɬibaŋebaŋ > *aliwombo* 'butterfly' *timba 'balance' > *mon-timba* 'weigh'

However, in a large number of cases *b is reflected as /b/ even though there is no preceding nasal. We say that these forms with /b/ do not evince the regular reflex because (1) many of them manifest other irregularities, (2) they are words of a sort easily subject to borrowing. For many of them, other reflexes of the same roots with /w/ also occur. Here is a sampling:

*banuwa 'land, place' > *banua* 'house, dwelling' *biɣengi 'night' > *bongi* 'dark' (also *wengi* 'night') *becuɣ 'satisfied, full' > *bosu* 'satisfied, full' *buleg 'single hill' > *buyu* 'mountain' *tahebu 'vessel to hold water' > *tabo* 'cup of half a coconut shell or gourd'

In one case, *b- is lost. There is no explanation:

*beli 'buy' > *oli* 'price'

C5.3.42 *d

PAn *d > /r/, except when there was a preceding nasal, in which case *d > /d/:

*daɣaq > *raa* 'blood' *depa > *ropo* 'a fathom' *diŋediŋ > *rindi* 'wall, partition' *duɣi > *rui* 'thorn' *ŋuda > *ngura* 'young, soft to the touch' *dem 'think' > *endo* 'remembrance' *tudaŋ > *tunda* 'sit'

In a few cases, *d is reflected as /d/ even though there is no preceding nasal. These forms are the result of dialect mixture. Many of the forms with /d/ manifest other irregularities or exist in addition to forms with /d/ as alternants or morphs with related meanings:

*deɣeqec 'move vigorously' > *da-dasa* 'run away in haste' (< *deceq < *deɣeceq) (also *karasa-rasa* and *kandasa-dasa*) *dusa > *dua* 'two' (also *rua* 'two')[10] *daɣeq > *daa* 'blood' (also *raa* 'blood (in particular contexts)') *dasedas > *dada* 'chest'

In two cases, *d is reflected as /j/:

*dilaq > *jila* 'tongue' *duyung > *juju* 'manatee'

There is no explanation for *juju* 'manatee'. In the case of *jila* 'tongue' there is contamination with a word 'lick' *jilat or *jilap, which has no reflexes in Pamona.[11]

---

[9] I characterize the process leading to two variant reflexes as 'dialect mixture', rather than as a case of a sound change that was not carried to completion. The two processes are different (§A2.3f.), although they may lead to similar results. Dialect mixture resulted in Pamona when speakers of other (closely related languages went over to Pamona and retained a substratum of vocabulary and articulatory habits that they carried over to Pamona and which became adopted by the wider speech community. Forms with the alternative reflex commonly show other irregularities

[10] The form *radua* 'two', which is a reduplicated form used in certain contexts, manifests both /r/ and /d/.

C5.3.43 *j

*j > /j/:

*jalan 'road' > *jaya* 'path, way' *jaqet > *jaʔa* 'bad' *qujaɬ 'rain' > *uja* 'rain' *saɣejaɬ > *eja* 'steps, ladder' *jaqewis *n-jaʔu* 'in the distance'

There are a few cases of reflexes of *j as /d/. None of these forms are directly inherited:

*jalikan 'trivet' > *dalika* 'hearth to cook salt' *jiɣuc 'bathe, sprinkle' > *man-diu* 'bathe' *isejam 'borrow, lend' > *indang-i* 'money lent'

The following form was secondarily and exists in several variants, all of which show irregularities of correspondence:

*ja-lateng > *jilata, gelata* 'nettle tree'

C5.3.44 *g

As onset of the penult or earlier, *g- > k-:

*gatel 'itch' > *kato* 'itch' *guɣita 'octopus' > *kuita* 'octopus'

Only a few forms with *-g- as onset of the final syllable are reflected in Pamona. The normal reflex is probably Ø:

*qaɬegaw 'day, sun' > *eo* 'sun' *igan > *p-ia* 'when?' *pagay > *pae* 'rice in field' *sapegiq > *poi* 'smarting'

Five forms have other reflexes of *-g- as onset of the final syllable. They are probably dialectal borrowings. Two forms manifest *-j-:

*paqegu > *apoju* 'gall' (< *qapegu) *laga 'weave mats' > *laja* 'loosely woven or stitched'

One form manifests /r/:

*maga > *mara* 'dried up'

Two forms reflect /y/:

*qageŋ 'charcoal' > *ayo* 'charcoal-producing tree' *qagan 'name' > *ngaya* 'kind'[12]

C5.3.45 *ɣ

*ɣ is lost without a trace in most cases, and we believe this to be the normal reflex:

*ɣakit 'planks or logs tied side by side' > *aki* 'raft' *ɣumaq 'house' > *uma* (in *uma uani* 'beehive') *ɣucuk > *usu* 'rib' *laɣiw 'flee' > *lai* 'leave a place' *duɣi > *rui* 'thorn'

In a fair number of cases, *ɣ is reflected as /g/. /g/ is apparently the normal reflex of *ɣ in many languages of central Sulawesi (as well as of northern Sulawesi and the Philippines),

---

[11]There is a fair number of languages in which the word for 'tongue' has an initial reflecting *j that is explained in this way. Some of these languages (e.g. ND) do have reflexes of *jilap or *jilat as well. The form with /j/ in the word for 'tongue' in fact spread to other languages from the language in which the original contamination occurred.

[12]There seems to be no semantic connection between the Pamona form and the forms in other An languages. However, Adriani (1928: 463) connects these, and since he was a solid scholar with a deep knowledge of the languages of the area, we have to take seriously his view that there is a connection in the meanings.

and the reflexes with /g/ are surely borrowings. Many of these forms manifest other evidence of borrowing. Here is a partial list:

*baɣu > *molobagu* 'a seashore shrub: *Hibiscus tileaceous*' *daɣat 'open area' > *daga* 'sea' (shamanic) *ɣabun 'mist' > *gawu* 'cloud' *ɣudang 'be grown' > *gura* 'old' *ɣumaq 'house' > *guma* 'sheathe of sword' (cf. *uma uani* 'beehive', above) *layaɣ > *layagi* 'sail' *paciɣ 'sand' > *pásigi* 'reef, sandbank' *paɣis > *pagi* 'ray' *qaɣaw 'snatch' > *ago* 'take s.t. that belongs to s.o. else' *suɣac 'wash' > *úgasi* 'wash off wounds'

In a few cases, *ɣ is reflected with /r/. These are clearly secondary forms:

*daɣa 'maiden' > *lun-dara* 'female buffalo that has not calved' *ɣambiya 'sago palm' > *rombe* 'k.o. palm' *sabaɣat 'strong monsoon wind' > *baráti* 'southwest wind in dry season' *teŋer 'tree of mangrove swamp: *Ciriops* spp.' > *tangári* '*Ciriops*'

C5.3.5 The liquids and nasals

C5.3.51 *l

In initial position, *l > /l/. (For exceptions see the fourth paragraph, below.)

*laɣiw 'flee' > *lai* 'leave a place' *liqeɣ > *leʔe* 'neck'

Medially, *l becomes /y/ and /l/. /y/ is reflected if the vowel before the *l was *a or *u and the vowel after the *l was *a, *e, or *u

*buleg 'single hill' > *buyu* 'mountain' *dalem 'beneath, inside' > *raya* 'inside part' *jalaɬ 'road' > *jaya* 'path, way' *mula 'plant' > *muya* 'plant' *pulut 'a tree yielding bird-lime: *Urena lobata*' > *puyu* 'glue, plants that yield it' *qaselu > *i-ayu* 'pestle' *qiteluɣ 'egg' > *toyu* 'egg, testicle' *walu > *uayu* 'eight'

This rule does not hold if an /e/ developed after the *l—i.e., for roots ending in *-lay or *leg (§C5.2.21):

*quleg > *ule* 'snake, worm'

In five cases, initial *l- > y- before *a or *u. The explanation may lie in the extension of the medial /y/ which developed after vowel-final prefixes.

*laban 'against' > *yawa* 'hold s.t. against' *lakaq 'step' > *yongko* 'step' *laɬa > *yana* 'oil' (also *lana*) *laŋit > yangi 'heavens' *lukut > *yuku* 'k.o. epiphyte' , *lumba 'race, vie' > *yumba* 'growing fast'

In other environments, *l > /l/:

*belaq 'split' > *bala* 'split into pieces' *beli 'buy' > *oli* 'buy' *ila 'mark' > *ila* 'mole' *qajelay '*Coix lachryma jobi*' > *jole* 'native corn' *qalíma 'hand' > *alima* 'take'

There are exceptions, some of which have other signs of being borrowed (found in shamanic texts or having other irregular reflexes):

*bulu > *wayo-wulu* 'k.o. bamboo' *kalacaɣ 'plaited bamboo' > *kalase* 'splint of woven bamboo' *qaluɣ 'deep place in river' > *alu* 'flow' (shamanic) *balu > *balu*'widow(er)' *palu > *palu* 'hammer' *culam > *sula* 'embroider' *culuq 'torch' > *sulu* 'eye' (shamanic) *tuluŋ > *túlungi* 'help' *teleɬ 'swallow' > *tolo* 'monstor that swallows the sun in an eclipse'

However, there are two forms that retain /l/ between *a and *u that except for the /l/ have nothing that would show them to be loan words:

*talun > *talu* 'fallow lands' *baluɬ 'wrap, pack' > *walu* 'wrap pack'

/l/ was lost entirely in the word for 'three', possibly because it is a generalization of a pretonic form:

*telu > *tou* 'three'

C5.3.52 *ɬ

*ɬ underwent the changes found throughout the MP languages (§§A1.1.32, 4th¶, A2.3.4). First, *ɬ falls together with *n—that is, becomes /n/:

*ɬam 'taste' > *nami* 'taste' *ɬecuŋ 'mortar' > *noncu* 'mortar' *qaɬitu 'evil spirit' > *anitu* 'spirit of the temple' *tuɬu 'roast' > *tunu* 'rost by the fire'

In some cases, ɬ > /l/. This is in forms with *ɬ-onset of an unstressed penult or earlier:

*ɬibú 'fenced in place' > *libu* 'ring around the moon' *ɬimác > *lime* 'bail water out of boat' *qaɬimatéq > *alinta* 'leech'

There are two cases of *ɬ-onset of unstressed penult that are reflected with /n/ in Pamona (and in a number of other eastern languages [cf. the comment in the glossary]):

*ɬaŋúy > *nangu* 'swim' *ɬecúŋ > *noncu* 'mortar'

In three forms, *ɬ is reflected by /ny/. These are borrowings, and there are cognate reflexes with /n/ for two of them:

*ɬepuq 'fish with poisonous dorsal spines' > *nyopu* 'lion fish', *ɬam 'taste' > *nyami* 'taste' (also *nami*) *qaɬuj > *anyu* 'earth carried by landslide' (also *andu* 'be carried by current')

In one case, *ɬ dissapears without explanation:

*qaɬegaw 'day, sun' > *eo* 'sun'

C5.3.53 Nasals

*m, *n, *ŋ > /m/, /n/, and /ng/ respectively.

*lima > *lima* 'five' *manuk 'bird' > *manu* 'chicken' *nunuk '*Ficus benjamina*' > *nunu* 'banyan' *ŋuda 'young' > *ngura* 'young, soft to touch' *taŋila > *talinga* 'ear'

Nasals in clusters assimilate to the consonant following them:

*timbaŋ 'balance' > *mon-timba* 'weigh' *lampiɬ > *lampi* 'cloth to cover' *diŋediŋ > *rindi* 'wall' *lakaq 'step' > *yongko* 'step' (with intercalated nasal [§C5.1.51])

In three cases not directly inherited, intervocalic /n/ (from *n or *ɬ [§C5.3.53]) became /nd/:

*linaw 'calm, unroiled' > *lindu* 'still water'[13] *linuɣ 'earthquake' > *líndugi* 'earthquake' qáɬuj 'be carried by the current' > *andu* 'carried by water'

---

[13] There is another reflex of this root that is probably directly inherited, *lindo* 'calm, at ease'. The development of the /d/ was probably a dialectal feature.

C5.3.54 *w and *y

C5.3.541*w

Initially, *w- > /u/

*walu 'eight' > *uayu* 'eight' *wałiw > *uani* 'honeybee' *wasiyeɣ > *ue* 'water'

Between two *a's, *w > /w/:

*qałiɣuwan 'bee'> *nyawa* 'k.o. small wasp' *sawak > *awa* 'waist, body' *sinawa 'breath' > *nawa* 'thoughts, heart'

Otherwise, medial *-w- was lost, including initially in roots that were preceded by petrified vowel-final prefixes:

*kawit 'hook' > *kai* 'hook into' *ka-wiɣi 'left' > *kaii* 'left, left hand'

The following root does not occur word initially and therefore the *w developed as in medial position.

*waɣi 'day, sun' > *mampo-ai* 'dry in the sun'

*-w- was also lost in the following form. This is probably a case of dialect borrowing:

*ka-wanał 'right' > *kana* 'right'

There are exceptions. None of these forms are directly inherited:

*cawa 'python' > *saoa* 'python' *lawa > *loa* 'spider'

For the diphthongs and *we, see §§C5.2.52 and C5.2.53.

C5.3.542 *y

Reflexes of *y are attested intervocallically and in dipthongs (§§C5.2.51 and C5.2.53). *-y- disappears after *i and e. Otherwise, *-y- > /-j-/ (i.e., falls together with medial *-j- [§C5.3.43]):

*buqaya 'crocodile' > *wuaja* 'cry upon being startled' *qayam 'pet' > *aja* 'dog, breeding animal' *liyus 'go around s.t.' > *liu* 'pass, passed by' *seyaq > *ea* 'shame'

After *y > /j/, /y/ developed again (§C5.3.51) and did not change.

CHAPTER SIX
Bugis

C6.0 Introduction

Bugis is a language that has spread widely from its original homeland in central Sulawesi and has been adopted by populations speaking other languages, many of which are now lost. For this reason, there is a great deal of variation in Bugis, caused by substratal influences of these various populations that adopted Bugis and much irregularity in the reflection of PAn phonemes as a result of the spread of variants beyond the original populations that employed them. (Cf. further discussion of this in the footnote to §C6.3.33, below.) Bugis has over the past century and a half or longer undergone strong influence from Ml, as is the case of most of the languages of this area. This influence is manifested not only in loan words but also apparently in the phonological shape of forms inherited from PAn that have Ml cognates of similar meaning. Inherited words similar in shape to their Ml cognates have been changed to conform to the shape of the Ml (§§C6.3.32, C6.3.33, and elsewhere).[1] Another source of irregularities was a style of speech employed by shamans for magical purposes. Their speech styles borrowed freely from surrounding languages and also employed purposely distorted forms. Some of these forms have worked their way into normal everyday styles. Finally, sound changes in progress are a source of variation. In some respects, the forms I elicited directly from my informants, young people in their twenties in the 1990s, evinced changes that are not noted in the published sources. A good example is the loss of final glottal stops, which originated in PAn final consonants. These are transcribed in some forms in the published sources, where they failed to appear in the speech of my informants. Oral versions of literary styles have far less phonological variation. The phonology recorded from recitation of classical texts by U. Sirk in Soppeng shows regularity where my oral sources and other written sources show a great deal of variation (U. Sirk, p.c.). (Cf. the discussion of final consonants in recitation of literary texts, §C6.41.)
Our sources are informants, students who are native speakers of Bugis and come from the area of Pare-pare and its surrounding villages, with whom I worked in the summers of 1993 and 1994. Additional citations come from the dictionary (Said 1977) and from Mills 1975.

[1] There is a fair amount of variation in the phonological make-up of Ml forms. I quote Ml forms with the pronunciation widespread in south Sulawesi, with which I acquired familiarity over two summers' residence. This is of importance for this study when it comes to Ml variation of /u/ and /o/. Almost always /o/ is the preferred variant in south Sulawesi.

The following chart lists the phonemes of Bugis:

CHART ONE. PHONEMES OF BUGIS

Consonants

voiceless stops	p	t	c	k
voiced stops	b	d	j	(g)
nasals	m	n	ñ	ng [ŋ]
liquids	w	r, l		
spirant		s		(h)

Vowels

high	i		u
mid	ɛ	e [ə]	o
low		a	

Stress falls automatically on the penult. There are no diphthongs, as is the case of the other languages of central and south Sulawesi, and /g/ and /h/ do not occur in forms inherited directly from PMP or PAn.

Bugis shows a remarkable number of innovations in common with other languages of the area, both in phonology and in the phonological developments of individual lexical items. The following chapter, which treats Salayar, repeats many of the rules given below for Bugis. I draw conclusions from this fact that are at variance from those of Mills (1975), which posits a protolanguage from which the languages of south Sulawesi derived. I say that Bugis, Salayar, and other languages of south Sulawesi do not constitute a subgroup as opposed to the languages spoken further north for two reasons: first, Bugis originated in central Sulawesi and spread south; second, Bugis' is a language that spread to new populations which imposed substratal features on Bugis. The parallel developments are ascribable to contact processes and not to common inheritance of innovations made by a protolanguage. This argument is supported by the fact a number of the forms that are identifiable as borrowings in one language occur also in other languages of the area, where they are also clearly marked as borrowings.

C6.1 Changes that characterize Bugis in general

A good portion of the rules detailed in the following subsections are shared by the languages of southwest Sulawesi.

C6.1.1 Disyllabization of trisyllables

Bugis tended to disyllabize roots that contained consonants that were lost or had *e. The particulars are given in the following subsections. Except in those cases of disyllabization, Bugis retains the trisyllabic shape of PAn roots faithfully. Here is a single example of some dozen or more trisyllabic PAn roots that have trisyllabic reflexes in Bugis:

*bituqen > *wittoɛng* 'star' (< *bintuqan)

Stems of four syllables reduced to three by losing the penult or antepenult:[2]

[2] The rules that governed which syllable was lost have not been identified. Positing metathesis in the development of *qusalipan 'centipede' obviates the necessity of assuming loss of *u in initial *qu- (the shortest and easiest route to producing *alipeng*. However, in §C6.1.12, we assume that an antepenult shaped *a- or *qa- was lost, so that the /a/ in *alipeng* requires explanation. A possible explanation is that metathesis that took place after the rule of antepenultimate *a loss ceased to be in effect, but more likely, this form developed in another unknown language and spread to Bugis. Trisyllabic reflexes with /a/ in the antepenult occur in many languages of south and central Sulawesi.

*qusalipan > *alipeng* 'centipede' (< *qasulipan) *qaɬipugu > *palɛsu* 'whorl' (< *paɬiugu) *qaɬimateq > *alitta* 'leech' (< *qalimteq)

C6.1.11 Syncope of the penult

*e in the penult of trisyllables was lost if the onset was *ɣ, *h, *ɬ, *s, or *q or if the onset of the final syllable was *s or *q. *e was also lost in the antepenult:

*basequ > *bau* 'smell' *beɣecay > *bisɛɛ* 'oar' *iseci > *isɛʔ* 'contents' *qaɬegaw > *esso* 'day, sun' (< *eggaw [§C6.1.3] < *eɬgaw < *eɬegaw [§C6.1.13, 4th¶]) *tahepa > *tapa* 'smoke to preserve'

An *i in the penult was elided before *y onset of the final syllable:[3]

*miniyak > *miñña?* 'oil' (also *miñaʔ*)[4] *peniyu > *peññu* 'sea tortoise'

C6.1.12 Loss of antepenult

The antepenult was lost in forms of three syllables with, *a-, *qa-, *qi- *sa- , *se- onsets.[5] Here are three examples:

*qalima > *lima* 'hand' *qamusa > *mua-mua* 'face, features' *qiteluɣ > *tello* 'egg'[6]

The antepenult was not lost if the penult had been lost by the rule of §C6.1.11, above:

*qaɣetaq 'person' > *ata* 'slave'*saɣejaɬ > *addeng* 'ladder'

C6.1.13 Other cases of disyllabization and weakening

Like vowels in trisyllables were contracted after the loss of an intervening consonant when they had been separated by a consonant that was lost:

*ɣabihi 'evening' > *ka-rawi-an* 'late afternoon' *palisi > *pɛ-mali* 'taboo'

Similarly, sequences *Ve, which developed, were contracted to /V/ (cf. §C6.1.21):

*betihec > *witi?* 'calf' (< *betis—§C6.2.32)

In the following case, metathesis took place before the rule of antepenultimate loss took effect (§C6.1.12). The antepenult was elided by the same rule that governed the loss of the penultimate *i before *y onset of the following syllable (§C6.1.11)—i.e., *i before *y was elided:

*sinawa > *ñawa* 'breath' (< *niyawa < *nisawa)

---

[3] Analogous elision of penultimate *u before *w does not seem to have taken place. In the first two of the following examples, we assume that two *u's developed and subsequently contracted to a single /u/. In the third case, we assume that the /u/ before the /w/ is not epenthetic but inherited unchanged:

*dasuwen > *raung* 'leaf' (< *dasuun) *taquweɬ > *taung* 'year' (< *taquun) *banuwa > *wanua* 'village'

[4] The double /ññ/ is unexplained. All the languages of the area have this /ññ/ reflex. Possibly it is the normal reflex of *niy as opposed to *ɬ, which is reflected with a single /ñ/. The variant *miñak* probably developed under Ml influence.

[5] Presumably, trisyllables with *e, *qe-, *i-, and *si-onsets have lost the first syllable as well, but reflexes of trisyllables with these onsets have not been found.

[6] Mills (1976: 855) reports a variant *itello?* with retention of the antepenult. Possibly the rule of loss of antepenults with /i/ nuclei developed later than the other antepenultimate losses in some dialects, so that the rule of penultimate loss (§C6.1.11) took effect (cf. the following ¶). Subsequently, epenthetic [e] was inserted to obviate the cluster [tl].

The following cases evince weakening of the antepenult as well as loss of the penult. The fourth example also is a unique case of loss of penultimate *a. These forms have probably been influenced by a dialect or neighboring language that was affected by stress in a way different from pre-Bugis. Note that in the case of *qaɬegaw 'day', the same sequence of changes occurred in languages of Sulawesi spoken to the north (Tondano *edo* §C4.1.12, Pamona *eo* §C5.1.14). Also note that the sporadic weakening of *a in the antepenult to /e/ took place before the changes of §§C6.1.1 and C61.1.2 had taken effect.

*biɣeŋi > *wenni* 'night' *binesiq > *wenɛ* 'seed for sowing'[7] *qaɬegaw > *esso* 'day, sun' (< *eggaw [§C6.1.3] < *eɬgaw [§C6.1.11] < *eɬegaw) *pacaqaɬ > *essang* 'carry over the shoulder' *paheɣaw > *perro* 'hoarse' *paqegu > *essung* 'gall' (< *epgung < *qapgu < *qapegu) *tineun > *tennung* 'weave'

Other trisyllabic loan words also show idiosyncratic syncope:

*paɬiki > *panning* 'bat' *paŋudaɬ > *panreng* 'pandanus'

The word for 'male' shows an idiosyncratic development of a petrified prefix coming four syllables from the end of the word:

*ma-ɣuqaɬay > *oroanɛ* 'male'

C6.1.14 Weakening of the first monosyllable in a root consisting of a two monosyllables

In some roots consisting of a doubled monosyllable, the vowel of the first monosyllable was weakened to /e/. This does not happen in all cases of doubled monosyllables, and there is variation in some roots. Dialect mixture is the probable explanation:

*bukebuk > *bebbuʔ* 'wood-borer' *cikecik 'search through' > *sessi* 'search for lice' (also *sissi*) *tacetac > *ma-tetta* 'come undone' *taketak > *tettaʔ* 'chop, hack'[8] *tuketuk > *tettu* 'pound'

C6.1.2 Contraction

C6.1.21

Vowel sequences with *e that arose from the loss of an intervening *s or *q lose the *e—i.e., *VCe > *Ve > /V/. The *e leaves a trace in lowering an adjacent *i or *u:

*túqed 'stump' > *to* (in *toaju* 'tree') *busuk > *ma-boʔ* 'drunk, seasick' *íseq > *tɛ-m-ɛ* 'urine'(< *-um- + iseq) *binesiq 'seed' > *binɛɛ* (< *binɛ [For doubling of the final vowel cf. §C6.1.51.]) *jaqet > *ma-jaaʔ* 'bad' (< *jaʔ [§C6.1.5])

---

[7] *binesiq is reported in our sources as reflecting the normal development, **binɛɛ* or *binɛ*. The dialectal form *wenɛ* is probably influenced by a neighboring language where the reflex underwent a weakening of the antepenult of the reconstructed PAn form. This development was widespread in the Hesperonesian languages, set forth in detail in Chapter Four of Part D (Malay), §D4.1.113b.

[8] The reconstructed root *teketek could also produce *tettaʔ* (§C6.2.31), and in fact the meaning of Bugis *tettaʔ* 'chop' is closer to the meaning reconstructible for *teketek 'chop up' than to the meaning reconstructible for *taketak 'fell, knock down'. However, there is no other attestation of a reflex of *teketek in a language outside of Taiwan, whereas *taketak is widely reflected both on Taiwan and in the MP languages. Further, at least one language has developed a meaning for the reflex of *taketak similar to the Bugis meaning—Kavalan *taktak* 'chop up'. For this reason I assume that Bugis *tettaʔ* remounts to *taketak.

The suffix *-eng* (< *-an) contracts with a preceding vowel by simple loss of /e/ with no other vowel change. This contraction takes place even if a /ʔ/ had developed at the end of the root, for the *ʔ was lost:

*kebel 'invulnerable'+ *-an 'adjective former' > *kebbeng* 'invulnerable' (< *kebeʔeng)

A sequence *au became /o/:

*naquɣ > *no* 'go down' (< *nauɣ)

A sequence *ao automatically became /au/ (but this rule came into effect after the rule above, whereby *au became /o/, had ceased to operate):

*basequ > *bau* 'smell'

C6.1.22

*uqu > /o/ . We have only one example:[9]

*punuq > *pong* 'tree trunk' (< *puqun)

C6.1.3 CC Simplification

Bugis allows no sequences of disparate consonants except for /ʔC/ and /NC/ (but not all consonants occur preceded by a nasal [see below]). Consonants also occur doubled. This situation was reached by the changes listed in the following subsections.

C6.1.31

$NC_1 > C_1C_1$, where C_1 is a voiceless consonant—a nasal followed by a consonant was changed to the consonant that followed it (§C6.1.8):

*qaɬimateq > *alitta* (< *alimta [with loss of the penult—§C6.1.11]) *gemegem > *kekkeng* 'hold in fist' (< *keŋkeŋ < *kemkem)

This probably also applies to the cases where C was a liquid, but there are only a very few attestations in forms inherited from PMP:[10]

*lapiɬ + *pan- > *pallapi* 'protective covering' *naquɣ + *man- > *mannoʔ* 'go down'

If C is *b or *g, the result is devoicing and assimilation of the nasal:

*bunebun > *wumpung* 'heap' *gemegem > *gengkeng* 'hold in the hand' (cf. §C6.3.34 for /k/ [This form is a variant of *kekkeng*, discussed in the first paragraph of this section.])

However, a nasal followed by *d became /nr/:

*diŋediŋ > *renring* 'wall' (< *dindiŋ)

Any nasal cluster in current Bugis that consists of a sequences other than /nr/, /mp/, or /ngk/ occurs in borrowed forms only:

*antiŋ 'hang down' > *anting* 'pendant' *biŋkuŋ > *bingkung* 'hoe' *cumbu > *sunggung* 'wick' *muntay > *amunte* 'citrus' *timbaŋ > *timbang* 'weigh'

---

[9] However, lowering of *i or *u when contracted with a following *e (§C6.1.21) offers a parallel that substantiates this rule.

[10] No doubt a lot of examples can be found in prefixed roots with a liquid onset.

C6.1.32

Other consonant sequences that developed by loss of the penultimate *e simplified by assimilating the first C to the C on the right:

*bedebed > *bebbeʔ* 'wind s.t. around' *bukebuk > *bebbuʔ* 'wood borer' *muɣemuɣ > *kali-mommo* 'gargle' *biɣeŋi > *wenni* 'night' *tacetac > *ma-tetta* 'come undone (stiches)' *ɬepeɬep 'suck on' > *ñoñño* 'slurp, suck on' *celecel > *sesseʔ* 'regret' *cikecik > *sissik* 'look for lice' *taketak > *tettaʔ* 'chop' *tuketuk > *tettuʔ* 'pound' *paqegu > *essung* 'gall' (< *epgung < *qepgu < *qepegu < *qapegu) *sapegiq > *pessi* 'smart, hot (like peppers)'

There are exceptions: *tC > /ʔC/:

*bitebit > *biʔbiʔ* 'take in fingers' *butebut > *buʔbuʔ* 'pull up (weeds)'

*q was lost entirely if it was the first C in the sequence, or it assimilated to the consonant on the left, if it was the second C:

*diqediq > *rɛdɛ* 'boil' *liceqes > *alissa* 'nit' (< *licqes—initial /a/ added by analogy[11])
*pacaqaɬ > *essang* 'carry over shoulder' (< *pesʔan < *pesaʔan)

C6.1.33

There are several forms in which the reflex of *ɣ in clusters does not follow the above rules. These forms probably are the result of borrowing from a dialect or language that treated clusters with *ɣ differently from the dialect that preceded current Bugis:

*qaɣetaq 'person' > *ata* 'slave' *beɣecay > *bisɛɛ* 'oar' *beɣunay > *buʔnɛ* 'k.o. bush' (< *buɣenay) *cuɣecuɣ 'follow behind to check' > *susuʔ* 'sail along the shore' (cf. Ml *susur* 'edge, move along edge')

C6.1.4 Assimilation of liquids

There are two rules of assimilation to the right detailed in the following subsections:

C6.1.41

/l/ onset of the penult is assimilated to /n/ when the final syllable had nasal onset. This is the case of /l/ <*l (§C6.3.42) and of /l/ < *ɬ (§C6.3.43):

*laŋaw > *a-nango* 'fly' *línuɣ > *ninoʔ* 'earthquake' *ɬaŋuy > *nangɛ* 'swim'

C6.1.42

/r/ (< *d, *j)[12] onset of the penult is assimilated to /l/ onset of the final syllable:

*jalan > *laleng* 'way' (<*raleng) *dilaq > *lila* 'tongue' *dalem > *laleng* 'inside'

C6.1.5 Disyllabization of monosyllabic roots

There is an on-going tendency to turn monosyllabic roots into disyllables. This process has affected inherited Pan monosyllabic roots and those that developed in pre-Bugis. This process takes place, as in other An languages, in one of three ways: (1) by stretching the

---

[11] PAn had an 'animal prefix' *qaɬi- > /ali-/, as in *alitta* 'leech' (< *qaɬimateq). Thus, *liceqes was changed to *aliceqes, as if it had had the initial 'animal prefix'.

[12] Presumably, /r/ < *ɣ would also be assimilated, but there are no examples inherited from PMP or PAn.

root to two moras by addition of a pretonic vowel /e/ or lengthening of the vocalic nucleus, (2) doubling of the monosyllabic root, (3) petrifaction of an affix—that is, reinterpretation of an affixed form as a single root. Examples of (1):

*túsud > *uttu* 'knee' (< *ettu[13] < *tu < *tuu) *nem > *enneng* 'six' *pat > *eppa* 'four'[14] *ɣiq 'imperata' > *dεa*[15] (< *rεa < *rε)

Examples of (2):

*gem > *kekkeng* 'hold in fist' (< *gemegem)

Examples of (3):

*busek 'drunk' > *ma-boʔ* 'drunk, seasick' (< *ma-busuk)[16] *íseq 'urine' > *tε-mε* 'urine' (*-mε < *-um- + iseq)

Monosyllabic roots that occur in compounds do not disyllabize:

*túqed 'stump' > *to* (in *toaju* 'tree')

C6.1.51 Other changes caused by metrics

A final /ε/ that had developed from a diphthong (§C6.2.51) or from an *i that had been lowered (§C6.2.1) was lengthened in roots that had been trisyllabic in An. This rule seems to be dialectal, as I have recorded it only in the speech of my informants. In the published documents final /ε/ is not recorded as lengthened:

*beɣecay > *bisεε* 'oar' *binesiq > *binεε* 'seed' *babinay (<*R-+-*in-+*bay) > *bainεε* or *bεnεε* 'woman'

The /ε/'s of the following root underwent lengthening with no explanation:

*beɣay 'give' > *bεεrεε* 'give' (The sources quote *wεrε* and *bεrε* with un-lengthened vowels.)

C6.1.6 Metathesis

Bugis evinces little metathesis aside from the metathesis that affected all of the MP languages—i.e., metathesis that occurred well before Bugis times. In a very few cases we assume metathesis peculiar to Bugis or to Bugis and to closely related languages:

*beɣunay > *buʔnε* 'k.o. bush' (< *buɣenay) *caŋeɣ > *canrε* 'lean on' (< *caŋer) *katu + *pa- > *kapatu* 'send' *qaɬipugu > *palεsu* 'whorl' (< *palεugu [§C6.2.1, 4th¶] < *paɬiyugu [y-insertion between *i and *u] *qusalipan > *alipeng* 'centipede' (< *qasulipan) *tidec > *teddiʔ* 'crush lice in fingernails' (< *tedic)

---

[13]This pretonic vowel originally was /e/ and changed to /u/ in the case of *uttu* 'knee' for unexplained reasons. We assume that the pretonic vowel was /e/ because of the doubling of the /t/ (§C6.1.8). The /u/ probably developed through contact with a language or dialect that assimilated *e to /u/ in the following syllable.

[14]The monosyllabic root is retained in compounds (as is the root-final consonant): *patappulo* 'forty' (<*pat 'four' + *aN 'linker' + *puluq 'tens').

[15] Initial /d/ in this word probably arose by analogy. Forms with /r/ vary with /d/, and in this case, a variant /d/ pronunciation arose that drove out the /r/.

[16] This is a disyllabic root that became monosyllabic when the medial *s was lost and the vowels on either side of the lost *s contracted. The monosyllabic root only occurred affixed, and when the prefix *ma- became nonproductive, the affixed form was reinterpreted as a root.

C6.1.7 Prenasalization of stop consonants

Bugis evinces sporadic prenasalization of the onset to the final syllable or to the penult, as is widespread in Hesperonesian languages (§A3.7.1). Note that prenasalization is reflected as a doubled consonant in the case of the voiceless consonants and as /mp/ in the case of prenasalized *b. (§§ C6.1.31, C6.1.8, C6.3.31, end.) For a large portion of the forms that show prenasalization, the cognates in Ml also evince prenasalization (i.e., Ml may well have been a catalyst to the development of prenasalization [§C6.0]). However, there are some cases that are unique to Bugis or to Bugis and other languages of central and south Sulawesi. Here are a few examples:

*agi > *anri* 'younger sibling' (also *ari*) *akat > *akka* 'lift' (< *aŋkat) (cf. Ml *angkat*) *bituqen > *wittoɛng* 'star' (< *bintuqen) (cf. Ml *bintang*) *puti > *utti* 'banana' (< *punti) *tabun > *tampung* 'pile up' *tapuc > *tappuʔ* 'finished' (< *tampus) *tiduɣ > *tinro* 'sleep' *udesi 'last, rear end' > *m-unri* 'behind, follow'

A sequence *mb is reflected as /mp/ (§C6.3.31, end).

C6.1.71 Nasal accretion at the end of a word

A handful of forms evince accretion of /ng/ at the end of the word. In some cases these can be explained as the reflex of a suffix *-an added to the final vowel of the root (§C6.1.21), but there are some examples of forms with accreted /ng/ that are unlikely to derive from a form suffixed with *-an. The following forms evince unexplained /-ng/ accretion. They are not inherited, and many evince other irregularities:

*baqebaq 'mouth' > *babang* 'door' *cela 'gap' > *sumellang* 'raise and lower alternate threads of the warp in weaving' *cumbu > *sunggung* 'wick' (the medial /ngg/ is also unexplained) *lalatu > *lalatung* 'spark' *pałiki > *panning* 'bat' *paqegu > *essung* 'gall' (also *essuʔ* [with unexplained /-ʔ/]) *tebas > *tebbang* 'cut down' *tilu 'earwax, deaf' < *culing* 'ear'

C6.1.72 Nasal substitution in the formation of active verbs

Bugis, like other Hesperonesian languages, forms active verbs by nasal substitution of the first consonant of the root.[17] Specifically, roots with initial *p- and *b- may substitute /m-/ in the active verb and in the case of vowel onset roots, may accrete /m-/. Also in rare cases, roots with other onsets may substitute /m-/ for the onset. There are a few cases where the sources quote only the affixed form—that is, the form where /m-/ has been added to the vowel onset or replaced the initial consonants. These are the examples attested in the data available to me:

*aɣi > *mai* 'come here!' *beli > *melli* 'buy' *kan + *dɛ > *man-rɛ* 'eat' *kilaw 'shine' > *milo-kilo* 'gleam' *palisi > *pe-mali* 'taboo' *piliq > *milɛ* 'choose' *qetuɣ > *motoʔ* 'penile erection' *udesi > *munri* 'behind'

[17] The process is discussed in greatest fullness for Kelabit (Part Four, Chapter One, §D1.1.5). Bugis evinces a parallel system. For the purposes of this study, the only case that need be discussed is that of /m-/ onset.

C6.1.8 Doubling of consonants

Doubled consonants have developed in several ways. First, consonants were doubled after /e/, which was inherited or had developed in the penult:[18]

*beɣac > *berreʔ* 'hulled rice' *elet > *elleʔ* 'interval' *paqegu > *essung* 'gall' (< *egung < *pegu < *qepegu < *qapegu) *sepat > *eppaʔ* 'four'

Second, consonant clusters that developed were assimilated to the right—i.e., $*C_1C_2 > /C_2C_2/$ (§C6.1.32).

Third, nasals before voiceless stops and *j changed to the stop—i.e., *NC > /CC/:

*cahebay > *sappɛ* 'hang' (< *sampay) *dapaɣ > *lappaʔ* 'flat' (< *dampaɣ) *paqah > *poppang* 'thigh' (/o/ in initial syllable unexplained < *pangpang [§C6.1.5] < *pang < *paʔa-an) *tapuc > *tappuʔ* 'finished' (< *tampus)

*bituqen > *wittoɛng* 'star' (< *bintuqen) *butu 'hillock' > *botto* 'high ground' (< *buntu) *puti > *utti* 'banana' (< *punti) *qaɬimateq > *alitta* 'leech' (< *alinta < *alimteq) *sated > *atteʔ* 'deliver' (< *anted)

*akat > *akka* 'lift' (< *aŋkat) *bukac > *wukka* 'remove covering' (< *buŋkac) *buŋkuk > *bukkuʔ* 'bent over' *cuŋkit 'pry up' > *sukkɛʔ* 'pry out thorns from skin' *gemegem > *kekkeng* 'hold in fist' *wakac 'cut free' > *wakka* 'remove lid from pot' (< *waŋkac)

*jak > *pɛjjak* 'step on' (< *pa-injak)[19]

Finally, several cases have doubled consonants that are unexplained:

*capaw > *sappo* 'bamboo fence erected for privacy (e.g., in bathing)' (also *sapo* 'fence' and *sao* 'house') *ciku > *sikku* 'elbow' *culuy 'shoot' > *colliʔ* 'bud of leaf' (/c/, /o/, and /ʔ/ are also unexplained) *ɣucuk > *russuʔ* ribs' *ikuɣ > *ikku* 'tail' *miniyak > *miññaʔ* oil' (also *miñaʔ*) *paɬid > *panni* 'wing' *sapaɣ > *appaʔ* 'unroll, spread out' *sated > *atteʔ* 'deliver'

Words meaning 'open' and the like with medial /k/ double it to /kk/. They have mutually influenced each other, possibly contaminated by *wekka* 'split' (< *beka):

*wakac 'cut free' > *wakkaʔ* 'remove lid from pot' *bukac 'remove covering' > *wukkaʔ* 'remove lid from pot'

C6.2 Vowels and diphthongs

Bugis has added two vowels to the PAn four-vowel system, /ɛ/ and /o/—i.e., the Bugis vowels are /i, ɛ, e [ə], a, o, u/. /ɛ/ and /o/ developed in a large number of the cases from the diphthongs *ay and *aw, respectively, and from lowering of *i and *u in certain environments. The following sections provide details.

---

[18] This case of doubling is referred to elsewhere as 'strengthening' and developed independently in many languages of SE Sulawesi and Kalimantan (cf. §§C7.1.8, D1.3.3).

[19] This is only the case of forms in which *j is reflected with /j/, and these forms had undergone change under the influence of Ml (§C6.3.33). The inherited *j that came to come after a nasal behaves like *d—i.e., *nj > /nr/:

*isejam > *inreng* 'borrow'

C6.2.1 *i

*i > /i/ in all positions with a few exceptions:

*cikecik 'search through thoroughly' > *sissi* 'look for lice'

*i in the final syllable is lowered before *q—i.e., *iq > /ɛ/:

*weliq 'do again' > *polɛ* (< *pa-uliq) 'return' *puɬetiq > *putɛ* 'white' (< *putiq [a PMP innovation]) *diqediq 'boil' > *rɛdɛ* 'boil'.

In one form, there is variation between lowered /ɛ/ and /i/. The /ɛ/ developed because of the final /-ʔ/, which is irregular. Dialect borrowing is the probable explanation:

*sapegiq 'burn, smart' > *pessɛʔ* 'smart, hot in flavor' (also *pessi*)

*i is also lowered before *y:

*tiyaŋ 'pole' > *tɛang* 'pole' *qaɬipugu > *palɛsu* 'whorl' (< *palɛugu[20] < *paɬiyugu [§C6.1.6])

In the following two forms, an open /i/ in the final syllable was lowered not by any of the above rules. In the first case, the accreted glottal stop and special intonation probably accounts for the lowered reflex.[21] The second case is probably not directly inherited:[22]

*indi > *dɛʔ* 'no' *juɣami > *daramɛ* 'straw'

There are cases where unstressed *i was weakened to /e/: (1) in the first monosyllable of a reduplicated monosyllabic root (§C6.1.14); (2) in the antepenult in irregular unexplained cases (§C6.1.13, end).

C6.2.2 *u

The most general case is that *u > /u/:

*buɣu > *buruʔ* 'broken into pieces'

*u is lowered to /o/ before *q or /ʔ/ that developed from another consonant (§C6.4) (cf. the analogous lowering of *i [§C6.2.1]):

*siɣup > *iroʔ* 'drink slurping' (also *iruʔ*) *diɣuq 'bathe' > *dio* 'bathe' *tuqas 'old' > *toa* 'old'

*u in root final syllable was lowered to /o/ before a velar consonant (*k, *q, *ɣ, *g). This lowering took place whether the final consonant became /ʔ/ (§C6.4) or was lost without a trace:

*qawuɣ 'k.o. bamboo' > *awoʔ* 'bamboo (general term)' *ɬámuk > *namoʔ* 'mosquito' *puluq > *pulo* 'tens' *timuɣ 'rain-bringing wind' > *timor-eng* 'east'[23] *tebug 'spring, well on beach' > *tompoʔ* 'well up, spring'

---

[20] I assume that the unstressed *u in this position (penult of a quadrisyllable) was elided [§C6.1.1]).

[21] At one time, a final glottal stop caused a preceding [i] to lower to [ɛ]. This was the case when *-q became *-ʔ. Subsequently, the rule ceased to operate, and this was before the other final consonants merged to /-ʔ/. Evidently, *indi developed a final glottal stop previous to the change of *iʔ > /ɛʔ/.

[22] Possibly < Mk *raramɛ* 'straw', where the reflex is regular.

In the following form, the *u was not lowered before root final *q because the reflex contains a petrified suffix:

*buq > *bui* 'pour' (< *buq + *-i, the local passive suffix, added to disyllabize the root [§C6.1.5])

In a few forms, *u was lowered to /o/ before a velar that was not at the end of the word. These are exceptions, not the rule. They are probably borrowings from a dialect that lowered the *u before velars in all positions:

*bituka 'stomach' > *bitokeng* 'have stomach worms' (< *bituka + *-an) *duɣi > *dori* 'thorn' (also *duri*) *ma-ɣuqaɬay > *o-roane* 'male' *tuqed 'stump' > *to-aju* 'tree' (< *toe < *toqe < *tuqe)

There are a number of exceptions to this lowering of *u for which there is no explanation:[24]

*buɣebuɣ > *bubuʔ* 'porridge' (Ml *bubur*) *lumpuq > *lumpu* 'lame' *manuk > *manuʔ-manuʔ* 'bird' *paɣimanuk > *parimanuʔ* 'manta' *nunuk > *nunu* 'a tree: *Ficus benjamina*' *nacuk > *nasu* 'cook in water' *puqepuq > *pupu* 'pluck' *tuk 'peck' > *tettuʔ* 'pound' (< *tuketuk)

In the following examples, *u > /o/ with no explanation:

*culuy 'shoot' > *colliʔ* 'leaf bud' *daqu > *dao* 'a tree: *Dracontomelon edule*' *kulit > *oli* 'skin' *qumaŋ > *kal-omang* 'hermit crab' *puceg > *posi* 'navel' *qaɬuwaŋ 'bovine' > *anoa* 'k.o. wild bovine' *qutiɬ > *oting* 'penis' *suni > *oni* 'noise' *suwab > *ting-oa* 'yawn'

Other cases with /o/ are clearly influenced by Ml:

*gucuk 'rub' > *gosoʔ* 'rub' (Ml *gosok*) *cudung > *sorong* 'shove forward' (Ml *sorong*) *lumba > *lompa* 'compete' (Ml *lomba*) *qutek 'brains' > *otaʔ* 'brains' (Ml *otak*) *tukup 'cover over' > *tongkoʔ* 'close with lid'

In one case, *u is reflected with /e/. There is no explanation:

*putuc 'cut off' > *pettu* 'severed'

C6.2.3 *e

The most general case is that *e >/e/:

*tebus > *tebbu* 'sugar cane' *teken > *tekkeng* 'prop' *laleg > *laleʔ* 'a fly'

C6.2.31

*e in final syllables is often affected by the coda. The coda may become glottal stop or not (§C6.4), and whether or not the coda becomes a glottal stop has an effect on the V that preceded.

Before *-q or *-s or before *-k if it becomes /-ʔ/, *e > /a/:[25]

---

[23] Failure of *u to lower to /o/ is an indication of secondary influence: e.g. *dapureng* 'place of cooking fire' is influenced by Ml *dapur* 'kitchen'. Cf. the remarks in §C6.3.32, 4th¶ about the possible influence of Malay cognates in favoring a /d/ reflex rather than an /r/ in reflexes of PAn roots with *d.

[24] In some of the cases there is a Ml cognate with a similar meaning that may have had an influence.

[25] Note that all these forms in which *eC is reflected as /aʔ/ also have Ml cognates that have undergone the same change (§D4.2.4). However, it is likely that the Bugis development was independent of the Ml because at least

*daɣeq > *dara* 'blood' *liceqes > *a-lissa* 'nit' *taneq > *tana* 'land, soil' *qutek 'brains' > *otaʔ* 'brains' *tałek 'boil starch' > *tanaʔ* 'make oil from coconut'

Before word-final *-p or *-k, *e > /o/ (but in the case of *-k, only if *-k does not become /-ʔ/ [cf. the paragraph immediately preceding]):

*cek 'wedge' > *po-so* 'constricted breathing' *pacek 'wedge' > *paso* 'stake, nail, peg' *cep + *ise- > *isoʔ* 'suck' (< *isecep) *dakep 'catch' > *rao* 'embrace'

There is one exception, where *e > /e/. Possibly this is borrowed from a dialect in which a final /ʔ/ prevented the *e from changing to /o/:

*qatep > *ateʔ* 'thatch'

Before word-final *ɣ or *g, *e > /i/, if they became Ø. This /i/ is lowered to /ɛ/ in some cases, and in some cases there is variation between /i/ and /ɛ/. This situation probably results from mixture of dialects that treated *e in this environment differently:

*caleɣ > *sali* 'flooring' *caŋeɣ > *sanrɛ* 'lean on' (< *saŋɛr [§C6.1.6] *puseg > *posi* 'navel' *wasiyeɣ > *waɛ* 'water' (also *wai*)

If *-ɣ or *-g became glottal stop, the change was blocked: *e > /e/:[26]

*laleg > *laleʔ* 'fly' *quleg > *uleʔ* 'worm'

C6.2.32

There are tendencies to make *e in a disyllabic root harmonize with the other vowel in the root, but evey rule of vowel harmony has numerous exceptions. This situation most likely is the result of dialectal diversity and dialect mixture.

*eCi > /iCi/; *eCɛ> /iCɛ/ or /ɛCɛ/:

*beɣecay > *bisɛɛ* 'oar' (< *beɣcɛ [The lengthening of /ɛ/ is discussed in §C6.1.51.]) *beɣay > *wɛrɛ* 'give' *betihec > *witiʔ* 'calf' (< *betis)

*uCe > /uCu/:

*buleg > *bulu* 'mountain'

The rule of §C6.2.31 is prior to rules of vowel harmony, so that its effects prevented vowel harmony from taking place:

*bugeq > *busa* 'foam' (*e changed to /a/ before vowel harmony could happen)

*eCo > /oCo/

*beɣaq 'abscess' > *boro* 'swelling' (the change of *aq to /o/ is unexplained) *qetuɣ > *m-oto* 'penile erection'

---

in one case (*tałek > Ml *tanak* 'cook starches' Bug *tanaʔ* 'make oil from coconut'), the Bugis form shows semantic divergence from Ml.

26 We assume that the development of /ʔ/ from *ɣ and *g was later than the development of /ʔ/ from *-q, *-s, or *-k because the preceding *e in the case of *eɣ and *eg did not change to /a/ as it did in the case of *-es, *-eq, and *ek (2nd ¶ of this section, above).

C6.2.33

There is a handful of forms with idiosyncratic reflexes of *e that are unexplained. Some are probably borrowings. Others may be contaminated. I have not been able to identify the source of the following irregularities:

*baɣeq 'abscess' > *boro* 'swelling' *bituqen > *wittoɛng* 'star' (also *wittoing*)[27] *cedu > *sidu* 'hiccough' *ceŋ > *essu* 'blow the nose' (< *cu) *cep > *isoʔ* 'suck' *ɬepeɬep > *ñoñño?* 'suck' *dakep 'catch' > *rao* 'embrace' *demedem 'feel' > *ranreng* 'yearn' *deŋ > *ped-dɛ* 'extinguish' (< *pa-dem)[28] *kepec > *keppɛ* 'deflated' (also *keppi*) *peɣec > *perra?* 'squeeze out'

C6.2.34

The sequence *we > /u/, as in most Hesperonesian languages:[29]

*dasuwen 'leaf' > *raung* 'leaf' (< *dasuun) *taqewen > *taun* 'year' *weliq 'do again' > *pole* (< *pa-uliq) 'return'

C6.2.4 *a

In general *a > /a/:

*ala> *ala* 'take' *balabaw > *balao* 'rat'

However, in final closed syllables that remained closed in Bugis, *a > /e/:

*salac > *ale?* 'forest' *qagan > *aseng* 'name' *pálag > *pale?* 'palm of hand' *uɣat> *ure?* 'vein'

In many cases, word-final C was lost, resulting in an open final syllable [§C6.4]). If the final consonant after *a was lost, *a remains /a/:

*dataɣ 'flat area' > *rata* 'level' *jilaq > *lila* 'tongue'

In several cases, *a in a closed final syllable remained /a/. The following forms were probably influenced by the Ml cognates in a process similar to described for /j/ in §C6.3.33:

*aɬak > *ana?* 'child' (Ml *anak*) *belaŋ > *belang* 'spotted' (Ml *belang* 'banded, spotted') *bilaŋ > *bilang* 'count' (Ml *bilang*) *dulang 'tray' > *dulang* 'water trough' (Ml *dulang* 'tray') *qúbaɬ > *ubang* 'white hair' (Ml *uban*) (sources from the mid-nineteenth century quote *ubeng*) *qudang > *urang* 'shrimp' (Ml *udang*) *sadang 'intercept' > *adang* 'lie in wait for' (Ml *hadang*)

The following two forms influenced each other. Possibly, the glottal stop had gotten lost and subsequently was replaced through contamination with *wekka* 'split'.

*bukac > *wukka?* 'open, uncover'*wakac > *wakka?* 'remove covering (e.g. lid of pot)'

In the following form there is no Ml cognate to account for the retention of *a:

*tacak > *tasa?* 'ripe'

---

[27] The irregular reflexes of the final syllable of this root are shared by all of the languages of south Sulawesi (cf. Mills 1975: 651).

[28] The loss of the final nasal and the change of *pa > /pe/ is best explained by taking this form to be a borrowing from a language or dialect that lost final nasals.

[29] The corresponding rule for *ey is probably also valid, but there are no Bugis attestations of forms with *ey inherited from PAn.

*a was syncopated in some trisyllabic roots, depending on their make-up (§§C6.1.12, C6.1.14).

In a few cases, *a in the penult > /e/ with no explanation:

*dem + *pa > *peddɛ* 'extinguish' (also *padeng* 'finish') *paheɣaw > *perro* 'hoarse' (< *paɣaw)[30]

In another case, *a in the penult harmonizes with the final syllable, but this is not a rule, as in most cases penultimate /a/ remains unchanged. Rather there was contamination with a reflex of *taytay, which is not reflected in Bug, but does occur in other languages of the area:

*latay 'pass across'> *lɛtɛ* 'a narrow bridge'[31]

C6.2.5 Diphthongs

Bugis has no diphthongs. Inherited diphthongs were monophthongized, as described in the following subsections.

C6.2.51 *ay

*ay > /ɛ/:

*cakay > *saɛ* 'climb' *matey >*matɛ* 'die' *qatay < *atɛ* 'liver'

*ay > /ai/ in monosyllables:

*bahi 'female' > *bai* 'female animal'[32]

C6.2.52 *uy and*iw

*uy and *iw > /i/:

*babuy > *bawi* 'pig' *sehapuy > *api* 'fire' *laɣiw 'flee' > *lari* 'run'

There are exceptions. In the word for 'wood', as in other languages, the *s became †h and syllabicity shifted. Subsequently, †h was lost. After that, medial *y developed and then was strengthened to /j/ (§C6.3.62):

*kasiw 'tree, wood' > *aju* 'wood, stick'

The following word developed an unexplained final glottal stop. Contamination with an unidentified form is the probable explanation. There are also irregularities in the vowel of the penult and the doubled medial consonant:

*culuy 'shoot' > *colliʔ* 'young leaf bud'

In the following case, the final /-i/, which had developed, was lowered to /ɛ/. There is no explanation:

*ɬaŋuy > *nangɛ* 'swim'

---

[30] Note that the cognate in other languages of Sulawesi and SE Kalimantan also have a reflex of *e in the first syllable of the cognate.

[31] Mills (1975:861) proposes that *lɛtɛ* remounts to *laytay < *talatay. This is hardly possible for two reasons: (1) loss of the antepenult is un-parallelled; (2) *látay is widely reflected in languages from the Philippines to Oceania, and surely Bugis *lɛtɛ* is cognate with those forms.

[32] In affixed forms, the root was *bay, which became /ɛ/:

*bahi + *R-in- > *bainɛɛ* 'woman' (< *bawinɛ < *babinay)

C6.2.53 *aw

*aw >/o/:

*balábaw > *balao* 'rat' (< *balabo [§C6.3.31, 3rd¶]) *qałegaw > *esso* 'day' *nakaw > *in-nau* 'steal' (< *in-nao < *in-nako)

/aw/ in monosyllables > /au/:

*taw > *tau* 'man'

/au/ that developed in monosyllables > /o/ when affixed or in compounds. In some cases, the allomorph that occurred in affixed forms was generalized:

*taw 'man' + *daya 'inland' > *toraja* 'mountaineer' *naquɣ '> *no* 'go down'

Pre-Bugis *ao (where the *o develops by contraction or by a normal lowering process) is automatically replaced with /au/:

*nakaw > *in-nau* 'steal' (< *in-nao < *in-nako) [33]

However, this process took place before the change of *-b- > *-w- , which became lost (§C6.3.31)—i.e., if the sequence /ao/ developed by the loss of a medial *-b-, the change to /au/ did not take place:

*balabaw > *balao* 'rat' (< *balawo < *balabo)

C6.3 Consonants in initial and medial position

In this section the reflexes of the PAn consonants in initial and medial position are discussed. The number of contrasts in word-final position has been considerably reduced. The reflexes of PAn final consonants are discussed in §C6.4.

CHART TWO. DEVELOPMENT OF THE BUGIS CONSONANTS FROM PAN

PAn	Bugis	PAn	Bugis
p	*p*	ɣ	*r*
t	*t*	l	*l*
k	*k, Ø*	ł	*n, l*
q, s, h	*Ø*	m	*m*
c	*s*	n	*n*
b	*w, b*	ŋ	*ng* [ŋ], *n*
d, j	*r, d*	w	*w*
g	*k-, -s-*	y	*j*

C6.3.1 Voiceless stops

C6.3.11 *p

The most general case is that *p > /p/:

---

[33] The difference in treatment of *nakaw 'steal' and *naquɣ 'go down' is explained by the temporal ordering of the changes: the change *au > /o/ came first. Only after that change had taken place and ceased to operate, did *ao become /au/:

*naquɣ > *nau- > *no-* *nakaw + *in- > *in-nako > *in-nao > *in-nau* 'steal' *pitu > *pitu* 'seven' *sehapuy > api 'fire'

Initial *pu- becomes /u/ variably.[34] In some cases, a form showing this innovation has spread through many of the Bugis dialects:

*pucuq 'heart' > *uso* 'banana blossom' *puti > *utti* 'banana' (< *punti)

Initial *p- was also lost sporadically before other vowels. There is no explanation for those cases:

*pagay > *asɛ* 'rice plant' *pacaqał > *essang* 'carry over shoulder' *pacegu > *essung* 'gall'

In one case medial *p is lost. There is no explanation:

*capaw 'field hut' > *sao* 'house' (also *sappo* 'flimsy walling erected to hide behind [e.g., for bathing]', *sapo* 'fence')

C6.3.12 *t

*t > /t/ in most cases:

*tacik > *tasiʔ* 'sea' *pakatu > *kapatu* 'send'

In a few cases *t is reflected with /c/. Some of these are variants of the root with /t/.

*puti 'banana' > *uci-uci* 'k.o. plant that resembles the banana' (also *utti* 'banana') *tapuc > *cappu* 'finished' (also *tappuʔ*) *tawa > *cawa* 'laugh' *tilu 'earwax, deaf' > *culing* 'ear' *tiŋadaq > *cɛnga* 'look up' (also *tingara*) *-metik > *la-mecciʔ* 'k.o. black ant' *tuŋaw 'k.o. flea' > *cungo-cungo* 'small red flea that inflicts an itchy bite' *tuqas > *ma-coa* 'old' (also *toa* 'old')

C6.3.13 *k

Most commonly, initial and medial *k > /k/, but there are cases, many of them forms of basic vocabulary, where *k in initial and medial position has disappeared without a trace:

*cakay > *sae* 'climb' *cakit 'sick' > *sai* 'plague, pestilence' *dakep 'catch' > *rao* 'embrace' *daki > *rai* 'dirt on skin' *dakis 'climb' > *o-rai* 'west' *gíta > *ita* 'see' (< *kita) *kasiw > *aju* 'tree' *kilat > *ileʔ* 'lightening' *kuduŋ > *urung* 'enclose' *kulit > *uli* 'skin' *kumpaC > *ma-umpeʔ* 'thick' *kutu > *utu* 'louse' *laki > *lai* 'male (animal)' *lakaw > *lao* 'go' *nakaw 'steal' > *in-nau* 'steal' *pakan > *pang* 'weft' *takut > *me-tau* 'be afraid'

In a larger number of cases, *k is reflected as /k/:

*kutała > *kutana* 'ask' *-ku > *-ku* 'my' *ikasu > *iko* 'you' *paku > *paku* 'k.o. edible fern'

It is impossible to say which the regular reflex is and which reflex has been borrowed. Forms that give no sign of being loan words, as well as forms that are loan words, evince the loss of *k and others evince retention of *k. Apparently, the loss of *k began in a dialect and spread, but only to some of the vocabulary. In the following form, the /i/ of the final syllable indicates that this form is not directly inherited. However, it has been subject to the loss of *k.

*kuden > *uring* 'pot'

---

[34] This loss probably originates in a postvocalic weakening of *p- to *b-, which then became generalized and subsequently weakened further to *w-. This *w- was lost variably, as is the case of *w < *PAn *b (§C6.3.31).

C6.3.14 *q

*q was lost entirely. In a few environments, *q affected the quality of the preceding vowel (§§C6.2.2, 2nd¶, C6.2.31), but otherwise *q left no trace:

*quway > *ue* 'rattan' *baqeɣu > *baru* 'new' *baseɣu > *bau* 'smell' *jaqet > *jaaʔ* 'bad' *dilaq > *lila* 'tongue'

C6.3.15 *c

In most cases, *c > /s/:

*caluɣ 'water course' > *salo* 'river' *acu > *asu* 'dog'

In three cases *c is reflected with /c/. These forms are not directly inherited, and there are other irregularities as well:

*culuy 'shoot' > *colliʔ* 'young leaf bud' *cuŋkit 'poke' > *cukki* 'pry up' (also *sukkɛʔ* 'pry thorn out of skin') *qapucuk > *pucuʔ* 'sprout' (< Ml)

C6.3.2 *h, *s

*h and *s were lost without a trace. *s left a trace in certain environments, where it affected the quality of vowels that preceded it (§C6.2.31).
Examples of *h-loss:

*bahi 'female' > *bai* 'female (animal)' *lahuj > *lauʔ* 'sea' *baɣah > *bara* 'embers'

Examples of *s-loss:

*baŋesis > *ma-wangi* 'fragrant' (also *mongi* [< *mawŋi[35]]) *qaselu > *alu* 'pestle' *salac > *aleʔ* 'forest' *sadiɣi 'post' > *aliri* 'pole'

C6.3.3 Voiced stops

PAN *b and *d have double reflexes: /b/ and /w/ and /d/ and /r/, respectively. *j has three reflexes /j/, /d/, and /r/. *ɣ is reflected with /r/. There is a near merger of *d, *j, and *ɣ (§C6.3.41), as all three protophonemes are reflected by /r/, but the number of contrasts was never reduced entirely because dialect mixture and borrowing from other languages has continually reintroduced the contrasts as they had been before. Bugis has a three-way contrast in the reflexes of these protophonemes: /d/, /j/, and /r/, with a certain amount of realignment in the reflected words, as described in the subsections that follow. *g is reflected as /k/ when onset of the penult or earlier and as /s/ when onset of the final syllable.
With the double reflexes, Bugis parallels the development of most of the other languages of central and south Sulawesi, where *b, *d, *j have double reflexes. The explanation for Bugis is likely to be similar to that for other languages of the area: namely, there was something about the articulation of *b, *d, and *j that set the stage for weakening these phonemes, especially in intervocalic position, and probably led to a complete phonemic change in some dialects. But dialect mixture, and leveling of the paradigm have led to the maintenance of the /b/–/w/ and the /d/–/r/ contrasts or the reintroduction of these contrasts. Cf. the second note to §C8.3 in the discussion of Muna, where similar phenomena in Muna are discussed.

---

[35] The elision of /a/ in the penult of a trisyllable is not a rule attested in other roots. It is probably a variable rule confined to rapid speech forms of roots with /w/ onset of the penult after vocalic prefixes.

C6.3.31 *b

In most cases, *b is reflected by /b/. There are fewer cases, but still many, in which *b is reflected by /w/. There are many doublets with /b/ and /w/, and some forms with two *b's show initial /b/ and medial /w/.

*beɣay > *bɛrɛ* and *wɛrɛ* 'give' *benang 'thread' > *wennang, bennang* 'thread' *batu > *batu* 'stone' (also *watu* in names) *bubu > *bubu* 'fish trap' *buqaya > *buaja* 'crocodile' *babuy > *bawi* 'pig'

In most cases in which *b became /w/ before /u/ or /o/, the /w/ was lost. *wu, which developed from *bu, became /u/.

*bulañ > *uleng* 'moon, month' *bucuɣ > *uso?* and *usoreng* (< *bucuɣan) 'bow' *tubuq > *tuo* 'grow' (< *tuwuq)

Further, if *b had become *w between *u or *o and *a, the *w was lost:

*balabaw > *balao* 'rat' *tuba > *tua* 'a plant furnishing fish poison' (< *tuwa)

However, in some cases, the /w/ that developed did not get lost or only was lost dialectally (cf. variable loss of *w in §C6.3.61):

*qabu > *awu* 'ashes' *bunuq > *wuno* (also *buno* and *uno*) 'kill'

*-w- that developed from *-b- in pre-Bugis was lost in words of three or more syllables when onset two or more syllables from the end of the root:[36]

*babaw 'above' > *wao* 'top' *baq 'down' > *iawa* 'below, under' (< *i-wawa [with doubling of the monosyllabic root]) *bahi > *bainɛɛ* (< *bawinɛ < babinay [*R- + *-in- + *bay]

Note that *b did not weaken when protected by a preceding consonant—i.e., *Cb > /bb/ or /ʔb/:

*budebud > *bebbe* 'wind s.t. around' *wɛrɛ* 'give' + *maʔ-* (< *maɣ-) > *maʔbɛrɛ* 'give'

Since many of the forms with initial /w/ from *b have allomorphs with initial /b/ because initial *b is protected after a consonant-final prefix, the number of forms with initial /b-/ tends to increase because of paradigm leveling.

In pre-Bugis, in clusters consisting of a nasal plus b, the voiced stop became voiceless—i.e., *mb > /mp/. I assign this change to pre-Bugis, because in current Bugis the sequence /mb/ has been reintroduced:

*bunebun > *wumpung* 'heap' (< *bumbun) *tabun > *tampung* 'heap' (< *tambun)

Borrowings into pre-Bugis evince the same change:

*ɣumbiya > *rumpia* 'sago palm' *qaɬi-baŋebaŋ > *kalu-bampa* 'butterfly'[37]

---

[36] This rule excludes words of three or more syllables if the penult contracted with the final syllable after medial -C- loss. In such cases , /w/ (< *b) has become the onset of the final syllable of the root and was not lost: although it may indeed be the onset of the penult of the word if it had been suffixed:

*ɣabihi + *ka-an > *ka-raweng* 'late afternoon' (< *ka-rawi-an*)

[37] The word for 'butterfly' *kalubampa* is clearly not directly inherited, but rather borrowed from a language or dialect that had lost the final nasal. However, it underwent the change of *mb > /mp/—either that, or the language from which *kalubampa* was borrowed has also made that change.

But later borrowings, which took place after this sound law ceased to be in effect, do not devoice the voiced consonants:

*timbaŋ > *timbang* 'weigh'

C6.3.32 *d

The basic reflex of *d is /r/:

*daki > *rai* 'dirt on skin' *dataɣ 'flat area' > *rata* 'level' *depa > *repa* 'fathom' *qudaŋ > *urang* 'shrimp'

However, *d is reflected with /d/ if it was protected (i.e., came immediately after a C, when an intervening *e was elided):

*diqediq > *rɛdɛ* 'boil' (< *diqdiq)

*n did not protect *d—i.e., /d/ does not occur following a nasal. PAn forms that developed a nasal before *d are reflected with a change of *d > /r/:

*diŋediŋ > *renring* 'wall' (< *dending)

In most cases in which unprotected *d is reflected with /d/, there are cognates in Ml. From this we conclude that /r/ is the normal reflex and /d/ arose through influence of Ml. In other words, under the influence of Ml, in cognates that have /d/ where Bugis has /r/, a process developed whereby the variant with /d/ was favored over /r/:

*daɣeq > *dara* 'blood' (Ml *darah* [cf. *rara* in 19th century manuscripts]) *dasedas > *dada* 'chest' (Ml *dada*) *damaɣ > *damaaʔ* 'damar resin' (Ml *damar*) *duɣi 'thorn' > *duri* 'thorn' (Ml *duri*) *dápuɣ 'place for cooking fire' > *dapur +eng* 'kitchen' (Ml *dapur)* *datu > *datu* 'chieftain' *dulaŋ 'tray' > *dulang* 'trough for drinking' (Ml *dulang* 'tray')

Other examples showing *d as a reflex are probably secondary:

*daɣa > *dara* 'maiden'[38] *dapit 'near' > *dapiʔ* 'connect' *daɣat 'open area' > *dareʔ* 'garden' *ɣiq > *dɛa* 'a saw grass: *Imperata cylindrica'* (< *rɛa < *rɛ) *tedec > *teddiʔ* 'crush lice between fingers' *teduŋ 'protect with a covering' > *teddung* 'umbrella'[39] *tudaŋ > *tudang* 'sit'

The following case with /d/ < *d is probably inherited. I have no explanation.[40]

*dusa > *dua* 'two'

The /r/ that developed from *d is dissimilated to /l/ before /l/ onset of the following syllable:

*dilaq > *lila* 'tongue' *dalem > *laleng* 'inside'

---

[38] This form occurs frequently in the sequence *anaʔdara* 'sister', a position in which the reflex of *d was protected. Likely, the allomorph with the protected /d/ spread to all positions.

[39] There are no other attested forms that reflect *ed except *teddiʔ* and *teddung*, nor are there any attestations of a reflex of *ej. Therefore, it is possible that these forms obey a rule that blocks *d from changing to /r/ after *e. However, it would be an idiosyncratic rule, for *eɣ > /err/:

*beɣac > *werreʔ* 'hulled rice'

[40] It is possible to speculate that the numbers typically occurred following a morpheme ending in a consonant, but I have found no evidence for that so far. Another speculative explanation, which probably can never be substantiated, is that there were dialects that did not weaken *d, and that current Bugis dialects have relexified from dialects that weakened *d, as explained in this section, but *dua* remained un-relexified.

In one other case, *d- > /l/. This probably arose by contamination, but the evidence has not been discovered:[41]

*dapaɣ > *lappa* 'flat'(< *dampag)

C6.3.33 *j

*j is scantily represented in forms that are directly reflected: in initial and medial positions, there are three reflexes: *d, *j, *r. For initial position, I assume that only one form reflects *j- directly. For medial position, there are two cases of /-r-/ reflex. All the other forms reflecting *j have in fact been reformed by the contact with Ml or by dialectal borrowing.[42]

In the only case of initial *j- that became*r, the *r was subsequently assimilated to an /l/ on the right (cf. other examples of assimilation in §C6.3.32):

*jalan > *laleng* 'road' (< *raleng)

The following are the three cases of medial *-j- reflected by /r/:

*qujaɬ > *ureng* 'rain' *sejam + *is- > *isejam > *inreng* 'borrow' *tajem > *tareng* 'sharp'

*j > /d/ if it was protected. Further, a cluster *Cj that developed by elision of the penult > /dd/:

*jeket > *maʔ-dekkɛ* 'stick' *saɣejaɬ > *addeng* 'ladder' (< *aɣjan)

In a fair number of other cases *j is reflected with /d/. These are secondary, and most of them evince other irregularities:

*juɣami > *daramɛ* 'straw' *juɣuq > *duro* 'broth' *jukut > *duʔ* 'grass' *sejen > *eddeng* 'press down in defecating, labor, etc.' *pejem 'close eyes' > *peddeng* 'sleep'

A number of forms reflect *j with /j/. In most cases in which PAN *j is reflected with Bugis /j/, there are cognates in Ml with /j/. From this we conclude that /j/ in these words arose through influence of Ml. In other words, under the influence of Ml cognates that have /j/ where Bugis has had a reflex of *j (presumably *r, possibly *d), a process developed whereby the variant with /j/ was favored over /r/ (or possibly /d/). (Cf. a similar case of reflexes of *d, §6.3.32, above.)

*jaqet > *ma-jaaʔ* 'bad' (Ml *jahat* 'bad') *jaɣum 'needle' > *jarung* 'needle'(Ml *jarum* 'needle') *jaqit 'sew' > *maj-jai* 'sew' (Ml *jait*) *jak > *pɛjjak* 'step on' (< *pa-injak) (Ml *injak*) *sijaw > *ijo* 'green' (Ml *hijau*) *sujung > *ujung* 'cape' (Ml hujung)

C6.3.34 *g

As onset of the penult or earlier, *g > *k:

---

[41] Tag also reflects initial /l/ in the cognate as a result of contamination (cf. the glossary under *dapaɣ).

[42] In saying that only four forms reflecting unprotected *j are in fact directly inherited and the fourteen others are all borrowed, I am assuming that current Bugis is the product of heavy relexification. This is in keeping with its history as a language that has spread widely. As the result of having been adopted by speakers of closely related languages in areas to which it spread, Bugis has undergone strong influence of substrata in various regions. My reason for fixing on /r/ as the normal reflex, and /d/ or /j/ as the result of contact, is that /r/ (or /l/ derived from /r/) occurs in reflexes of two basic PAn forms that are almost universally directly inherited—they have been stable in practically all of the languages studied in detail in this work, *jalan > *lalan* 'way' and *qujaɬ > *ureng* 'rain"

*gatel 'itchy' > *ma-kateʔ* 'itchy' *gemegem > *kekkeng* 'hold in fist'

Mills (1976:702) quotes *gengkeng* as a reflex of *genggeng (< *gemgem). The development of /ngk/ in this form is parallel to the development of /mp/ from prenasalized /b/ (§C6.3.31). I can only conclude that Bugis is an amalgamation of two dialects: one, in which *g- > /k-/ and the other in which *g- /g-/, There are plenty of variants, not reflexes of PMP forms, listed in the dictionary, one of which evinces /k-/ and the other of which evinces /g-/. The following forms show initial /g-/ in all dialects, as far as the published materials provides information—i.e., these are forms where the /g-/ variant has won out. Clearly in some of these cases, the Ml or Mk cognate was catalytic to the demise of the /k-/ variant (which we assume did develop, if we hold /k-/ to be the normal reflex of *g-):

*gadic 'scratch > *garisiʔ* 'draw a line' (Ml *garis*, Sal *garisi* 'line') *giliŋ 'roll over something' > *giling* 'grind' (Ml *giling*) *gucuk > *gosoʔ* 'rub'[43] (Ml *gosok*) *gusam 'thrush' > *guameng* 'bitter taste after having been sick'

As onset of the final syllable, *-g- > -s-:

*qagan 'name' > *aseng* 'name'

There are three exceptions in which *g-onset of the final syllable is reflected with /r/. /s/ is the regular reflex—in fact, Sa'dan (To Raja) is the only other documented language in the area that reflects *g- onset of the final syllable with /s/. The languages in south Sulawesi with which Bugis is in contact reflect *g- onset of the final syllable with /r/. The following forms are borrowings, but the source is unknown.[44]

*lugan > *lureng* 'load' *ɬagam > *ñareng* 'tame' *suwagi > *anri* 'younger sibling'

C6.3.4 Voiced continuants

C6.3.41 *ɣ

*ɣ is reflected as /r/ except when it came to be in a consonant cluster:

*beɣac > *berreʔ* or *werreʔ* 'rice' *ɣakit > *rakiʔ* raft'

In clusters, the normal development was to assimilate to the right, but there are several examples, probably in forms not directly inherited, where the outcome is different (cf. §C6.1.33).[45]

C6.3.42 *l

*l remained unchanged in most environments:

*laɣiw > *lari* 'flee' *ala > *ala* 'take'

/l/ onset of the penult is assimilated to /n/ when the final syllable has /n/ or /ng/onset. This is the case of /l/ <*l and of /l/ < *ɬ (§C6.3.43):

---

[43] A number of words for 'rub' begin with /g-/ and have variants beginning with /k-/. There has been a great deal of mutual influence among these forms.

[44] None of the forms listed in Mills 1976 shows a palatal initial reflex of *ɬagam. The protoforms listed here all have reflexes in numerous languages listed by Mills, and in all of them *g is reflected with /r/.

[45] Evidently, *-ɣ as coda of a prefix was treated as if it were word final. Thus, the prefix *maɣ- may be reflected as *maʔ-* (§C6.4):

*beɣay + *maɣ- > *maʔbɛrɛ* 'give'

*laŋaw > *a-nango* 'fly' *línuɣ > *nino?* 'earthquake' *ɬaŋuy > *nangɛ* 'swim'

This assimilation does not take place in two cases. Very likely these forms were reshaped on the influence of another language:

*laŋit > *langi* 'sky' *linaw > *lino* 'calm'

C6.3.43 *ɬ

*ɬ underwent the changes found throughout the MP languages (§§A1.1.32, 4th¶, A3.3.4). In addition, PMP †ñ < *ɬ underwent depalatalization, as it did in many of the MP languages.[46] As onset to an unstressed penult or earlier syllable, *ɬ- becomes /l-/. Otherwise, *ɬ > /n/. This rule can be restated as follows:

Preceding the unstressed penult or earlier syllable, *ɬ > /l-/, as is the case of most western An languages.[47]

*qaɬimatɛq > *alitta* 'leech' *ɬemɛc 'disappear' > *lemme?* 'drown' *ɬaŋuy > *nangɛ* 'swim' (< *laŋɛ—§C6.3.42)

Otherwise, *ɬ > /n-/ and /-n-/.

*aɬák > *ana?* 'child' *áɬay > *anɛ-anɛ* 'termite' *ɣuqaɬáy > *oroanɛ* 'male' *keɬa > *kenna* 'hit the mark' *ɬámuk > *namo?* 'mosquito'

In final position, *ɬ > /ng/:

*saɣejaɬ > *addeng* 'ladder' *buɬebuɬ > *bubung* 'fontanelle'

In a few cases, *ɬ is reflected as /ñ/. However, these forms are secondary. /ñ/ is part of the inventory of Bugis, but it developed from syncope of *niy (cf. the first footnote to this section). In one case, the influence of Ml accounts for the occurrence of /ñ/:

*ɬam 'taste' > *ñam-eng* 'delicious' (Ml *nyaman* 'delicious')

In two other cases, there are other irregularities, indicating that these forms were not directly inherited. The source has not been identified:

*ɬepeɬep > *ñoñño?* 'slurp, suck on s.t.' *ɬagam > *ñareng* 'tame'

In two other cases, there are no other irregularities. Note that the first example is not securely reconstructed. It is probably borrowed from Ml. The second example is also secondary, but there is no other evidence for this except the reflex /ñ/:

*leɬeb > *leñña?* 'disappear' *qaɬit 'skin, bark, pelt' > *añi?* 'peel'

---

[46] *ñ that arose by syncope from *niy did not undergo depalatalization (as did happen in other languages, e.g., Muna—cf. the footnote to §C8.3.43)

sinawa > *ñawa* 'breath' (< *niyawa < *nisawa) *peniyu > *peññu* 'sea turtle' (< *penyu) *miniyak > *miñña?* 'oil'

[47] The following forms are spread throughout the languages of south Sulawesi and evince /n/ as the reflex of *ɬ when onset to the penult. The /n/ developed in a dialect in which the stress had moved to the penult in these words before change of *ɬ > /l/ before unstressed penults:

*qaɬuwaŋ 'bovine' > *anoa* 'k.o. wild bovine: the anoa' *kaɬuskus > *kanuku* 'nail'

C6.3.5 *m, *n, *ŋ

The nasals remained unchanged in most environments:

*mata > *mata* 'eye' *lima > *lima* 'five' *naquɣ > *no* 'go down' *manuk 'bird' > *manuʔ* 'chicken' *ŋaŋa > *nganga* 'open mouth'

In final position, they merge to /ng/:

*inum > *m-inung* 'drink' *saŋin > *anging* 'wind' *tutuŋ > *tutung* 'burn'

In a handful of unexplained cases, the final nasal was lost entirely, doubtlessly under the influence of a neighboring language that lost final nasals entirely:

*ceŋ 'stop up' > *essu* 'blow nose' *lapiɬ > *pal-lapi* 'protective cloth' (< *panlapi*)

In one case *-ng- is reflected with /-n-/. This form has several irregularities and has been subject to unidentified influence:

*biɣeŋi > *wenni* 'night'

The nasals have special outcomes in clusters. These are detailed in §C6.1.31).

C6.3.61 *w

*w > /w/ in initial and medial positions, except when abutting on /u/ or /o/:

*wasiyeɣ > *waɛ* 'water' *tawa > *cawa* 'laugh'

In the environment of /u/ or /o/ *w is lost variably. In some forms the reflex is /w/ and in other forms *w > ∅. (Cf. a parallel treatment of /w/ < *b, §C6.3.31.)

*qawuɣ > *awoʔ* and *aoʔ* 'bamboo' *luwa > *lua* 'vomit' *qisuwab > *ting-oa* 'yawn' *waɬi + *au-[48] > *o-wani* 'bee' (also *a-wani* and *u-wani*)

The sequence *we became /u/, as in most languages (§C6.2.34).
For *w at the end of words, cf. §§C6.2.52, C6.2.53.
In one case, *w occurred as onset of the penult in a trisyllable. In this position, *w was lost (like *w < *b [§C6.3.31, 5th¶]):

*kawiɣi > *kairi* 'left (hand)'

C6.3.62 *y

*-y- > *-j-. This change also affects a [y] that developed intervocalically in pre-Bugis.

*buqaya > *buaja* 'crocodile' *mayaŋ > *majeng* 'stem with young areca fruit' *kasiw 'tree' > *aju* 'tree' (< *kayu < *kaiw)

*y was lost between *i and back vowels:

*liyan > *laing* 'other' (< Ml)

For *y at the end of a word, see §§C6.2.51, C6.2.52.

C6.4 The fate of word-final consonants

Bugis is well on the way to losing all word-final consonants. Only glottal stop and nasals occur in word-final position currently,[49] and the final glottal stop is variable in some

---

[48] I speculate that this prefix eventually remounts to the animal prefix *qaɬi-, but there is no confirmatory evidence.

forms: forms transcribed with a final glottal stop in the published sources in many cases lack the glottal stops in the speech of informants born after 1970, whom I recorded.
The following list gives a selection of forms that originate in PAn forms reconstructed with final voiced stops. Some have final glottal stops, others have open codas, and many vary:

*suwab > *ting-oa* 'yawn' *leɬeb > *leññeʔ* 'disappear' *paɬid > *panni* and *panniʔ* 'wing' *sated > *atteʔ* 'deliver' *idid 'move rapidly' > *iri* 'breeze' *laleg > *laleʔ* 'fly' *buleg > *bulu* 'hill' *lahuj 'seaward' > *a-lau* 'east' *lauʔ* 'sea'

The voiceless stops except for *q behaved in the same way as the voiced, as did the continuants *ɣ and *l. First, examples of the voiceless stops:

*qatep > *ateʔ* 'thatching' *dakep > *rao* 'embrace' *sabaɣat > *bareʔ* 'west monsoon' *sepat > *eppa* 'four' *berac > *berreʔ* 'rice' *ɬisebic >*nipi* 'thin' *tacetac > *ma-tetta* 'get undone' also *tettaʔ* 'cut into pieces' *buɣuk 'rotten' > *buruʔ* 'broken into little pieces' *nasuk > *nasu* 'cook in water'

Now, examples of final *ɣ and *l:

*aliɣ 'flow' > *ali* 'be carried by the current' *qawuɣ > *awoʔ* 'bamboo' *kasepal > *kapeʔ* 'thick' *pundul > *ma-kunru* 'dull'

Final*-q was lost entirely, but had an effect on the preceding vowel (§§C6.2.1, C6.2.2, C6.2.31):

*bunuq > *wuno* 'kill' *binesiq > *binɛɛ* 'seed' *ɬiteq > *lita* 'sticky sap'

C6.41 Pronunciation of the final consonants in text recitation

The pronunciation of the reflexes of the final consonants in readings of texts is far more regular than the variability described above. The following information summarizes what is presented in Sirk 1983: 29–37.[50] These rules apply for the most part, but there are exceptions (due to analogy):

(1) Final *-k > /ʔ/

*aɬak > *anaʔ* 'child' *manuk > *manuʔ* 'chicken'

(2) Final *eC$_{\text{not nasal}}$ is reflected with /eʔ/:

*beɣac > *berreʔ* 'rice'

(3) Other final consonants, apart from nasals, are lost with compensatory lengthening on the preceding vowel, except for *e (cf. (2), immediately preceding):

*akat > *akkā* 'lift' *caluɣ 'watercourse' > *salō* 'river'

There are exceptions: *buluʔ* 'mountain' has a final glottal stop and is not lengthened:

*buleg 'single hill' > *buluʔ* 'mountain'

---

[49] My informants identified a few MI borrowings with /-l/ as Bugis words. The borrowings are recent, and it is hard to know if monolingual speakers use them pronouncing /-l/. But certainly /-l/ is being reintroduced into the language:

*kumbal > *kumbal* 'stem of the leaf of a sago palm'

[50] I am grateful to U. Sirk for a long letter, expanding and clarifying this material for me in a personal communication.

CHAPTER SEVEN

Salayar

C7.0 Introduction

Salayar (Sal) is one of three closely related languages (or perhaps dialects of a single language), spoken in southwest Sulawesi: Macassarese (Mk), Konjo, and Sal, of which Mk has been a language of literature since the eighteenth century. Sal is spoken on the northern two-thirds of Salayar Island off the southwest coast of Sulawesi. Our sources are college students from Salayar, resident in Macassar in the summers of 1993 and 1994. The forms have been checked by Dr. Hassan Basri, a linguist of Hassanuddin University and a native speaker of Salayar. Since there is little published information on Salayar, and I was not destined to have direct access to Salayar informants again, in preparing this Chapter, I relied on Mk to fill in the gaps where I did not have Salayar citations. It turns out that Mk and Salayar largely underwent the same changes, and Mk citations from published sources can provide attestations.[1] Our Mk citations come from the dictionary (Cense 1994) and from Mills 1975.

Like other languages of the area, Sal has been strongly influenced by Ml and Bugis. Contact with both languages dates back several centuries as a result of Macassar's position as an entrepôt in the spice trade. There was apparently a great deal of population movement between the peripheral areas and Macassar, leading to linguistic and cultural influence over their population. Sal has made innovations together with Bugis, both on the level of phonology and in the make-up of individual lexical items. Cf. the comments at end of §C6.0, where the source of these common features is discussed.

The following chart lists the phonemes of Sal:

CHART ONE. PHONEMES OF SALAYAR

Consonants

voiceless stops	p	t	(c)	k
voiced stops	b	d	j	(g)
nasals	m	n	ñ	ng [ŋ]
liquids	w	r, l		
spirant		s		h

Vowels

high	i		u
mid	e [ɛ]		o
low		a	

Stress falls automatically on the penult or antepenult (as specified in §C7.4, below). There are no diphthongs, as is the case of the other languages of central and south Sulawesi. /g/

[1] Somewhat more than ninety of more than six hundred citations come from Mk.

does not occur in forms inherited directly from PMP or PAn. /c/ occurs only after /n/ in inherited forms.

C7.1 Changes that characterize Sal in general

A good portion of the developments detailed in the following sections also took place in Bug and other SW Sulawesi languages. (Cf. §C61.1ff. in Chapter Six.)

C7.1.1 Disyllabization of trisyllables

Sal tended to disyllabize roots, as did the other languages of the area. However, many trisyllabic roots remained trisyllabic. Further, the addition of echo vowels caused new trisyllabic roots to develop (§C7.1.74). Here is an example of the approximately fifteen trisyllabic roots that remained trisyllabic in Sal:

*bituqen > *bintoeng* 'star' (< *bintuqan)

Stems of four syllables are reflected as trisyllables, and in some cases, are reduced further to disyllables (§C7.1.12).

*ɣuqaɬay + *ba- > *buraʔne* 'male' *qaliɣuwan 'k.o. bee' > *beroang* 'beehive' *qaɬimateq > *linta* 'leech' (Mk *alinta*) *qaɬipugu > *tam-palesu* 'whorl' (< Bugis?) *qusalipan > *lipang* 'centipede' (< *alipang < *qasulipan)

C7.1.11 Syncope of the penult

*e in the penult of trisyllables was lost:

*baqeɣu > *bau* 'new' *beɣecay > *bise* 'oar' *qaɬegaw > *allo* 'day' (< *algaw < *alegaw) *qetaq + *ma- > *mata* 'raw' (< *maqetaq) *tahepa > *tapa* 'smoke to preserve' *tapes + -i > *tapi* 'winnow' (< *taspi < *tasepi)[2]

An *i in the penult was elided before *y onset of the final syllable:[3]

*miniyak > *miñña?* 'oil' *peniyu > *paññu* 'sea tortoise'

In sporadic cases, a penult with other vowels was lost. The first example reflects a change that happened in all of the MP languages that reflect the root—i.e., it took place in PMP. The other two cases are stems of four syllables, which evidently treated the penult differently from trisyllables.

*paŋudaɬ > *pandang* 'pandanus' *qalimateq > *linta* 'leech' (< *alinta) *ɣuqaɬay + *ba- > *buraʔne* 'male' (< *buɣaqnay < *buɣaqaɬay [§C7.1.6] < *baɣuqaɬay)

C7.1.12 Loss or weakening of the antepenult

The antepenult was lost in forms of three syllables with, *a-, *qa-, *i-, *qi-, *sa-, or *se- onsets.[4]

[2] We assume that metathesis of *tapes > *tasep occurred in PMP—i.e., pre-Salayar underwent the same metathesis undergone by other MP languages.

[3] Analogous elision of penultimate *u before *w does not seem to have taken place. In the first two examples, we assume that two *u's developed and subsequently contracted to a single /u/. In the third case, we assume that the /u/ before the /w/ is not epenthetic but inherited unchanged. This development was shared by Bug (§C61.11, footnote).

*dasuwen > *raung* 'leaf' (< *dasuun) *taquweɬ > *taung* 'year' (< *taquun) *banuwa > *wanua* 'village' *aqetih 'recede (water)' > *atti* 'low tide' *qapucuk > *pusuʔ* 'top of tree' *ikasu > *kau* 'you (sing)' *qalima > *lima* 'hand' *qiteluɣ > *tannoro* 'egg' *di + *atac > *rate* (< *irate < *riate) *sapegiq > *passe* 'smart (pain)' *sehapuy > *api* 'fire'

This also applies to trisyllables that developed from stems of four syllables:

*qałimateq > *linta* (< *alinta [Mk *alinta*]) *qusalipan > *lipang* 'centipede' (< *alipang < *qasulipan)

The antepenult was also lost in the following form, but there is no evidence that this exemplifies a regular sound change:

*ulun + *-an > *lungan* 'head-rest' (< *ulungan < *ulung + *-an—i.e., the root developed a final /ng/ [§C7.3.5] before the suffix was added)

In a number of cases, the antepenult was weakened rather than lost. In forms with *e in the penult, the *e of the penult was lost after the antepenult had been weakened. Some of these forms show the same development across a wide range of MP languages, while others are confined to Sal or to Sal and neighboring languages.
With loss of *e and weakening of the antepenult:

*biɣeŋi > *bangngi* 'night' *binesiq 'seed for sowing' > *banne* 'millet' *paqegu > *pidu* 'gall' (< *epegu ?) *iseci > *assi* 'contents, flesh' *paheɣaw > *parro* 'hoarse' (< *peɣaw)[5] *tineun > *tannung* 'weave'

Other cases of antepenult weakening:

*taseyup > *tui* 'blow' (< *tiu < *tiup < *teyup < *taeyup)

In the following case, metathesis took place before the rule of antepenultimate loss took effect. The antepenult was elided by the same rule that governed the loss of the penultimate *i before *y onset of the following syllable (§C7.1.11)—i.e., *i before a nonfront vowel was elided:

*sinawa 'breath' > *ñaha* 'soul' (< *ñawa < *niawa < *nisawa)

C7.1.2 Contraction

In some cases, when vowels came to abut after loss of intervening consonants or in affixation, contraction took place. Like vowels became single vowels if the contraction would not have produced a monosyllabic root—i.e., like vowels in stems of more than two syllables contracted:

*tusud > *kalan-tuʔ* 'knee' (< *tuud) *wanał + *ka- > *kanang* 'right side' (< *kaanan)

In the following case, the prefix was petrified and became part of the root so that contraction did not produce a monosyllable:

*busuk > *ma-boʔ* 'drunk'

Sequences *Ve that developed were contracted to /V/:

*betihec > *witiʔ* 'calf' (< *betis [§C7.2.36])

---

[4] Presumably, trisyllables with *e, *qe-, and *si- onsets lost the first syllable as well, but reflexes of trisyllables with these onsets have not been found.
[5] *Parro* must derive from *peɣaw because of the strengthened /rr/ (§C7.1.8).

*a + *i contracted to /e/, and *a + *u contracted to /o/:

*iseq + ma- > *mea* 'urine'(< *ma-ia) *qawuɣ > *oro* 'k.o. bamboo' *weliq + *pa- > *pole* 'again' (< *pa-uliq)

If the vowel sequence occurred in a root that was not affixed, the monosyllable that developed was disyllabized or contraction did not take place at all, for contraction was impeded by the rule that monosyllables are not tolerated (§C7.1.5):

*punuq 'brain' > *poʔong* 'trunk of tree (< *pong < *puqun [§C7.1.6]) *pasuq > *pao* 'mango'

C7.1.3 CC simplification

Sal allows no sequences of disparate consonants except for /ʔC/ and /NC/. Consonants also occur doubled. This situation was reached by the changes detailed in the following subsections:

C7.1.31 Nasals assimilated to the following consonant except *c and *d:

*biŋebiŋ > *bimbing* 'guide, lead by hand' *apu > *ampu* 'grandchild' (with nasal intercalation) *cumbu > *sunggu* 'wick' (change of *b > /g/ unexplained) *qaɬimateq > *linta* 'leech' (< *alimta)

Nasal + *d > /nr/:

*diŋediŋ > *rinring* 'wall' *isejam > *inrang* 'borrow' *kan > *-de > *kanre* 'eat' *tiduɣ > *tinro* 'sleep'

Nasals before *c were lost:

*cuɬ > *susung* 'stack up' (< *sunsun [§C7.1.5] < *sun)

The following forms are borrowed:

*diŋediŋ > *dinging* 'cold' (Ml *dingin*) *paŋudaŋ > *pandang* 'pandanus'

C7.1.32 Clusters that developed from a voiced stop or *ɣ coda followed by a consonant onset, changed the coda to /ʔ/:[6]

*qaɬi-muɣemuɣ > *kali-moʔmoro* 'rinse out mouth' *luɣeluɣ > *loʔloro* 'move fast (as water in a river)' *buɣebuɣ 'break into small bits' > *boʔboroʔ* 'corn or rice porridge' *bedebed 'wind' > *baʔbaʔ* 'bind by winding around'

The following form is not an exception. The coda *-b of the doubled monosyllabic root was changed to *w (§C7.3.31) before assimilation had taken place:

*lebeleb 'hidden by being covered' > *lullung* 'cover with cloth'

C7.1.33 *c assimilated to a following C, except when preceding *q, in which case *q > /s/—i.e., assimilated to the *c, which had become /s/. Further, a C (including *w) preceding *c (which became /s/) was assimilated to the /s/—i.e., *Cs, which developed from *Cc > /ss/:

[6] A *-ɣ coda becomes a glottal stop only in doubled monosyllabic roots. Otherwise *ɣ was lost when it had come to abut on a following C onset (§C7.3.41).

*liceqes > *ku-lissa* 'nit' (< *licqes) *kicekic 'grate, file' > *kekkese* 'remove bit by bit, dig' *cakecak > *sassaʔ* 'chop up' *cawcaw > *sassa* 'wash'

C7.1.34 *l assimilated to a following *c, but other consonants following *l became /l/:

*celecel > *sassala* 'regret' (< *selsel) *caleŋaɣ > *sallara* 'cook in pan without water' *qaɬegaw > *allo* 'day'

C7.1.35 Coda *t (and presumably *-p [§C7.41]—there are no attestations) became /ʔ/ before another consonant. Coda *-k assimilated to a following stop:

*butebut > *buʔbuʔ* 'pluck out' *tuketuk > *tottoʔ* 'peck (e.g., chicken)'

C7.1.36 Coda *q became /ʔ/ if abutting on a consonantal onset:

*diqediq > *reʔre* 'boil' *ɣuqaɬay + *ba- > *buraʔne* 'male' (< *buɣaqɬay < *buɣaqaɬay [§C7.1.6] < *baɣuqaɬay) *kaqekaq > *kaʔkaʔ* 'split open' (final /-ʔ/ by contamination) *basaq > *aʔba* (< *baʔah [§C7.1.6] < *baqas)

There are two exceptions, where the glottal stop, which presumably had developed from *-q, was lost. In the first case, possibly the final *-ʔ was lost to make the initial syllable like the final.[7] In the second case, the development is shared by other languages of Sulawesi and Kalimantan—i.e., the innovation occurred at a stage long before pre-Salayar:

*baqebaq > *baba* 'mouth' *qetaq + *ma- > *mata* 'raw' (< *maqtaq < *maqetaq)

C7.1.4 Assimilation of liquids

/r/ (< *d, *j)[8] onset of the penult is assimilated to /l/ or /ng/ onset of the final syllable:

*dalem > *lalang* 'inside' *dilaq > *lila* 'tongue' *deŋeɣ > *langngere* 'hear' *jalan > *lalang* 'road'

C7.1.5 Disyllabization of monosyllabic roots

There is an on-going tendency to turn monosyllabic roots that were not enclitic into disyllables. This process has affected inherited Pan monosyllabic roots and those that developed in pre-Salayar. This process took place, as in other An languages, in one of three ways: (1) by stretching the root to two moras by addition of a pretonic vowel, a reflex of *e, or lengthening of the vocalic nucleus, (2) doubling of the monosyllabic root or (2a) reduplication of the root, (3) petrifaction of an affix—that is, re-interpretation of an affixed form as a single root. Examples of (1):

*bukes > *uhuʔ* 'hair' (< *ubuk < *buuk < *buk < *busek) *sepat > *appa* 'four'[9] (< *pat) *ɣiq > *rea* 'saw grass' (< *re) *taw > *tau* 'person'

Examples of (2):

*cuɬ > *susung* 'stack up' (< *sunsun < *sun) *kud > *kukkuru* 'grate'

Examples of (2a):

---

[7] A parallel development is the case of *palopa* 'palm frond' < *palaqpaq, but this form is probably secondary (§C7.2.4), and there is a countercase, *reʔre* 'boil' < *diqediq, where the /ʔ/ is not lost.

[8] Presumably, /r/ < *ɣ would also be assimilated, but there are no examples inherited from PMP or PAn

[9] The enclitic allomorph *pat, which developed from *sepat in prothetic position, was generalized.

*tec > *tetese* 'undone' *tup > *tutuʔ* 'closed'

Examples of (3):

*busuk 'drunk' > *ma-boʔ* 'drunk, seasick' (< *ma-busuk)[10] *kan + *de > *kanre* 'eat'

Monosyllabic roots that occur in compounds do not disyllabize:

*tusud > *kala-tuʔ* 'knee' (< *tud [§C7.1.2] < *tuud) *pat 'four' + *aN 'linker' + *puluq 'ten's' > *patampulo* 'forty'

C7.1.6 Metathesis

Sal evinces the metathesis that affected all of the MP languages—i.e., metathesis that occurred well before Sal times and a fairly large number of cases of metathesis that occurred only in Sal or in Sal and neighboring languages. In many cases we can only infer the metathesis from the other sound changes the root underwent. Some of the following forms are in fact not directly inherited, and it is unknown if they were borrowed in metathesized form of if they were metathesized in Sal after having been borrowed:

*basaq > *aʔba* 'flood' (< *baʔa < *baa) *bukes > *uhuʔ* 'hair' (< *ubuk < *buuk < *buk < *busek) *di atac > *rate* 'up' (< *irate < *riate) *ɣuqaɬay + *ba- > *buɣaʔne* 'male' (< *buɣaqɬay < *buɣaqaɬay < *baɣuqaɬay) *kakac 'undone' > *kiakkasa* 'open (flower) (< *ki-kakasa) *labeɣ > *laʔbaʔ* 'wide' (< *lebaɣ [influenced by Ml *lebar*]) *lubaŋ > *balo* 'hole' (loss of *-ŋ unexplained) *mula > *lamung* 'to plant' (for /-ng/, cf.§C7.1.72) *punuq 'brain' > *poʔong* 'tree trunk' (< *puung < *puqun) *qawec > *soso* 'worn down' (< *osos < *os) *qudaŋ > *dowang* 'shrimp' *sinawa 'breath' > *ñaha* 'soul' (< *niawa < *nisawa) *taseyup > *tuiʔ* 'puff, blow' (< *tiup < *teyup < *taeyup)

C7.1.7 Accretion of consonants and vowels

C7.1.71 Prenasalization of consonants

Sal evinces sporadic prenasalization of the final syllable of the penult, as is widespread in Hesperonesian languages (§A3.7.1). Some of these cases of prenasalization are shared by many of the Hesperonesian languages, but a few of them are peculiar to Sal or Sal and its neighboring languages. Here are a few of them:

*apu > *ampu* 'grandchild' *bituqen > *bintoeng* 'star' *cek 'cram' > *onco* 'squeeze in between' (< *um- + *cek) *metik > *kalu-manti* 'k.o. ant' *nituq > *nintu* 'a vine used for tying' *qabuk 'dust' > *ambu* 'smoke' *tiduɣ > *tinro* 'sleep'

C7.1.72 Nasal accretion at the end of a word

A few forms evince accretion of /ng/ at the end of the word. Some of these forms had previously ended in a vowel, but some had ended in a consonant and substituted /ng/ for the final consonant. There is no environment that determines the occurrence of /-ng/, and there is no explanation. (Cf. §C6.1.71, where the same phenomenon is described for Bugis, but note

[10] This is a disyllabic root that became monosyllabic when the medial *s was lost and the vowels on either side of the lost *s contracted (§C7.1.2). The monosyllabic root only occurred affixed, and when the prefix *ma- became nonproductive, the affixed form was reinterpreted as a root.

that the Bugis forms that have the /-ng/ accretion are not cognate.) Here are the attestations in my Sal data. There are others that occur in Mk:

> *kutała > *kutaʔnang* 'ask'(/ʔ/ also unexplained) *lebeleb 'hidden by being covered' > *lullung* 'cover over' *limpa > *lempang* 'spleen' *mula > *lamung* 'plant' *naquɣ > *naung* 'decend'

C7.1.73 Accretion of /ʔ/

In disyllables,[11] when a sequence of like vowels developed from loss of a medial consonant or semivowel, a glottal stop was intercalated between the two vowels to separate them.[12] Similarly, if a monosyllable was disyllabized by lengthening the vowel nucleus, a glottal stop developed between the two moras. If *ʔ had developed at the end of the root, it was lost in most cases:

> *cawa 'python' > *saʔa* 'snake' *dasak > *ka-raʔaʔ* 'phlegm' *jaqet > *daʔa* 'bad' (< *da [/d/ unexplained]) *punuq > *poʔong* 'tree trunk' (< *puun < *pun < *puqun) *tuqed > *toʔo* (< *tooʔ [§C7.2.25)] < *tuuʔ < *tuʔ)

The following example lost medial *-c and did not develop a medial glottal stop. It is a word that has spread secondarily:

> *pacu > *pooʔ* 'pot'

/ʔ/ was added sporadically at the end of forms ending in a vowel or in the consonants that accreted an echo vowel (*ɣ,*l, *q, or*c).[13] These are, for the most part, forms that evince other irregularities and are either borrowed or were influenced by other words of similar meaning:

> *baɣaq > *parruʔ* 'lungs' *bakul > *bakuʔ* 'basket' *bukul 'knob-shaped protrusion' > *bukkuʔ* 'hunchback' *kaqekaq > *kaʔkaʔ* 'split open' *labeɣ > *laʔbaʔ* 'wide' *lawa 'spider' > *lawaʔ-lawaʔ* 'spider-web' (-ʔ on contamination with word for 'net', *lawaq [no reflex in Sal attested]) *caluɣ 'watercourse' > *saloʔ* 'water conduit on roof' *luwaq > *me-ruaʔ* 'vomit' *palisi > *ka-palliʔ* 'taboo' *lapił > *lapiʔ* 'cloth' *putaq > *pitaʔ* 'foam' *seqałi 'string a loom' > *ng-anniʔ* 'make threads' *ɣetac 'break open' > *rontoʔ* 'take seeds out (beans)' *tebas > *teʔbaʔ* 'hit with machete' *titic > *mattiʔ* 'drip' *wakaɣ > *akaʔ* 'root'

The following form has an unexplained /ʔ/ that developed before a medial consonant:

> *kutała > *kutaʔnang* 'ask'

C7.1.74 Echo vowels

The consonants that developed into continuants in Sal—PAn *-c, *-ɣ and *-l, developed echo vowels at the end of the root that are the same as the vowel of the final syllable. (Cf. §§C7.4ff. for a discussion of the fate of the final consonants in general.) In Mk, a glottal stop developed after the echo vowel, but in Sal there is no final glottal stop after an echo vowel except in forms borrowed from Mk. The stress, which had fallen on the root

---

[11] In the case of stems of more than two syllables or in compounds, the like vowels contracted (§C7.1.2)

[12] At a later stage, /h/ was intercalated rather than /ʔ/. Cf. the discussion in §§C7.3.31, C7.3.61.

[13] In those cases, /ʔ/ replaced the consonant plus the echo vowel.

penult in pre-Salayar, remained in the same position after the echo vowel had been added, giving rise to antepenultimate stress in the case of forms with echo vowels. Here are three examples:

*besuɣ > *bássoro* 'sated' *kasepal > *kápala* 'thick' *salac > *álasa* 'forest'

There are a few exceptions to the addition of echo vowels discussed in §§C7.4ff.

C7.1.8 Strengthening of consonants

The syllable onset is STRENGTHENED[14] after an *e that was not lost by syncope (§C7.1.11). Strengthening also took place in the simplification of CC's (§§7.1.3ff.). In Sal strengthening involves insertion of a glottal stop before a voiced onset[15] after an *e or after a C that was lost and involves doubling after an *e or a lost C before the other consonants:

*kebel > *kaʔbala* *qadep > *m-aʔraʔ* 'to face' (< *m-edap) *sejen > *m-aʔrang* 'strain in defecating'

Other consonants (except the consonants that were lost *q, *s, and *h and the semivowels *y and *w) strengthened by doubling:

*sepat > *appaʔ* 'four' *betehus > *battu* 's.o. who has just appeared' (< *betu) *jeket > *dakkiʔ* 'stick, adhere' (/d/ and /i/ by contamination) *keɣet 'cut off' > *karraʔ* 'cut into slices' *beli > *halli* 'buy' *peɬuq > *pannu* 'full' *becuɣ > *bassoro* 'sated' *iseci > *assi* 'contents, flesh' (< *eci) *lemaq > *lamma* 'weak' *enem > *annang* 'six' *deŋeɣ > *langngere* 'hear' *peniyu > *paññu* 'sea tortoise' (< *peñu)

In one case /l/ is strengthened to /ʔl/ instead of being doubled. Probably this is a dialect borrowing:

*celat > *saʔlaʔ* 'straits'

If prenasalization of the penultimate or earlier onset developed (§C7.1.71), strengthening did not take place:

*-metik > *kalu-manti* 'k.o. ant'

There are a few cases where strengthening failed to take place. There is no explanation as to why strengthening failed to take place:

*celem 'sink' > *selang* 'be under water' *baɣehat > *beraʔ* 'heavy' *beɣac > *berasa* 'rice' *peɣaq > *pera* 'squeeze out, wring out' *teɣac 'k.o. hardwood' > *terasa* 'hard' *tec + R- > *tetese* 'come undone'

---

[14] I use the term 'strengthen' in the discussion of several languages. The process is similar phonetically in the various languages in which strengthening occurs, but the processes developed independently and took place independently (cf. §C6.1.8, first footnote).

[15] There are in fact no attestations of an inherited from reflecting *e before a *d or a *g onset. The one form that reflects *egV in the penult and final syllable reflects /ssV/, very likely to have been borrowed from Bugis, for *g only becomes /s/ in Bugis when onset to the final syllable:

*sapegiq > *passe* 'smart, stinging (pain)'

C.7.1.81 Cases of irregular strenghthening

There are a few cases where strengthening took place in environments other than after *e or in a CC that was simplified. In some cases, the form reflects prenasalization of a syllable onset influenced by Bugis or another language in which prenasalized consonants are reflected as doubled consonants (§C6.1.8, 3rd¶):

*baŋkay > *bakke* 'corpse' *bukul 'knob-shaped protrusion' > *bukku?* 'hunchback'

Metathesis accounts for one case:

*kakac 'undone' > *kiakkasa* 'open (flower) (< *ki-kakasa)

For some cases, there is no explanation. Some of these forms have probably been contaminated by other forms of similar meaning with doubled consonants:

*ala > *alle* 'take' *ama > *amma* 'father' *bulehaɣ > *bulla?* 'cataract' *cicik 'scales' > *sissi?* 'k.o. turtle with thick shell' *dakat 'take a step' > *dakka* 'walk' *ini > *inni* 'this' *tu + *i- > *ittu* 'that'[16] *lilin > *lilling* 'beeswax' *palisi > *ka-palli?* 'taboo' *pilit > *pilli?* 'sticky' *sacaŋ > *assang* 'gills' *seqaɫi 'string a loom' > *ng-anni?* 'make thread'

C7.2 Vowels and diphthongs

Sal has added two vowels to the PAn four-vowel system, /e/ ([ɛ]) and /o/ and lost *e—i.e., the Sal vowels are /i, e ([ɛ]), a, o, u/. /e/ and /o/ developed in a large number of the cases from the diphthongs *ay and *aw, respectively, and from lowering of *i and *u in certain environments. The following sections provide details.

C7.2.1 *i

The most general case is is that *i > /i/:

*biŋebiŋ > *bimbing* 'guide, lead by hand' *inum > *inung* 'drink' *binaŋa > *binanga* 'mouth of river' *kawiɣi > *kairi* 'left' *nasik 'go up'> *nai?* 'climb'

*i is lowered before *-q (which subsequently was lost at the end of a word):

*diqediq > *reʔre* 'boil' *piliq > *pile* 'choose'

Penultimate *i is sporadically lowered before /a/ and /o/ in the following syllable. The explanation probably lies in dialect mixture—i.e., these forms came into Sal by contact with an unidentified language or dialect that had vowel harmony:

*balikat > *baleka?* 'shoulder blade' *biluk > *belo?* 'veer' *iɣaq > *eja* 'red' *qitem > *etang* 'black' *limpa > *lempang* 'spleen' *timpaŋ > *kempang* 'lame' (/k/ unexplained)

The normal reflex of penultimate *i before /a/ or /o/ in the final syllable is /i/:

*ina > *ina* 'mother' *diɣuq > *rio* 'bathe'

There are several other cases of lowering of /i/ that are unexplained. These case are in forms borrowed from an unidentified source:

---

[16] *Inni* 'this' and *ittu* 'that' developed prenasalization of the final syllable onset (§C7.1.71). *Ittu* developed under the influence of a language or dialect that changed *nt > /tt/ (as, for example, Bugis). There is a variant *intu* 'that', which reflects the normal Sal reflection of a nasal cluster with /t/.

*balik > *bale?* 'return' *kicekic 'grate, file' > *kekkese* 'remove bit by bit, dig' *kitiŋ 'tendon at wrist or heel' > *keteng-keteng* 'connection between the foot and the leg (the analog of the wrist)' *qaɬipugu > *tam-palesu* 'whorl' (cf. Bugis *palɛsu* [§C6.2.1, 4th¶]) *saɬid > *aññere* 'fetid, smell of fish'

The *i that developed from *uy (§C7.2.52) also lowered in one unexplained case. Note that the Bugis cognate also lowered the *i unexpectedly:

*ɬaŋuy > *lange* 'swim' (cf. Bugis *nangɛ* 'swim')

C7.2.2 *u

C7.2.21 The most general case is that *u > /u/:

*ɣucuk 'ribs' > *rusu?* 'ribs' *bukebuk > *bu?bu?* 'wood-borer'

C7.2.22 *u was lowered to /o/ before *q (cf. the lowering of *-i before *q [§C7.2.1, above]):

*bunuq > *huno* 'kill' *peɬuq > *panno* 'full'

In the following cases, *u was not lowered before *q. The first three of the following examples, were probably influenced by Ml. The last is borrowed from neighboring language. In them, *u failed to lower:

*aɣusuq > *eru* 'the Australian pine' (cf. Ml *eru*) *ɬabuq 'fall' > *labu* 'anchor, sink' (cf. Ml *labuh* 'anchor') *lumpuq > *lumpu* 'lame' (cf. Ml *lumpuh*) *nituq > *nintu* 'k.o. vine used for tying'

C7.2.23 In sporadic cases, *u was lowered to /o/ before /a/ in the following syllable. Some of them have Ml cognates with /o/ in the pronunciation normal in south Sulawesi, and are probably influenced by that. Others are probably cases of dialect mixture, but no evidence has been published to substantiate that hypothesis:

*ɣuwaŋ > *a-roang* 'ship's bilge' *qaɬiɣuwan 'bee' > *beroang* 'beehive' *buŋkaɣ > *bongkara* 'take apart' (Ml *bongkar*) *busekag > *bongkara* 'open (flower)' (this form may have been contaminated by *bongara* 'take apart' [also *bungkara*]) *qudaŋ > *dowang* 'shrimp' *ɬuwaŋ 'opening' > *ga-lowang* 'hole' *qumaŋ > *kala-omang* 'hermit crab' *gusam > *kosang* 'thrush' *lumba > *lomba* 'race' (Ml *lomba*) *tulak 'push away' *tolla?* 'refuse' (Ml *tolak* [tola?] 'refuse') *tuqas > *towa* 'old' *tunac 'sucker, shoot from bottom of tree' > *tonasa* 'heartwood'

C7.2.24 *u was normally lowered to /o/ before final *-ɣ.

*qapuɣ > *kaporo* 'lime' (influenced by Ml *kapur* 'lime') *qatuɣ 'arrange in a stack, line' > *atoro* 'form a row' *qiteluɣ > *tannoro* 'egg' *suluɣ > *uloro* 'lower rope' *tiduɣ > *tinro* 'sleep' *timuɣ > *timoro* 'east wind'

There are a few cases in which the lowering does not take place in this environment. In some cases, it is likely that contact with Ml was part of the cause of the failure of *u lower in this environment.

*becuɣ > *bassoro* 'sated' *dapuɣ > *dapuru* 'stove' (cf. Ml *dapur* 'kitchen') *ɬuɣ > *ñiuru* 'k.o. small areca' (but also *ñjoro* 'coconut') (Ml *niur* 'coconut') *qaɬi-muɣemuɣ > *kalimo?moro* 'rinse out the mouth'

C7.2.25 *CuCe(C) > /CoCo(?)/—i.e.,*u in the penult and *e in the final syllable changed to /o/:

*cequɬ > *soʔong* 'carry on the head' *kuden > *korong* 'cooking pot' *puceg > *posoʔ* 'navel' *quleg > *oloʔ* 'worm' *qutek > *otoʔ* 'brains' *tuqed > *toʔo* 'stump'

The following two cases are exceptions. The third example is influenced by Ml:

*buleg > *buluʔ* 'high mountain' *buɣes > *burusang* 'spill out' (/s/ also unexplained. It is probably a contaminated form.) *puket > *puka* 'large hauling net' (Ml *pukat*)

The following rule is a corollary: if a root developed two /u/'s separated by hiatus or a glottal stop, the /u/'s were lowered to /o/:

*busuk > *ma-boʔ* 'drunk' (< *ma-buuk) *punuq > *poʔong* 'tree trunk' (< *puqun)

C7.2.26 If /o/ developed in the final syllable, penultimate /u/ was lowered. However, this process occurred before the change of *u of the final syllable to /o/, as described in §§C7.2.22 and C7.2.23, above, or before the change of *aw > /o/ (§C7.2.53)—i.e., *u in the penult was not lowered before final syllables with *uq, *uɣ, or *aw. The rule of vowel harmony only affected the cases of final /o/ that were not regular—i.e., forms that had been borrowed or had been affected by analogies. The /o/ of the final syllables in these words is unexplained:

*ɬuka > *loko* 'wound' *tudaŋ > *tolong* 'sit' *tuketuk > *tottoʔ* 'peck' *tukup > *tongkoʔ* 'cover, lid'

C7.2.27 In the following examples, *u > /o/ with no explanation. In some case there was Ml influence, but not in all of them:

*biluk > *beloʔ* 'veer' (Ml *bɛloʔ*) *bituqen > *bintoeng* 'star'[17] *bunag > *bone* 'sand' (contaminated with *qenay 'sandy soil', not attested in Sal) *cuduŋ > *sorong* 'push forward' (Ml *sorong*) *lubaŋ > *balo* 'hole' (§C7.1.6) *suni > *oni* 'noise'

C7.2.28 In three cases, *u is reflected with an unexplained /i/. In the last case, a reflex with /i/ is so widespread among the Hesperonesian languages, that I hypothesize a variation in PMP (cf. †tiduɣ in the glossary):

*duyuŋ > *diyung* 'sea cow' *tubuq > *timbo* 'grow' (Konjo *tuho*) *tuduɣ/†tiduɣ > *tinro* 'sleep'

C7.2.3 *e

The following rules govern the development of *e's that were not elided (§C7.1.11):

C7.2.31 *e >/a/ in closed final syllables[18] or in nonfinal syllables that came to be closed by medial consonant strengthening (§C7.1.8), by loss of the epenthetic vowel in doubled monosyllabic roots, or by insertion of a nasal (§C7.1.71):

---

[17] Note that the /e/ of the final syllable is also irregular. Bugis *wittoɛng* shares this innovation (§C6.2.33), as do reflexes in all of the languages of S. Sulawesi (as is noted by Mills 1975: 651). The source of the innovation is unknown. The lowering of the /o/ is normal in Bugis.

[18] With the exception of closed final syllables that developed echo vowels (§§C7.2.32, C7.42, C7.44).

*bedebed 'spool, wind' > *ba?ba?* 'bind by winding s.t. around' *becuɣ > *bassoro* 'sated' *deŋeɣ > *langngere* 'hear' *qetut > *attu* 'break wind' *sejen > *m-a?rang* 'strain to move bowls, give birth' *tałek 'boil starch' > *tana?* 'make oil out of coconut' *tałem > *tanang* 'plant'

As a corollary to this rule, *e in final syllables became /a/ before *l, *q, or *s. *l developed an echo vowel (§C7.1.74); *q and *s were lost:

*celecel > *sassala* 'regret' *gatel > *katala* 'itchy' *kebel > *ka?bala* 'invulnerable' *liceqes > *ku-lissa* (< *ku-licqes) *iseq > *m-ea* 'urine' (< *ma-ia [§7.1.2] < *ma-ieq) *łiteq 'sticky sap' > *rita* 'k.o. tree that produces a sticky sap' (borrowed) *qałimateq > *linta* 'leech' *tałeq > *tana* 'earth' *tumes > *tuma-tuma* 'clothes louse'

In a few cases, *e failed to change to /a/ in a closed syllable. In the first two cases, Ml influence is the probable explanation. The third was probably contaminated, and the last three were probably influenced by a neighboring language or dialect that reflected *e with /e/:

*batek 'splotch' > *bate?* 'batik' (Ml *batik*) *tapel > *tempele* 'stick on to s.t.' (Ml *tεmpεl*) *pekuq > *pekko?* 'bent' *tebas > *te?ba* 'cut with a machete' *tepak > *tempa* 'slap' *pan > *eppang* 'bait' (< *epan [§C7.1.5])

C7.2.32 *e became /e/ before final *-c and*-ɣ, which developed echo vowels:

*deŋeɣ > *langngere* 'hear' *kepec > *kempese* 'deflated' *tecetec > *tetese* 'for stitches to become undone'

C7.2.33 *e >/e/ in syllables that remained open in Sal. The following examples show an /e/ in the penult that failed to cause doubling of the onset of the final (§C7.1.8). The *e became /e/ because the penult remained open:

*baɣehat > *bera?* 'heavy' (< *beɣehat) *beɣac > *berasa* 'hulled rice' *celem 'sink' > *selang* 'be under water' *peɣac > *pera* 'wring out' *teɣac > *terasa* 'hard'

C7.2.34 *e in the final syllable became /a/ before other consonants in other cases where there was Ml influence:

*balec > *balasa* 'answer' (Cf. Ml *balas*)

C7.2.35 Vowel harmony affected *e in stems that had *u and *e as described in §C7.2.25. The *u was lowered to /o/ and /e/ became assimilated to /o/:

*kuden > *korong* 'clay cooking pot' *puceg > *poso?* 'navel' *quleg > *olo?* 'worm' *cequł > *so?ong* 'carry on head'

There are a few other cases in which *e > /o/. They are probably borrowed from an unidentified source. Note that in some of these cases, the Bugis cognate also evinces an irregular /o/:

*baɣeq 'abcess' > *amboro* 'swell' *beŋel > *bongolo* 'deaf' *cek 'stuff, chock full' > *osso?* 'push, shove through' (< *ecek [§C7.1.5]) *ɣetac 'break through' > *ronto?* 'take out the seed (e.g., of a dry bean)' *łepełep 'suck on' > *ño?ño?* 'slurp (as water from plate)' (*ɬ reflected with /ñ/ is irregular [§C7.3.43, 4th¶]) *pacek 'wedge' > *pasoʔ* 'peg' *teken > *tokong* 'pole for pushing a boat'

C7.2.36 There are a few unexplained cases in which *e became /i/. These forms are very likely to have been borrowed, but the source has not been identified. In the case of the first example, the change of *e > /i/ is found in Bugis and Mgg as well (and is not a normal development in any of them); the second example has an irregular /i/ in cognates ranging from the Philippines through southeast Sulawesi.[19] Note that all three of the first three examples have *e in the antepenult of a trisyllabic root, which possibly might be the environment that caused the change of *e to /i/ (although this is not a general rule for Sal):

*beɣecay > *bise* 'oar' *betihec > *bitisi* 'calf' (for /i/ < *ihe, cf. §C7.1.2) *ceŋet > *sangngi* 'smell of urine'

C7.2.37 The sequence *ew > /u/ and *ey > /i/. Also *ew that developed from syllable final *eb became /u/ (i.e., *eb > *ew > /u/):

*lebeleb 'hidden by being covered' > *lullung* 'cover over with cloth, water, etc.' (< *lewlew + ng [§C7.1.72]) *caweŋ > *sawung* 'sun hat' *taquweɬ > *taung* 'year' *laqeya > *laia* 'ginger' *taseyup > *tuiʔ* 'blow' (< *tiup < *teyup < *taeyup)

C7.2.4 *a

In general *a > /a/:

*aɬak > *ana* 'son, daughter' *salac > *alasa* 'forest'

There are a very few exceptions, all of them in words that have been reformed or borrowed. First, there are two forms, probably influenced by Bugis, where /e/ is the normal reflex of /a/ in a closed final syllable (§C6.2.4):

*agan > *areng* 'name' (Bugis *aseng*) *bulawan > *bulaeng* 'gold' (Bugis *bulaeng*)

In the following form there is no attestation in any language to account for the /e/ nor of the double /ll/:

*ala > *alle* 'take'

In a couple of roots consisting of doubled monosyllables with an *a-nucleus, the first *a is changed to /o/ (probably from *ə), a development characterizing some languages with which this group was in contact directly or indirectly (e.g. Pamona, §C5.2.41). This development is not the normal development in Sal:

*dapedap > *dodaʔ* 'k.o. tree: *Erythrina* sp.' *paqepaq + -al- > *palopa* 'palm branch' (< *palaqpaq) (loss of *q also not explained [§C7.1.36])

There are three cases where *a was in a disyllabic root with *u or *e in the other syllable that developed irregularily to /o/. In those cases, the *a assimilated to the /o/ (i.e., > /o/):

*baɣeq 'abscess' > *amboro* 'swell' *ɣetac 'break through' > *rontoʔ* 'take out (e.g., seed from pod)' *ɬuka > *loko* 'wound'

[19] Cb has irregular *bitiʔis* as a variant of the form with the normal reflex *batiʔis*. The development of /i/ in the antepenult there is likely to be connected with the /i/ in languages of south and southeast Sulawesi, for some of the languages in between also show /i/ in the antepenult (cf. the listing in the glossary under *betihec).

In one case, *a irregularly assimilated to the /e/ that had developed in the final syllable. This innovation also affected Bugis and is probably borrowed from there (or possibly Bugis borrowed from Sal or both borrowed from another language) (cf. §C6.2.4, end):

*latay > *lete* 'narrow bridge'

In one case, *a seems to have been replaced by /i/ by some unknown analogy:

*paqegu > *pidu* 'gall (< *paqgu [cf. the 2nd footnote to §C7.3.33])

*a is also replaced by /i/ in a word of secondary spread:

*lampuyaŋ > *limpuyang* 'k.o. ginger'

C7.2.5 Diphthongs

Sal has no diphthongs. Inherited diphthongs were monophthongized, as described in the following subsections.

C7.2.51 *ay

*ay > /e/:

*cakay > *sake* 'climb' *matay > *mate* 'die' *qatay < *ate* 'liver'

*ay > /ai/ in monosyllables:

*cay > *nai* 'who?' (nasalized initial [§A3.7.1])

C7.2.52 *uy and*iw

*uy and *iw > /i/:

*babuy > *bahi* 'pig' *sehapuy > *api* 'fire' *laɣiw 'flee' > *lari* 'run'

There are exceptions. In the word for 'wood', as in other languages, the *s became †h and syllabicity shifted. Subsequently, †h was lost. After that, medial *y developed and then was strengthened to /j/ (§C7.3.62):

*kasiw 'tree, wood' > *kaju* 'wood, stick'

In the following case, the final /-i/, which had developed, was lowered to /e/. This development was shared by Bugis. There is no explanation for it in either Bugis or Sal:

*łaŋuy > *lange* 'swim'

C7.2.53 *aw

*aw >/o/:

*balábaw > *balaho* 'rat' *qałegaw > *allo* 'day' *capaw 'hut > *sapo* 'house'

/aw/ in monosyllables > /au/:

*taw > *tau* 'man'

The following form is an exception, probably due to contact with an unidentified language or dialect:

*liŋaw 'confused' > *lingu* 'make an error' (Mk *lingu* 'confused, feverish')

The following form, consisting of a doubled monosyllable, possibly simplified the final diphthong to bring it into conformity with the initial syllable:

*caw > *sassa* 'wash out (body orifices)' (< *cawcaw)

C7.3 Consonants in initial and medial position

In this section and its subsections, the reflexes of the PAn consonants in initial and medial position are discussed. Like other languages of central and south Sulawesi, Sal is moving toward developing open syllables, and the number of possible final contrasts has been reduced to three: glottal stop, /-ng/ or ∅ (final vowel). The reflexes of PAn final consonants are discussed in §C7.4.

CHART TWO. DEVELOPMENT OF THE SALAYAR CONSONANTS FROM PAN

PAn	Sal	PAn	Sal
p	*p*	ɣ	*r*
t	*t*	l	*l*
k	*k*	ɬ	*n, l*
q, s, h	*∅*	m	*m*
c	*s*	n	*n*
b	*b-, -h-*	ŋ	*ng* [ŋ], *n*
d, j	*r*	w	*w*
g	*k-, -r-*	y	*j*

C7.3.1 Voiceless stops

C7.3.11 *p

Except when changed in clusters (§C7.1.35), *p > /p/:

*pan > *eppang* 'bait' *pitu > *pitu* 'seven' *sehapuy > *api* 'fire'

C7.3.12 *t

Except when changed in clusters (§C7.1.35), *t > /t/:

*taqi > *tai* 'feces' *telu > *tallu* 'three' *qatep > *ataʔ* 'thatch' *batu > *batu* 'stone'

An exception is *talicay > *dalise* 'a tree: *Terminalia*'. This is not directly inherited.

C7.3.13 *k

Except when changed in clusters (§C7.1.35), *k > /k/:

*kasiw > *kaju* 'tree, wood' *kasu > *kau* 'you (sg)' *kaɬuskus > *kanuku* 'finger- or toenail' *wakaɣ > *akaʔ* 'root' *pukuh > *buku* 'knuckle, knot, bone'

C7.3.14 *q

*q was lost entirely, except (a) that final *-q affected a preceding *e (§C7.2.31) and (b) in clusters that developed (cf. §C7.1.36):

*paqit > *paiʔ* 'bitter' *panaq > *pana* 'arrow' *qatep > *ataʔ* 'thatching' *pasuq > *pao* 'mango'

C7.3.15 *c

Except when changed in clusters (§C7.1.33), *c > /s/:[20]

*becuɣ > *bassoro* 'sated' *liceqes > *ku-lissa* 'nit' *cakay 'climb up onto'> *sake* 'climb (mountain)' *cequɬ > *soʔong* 'carry on the head'

In one case *c is reflected in a nasalized form (§A3.7.1):

*cay > *nai* 'who?'

C7.3.2 *h, *s

*h and *s were lost without a trace, except that final *-s affected a preceding *e (§C7.2.31):

*lahuj > *lauʔ* 'sea' *tahepa > *tapa* 'smoke to preserve' *baɣah > *bara* 'embers'

*sapaɣ > *apara* 'spread out (mat)' *sepat > *appaʔ* 'four' *basequ 'smell' > *hau* 'sniff' *busat > *buaʔ* 'make' *kasepal > *kapala* 'thick' *tuqas > *towa* 'old'

C7.3.3 Voiced stops

The languages of the Macassarese group do not evince the double reflexes of voiced *b, *d, and *g, manifested in Bug and Muna (and in the other languages of south Sulawesi).

C7.3.31 *b

PAn *b > initial /b-/ and medial /-h-/:[21]

*babuy > *bahi* 'pig' *bahi + R-in > *bahine* 'woman' *bubu > *buhu* 'fish trap' *balabaw > *balaho* 'rat' *ɣabun > *rahung* 'fog' *qubi > *uhi* 'yam'

However when protected by /ʔ/ (§C7.1.8) or /m/ (§C7.1.71), *b remains /b/:

*bedebed 'wind around' > *baʔbaʔ* 'bind by winding twine around' *ɣebaq 'fallen in' > *raʔba* 'fall from standing position' *tabun > *tambung* 'pile up'

There is one example that makes it seem likely that a preceding *q also protected *b:[22]

*baqebaq > *baba* 'mouth' (< *baʔbaʔ < *baqbaq)

Roots that occur with vowel-final prefixes may generalize the /h/ that developed from the initial *b- that occurred in a prefixed form:

*beli > *halli* 'buy' *basequ 'smell' > *hau* 'sniff'

Metathesis of the penult and the final syllables caused medial *-b- to become initial *b- in the following case:

*lubaŋ hole'> *balo* 'hole'(< *baŋlo [with unexplained loss of *-ŋ] < *baŋlu)

---

[20] However, when prenasalized (§C7.1.71), the /s/ that had developed became /c/.

*cek 'cram' + *um- > *onco* 'squeeze in between in a tight place'

[21] /h/ developed from /w/—i.e. *-b- > -w- (as in Mk). Subsequently intervocalic *w (< *w [§C7.3.61] as well as from *b) was lost, and [h] developed as a transition in the hiatus that had been left by the loss of *w.

[22] We hypothesize that *q > *ʔ, which subsequently was lost (although it is unknown why *ʔ was lost [§C7.1.36, end]). Before [ʔ] was lost, the change of *-b- > [w] took place, so that the *ʔ < *q protected the *b.

A couple of forms that evince intervocalic /b/ < *b have been borrowed from Ml or influenced by Ml:

*labuq > *labu* 'anchor, sink'[23] *busuk > *mabo?* 'drunk' (Ml *mabuk*)

In one case of a form borrowed from Ml, the loss of *-b- took place but transitional /h/ did not develop. This is probably accounted for by a hypothesis that this form was borrowed via Mk:

*cabung > *saung* 'cockfights'

C7.3.32 *d *j

*d and *j fell together as /r/.

*d > /r/:

*dakep 'catch' > *raka?* 'hold in embrace' *daki > *raki* 'dirt on skin' *depa > *rappa* 'fathom' *diɣuq > *rio* 'bathe' *dusa > *rua* 'two' *kuden > *korong* 'cooking pot' *seden > *m-aʔrang* 'strain in childbirth' *tingadaq 'look upwards' > *tingara* 'facing upwards' *tiduɣ > *tinro* 'sleep' (with development of nasal before the medial consonant and loss of final *-ɣ [§C7.44])

There are very few forms that reflect *j, but I assume that /r/ is the regular reflex:

*jukut > *ruku?* 'grass' *isejam 'borrow'> *inrang* 'borrow' *tajem > *tarang* 'sharp'

Before a syllable with /l/ or /ng/ onset, the *r (from initial *d- or *j-) was assimilated becoming /l-/ (cf. a similar development in Bugis §C6.3.32):

*dalem > *lalang* 'inside' *dilaq > *lila* 'tongue' *jalan > *lalang* 'road' *deŋeɣ > *langngere* 'hear'

Some forms show /d/ from *d or *j. Most of them were influenced by Ml, but some have been influenced or borrowed from another unidentified language:

*dakat > *dakka* 'walk' *damaɣ 'torch' > *damara* 'damar resin' (Ml *damar*) *dapedap > *doda?* 'a tree: *Erythrina*' *dapuɣ 'place for cooking fire' > *dapuru* 'stove' (Ml *dapur* 'kitchen') *dataɣ 'flat area' > *datara* 'plain' (Ml *dataran* 'level land') *datu > *dato?* 'title for older person' *diŋediŋ > *dinging* 'cold' (Ml *dingin*) *qudaŋ > *dowang* 'shrimp' *dulaŋ > *dulang* 'tray' (Ml *dulang*) *duyuŋ > *diyung* 'sea cow' *qajay > *ade* 'chin' *sadaŋ > *adang* 'intercept' (Ml *hadang*)

In one puzzling case, initial *d- has been replaced by /b/. The explanation is most likely contamination, but the source has not been discovered.[24]

*daɬih > *bani* 'near'

---

[23] The meaning 'sink' is from the directly inherited form, which has been replaced by *labu* under the influence of Ml. However, the meaning 'anchor' is borrowed from Ml.

[24] The reconstructed form *daɬih is an innovation resulting from the petrifaction of the locative prefix *d-. Paz and St both reflect a cognate without the initial *d-, Paz *alih* and St *ʔalʔalihan*. But south of those languages, reflexes show the petrified *-d. It is highly unlikely that Sal *b remounts to a petrified prefix and that *aɬih comes down to PMP or pre-Salayar, for the form no language located between Paz or St and Sal has anything but a reflex of *d- in this root.

Similarly, there are exceptions where *j is reflected as /j/. These are borrowings from or influenced by Ml:

*jaqit 'adjacent' > *jaiʔ* 'sew' (Ml *jahit*) *jaɣum > *jarung* 'needle' (Ml *jarum*) *sijaw > *ijo* 'green' (Ml *hijaw*) *sujuŋ > *ujung* 'end' (Ml *hujung*)

A few forms reflect *j- with /d/. I hypothesize that these are not directly inherited, but the source is unidentified. Note that Bugis cognates of these forms also manifest an irregular onset (§C6.3.33):

*jaqet > *daʔa* 'bad' *jeket 'stick' > *dakkiʔ* 'stick'

C7.3.33 *g

As onset of the penult or earlier, *g > *k:

*galaŋ 'wedge' > *kalang* 'restraining wood or rope' *gatel > *katala* 'itchy' *guɣita > *kurita* 'octopus' *gusam > *koang* 'thrush'

In a few cases, *g- is reflected as /g-/ initially, as is the case of the cognates in neighboring languages. The forms originated in Ml and spread in the area (cf. the Bugis cognates §C6.3.34):

*gadic > *garisi* 'scratch' *giliŋ 'roll over s.t.' > *giling* 'crush by rolling something over it' *gucuk > *gusuʔ* 'rub' (Ml *gosok*)

Medially, *-g- > /r/:

*lugan > *lurang* 'load' *ɬagam > *naram* 'tame' *maga > *mara* 'dry'

In the following case, the *r that developed from *g was assimilated to a preceding /l/ (< *ɬ), after *g had become the second phoneme in a CC:

*qaɬegaw > *allo* 'day' (< *algaw < *alegaw)

In the following unique case *-g- > /d/, perhaps because it was protected by a preceding *ʔ that later became lost:[25]

*paqegu > *pidu* 'gall' (< *paʔgu < *paqegu < *qapegu)[26]

In a few cases, *-g- is reflected with /s/. These forms are borrowed or were influenced by Bugis or some other language in the area that reflects medial *-g- with /s/:

*sapegiq > *passe* 'smart, biting' (Bugis *pessi*) *qugiŋ > *osang* 'charcoal' (Bugis *using*) *qaɬipugu > *tampalesu* 'whorl' (Bugis *palɛsu*)

---

[25] I hypothesize that medial *-g- > /r/ via *d—i.e., *g > *d > /r/).

[26] The development of this form is puzzling. The evidence from languages other than those of south Sulawesi is clear that PAn *paqegu metathesized to *qapegu prior to the development of PMP. The south Sulawesi cognates, thus, must have undergone a second metathesis. The reconstruction of *paʔgu (or *paʔdu) is substantiated by the cognates aside from Bugis, that show a reflex of *-g- (e.g. Sa'dan Toraja *paʔsu* 'gall'). Why /a/ should have changed to /i/ remains unexplained. This change is unique to Sal, to my knowledge.

C7.3.4 Voiced continuants

C7.3.41 *ɣ

*ɣ is reflected as /r/ except when it came to be in a consonant cluster:

*ɣebaq > *raʔba* 'fall from standing position' *ɣiq > *rea* 'saw grass: *Imperata cylindrica*' *ɣucuk > *rusuʔ* 'ribs' *baɣiw > *hari* 'spoiled' *laɣiw > *lari* 'run, flee' *kawiɣi > *kairi* 'left' *baɣu > *baru* 'a bush: *Hibiscus tiliaceus*'

When abutting on another consonant in a cluster that developed, *ɣ was lost, with the exception of monosyllabic roots, as discussed in §C7.1.32):

*baqeɣu > *bau* 'new' (< *baʔu < *baʔɣu) *beɣecay > *bise* 'oar' (< *beɣsay) *biɣeŋi > *bangngi* 'night' (< *beɣŋi < *beɣeŋi)

In the following cases, *-ɣ- was unaccountably lost:

*diɣuq 'bathe' > *rio* 'bathe'[27] *iɣaq > *ɛja* 'red' (< *-iya < *ia)

C7.3.42 *l

*l remained unchanged in all but one case:

*laŋit > *langiʔ* 'sky' *leŋa > *langnga* 'sesami' *laqeya > *laia* 'ginger' *balik 'go back' > *baleʔ* 'return' *bulu > *bulu* 'body hair' *beli > *halli* 'buy' *telu > *tallu* 'three'

/l/ onset of the penult dissimilated to /n/ before a *ɣ coda. This is a unique case, and other cases of /l/ to the left of /ɣ/ did not assimilate or dissimilate. The form is probably borrowed, but the source is unidentified:

*qiteluɣ > *tannoro* 'egg'

In one irregular case, *l is reflected with /r/. The form also shows an irregular final /-ʔ/. No source has been identified:

*luwaq > *me-ruaʔ* 'vomit' (Mk *lua* 'vomit' is regular)

C7.3.43 *ɬ

*ɬ underwent the changes found throughout the MP languages (§§A1.1.32, 4th¶, A3.3.4). In addition, PMP †ñ < *ɬ underwent depalatalization, as it did in many of the MP languages.[28] As onset to an unstressed penult or earlier syllable, *ɬ- becomes /l-/. Otherwise, *ɬ > /n/. This rule can be restated as follows:
Preceding the unstressed penult or an earlier syllable, *ɬ > /l-/, as is the case of most western An languages.[29]

---

[27] Possibly the occurrence of /r/ to the left in this case influenced the loss of the *ɣ- onset to the final syllable, but in another case, the *ɣ was not lost following an /r/:

*daɣaq > *rara* 'blood'

[28] *ñ that arose by syncope from *niɣ did not undergo depalatalization. (Cf. the 5th¶ of this section.)

[29] The following forms are spread throughout the languages of S. Sulawesi and evince /n/ as the reflex of *ɬ when onset to the penult. The /n/ developed in a dialect in which the stress had moved to the penult in these words before change of *ɬ > /l/ before unstressed penults:

*qaɬimateq > *linta* 'leech' *ɬaŋúy > *lange* 'swim' *qáɬegaw > *allo* 'day' (< *algaw < *alegaw)

Otherwise, *ɬ > /n-/ and /-n-/:

*ɬágam > *narang* 'tame' *aɬák > *ana?* 'son, daughter' *ɣuqaɬáy > *buraʔne* 'male' *peɬúq > *panno* 'full' *taɬéq > *tana* 'earth, soil'

In one case, *ɬ- was lost unaccountably (as it was in many languages [cf. the commentary to the entry *ɬecuŋ in the glossary]):

*ɬecuŋ > *assung* 'mortar'

In a few cases, *ɬ is reflected as /ñ/. However, these forms are secondary. /ñ/ is part of the inventory of Sal, but it developed from syncope of *niy. /ñ/ that arose by syncope from *niy did not depalatalize (as happened elsewhere—e.g., Muna, cf. the first footnote to §C8.3.43):

*sinawa 'breath' > *ñaha* 'soul' (< *ñawa < *niyawa < *nisawa) *miniyak > *miñña?* 'oil' *peniyu > *paññu* 'sea tortoise'

Cf. the very same phenomenon in Bugis, where some of the cognates of the forms discussed here also manifest /ñ/ (§C6.3.43).
In one case, *ñ developed in a process of assimilation when the root was disyllabized:

*ɬuɣ > *ñjoro* 'coconut' (< *niyuɣ)

In three cases, the influence of Ml accounts for the occurrence of /ñ/:

*ɬam 'taste' > *ñam-ang* 'delicious' (Ml *nyaman* 'delicious') *qaɬuj > *m-añu?* 'be carried by the current' (Ml *hanyut*) *saɬid 'rancid' > *aññere* 'fetid' (Ml *hañir* 'fetid')

In one case, Ml is not the source of /ñ/, and its occurrence cannot be ascribed to assimilation. The source of /ñ/ is unidentified (as is the case of the Bugis cognate):

*ɬepeɬep 'suck on s.t.' > *ñoʔño?* 'slurp'

In final position, *ɬ > /ng/:

*bulaɬ > *bulang* 'moon' *buɬebuɬ > *buhung-buhung* 'fontanelle' < *bungbung-bungbung)

*ɬ is reflected as /r/ unaccountably in the following form (cf. the reflection of /l/ as *r listed in §C7.3.42, end, above):

*ɬiteq > *rita* 'sticky sap'

C7.3.5 *m, *n, *ŋ

The nasals remained unchanged in most environments:

*mata > *mata* 'eye' *lima > *lima* 'five' *nakis > *nai?* 'go up' *suni > *oni* 'noise' *ŋaŋa > *nganga* 'open mouth'

In final position, they merge to /ng/, unless they occur only followed by a suffix:

---

*qaɬuwaŋ 'bovine' > *anoa* 'k.o. wild bovine: the anoa' *kaɬuskus > *kanuku* 'finger- or toenail' *dalem > *lalang* 'inside' *saŋin > *anging* 'wind' *tisaŋ > *tiang* 'pole'

In one case, *ŋ dissimilated to to /n/ when onset to a syllable with /r/ coda (< *ɣ). There are counterexamples where dissimilation does not take place, and this form is secondary in Sal. There was also a voiced stop intercalated after the nasal before /e/, an innovation made before the form was borrowed by Sal:

*caŋeɣ > *sandara* 'lean on' (< *sander < *saner)

In one case *-ŋ- onset of the final was lost before a nasal coda, but in another case it was not lost. Perhaps there was a rule that *-ŋ- between *a in the penult and *u in the final syllable was lost:

*baŋuɬ 'raise, rise' > *baung* 'build, get up from sleep' *saŋin > *anging* 'wind'

The nasals have special outcomes in clusters. These are detailed in §C7.1.31.

C7.3.61 *w

*w was lost:

*wakaɣ > *akaʔ* 'root' *ka-wiɣi > *kairi* 'left' *buwaq > *bua* 'fruit'

Like vowels separated by *w contracted when *w was lost (cf. §C7.1.2):

*ka-wanaɬ > *kanang* 'right (side)'

However, if the contraction would have produced a monosyllabic root, contraction did not take place. Subsequently, an /h/ developed in the hiatus between the two vowels (cf. the discussion in the next paragraph):

*sinawa 'breath' > *ñaha* 'soul' (< *ñaa < *ñawa < *niawa < *inawa)

In pre-Salayar a rule of laryngeal transition developed (§C7.1.73), so that loan words that came into the language at the time that Sal did not tolerate *w, developed /h/ or /ʔ/ transition:

*cawa 'python' > *saʔa* 'snake' *tawaɣ > *tahari* 'offer a price' (Ml *tawar-i* 'offer to s.o.')

In recent times, /w/ was reintroduced through loan words. Further, /w/ developed between an *u that had been lowered to /o/ (§C7.2.23) and a following /a/:

*qudaŋ > *dowang* 'shrimp' *ɬuwaŋ 'opening' > *ga-lowang* 'hole' *tuqas > *towa* 'old'

Dialect mixture has given rise to reflexes with medial *-w-:

*caweŋ > *sawung* 'sun hat' *lawa > *lawaʔ-lawaʔ* 'spider web'

In one case, initial *w- was changed to /b/. There is no explanation:

*waɬiw > *bani* 'bee'

*we > /u/, as exemplified in §C7.2.37, end.
For *-w, cf. §§C7.2.52, C7.2.53.

C7.3.62 *y

*-y- > *-j-. This change also affects a [y] that developed intervocalically in pre-Salayar:

*buqaya > *buaja* 'crocodile' *mayaŋ 'stem of palm with young fruit' > *majang* 'young beans before they are mature' *iɣa > *eja* 'red' (< *ɛya [change of *ɣ > /y/ unexplained) *kasiw 'tree' > *kaju* 'tree' (< *kayu < *kaiw) *lampuyaŋ > *limpujang* 'k.o. ginger' (/i/ unexplained)

This change did not affect inherited forms that had *iy if the /i/ was not lost by elision:[30]

*tiyaɬ > *tianang* 'pregnant'

In the penults consisting of *niy, where the /i/ is elided, there are two outcomes depending on the number of syllables in the root. In inherited trisyllables, the sequence became /ññ/, and in inherited disyllables or disyllabized monosyllables, it became /ñj/:

*miniyak > *miñña?* 'oil' *peniyu > *paññu* 'sea tortoise' *ɬuɣ > *ñjoro* 'coconut' (< *ñiyuɣ [§C7.1.5])

The sequence *ey > /i/ (§C7.2.37). In the penult /i/ < *ey was stressed and did not merge with *y (i.e., it remained /i/):

*laqeya > *laia* 'ginger'

There are a few irregular reflexes. They are in words that have been borrowed or affected by a language with which Sal was in contact:

*duyuŋ > *diyung* 'sea cow' (/i/ of the first syllable irregular) *payuŋ > *paiung* 'umbrella'

For *y at the end of a word, see §§C7.2.51, C7.2.52.

C7.4 The fate of word-final consonants

Sal is well on the way to losing all word-final consonants. Only glottal stop and /ng/ occur in word-final position currently. In some cases, the final root consonant was preserved and an echo vowel developed (§C7.1.74). In some cases a petrified suffix forestalled the loss of a final consonant:

*baɣat 'athwart' + *an > *baratang* 'outriggers'

C7.41 Final voiceless stops

Final *-p, *-t, *-k became /-ʔ/:

*dakep 'catch' > *raka?* 'hold in embrace' *paqit > *pai?* 'bitter' *qapucuk > *pusu?* 'top of a tree'

The following form evinced metathesis of the final /ʔ/ that developed:

*kabut > *kaʔbu* 'fog'

Exceptions are forms that were not directly inherited. Most of these forms evince other irregularities, as well:

*bulut > *bulu* 'fibre' (contamination with *bulu* 'body hair') *ceŋet > *sangngi* 'stench of urine' *dakat 'step' > *dakka* 'walk' *jaqet > *daʔa* 'bad' *metik > *kalu-manti* 'k.o. ant' *paɣatpat > *parapa* 'k.o. tree' *puket > *puka* 'net' *qabuk 'dust' > *ambu* 'smoke' *tepak > *tempa* 'slap lightly'

[30] A possible countercase is *ɛja* 'red' (< *iɣaq) (§C71.3.41).

Word-final *-q was lost with little a trace in most cases. However, the *-q did affect the quality of certain preceding vowels (§§C7.2.1, C7.2.22, C7.2.31):

> *daɣaq > *rara* 'blood' *puluq > *pulo* 'ten's' *qaɬimateq > *linta* 'leech'

The final *-q was changed to glottal stop before it was lost. In one case metathesis occurred after the change to /ʔ/ but before the loss of final *-ʔ, so that it remained:

> *basaq > *aʔba* 'flood' (< *baaʔ)

There is a handful of other forms that reflect final *-q with /ʔ/. For the most part, they evince other irregularities and must have come into or developed in Sal after the loss of final *-ʔ (< *-q) had been completed. In the first four cases, contamination is probably the explanation. In the other case, the source is probably borrowing from an unidentified source:

> *baɣaq > *parruʔ* 'lungs' *kaqekaq > *kaʔkaʔ* 'split open' *pekuq > *pekkoʔ* 'bent' *putaq > *pitaʔ* 'foam' (cf. *rita* 'tree that produces sticky sap' < *ɬiteq) *luwaq > *me-ruaʔ* 'vomit'

C7.42 Final *c and *s

At the end of a word, *c developed an echo vowel of the same quality as the vowel of the final root syllable:

> *beɣac > *berasa* 'hulled rice' *ɬisebic > *nipisi* 'thin' *qaɣuc > *arusu* 'current' *tec > *tetese* 'undone (stitches)'

There are a two exceptions, possibly due to dialect mixture. These forms also show apocope of *i and change of *a to /e/, not otherwise attested for Sal:

> *titic > *ma-ttiʔ* 'drip' *di 'at' + *atac 'above' > *rate* 'above' (< *irate < *riate)

Final *-s disappeared in Sal, as was the case of all MP languages with a small number of exceptions in roots consisting of reduplicated monosyllables. However, final *-s left a trace in the quality of a preceding *e (§C7.2.31).

C7.43 Final voiced stops

The final voiced stops became glottal stops. *-b reflected as a glottal stop is not attested in our data. I only have an attestation from Mk. Here some examples:

> *suwab > *ng-oaʔ* 'yawn' (Mk) *bedebed 'wind' > *baʔbaʔ* 'bind s.t. by winding' *tusud > *kalan-tuʔ* 'knee' *lahuj 'seaward' > *lauʔ* 'sea' *quleg > *oloʔ* 'worm'

*-eb > *ew:

> *lebeleb 'hidden by being covered' > *lullung* 'cover over' (< *lullu [with /-ng/ accretion—§C7.1.72]) < *lewlew)

In a couple of cases, the final glottal stop that had developed was lost. There is no explanation:

> *luhab > *lua* 'boil over' *timid 'jaw, chin' > *timu* 'mouth' (/u/ also unexplained) *tuqed > *toʔo* 'stump (possibly *-ʔ was lost after the /ʔ/ onset)

In a few cases, an echo vowel developed and the final voiced consonant developed as it did in intervocalic position. All of these forms except the last one are clearly borrowed from Ml:

*bayad > *bajara* 'pay' *busekag > *bongkara* or *bungkara* 'open (flower)' (Ml *bongkar* 'undo') *saɬid > *aññere* 'fetid, smell of fish' (Ml *hañir* 'fetid') *sated > *antara* 'deliver' (Ml *hantar*) *kudekud > *kukkuru* 'rasp'

C7.44 Final *ɣ and *l

Both final *ɣ and *l added an echo vowel and developed the same way as medial *ɣ and *l—i.e., became /r/ and /l/, respectively:

*celecel > *sassala* 'regret' *kasepal > *kapala* 'thick' *ipil > *ipili* 'k.o. tree' *pupul > *puppulu* 'pluck little at a time'

*quciɣ > *usiri* 'chase away' *dengeɣ > *langngere* 'hear' *sapaɣ > *apara* 'spread out (like a mat)' *muɣemuɣ > *kali-moʔmoro* 'rinse out mouth' *qawuɣ > *oro* 'k.o. bamboo' (< *auɣ)

There are some exceptions: in one case, development of a final /-ng/ (§C7.1.72) prevented *ɣ from becoming /r/:

*naquɣ > *naung* (possibly from*nauɣan)

Several cases were either influenced by a Ml cognate or directly borrowed from Ml:

*wakaɣ > *akaʔ* 'root' (Ml *akar*) *bakul > *bakuʔ* 'basket' *labeɣ > *laʔbaʔ* 'wide' (< *lebaʔ < *lebar (Ml *lebar* [/lebaʔ] [§D4.3.32]) *pakeɣ > *paku* 'nail' (Ml *paku*)

In one case, contamination is the probable explanation:

*bukul 'knob-shaped protrusion' > *bukkuʔ* 'hunch-backed' (cf. *bungkuʔ* 'bent')

There are three other unexplained exceptions, where *-ɣ became /ʔ/ or was lost:

*bulehaɣ > *bullaʔ* 'cataract' (/ll/ also unexplained) *caluɣ 'watercourse' > *saloʔ* 'conduit for water on roof' *tiduɣ > *tinro* 'sleep' (probably borrowed from a neighboring language [e.g., Bugis *tinro*])

CHAPTER EIGHT
Muna

C8.0 Introduction

Muna is spoken by some 230,000 people in southeast Sulawesi on the island of Muna and on the northwestern portion of the neighboring island of Buton, facing Muna. Some of the innovations that have affected languages of Central and South Sulawesi discussed here (Pamona, Bugis, and Salayar) have also affected Muna (e.g., the development of double reflexes of Pn *b [§C8.3.31]), but on the whole Muna has developed rather differently from those languages and shows innovations quite separate from those made by other languages studied here.

Muna has been well documented. There is a full grammar and extensive dictionary complied by René van den Berg and a team of Muna-speaking linguists (van den Berg 1996). In addition van den Berg (1991) has published a history of Muna phonology, which to a large extent treats the same phenomena treated here.[1] Muna has a good deal of dialect variation. It is mainly the northern dialect, considered the standard, that is documented, and there is little information available on variants that occur in the dialects. Multiple reflexes of the stop consonants and certain vowel sequences are a strong indication that there is (or at least was) dialectal variation.

The following chart lists the phonemes of Muna:

CHART ONE. PHONEMES OF MUNA

Consonants

voiceless stops	p	t	k	
voiced stops	b	d, (d^y)		
imploded voiced	bh			
spirants	f	s	h	ɣ
nasals	m	n	ng [ŋ]	
glides and laterals	w	l, r		

Vowels

high	i		u
mid	e		o
low		a	

The transcription here follows the transcription given in the dictionary, except that /d^y/ and /ɣ/ are transcribed as *dh* and *gh*, respectively, in the dictionary. We do not use the digraphs *dh* and *gh* in order to avoid the impression that /d^y/ and /ɣ/ share articulatory features with the imploded stop /bh/. /bh/ is a voiced imploded labial stop. /d^y/ is a fronted apico-dental voiced stop. /d^y/ does not occur in words that derive directly from PAn (§C8.3.32). /ɣ/ is a voiced

[1] I could not have been able to treat the complex problems that Muna phonology presents with decisiveness and accuracy without the guidance of this ground-breaking and thorough-going study.

velar spirant. Stress is always on the penult. Muna has no diphthongs, and sequences of all vowel combinations occur.

C8.1 Changes that characterize Muna in general

Syncope has had an important role in the phonological history of Muna. It should be noted that the forms showing the effects of syncope are those for which cognates in other An languages also show similar syncope. These processes of syncope may in fact have been operative very early when Muna and the other languages that evince them were not differentiated. Cf. the discussion in §§A3.5.1–A3.5.3. Vowel contraction due to the loss of consonants and consonant cluster simplification have also been important forces in shaping Muna reflexes. But these changes are peculiar to Muna and not just like processes of contraction and simplification that took place in other languages. In short, they are fairly recent in the history of Muna, and some of them may in fact still be in progress.

C8.1.1 Disyllabization of trisyllables

Syncope of unstressed syllables was an important process in Muna, and Muna evinces the tendency to develop disyllabic roots, much as most of the MP languages do. Although the rules in some cases are similar to those that obtain in other MP languages, the development in Muna was probably independent in most cases.

C8.1.11 Loss of antepenult

Antepenults consisting of *qa in trisyllabic roots were lost:

*qajelay > *sole* 'a grain: *Coix lacryma jobi*' *qaɣucuq > *guu* 'the Australian pine: *Casuarina equisetifolia*' (for /g/ cf. §C8.3.41, 4th¶) *qapucuk > *pusu* 'tip, top' *qalima 'hand' > *lima* 'hand' *aqetih 'for water to recede' > *ɣoti* 'ebb tide'

In the following two examples, the antepenult was not lost, however. There is no definitive explanation as to why some trisyllables lost an initial *qa- and others retained it (albeit with a weakened vowel [§C8.1.21]). Probably these two forms are inherited, and those that lost the antepenultimate syllable entirely are, in fact, secondary.[2] For the change of *a to /o/ in these words, cf. §C8.1.21, immediately below.

*páqegu > *ɣofei* 'gall' (< *qapegu [§C8.1.6]) *qałegaw > *ɣoleo* 'day' (for the reflex of *e before *g, cf. §C8.2.32)

An initial syllable *se is lost, both in trisyllabic and in disyllabic roots. If a monosyllabic root resulted from the loss of *se, it was disyllabized subsequently (§C8.1.5):

*sehapuy > *ifi* 'fire' *sejam > *ada* 'borrow' (< *ajam < *jam) *sepat > *paa* and *fato-* 'four' *seqeɣet 'tight, firmly tied' > *kee* 'tight, packed' (< *skeet < *saqɣet)

---

[2] My reason for thinking the forms that lost the *qa- to be secondary is that the loss of *qa- is reflected in the other languages of central and S. Sulawesi precisely in the reflexes of these same protoforms (whereas antepenultimate *qa is not lost in other reflexes. Cf. the following sections: §§C4.1.1.2, C5.1.11, C6.1.12, C7.1.12). There is no other evidence that these languages form a subgroup. Either these facts reflect variation in Proto-Sulawesi (if there was such a protolanguage) or these forms have spread secondarily after these languages separated. In the case of *qalima 'hand', languages from N Formosa through the gamut of the MP languages show reflexes without *qa-. It could be argued that *qa- was a prefix—i.e., Muna and the other languages did not lose the antepenult: the current form was derived from a protoform that did not have the prefix.

C8.1.2 Syncope and vowel weakening

Trisyllabic roots with *e as the vowel of the penult other than those with *qa- in the antepenult lose the penult:

> *baɣeqaŋ > *bhaga* 'molar' *basequ > *wo-no* 'smell' and *kom-bo* 'putrid, stink' (< *bau < *baqesu) *beɣekec 'bundle' > *bhoke* 'bind together' *beɣecay > *bhose* 'oar' *binesiq 'seed'> *wine* 'seed, seedling' *kasepal > *kapal* 'thick' *liceqes > *liko* 'nit' (< *licqes [§C8.1.4]) *ɬisebic > *nifi* 'thin' (< *nipi < *nispi < *ɬisbic) *ma-qetaq > *ngkala-mata* 'raw' (< *maqetaq) *isepi + maN- > *mon-ifi* 'dream' (< *maŋispi) *seqeɣet 'tight, firmly tied' > *kee* 'narrow, tight' (< *skeet < *saqɣet)

Similarly, in trisyllabic roots, *i before a final syllable with *y onset and *u before a final syllable with *w onset were elided:

> *miniyak > *mina* 'oil' (< *minyak) *peniyu > *ponu* 'sea turtle' (< *penyu [for loss of *y, cf. §C8.3.41, footnote]) *wasiyeɣ 'water' > *oe* 'water' (< *woeɣ [§C8.3.62] < *woyeɣ < *woiyeɣ [§C8.1.21] < *waiyeɣ)

A medial /u/ is lost in the following form. The form is probably secondary, as it is in most languages that reflect it:

> *paŋudaɬ > *ponda* 'pandanus' (showing weakening of the antepenult prior to the syncope)[3]

There are exceptions to this rule of penultimate *e loss. These may possibly be explained by the accentual pattern of the root in PAn.[4] The following forms manifest a weakening of the antepenult (as in the forms listed in the next paragraph, below) with a reflex of penultimate *e retained:

> *báqeɣuh > *buɣou* 'new' (< *beqeɣu) *páqegu > *ɣofei* 'gall'(< *qopegu < *qapegu) *qáɬegaw > *ɣoleo* 'day'(< *qelegaw) *qitelúɣ > *ɣunteli* (< *qeteluɣ) 'egg' *tiqeɣáb > *ɣontea* 'belch' (< *qeteɣab < *qiteɣab)

Trisyllabic roots with vowels other than *e in the penult (or *i before *y or *u before *w) weakened the antepenult.

C8.1.21

*a > /o/ (from earlier *e—*[ə]) in the antepenult or earlier:

---

[3]There is evidence that syncope is an early process in that the same syncopation occurs over a wide range of languages. Muna shows less syncopation than other languages, and if syncopation occurs in Muna, it is almost always in forms the cognates of which are also syncopated over a wide geographical range of languages. This I take to be evidence that syncopation is a process that happened early. Vowel weakening, on the other hand, seems to be a recent change. This form, showing a vowel weakening prior to syncopation, is therefore very likely not directly inherited. An additional argument against direct inheritance of this form is that it is the only form which shows the loss of /u/ in the penult.

[4] There is evidence outside of Muna to reconstruct end stress in *qitelúɣ and *tiqeɣáb (cf. the entries in the glossary). I assume that in the protolanguage that gave rise to the languages of SE Kalimantan and Sulawesi the stress shifted to the final syllable (§A3.5.3, 1st footnote). If so, then stress on the final syllable is the factor that blocked elision of penultimate *e.

*balabaw > *wolawo* 'rat' *laqeya > *loɣia* 'ginger' *pa- > *fo-* 'causative prefix' (e.g. *fo-ada* 'lend' < *ada* 'borrow') *qabaɣa > *ɣowea* 'shoulder' *qaciɣah > *ɣohia* 'salt'

In the case of doubled monosyllables with a vowel nucleus of /a/, the epenthetic vowel that had developed between the two monosyllables was elided and the vowel of the first of the two monosyllables was changed to /o/:

*baqebaq > *wobha* 'mouth' (< *bobaq) *paqepaq + *-al- > *polopa* 'midrib' (with the *a of the leftmost syllable changed to /o/ by the rule of the first paragraph of this section) *dapedap > *roda* 'k.o. tree: *Erythrina*)

C8.1.22

In some cases, the *e in the antepenult or earlier became a front vowel, /e/. The conditions for development of /e/ rather than /o/ are unknown:

*paka- 'causitive prefix' > *feka-* 'causitive prefix with stative verbs'

C8.1.3 Contraction

The loss of medial *s, *ɣ, and *g led to vowel sequences that contracted in some cases. First, like vowels contracted, including sequences of unlike vowels that had developed into sequences of like vowels:[5]

*basaq 'flood' > *mawa* 'flood' (< *wawa with doubling of a monosyllabic root [§C8.1.5])

When *u and *a came to abut on each other, *u contracted with the *a to form /o/:

*ɣuqaɫay + *ma-> *moɣane* 'male' *qusalipan > *ɣolifa* 'centipede'

The resulting /o/ is lengthened to two moras if the loss of the intervocalic consonant forms a monosyllabic root (§C8.1.5):

*dasuwen > *roo* 'leaf' (< *daun < *dauun [§C8.2.34]) *pasuq 'k.o. mango' > *foo* 'mango' *qawuɣ > *koo* 'k.o. large bamboo'

*ue (like *we [§C8.2.34]) contracts to /u/. (This is an example of assimilation of *e to the preceding *u [§C8.2.35, 5th¶].)

*luseq > *luu* 'tears' (< *lu with lengthening of the vowel after a monosyllable had developed [§C8.1.5])

In the following example, *ue contracted to /o/ There is no explanation. There is semantic contamination with *bacaq 'wet', not attested in Muna.

*bacuheq 'wash' > *bhaho* 'wet by splashing water on'

*ae > /a/:[6]

---

[5] However, sequences of like vowels in disyllabic roots are often not contracted, for this would have given rise to monosyllabic roots, which Muna avoids.

[6] There is only one example. In effect, this rule only applies to forms that have *ase in the penult and final syllable. If this sequence came earlier in the word, the *e was syncopated (§C8.1.2). In the case of a sequence *aɣe or *age, the *a was fronted to /e/ (§C8.2.411 [cf. the examples there]), so that contraction did not take place after the loss of the medial *ɣ and *g.

*tapes 'chaff' > *uta* 'rice husk' (< *utap [disyllabization by /u/-prothesis] < *tap < *taep < *tasep)

*ei, *ie > /i/:

*deŋeɣ 'hear' + *peN-i > *pendengi* 'listen (< *pendeŋei) *nakis + *pa- > *fo-ni* 'climb' (< *paneik [§C8.2.413]) *betihec > *folo-bhiti* 'calf' (< *betiec [The change of *e to /i/ in the antepenult is unexplained.[7]])

C8.1.4 CC simplification

Muna tolerates no consonant clusters other than homorganic nasal plus stop. When two consonants came to abut through elision of a medial vowel, the sequence was simplified by loss of the first consonant. The lost consonant, protected the onset of the final syllable (cf. §C8.3.41):

*beɣekec 'bundle' > *bhoke* 'bind together' *beɣecay > *bhose* 'oar'

In a sequence consisting of a consonant plus *q, the *q was protected but changed to /k/ (i.e., the consonant was lost, and *q > /k/):

*liceqes > *liko* 'nit' (< *licqes [§C8.1.2])

In the following form, the first consonant in the sequence was lost after elision of the penultimate vowel, but *q is reflected as /ɣ/. There is no explanation as to why /k/ did not develop in this word (§C8.3.41, 2nd¶):[8]

*biceqak 'split' > *weɣa* (< *biqak < *bicqak)

In the following case, metathesis caused the *q to protect the *ɣ that had preceded it (i.e., *q–*ɣ > *ɣ–*q), and with the loss of the intervening vowel, a consonant cluster developed that was simplified by loss of the first C. *ɣ, when protected, became /g/ (§C8.3.41):

*baɣeqaŋ 'molar' > *bhaga* 'molar' (< *baqɣaŋ < *baqeɣaŋ)

The following form is also an exception. The contraction of the prefix and the root occurred in PAn times (i.e., it is reflected in many of the Formosan languages) and was inherited by Muna as a disyllabic root:

*ma-qetaq 'raw' > *mata* in *ngkala-mata* 'raw' (< *mataq)

Doubled monosyllabic roots, which are reconstructed with an epenthetic *e between the monosyllables, lost the epenthetic *e by the rule of §C8.1.2, above. The CC's that developed were treated like the other CC's that developed—that is, doubled monosyllables lost the coda of both monosyllables. The onset of the second was protected:[9]

*bukebuk > *bubu* 'wood borer' *bułebuł > *tanam-bubu* 'fontanel' *celecel > *soso* 'regret' *cepecep > *soso* 'suck' *dapedap > *roda* 'a tree: *Erythrina*' *demedem 'dark,

[7] /i/ in the antepenult of this word is reflected in some but not all of the other languages in Sulawesi and also to the north in the Philippines (cf. *betihec in the glossary).

[8] *c is also unaccountably lost in the Mgg cognate of this form *wiʔak* 'spit with a wedge' (§F1.1.11). This was probably a development in a neighboring language that spread to Muna and Mgg.

[9] If there was a suffix, the coda of the second monosyllable was often preserved:

*bucebuc > *bubusi* 'pour water over grave'

cloudy' > *rondo* 'be night' *dicedic > *didi* 'slice' *diŋediŋ > *rindi* 'cold' *palaqepaq > *polopa* 'midrib'

C8.1.5 Disyllabization of monosyllabic roots

Muna avoids monosyllabic roots. Monosyllabic roots may become disyllabized by the processes that are general throughout the An languages (§A3.6.2): doubling, stretching the vowel nucleus to two moras or two syllables, or reinterpreting an affixed form as a root. Disyllabization by doubling:

*cuɬ 'stack up' > *sunsu* 'stack up, layer'

Disyllabization by adding a mora:

*daŋ 'heat' > *rana* 'warm oneself near fire' (with /a/ paragoge) *kud 'grate' > *kuru* 'scrape' (with /u/ paragoge) *peŋ 'dam, fence' > *ompu* 'fish trap in shallow part of sea' *pu > *ompu* 'lord, God' (with a prothetic vowel. This form is probably not inherited.) *cay 'who?' > *hae* 'what?' *tan > *taɣo* 'set trap' (< *taʔen[10])

Disyllabization by petrifaction of an affix:

*ɬam > *nami* 'taste'(with petrifaction of the local passive suffix *-i)

There is a small number of examples that manifest disyllabization of monosyllabic roots that had developed in the recent history of Muna as a result of consonant loss and contraction.

*basaq 'flood' > *mawa* 'flood' (< *wawa < *wa [with loss of intervocalic *s and subsequent contraction—§C8.1.3]) *basequ 'smell' > *wo-no* 'smell' (where the suffix *-no* is reinterpreted as part of the root after the development of /wo/ from *basequ [§C8.1.2]) *buɣuk > *wuwu* 'rotten' *seqeɣet 'tight, firmly tied' > *kee* 'narrow, tight' (< *ket [§C8.1.11, end] < *seket < *seqɣet) *sepat > *paa* 'four' *tapes 'chaff' > *uta* 'rice husk' (< *utap [disyllabization by /u/-prothesis] < *tap < *taep < *tasep)

The numerals that became monosyllabic disyllabize by suffixing a vowel /o/ (< *e). This developed from an epenthetic vowel that had been intercalated between a numeral and the noun following it:

*enem 'six' > *nomo-* 'six' *sepat 'four' > *fato-* 'four'

C8.1.6 Metathesis

Muna reflects the cases of metathesis that occurred in late PAn and in PMP times (§A1.1.32, 3rd¶). We give a couple of examples of many:

*bukes 'hair on head' > *wuu* 'body hair, fur' (< *busek) *paqegu > *ɣofei* 'gall' (< *qapegu)

Otherwise, metathesis was not an important process in the development of Muna. I have assumed metathesis in the case of the following forms in order to explain their development. They all involve syllables with *q or *s onset.

---

[10] Muna did not develop glottal stops between vowels. This form is borrowed from an unknown source that stretched the nucleus of the monosyllabic roots and developed a glottal stop between the two moras. The glottal stop was reinterpreted in Muna as /ɣ/.

*bayeqaŋ 'molar' > *bhaga* 'cheek, molar' (< *baqyaŋ < *baqeyang) *basequ > *wo-no* 'smell' (< *bau < *baesu < *baqesu) *deyeqec > *ka-dei-dei* 'hurriedly' (< *deqeyec) *tiqeyab > *yontea* 'belch' (< *qetiyab) *aqetih > *yoti* 'ebb tide' (< *qaeti)

There are a few cases of metathesis, not involving forms with *q: [11]

*lakaq 'step' < *kala* 'go' *gamay 'hand' > *kema* 'left side'

C8.1.7 Prenasalization stop consonants

Muna, like the other western An languages, shows sporadic prenasalization of the onset of a syllable that was not initial:

*bakesaw > *bhangko* 'k.o. mangrove' *ijak > *f-inda* 'step on' *qiteluy > *yunteli* 'egg' *tiqeyab > *yontea* 'belch'

Muna also developed prenasalzation of the onset of the first syllable of a root.[12]

*baliw 'one of two' > *mbali* 'side, half of two' *dabuq > *ndabu* 'fall' *dalem > *ndalo* 'deep' *tabun > *ntawu* 'in heaps'

C8.1.8 Raising of /e/ and /o/

/e/ and /o/ are raised variably to /i/ and /u/, respectively, in certain lexical items under certain conditions. In most of the forms in which /e/ and /o/ are raised, variants without the raised phoneme also occur—i.e., there are double reflexes. Further, not all protoforms that had the sequences leading to variable raising did in fact develop doublets.

First is raising of /e/ to /i/. This phenomenon occurs with /e/ that developed from the raising of *a to /e/ or the fronting of *e to /e/ preceding a medial *ɣ or *g: §C8.2.411, 4th¶, e.g. *bayeq 'abscess' becomes *weo*, which subsequently is raised to *wio*. (See further examples in the referenced section.)

Second is raising of /o/ to /u/ in the antepenult of forms that were inherited from PAn with *e or *a in the antepenult (§C8.1.21). In this case, it is possible that /u/ and /o/ are neutralized in the antepenult in current Muna.[13] If these vowels do, in fact, contrast, we may interpret the facts as follows: the /o/ that developed from *e and *a had allophones of different heights in different dialects. Contact between dialects with higher allophones and lower allophones produced the situation in which speakers of the dialect with the lower allophones perceived the /o/ with the higher allophones in the other dialects to be allophones of /u/. Dialect borrowing gave rise to variants for some of the forms—that is, doublets: one with /u/ and the other with /o/. Examples of doublets:

---

[11] In these two cases I am presenting van den Berg's hypothesis (1991:17). the forms may, in fact, not be connected, for metathesis of this sort is porly attested. There are other examples aside from these two, but they do not remount to PAn or PMP.

[12] Prenasalization of the initial consonant of the word resulted from prefixes, the first parts of which were elided (Van den Berg 1991: §5.2).

[13] Van den Berg (1991: 7) states, "..it may even be that there is no phonemic contrast between /o/ and /u/ in that [antepenultimate] position." In this same paragraph van den Berg points out that the change of *a to /o/ in this position is a weakening due to the stress placement to the right. In §C8.1.21 the same point is made. I believe that the change was as follows: *a > [ə], and subsequently [ə] > /o/ as was the case of the reflexes of PAn *e (*[ə]).

*balabaw > *wolawo* and *wulawo* 'rat' *baqebaq > *wobha* and *wubha* 'mouth' *paqegu > *ɣofei* and *ɣufei* 'gall' (< *qapegu)

In three cases, only the form with /u/ in the antepenult survives.

*baqeɣu > *buɣou* 'new' < (< *boqou < *beqeɣu) *kawanaɬ > *suwana* 'right' *qiteluɣ 'egg' > *ɣunteli* 'egg' (< *qateluɣ)[14]

There are doublets with /u/ and /o/ in the final syllable (from *aw), but this phenomenon has nothing to do with the raising of /o/, described here. (Cf. the examples in §C8.2.53.)

C8.1.9 Vowel harmony or assimilation

Assimilation of vowels to what preceded or followed was an important process in the development of Muna. In this section we list the various types of vowel harmony and assimilation that occurred with reference to the section in which the process is exemplified and exceptions are discussed.[15]

(1) First is lowering of vowels involving assimilation to the right:

*i > /e/ before *ɣ: §C8.2.1, 6th¶;

*e > /a/ before *k, *q, and *s:[16] §C8.2.33.

(2) Second is fronting involving assimilation to the right:

*uɣ > /i/: §C8.2.2;

*aɣ *or* *eɣ > /e/: §C8.2.411, §C8.2.32;

*ay (not final)[17] > /e/: §C8.2.413a;

*a before Ci *or* Cuɣ *or* Cuy *or* Ciw > /eCi/: §C8.2.413;

*ey (not final) > /i/: §C8.2.34;

*eCuɣ > /eCi/: §§C8.2.2, C8.2.35.

(3) Third is fronting involving assimilation to the left:

*eCu > /eCi/: §C8.2.21;

*eCe > /eCe/:[18] §C8.2.35, 2nd¶;

*u *or* *i before Caɬ >/uCe/ *or* /iCe/: §C8.2.412.

(4) Fourth is backing of *e before or after *u:

*eCu *or* *uCe > /uCu/ §C8.2.35, end.

---

[14] The change of the initial *qi- in this root to *qa- characterizes the reflexes of this protoform in all the MP languages outside of the Philippines, except in those cases where the initial syllable was elided.

[15] The statement, *e > /e/, describes a fronting: *[ə] > [ɛ]. It is somewhat confusing that we have chosen the symbol *e to represent what is reconstructed as *[ə], whereas /e/ is a lower front vowel [ɛ].

[16] *e was lowered before PAn *s because *s had already made the MP change to [h].

[17] Final *ay also becomes /e/ (§C8.2.51).

[18] After *e of the final syllable had moved to the front, the *e of the penult became /o/ (cf. the examples in §C8.2.315, 2nd¶).

C8.2 Vowels and diphthongs

Muna has added two vowels to the PAn four-vowel system, *i, a*, *e, and *u and lost the central vowel *e—that is, Muna has a five-vowel system: /i, e, a, o, u/. /e/ developed in a large number of the cases from *e and *a by assimilation to the following consonant or the vowel of the following syllable (§§C8.2.3ff.). /o/ developed from *aw and from *e. The following sections provide details.

C8.2.1 *i

*i > /i/ in all positions:

*iseci > *ihi* 'contents' *biɣebiɣ > *wiwi* 'lips'

When two /i/'s come to abut each other because of consonant loss, the two /i/'s contract:

*palisi > *fali-a* 'taboo' *ɣabihi 'night > *in-dewi* 'yesterday'

*i in the antepenult remained /i/:

*miniyak > *mina* 'oil' *qaɬiɣuwan 'bee' > *ka-eniua* 'k.o. small bee' *sinawa 'breath' > *inawa* 'life sustaining force'

Normally, *i > /i/ before *q:

*piliq 'choose' > *pili* 'choose' *tapiq 'skirt' > *tapi* 'layer' *weliq 'repeat, go back' > *s-uli* 'return home'

In three cases, *i is lowered to /e/ before *q in borrowings from a neighboring language:[19]

*biceqak 'split' > *weɣa* (< *biqak [§C8.1.2]) 'cracked (of pots)' *binesiq > *wine* 'seed, seedling' *puɬetiq > *pute* 'white' (< *putiq)

*i > /e/ before *ɣ:

*iɣaq > *d-ea* 'red' *tiqeɣab > *ɣontea* 'belch' (< *qetiɣab)

In five cases, *i > /e/ with no explanation. They are probably not directly inherited:

*biluk 'veer' > *belo* 'turn aside' *dilaq > *lela* 'tongue' *jilaq > *selaɣ-i* 'lick something' *biɣeŋi 'night' > *nae-wine* 'tomorrow'

The words for 'lick' and 'tongue' just cited, *selaɣi* and *lela*, have probably influenced each other, but how /e/ developed in the first place is unknown.

C8.2.2 *u

In most cases, *u is reflected with /u/:

*itu > *itu* 'that' *dusa > *dua* 'two' *puluq > *fulu* 'unit of ten'

At the end of a word, *-uɣ > /i/:[20]

*becuɣ > *wehi* 'sated' *qapuɣ 'lime' > *ɣefi* 'lime' *qiteluɣ > *ɣunteli* 'egg'

[19] Sirk (1989: 56-57) points out that *i lowered to *ɛ before *q in many of the languages of S. Sulawesi. Muna did not make this change, however.

[20] Van den Berg (1991:§2.6) shows that *ɣ > *y in pre-Muna. Thus, *uɣ > /i/ just as *uy does (§C8.2.52).

However, in the following case *-uɣ > /u/, possibly because the vocalism that occurs when the *uɣ is not word final was generalized:

*tuduɣ 'sleep' > *tuturu mata* 'sleepy'

In one case *-uɣ is reflected with /e/ (if the forms are cognate):

*uyuɣ > *ue* 'rock, swing'

When a sound change took place that caused an *u and an *a to abut on each other, *u contracts with the *a to form /o/ (§C8.1.3, 2nd¶):

*dasuwen 'leaf' > *roo* 'leaf' *maɣuqaɬay > *moɣane* 'male' *qusalipan > *ɣolifa* 'centipede'

The resulting /o/ is lengthened to two moras if the loss of the intervocalic consonant forms a monosyllabic root (§C8.1.5):

*pasuq 'k.o. mango' > *foo* 'mango' *qawuɣ 'Bambusa sp.' > *koo* 'k.o. large bamboo'

In a few cases, *u > /o/. Most of these forms show other irregularities and are borrowings, some from Malay and others, from an unknown source.

*biluk 'veer' > *belo* 'turn aside' *buŋkaɣ 'take apart' > *bhongka* 'crack, smash, break' *buɣaw 'chase' > *bhora* 'shout to shoo away' (with irregular reflex of *ɣ as well) *buleg > *molo* 'hill' (possibly unconnected) *bunag > *bhone* 'sand' *ɣugan > *owa* 'load' (with unexplained failure of *owa to contract) (< *laɣugan) *kutu > *otu* 'louse' (with unexplained loss of *k)

C8.2.21 Vowel harmony involving *u

After a penult with /e/ nucleus, *u in the final syllable > /i/ by assimilation. In the following examples, /e/ developed in the penult (before *g and *ɣ [§§C8.2.32, C8.2.411]) and *u > /i/. Note that this change took place at a time when the rule of contraction was no longer in effect—i.e., the /ei/ that developed did not contract (§C8.1.3, end):

*qapegu > *ɣofei* 'gall' *taɣuq > *tei* 'put'

C8.2.3 *e

C8.2.31

The most general case is that *e > /o/:

*teleɬ > *tolo* 'swallow' *cedu > *hodu* 'hiccough' *qatep > *ɣato* 'roof'

Occasionally, *e is reflected with /u/ instead of /o/. (cf. §C8.1.8).

C8.2.32

Before *ɣ and *g, *e > /e/:[21]

*caleɣ 'flooring' > *hale* 'floor' *peɣec > *feo* 'squeeze out' *puceg > *puhe* 'navel' *qaɬegaw 'day, sun' > *ɣoleo* 'day' *qapegu > *ɣofei* 'gall, *quleg 'worm' > *ɣule* 'snake,

[21] Note that *eɣ > /e/ whereas *ey > /i/ (§C8.2.34).

worm' *seqeɣet > *kee* 'tight'[22] *wasiyeɣ 'water' > *oe* 'water' (< *woeɣ [§C8.3.62] < *woyeɣ [§C8.1.2, 2nd¶] < *woiyeɣ [§C8.1.21] < *waiyeɣ)

However, there are a few forms in which *e before /ɣ/ became /o/. Two of these are explained by the fact that there was syncope in the penult yielding a consonant cluster that was simplified by loss of *ɣ, which took place before the rule of the change of *e to /e/ before *ɣ had come into effect.

*beɣekec 'bundle' > *bhoke* 'bind into a bundle' (< *bekec < *beɣkec) *beɣecay 'oar' > *bhose* 'oar' (< *becay < *beɣcay)

In the following case, *e did not develop into /e/ probably because the form only occurred with a suffix—i.e., the *e was in the antepenult. This does not explain the loss of the penultimate *a, and there is no explanation:

*beɣac 'husked rice' > *wo-ne* 'small rice pieces' (< *woa-ne [loss of *a unexplained])

C8.2.33

*e in the final syllable > /a/ before *-k, *-q, and *-s (which were subsequently lost):

*bureq > *bura* 'foam' *daɣeq > *rea* 'blood' *qaɬimateq > *rinta* 'leech' *tabeq > *tabha* 'fat' *taneq 'earth' > *lilin-tana* 'travel around the country' *tumes > *tuma* 'clothes louse'

The following forms are exceptions. There is no explanation:

*liceqes > *liko* 'nit' *baɣeq > *weo* 'abscess'

In other cases, vowel assimilation (§C8.2.35, end) blocked the development of /a/:

*bukes > *wuu* 'hair' (< *buek < *busek) *luseq > *luu* 'tears' (< *lueq)[23]

C8.2.34

*ey > /i/, *we > /u/:

*seyup > *f-iu* 'blow' *laqeya > *loɣia* 'ginger' *dasuwen 'leaf' > *roo* 'leaf' (< *dau) *weliq 'repeat'> *s-uli* 'return home' *taquwen > *taɣu* 'year'

The following example shows development of *we to /o/. There is no explanation:

*lahuwen 'long time' > *lao* 'long (of the dry season)'

C8.2.35 Vowel harmony involving *e

*e > /e/ preceding a final syllable with *-uɣ, which became /i/ (§C8.2.2):[24]

---

[22] A variant *kii* 'firm' developed, where the /e/ was raised to /i/. Cf. the parallel variable raising of /a/ to/i/ described in §C8.2.411, 4th¶.

[23] In some dialects *e changed to /a/ before assimilation could take place:

*luseq > *lua* 'tears'

[24] There are only two examples. There is counterevidence in that penultimate *e does not become /e/ before an *i in the final syllable:

*beli > *bholi* 'buy' *gemi 'hold on to' > *komi* 'suck'

For this reason, it seems unlikely that *uɣ in the final syllable should have provided the impetus for *e to become /e/. There is no better explanation, however.

*becuɣ > *wehi* 'full, satisfied' *qiteluɣ > *ɣunteli* 'egg'

*e in the final syllable became /e/ by vowel harmony when a penult had or developed *e:

*beɣekec 'bundle' > *bhoke* 'tied in a bundle' (<*beɣkec) *seqeɣet 'tight' > *kee* 'tight, narrow'

Roots consisting of doubled monosyllables with *e nucleus were not affected by this rule:

*celecel > *soso* 'regret'

The following three forms also failed to undergo this change—i.e, failed to develop /e/ in the final syllable. There is no explanation:

*peɣec > *feo* 'squeeze' *qaɣeŋ > *ɣeo* 'charcoal' *teleɬ > *tolo* 'swallow'

*e > /u/ before or after an *u that had not changed:

*bukes 'hair on head' > *wuu* 'body hair, fur' (< *busek) *luseq > *luu* 'tear'[25] *cequɬ 'carry on head' > *suɣu* 'carry over shoulder on pole'

C8.2.36 Unexplained changes of *e

There are some exceptions to the above rules. Most of them involve forms that are not directly inherited. Some of them manifest other irregularities besides the reflex of *e. The first four forms may well be Ml borrowings, but the other forms listed below do not have a Ml origin:

*puket > *puka* 'drag net' *celem > *sela* 'dive to the bottom' *tiɣem 'oyster' > *tira* 'kind of oyster' *teŋaq > *tanga* 'middle, half'[26] *betak 'split, tear apart' > *weta* 'side, half' *kamet 'grab' > *kama* 'grip, squeeze' *jaqet 'bad' > *dai* 'broken, bad'

C8.2.4 *a

In general, *a > /a/.

*alap > *ala* 'take' *bulaɬ > *wula* 'moon, month' *alem > *alo* 'night' *waɬiw > *ani* 'bee'

C8.2.41 Fronting of *a

*a was fronted in harmony with what followed, in some cases in the same syllable and in other cases in the following syllable. There are many countercases, and these forms possibly exemplify sound changes that were not carried through to completion. Another possibility is that these result from dialect mixture—that is, some dialects fronted *a in these environments, and other dialects failed to front in some or all of these environments.

C8.2.411

*a > /e/ before medial *ɣ and *g if the following syllable did not contain *u (cf. the change of *e to /e/ before /ɣ/ (§C8.2.32):

---

[25] This change took place before the lowering of *e before *q (§C8.2.33), but note that a variant occurs in which the *e was lowered and assimilation did not take place: *lua* 'tears'.

[26] Since there are no other attestations of forms reflecting *e in the penult and *a in the final, it is possible that the development of /a/ in the penult of this form is a case of vowel assimilation. However, the meaning of this word 'in the process of' (as well as 'middle') evinces a semantic innovation made by Ml. This makes it likely that the form *tanga* was in fact borrowed from Ml.

*baɣeq 'abscess' > *weo* 'swell, swollen' *baɣiw > *bhei* 'spoiled food' *daɣaq > *rea* 'blood' *laɣiw > *fi-lei* 'run, flee' *ɬagam 'accustomed, tame' > *nea* 'accustomed to doing' *ŋagan > *nea* 'name'

Otherwise (i.e., in final position and before *u), *aɣ is reflected with /a/:

*bulaɣ > *tam-bula* 'cataract' *buŋkaɣ 'take apart' > *bhongka* 'crack, smash, break' *dataɣ 'flat area' > *rata* 'level' *jaɣum 'needle' > *ka-sau* 'thread on needle'

The following forms are exceptions. There is no explanation:

*agi > *ai* 'younger sibling' *aɣi + *m-> 'come' > *mai* 'come hither'

In the case of a few forms, *a is raised to /i/ before *ɣ or *g (§C8.1.8). In most cases these are variants of forms with /e/:

*baɣeq > *weo/wio* 'abscess' *kaɣat > *sia* 'bite' (and also *sea-kito* 'a k.o. biting ant') *peɣec 'squeeze' > *feo/fio* 'hold by pinching' *qageŋ > *ɣeo/ɣio* 'charcoal' *taɣaq 'chop' *tea/tia* 'shape a piece of wood into an object'

In at least two cases, only the higher variant is attested:

*baheɣat > *bhie* 'heavy' *kapit > *simpi* 'pick up with the finger tips'

The following forms show a change of *a > /e/ before *ɣ when the final syllable had /u/. The first example is not inherited. The initial /d/ is also irregular (§C8.3.33). There is no explanation for the second:

*jaɣum > *deu* 'needle' (A regular reflex is also attested: *ka-sau* 'thread a needle'.) *taɣuq < *tei* 'put, store'

C8.2.412

*a in the final syllable before *ɬ > /e/ if the penult had a high vowel:

*qujaɬ 'rain' > *ɣuse* 'rain' *tiyaɬ 'belly' > *tie* 'womb'

However, the following form does not follow this rule. There is no explanation:

*qubaɬ > *ɣua* 'grey hair' (The loss of *b is also unexplained.)

*a of the final syllable was not assimilated to a preceding high vowel when the coda was other than *ɬ. Here are a few examples of many:

*ina > *ina* 'mother' *qaciɣa > *ɣohia* 'salt' *qusalipan > *ɣolifa* 'centipede'

However, in several cases, *a was assimilated to a preceding high vowel when not followed by *ɬ. In two cases, perhaps the preceding *ɣ caused the *a to change to /e/. In the other cases, there is no explanation:

*uɣat > *ue* 'vein, tendon' *baheɣat > *bhie* 'heavy' *igan > *nae-f-ie* 'when?' *ica > *ise* 'one'

C8.2.413

*a > /e/ before a high vowel in the following syllable (other than before *ɣ or *g [§C8.2.411]):

*gali 'dig, excavate' > *seli* 'dig up' *ɣabihi > *in-dewi* 'yesterday' *pa- 'verbal prefix' > *fe-* 'verb-forming prefix' (e.g. *fembula* 'cultivate, grow' < *pa-+ *mula 'plant') *qaɬiɣuwan > *ka-eniua* 'k.o. bee' *tapes 'winnow' > *tepi* 'winnow' (< *tapi < *tapes-i) *tacik 'sea' > *tehi* 'sea'

Similarly, *a > /e/ before /i/ in the final syllable that developed from *-uy, *uɣ, and *-iw (§§C8.2.2, C8.2.52). Cf. the change of *e to /e/ before *uɣ in the final syllable, §C8.2.35.

*babuy 'pig' > *wewi* 'pig' *ɬaŋuy > *leni* 'swim' *qapuɣ > *ɣefi* 'lime' *cabuɣ 'scatter' > *hewi* 'plants that grow by themselves without being sown' *baɣiw > *bhei* 'spoiled food' *laɣiw > *fi-lei* 'run, flee'

Contraction blocks the change of *a to /e/ in a syllable before *-uɣ:

*qawuɣ > *koo* 'k.o. large bamboo' (< *ko with doubling of the vowel after development of a monosyllable [§C8.1.5]) *basuɣ > *so-bho* 'mix'

Note that there were exceptions where *a did not assimilate to *i in the following syllable. This sound change affected the vast majority of the examples, but there were a few forms of high frequency that remained untouched by the rule:

*laŋit > *lani* 'sky' *paɬid > *pani* 'wing' *paqit > *paɣi* 'bitter'

C8.2.413a

Similarly, *a > /e/ before *y, which was subsequently lost (cf. §C8.2.51):

*buqaya > *buea* 'crocodile' (loss of *q unexplained)

The following word is a loan word that was borrowed at a time when Muna had lost *y. It was borrowed without /y/, and the /a/ was not fronted:

*payuŋ < *pau* 'umbrella' (Ml *payung* 'umbrella')

C8.2.42 Other irregular reflexes of *a

In a few forms, *a has irregular reflexes. There is no explanation for any of them. In the following form, *a assimilated to the /i/ of the following syllable. It is a unique example:

*sehapuy 'fire' > *ifi* 'fire'

Cf. §C8.2.413, above, which describes the change of *a > /e/ before /i/ in the following syllable. However, note that there are several examples where /i/ varies with /e/ in forms that reflect *a before *ɣ or *g (§C8.2.411, 4th¶) Further, there is a case where /e/ < *e was raised variably to /i/ and subsequently the variable with /i/ underwent semantic shift (§C8.2.32, 2nd footnote).

In the following three forms, *a > /o/ with no explanation:

*dapat 'meet' > *rafo* 'catch up with' *leŋa 'sesame' > *longo* 'sesame' *paheɣaw 'hoarse' > *pooro* 'hoarse' (< *paɣaw) (/r/ is also irregular [§C8.3.41, end])

C8.2.5 Diphthongs

Muna has no diphthongs. Inherited diphthongs were monophthongized, as described in the following subsections.

C8.2.51 *ay

*ay > /e/

*bahi + *-in- 'woman' > *ro-bhine* 'woman' (< *binay) *matay > *mate* 'die' *qajelay > *sole* 'a grain: *Coix lachryma-jobi*'

In monosyllabic roots, *ay > /ae/.

*cay 'who?' > *hae* 'what?'

One form with /ay/ had an idiosyncratic development. There is no explanation:

*beɣay 'give' > *waa* 'give'[27]

C8.2.52 *uy and*iw

*uy and *iw > /i/:

*babuy > *wewi* 'pig' *łaŋuy > *leni* 'swim' *sehapuy > *ifi* 'fire' *baɣiw > *bhei* 'spoiled food' *laɣiw > *fi-lei* 'run, flee' *wałiw > *ani* 'bee'

In one case, *iw > /u/. There is no explanation for /u/ instead of /i/.

*baliw 'change, return' > *bhalu* 'buy'

In the third case, the *s became *h and syllabicity shifted, as was the case in many of the An languages. Subsequently, the medial *y that had developed was lost (§C8.3.62):

*kasiw 'tree, wood' > *sau* 'wood, stick' (< *kahu < *kahyu)[28]

C8.2.53 *aw

In most cases, *aw > /o/:

*balabaw 'rat' > *wolawo* 'rat' *qałegaw > *ɣoleo* 'day' *línaw > *lino* 'calm' *babaw 'above' > *wawo* 'top'

In two cases, *aw > /u/. The first example probably was contaminated by an unidentified form. The second example, referring to a disease, probably spread through borrowing throughout the MP languages:

*baław 'wash' > *fe-wanu-i* 'wash hands or feet' *panaw > *panu* 'white fungus splotches on the skin'

A sequence *a plus *u which developed when an intervocalic consonant was lost develops like *aw (i.e., becomes /o/). Cf examples in §C8.1.3, above.

C8.3 Consonants

The most profound phonological development of recent times affecting Muna independent of other languages is consonantal weakening. First, all word-final consonants have been lost. Second, many of the stop consonants have been weakened to spirants when not

[27] The root *beɣay developed a monosyllabic allomorph before suffixes (as attested by the variant **wahi* 'give' [< *wa* +*i* 'local passive' + transitional /h/]. The rules for the development of this allomorph are unknown, however. We may hypothesize that this monosyllabic allomorph was generalized throughout the paradigm, and the vowel nucleus doubled for the root to attain disyllabicity (§C8.1.5).

[28] *s > †h in PMP (§A3.3.32). The *h that developed from *s in this form blocked fronting of the *a that preceded, as normally would have happened to *a before *y (§C8.2.413a).

protected as the second element of clusters. Specifically, *p > /f/, *k > /s/ (only before a), *q > /ɣ/, *b > /w/, *d > /r/, *j > /s/, and *g and *ɣ have been lost entirely.[29] This weakening process did not affect *t at all, nor did it affect *k in most environments. Apparently, in some dialects *d and *j were not weakened. My reason for saying this is that *d in fact has two reflexes /r/ and /d/ and the distribution is such that we can only conclude that current Muna manifests a mixture of two dialects that had two different reflexes of *d. Similarly *j is reflected as /d/ as well as /s/, again the result of dialect mixture.[30] Consonants were not weakened when protected by a preceding consonant. Thus, in roots to which a prefix ending in a consonant was added, the initial consonant was not weakened—i.e., it remained a stop. In some cases, the allomorph with an initial stop was generalized throughout the paradigm, so that there are examples that show root initial stop reflexes of the PAn stops rather than spirant reflexes. The following chart summarizes the PAn consonants and their reflexes in Muna:

CHART TWO. DEVELOPMENT OF THE MUNA CONSONANTS FROM PAN

PAn	Muna	PAn	Muna
p	*f, p*	g	*k-, Ø*
t	*t*	ɣ	*Ø*
k	*k, s*	l	*l*
q	*ɣ, k*	ɬ	*n, l*
s, h	*Ø*	m	*m*
c	*h, s*	n	*n*
b	*w, bh* or *b*	ŋ	*ng* [*ŋ*], *n*
d	*r, d*	w	*Ø*
j	*s, d*	y	*Ø*

C8.3.1 Voiceless stops

C8.3.11 *p

The most general case is that *p > /f/:

*palisi > *fali-a* 'taboo' *apa 'what?' > *afa* 'do what?' *qapuɣ > *ɣefi* 'lime' *qusalipan > *ɣolifa* 'centipede'

When protected *p > /p/:

*kasepal 'thick' > *kapa* 'thick' (< *kaspal) *lampin 'wrapper, diaper' > *lampi* 'to line, coat' *paŋa 'forking' > *kam-panga* 'fork in river'

---

[29] Note that /ɣ/ is written as *gh* in the Muna orthography and derives from PAn *q (not PAn *ɣ).

[30] Dialect mixture is perhaps a simplified explanation of the historical origin of these double reflexes. Languages throughout southern Sulawesi (SW as well as SE Sulawesi) evince double reflexes of PAn *b, *d, and *j: one reflex is a stop and the other a continuant. (Cf. Mills 1976: §§4.3a, and 4.3b; also van den Berg 1991: 12) There is no matching up of weakened reflexes and unchanged reflexes in cognates in the various languages. That is, for a form that shows up with a weakened reflex in Muna, the cognate in another language of the area may very well not have a weakened reflex, and for a form that shows an unweakened reflex in Muna the cognate in another language of the area may well have a a weakened reflex. This leads to the conclusion that there was an articulatory feature shared by the languages of this area that led to a weakening of stops and that the process of weakening to a large extent took place independently in several languages (although surely weakened forms or unweakened forms also spread from one language to another in some cases, as well).

There are cases when *p > /p/ in unprotected environments: first, as onset of the first syllable in a disyllabic stem, if there is a C-onset of the final syllable, but not if there is a suffix:

> *panac > *pana* 'hot' (as well as *fanaha* 'warm' and *fanahi* 'heat' [where the /f/'s are onset in a suffixed stem) *pat > *paa* 'four' (as well as *fato* 'four'[which occurs only as a clitic—i.e., the form following *fato* acts like a suffix. The doubled /a/ of *paa* is a disyllabization of a monosyllable [§C8.1.5]) *paqit > *paɣi* 'bitter' *piliq > *pili* 'choose' *pitu > *pitu* 'seven' (when an independent word, but *fitu-* as a clitic) *pucuq 'heart' > *ko-puhu* 'banana blossom'

Second, initial *p in a disyllable is reflected as /f/ if the final syllable is vowel initial (had had a consonant that had been lost as onset):

> *pasuq > *foo* 'mango' *peɣes > *feo* 'squeeze'

There are exceptions, where *p as onset of the final syllable is reflected as /p/, or where *p as onset to a disyllable containing a medial consonant that was lost, is nevertheless reflected as /p/. Most of these irregular forms are loan words and evince other irregular reflexes, but a couple have no other irregularities. In the first case, possibly the initial /h/ < *c of the root blocked the weakening of the *p. (It is the only example of an inherited root with *c onset of the penult and *p onset of the final syllable.)

> *capus > *hapu-i* 'wipe clean'

In the following case, perhaps an earlier prenasalization of the medial *p protected it:

> *tapes + *i > *tepi* 'winnow' (possibly < *tampi < *tapesi [cf. Ml *tampi* 'winnow'])

The following forms with irregular reflexes of *p are clearly loan words:

> *kuɣapu > *korapu* 'grouper' *ɬepuq > *nopu* 'lion fish' *pagay > *pae* 'rice' (/a/ of the penult is irregular as well [§C8.2.411]) *paɣis > *pagi* 'stingray' *payuŋ > *pau* 'umbrella' *paheɣaw > *pooro* 'hoarse' *tapay 'fermented rice cake' > *tape* 'k.o. sweet cake' *tapiq > *tapi* 'layer'

There are examples of a disyllable with initial /f/ and C-onset of the final syllable that developed from *p-.[31] Such a form could have developed by generalizing the allomorph that occurred in a suffixed form (where the initial *p would have developed into /f/).

> *pulut > *fulu* 'sticky' (a back-formation from *fuluti* 'catch (birds) with lime'. Cf. *pulu* 'a tree producing sticky substance.)

In the following case, no suffixed form of the root is found in the sources that would explain the change of *p > /f/:

> *paqa > *faɣa* 'thigh'

As coda, *-p is lost, but it may be reflected as /f/ before suffixes:

> *qatep 'thatching' > *ɣato* 'roof' *dakep > *rako* 'catch (singular)' *and rakof-i* 'catch (plural)' *cepecep > *soso* 'suck'

In one case initial *p- disappears. There is no explanation:

---

[31] There are plenty of disyllabic roots not derived from the protolanguage that have initial /p/ and a consonant onset of the final syllable. In other words, the rule that determines the distribution of the development of /f/ or /p/ from *p is currently not operative.

*pulec 'twist' > *ulo* 'twisted, tangled'

C8.3.12 *t

*t > /t/ in initial and medial position. Like the other consonants, *-t is lost in final position, but occasionally retained before the vowel of a suffix:

*taqi 'feces' > *taɣi* 'dregs' *tebus > *towu* 'sugar cane' *tuqus 'true' > *ko-tuɣu* 'right, true' *batu > *bhatu* 'stone' *qatay > *ɣate* 'liver' *qitem > *ɣito* 'black'

Examples of *-t:

*kulit > *kuli* 'skin' *libut 'surround, demarcate an area' > *liwu* 'village' (also *libuti* 'surround') *pat > *paa* 'four' (but also *fato* 'four') *paqit > *paɣi* 'bitter'

C8.3.13 *k

*k > /k/ in initial and medial position. Like the other consonants, *-k is lost in final position, but occasionally retained before the vowel of a suffix:

*kima > *kima* 'k.o. large shellfish' *beɣekes > *bhoke* 'bind together' *laki 'male' > *laki* 'leading bull in the herd' *tangkay 'stem of leaf' > *tangke* 'sheet (classifier)'

Exmples of *-k:

*bukebuk > *bubu* 'wood borer' *manuk 'bird' > *manu* 'chicken' *cucuk 'make go through by piercing' > *susuki* 'fill completely' (semantic contamination with a reflex of *cek, not attested in Muna)

*k- as onset to a non-final syllable with *a as its nucleus is weakened to /s/

*gali 'dig' > *seli* 'dig up' (< *kali [§C8.3.34]) *kacaw > *saho* 'rafter' *kasiw 'wood' > *sau* 'wood, stick' *kawanał > *suwana* 'right side' (< *sawana [§§C8.1.121, C8.1.8])

However, *ka- > /ka-/ in the following case. The word is probably borrowed:

*kawit > *kai* 'hook'

In one case *k- is lost with no explanation. The vowel of the first syllable is also not the regular reflex:

*kutu 'head louse' > *otu* 'louse'

C8.3.14 *q

*q > /ɣ/ except when protected by a preceding consonant:

*qatay > *ɣate* 'liver' *qitem > *ɣito* 'black' *qetut > *ɣotu* 'break wind' *quway > *ɣue* 'rattan' *baqeɣu > *buɣou* 'new' *ɣuqałay + *ma- > *moɣane* 'male' *punuq 'tree trunk' > *puɣu* 'classifier for trees' (< *puqun)

*q > /k/ when protected. In the first example, the first C of a cluster that had developed was lost. The other examples are nasal clusters. In several cases, a form with /k-/ is an prefixed allomorph of a root that occurs with /ɣ/ when not prefixed:

*liceqes > *liko* 'nit' (< *licqes) *qabu 'ashes' > *ngkabu* 'grey', *kang-kabu* 'roast in ashes' (cf. *ɣabu* 'ashes') *quluh > *padang-kulu* 'head (coarse)' (cf. *ɣulu* 'body') *qatep > *ɣato* 'roof' + *turu* 'drip' (< *tuduq) + linker > *turung-kato* 'eaves' *qałegaw > *ɣoleo* 'sun' + *kang-ha* > *kang-koleo-ha* 'frame or line to hang clothes' *q > /k/ sporadically[32] when there was a *ɣ to the right:

> *qawuɣ 'Bambusa sp.' > *koo* 'k.o. large bamboo' *seqeɣet > *kee* 'tight' (< *qeɣet)

*q is lost if it is the onset of the penult or earlier, unless it is initial in the word, in which case it is reflected with /ɣ/.[33]

> *basequ 'smell'> *wo-no* 'smell' (< *bou < *boesu < *baqesu) *buqaya > *buea* 'crocodile' *deɣeqac 'move vigorously and rapidly' > *ka-dei-dei* 'hurriedly' (< *deqeɣac)[34] *jaqet 'bad' > *dai* 'bad' *qałiɣuwan 'bee' > *ka-eniua* 'k.o. bee'

In two cases, a *q- onset of the penult in trisyllabic roots is reflected by /ɣ/. There is no explanation as to why the *q was not lost in these forms:

> *baqeɣu > *buɣou* 'new' *maɣuqałay > *moɣane* 'male'

C8.3.15 *c

There are two reflexes of *c: /s/ and /h/. There are rules for which of these two reflexes should occur, but the rules have numerous exceptions:
*c > /s/ word initially when not before *a, including the onset of the final syllable in reduplicated or doubled monosyllables:

> *ciwa > *siua* 'nine' *celecel > *soso* 'regret' *ciku > *siku* 'elbow' *cunecun > *sunsu* 'stack up'

In monosyllabic roots beginning in *c that occur with a petrified prefix, the *c also becomes /s/:

> *pacek 'wedge' (< *pa-'causative' + *cek) > *paso* 'nail' *tucuk (< *tu- + *cuk) > *tusu* 'pierce'

*c > /s/ when protected:

> *beɣecay > *bhose* 'oar' (< *beɣcay) *ŋucuq 'snout' > *nunsu* 'mouth' *sacaŋ > *ansa* 'gills'

Otherwise, *c > /h/—that is, initially before *a and medially, *c > /h/:[35]

> *caleɣ 'flooring' > *hale* 'floor' *cabuɣ 'scatter' > *hewi* 'plants that grow by themselves without being sown' *iseci > *ihi* 'contents' *puceg > *puhe* 'navel' *tacik > *tehi* 'sea'

---

32 This rule of dissimilation was not carried through to all cases of *q followed by *ɣ in the same word. Or possibly, the rule of dissimilation was dialectal, and in the case of these items, Muna reflects forms from the dialect that dissimilated the *q and other forms from the dialect that did not have this rule of dissimilation. The number of forms that fail to show dissimilation is far greater than the forms that show dissimilation. Here is one example:

> *qapuɣ > *ɣefi* 'lime'

33 In the following case, metathesis prevented the *q-onset of the penult from being lost. After metathesis, *q moved to initial position in the root and in that position is reflected with /ɣ/:

> *paqegu > *ɣofei* 'gall' (< *qapegu)

34 How the final syllable was changed to /i/ in *ka-deidei*, and *dai* is unknown.

35 Note the parallelism between *c and *k: both have the weakened reflex initially before *a and not before other vowels (§C8.3.13).

There are a few exceptions. Probably none of them, except for the word for 'one', are inherited from the protolanguage. Why the word for 'one' should be irregular is a puzzle.[36]

Examples of *c initially before /a/:

*cakit > *saki* 'illness' (probably borrowed) *caŋeɣ > *sande* 'lean on' *cahebay > *sampe-lao* 'hang down'

Examples of *c medially:

*aciq > *asi* 'like, love' (probably borrowed) *ica > *ise* 'one' *pacaŋ 'pair' > *pasa* 'equal' *paciɣ 'sand' > *pasi* 'coral' *picaw > *piso* 'knife' *qapucuk > *pusu* 'top, tip'

In two cases an /h/ is reflected where /s/ is expected. The first case is probably contaminated with an unidentified form. In the second case, the root only occurs prefixed or reduplicated or doubled. In the reduplicated or doubled form, the *c was medial (and thus became /h/), and the initial consonant of the word was brought in line with the initial consonant of the root:

*cilaw 'glare' > *hido* 'shine, sparkle' *cedu > *ho-hodu* or *hodu-hodu* 'hiccough'

In syllable-final and word-final position *c is lost except that when there is a suffix, *-c > /-h/:

*balec > *bhalo* 'answer, reply' *dicedic 'cut, lance' > *didi* 'slice' *liceqes > *liko* 'nit' (< *licqes) *panac > *pana* 'warm' and *fanah-a* 'hot'

C8.3.2 *h, *s

*h and *s were lost without a trace:

*sawak 'body' > *aa* 'waist'*dusa > *dua* 'two *bukes 'hair on head' > *wuu* 'body hair, fur' (< *busek) *tebus > *towu* 'sugar cane'

Examples of *-h loss:

*bahi + -in- > *ro-bhine* 'female' (< *binay < *binahi) *tuɫuh > *tunu* 'roast'

C8.3.3 Voiced stops

C8.3.31 *b

PAn *b has three reflexes in non-final position: /b/, /bh/ and /w/. /bh/ is the transcription of an imploded [bʔ]. In protected position *b is reflected with /b/. Otherwise, *b may be reflected by a stop (/b/ or /bh/ depending on the environment) or by a semivowel /w/, and there is no rule for determining whether *b is reflected with a stop consonant or with /w/. In the basic vocabulary, forms both with a stop consonant and with /w/ reflect PAn forms with *b. The best hypothesis to explain the double reflexes is that *b > /b/, and that /b/ subsequently weakened (as is the case of most of the other stop consonants), but that the weakening was not carried through all instances. There are numerous doublets with a stop, /b/ or /bh/, and /w/.[37] First, forms manifesting /w/:

---

[36] Van den Berg (1991: §§6,7) points out that the pronouns and the numbers do not reflect the PMP phonemes regularly.

[37] Note that other languages of central and south Sulawesi also evince double reflexes of *b (Pamona: §C5.3.41, Bugis §C6.3.31) Salayar does not have double reflexes, but many other languages of the area aside from Muna, Bugis, and Pamona do. (Cf. the second footnote to §C8.3.)

*balay 'large open house'> *wale* 'small house' *becuɣ > *wehi* 'full, satisfied' *binesiq 'seed' > *wine* 'seed, seedling' *bulaɫ > *wula* 'moon' *balabaw > *wolawo* 'rat' (but also *kuambo* 'rat' [with /b/ in protected position]) *ɣabuk 'pulverized' > *awu* 'destroyed, dissolved' *tuba > *tuwa* 'a bush: *Derris elliptica*'

In two cases *b was lost entirely. Possibly there are dialects which lost the contrast between /w/ and its absence between /u/ and /a/. In this case, *b > *w, which was subsequently lost dialectally:

*babaw + *ku- > *kuambo* 'rat' (< *ku-babaw) *qubaɫ > *ɣua* 'grey hair'

In cases where *b did not become /w/, *b > /b/ before /u/ and in protected position. Otherwise *b > /bh/. The following forms reflect a stop from *b, with /b/ in protected position and before /u/, and /bh/ elsewhere:

*bubu > *bubu* 'fish trap' *pukuh 'node, knot' > *buku* 'bone' (< *bukuh [cf. the entry in the glossary for the change of *p > *b]) *qabu 'ashes' > *ɣabu* 'ashes' *libut > *libut-i* 'surround' (also *liwu* 'village') *bukbuk > *bubu* 'wood borer' *tambal > *tamba* 'patch' *balec > *bhalo* 'reply' *batu 'stone' > *bhatu* 'stone' *beŋel 'deaf' > *bhongo* 'dumb, mute' *bahi + *-in-) > *ro-bhine* 'woman' (< *binay)

However, *qb > /bh/:

*baqbaq 'mouth' > *wobha* 'mouth' (with /bh/ in protected position)

In a form probably not directly inherited, *b is reflected with /b/ before a front vowel:

*biluk 'veer' > *belo* 'veer'

C8.3.32 *d

PAn *d, like many of the other stop consonants, has two reflexes in Muna, a strong stop reflex /d/ and a weakened reflex /r/. The strong reflex occurs in protected position. In most cases intervocalic *-d- is reflected by /r/. In initial position *d is reflected by both /r/ and /d/, and there are examples of doublets. As is the case of the other stops, the best hypothesis to explain the two reflexes is that there was a sound change that involved weakening of the *d and that this change was not carried through. In the case of *d, for all but a few examples, it would be far-fetched to explain the occurrence of /d/ instead of /r/ as a generalization of the reflex of the protected position.

The following forms exemplify /d/ in protected and in initial position:

*dicedic 'cut, lance' > *didi* 'slice'[38] *dusa 'two' > *dua* 'two' *dalem 'beneath, inside' > *ndalo* 'deep' *daqis > *kon-daɣi* 'forehead'

In initial position *d- is most often reflected with r-.

---

[38] The initial /d/ in this root might be explained by the fact that this root derives from a doubled monosyllable: the *d-onset of the second monosyllable became /d/ because it was protected by the coda of the first, and the first *d-onset was made to harmonize with the second:

*dicedic > *dicdic > *ridi > *didi* 'slice'

However, note that in the case of *demedem and *dapedap, the first *d became /r/ and was not brought into harmony with the onset of the second monosyllable.

*dayeq > *rea* 'blood' *demedem > *rondo* 'dark, be night' (note that the second occurrence of *d in this root is protected) *dapedap > *roda* 'a tree: *Erythrina* sp.'(The second *d is reflected with /d/ because it was protected by the coda of the first monosyllable, which was lost.)

Medially, *d is reflected with /-r-/ in almost all cases.

*qudip > *yu-yuri* 'alive' *kiday > *kire* 'eyebrow' *tuduq > *po-turu* 'leaking'

Before a suffix or paragoge, final *d was treated like medial *d:

*kid 'file' > *kiri* 'scrape' *kud 'grate' > *kuru* 'shave off'

An unprotected *d-onset of the penult us assimilated to an *l-onset of the final syllable:

*dalem 'inside' > *lalo* 'heart, set of emotions' *dilaq > *lela* 'tongue' (/e/ developed by contamination with *selayi* 'lick')

There is one case in which *-d- is reflected with a stop. There is no explanation:

*cedu 'hiccough'> *hodu* 'hiccough'

In one case, *d is reflected with the apico-dental voiced stop /d^y/), a loan from an unknown source:

*damay 'torch' > *pa-d^yamara* 'traditional oil lamp'

In at least one form, a cluster with *nd was simplified to /-d-/ (with the /-d-/ retaining its stop character in protected position):

*tindec 'press flat, crush' > *tido* 'kill lice by squeezing them with the nails'

In final position, *d was lost, as is the case for all consonants:

*pańid > *pani* 'wing' *sated 'deliver' > *ato* 'bring s.o. to a destination'

C8.3.33 *j

Like *b and *d, *j also has two reflexes: a weak reflex—i.e., a spirant /s/, and strong reflex—i.e., a stop /d/. The one example of *j in protected position manifests the strong reflex. In initial and intervocalic position, both /s/ and /d/ reflect *j. However, reflexes of /d/ from *j are not numerous, and the forms with /d/ may be borrowings.

*jalan > *sala* 'road, path' *jilat > *sela-yi* 'lick s.t.' *qajelay > *sole* 'a grain: *Coix lachryma-jobi*' *qujał > *yuse* 'rain' *tujuq 'point' > *tusu* 'point toward'

Examples of *j > /d/:

*jaqet 'bad' > *dayo* 'stingy' *jiyuq > *ka-diu* 'bathe' *sejam > *ada* 'borrow' *ijak 'tread on' < *f-inda* 'step' (with sporadic nasal insertion) *jayum 'needle' > *deu* 'needle' (also *ka-sau* 'thread on a needle')

There are three cases in which *j is reflected with /d^y/. In these cases, however, it is unlikely that the environment had anything to do with the development of /d^y/ (as is the case of the development of /bh/). I say this because *d does not have fronted reflexes: if the following vowel affected the articulation of the reflex of *j, the analogous thing should have happened with the reflexes of *d. Therefore, it is most probably the case that these forms are not directly inherited. In the case of the second and third examples, there are also a reflexes of the PAn root with /d/ or /s/:

*sijaw 'green' > *iďo* 'green' *ijak 'tread on' > *fiďa* 'stamp the feet' (also *finda* 'step, tread') *jalan > *ďala* 'way, method' (cf. *sala* 'road')

In final position, *j is lost entirely:

*penej 'plugged up' > *pono* 'full' (meaning influenced by *peɫuq 'full', which has no direct reflex in Muna) *qalaj > *ka-ɣala* 'pen' *tukej > *tuko* 'prop, support'

C8.3.34 *g

When it was the onset to the penult or earlier and to monosyllables, *g- > k-.

*gemi 'sucker fish' > *komi* 'suck' *gaɣut 'scrape' > *kau* 'grate'[39] *guɣita > *kuita* 'octopus'

The change of *g- > /k-/ preceded the change of *ka > /sa/ (§C8.3.13), so that *ga also changes to /sa/:

*galih > *seli* 'dig, dig up' (For /e/, cf. §C8.2.413.)

When it was onset or coda of the final syllable. *g was lost. Note that in some environments, *g affected the vowels with which it had been in contact (§§C8.2.32, C8.2.411).

*qapegu > *ɣofei* 'gall' *qaɫegaw > *ɣoleo* 'day' *quleg 'worm' > *ɣule* 'snake, worm' *puceg > *puhe* 'navel'

There are a few forms in which *g is changed to a reflex other than initial /k-/ or medial Ø. These are not directly inherited:

*baliga > *bhalida* 'weaver's sword' *bugeq > *bura* 'lather, foam, scum' *maga 'dry' > *mala* 'blazing, red hot' *gemi 'hold on to' > *ɣomi* 'sucker fish' (in addition to the regular *komi* 'suck') *giliŋ 'roll over s.t.' > *gili* 'grind, mill'

C8.3.4 Voiced continuants

C8.3.41 *ɣ

*ɣ was lost in all environments, except when protected. In initial position, we have found only two forms that are directly inherited.

*ɣabuk 'pulverized' > *awu* 'destroyed, dissolved' *ɣugan 'load' > *owa* 'load, bringing, carrying' (the /w/ is unexplained)

In medial position, there is any number of inherited forms showing loss of *ɣ. There is a trace of the *ɣ, in that the *ɣ often affected the quality of the preceding vowel before it was lost (§§C8.2.32, C8.2.411):

*laɣiw > *fi-lei* 'run, flee' *jaɣum > *ka-sau* 'thread on the needle' *maɣi > *mai* 'come' *guɣita > *kuita* 'octopus'

In protected position, *ɣ is reflected with a /g/. In the first example, below, the *g that had developed from *ɣ was assimilated to the preceding /n/ of the prefix; in the second, metathesis took place causing *q to precede *ɣ and protect it (§C8.1.6). *ɣ then became /g/ and *q was lost:

[39] Why /kau/ did not change to *sau (§C8.3.13) is unexplained.

*ɣabihi 'night' > *in-dewi* 'yesterday' (< *in-gabi) *baɣeqaŋ 'molar' > *bhaga* 'molar' (< *baqɣaŋ < *baqeɣaŋ)

The /g/ in the following two forms may also have developed from *ɣ. The first may have developed by metathesis, but this is speculative, for there is no other example of a parallel metathesis. The second may be a generalization of the allomorph that occurred after the prefix *mang-*.[40]

*aɣusuq > *guu* 'the Australian pine: *Casuarina*' (< *saguu < *saqɣuu) *ɣabun > *gawu* 'mist, fog' (cf. *manggawu* 'distant, invisible')

In the following examples, *ɣ is reflected with /r/, with /g/, or with /l/ in one case. These forms are not directly inherited:

*buɣaw 'chase away' > *bhora* 'shout to shoo away'(with irregular reflexes of *u and *-aw, as well), *ɣakit > *raki* 'raft' *iɣiŋ > *m-iri* 'aslant' *kuɣapu > *korapu* 'grouper' *paheɣaw > *pooro* 'hoarse' (/oo/ also irregular) *sabaɣat 'strong monsoon' > *bhara* 'season of westerly rains' *tiɣem > *tira* 'k.o. oyster' *paɣis > *pagi* 'stingray' (also *pai-pai-ta* 'fish resembling the stingray' [with the regular reflex of *ɣ]) *taɣa 'wait' > *ntaga* 'hover in sky' *paɣa 'large shelf, rack' > *pala-pala* 'low bench near hearth'

C8.3.42 *l

*l > /l/ in initial and medial position. In final position it was lost, just as the other consonants were:

*laŋit > *lani* 'sky' *lima > *lima* 'five, hand' *alem > *alo* 'night' *piliq > *pili* 'choose' *telu > *tolu* 'three' *celcel > *soso* 'regret' *tambal > *tamba* 'patch'

As second C in a cluster that developed, *l is strengthened (> /d/):

*lebeleb 'hidden by being covered' > *lodo* 'sleep' (< *lebleb)

In another case, *l is reflected with /d/. This form is not directly inherited, for otherwise *l between like vowels is reflected with /l/:

*cilaw 'shine' > *hido* 'shine, sparkle'

C8.3.43 *ɬ

*ɬ underwent the changes found throughout the MP languages (§§A1.1.32, 4th¶, A3.3.4). In addition, PMP †ñ < *ɬ underwent depalatalization, as it did in many of the MP languages.[41] As onset to an unstressed penult or earlier syllable, *ɬ- becomes /l-/. Otherwise, *ɬ > /n/. This rule can be restated as follows:

Preceding the unstressed penult or earlier syllable, *ɬ > /l-/, as is the case of most western An languages. Otherwise, *ɬ > /n-/ and /-n-/.

---

[40] More likely, this form is secondary. It also is attested in other languages of south Sulawesi with an initial /g/, where it is also not the regular reflex, e.g. Pamona *gawu* 'cloud' (§C5.3.45).

[41] In fact, any occurrence of [ñ], whether it arose from *ɬ or by syncope from *niy, depalatalized (> [n]):

*peniyu > *ponu* 'sea turtle' (< *penyu)

*ɬágam 'tame > *nea* 'accustomed to doing' *ɬaŋúy > *leni* 'swim' *qáɬegaw > *ɣoleo* 'day' *aɬak > *ana* 'child' *waɬiw > *ani* 'bee' *tuɬu > *tunu* 'burn, roast'

There are two exceptions. The first is probably not directly inherited. In many of the MP languages, this form manifests the expected initial /l/, but in other languages, it shows an unexpected /n/, and it is clear that the form with /n/ spread secondarily. (Cf. *ɬepuq in the glossary.) In the second case, the *ɬ is onset to the antepenult. In other Hesperonesian languages, *ɬ > /l/ as onset to the antepenult (e.g. Tagalog *ligwan* 'bee' [§C1.3.43]). It is a mystery why Muna should evince an /n/ in this form rather than /l/.[42]

*ɬepúq 'lion fish' < *nopu* 'stone fish with poisonous spines' *qaɬiɣuwan > *ka-eniua* 'k.o. bee'

One form manifests /r/ as the reflex of *ɬ instead of the expected /l/. It also shows loss of the penult and of the initial syllable of the root, not a normal development in Muna. The form is probably not directly inherited:

*qaɬimataq > *rinta* 'leech'

C8.3.5 *m, *n, *ŋ

In general, *m and *n remain unchanged in initial and medial position and in clusters—that is, *m, *n > /m/, /n/, respectively, in initial and medial position:

*manuk 'bird' > *manu* 'chicken' (*manu-manu* 'bird') *lima > *lima* 'five, hand' *naɬaq < *nana* 'pus' *nem > *nomo* 'six'

In final position, the nasals are lost (except on occasion when protected by the vowel of a suffix):

*qitem > *ɣito* 'black' *jalan > *sala* 'road, way' *qusalipan > *ɣolifa* 'centipede' *qumaŋ > *kala-ɣuma* 'hermit crab'

Nasals are also preserved in clusters, but assimilated to the articulation of the following consonant. In the doubled monosyllables in the following list, the epenthetic vowel was syncopated:

*demedem 'dark, cloudy' > *ronda* 'dark, be night' *tumbuk 'hit hard with thump' > *tumbu* 'pound, strike' *tunetun 'lead on rope'> *tuntu* 'continue, prolong', *paŋepaŋ > *pampa* 'steep slope, cliff' *taŋkay 'stem of leaf' > *tangke* 'leaf (classifier)'

Between a high vowel and /u/ in the following syllable, intervocalic *-m- >/-mb-/:

*timuɣ > *timbu* 'east wind' *mula 'plant' > *fe-mbula* 'cultivate, raise, breed'

Similarly, *n > /nd/ between a low vowel and a high front vowel:

*caŋeɣ 'lean on' > *sande* 'lean on' (< *saneɣ by the rule immediately following)

---

[42] Other Hesperonesian languages outside of the Philippines also show the reflex that is normal after a stressed vowel (e.g. ND *ñuan* 'k.o. biting ant' [§2.3.43, footnote]), and it is possible that this word underwent a shift of stress in the ancestor of the languages that show the /ñ/ reflex. In other words, it is possible that the protoform had antepenultimate stress *qáɬiɣuwan, which shifted to the penult in the ancestor of Muna and ND, but not in the ancestor of Tag. Another possibility is that the development of the /ñ/ reflex occurred at a later time in one language and subsequently spread to other Hesperonesian languages.

*ŋ is reflected as /n/ unless coming to abut on /k/:

*ŋagan > *nea* 'name' *ŋucuq 'snout' > *nunsu* 'mouth' *baŋuɬ > *wanu* 'rise' *buŋa > *wuna* 'flower' *daŋ > *rana* 'warm oneself near fire' (< *daŋa with /a/ paragoge) *laŋit > *lani* 'sky' *liŋaw 'bewildered' > *koli-lino* 'lost, astray' *ɬaŋuy > *leni* 'swim'

Words with an *-ŋ coda in the protolanguage that are attested in Muna with a petrified suffix retain /ŋ/:

*timbaŋ 'balanced' > *timbangi* 'weight' *tuluŋ > *tulungi* 'help'

In the case of the following form, the *ɣ on the right probably blocked the change of *ŋ to /n/:

*deŋeɣ > *ndenge* 'listen while sleeping'

There are other forms that reflect *ŋ with /ng/. They are secondary, although the source is unknown in most cases:

*ŋa > *ma-nga* 'be wide agape' *banguɬ 'rise' > *bhangu* 'shape' *beŋel 'deaf' > *bhongo* 'dumb, mute' *leŋa > *longo* 'sesame' *paŋa 'forking' > *kam-panga* 'fork in the river' *teŋaq > *tanga* 'half, middle, in the process of'

C8.3.61 *w

Initial *w was lost:

*wañiw 'bee' > *ani* 'k.o. honey bee' *walu 'eight > *alu* 'eight' *walu + R- > *oalu* (< *aalu [C8.1.21]) *wasiyeɣ 'water' > *oe* 'water' (< *woeɣ [§C8.3.62] < *woyeɣ [§C8.1.2, 2nd¶] < *woiyeɣ [§C8.1.21] < *waiyeɣ)

Intervocalic *-w- was lost in most cases:

*sawak 'body' > *aa* 'waist' *tawa 'laugh' > *fu-taa* 'laugh' *kawit 'hook' > *kai* 'hooked' *buwaq 'fruit' > *bua* 'classifier for large fruits and other round empty objects'

There are two cases in which *w is reflected by /w/ or syllabic /u/, and these probably are not directly inherited, although there may be another explanation for the retention of *w:

*nisawa 'breath' > *inawa* 'life sustaining force, breath' *ciwa > *siua* 'nine'

In one case *-w- is reflected with /bh/. The form is not directly inherited:

*kawil 'hook'> *ko-kabhi* 'fishing hook'

For the diphthongs and *we see §§C8.2.34, C8.2.52, C8.2.53.

C8.3.62 *y

*y was lost but caused a preceding *a become /e/ (§C8.2.413a).

*buqaya 'crocodile' > *buea* 'crocodile' *iyu 'second plural' > *m-iu* 'you plural (genitive)' *payung > *pau* 'umbrella' *tiyaɬ 'belly' > *tie* 'uterus' *uyuɣ > *ue* 'rock, swing' *wasiyeɣ 'water' > *oe* 'water' (< *woeɣ < *woyeɣ [§C8.1.2, 2nd¶] < *woiyeɣ [§C8.1.21] < *waiyeɣ)

For the diphthongs and *ey, see §§C8.2.34, C8.2.51, C8.2.52.

Part D. Developments of the languages of Kalimantan, Malagasy, and Malay

These languages are treated together in one section because they all originate on Kalimantan. Although they share some vocabulary innovations that spread over the languages of the island, they make no innovations in common not made by other MP languages as well. Kelabit and other languages of N. Sarawak belong in one group (Blust 2006), and Malagasy and Ngaju Dayak both are in a subgroup together with other languages of the southwest Barito basin. No evidence has turned up to show that the southwest Barito and the N. Sarawak languages belong in a subgroup. Nor has any evidence turned up to show that Malay subgroups with other languages in Kalimantan.

Map 7. Kalimantan and location of Kelabit, Iban, Ngaju Dayak, Malay.

CHAPTER ONE

Kelabit

D1.0 General background

Kelabit (Kel) is the name given to a number of closely related dialects spoken in upriver portions of the Fourth and Fifth Divisions of Sarawak and in neighboring areas of Indonesian Kalimantan, generally at altitudes above 2,000 feet. There is no information on the total number of speakers, but it is small (Blust 1993: 141). The data here relies mainly on Blust 1993 and Amster 1995. I also took down a list from a native speaker of Kelabit, Poline Bala, who studied at Cornell University in 1996-1999. The following chart shows the inventory of Kel phonemes. There is apparently a difference in vowel inventory among the dialects. Amster reports both /ʌ/ and /ə/,[1] whereas Blust reports only /ə/. The phonemes or sequences in parentheses are not found in inherited forms. Stress is predictably on the penult of the word unless the vowel of the penult is *e, in which case the stress is on the final syllable.

CHART ONE. PHONEMES OF KELABIT

Consonants

voiceless stops	p	t	k	ʔ
voiced stops	b	d	g	
aspirated stops	b^h	d^h	(g^h)	
spirants		s		h
nasals	m	n	ng [ŋ]	
liquids	w	l, r	y	

Vowels

high	i		u
mid	ɛ	e [ə]	o
low-mid		ʌ	
low		a	
diphthongs	iw	(ay, aw)	uy

D1.1 Changes which characterize Kel in general

D1.1.1 Treatment of trisyllabic roots

Trisyllabic roots were shortened when a medial consonant was lost and the resulting abutting vowels contracted or when a penultimate *e was syncopated and the resulting CC simplified. This is described in §§D1.1.14 and D1.1.15, below. If a trisyllabic root did not lose a medial consonant or elide a penultimate *e, then the first syllable was lost if it began with a vowel or had had a C onset that was lost—i.e., *q, *h, *s, and *c, as detailed in §§D1.3.14 and D1.3.2ff.

[1] Both /ʌ/ and /ə/ occur in inherited forms, but /ʌ/ is reported in only a very small number of them. There is no environment that determines when /ʌ/ occurs, and here I treat both as a single reflex, ignoring the fact that some dialects have /ʌ/ in place of /ə/ in a few forms.

D1.1.11 Loss of a syllable

If the penult onset was lost, the abutting vowels contracted by loss of *e or loss of the first of two succeeding vowels:

> *baɣehat > *berat* 'heavy' (<*beɣehat [cf. 3rd ¶, below]) *buqaya > *bayeh* 'crocodile' *kasepal > *kapal* 'thick' *seqeɣet 'tight' > *eret* 'man's belt' *laqeya > *lieh* 'ginger' (< *laia < *layiʔa [§D1.13] < *laʔiya)

If the root initial was a vowel, *q,[2] or *s, the initial syllable was lost:

> *aluten > *luten* 'half-burnt wood' *paqegu > *pedʰuh* 'gall' (< *qapegu) *qisuwab > *uab* 'yawn' *qiteluɣ > *terur* 'egg' *sadiɣi > *diri* 'house post' *sapegiq 'causing sharp pain' > *pedʰih* 'salty' *sehapuy > *apuy* 'fire'

If the trisyllabic root did not lose a consonant onset of the penult (*h, *s, or *q), the vowel of the antepenult was weakened to /e/:[3]

> *balatik > *belatik* 'spring arrow trap' *bikaŋekaŋ > *bekakang* 'with legs spread apart' *bituka > *betueh* 'stomach' *juɣami > *derami* 'straw' *pacaqaɬ > *maʔen* 'carry over shoulder' (< *paaʔen < *pacaʔen < *pecaʔan) *qalima 'hand' + N- verb former' > *ngelima* 'rub between the palms or the hands) *qaɬimátek > *lematek* 'leech' (*qa- is lost, but *ɬi is only weakened) *tinaqi > *senaʔih* 'intestines'

There are two exceptions in which the antepenult was not weakened. They are secondary forms:

> *binuwaŋ > *binuang* 'k.o. tree' *bituqen > *gituʔen* 'star' (also *getuʔen*)

The antepenult was lost entirely in the following forms, even though they did not contain one of the lost consonants. The explanation is probably dialect mixture:

> *kulabaw > *labo* 'rat' *tened 'sink' > *mened* 'drown' (< *tumened)[4]

D1.1.12 Loss of the penult with an *e nucleus in trisyllables

The penult was lost in forms that had an *e nucleus in the penult, and the resulting CC was simplified by losing the first C:

> *layehu > *layuh* 'withered' (< *laheyu) *liceqes > *liʔa* 'nit' *pakehu > *paʔuh* 'fern' *qaselu > *aluh* 'pestle' *tuqelaɬ > *tulang* 'bone'

If the second C (onset of the final syllable) was a voiced stop, it became aspirated (§D1.3.3):

---

[2] In two cases the antepenult with initial *q was not lost: *qaselu 'pestle' and *qaɬegaw 'day'. In the case of *qaselu, the loss of the *s probably caused the penultimate vowel to contract before the initial *qa- could get lost, and it did not get lost, because after the loss of the *e, the root became disyllabic. The antepenult of *qaɬegaw weakened, but was not lost, whereas the penultimate *e was lost with subsequent simplification of the resultant consonant cluster (*-lg- < *-ɬeg-). This form may well be a borrowing in Kel. (Cf. a similar process in §D1.1.12a.)

[3] This rule also applies to doubled monosyllabic roots with an *a nucleus (but not to roots with an *i or *u nucleus). Doubled monosyllabic roots had an epenthetic *e (§A3.6.1).

> *bakebak 'remove outer layer' > *bebʰak* 'torn' *bunebun > *bubʰun* 'heap, pile'

[4] *Mened* 'drown' could be compared to *temaraʔ* 'clear the forest' (< *tumaɣaq 'cut') *temurun* 'go down' (< *tumuɣun), which did not lose the antepenult, but weakened it to /e/.

*qałegáw > *ed^{h}o* 'day' (< *qeld^{h}aw < *qeldáw < *qełegáw) *saɣejał > *ed^{h}an* 'ladder'

D1.1.12a

In some cases of roots with a penult that had *h, *s, or *q onset, the antepenult was weakened first (as in (D1.1.11, 3rd¶), above) before contraction of the vowel of the penult with the vowel of the antepenult took place (as in (D1.1.11, 1st¶), above). That is, the Kel reflex has /e/ in the first syllable. It is unknown why some roots weakened the antepenult first before the *h-, *s-, or *q- onset of the penult was lost, and why others failed to do so.

*busekag 'unfold (of flower)' > *bekad* 'split' (< *besekad) *baqeɣuh > *beruh* 'new' *basequ > *bu-en* 'a smell' (< *bequ-en[5] < *besequ-) *saɣejał > *ed^{h}an* 'ladder' (< *seɣjał < *seɣejał)

D1.1.13 Contraction of the penult and final syllables

If the onset of the final syllable was lost, the vowels of the final two syllables were contracted. The resulting vowel sequences contracted as follows: *e was lost, two like vowels were contracted to a single vowel, *u and *i formed diphthongs with the vowel that preceded them. Further, *aw and *ay that developed from this changed to /o/ and /ɛ/ respectively [§D1.2.4]):

*aɣusuq > *aruʔ* 'Australian pine' *baɣiyus > *bariw* 'storm' *betihec > *beti* 'calf of leg' *dasuwen > *daʔun* 'leaf' *ikasu > *iko* 'you' (< *ikaw) *jaqewis > *ma-do* 'far' (< *ma-jaw > *ma-jau < *ma-jaweq < *ma-jawiseq) *lahuwen > *aʔun* 'long time' (loss of *l unexplained) *palisi 'taboo' > *alih* 'pregnant'

D1.1.14 Contraction of vowels

The changes outlined In §D1.1.1ff, above, led to vowel contractions. Like vowels that come to abut as a result of loss of an intervening consonant contract (cf. D1.1.13):

*aɣusuq > *aruʔ* 'the Australian pine: *Casuarina*' *palisi 'taboo' > *alih* 'pregnant' *piya + *-an > *piyan* 'desire, want'

When *q, *s, *h, or *c abutting on *e were lost, the *e disappeared (was elided or absorbed by the other vowel in the root). See the examples under §§D1.1.11 and D1.1.12, above. Other contractions are specified in §D1.1.13, above. In the following case, a monosyllabic root resulted from loss of *q and *c, and the vowel was doubled to retain disyllabicity (§§D1.1.2):

*leqacem > *laam* 'sour' (< *lam < *leaem)

Forms that typically occurred in atonic position (formed a stress-group with the word immediately following) underwent elision and vowel contraction:

*dalem > *lem* 'inside' *bayaq > *mɛ* 'go' (<*mayaʔ[6]).

---

[5] When the suffix /-en/ was added, the word became trisyllabic and weakened the antepenult by the rule of §D1.1.11. Cf. §D1.3.14 for the loss of *q onset of the penult in trisyllabic forms.

[6] Syllables prior to the antepenult were lost in a stress-group. I assume that *dalam + (C)VCV(C) > *lem + (C)VCV(C). But in some cases, phonologically determined, it was the antepenultimate vowel that was lost: *mayaʔ + (C)VCV(C) > *may + (C)VCV(C) with the loss of *ʔ in the CC or in the onset of the penult, as well. Subsequently *may > *mɛ* (§D1.2.4).

D1.1.15 Simplification of consonant clusters

Consonant clusters that resulted from the elision of a penultimate *e in trisyllabic roots (§D1.1.12, above) were simplified by the loss of the first consonant in the sequence (cf. the examples of §D1.1.12). This rule also applies to doubled monosyllabic roots: the epenthetic *e in the penult was lost and the final consonant of the first doubled element (that is, the first C of the cluster that had developed) was lost:

> *butebut > *bub^{h}ut* 'pluck out' (< *butbut) *tuketuk 'strike' > *tutuk* 'pestle'

Although PMP had nasal clusters, these have become simplified in Kel: *mb > /b^h/; *nd, *nj > /d^h/; *nt > /t/:

> *bunebun > *bubhun* 'heap' (< *bumbun)[7] *tinjak 'step on' > *tid^{h}aʔ* 'footprint'[8] *bintiq 'shins' > *meti* 'kick'

D1.1.2 Disyllabization of monosyllabic roots

Kel like most of the An languages disyllabized monosyllabic roots that were not atonic. Disyllabization took place in one of three ways: (1) stretching the root by doubling the vowel nucleus or by addition of a prothetic /e/, (2) doubling or reduplicating the monosyllabic root, or (3) petrifaction of an affix:
(1) addition of a prothetic /e/ or doubling the vowel nucleus:

> *teb 'cut off' > *eteb* 'action of cutting off' *keb 'cover' > *ekeb* 'a cover, lid' *cak > *l-aak* 'ripe'

(2) doubling or reduplicating a monosyllabic root:

> *ba > *babeh* 'carry on back' *biɣ 'lip-like growth' > *bibir* 'lips' *daɬ > *dadan* 'old' *kuj 'lower shank' > *kukud* 'leg' *gap > *ngakap* 'grope' (< *kapkap plus nasalization)

(3) by adding an affix that became petrified:

> *busuk + *ma- > *mabuk* 'drunk' *kab + *ise- > *ikab* 'opening in roof to provide light, emit smoke, etc.' *kab + *um- > *ng-ukab* 'open (a door, etc.)' *met + *ise- > *imet* 'seize' *pan + *um- > *upan* 'bait'

Monosyllabic roots that form verbs with /nga/[9] developed disyllabic back formations consisting of /a/ + root: the /ng/ of the prefix was taken to be the verbal prefix. The following forms are examples:

> *baŋ > *abang* 'ditch', *ngabang* 'make a ditch' *tay > *atɛ* 'death', *ngatɛ* 'kill'

Monosyllabic roots that developed from disyllabic roots that lost a syllable also disyllabized by the same processes:

---

[7] The aspiration of the medial *b took place before the loss of the epenthetic *e in *bunebun (cf. the discussion in the second footnote to the third paragraph of §D1.3.3.) There are no other examples of the change of *mb > /b^h/ in inherited forms. Nevertheless, we assume this to the rule, and a form like *timang* 'weighing scale' < *timbaŋ is borrowed.

[8] The development of /d^h/ indicates that prior to the loss of the nasal, *tinjak developed an epenthetic *e (i.e., > *tinejak), which subsequently was elided (§D1.3.3).

[9] /nga-/ itself is formed by nasal substitution (§D1.1.5) of a petrified form with a prefix *ka- which, to my knowledge, does not occur with the roots discussed in this section. A cognate with /ka-/ is found in other languages of the area, e.g. Mukah *katay* 'turn off (light, etc.)'

*sejen > *ded^h^en* 'press down' (< *jen) *basaq 'flood' < *eb^h^aʔ* 'water , liquid coming out of something' (< *baq) *bayaq 'leave' > *emɛ* (when occurring as an independent word) 'go' (< *mɛ* [in atonic position] < *mayaq [also attested as *mayaʔ* 'follow']) *bukes > *eb^h^uk* 'hair on head' (< *buk < *busek) *leqacem > *laam* 'sour' (< *lam < *leaem) *tucuk 'pierce' > *nuuk* 'thread a needle (< *tuk) *basequ > + *-en* > *buen* 'a smell' *jaqewis + *ma-* > *mado* 'far'

D1.1.3 Metathesis

Except for the metathesis that took place in PMP or earlier, Kel reflects little metathesis. Here are the only examples found in the data. They most involve vocalic metathesis:

*baɣeqaŋ > *beraʔang* 'molar' *qaɬiɣuwan > *berinuan* 'bee' (metathesis precedes the rule that *ɬ > /l/ [§D1.3.43]) *qaɣuc > *awer* 'current' (< *aur[10] < *aru) *keɬaŋ + *ta-[11] > *sekanan* 'remember' (> *ta-kenan) *laheyu > *layuh* 'withered' (< *layehu) *lepit 'fold' > *lipet* 'manifold' *pacaqaɬ > *maʔen* 'carry over the shoulders' (< *paaʔen < *pacaqen < *pecaqan [§D1.1.11, 3nd ¶]) *tusuq > *tuʔuh* (< *tuqus) 'true'

D1.1.4 Insertion of laryngeals

When a consonant was lost in the onset of the root-final syllable of a disyllabic root, a glottal stop was intercalated in the hiatus that developed:[12]

*lahuj 'seaward' > *laʔud* 'downriver' *lahuwen > *aʔun* 'long time ago' (< *laʔun [loss of /l/ unexplained] < *lahun)

Note that no hiatus developed with the loss of a consonant onset of the final syllable in a trisyllabic root (cf. the examples in §D1.1.13, above).

D1.1.41 Addition of /-h/ after final vowel

In words with inherited final vowels (but not final diphthongs) or ending in PAn *-Vh or in *-Vs, an automatic [h] was added at the end of the root (that is, final vowels became voiceless). The [-h] became contrastive when *ay and *aw monophthongized (§D1.2.4), when *-c was lost, creating a new group of vowel final stems, and when loan-words with final vowel were borrowed without accreting an [-h].

mata > *mateh* 'eye' *aɣi > *marih* 'come here' *bubu > *bubuh* 'k.o. fish trap' *baɣah > *bareh* 'glowing coals' *capuh 'sweep' > *apuh* 'broom' *tebus > *teb^h^uh* 'sugar cane'

There are cases where an inherited final vowel did not develop an /-h/. There is no explanation:

*ŋaŋa 'mouth agape' > *nganga* 'open mouth'

---

[10] A sequence *VuC normally becomes /VʔuC/ in Kel (§D1.1.4, below). The change to /VweC/ indicates that this form is a borrowing. The source is unknown.

[11] The prefix was probably *ta-, and *t > /s/. Cf. the discussion in §D1.3.12, footnote.

[12] Note, however, that loss of /k/ did not invariably give rise to a glottal stop (§D1.3.13).

D1.1.5 Nasal substitution and *-um-* infixation

Verbs are sometimes quoted in affixed form in the sources. There are two types of verbal affixation that cause morphophonemic alternations, as is common in Hesperonesian languages: nasal substitution and *-um-* infixation (which arose from *um*-prefixation [§A3.7.1]). Nasalization consists of the substitution of a homorgnic nasal for the initial consonant of the root (cf. §A3.7.1 for a discussion of this process in An languages in general). The following chart shows this process in Kel:

CHART TWO. NASAL SUBSTITUTION IN KELABIT ONSETS

initial C	p, b	t, d, *c[13]	k, g	vowel[13]
nasal sub.	m	n	ng	ng

Examples:

*pacaqaɬ > *maʔen* 'carry over shoulder' *bayaʔ 'leave' > *mayaʔ* 'follow', *mɛ* 'go' *dakep > *nakep* 'catch' *tucuk 'pierce' > *nuuk* 'thread a needle' *gemel > *ngumel* 'squeeze in hand' *alap > *ngalap* 'take'

The affix *-um-* is infixed following the initial consonant of the stem, but if the initial is /b/ or /p/, there is no infixation, and /p/ or /b/ get substituted for by /m/ (that is, *-um-* in those cases is indistinguishable from nasalization). If a stems begins in a vowel, /m-/ is prefixed in place of *um-* (that is, the /u/ of the affix is elided):

*tened 'sink' > *mened* 'drown' (< *tumened with loss of the antepenult [§D1.1.11, 3rd footnote]) *tuɣun > *temurun* 'go down'[14] *siɣup 'slurp' > *mirup* 'drink' (< -um- + *irup < *sirup)

D1.1.51 Back formations

Since initial /m/ in a verb may be in a paradigm with either /p/ or initial vowel, back formations have occurred in Kel, as has been the case of other Hesperonesian languages. The following form is an example:

*weliq > *muliʔ* 'return home' (< *um- + *uliq), *puliʔ* 'coming back together' (back formation from *muliʔ*)

Similarly a stem beginning in *p- may be reanalyzed as beginning in a vowel:

*palisi > *alih* 'taboo, pregnancy' (back formation from *malih* 'be pregnant')

---

[13] *c was lost in Kel, but it left traces in the nasalization process: if the initial vowel is in a root that has lost initial *c, the nasalization process produces /n/:

*capuh > *apuh* 'broom' *napuh* 'sweep'

[14] Why the antepenult is lost entirely when *-um- was added to *tened, but only weakened to /te/ in the case of *tuɣun is unknown.

D1.1.6 Accreted consonants

Several vowel-final roots occur with accreted /-n/ or /-ʔ/. The /-n/ either remounts to a suffix *-en or *-an, where the vowel of the suffix contracted with the final root vowel, or it is a petrified linker, such as is productive in many of the Philippine languages and is found petrified across the board in MP languages:

anu > *anun* 'what' (< *anu + linker) *qacawa 'in-law' > *awan* 'spouse' (possibly from *qacawa + *-an) *piya 'desirous' > *piyan* 'desire, want s.t.' (< *piya + *-an)

In the case of terms of relations the final /-ʔ/ derives from the use of the term as a vocative. Other cases are borrowed from or influenced by Ml.

*ama > *t-amaʔ* 'father' *ina > *s-inaʔ* 'mother' *beraniʔ* 'daring' < Ml *berani* 'dare' *belangaʔ* 'k.o. jug' (< *balanga,* a word that has spread to many of the Hesperonesian languages) *buŋa > *bungaʔ* 'flower' *iseci > *isiʔ* 'contents' *tambuɣi 'triton shell' > *buriʔ* 'someone's words'

Contamination accounts for /-ʔ/ in some cases:

*lawa > *kelawaʔ* 'spider' (contamination with the word for 'net' *lawaq, not attested for Kel) *kiluŋ > *kiluʔ* 'crooked' (contamination with other words meaning 'bent, crooked' ending in /-ʔ/)

Other cases are unexplained:

*baluɬ 'rolled in a bundle' > *baluʔ* 'provisions' *ciwa > *iwaʔ* 'nine' (perhaps /-ʔ/ developed in counting)

D1.2 Vowels and diphthongs

D1.2.1 *i, *u

When not syncopated (§D1.1.1ff.), *i > /i/:

*piliq 'choose' > *piliʔ* 'choice'

In one case, *i is lowered to /ɛ/. There is no explanation. Probably this is a dialect borrowing:

*taŋic > *nangɛ* 'weep'

When not syncopated, *u > /u/:

*puluq > *puluʔ* 'ten'

In two cases, *u is reflected with /e/. In the first case, there is no explanation. In the second, the /u/ has been centralized because the form occurs most frequently in pretonic position.

*qulun 'rest head' > *elen* 'pillow of wood or corn silk' *kunu > *ken* 'it is said'[15]

In one case *u is reflected by /i/. There is no explanation:

*ludaq > *lidʰaʔ* 'spit'

---

[15] The loss of the final *u is also due to the pre-tonic position of this word. The final vowel of the root came to be unstressed as the second syllable of the stress-group of three or more syllables.

D1.2.2 *e

*e in the penult of trisyllabic stems is elided, and the resulting CC simplified (§D1.1.15). Otherwise, *e > /e/ (remains a central vowel) in most cases:

*seqeɣet 'firmly tied, tight' > *eret* 'man's belt' *gatel > *gatel* 'itchy' *dalem 'inside' > *lem* 'in'

*e before final *s, *q > /a/:

*baɣeq > *baraʔ* 'swelling' *liceqes > *liʔa* 'louse egg' *puteq > *butaʔ* 'secretion from eyes' *taɬeq > *tanaʔ* 'earth' *tumes > *tumeh* 'clothes louse'(< *tuma[16])

The sequence *we > /u/

*weliq 'do again, do back' > *m-uliʔ* 'go home' *lahuwen > *aʔun* 'long time' (< *lauun [loss of *l unexplained)

There is some evidence that *ey > /i/, as in many languages, but it is not conclusive:[17]

*laqeya > *lieh* 'ginger' (< *leiya [§D1.1.11, 3rd¶] < *laiya [§D1.3.14] < *laʔiya) *iseyup > *iup* 'blow' (< *iiup < *ieyup)

In some cases, /e/ was changed to /i/ as part of the morphological process of forming the past tense. Thus, the substitution of /i/ for /e/ is said to be a past-tense morpheme (Amster: 24):[18]

*seqeɣet > *iret* 'tightly tied' (< *i + *eret)

In one case, *e is reflected as /u/ before a syllable with /u/ nucleus. This is probably a borrowing, as normally *e does not assimilate to the vowel of the following syllable. In another case *e is reflected by /u/ before /e/ of the final syllable:

*bekut > *bukut* 'bent' *gemel > *ngumel* 'squeeze in the hand' (< *gumel + nasalization)

In one case, *e is reflected as /a/. There is no explanation. The accretion of final /ʔ/ is also irregular. In another case, *e is reflected as /a/ dialectally:

*jaqet > *daʔat* (Amster: 14)/*daʔet* 'bad' *iqetah > *ataʔ* 'left-over rice hulls after pounding' (< *qeta[19]) (Blust: 166)

In one case, *e is reflected by /i/. The explanation is unknown:

*deŋeɣ 'hear' > *dinger* 'way of listening'

D1.2.3 *a

*a > /a/ in most environments:

---

[16] Note that *-es is reflected as /eh/ in the case of *tumeh*, but as /a/ in the case of *liʔa*. A possible explanation is that dialectally the glottal-stop onset blocked the development of /e/ in the final syllable (§D1.2.3, 2nd ¶). There is a counterexample (*paqah > *paʔeh* 'thigh'), and therefore this rule , if it is correct, must be dialectal (cf. the footnote to the following section).

[17] I say the evidence is inconclusive because *iup* may have developed by loss of the penult of *iseyup, rather than the sequence given here, and *lieh* 'ginger' may be a loan word, as is the word for ginger in many Hesperonesian languages.

[18] Another possible explanation is that *iret* contains a petrified instrumental passive prefix, not the past- tense morpheme—i.e., *seqeɣet + *ise- > *eret + *i- > *ieret > *iret.*

[19] I assume that the Kel form derives from *qeta because the MP languages otherwise all reflect this—i.e., they have lost the initial *i and the final *-h.

*alap 'take' > *ng-alap* 'take'

In some environments, however, *a > /e/. First, *a > /e/ in the antepenult (§D1.1.11, 3rd¶), if it is not lost entirely (§D1.1.11, 2nd¶). This rule also applies to doubled monosyllabic roots with *a:

*bakebak 'remove outer layer > *beb^h^ak* 'torn' *baqeɣuh > *beruh* 'new' *qaɬibaŋebaŋ > *keleleb^h^ang* (< *kelebeb^h^aŋ) *qalima 'hand' > *ngelima* 'rub in palms'

*a > /e/ in word-final position. An /h/ is automatically accreted after the /e/ (§D1.1.41):

*buqaya > *bayeh* 'crocodile' *mata > *mateh* 'eye'

If a stem ended in PAn *-ah, the *a > /e/—i.e., the change occurred after the loss of *-h (§D1.3.21). On the other hand, if a stem ended in *ac, *a remains /a/—i.e., the change occurred before the loss of *-c (§D1.3.22). (The one attested Kel reflex of a PAn form that ended in *as [*mɛ* < *mas 'and'] is irregular [cf. the entry *mas in the glossary].)

*baɣah > *bareh* 'embers' *paqah > *paʔeh* 'thigh'[20] *beɣac > *bera* 'hulled rice'

In one unexplained case, final *a did not change to /e/ and /ʔ/ was accreted:

*ciwa > *iwaʔ* 'nine'

In a few cases, *-an is reflected as /-en/ and *-aŋ is reflected as /eng/. There is no explanation. These forms may have arisen though dialect mixture:

*ɣaqan > *raʔen* 'light in weight' *puɬaŋ 'origin' > *puneng* 'headwaters'

In several cases, *a in the penult of a disyllabic form is reflected as /e/. This is a weakening of the penult, a process that normally does not occur in disyllabic roots, but occurs only with the antepenult in trisyllabic roots. There is no explanation:

*dapaɣ 'flat' > *depar* 'back of hand, top of foot' *ɣabun 'mist' > *reb^h^un* 'smoke' *kaɣuc > *kerud* 'scrape' *kan + *-en > *kenen* 'eat it' (but *k-um-an* 'to eat') *sapiɬ 's.t. placed underneath to protect' > *epin* 'sleeping mat' *anu > *enun* 'what' (also *anun*)

The following form evinces the same weakening of the penult of a disyllabic root as the examples immediately preceding:

*sejen > *ded^h^en* 'pressing down' (< *jen + doubling)

The following form also shows *a of the final syllable changed to *e. This form may be unconnected with the forms in other languages listed under the entry, but if there is a connection, the occurrence of /e/ and the initial /b/ is unexplained:

*dasak 'phlegm' > *bedhek* 'nasal mucus' (possibly < *edhak < *dhak)

The following form shows a weakening of *a to /u/ before *wi:

*kawit + *-al- > *keluwit* 'hook' (< *kalawit)

D1.2.4 Diphthongs

*ay and *aw monophthongized to /ɛ/ and /o/ respectively:

---

[20] Amster (64) lists *paʔah* 'thigh'. This must be borrowed from a dialect that did not change *a to /e/, or possibly it has been influence by Ml *paha* 'thigh'. The development of *liʔa* (< *liceqes) is a parallel (footnote to §D1.2.2, above), but is from a dialect that did not develop /-h/.

*aɣaw > *ng-aro* 'snatch' *pagay > *padɛ* 'rice plant'

There are two exceptions. These forms are borrowings. The first evinces other irregularities as well. The second is irregular in many languages and the type of thing that is spread from community to community:

*beɣecay > *besay* 'oar' *wacay > *uay* 'native axe'

*iw > /iw/:

*baliw > *baliw* 'transform'

In the case of *kasiw 'tree', after *s was lost, /i/ became a glide and /w/ became vocalized:

*kasiw > *kayuh* 'tree'

*uy > /uy/:

*sehapuy > *apuy* 'fire'

D1.3 Consonants

The following chart shows the Kel reflexes of the PAn consonants:

CHART THREE. DEVELOPMENT OF THE KELABIT CONSONANTS FROM PAN

PAn	Kel	PAn	Kel
p	*p*	g	*g-, d, dʰ*
t	*t*	ɣ	*r*
k	*k*	l	*l*
q	*ʔ*	ɬ	*n, l*
h	*∅*	m	*m*
s	*∅*	n	*n*
c	*∅*	ŋ	*ng* [ŋ]
b	*b, bʰ*	w	*w*
d, j	*d, dʰ*	y	*y*

Kel permits no consonant clusters. CC's that developed through vowel syncopation are simplified (§D1.1.15).

D1.3.1 Voiceless consonants

The voiceless consonants except for *q were stable in Kel and remain except where they are lost in simplification of CC's that developed (§D1.1.15).

D1.3.11 *p

*p remained /p/ in all positions:

*pagay > *padɛ* 'rice plant' *depa > *depeh* 'fathom' *alap > *ng-alap* 'take'

In one case, *p is reflected by /b/ in a word that was contaminated by another form of similar meaning. This innovation was shared by Paiwan and all the MP languages:

*pukuh > *bukuh* 'knot, joint in finger' (contaminated in PMP or earlier by *bukul 'knob shaped' Cf. Tg *búkol* 'boil, tumor', Cb *bungkul* 'bulging bones in joints')

The process of nasalization has led to the reflection of *p as /m/ in a small number of cases (see the examples in §D1.1.5).

D1.3.12 *t

*t remained /t/ in almost all cases:

*telu > *teluh* 'three' *tinjaq > *tidaʔ* 'step on' (also *tidʰaʔ*) *betihec > *beti* 'calf' *qatay > *atɛ* 'liver' *jeket > *deket* 'stick, adhere'

In a few cases, *ti > /si/. These may be cases of dialect mixture or in fact cases of a normal Kel change in progress that may be more widespread than dictionary entries would make one believe.[21]

*t-ina > *sinaʔ* 'mother' *tinaqi > *senaʔi* 'intestines' (< *sinaʔi) *qatimun > *simun* 'cucumber' *tinjak + *-in- > *senidʰaʔ* 'tracks' (< *tinidʰaʔ cf. *tidʰaʔ* 'footprint') *qatimela > *gesimel* 'flea'

The process of nasalization has led to the reflection of *t as /n/ in a small number of cases (see the examples in §D1.1.5).

D1.3.13 *k

*k remains /k/ in all environments:

*kasiw > *kayuh* 'wood, tree' *ɬeket > *neket* 'stick' *manuk > *manuk* 'bird'

In a few cases, *k has been lost. Intervocalically, in three cases a glottal stop developed by the rule of §D1.1.4 and in two others a glide developed. In final position, it was replaced by a glottal stop. These forms are probably loan words. There is no other explanation:

*bituka > *betueh* 'stomach' *cakit > *aʔit* 'sickness' *ikuɣ > *iur* 'tail' *pakehu > *paʔuh* 'k.o. fern' *ɣakit > *raʔit* 'raft' *sawak > *awaʔ* 'waist' *takut > *taʔut* 'fear' *tinjak 'step on' > *tidʰaʔ* 'footsteps'

The process of nasalization has led to the reflection of *k as /ng/ in a small number of cases (see the examples in §D1.1.5).

D1.3.14 *q

*q > Ø- in initial position. In general, in medial and final positions, *q > /ʔ/:

*baɣeqaŋ > *beraʔang* 'molar' (< *beɣaqaŋ [§D1.1.3])

However, *q onset to the penult in trisyllabic roots was lost:

*buqaya > *bayeh* 'crocodile' (< *beaya < *beqaya) *baqeɣu > *beruh* 'new' (< *beqeɣu) *laqeya > *lieh* 'ginger' (< *leia [§D1.2.2, middle])

---

[21] *t in most cases *t remains /t/ before /i/. However, in a suggestive note Blust (1993:147) states that *tinebakang* 'spread wide apart, as legs, forceps, etc.' is pronounced [simbakang]. The change of /t/ > /s/ before /i/ happens to be exemplified here but is not discussed. In fact, there is evidence that /t/ > /s/ in other environments, as well. Cf. *sekanan* 'remember' (< *keɬaŋ) and *segerang* 'ribs' (< *ta-geɣaŋ), which probably derive from roots with a prefix *ta-. There is no directly inherited form with /s/ (§D1.3.22), a fact that indicates that [s] and [t] did not contrast at an earlier stage of Kel. This explains a situation in current Kel where some forms with *t are manifested with /s/ and there is variation between /s/ and /t/ in some forms.

In the following four cases, a final *q was lost entirely. They were most likely influenced by other languages with which Kel is in contact:

*qabiq 'all' > *abi-abi* 'do to all' *m-abi* 'finish' *ɣataq > *rata* 'milk' *panaq 'shoot' > *pana* 'slingshot' *sacaq > *ng-asa* 'whet'

In the following case, contamination or some other unidentified analogical process has accreted initial /g-/. It also lost the final vowel, as happened sporadically in other languages of the Philippines and Kalimantan. This form has spread secondarily:

*qatimela > *gesimel* 'flea'

In many languages of northern Kalimantan and Sulawesi, the prefix *qaɬi-, a prefix referring to animals and other similar phenomena (cf. Blust 2001), is reflected with intial /k-/, presumably the result of a neutralization between *q and *k in the onset of the antepenult or earlier before *q changed to [ʔ]. This is reflected in Kel in the form *kelelebʰang* 'butterfly' < *qaɬibaŋebaŋ. The prefix *qaɬi > *kaɬi, and in Kel the vowels were reduced to /e/. This yields *kelebaŋbaŋ. This became *kelebebʰaŋ (§D1.1.11, 2nd footnote), which by dissimilation became *kelelebʰang.*

D1.3.2 *h, *s, *c

D1.3.21 *h, *s

*h was lost for the most part, but the presence of an intervocalic glottal stop in roots that had *h-onset of the final syllable may reflect *h, analogous to the development in the Philippine languages (§C1.3.21):

*lahuj 'seaward' > *laʔud* 'downriver' *lahuwen > *aʔun* 'long time (< *laun < *lahun [loss of *l unexplained])

Otherwise, *h was lost without a trace:

*capuh > *apuh* 'broom' (/h/ in Kel is not connected with PAn *h [cf. §D1.1.41])

*s was lost almost without a trace:[22]

*saɣejaɬ > *edʰan* 'ladder' *dusa > *dueh* 'two' *kasepal > *kapal* 'thick' *tebus > *tebʰuh* 'sugar cane'

The *s may possibly have left a trace in roots that have *s followed by *c, in that the *c was not lost, as is the case with forms that had no *s to the left. (Cf. the examples in §D1.3.22, immediately following.)

D1.3.22 *c

For the most part, *c was lost:

*ciwa > *iweh* 'nine' *cuɣuq > *uruʔ* 'order, direct' *nacuk > *nauk* 'to boil' *bacaq > *baaʔ* 'wet' *beɣac > *bera* 'hulled rice'

However, if there had been an *s to the left in pre-Kelabit (< PAn *s), *c > /s/.[23]

---

[22] Blust (1969) put forward a hypothesis that Kel and other languages of northern Kalimantan reflected *s in the strengthened reflexes of voiced onset of the word-final syllable in some roots. There is a more persuasive explanation that can account for the strengthened reflexes, and here we assert that Kel and the other languages of northern Kalimantan have lost *s without a trace (cf. the discussion in §D1.3.3).

*iseci 'contents, flesh' > *isiʔ* 'contents' *sacaq > *asa* 'whet' *sacaŋ > *asang* 'gills' *sicaŋ 'jaw' > *isang* 'gills'

If a root had two syllables with *c onset, the first became /t/ and the second, /s/:

*cucu > *tusu* 'milk'[24]

There are a number of additional forms in which *c is reflected by /s/. These are most likely loan words in Kel:

*becit > *besit* 'spurt' *beɣecay > *besay* 'oar' (/ay/ is also irregular) *calaq > *salaʔ* 'wrong' *calin > *salin* 'translate' *cepaq 'chew' > *sepaʔ* 'quid' *cikep 'seize' > *sikap* 'find' *cilaw 'glare' > *silo* 'shiny' *tucuk 'pierce' > *nusuk* 'inject' (cf. the regular reflex *nuuk* 'thread a needle')

D1.3.3 Voiced consonants stops in Kel

The PAn *b remained *b. *d, *j, *g merged in the onset and coda of root-final syllables and became *d. Subsequently the *b and *d each spilt into voiced unaspirated and voiced aspirated phonemes: *b > /b/, /b^h/; *d, *j, *g > /d/, /d^h/. This development of aspiration is a strengthening of the voiced stop. Strengthening of the voiced stops is an areal feature that characterizes most of the languages of northern Kalimantan and has been taken as evidence that these languages constitute a subgroup (Blust 2006).[25] However, strengthening obtains only in the onset of the root-final syllable. Zorc (1983: §8.3) hypothesized that stress was the conditioning factor: if the final syllable of a root was stressed and had voiced stop onset, the onset was strengthened. In other cases strengthening did not occur.[26] Morphophonemics supports this hypothesis: when a suffix is added to a stem with a strengthened onset of final syllable, the strengthening is lost (fails to take place), for what was the final syllable in the unaffixed form became the penult in the suffixed form:

teb^{h}uʔ 'cut down' + *-en* 'passive' > *tebuʔen* 'clearing

Similarly, when a final voiced stop in roots with former end stress comes to stand before a suffix, the voiced stop is strengthened, for the stress would have shifted to the suffix (§A3.5, 2nd ¶):

---

[23] This may in fact not be a rule of Kel, for *isiʔ* and *asa* are loan-words (reflecting other irregularities), and the two words for 'gills' may also be secondary.

[24] There is no other example. Since there is another word for 'milk' *rata* (< *ɣatac), this may in fact be a loan word. Further, other languages of Kalimantan manifest *tusu* 'milk' (e.g. ND [cf. §D2.3.15]).

[25] In Kel strengthening is aspiration. In other languages strengthening may have other characteristics: devoicing, implosion, or change to [s], and others, as described by Blust 1969, 2006.

[26] Zorc analyzes this development in terms of short penults rather than stress on the final syllable, and this way of looking at the phonetic facts explains why strengthening can have taken place. From the point of view of phonology, a short penult is tantamount to final stress and a long penult is tantamount to penultimate stress (for the antepenult was never stressed in pre-Kelabit because it was always weakened or lost [§D1.1.1ff.], although the antepenult could be stressed in PAn [§A3.5.3]). This does not imply that pre-Kelabit had contrastive stress. The rule of current Kelabit (§D1.0) is that stress is on the penult of the word unless the penultimate vowel nucleus is /e/, in which case stress is on the final syllable, and this rule was operative in Pre-Kelabit: Pre-Kelabit had lost the PMP contrastive stress. This conclusion is based on the fact the PMP or PAn forms with end stress do not cause a medial voiced stop to strengthen, if the penultimate vowel was other than *e:. E.g., *qujáɬ 'rain' with a stressed final syllable did not strengthen the medial *j. The Kel reflex is *udan* 'rain'.

m-eleg 'cease' + *-en* 'passive' > *leg^hen*[27] 'cease it' (Blust 1993: 148) *tuked* 'climb' + *-en* > *tuked^hen* 'slope' (Zorc 1983: 18)

Further support is offered by the fact that all stems with voiced stop onsets in the final syllable following a penult with /e/ nucleus are strengthened: stress fell automatically on the final syllable in roots with *e penult in PMP—that is, penultimate /e/ causes the stress to fall on the end syllable in all MP languages, if not currently, at least at an earlier stage. Additionally, stems consisting of doubled monosyllabic roots also had final stress,[28] and such forms also have strengthened onsets of the final syllable in Kel.[29]
Strengthening also takes place in forms that did not have *e in the penult. These are forms that had developed CC's through syncopation or had developed a nasal coda of the penult (or what is tantamount, prenasalization of the onset of the final syllable). The assumption is that closed penults also had stress on the final syllable (much as is the case in current Tag).[30]

D1.3.31 *b

*b > /b/ and /b^h/ in the environment described in §D1.3.3, above:

*baliw 'change, return to previous' > *baliw* 'transform' *betihec > *beti* 'calf of leg' *qabú > *abuh* 'ashes' *qaleb > *aleb* 'knee' *bekebek 'pulverize' > *beb^hek* 'crushed into fine particles' *basaq > *eb^ha?* 'flood'

---

[27] A /g/ that developed in Kel and the other languages that evince this phenomenon also developed a strengthened phoneme /g^h/. No Kel forms with /g^h/ remount to PAn or PMP.
[28] Reduplicated monosyllabic roots probably retained the epethetic *e between the two monosyllabic elements that we reconstruct for PAn (§A3.6.1). This hypothesis is supported by the weakening of an *a in the first reduplicated element. If Kel had already lost the epenthetic medial vowel, the motivation for the development would be the rule that closed penults had end stress (cf. the following ¶):

*dakedak 'slam s.t. down' > *ded^hak* 'tamp down earth'

Blust (2006: 327, 333) has a different hypothesis: he attributes the weakening of the first *a to the character of the following consonant, and attributes the strengthening of the medial consonant to a simplification of the CC – e.g, he reconstructs *dakdak, which became *dad^{h}ak, and then *a > /e/ before the following /d^h/.
[29] However, in three cases the initial *d of the first syllable of a disyllabized monosyllabic root was not strengthened. This may be because in those cases the monosyllabic roots were not doubled but rather reduplicated (R)—that is, not the whole root was doubled, but rather just the initial consonant of the root plus the first vowel were prefixed to the root. In the case of reduplication, no medial CC's developed to simplify. I assume that reduplicated forms came to be stressed on the penult, e.g., *bibíɣ > *bibir* 'lips' (< *bíbiɣ). There are three other examples:

*dab + R > *dádab > *dadab 'set on fire'* *daŋ + R > *dádaŋ > *dadang* 'warm oneself by the fire' *daɬ + R > *dádaɬ > *dadan* 'old'

[30] Blust (2006:329-300) proposes that aspirated voiced stops arose in Kel as a result of the simplification of prenasalized stops. The rule is tantamount to ours, but Blust does not assume end stress in roots with closed penults but rather assumes that development of aspiration was motivated by the simplification of the cluster. The hypothesis that prenasalization (which subsequently was lost) led to the development of aspiration of the following C is supported by three facts: (1) prenasalization of medial stops was a sporadic process in MP languages (§A3.7.2) and that explains why only a few medial voiced stops are strengthened; (2) some of the forms that show strengthening after a vowel other than *e manifest prenasalization of the medial stop in closely related languages; (3) Kelabit permits no nasal clusters.
In an earlier article, Blust (1969) hypothesized that the environment for strengthening was an *s elsewhere in the root. This hypothesis does not hold water, and Blust 2006 provides an account of the development of the aspirated stops that is unexceptional (as is the account we present here)p.

The process of nasalization has led to the reflection of *b as /m/ in a small number of cases (see the examples in §D1.1.5).
In one case, initial *b was replaced by /g/. This: form is not directly inherited. The /i/ of the antepenult is also irregular (§D1.1.11):

*bituqen > *gituʔen* 'star' (also *getuʔen*)

Reflexes of *sebic 'thin' are reflected with *pic, as in all languages apart from Bunun:

*ɬisebic > *nipi/lipi* 'thin'

D1.3.32 *d *j

*d and *j merged and became /d/ and /dʰ/ in the environments specified in §D1.3.3, above:

*daqaɬ > *daʔan* 'branch' *qudaŋ > *udang* 'shrimp' *udesí 'last, rear end' > *m-udʰih* 'behind'[31] *ɬatad > *natad* 'yard' *jalan > *dalan* 'road' *saɣejáɬ > *edʰan* 'ladder' *qujaɬ > *udan* 'rain' *qaɬuj 'be carried by current' > *anud* 'current'

D1.3.33 *g

The reflex of *g as onset of the penult or earlier and of monosyllabic roots is both /g-/ and /k-/. The two reflexes no doubt have resulted from dialect mixture. In two cases, *g- is reflected with /g-/. In two other cases, *g- is reflected by *k-. Other reflexes of PAn forms with *g- are nasalized, so that it is indeterminate whether Kel has /k-/ or /g-/:

*gatel > *gatel* 'itchy' *geɣaŋ > *se-gerang* 'ribs' *gap > *ngakap* 'grope' *gemegem > *kekem* 'hold in palm of hands'

As onset or coda of the final syllable, *g merged with *d and *j (> /d/). /d/ < *g was strengthened under the conditions cited in §D1.3.3:

*ŋagan > *ngadan* 'name' *quleg > *uled* 'worm'*isegúŋ > *idʰung* 'nose' *qaɬegáw > *edʰo* 'day'

D1.3.4 Voiced consonants, continuants

D1.3.41 *ɣ

*ɣ > /r/ in all positions:

*ɣabut > *rabut* 'uproot' *ɣeken > *reken* 'coiled base to rest things on' *ɣik > *rumik* 'thresh by trampeling' *ɣumaq > *rumaʔ* 'house' *baɣiyus > *bariw* 'storm' *qaɣem > *arem* 'pangolin' *beɣay > *berɛ* 'give' *pataɣ > *patar* 'flat area'

When *ɣ came to abut on another consonant through syncope of the penult, *ɣ was lost:

*saɣejáɬ > *edʰan* 'ladder' (<eɣdán < *eɣeján) *beɣecay > *besay* 'oar'

In one other case *ɣ was lost. It is unexplained, and the form is probably a borrowing:

*diɣuq > *diuʔ* 'bathe'

---

[31] /dʰ/ developed because the root had end stress (D1.3.3):

*qudesí > *udhí > *-udʰih* 'behind'

D1.3.42 *l

*l remained /l/ in almost all positions:

*lahuj 'seaward' > *la?ud* 'downstream' *liceqes > *li?a* 'louse egg' *kulit > *kulit* 'skin' *gatel > *gatel* 'itchy'

/l/-onset assimilated to an /r/ on the right (> /r/):

*liqeɣ > *ri?er* 'neck' *qaluɣ 'deep place in river' > *arur* 'branch, small stream' *qiteluɣ > *terur* 'egg'

D1.3.43 *ɬ

*ɬ became /n/ and /l/ as described in §A3.3.4:

(1) *ɬ > /l/ when onset of an unstressed (short)[32] penult or earlier syllable:

*ɬaŋúy > *languy* 'swim' *qaɬibaŋebaŋ > *kelelebang* 'butterfly' (cf. §D1.3.14, end, for a complete account of this form) *qaɬimátek > *lematek* 'leech'

(2) *ɬ > /n/ otherwise—i.e., when onset of a stressed (long) penult, when onset of a final syllable (including onset of monosyllabic roots), and in stem-final position:

*ɬátad > *natad* 'yard' *aɬák > *anak* 'son, daughter' *áɬay > *anɛ* 'termite' *bulaɬ > *bulan* 'moon'

Occasionally, *ɬ in the onset of an unstressed (short) penult is reflected as /n/. There is no explanation for these forms, other than that the change of *ɬ > /l/ (¶1, above and §A3.3.4) was not completed:

*ɬekét > *neket* 'stick' *ɬisebíc > *nipi* 'thin' (but also *lipi*)

In one case, *-ɬ is reflected as /ng/, as is the case of cognates in several languages:

*tuqelaɬ > *tulang* 'bone'

In the following example, the *l that developed from *ɬ formed a cluster by syncope of the medial syllable. Subsequently the cluster was simplified by dropping the *l:

*qaɬegáw > *edʰo* 'day, sun' (< *eldáw < *eledáw < *qeɬegáw [§D1.1.12])

*ɬ was lost in one other unexplained case: There is no explanation:

*ɬecuŋ > *iung* 'mortar' (/i/ of the first syllable is also unexplained)

D1.3.44 *m, *n, *ŋ

*m, *n, *ŋ remained unchanged in all positions:

*mata > *mateh* 'eye' *lima > *limeh* 'five' *demedem > *dedʰem* 'darkness' *salem > *alem* 'night (length of time)' *naɬaq < *nana?* 'pus' *enem > *enem* 'six' *jalan > *dalan* 'way' *ŋaŋa > *nganga* 'open mouth' *laŋit > *langit* 'sky' *baɣeqaŋ > *bera?ang* 'molar' *beŋ 'block' > *ebʰeng* 'bund in rice paddy'

---

[32] That is, unstressed in PMP. The change of /ɬ/ to /l/ or /n/ took place when the forerunner of Kel still had contrastive stress.

However, in nasal clusters that developed by syncopation, the nasals were lost (except that *mb > /m/ (§D1.1.15).

*keŋekeŋ 'tight, cramped' > *pe-kekeng* 'stiff after sitting' (< *keŋkeŋ) *tinjak > *tid*^{h}*a?* 'footprint' (< *tinejak [cf. §D1.1.15, footnote])

D1.3.45 *w and *y

*w is reflected by /w/ in all positions, except that the sequence *we has a special outcome (§D1.2.2, middle). Cf. §D1.2.4 for diphthongs with *w.

*walu > *waluh* 'eight' *ciwa > *iwa?* 'nine' *qacawa 'in-law' > *awa-n* 'spouse' *quway > *uwɛ* 'rattan'

A glide [w] between /u/ and /a/ does not contrast with its absence:

*buwaq > *bua?* 'fruit'

*y > /y/ in medial position. For diphthongs with *y, see §D1.2.4. There are no attestations of *y in initial position.

*buqáya > *bayeh* 'crocodile' *laheyu > *layu* 'wither'

A y-glide between /i/ and /u/ or /a/ (/eh/) is not contrastive:

*iseyup > *iup* 'blowing' *piya > *pia-n* 'desire' *leqeya > *lieh* 'ginger' (< *lia)

CHAPTER TWO
Ngaju Dayak

D2.0 Background and cultural factors that influenced the history of Ngaju Dayak

Ngaju Dayak (ND) is spoken by more than 300,000 people in Central Kalimantan in the Kapuas and the Katingan river valleys. The language is still very much alive and spoken by young people, although it is not a medium of instruction. As the largest Dayak language, spoken over the widest area and by the largest number of people, ND is widely understood and influential throughout Central Kalimantan. ND has been in close contact with Malay since prehistoric times, and both Banjarese Malay (MlBjr) and Indonesian have had an overwhelming influence on the vocabulary of ND. ND shares a great number of structural innovations in common with Malay, many of which have surely come about through the centuries of contact. Another strong influence on the history of ND has been the *Basa Sangiang* 'the language of the gods' of the Kaharingan religion, which plays a central role in the rituals of this religion, the focus of traditional ND culture. The *Basa Sangiang* is an artificial register employed by shamans, consisting of a special vocabulary either created or taken from other languages of the region, with normal ND grammar, similar in character to the shamanic registers of speech found throughout the region. Forms from the *Basa Sangiang* have moved into normal speech styles. This has been a source of borrowing from neighboring languages. In the times before colonial control, the practice of slavery probably also led to borrowings from neighboring language as well.

ND is documented from the middle of the nineteenth century from the work of August Hardeland, a German missionary, who translated the Bible into ND and prepared a dictionary and grammar book, which was the source of Dempwolff's study of ND. Hardeland worked at the mouth of the Kapuas river, which is at the language border between MlBjr and ND. It was a melting-pot area, to which immigrants from all over the region came, and the ND recorded by Hardeland is strongly marked by diverse dialectal influences. Nevertheless, Hardeland's translation of the Bible was influential throughout the ND area because his Bible was widely used in Christian communities, and subsequent translations were influenced by Hardeland's version. In this study, we quote forms from Ben Abel, a native of the upper Katingan valley, far inland from the area of Hardeland's dialect. We quote Hardeland's forms only when they are unknown to Mr. Abel, and mark them as such. The only substantial phonological difference between our consultant's speech and the forms quoted by Hardeland is in the vowels, particularly /o/, which is a marginal phoneme in our consultant's speech, but which is a prominent phoneme and frequently reflects PAn *u in Hardeland's transcription.

ND has borrowed a substantial number of words from Ml, many of which have PAn or PMP etyma. The forms from Ml evince the sounds of the Ml reflexes, some of which are different from the ND reflexes. Dempwolff (1938: §86a) hypothesized that ND incorporated a stratum of vocabulary from a lost language to account for the two different sets of reflexes of PMP forms in ND. In an important article, Dyen (1956) pointed out that the forms that Dempwolff had thought to be inherited in ND were in fact Ml borrowings and the forms that Dempwolff had thought to derive from a lost language were in fact the forms inherited directly from PMP. The forms of Ml origin have the reflexes evinced by MlBjr, which retains /h/ where standard Ml has Ø (§§D2.3.14, D2.3.2) and which shows /a/ where standard Ml has /e/ [ə] (§D2.2.3). The following sound correspondences are hallmarks of MlBjr provenience:

CHART ONE. PHONEMES SHOWING BANJARESE PROVENIENCE

PAn	ND (borrowed)	MlBjr	ND (inherited)
*e	*a*	*a*	*e*
*ay	*ay*	*ay*[1]	*ey*
*iw	*i*	*i*	*uy*
*q, *s	*h*	*h*	*Ø*
*ɣ	*r*	*r*	*h*

An example: of *e and *q in a borrowed word:

*qatep > *hatap* 'thatching' MlBjr: *hatap* 'roof, thatching'

An example of *s in a borrowed word:

*tisaŋ > *tihang* 'pole, mast' MlBjr: *tihang* 'pole, mast'

An example of *e and *ɣ in a borrowed word:

*keɣet > *karat* 'cut off' MlBjr: *karat* 'cut off'

An example of *ay in a borrowed root:

*tapay > *tapay* 'fermented rice' Ml: *tapai* 'fermented rice'

An example of *iw in a borrowed root:

*baliw 'the one of two things that evens things out' > *bali* 'blood money' (not attested in Ml)

Word taboo has influenced the development of the vocabulary of languages in the region. It has been a force in the borrowing of forms from Ml and from *Basa Sangiang* into normal speech. In some cases, a special form may have been created to meet the requirements of word taboo. One such form is the reflex of *buqáya 'crocodile' (a sacred animal in the Kaharingan religion), which has the shape /bajai/ in current ND.

[1] /ay/ is not the reflex of PAn *ay in inherited words in Ml. Ml forms that have been borrowed with /ay/ into ND are themselves loan words in Ml (§D4.2.5).

CHART TWO. NGAJU PHONEMES

Consonants

voiceless stops	p	t	(c)	k	
voiced stops	b	d	j	g	
spirants		s			h
nasals	m	n	ñ	ng [ŋ]	
glides and laterals	w	l, r	y		

Vowels

high	i		u
mid	e		o
low		a	
diphthongs	ey	aw, ay	uy

/c/ does not occur in directly inherited forms.

D2.1 Changes that characterize ND in general

D2.1.1 Tendencies to form disyllabic roots

ND has a strong tendency to form disyllabic roots (§A3.6.2). First, roots of more than two syllables were reduced to two syllables by the process of syncope or other types of syllable loss, with the exception of some of the stems of four syllables, which were reduced to three syllables. Second, roots that became monosyllabic because of sound changes or roots that were inherited as monosyllabic roots from PAn were disyllabized by processes that are widespread throughout the Austronesian area (§A3.6.2).

D2.1.11 Disyllabization of roots of three or more syllables

Syncope and vowel contraction figure prominently in processes of disyllabization of roots of three or more syllables. Trisyllabic roots elided an *e (or an *i before *y or *u before *w) in the penult. In some cases this elision happened well before ND became a separate language, and it is found over a large range of languages (§A3.5.1):

*básequ 'smell' > *ewaw* 'smell' (< *bau [addition of prothetic /e/ is discussed in §D2.1.2]) *binesiq > *biñi* 'seed' *dásuwen 'leaf' > *dawen* 'leaf' (< *dauwen) *deɣeqéc 'move vigorously' > *dehes* 'current' *jáqewis 'far' > *ke-jau* 'go to distance' (< *jaqus < *jaqwis) *leqacem > *m-asem* 'sour' (< *qalcem < *qalecem) *qáłegaw > *andaw* 'day' *túqelał 'bone' > *tulang* 'bone' *ma-qetáq > *manta* 'unripe'

There are three trisyllables reconstructed that elide the medial syllable and also change the antepenult to /e/. The explanation probably lies in metathesis (§D2.13):

*baɣehat > *behat* 'weight' (< *beɣehat) *búɣesu > *pam-behu* 'o. who is jealous' (< *beɣusu) *paheɣáw > *pehaw* 'hoarseness' (< *peɣahaw)

A single example shows elision of medial /u/, as do all the other extra-Formosan languages that have reflexes of this root. This form has probably spread from language to language:

*paŋudał 'pandanus' > *pandan* 'pandanus'

In trisyllabic roots, antepenults that had *a onset or *a onset after the loss of *s and *q, became lost. If the antepenult had been stressed, the stress shifted to the final syllable in pre-Ngaju. The following list gives some examples:

*qabaɣa > *baha* 'shoulder' *páqegu > *peru* 'gall' (< *qapegú) *qacáwa 'in-law' > *sawe* 'wife' *saɣejáł > *hejan* 'ladder, steps'

If the onset of the final syllable was lost, the vowels of the penult and final syllable contracted:

*batihec > *buntis* 'calf' *lasuwek 'mix other food into staple' > *lauk* 'fish' *ikasu > *ikaw* 'you (sg.)' *palisi > *pali* 'taboo'

Vowels in the antepenult were neutralized and became /a/.[2] This change took place before the elision of penultimate *e and the metathesis and disyllabization of *buɣesu, and *paheɣaw listed in this section, above.

*binuwaŋ > *banuang* 'k.o. tree with light wood') *ɣuqáɬay 'male' > *hañi* 'spirit, bravery'[3] (< *ɣaɬi < *ɣaqaɬi) *qaɬimátek > *lamantek* 'upland leech' *tinaqi > *kanai* 'intestines' (Initial /k/ is unexplained.)

The following form, however, is a counterexample, for *i in the antepenult apparently remained [i]. The form may well be borrowed, although the source is unknown:

*qaɬíɣuwan 'bee'> *ñuan* 'k.o. ant' (< *ñiuwan < *ɬihuwan)

The following form also lost the antepenult, and as they are the only trisyllabics with an antepenult consisting of *da, it is impossible to conclude that the loss of the antepenult here is a sound law. It is likely, however, that these forms are not directly inherited, for an antepenult consisting of *ba is not lost.

*dalukap > *lukap* 'palm of hand' (cf. *balatuk > *balatok* 'woodpecker')

Forms of four syllables lost the vowel the first syllable and a *q- or *s- onset, if there was one:

*basequ 'smell' + *-an 'adjective former' > *bewan* 'smelly' (< *baeuan) *qaɬimátek > *lamantek* 'upland leech' *qaɬíɣuwan 'bee'> *ñuan* 'k.o. ant' (< *ñiuwan < *ɬihuwan) *qusalipan > *halalipan* 'milliped' (< *halilipan. with reduplication of the penult in animal names[4])

D2.1.12 Consonant clusters

ND only permits nasal clusters and clusters formed by affixing the genitive pronouns to words ending in a consonant. In other words, all clusters that developed in inherited forms except for nasal clusters and clusters at morph boundaries were simplified. In the case of roots consisting of reduplicated monosyllables, the penultimate epenthesized vowel, which we hypothesize for PAn, was lost, as is the case of all MP languages (§A3.6.1). Further CC's were simplified according to sonority: the spirants or liquids were lost. Otherwise, the coda of the first syllable was lost. The following list gives some examples:

---

[2] Most derivative prefixes and proclitics (prepositions) have /a/ as their vowel, and borrowed forms with three syllables neutralize the initial syllable to /a/:

*γumbiya (an early borrowing into Ngaju from an unknown source) > *hambia* 'sago' *ke 'location, motion marker' > *ka* 'to'

[3] It is possible that *hañi* 'bravery' is borrowed from Ml *berani/barani*, but the question arises why the first syllable was lost, when antepenultimate *ba in inherited trisyllables is not lost. Further, Ml /r/ is normally borrowed with /r/ in ND (§D2.3.41, last ¶). The Ml cognate probably did influence the meaning of the ND form.

[4] This form was borrowed from Ml *halipan* 'milliped'. The root was felt to be /lipan/ and therefore the 'animal reduplication' affected the penult /li/.

*biɣebiɣ > *biwih* 'lips' *beɣecay 'oar'> *besey* 'short paddle' (< *beɣcay) *buteliɣ 'cyst' > *butih* 'wart' *dukeduk 'sit' > *duduk* 'live somewhere'(probably < Ml) *gapegap > ngakap '*grope*'[5] *kid + doubling > *kidekid 'file, rasp' > *kikir* 'file'

Nasal clusters were not normally simplified, except that nasals were assimilated to the following consonant:

*baŋkuwaŋ > *bangkuang* 'thorny pandanus of the swamps' *diŋediŋ > *dinding* 'wall, partition, screen against wind'

Occasionally, however, nasal clusters were simplified:

*aŋkup 'put in cupped hands' > *akup* 'take in cupped hands' *dem + doubling > *demedem 'dark cloudy' > *derem* 'dark, cloudy' (but also *ba-rendem* 'begin to be dark'

Like other languages of the area, ND sporadically inserted a nasal before the onset of the final syllable. (Cf. the discussion in §D2.14, below.)

D2.1.121 Loss of -C in doubled roots

Doubled roots normally lost the final C of the first of the two repeated roots:

*qaluɬ 'wave' > *m-alu-alun* 'fata morgana'

D2.1.13 Loss of initial syllable

Loss of initial syllable has been described for stems of three or more syllables (§D2.1.11, above). In fact, this process also affects proclitics as well, for proclitics form a phonological word together with the following word. For example, *ije* 'one' (< *ica) typically occurs followed by a word it modifies. In those context *ije* 'one' loses the first syllable and is manifested as /je/.

D2.1.2 Disyllabization of monosyllabic roots

Inherited monosyllabic roots or monosyllabic roots that developed as a result of sound changes in the prehistory of ND were disyllabized. The most widespread process is addition of a prothetic /e/ to the root:

*daqaɬ 'branch' > *edan* 'branch' *ɬuɣ 'coconut' > *eñuh* 'coconut' *sepat 'four' > *epat* 'four' (< *pat[6])

In some cases of PAn monosyllabic roots, a petrified prefix was interpreted as part of the root:

*baw 'above' > *timbaw* 'side plank of boat' *binit 'carry hanging > *imbit* 'carry with fingers' (< *in- + *bit) *biŋ 'hold, guide' > *imbing* 'held fast' (< *in- + *biŋ) *bun >

---

[5]The reflex of *g- as /k-/ is irregular (§D2.3.34). It can be explained as follows: in a cluster consisting of a voiced consonant preceded by a voiceless, the voiced became assimilated to the voiceless consonant—that is, *gapegap > *gapgap > *gapkap. This is an aberrant shape, for in reduplicated monosyllables both the monosyllables normally begin the same manner of voicing. Both are either voiced or both are voiceless. In the case of *gapgap, the initial /k/ was regularized rather than *g-. An alternative explanation would be borrowing from a neighboring language that reflects *g- with *k-.

[6] *sepat lost the first syllable in all MP languages.

tawon 'heap' *ɣik > *ihik* 'be threshed by trampling' (< *ise- + *ɣik) *kaŋ 'spread egs' > *ingkang* 'step' (< *ise- + *kaŋ) *pan 'bait' > *um-pan* 'bait' (< *um- + *pan) [7]

The following two forms are irregular in the formation of the disyllabic root and probably not directly inherited:

*bun > *ambun* 'dew, fog' *ceŋ 'stop up' > *aseng* 'breath'

D2.1.3 Metathesis

Metathesis is a minor process in the history of ND, but there are forms that clearly show metathesis. First, the prefix *in- is metathesized to a prefix *ni- which later became /i-/ in the verbal system.[8] With monosyllabic roots this prefix is unchanged (§D2.1.2, 2nd¶):

*binit 'carry hanging > *imbit* 'carry with fingers' (< *in- + *bit) *biŋ 'hold, guide' > *imbing* 'held fast' (< *in- + *biŋ)

Other forms also show consonantal metathesis. One group is those that are metathesized in all MP languages (e.g. the cases discussed in §A1.1.32, 4th¶). Some of these forms underwent a second metathesis. The following list gives examples of those that underwent the ND metathesis, some of which had been metathesized in the general metathesis that affects all MP languages:

*buɣesu > *pam-behu* 'one who is jealous' (< *beɣusu) *liceseq > *lies* 'nit' (< *liseqec < *liceqes [§A1.1.32, 3rd¶]) *paheɣaw > *pehaw* 'hoarseness' (< *peɣahaw) *púnuq 'head as the main part of s.t.' > *púqun (§A1.1.32, 7th footnote to the 3rd¶) > *puun > *upun* 'origin, beginning' *qáɣuc 'current' > *m-asuh* 'flow downstream' (< *-um- + *qacuɣ) *qaciɫ 'salt' > *anis* 'sweet' *qilaw 'light' > *liau* 'the departed soul' *tepak 'slap' > *tekap* 'be hit' *tusud > *utut* 'knee' (< *tuut)

One form shows metathesis of vowels:

*lepit > lipet 'folded'

D2.1.4 Prenasalization of medial stop consonants

Like other Hesperonesian languages, ND evinces a tendency to add a nasal to close a penult or earlier syllable that is open (§A3.7.2). The number of forms that undergo prenasalization of medial consonants is smaller than in Ml. Many of the forms that show this sporadic nasal insertion are cognates with Ml forms that show sporadic nasal insertion, and it is highly probable that in most of these cases, contact with Ml has influenced the process of medial nasal insertion. However, a certain number of those with nasal insertion do not have inserted nasals in the Ml cognate, and it is clear that ND nasal insertion was in some cases independent of language contact.

*agi 'younger sibling' > *andi* 'younger sibling' *beteŋ 'stomach' > *benteng* 'middle point of a long thing' *betihec > *buntis* 'calf' *bukul 'knob-shaped' > *bungkul* 'knob-shaped protusions of new growth' *dapaɣ > *dampah* 'flat' *liduŋ > *malindung* 'hide' *mayaŋ 'stem of palm inflorescence' > *mañang* 'areca palm blossom' *qaɫimátek 'upland leech'

[7]This form may well be a borrowing from Ml *umpan* 'bait'—i.e., it has gone through a process similar to the one discussed here in pre-Ml (§D4.1.2, 2nd¶) and then was borrowed into Ngaju.

[8] It is not clear whether the past-tense morpheme was a prefix *in- or an infix *-in-. Cf. the commentary to *in in the glossary.

> *lamantek* 'upland leech' *qudaŋ 'lobster, crayfish' > *undang* 'shrimp' *qutek > *untek* 'brains' *sejam + ise- > *isejam > *injam* 'be borrowed, lent' *tukej > *tungket* 'support'

In some cases, the prenasalized final syllable is the remnant of a petrified infix *-um-:

*tebuk 'hit with a thump' > *tumbok* 'pole to hit a fish in the water to stun it' (< *tumebuk) *tubuq > *tumbo* 'sprout' (< túmubuh)

D2.1.5 Forms with final syllables similar to final syllables in other languages

There are some roots whose final syllables correspond regularly to final syllables of roots in other languages with similar meanings, but whose initial syllables are different. There is no evidence to reconstruct these final syllables as monosyllabic roots, and no explanation can be found for the first syllables. In some cases these forms are probably inherited by some language in the area but not directly inherited in ND and rather borrowed from that neighboring language. In other cases they have been formed by analogies (§A3.6.3):

*tip 'pinch off' + *ka- > *katip* 'tongs' *qaluɣ 'deep water in river or pool' > *laloh-an* 'place where water is deepest' *cepit > *sipit* 'narrow'

Two roots clearly must have a PAn etymology but have lost their initial consonant. There is no explanation why, but the forms are probably inherited:

*layaŋ 'fly' > *b-ayang* 'fly' (< *ba-layang) *miniyák 'fat' > *eñak* 'fat, bacon' (< *meñak)

D2.2 Vowels and diphthongs

ND reflects the inherited PAn vowel system fairly faithfully. What is reconstructed as a central vowel *e is reflected as a mid-front vowel [e] in ND and is symbolized /e/.

D2.2.1 *i

*i > /i/ in all positions except the antepenult:

*biɣ + doubling > *biɣebiɣ > *biwih* 'lips' *bilit > *bilit* 'wind, go around' *buteliɣ 'cyst' > *butih* 'wart' *puɫetiq > *puti* 'white'

Vowel sequences with *i whether inherited or developed with the loss of an intervening consonant, contract to /i/:

*betíhec 'calf' > *buntis* 'leg between knee and foot' *palisi > *pali* 'taboo' *tiɣic > *han-tis* 'drip'

Unstressed *i is elided after *u or *w:

*jáqewis > *ke-jau* 'go far' (< *jaqus < *jaqwis)

In antepenultimate position, *i > /a/ (§D1.1.11). In two cases, *i in antepenult is reflected as /u/. There is no explanation:

*betíhec > *buntis* 'leg between knee and foot' *iseguŋ 'nose' > *urung* 'nose'

In one case, *i is reflected with /e/. This is a contamination with *jelap* 'lick', which is not inherited from PAn.[9]

*dilaq > *jela* 'tongue'

---

[9]Dempwolff reconstructed a form *dilap, but there is no good evidence that *jelap* is inherited from PMP, for the only good cognate is the closely related Mlg *lelafina* 'licked'

D2.2.2 *u

*u > /u/ in all environments:

*baluɬ 'fold over, wrap' > *balun* 'what has been rolled up' *becuɣ > *besuh* 'full, sated' *pukuh 'knot, node' > *buku* 'knuckle, nobs on fingers' (§D2.3.31, end) *manúk 'bird' > *manuk* 'chicken'

Unstressed /u/ was elided before a w-onset of the following syllable (§D2.1.11):

*dásuwen 'leaf' > *dawen* 'leaf'

A sequence of two /u/'s that developed from the loss of an intervening consonant contracted:

*buɣesu > *pam-behu* 'one who is jealous' (< *beɣusu) *tuqus 'true' > *tu-tu* 'truly'

In one case, metathesis prevented the contraction of two *u's.

*tusud > *utut* 'knee' (< *tuut)

In a couple of forms, *u is reflected with /i/. There is no explanation. These forms have the look of forms that are of secondary origin.

*kútu > *guti* 'head louse' *tuɬuh ' roast' > *tino* 'roasted over coals'

In Hardeland's dictionary, *u sporadically is reflected as /o/. However, our consultant has /u/ in almost all cases in which Hardeland reports /o/. The following example manifests /o/ from *u in our consultant's speech. This form is probably not directly inherited:

*cuɣuq > *soho* 'message, order'

*u > /w/ when it comes between two vowels as a result of consonant loss.

*basequ 'smell' + *-an > *bew-an* 'smelly' (< *beu-an [cf. §D2.1.11, end])

D2.2.3 *e

*e in most positions is reflected as /e/:

*beɣac > *behas* 'husked rice' *dasuwen 'leaf' > *dawen* 'leaf' *deɣeqec 'move rapidly' > *dehes* 'current' *teken 'stick to lean on' > *teken* 'pole to push boat' *tumes 'body louse' > *tume* 'body and clothes louse'[10]

*-eq > /-a/. This change took place after the change of §D2.2.4, 1st¶, whereby final *-a > /-e/.

*baɣeq 'abscess' > *baha* 'large boil' *taɬeq 'earth' > *tana* 'dry field'

An exception is the following form, where the loss of *-q took place after the change of *e > /a/, described above. This form is the result of dialect mixture and was unknown to our consultant.

*bugeq > *bure* 'foam'

*e in the penult of trisyllabic forms is elided (§D1.1.11). *e in the penult of disyllabic roots assimilates to the /i/ of the final syllable:

*tebiŋ > *tiwing* 'embankment of a river'

There are a few other cases in which /e/ is reflected as /i/. There is no explanation for them:

[10]In fact, *-es > *-a > /-e/ by the rule of §D2.2.4, 1st¶. The evidence is that if an affix is added to *tume*, an allomorph *tuma-* occurs: *tuma-m* 'your louse'. However, an alternative explanation is analogy with other roots ending in /-e/, which also have an allomorph with /-a/ before a suffix.

*ɣamec 'crush, crumble' > *hamis* 'wring out clothes, squeeze juice' *łecuŋ 'mortar' > *lisung* 'mortar' *qageŋ 'charcoal' > *aring* 'coals left over after s.t. has been burnt'[11] *tajem 'sharp' > *tajim* 'sharp'

There are many cases where /e/ is reflected with /a/. These forms are borrowings from MlBjr, which reflects all *e's as /a/. Many of these forms also show Ml reflexes of other phonemes that are reflected differently in Ml than in ND.

*bedebed 'spool, wind' > *babat* 'belt, shash' *qatep 'thatch' > *hatap* 'thatch' (with /h/ from *q- [§D2.3.14])

In one case, *we- is reflected as /u/ in a form borrowed from a neighboring language. The change of *we > /u/ happened independently in many MP languages (but not in ND).

*weliq > *b-uli* 'return home'

D2.2.4 *a

*a > /a/ except in open final syllables, in which case *-a > /e/.

*qaɣem 'ant eater'> *ahem* 'ant eater' *tabaɣ 'insipid' > *ba-tawa* 'be weak'

Examples of the change of *-a to /e/ at the end of a word:

*buta 'blind' > *bute* 'blind' *depa 'fathom' > *depe* 'fathom'

In ND open final syllables that had been closed by consonants that were lost, *a remains /a/:

*daɣaq > *daha* 'blood' *maqetaq 'raw' > *manta* 'unripe'

In the morphophonemics of ND the syllable final *-a in suffixed forms beginning with a C remains /a/—i.e., the change to /e/ does not take place when there is a suffix beginning with a C:

*mata 'eye' > *mate* 'eye' *mata-ŋku > *mata-ngk* 'my eye'

Word-final *qa, *ɣa > /i/:

*ɣaɣa 'great ' > *hai* 'large' *láqeɣa 'ginger' > *lai* 'ginger' *paqa 'thigh' > *pai* 'leg, foot'

Occasionally, final *-a is reflected as /a/, and in some cases *-a is reflected as /-ah/. These exceptions are unexplained:

*kita 'we' > *itah* 'we' *baŋa 'gap' > *bangah* 'stand open' *paŋa 'forking' > *paŋa* 'stocks'

There are also two unexplained cases in which the *a of the first syllable is reflected as /i/:

*bacaq > *bisa* 'wet' *ɣaqan > *ma-hian* 'light, not heavy'

D2.2.5 Diphthongs

D2.2.51 *ay

*-ay is reflected as /ey/ when it was stressed in PAn:

*beɣecáy 'oar' > *besey* 'short paddle' *matáy 'die' > *matey* 'die' *págay > *parey* 'rice plant' (< *pagáy) *qatáy 'liver' > *atey* 'heart, mood' *cakáy > *sakey* 'climb, go into house'

[11] There may be contamination with the reflex of *qugiŋ 'charcoal', *buring* 'charcoal to make s.t. dark'.

In two cases, *-ay is reflected as /i/. The explanation of the reflex /i/ probably has to do with the fact that these two roots had penultimate stress, but evidence to support this has not turned up:

* ɣuqáɬay 'male' > *hañi* 'spirit, bravery' *báhi 'female' + R > *babáhi > *bábay > *bawi* 'female'

In a few cases, *ay is reflected as *ay. Most of these forms have Ml cognates with /ai/ and are probably borrowings from Ml.[12]

*baŋkay > *bangkay* 'corpse *lantay 'bamboo, lathes > *lantay* 'lattice work on the bottom of boats or huts' *cahebay 'hang' > *campay > *sampay-an* 'place to hang things on' *qajelay > *jelay* 'a grain: *Coix lachryma-jobi*' *taŋkay 'leaf stem' > *tangkay* 'twig and its leaves' *tapay 'ferment' > *tapay* 'fermented rice'

In the following cases, the form with *ay does not have a Ml cognate with /ai/. The first is probably a borrowing from Ojv, and the second can be explained as borrowing from a neighboring language:

*lábay 'yarn' > *laway* 'yarn' *santay 'wait' > *entay* 'wait'

In one case,*-ay is reflected with /e/. This form is not inherited directly:

*baláy 'building, constructed part of building' > *bale* 'work table made with bamboo slats'

D2.2.52 *uy and *iw

*iw and *uy fall together as /uy/:

*báliw 'change, return to previous' > *baluy* 'often tell the same thing' *bábuy > *bawuy* 'pig' *sehapúy 'fire' > *apuy* 'fire'

*iw > *yu after a spirant, and the CC consisting of the spirant + *y became simplified to /y/:

*baɣiw 'spoiled staple' > *bayu* 'spoilt' *kásiw > *kayu* 'wood'

D2.2.53 *aw

*aw is reflected with /aw/:

*buɣaw 'chase: > *buhaw* 'send s.o. away' *betaw > *betaw* 'female relative' *danaw 'lake, pond' > *danaw* 'fairly big lake'

In one case *aw is reflected with /u/. There is no explanation.

*sambaw 'raise' > *ambu* 'on the very top'

D2.3 Consonants

ND reflects the PAn consonants fairly faithfully in initial and medial position with the following exceptions: *q and *s have been lost entirely, and *g has merged with *d (> /r/) when onset or coda or the final syllable. In medial position, *-b- and *-d- have become weakened to /-w-/ and /-r-/. In final position, the contrast between voiced and voiceless stops was lost (they have become devoiced), and CC simplification took place as outlined in §D2.1.12, above.

---

[12]An alternative explanation is to say that these forms reflect a contrast that existed in PAn—i.e., to conclude that those forms with /-ey/ reflect PAn *-ey and those with /-ay/ reflect PAn *-ay. We do not make this assumption. Rather we assume that these forms are secondary in ND. The lack of contrast between *ay and *ey is discussed in §A3.4, 2nd¶.

CHART THREE. DEVELOPMENT OF THE NGAJU CONSONANTS FROM PAN

PAn	ND	PAn	ND
p	*p*	g	*g-, -r-*
t	*t*	ɣ	*h*
k	*k*	l	*l*
q	*ø*	ɬ	*ñ, n, l*
s, h	*ø*	m	*m*
c	*s*	n	*n*
b	*b, -w-*	ŋ	*ng* [ŋ]
d	*d-, -r-, -r*	w	*w*
j	*j*	y	*y*

D2.3.1 Voiceless consonants

*p *t, *k have remained stable and are reflected as /p, t, k/ respectively everywhere except in the case of roots consisting of reduplicated monosyllables, which lost the coda of the first of the monosyllables (§D2.1.12). The following subsections give examples in a variety of positions.

D2.3.11 *p

*p remained /p/ in all positions:

*páqa 'thigh' > *pai* 'leg, foot' *piga > *pire* 'how many?' *púluq > *pulu* 'tens' *dapuɣ 'place for cooking fire' > *dapuhan* 'cooking hearth' *depa > *depe* 'fathom' *kasepál > *kapal* 'thick' *lekep 'do completely' > *lekep* 'join two pieces of wood so that the connection does not appear' *síɣup 'slurp' > *ihup* 'drink' *dapedap > *dadap* 'a tree: *Erythrina* sp.' *sacep > *asep* 'smoke'

Some reflexes of *-p- manifest sporadic prenasalization (§D2.1.4):

*ísepun 'gather' > *impun* 'collect, pick up, glean' *pu 'grandparent' > *empu* 'parent-in-law' (with disyllabization with prothetic /e/ [§D2.1.2])

D2.3.111 Accretion of /p-/

Occasionally /p-/ is accreted to a root beginning with a vowel by an analogy involving the verbal conjugation. A prefix /m-/ forms verbs from roots beginning with a vowel and also from roots beginning with a /p-/ with the /p-/ lost. Thus, a verb beginning with /m-/ may be either to a root with an initial V or with an initial /p-/, and in some cases /p-/ has been added to a V-initial root by analogy:

*úɬah 'be original, thing that came first' > *puna* 'actually, be the real thing'

D2.3.12 *t

*t remains /t/ in almost all cases:

*talís > *tali* 'rope, chord' *tay + doubling > *taytay 'go over narrow passage' > *tatey-an* 'footbridge' *teken 'stick to lean on or propel' > *teken* 'pole to push boat off' *túba > *tuwe* 'a vine: *Derris elliptica'* *qatáy 'liver' > *atey* 'heart, mood' *butá > *ba-bute* 'blind' *báɣat 'athwart' > *bahat* 'thickest and bottommost supporting posts in house' *bilit > *bilit* 'wind, go around s.t.' *buteliɣ 'cyst' > *butih* 'wart'

In one case, an initial *t in the antepenult has been replaced by /k/. There is no explanation:

*tináqi 'intestines' > *kanai* 'stomach'

D2.3.13 *k

*k remains /k/ in almost all cases:

*kan > *kuman* (kan + -um-) 'eat' *kasepál > *kapal* 'thick' *kílat > *kilat* 'lightening' *kubu 'hut' > *kuwu* 'be enclosed, shut in prior to marriage' *aku > *aku* 'I' *búkij > *bukit* 'hill' *qekuŋ 'owl' > *ekung* 'echo' *ɣakit > *hakit* 'raft' *balik 'return' > *balik* 'backwards first, wrong way' *qaɬimátek > *lamantek* 'upland leech' *baŋkuwaŋ > *bangkuang* 'thorny pandanus' *baksaw > *bakaw* 'tree of mangrove forest'

The *k is inexplicably lost in the following form. The final /h/ is also unexplained:

*kita 'we' > *itah* 'we'

There is an analogical process by which some verbal roots with initial vowel develop an initial /k-/.[13]

*jek + *ise > *isejek 'step on' > *ijek > *kijak* 'step on' (The /a/ of the final syllable indicates secondary origin.)

There is another analogical process whereby verbs with *k- may lose the *k-. A verb forming prefix /m-/ substitutes for the /k-/ in verb formation and a verbal prefix /m-/ is added to vowel initial roots as well. This leads to the reinterpretation of roots with /k-/ as roots with vowel initial:

*kawit 'hook' > *-awit* 'bent' (the root of *mawit* 'bend')

D2.3.14 *q

*q has disappeared without a trace in all positions.[14] The following list gives examples in a variety of positions:

*qaɣem > *ahem* 'ant eater' *qatáy 'liver' > *atey* 'seat of emotions mood' *deɣeqéc 'move vigorously' > *dehes* 'current' *páqa 'thigh' > *pai* 'leg, foot' *tuqus 'true' > *tu-tu* 'truly' (with doubling of monosyllabic root that developed [§D2.1.2]) *baq + doubling > *baqebaq 'mouth' > *bawa* 'be called' *buwaq > *bua* 'fruit'

In three instances, initial *q- is reflected with initial k-. The Ml cognates also have an initial /k-/ and show the same meaning. These forms are either borrowed from or influenced by Ml:

---

[13]This process is that the addition of a prefix *maN-* at an earlier stage of ND to roots with initial /k-/ resulted in a form with a prefix shaped /mang-/ and a loss of the initial /k-/. Further, the addition of this prefix to vowel-initial roots resulted in /mang-/ plus the root. In other words, a verb shaped /mangVCV(C)/ could be either with a root shaped /kVCV(C)/ or a root shaped /VCV(C)/, and roots with the shape /VCV(C)/ were reinterpreted as having the shape /kVCV(C)/. This is a process that is widespread in languages of the area, but in Ngaju itself this process is no longer active, although the results of the former working of this process are widely manifested.

[14]The only qualification to this statement is that *q affected the *-e of final syllables that it closed—i.e., *-eq > /a/ (§D2.2.3).

*qabu > *kawu* 'ashes, dust' *qapuɣ > *kapur* 'lime' (with irregular /r/ as well) *qetut > *ketut* 'flatus ventris' (cf. §D4.1.13, end)

There are many examples of *q reflected as /h/. These forms are all borrowings from Ml, mostly from MlBjr, which is conservative in retaining /h/ as a reflex of *q (§§D4.3.21, D4.3.22):

*qaɬuj > *hañut* 'be carried by water' *quluh > *hulu* 'upper part of river' *panaq > *panah* 'arrow'

D2.3.15 *c

*c is reflected as /s/ in almost all positions.

*cakáy > *sakey* 'climb, go up into' *cíku > *siku* 'elbow' *cuɬ + R- >*cucuɬ 'stack up' > *susun* 'set of things that go together' *qacíɬ 'salt' > *anis* 'sweet' (§D2.1.3) *becuɣ > *besuh* 'full, sated' *isecí 'contents, flesh' > *isi* 'meat' *puceg > *puser* 'navel' *beɣac > *behas* 'husked rice' *kicekic 'grate, file' > *kikis* 'filed down' *beɣecay 'oar' > *besey* 'short paddle'

However, initial *c > /t/ if the following syllable begins with *c:

*cicik > *tisik* 'fish scales' *cucu > *tusu* 'teat'

There are two cases where *c > /h/. The first example was borrowed from a neighboring language in which *c is reflected with /h/. The third case may have been contaminated by *hela* 'between'.

*balec > *baleh* 'retribution, revenge' *cela 'gap' > *hela* 'between' *celat 'slit, straits' > *helat* 'space between' (also *selat* 'go through between two rocks')

In one case, *c is reflected with /j/. The explanation may reside in the accentual pattern of an environment in which this root commonly occurs, but the nature of this pattern has not been ascertained.

*ica > *ije* 'one'

In one case, *c is inexplicably reflected with /c/. The final /-k/ in this root is also unexplained:

*culuq > *culuk* 'torch'

*c is replaced by /ñ/ when nasalized by the process described in §A3.7.1:

*cakáy 'climb' > *ñakey* (short for *mañakey)* 'climb, go up or in somewhere (for sex)'

D2.3.2 *h, *s

*h disappeared without a trace:

*lahuj > *laut* 'seaward' *paheɣaw > *pehaw* 'hoarse' *capuh 'wipe' > *sapu* 'color'

*s disappeared without a trace.

*sacep > *asep* 'smoke' *suɣac 'wash s.t.' > *uhas* 'wash by rubbing' *kasepál > *ba-kapal* 'be thick' *nakis > *naik* 'rise climb' *tebus > *tebu* 'sugar cane'

In several cases, *s is reflected with /h/. These forms are borrowings from Ml (§D4.3.22):

*siyaŋ 'divine being' > *hyang* 'divine' *tasaɬ 'remain, stay' > *tahan* 'not vulnerable to s.t.'

D2.3.3 Voiced stops

In initial position, the voiced stops are reflected faithfully. In medial position, they were weakened to spirants, except for *j, and in final position, they became devoiced. *d and *g fell together as onset of the final syllable, and *d and *j fell together in final position.

D2.3.31 *b

*b > /b-/ in initial position and after nasals, /-w-/ in medial position, and /-p/ in final position:

*bałbał > *bamban* 'k.o. reed used for mats: *Donax canniformis*' *baɣeq 'abscess' > *baha* 'large boil' *basequ 'smell'> *bew-an* 'smelly' *becuɣ > *becuh* 'full, sated' *butá > *ba-bute* 'blind' *balábaw > *balawaw* 'rat' *bábuy > *bawuy* 'pig' *tebek > *newek* 'stab to slaughter' (< N- [§A3.7.1] + *tebek) *ibeɣ 'salivate' > *iweh* 'saliva' *tuba > *tuwe* 'a vine: *Derris elliptica*' *gilab 'shining' > *kilap* 'whet, sharpened' (§D2.3.34)

In roots consisting of reduplicated monosyllables, the final consonant of the first monosyllable is lost:

*lebeleb 'hidden by being covered' > *lelep* 'be flooded' (semantic contamination with *lem)

In a few cases, medial *-b- is reflected with /b/. These words are loan words, probably from Ml:

*tabułi > *tabuni* 'afterbirth'

Before *u (but not before *uy), *-b- is lost:

*busuk 'drunk' > *mauk* in *mauk dan muntah* 'severe diarrhea' (calque from MlBjr) (< *ma-buk < *ma-busuk)

In the case of *pukuh 'knob, node', ND, like all the MP languages, voiced the intial C (> *buku* 'knuckle')

D2.3.32 *d

*d > /d-/ in initial position and after a C, /-r-/ in medial position, and /-t/ in final position:

*daɣeq > *daha* 'blood' *depa 'fathom' > *depe* 'fathom' *diŋediŋ > *dinding* 'wall, partition' *dusa 'two' > *due* 'two' *wada 'there is' > *are* 'many' *caduŋ > *sarung* 'sheathe' *likud 'back, behind' > *likut* 'back, behind' *lilid > *lilit* 'be wound round' *dapdap > *dadap* 'a tree: *Erythina*' *anduy > *anduy* 'bathe'

There are four cases in which *d is reflected with *j. There are two possible explanations. In some of these cases, there may be contamination with a word of similar meaning with a /j/.[15] However, there are languages in the region that reflect *d with /j/, and these forms may be borrowings from one of these languages.

*sadiɣi > *jihi* 'post' *dilaq > *jela* 'tongue' *ludaq > *luja* 'spit' *qedipen 'slave' > *jipen* 'people held for ransom'

---

[15]The /j/ in *jela* 'tongue' is best explained by contamination with *jelap* 'lick', which has no PAn etymology (cf. §D2.2.1, end).

There are examples of medial *-d- reflected with /-d-/. These forms have Ml cognates and are borrowings from Ml.

*uda > *muda* 'unripe' *sapedec > *padas* 'sharp, biting' *cudu 'scoop' > *san-sudu* 'spoon'

Final *-d > /-t/:

*tukad > *manukat* 'go up ladder' (*maN-* + *tukat*) *tusud > *utut* 'knee'

There are cases of *-d reflected with /-r/. With one exception, all of the examples are demonstrably borrowed, mostly from Ml. The following forms may also be of Ml origin, but it cannot be demonstrated:

*kid + doubling > *kidekid 'file, rasp' > *kikir* 'file' *kud 'grate, scratch, rasp' > *kukur* 'rasp'[16]

D2.3.33 *j

*j > /j/ in initial and medial position and /-t/ in final position. There are no unequivocal forms inherited from PAn that show a reflex of *j after a nasal. However, the form *isejam 'borrow' developed a nasal and retains /j/:

*jalan > *jalan* 'way' *jaqewis > *ke-jau* 'far' *juɣuq 'broth, liquid material' > *juhu* 'brew, soup' *saɣejaɬ > *hejan* 'steps, ladder' *isejam > *injam* 'borrow' *qujaɬ > *ujan* 'rain' *bukij > *bukit* 'hill' *lahuj > *laut* 'seaward' *tukej 'support, prop' > *tungket* 'support'

In the following example, *-j is reflected with /-r/. The form with /-r/ is clearly not directly inherited:

*likuj 'back, behind' > *ba-rikur* 'on the back' (but also *likut* 'behind, back', directly inherited)

D2.3.34 *g

Except in three cases, *g-onset to the penult or earlier is reflected with /g-/:

*galaŋ 'something wedged underneath to support' > *galang* 'fundament on which s.t. stands' *gatel > *gatel* 'itchy' *gusam > *guam* 'thrush'

The exceptions are the following forms. In the first case, there is contamination with *kilat* 'lightning'. The other two exceptions have no explanation. They are probably borrowings from a neighboring language that reflects *g with /k/.

*gilab 'shining' > *kilap* 'whet, sharpened' *gac + doubling > *gacegac 'scratch' > *kakas* 'for a chicken to scratch' *gap > *mangap* (root: *-kakap*) 'grope' (cf. §D2.1.12, footnote) *gilig > *kilir* 'side'

The form *gita* 'see' also shows morphophonemic alternants that presuppose a variant with /k-/.

*gíta 'see' > *ita* 'see' (where the /k-/ was lost by the processes described in §D2.3.13, end)

As onset or coda of the final syllable, *g > /r/:

*qagan > *ara* 'name' *págay > *parey* 'rice plant' *piga > *pire* 'how many' *puceg > *puser* 'navel' *gilig > *kilir* 'side'

---

[16] Clearly *kikir* and *kukur* have influenced each other. It is unknown which form influenced the other.

There is only one example of a cluster with *g, and this shows the *g merging with the reflex of *d, as is the case of other reflexes of *g as onset of the final syllable:

*qałegaw > *andaw* 'day'

D2.3.4 Voiced continuants

D2.3.41 *ɣ

*ɣ is reflected as /h/ everywhere but in clusters:

*ɣaya 'great' > *hai* 'big' *ɣíbay 'oscillate' > *hiwey* 'hang down (like cloth from a table)' *ɣumaq > *huma* 'house' *qaɣem > *ahem* 'pangolin' *beɣac > *behas* 'husked rice' *biɣaq > *biha* 'k.o. arum' *uɣát > *uhat* 'root, vein, artery' *becuɣ > *besuh* 'full, sated' *buteliɣ 'cyst' > *butih* 'wart' *dátaɣ 'flat area' > *datah* 'slope, plain'

*ɣ was lost in clusters or in clusters that developed by elision of a vowel:

*beɣecáy 'oar' > *besey* 'short paddle' *biɣ + doubling > *biɣebiɣ > *biwih* 'lips' *baɣiw > *bayu* 'spoiled food' (< *baɣɣu)

*ɣ was lost in the following form, perhaps because of its position as onset of the final syllable of a trisyllabic stem between two /i/'s:

*tiɣic 'drip' > *han-tis* 'drip' (also *pan-tis* 'drip')

*ɣ was also lost when onset of the penult of forms that retained more than two syllables after the processes of elision had taken place:

*qałiɣuwan 'bee' > *ñuan* 'k.o. ant' (< ñiuwan)

*ɣ was lost in the following form without explanation:

*ɣúcuk 'ribs' > *usuk* 'ribs'

In one case, *-ɣ was lost, and in another, *-ɣ is reflected with /l/. These forms are not directly inherited.

*kátiɣ 'outrigger' > *katil* 'seat in a canoe' *caŋelaɣ > *sanga* 'fry with little oil'

In a large number of cases, *ɣ is reflected with /r/. These have, for the most part, been borrowed from Ml, but some may have other origins. In any case, they are not directly inherited. The following list gives examples:

*baɣu > *waru* 'a shrub: *Hibiscus tileaceous*' *dámaɣ 'torch' > *damar* 'damar resin' *ɣatúc > *ratus* 'hundreds'

D2.3.42 *l

*l is reflected as /l/ everywhere but in clusters:

*laŋaw > *langaw* 'a fly' *lima > *lime* 'five' *lúmut > *lumut* 'moss, slime in water' *salem 'night' > *ha-m-alem* 'night' *balik 'return' > balik 'inside out, backwards first' *bilit > *bilit* 'wind about, go around' *bulu 'body hair > *bulu* 'hair, feathers, fur' *kasepál 'thick' > *ba-kapal* 'be thick' *gatél > *gatel* 'itchy' *kawil > *kawil* 'k.o. fish hook'

In clusters (which developed by elision of an intervening vowel), *l was lost, except for *ql, in which case *q was lost:

*buteliɣ 'cyst' > *butih* 'wart' *túqelaɬ > *tulaŋ* 'bone'

*l was not lost in the case of roots consisting of reduplicated monosyllabic elements:

*lebeleb 'hidden by being covered' > *lelep* 'flooded' (< *lebleb)

There are cases in which *l is reflected with /r/. These forms are clearly not directly inherited:

*láyaɣ 'sail' > *rayar* 'sail' *likuj 'back' > *ba-rikur* 'on the back' (but also *likut* 'behind')
*qúleg 'worm' > *uret* 'worm'

D2.3.43 *ɬ

*ɬ underwent the changes found throughout the MP languages (§§A1.1.32, 4th¶, A3.3.4): *ɬ > /ñ/ initially preceding a stressed syllable (including monosyllabic roots). As onset to an unstressed penult or earlier syllable, *ɬ- became /l-/. Following an unstressed penult and finally,*ɬ > /n/.

As onset to a stressed penult or monosyllabic root, *ɬ > /ñ/:

*ɬámuk > *ñamuk* 'mosquito' *ɬála > *ñala* 'flame' *ɬuɣ > *eñuh* 'coconut'

As onset to an unstressed penult, * ɬ > /l/:

*ɬabúq > *lawu* 'fallen'

This development affects most of the forms that reflect roots affixed with *qaɬi-. The first syllable was lost by the rules of §D2.1.11, above: [17]

*qaɬimátek > *lamantek* 'upland leech' *qaɬisípec > *lipes* 'roach' (with loss of the initial syllable, *s, and contraction of *isi)

In final position, * -ɬ > /-n/:

*qaciɬ 'salt' > *anis* 'sweet' (< *qanic [§D2.1.3] < *qacin) *bulaɬ > *bulan* 'moon' *qujaɬ > *ujan* 'rain'

In clusters, including clusters that developed, *ɬ > /n/:

*baɬebaɬ > *bamban* 'k.o. reed' *qaɬegaw > *andaw* 'day'

Exceptions to these rules are forms not directly inherited or that were changed by analogy (§A3.8):

*ɬaŋúy > *hananguy* 'swim' *ciɬaɣ 'shine, ray' > *singah* 'torch'

The following form, reconstructed with *-ɬ, is reflected with /ng/, as is the case of the cognates over a wide portion of western An languages:

*túqelaɬ 'bone' > *tulang* 'bone'

The following form can be explained as a replacement by analogy of *n by /t/, but a reflex *n from *ñ in this position indicates that the form must have been borrowed:

---

[17] However, the word for 'bee' evidently developed a stress on the antepenult in pre-Ngaju, causing *ɬ > *ñ:

*qaɬíγuwan 'bee' > *ñiγuwán > *niyuwán > ñuwan 'k.o. ant'

*ɬisebic > *tipis* 'thin'

D2.3.5 *m, *n, *ŋ

The nasals reflected with little change.

D2.3.51 *m

*m is refected as /m/ everywhere:

*manúk 'bird' > *manuk* 'chicken' *ɣumaq > *huma* ' house' *daɬúm > *danum* 'water'

D2.3.52 *n

*n is reflected as /n/ in most environments:

*naɬáq > *nana* 'pus' *ina > *ine* 'mother' *dásuwen > *dawen* 'leaf'

Before *i, *n is palatalized (> /ñ/):

*binesíq 'seed' > *biñi* 'seed rice' *ɣínu 'winnowing tray' > *ñiro* 'rice tray' (not inherited)

There is a morphophonemic process such that when the third singular genitive ending /-a/ is added to stems ending in /-n/, the /-n/ is lost. In some cases, the form without /-n/ has been generalized throughout the paradigm. This is the case of the following form:

*qagan > *ara* 'name'

In one case, *n- is lost, but this root also shows other irregularities, and it is clearly not directly inherited.

*nipaq > *ipah* 'a palm: *Nypa fruticans*'

In at least two cases, a /d/ was intercalated between /n/ and a following vowel:

*qaɬup > *andop* 'pursue game' *aɬipa 'k.o. snake' > *handipe* 'snake' (/h-/ is an indication that the word is secondary)

D2.3.53 *ŋ

*ŋ > /ng/ in all positions except that in clusters where the *ŋ is the final C of a monosyllabic root, *ŋ assimilates to the following C.

*ŋaŋa > *ka-nganga* 'open mouthed' *deŋan > *dengan* 'with' *láŋit > *langit* 'sky' *lutúŋ > *lutung* 'k.o. ape' *puŋ + doubling > *puŋpuŋ > *pumpung* 'gather', *diŋediŋ > *dinding* 'wall, shield against wind, screen'

There is one unexplained exception, in which case *ŋ > /ñ/. It is the only form inherited from PAn that reflects *ŋ to the left of *l in the next syllable. There may be a regular sound change of *ŋ > /n/ when the next syllable begins with *l, and the *n is further changed to /ñ/ before /i/ by the rules of §D2.3.52, 2nd¶, above.

*ŋilu 'throbbing pain' > *ñilu* 'pain in the bones'

D2.3.61 *w

In initial position, *w was lost:

*wada 'there is' > *are* 'many'

Intervocalically, *-w- is retained except between *u and *a (including when *s or *q were lost in the sequences *usa and *uqa):

*kawit 'hook' > *m-awit* 'crooked, bent' *qacáwa 'in-law' > *sawe* 'wife' *dásuwen > *dawen* 'leaf'

The following forms reflect Ø < *w or < *w that had developed between *u and *a:

*buwaq > *bua* 'fruit' *lahuj > *laut* 'seaward' *dusa > *due* 'two' *tuqas 'old' > *mama tue* 'middle uncle'

There is one example of *uwa reflected as /uwa/. In this case, our consultant insists on /uwa/ although Hardeland lists the root with /ua/. The form may well be a Ml borrowing:

*busat 'lift' > *muwat* 'load' (Hardeland lists the root: as *-buat* or *-puat.*)

In trisyllabics, *w onset of the final syllable was lost:

*babaw + *an (or *-en) > *bawan* 'to weed' (< *babawan or < *babawen)

For *w at the end of a syllable, see the diphthongs §§D2.2.52, D2.2.53).

D2.3.62 *y

Intervocalically, *-y- is reflected with /-y-/, but not after *i, except when protected by a nasal (forming /ñ/):

ayaw > *mang-ayaw* 'head hunting' *dayuŋ > *dayung* 'k.o. long rudder' *iya > *ie* 'he, she' *miniyak 'fat' > *eñak* 'fat, bacon' (§D2.1.5, end)

The sequence *-ey- medially is reflected with /i/ if the *e is not elided:

*iseyup 'blow' > *tar-iup* 'blown away' *láqeya > *lai* 'ginger' (< *laqiya) *laheyu > *ba-layu* 'withered'

For forms ending in *-ya, see §D2.2.4. For *-y at the end of the syllable, see the diphthongs, §D2.2.51, D2.2.52.

CHAPTER THREE
Malagasy

D3.0 General background

Malagasy (Mlg) is spoken throughout the island of Madagascar. As a consequence of the long period over which the island was settled, the language that was brought to Madagascar developed a great deal of dialectal diversity. The Merina dialect of the central plateau, the seat of the central government, is the official language of the Malagasy Republic, and the forms considered in this study are taken from Merina. Forms from another dialect are quoted only when no Merina cognate occurs in the data. Dempwolff (1934-38) used Merina Malagasy (referring to it by its other name 'Hova') as one of the languages to test his reconstructions and discussed the correspondences in detail. Our conclusions here agree in many respects with Dempwolff's, but there are differences in detail, and of course here, the development of the Mlg phonemes from PAn is described in terms of a sound system very different from the one Dempwolff posited. Mlg has been widely described since Dempwolff's time, including its history, most importantly by Mahdi 1988, and much of what is said here relies on the literature cited in these studies and the others listed under Malagasy in the bibliography. The primary sources are both Richardson (1885) and Abinal-Malzac (1888). When these two sources do not coincide in their interpretation of the meaning of a root, I have followed Richardson.

Malagasy is the westernmost outpost of the An languages. It was brought to the western end of the Indian Ocean after the An languages had spread throughout Indonesia and onto mainland Southeast Asia. The language was brought westward as a consequence of the trade between Indonesia and East Africa, most likely by ship crews, military personnel, and others who were involved in the trade and remained in the new land. However, there is no good evidence that ancestors of the present-day Malagasy's were present in this trade at its inception, and it is unknown when the first Austronesian settlements in the west were made. Although there are estimates as early as 2,000 years ago (Mahdi 1988: 219–220), there is no evidence that the An migrations date back that far. The earliest systematic human settlement in Madagascar is only after the 8th Century AD (Adelaar 2009) , and if it is true that Austronesians were the first people to settle there, then they must have arrived in the west at least by that time.[1] Austronesian settlement may well have begun in East Africa or on the

[1]Dahl (1951:36-369) suggests that since Mlg has words of Sanskrit origin, the migration to the west must have been after the earliest Hindu influence in Kalimantan. This can be dated on the basis of an inscription found in east Kalimantan to 400AD. This inscription contains the names of three generations of kings, the earliest of whom has a name of An origin and the next two generations of whom have names of Sanskrit origin. The beginnings of Hindu influence can therefore be dated accurately. Dahl argues further that the number of Sanskrit loans in Mlg is limited, and therefore the migration to the west was at the beginnings of Hindu influence—i.e., it can be dated to around 400 AD. On the other hand Adelaar (2009) argues for a later date on the grounds that the Indic influence on Mlg is not at all limited and the forms in Mlg were introduced via Ml or

Comoro Islands, but there is no evidence for it. The extent of the Bantu influence on Mlg vocabulary indicates intimate contact, but does not necessarily imply Mlg settlement in Bantu areas. This influence could be explained by slavery and intermarriage (or both), as well. Africans who came to Madagascar over the years mainly integrated and intermarried with Austronesians. Cf. further discussion Bantu influence in §D3.1.13, below.

The geographical origin of Mlg has been a subject of intense speculation since it was first known that Mlg clearly has connections with the Indonesian languages. In 1951 O. Dahl published a study that compared Mlg with Maanyan and hypothesized that Mlg originated in early Maanyan (Dahl 1951). He was certainly correct in his thesis that Mlg comes from the Barito River basin in southeast Kalimantan, but it is not at all certain that Maanyan is the language most closely related to Mlg. There is a number of only slightly known languages of southeast Kalimantan that in fact exhibit features in common with Mlg of the same sort that Maanyan exhibits. In any case, innovations made by Mlg in common with languages of this area, especially in vocabulary, make it almost certain that Mlg originates there. This makes sense from what is known about the history of the area. The languages of southeast Kalimantan are located in the hinterlands of Banjarmasin, which was an important entrepot well before Majapahit times.[2] The most likely scenario is that Malay ships sailed from this harbor, manned by personnel originating in the hinterlands and guarded by soldiery from that area. It is hypothesized that these people spoke the ancestor of modern Mlg, and this hypothesis is supported by the fact that Mlg itself is replete with loan forms from Ml (Adelaar: 1989). It is telling that terms for seafaring in Mlg are almost entirely loan words from Ml.

The extent of borrowing from Ml in Mlg is immense and not entirely determinable, for any number of forms that descend from PAn or PMP found in both Mlg and Ml contain no phonemes or any other characteristics that would enable us to identify the Mlg form as originating from Ml.[3] Some of the Ml loan words in Mlg are likely to be of Banjarese origin, as shown by having /a/ in the final syllable where Banjarese also has /a/ and where the Ml of eastern Sumatra has retained the inherited /e/ in that position . That Mlg should have borrowed from Banjarese makes sense, for Banjarese Ml was probably the lingua franca in southeast Kalimantan even before Majapahit times, as it is today. The ship captains were not necessarily Banjarese and the lingua franca on the boats must have been the Ml of Sumatra, as a large portion of the Ml vocabulary is clearly not of Banjarese orgin.

The following chart shows the phonemes of Mlg. A number of them are confined to specific environments, due to the changes discussed in §D3.1.1ff., below, but recent additions, dialect mixture, and analogical changes have caused these formerly restricted sounds to occur in a much larger variety of environments

---

OJv. Loan words from Ml were introduced over a long period of time, from before the migration and continuing for centuries thereafter, for contact with Asia continued until the arrival of the Europeans. Adelaar (1989: 33, 35) gives evidence for borrowing of Ml that took place after the coming of Islam to Indonesia.

[2] I have found little information on history of Banjarmasin prior to Majapahit times, and it is unknown how early this port gained importance. Most certainly it was an entrepot at the time of the early east Africa trade.

[3] Many of the forms of Ml origin were borrowed in pre-Mlg times and participated in the sound changes described in §§D3.2ff. and D3.3ff. The examples illustrating these changes in some cases are in fact not inherited but borrowed from Ml.

CHART ONE. PHONEMES OF MALAGASY

Consonants

voiceless stops	p	t	k	
voiced stops	b	d	g	
voiceless spirants	f	s		h
voiced spirants	v	z		
affricates		j [j], ts [c], tr [č]		
nasals	m	n	[ŋ][5]	
liquids		l, r		

Vowels[4]

high	i		o
mid	e		ɔ
low		a	

We follow Mlg orthography in transcriptions. /i/ is written *y* at the end of a word. /o/[6] is written *o*. Occasionally, in Mlg orthography /ɔ/ is written *o* (confusing it with the transcription of /o/—[u], which is also written with *o*), but the pronunciation of /ɔ/ is in fact lower than /o/. In inherited forms /ɔ/ only occurs as an alternant of /ao/, and here both /ɔ/ and /ao/ are written the same way as *ao*.

Stress in current Mlg is contrastive. However, in inherited forms, stress is predictable in terms of the make-up of the word: (1) words ending in *-tra, -ka,* or *-na* are stressed on the antepenult—i.e., on the penult prior to the addition of the endings (§D3.1.11, below). Otherwise stress is on the penult, with the exception of words containing monosyllabic roots, where the root is always stressed, and of a small number of morphological formations, where the affix is always stressed.

ándro 'day' + *man-* 'verb former' + *-a* 'imperative' > *manandróa* 'tell whether a day is lucky or not (imperative)'; *ándro* 'day' + *fan-a* 'nominal former' + *-na* (ending [§D3.1.11]) > *fanandróana* 'telling whether a day is lucky or not'

In short, PAn and PMP stress is not directly reflected in Mlg.

D3.1.1 Morphophonemic alternations and their historical source

D3.1.11 Development of final *-na, -tra,* and *-ka.*

Proto-Malagasy—that is, the language that was first brought west and became the ancestor of the modern dialects, had articulatory characteristics that led to innovations, giving the language a substantially changed aspect and making its phonology typologically rather different from the other languages spoken in southeast Kalimantan. First, the word stress moved away from the final syllable in those cases where it had been final. Penultimate or earlier stress led to weakening of the end of words. This led to the weakening and loss of word final consonants in two stages: word final nasals and final *l first merged to [n] and then in stage two, were lost entirely in the dialect from which current Mlg derives; the stop

---

[4] Contemporary Malagasy arguably also has two diphthongs /ai/ and /ao/ (written *ay* [because this diphthong occurs at the end of a word] and *ao*, respectively), which derive from what was historically vowel sequences. However, the evidence for the phonological status of *ay* and *ao* is contradictory, and it would be tangential to discuss here the details of the facts involved. The phonological history of the vowels can be described exhaustively if /ai/ and /ao/ are treated as vowel sequences, without resolving the question of whether in the phonology these are sequences or diphthongs.

[5] In Merina [ŋ] only occurs as an allophone of /n/ before /g/ and /k/. In other dialects it is a phoneme (§D3.3.44).

[6] /o/ is a high back rounded vowel. Mlg orthography has traditionally used *o* rather than *u* to represent this sound under the influence of French orthography. Mlg does not use the letter *u*.

consonants were devoiced. In stage one *t and *d merged and then in stage two, were lost entirely in the dialect from which modern Mlg derives. The labials merged with *k and then in stage two, were lost. Final *h, *q, and *c were lost entirely in the first stage. In this way a structure of open final syllables emerged. There were, however, dialects in which only the first stage changes took place (the mergers and loss of final *h, *q, and *c), but not the second stage, the loss of the final nasal, the final *t and the final velar *k (including the final labials that had merged with it). The dialects that retained the second stage finals influenced the dialects that had developed open final syllables—i.e., forms from the dialects that had retained a few final consonants were taken back into the main dialect from which the current Mlg derives. The open syllable structure was retained by adding a vocalic release to word final consonants. The stress had shifted to the penult in all roots, and when the final consonant with the vocalic release was added, the stress remained where it had been. For example. *búlan > *vúla and then > *vólana* 'moon'; *sabáɣat 'monsoon wind' > *avára > *aváratra* 'north';[7] *dábuk 'pound' > *rávu > *rávoka* 'pound (rice)'; *kúbekub > *húhu > *hóhoka* 'cover by something turned over'; *sáted > *áte > *man-átitra* 'conduct, convey'; *láleg > *eále > *lálitra* 'fly' (the merger of *g with *d, *j [§D3.3.33] preceded the devoicing and merger of the finals in 'stage one', so that the final of *lalitra* < *laleg is *-tra* and not *-ka*). The evidence that the Mlg endings of roots, *-na, -tra,* or *-ka*, developed by contact in the way here described comes from the fact that not all of the roots that had ended in nasal or a labial, alveolar, or velar stop developed these endings, and in some cases there are doublets, with and without the final syllable: *qaɬimatek > *dimaty* 'leech' (and not the expected *dimatika), *ipen > *ify* 'tooth', *daɬum > *rano* 'water', and others. *baŋkuwaŋ is reflected by both *vakoa* '*Pandanus* sp.' and *vakoana*. The Sakalava dialect of western Madagascar shows reflexes of a large number of forms ending in PAn stop consonants that never developed *-na, -tra,* or *-ka.*[8] These forms that failed to develop the endings *-na, -tra,* and *-ka* or that developed doublets can best be explained if the endings had been added word at a time through Mlg contact with a dialect that had preserved final consonants reduced to three in number. Further evidence that the endings developed in this way is provided by words borrowed from Ml that get endings attached to them even though they do not end in any of the consonants that gave rise to the endings *-na, -tra,* and *-ka.* (See the examples in §D3.3.41, ff.) Finally, the fact that some roots add the wrong ending—that is, add *-tra* instead of *-ka*, further indicates that these endings were added word at a time as a result of contact with a dialect that retained the finals:

*tup + R- 'close' > *mi-tototra* 'be covered over' *totof-ana* 'be covered'

Note that root final stop consonants in affixed forms have their intervocalic reflexes (that is, when they are followed by a vowel and are not at the end of the word). E.g. *inum > *inona* 'drinking' (in word final position). But *inum-en became *inom-ina* 'drink it'. The *-m remains unchanged intervocalically. More examples are given in the discussions of the development of the individual consonnants, §§D3.3ff., below.

---

[7] The form *avaratra* 'north' is in fact of Ml provenience. The loss of the final consonants and subsequent accretion of the endings took place after pre-Mlg had already incorporated a number of Ml borrowings.

[8] In some dialects the endings *-na, -tra,* and *-ka* developed centralized ([ə]) releases, which subsequently became /i/ (§D3.2.2). What is said here about the endings with /a/ goes also for the endings with /i/.

D3.1.12 Change of stop consonants to continuants

In initial and medial positions, the stop consonants other than *t and *q became continuants: *b > /v/; *d, *j, *g (medially) > /r/; *p > /f/; and k > /h/. *t remained /t/, *c and *ɣ were lost in some environments, but in others became /s/ and /z/ respectively, and *q was lost entirely. Examples are given in the sections discussing the development of the individual phonemes, §§D3.3ff., below.

The change to a continuant did not take place when the phoneme was protected—that is, when it came to be the second consonant in a sequence. In the following examples, the initial consonant of the second word of a phrase was protected by a nasal linker that came between the two words of the phrase:

tady 'rope + linker + *foitra* 'navel > *tadi-m-**p**uitra* 'navel chord' (< *puseg)

tay 'feces' + linker + *huhu* 'the nails' > *tai-n-**k**uhu* 'dirt under the nails' (< *kuku)

If the first word in the phrase ends in *-na, -tra,* or *-ka*, the endings meld with the linker (*na-* becomes a homorganic nasal, *-tra* and *-ka* are lost):[9]

tolana 'bone' + *fe* 'thigh' > *tolam**p**e* 'thigh bone' (< *paqa)

hoditra 'skin' + *hazu* 'tree' > *hodi**k**azo* 'bark of tree' (< *kasiw)

hoditra 'skin' + *fotsi* 'white' > *hodi**p**otsy* 'white spots on the skin' < *putiq < *puɬetiq)

lelaka 'lick + *fala-dia* 'sole of foot' > *lela**p**ala-dia* 'ask humbly for pardon (lit. lick the soles of the feet)' (< *palag)

araka 'follow' + *vavy* 'female' > *man-ara**b**avy* 'live with the wife's family'

mpivarotra 'seller' + *satroka* 'hat' > *mpivaro**ts**atroka* 'seller of hats'

Although the alternation between /h/ and /k/, /f/ and /p/, /v/ and /b/ originated when stops were protected by an adjacent preceding consonant—i.e., kept from spirantizing, a process of strengthening also developed in Mlg, whereby continuants were changed to stops when a nasal or other consonant came to precede them immediately. Thus *s < *c (§D3.3.22) is strengthened to /ts/;[10] /r/ < *d (§D3.3.32) is strengthened to /dr/; /v/ < *w is strengthened to /b/; /z/ < *y or *ɣ is strengthened to /j/; /l/ < *l is strengthened to /d/:

lalana 'road' + *ra* 'blood' > *lalan**dr**a* 'veins' (< *daɣaq)

taolana 'bone' + *valo* 'eight' > *taolam**b**alo* 'the eight bones (that have to be buried after death)'

tai 'feces' + linker + *zaza* 'child'+ > *tai-n-**j**aza* 'k.o. small bead'

tai 'feces' + linker + *lalitra* 'fly'+ *-ina* 'adjective suffix' > *tai-n-**d**alerina* 'fly specks'

If the first word in the phrase ended in *-tra* or *-ka,* the initial consonant of the second word is protected or strengthened, but the final of the first word is lost:

---

[9] The rule is that the linker is retained overtly only after a vowel. The *-na* final absorbs the linker—that is, the two together become a nasal homorganic with the consonant that follows (in its protected or strengthened form [see the following paragraph for a discussion of strengthening]). The finals *-tra* and *-ka* are lost entirely and leave their trace in that the consonant of the following word is protected or strengthened, but there is no trace of any linker.

[10] The alternant /ts/ originates in strengthening, rather than as a protection of *c, for it is likely that PAn *c > /s/ earlier than Proto-Mlg times. /ts/ is not inherited directly from *c, but is a development when the *s was the second consonant in a cluster.

zaitra 'sew' + *zaitra* > *zaijaitra* 'keep sewing' (< *jaqit-jaqit: the first *t is lost but the /z/ < *j is strengthened))

lanitra 'heavens' + *latsaka* 'fallen' > *lanidatsaka* 'innumerable, immense' (lit. 'fallen sky') (< *langit + *latsaka*: the final *t of *langit was lost, but not before the /l/ of *latsaka* was strengthened)

Strengthening also takes place morpheme internally when a nasal coda of the penult develops (§D3.1.5) or a nasal cluster develops in other ways:

*paya > *fanja* 'swamp' (< *faza) *qulun + *-an > *ondana* 'pillow' (§D3.1.4)

Nasal clusters that developed were retained in Mlg. There are no examples of [ŋk] that look to be inherited,[11] but in compounds with a linker, the cluster /nk/ develops when the second member had inherited /h/ from initial *k-:[12]

tay 'feces' + linker + *huhu* 'the nails' (< *kukuh) > *tainkuhu* 'dirt under the nails'

There are several examples of /k/ in forms reflecting a protoform, and the Ml cognate reflects /ŋk/. Since known Ml borrowings have /k/ for Ml /ŋk/ (Adelaar 2009, Appendix), I hypothesize that the forms evincing /k/ are in fact from earlier *ŋk and are not inherited but borrowed.[13]

*akat 'lift' > *akatra* 'ascent' (Ml *angkat* 'lift') *baŋkuwaŋ > *vakoana* 'k.o. pandanus' (Ml *bengkuang* '*Pandanus furcatus*') *caŋkal 'handle' + *-an > *akalana* 'cutting board' (Ml *sengkalan* 'cutting board') *cuŋkit 'poke with s.t. sharp' > *sokitra* 'work with a pointed instrument' (Ml *sungkit* 'k.o. embroidery') *lakaq 'step' > *laka* 'lines in a board game' (Ml *langkah* 'step') *taŋgap 'grab with hands' > *takatra* 'seize, get by reaching' (Ml *taŋkap* 'catch') *takub > *takofana* 'covered with s.t. hollow' (Ml *tangkup* 'hollow cover')

D3.1.13 Bantu influence on Mlg

It has been speculated that the phonological developments in Mlg discussed in §D3.1.11 and D3.1.12, above, came about due to a Bantu substratum (Dahl 1988). The notion 'Bantu substratum' implies that the language was adopted by a Bantu population that altered structures and that these altered structures were subsequently spread to the entire community. Dahl adduces three factors to substantiate this, none of which do in fact provide evidence for a Bantu substratum in the sense here defined. First is the existence of Bantu loan words, some of them intimate. These loans are evidence for contact with Bantu, but not for a Bantu substratum. Second is the development of open syllables. In §D3.1.11 I attributed this to the accentual pattern that had developed in pre-Mlg. Certainly open syllables have developed widely and spontaneously across the world's languages without input from a substratum. As Mahdi points out (1988: 213–215), the changes that Mlg underwent are widespread over the range of the An languages, especially in eastern Indonesia and Oceania, so that the open syllable feature of Bantu is no evidence that Mlg developed open syllables

---

[11] There are a few examples of morpheme internal clusters /ŋk/. Their source is unknown, but they are not inherited, for they exhibit irregularities:

*biŋkuk 'crooked' > *bingo* 'bow-legged' *beŋkeŋ > *vonkina* 'shrivel'

[12] The grammar books often consider the linker to be a shortened form of the marker *ny*, but at the time of the change of stops to continuants, the linker had no final vowel (if it ever had had), for the linker protects the stops.

[13] It is assumed that Bantu influence led to the development of /k/ in borrowing forms with /ŋk/ (Dahl 1953: 114, Adelaar 2009, Appendix), but for the reasons given in §D3.1.13, below, that is highly unlikely.

due to a Bantu substratum. Third, Dahl adduces the development of continuants from stops in Mlg as evidence. Indeed, the Sabaki languages (which include the Bantu languages that could have had contact with Mlg) developed continuants from stops, but the phonetics of the Bantu developments are totally incongruent with those of Mlg with the exception that proto-Bantu *k develops into [h] in Comoro just as PAn *k develops to [h] in Mlg (Nurse and Hinnebusch 1993: 73). There is no reason why the Comoro and the Mlg developments of *k cannot have been independent of each other. In fact, they certainly must have been independent, for the other changes of the stops in Bantu and Mlg were completely different in their phonetics. Further, there is evidence that the change of *b and *d to continuants (to /v/ and /r/ respectively [§§D3.3.31 and D3.3.32]) took place before the migration to the west. The evidence comes from loan words with /b/ that cannot derive from Ml, e.g. *baby* 'carry on the back' (< PAn *baba) must have been borrowed from a language near Mlg in the homeland, for the Ml reflex is *bawa.*[14] Further, Ml forms reflecting *d are borrowed into Mlg with //tr/. Therefore, a form like *daboka* 'beat' (< PAn *dabuk) either was borrowed from a neighboring language in the homeland or was borrowed from Ml at a time earlier than the other loan words borrowed with /tr/. In any case Mlg borrowings with /b/ and /d/ must have taken place after the spirantization of inherited *b and *d, and this must have been before the migration west. In short, spirantization of *b and *d cannot have been under Bantu influence. Bantu languages developed strengthening, as did Mlg, but the conditions were totally different. For this reason, it is impossible that Bantu had anything to do with the development of continuants in Mlg. In fact, there is evidence internal to Mlg to the contrary—that is, that a Bantu substratum cannot have caused the development of continuants. Namely, evidence is furnished by the sandhi rule whereby initial consonants in the second member of a compound or a phrase are protected from developing into continuants by the final consonant of the first word in the phrase—e.g., *kayu 'wood' developed into /hazu/ but when coming after /hoditra/ 'skin' (< *kulit), the *k did not change to /h/. Thus, the phrase is /hodikazu/ 'bark' (cf. §D.3.1.12, above). This rule proves that the development of continuants from stops preceded the loss of the word-final consonants. Since the very first thing that would happen in substratum effects would have been the loss of word-final consonants, especially in a phrase preceding another consonant, it is virtually impossible that the development of continuants had anything to do with substratum effects.

There is one piece of evidence adduced to prove Bantu influence on Mlg phonology that at first sight seems persuasive. Namely, it was thought that Comoro was the most likely source of Bantu influence, and the fact that Ml /ŋk/ is borrowed with /k/ is adduced as evidence (Dahl 1951: 114). Indeed there are Sabaki languages that reflect earlier *ŋk with /k/ or /kh/. However, this is the case of only one of the Comoro dialects, Maore (Nurse and Hinnebosch: 156). Further, this dialect and the other languages that simplify *ŋk also simplify *mp and *nt, whereas Mlg does not simplify these clusters in loan forms from Ml or in inherited forms. Although it remains a mystery why Mlg should have borrowed Ml forms containing /ŋk/ with /k/, it is not likely that the developments in the Maore dialect or any of the other Sabaki languages had a hand in it if the other clusters were not simplified as well.

It is certainly possible that a Bantu language was catalytic in the change of *p and *k to /f/ and /h/ in the sense that the borrowing of Bantu forms with /f/ or /h/ facilitated the tendency

[14] If the change of *b > /v/ had occurred after Mlg was in contact with and affected by a Bantu language, then *baby* should have participated in this change. It did not. Therefore, the change *b > /v/ took place before the period of Mlg–Bantu contact.

of pre-Mlg phonemes to develop spirantal allophones of inherited *p, *k. But there is no evidence that Mlg was adopted by a population that turned stops into continuants (because they lacked stops in their original language) and then spread their pronunciation to the rest of the community. Similarly, the development of open syllables could well have been facilitated by the presence of Bantu speakers in the community who dropped word-final consonants. The number and character of the loan words from Bantu present a scenario of close contact, and this jibes with the genetic make-up of the Mlg population, which evinces a combination of Asian and Bantu features. The picture is one of a Bantu population that lived in Mlg communities and integrated into them. It is totally possible and in fact likely that Bantu-speaking care-givers raised children in some of the Mlg communities. Bantu speakers were numerous and influential enough to have supplied an important amount and quality of vocabulary and to have influenced Mlg phonology in ways described above.

There remain unexplained mysteries about Mlg developments. First is the borrowing of Ml words with syllable onset /d-/ into Mlg with /tr/ (e.g. *tratra* from Ml *dada* 'chest'). Second, is the borrowing of Ml /ŋk/ with Mlg /k/ (cf. the second and third paragraphs of this section, above). Dahl (1951: 117) and Adelaar (2009: Appendix) suggest that Bantu influence might explain these mysteries, but as discussed two paragraphs above, the scenario presented by Dahl is unlikely in the case of Mlg /k/ from *ŋk. No facts are cited to explain why Bantu should be responsible for the development of /tr/ < Ml /d/. In short, the hypothesis of Bantu influence on the phonology remains unproven. There is another Mlg mystery for which no explanation has been offered so far: why are words ending in *-t reflected in Mlg with final /tra/ rather than /ta/, when intervocalic /t/ is a widely attested (and *t is retained in stem final position before suffixes [§D3.3.12])? Bantu influence may well explain these mysteries, but decisive evidence remains to be marshaled.

D3.1.2 Processes of syncopation and CC simplification

Prior to the change of the stops to continuants, pre-Mlg made some of the changes made by other An languages in disyllabizing trisyllabic roots and simplifying CC's that resulted. That these changes were prior to the change of stops to continuants is proven by the treatment of doubled monosyllabic roots. The epenthetic *e between the two repeated monosyllabic roots was lost and the resulting cluster was simplified if the root had a consonant coda. But the change of stops to continuants had not yet occurred, so that the morphophonemic changes of the root-final consonant of the first syllable like the root final changes described in §D3.1.11, above, did not take place:[15]

*bukebuk > *vovoka* 'decayed, worm-eaten' (< *bukbuk) *cekecek > *sesika* 'cram s.t. into place' *kubekub > *hohof-ana* 'covered by s.t. turned over'

After the loss of medial consonants, trisyllabic roots became disyllabic by contraction of the vowels that had come to abut. With a handful of exceptions the contractions involve the merger of like vowels or the absorption of *e into a vowel on which it came to abut:[16]

---

[15] In the case of a nasal coda the final nasal of the first occurrence of the root was not lost (because the language allowed sequences of nasal plus consonant) and the result is indistinguishable from that produced by the rule of §D3.1.12:

*diŋediŋ > *rindrina* 'wall'

[16] A sequence /aa/ that developed at the end of a word became /e/. Cf. §D3.2.3, where the change of *-a > /-i/ is discussed:

*iseci 'contents' > *isy* 'there is, exist' (< *ieci) *qetaq + *ma- > *manta* 'raw' *qaselu > *alo* 'pestle' (< *aelu) *pakehu 'k.o. edible fern' > *faho* 'k.o. shrub yielding sago' *palisi > *fady* 'taboo' *seqeɣet 'tight' > *etra* 'girdle, belt' (< *eeet) *pacaqaɬ > *mi-ana* 'carry over shoulder' (< *paaan, where *p was replaced by the productive verbal affixes) *pucuq > *fo* 'heart' *taseyup 'blow' > *tsioka* 'wind'(< *taiup [*ai > /i/—§D3.2.4])

In some cases, the sequences *ie that developed from consonant loss are reflected with /o/. Similarly, a sequence *ei that developed in one case contracted to /oi/ in one case.[17] The precise rule has not been worked out:

*isegun̥ > *orona* 'nose' *isepi > *n-ofy* (< *inisepi < *sinepi) *beɣecay > *fi-voy* 'paddle' (< *pi-bei < *pi-beay)

Similarly, the sequences *ue and *eu that developed from consonant loss became /ao/ in some cases:[18]

*tuqelaɬ > *taolana* 'bone' *ɬecuŋ > *laona* 'mortar'

In trisyllabic roots with penult having a a nasal onset followed by *e, the *e was lost, and the nasal became homorganic with the following consonant. Similarly, in trisyllabic roots with an *e in the penult and with an *l onset of the penult or the final syllable, the *e was lost and the CC with *l is simplified by losing the *l.

*buteliɣ > *votsy* 'cyst' (< *butliɣ) *qaɬegaw > *andro* 'day' (< *andaw < *angaw)

In trisyllabic roots, *u before *w (and *i before *y[19]) were elided:

*dasuwen > *ravina* 'leaf'

In a few cases, the antepenult was lost. The first case is clearly a borrowing (it also has other irregular correspondences). The second case reflects a change that took place in PMP or earlier times. The other two cannot be explained:

*qaciɣah > *sira* 'salt' *sehapuy < *afo* 'fire' *sapegiq 'sharp, biting' > *fery* 'wound' (The /e/ is also unexplained.) *iceŋet 'stinger' > *fanenitra* 'k.o. wasp' (< *faN- + *senitra)

There are two inherited forms that reflect PAn stems of four syllables, and in them, the fourth syllable from the end is lost:

---

*paqa > *fe* 'thigh' (< *pai < *paa)

[17] Only one form exemplifies this change, and this form may not be directly inherited, for there is a countercase discussed in §D3.2.4: *ome* 'give' (< *um-bei < *um-beay). There are other examples where *e > /o/ discussed in §D3.2.2.

[18] Loss of *h took place much earlier than the loss of the other consonants, so that with the loss of medial *h, a preceding *e contracted with a following *u:

*pakehu 'k.o. edible fern' > *faho* 'k.o. palm with edible pith'

[19] The only forms that reflect *i before *y in the penult of trisyllabic roots are borrowed from Ml:

*meniyak > *menaka* 'fat' *peniyu > *fano* 'sea turtle'

*qaɬimateq > *dimaty* 'k.o. leech' *ɬiki-ɬiki > *helika* 'armpit' (< *ki-liki[20])

The form *tenona* 'weave' (< *tineun) reflects a weakening of the antepenult that took place in PMP or earlier.

D3.1.3 Disyllabization of monosyllabic roots

Although present-day Mlg tolerates monosyllabic roots, pre-Mlg, like most of the An languages, disyllabized monosyllabic roots that were not atonic. Disyllabization took place in one of three ways: (1) stretching the root by addition of a prothetic /e/, (2) doubling or reduplicating the monosyllabic root, or (3) petrifaction of an affix.

(1) addition of a prothetic /e/:

*lak 'separated > *elak-elaka* 'intermediate space' *but 'pluck out' > *evotra* 'plucked up, retracted'

(2) doubling or reduplicating a monosyllabic root:

*ceŋ > *tsentsina* 'stopper' *put 'blow on s.t.' > *fofotra* 'blow up bellows'

(3) adding an affix that became petrified:

*but + *um- > *ombotra* 'plucked out' *ɣaŋ 'heat' + *ka- > *hazana* 'dry' *mic + *ma- > *mamy* 'sweet' *kan + um- > *homana* 'eat'[21]

D3.1.4 Metathesis

Except for the metathesis that took place in PMP or earlier, Mlg reflects little metathesis. There is only a handful of examples found in the data, and the forms all involve vocalic metathesis:

*baliw 'change' > *valo* 'change of sentiment' (< *baluy) *ikuɣ > *ohy* 'tail' *qiteluɣ > *atody* 'egg' (< *atuleɣ [/a/ of the antepenult and the /d/ are unexplained [cf. §D3.3.42, footnote]) *qaɬiŋu 'shadow' > *onina* 'shape or appearance of s.t.' (< *aninu) *tiduɣ > *ma-tory* 'sleep' (< *tiru)

The following forms reflect metathesis of consonants, but the metathesis probably occurred early well before pre-Mlg times. The last form also shows elision of the penult that is otherwise unattested in Mlg. There is no explanation:

*jaqet > *ratsy* 'bad' (< *jateq) *ɬicebic > *ify* (< *ipis < *impis < siɬpic < ɬispic)[22] *paqegu > *afero* 'gall' *taŋila 'ear' > *tadiny* 'foramen of ear' (< *taliŋa) *qulun+an > *ondana* 'pillow' (< *unlan < *qunulan)

D3.1.5 Addition of nasal coda in the penult

Like other Hesperonesian languages, Mlg sporadically developed a nasal coda in the penult. In many cases, the root with the penultimate nasal coda is cognate with forms

---

[20] The weakening of *ki- to /he/ in the antepenult may in fact be the normal development in Mlg. Except for doubled monosyllabic roots there are no other cases of *i in the antepenult that are not contracted with what follows due to the loss of the intervening consonant. The substitution of the original final syllable *hi by /ka/ and the retraction of the stress to the first syllable is probably due to the rarity of words ending in /hi/.

[21] Many languages of Kalimantan reflect *kuman 'eat' with a petrified inflix *-um-*. Cf. Kel *kuman*, ND *kuman* 'eat'. This is clearly a Kalimantan innovation and one of the many features that show Mlg to have originated in Kalimantan.

[22] This is an innovation that Mlg shares with Ml and not with any other of the languages considered here.

manifesting the same in other Hesperonesian languages, but in other cases Mlg is the only language of the ones studied here that shows this:

*suwagi > *andry* 'younger sibling' *cahebay > *sampy* 'hang' *isejam > *indram-ina* 'be borrowed' *kutała > *ontany* 'question' *qetaq + *ma- > *manta* 'raw' (< *mataq) *pudul > *mondro* 'blunt' *qitem > *ma-inty* 'black' *sadiɣi > *andry* 'pillar, post' *tidec > *tsindri-ana* 'be squeezed' *tipun > *tsimpona* 'gather one at a time'

D3.2 Vowels and diphthongs

D3.2.1 *i, *u

*i > /i/ in all positions:

*saŋin > *anina* 'wind' *qałimateq > *dimaty* 'leech'

In a few cases, *i is reflected with /e/. In two of these cases contamination with a word of similar meaning is the explanation. For the others, there is no good explanation.[23]

*dilaq > *lela* 'tongue' *jilap > *lelaf-ina* 'be licked at' (contamination with *lela* 'tongue') *kilat > *helatra* 'flashing light' (contamination with *tselaka* 'lightening') *tidec > *tery* 'pressed' (cf. *tsindr-iana* 'squeezed') *titic > *mi-tete* 'drip' *tiŋeɣ 'voice' > *teny* 'word'

The sequence /ai/ may variably be contracted to /e/, and in some cases has been contracted absolutely (the original *ai, no longer occurs):

*ina > *reny* 'mother' (< *ra ina) *ina-ina > *ineny* 'mother' *ma-iɣaq > *me-na* 'red' (< *maia- + *-na < *maiɣa)

In one case, *i is reflected with /a/. The /a/ is probably the result of contamination with *fampana* 'precipice' (< *paŋepaŋ)

*cimpaŋ 'veering off' > *sampana* 'branch (of road, river), embankment'

*u is reflected by /o/ in almost all cases:

*nunuh > *nono* 'breast'

The sequence /ao/ may variably be contracted to /ɔ/.[24] In some cases the contraction is obligatory:

*lahuj > *laotra* 'sea' *ta-lɔtra* 'Arab' (< *tawu 'man' + *lahuj) *tuqelał > *taolana/tɔlana* 'bone'

In one case *-u is reflected by /-y/. This may have come about from its use as a vocative (where the final *-u became weakened to *[ə], which became /y/ [cf.§D3.2.2, below]):

*apu > *afy* (also *zafy* < *i+apu) 'grandchild'

D3.2.2 *e

*e has two outcomes when it is not lost (§D3.12, above): /i/ (written *y* in word-final position) and /e/. *e becomes /e/ in the penult or earlier and /i/ (*y*) in the final syllable or the syllable before the endings *-na, -tra,* or *-ka*.

[23] Borrowing or influence from a neighboring language when pre-Mlg was located in Kalimantan is a possible explanation.

[24] Cf. the statement in the footnote at the end of D3.0, as to why /ɔ/ is transcribed as /ao/.

*qałimatek > *dimaty* 'k.o. leech' *salem > *alina* 'night' *penet 'plugged up' > *feny* 'enclosure, hedge' *qelag > *elatra* 'wing'

When a stem is affixed, the *e that had been in the final syllable or in the syllable before the endings *-na, -tra,* or *-ka* comes to be the penult and there the *e is reflected with /e/:

*enem > *enina* 'six' *enem-ina* 'divided into six' (< *enem-en) *sated > *atitra* 'act of delivering' *ater-ina* 'be delivered'

*e in the penult was raised by assimilation to /i/ < *i in the final syllable or in the penult before *-na, -tra,* or *-ka*:

*beli 'buy' > *vidy* 'price' *beŋic 'cruel' > *vinitra* 'angry in looks' *betihec > *voa-vitsy* 'calf' (< *betic) *lepit 'fold' > *dify* 'a fold, seam'[25]

The *e in the penult was not assimilated to an /i/ on the right that originates in *e. (The assimilation of *e to a following *i took place before the raising of *e in the final syllable, as discussed in the first paragraph of this section.)

*enem > *enina* 'six' *enem-ina* 'divided into six' (< *enem-en)

Contraction of two or more *e's yielded /e/:

*seqeɣet 'tight' > *etra* 'belt'

*e is occasionally reflected by /o/. There is no explanation. Forms evincing this must be borrowings, but the source is unknown

*beɣecay > *fi-voy* (< *pi-vei) *beŋkeŋ > *vonkina* 'shrivel' *teŋaq 'half' > *ma-tona* 'center' (also with the regular reflex: *tena-tena* 'middle')

D3.2.3 *a

*a > /a/ in most environments:

*ałak > *anaka* 'child, offspring' *qanibuŋ 'k.o. tree' > *anivona* 'k.o. palm, the leaves of which are used for thatching'

*a at the end of a root, and also *a at the end of a root followed by *s, *ɣ, or *h, is reflected as /i/ (written *y* in word-final position):

*lima > *dimy* 'five' *tuqas > *ma-toy* 'old' *damaɣ 'light, torch' > *ramy* 'k.o. tree producing incense' *baɣah > *vai-nafu* 'embers'

If final *a was followed by *c or *q, *a remains /a/. (The loss of *q and *c occurred after the change of word-final *-a to /i/):

*ludaq 'spit' > *rora* 'spit, spittle' *suɣac > *oza* 'wash (body part)'

The /i/ < *a caused a preceding *y to become lost:

*buqaya > *voay* (< *buayi) *layaɣ < *lay* 'sail' (< *layi)

A sequence /aa/ at the end of a word became [ai] and subsequently /e/:

*paqah > *fe* 'thigh' (< *pai < *paa)

---

[25] However, when the inherited *e comes to be in the antepenult, it reverts to /e/ before /i/ in the following syllable:

*lepit > *lefitra* 'to fold'

There are a number of exceptions in which final *-a is not weakened to /y/. The vast majority of them are loan words. In fact, the occurrence of /-a/ at the end of a root that did not lose a final consonant is one of the hallmarks of a loan form. However, the following form is not likely to be a loan. It can be explained as occurring typically in proclitic position—i.e., not finally:

*dusa > *roa* 'two'

There is no evidence other than the final /-a/ in the following forms to show that they are loan words, and indeed they do not have the semantic character of learned borrowings. However, there is no other explanation for the final /-a/:

*paya > *fanja* 'swamp' *gita > *hita* 'see' *ki-ɬala 'perceive' > *maha-lala* 'know, recognize' *kima 'giant clam' > *hima* 'k.o. shell'

D3.2.4 Diphthongs

*ay and *aw monophthongized to /i/ and /o/ respectively:

*qatay > *aty* 'liver' *qaɬegaw > *andro* 'day'

In the following reduplicated monosyllabic root with *ay, the first *ay is reflected with /e/, and the final *ay with /i/. Why the first *ay should have become /e/ is unknown:[26]

*taytay > *mi-tety* 'pass over'

A sequence /ai/ that developed from /aa/ at the end of a word,[27] monophthongized to /e/:

*paqa > *fe* 'thigh' (< *pai [§D3.2.3])

However, /ai/ that developed from an earlier /ayi/ (§D3.3.45, 8th¶) did not monophthongize:

*layaɣ > *lay* 'sail' (< *layi > *laya) *taqi > *tay* 'feces' (< *tayi)

The sequence *eay that developed by the loss of an intervening consonant contracts to /e/ in one case:[28]

*beɣay + um- > *ome* 'give' (< *umbeay)

*uy > /o/

*ɬaŋuy > *lano* 'swim' *sehapuy > *afo* 'fire'

The reflex of *iw is uncertain. In one case, *iw is reflected with /o/ (as if *iw had merged with *uy); in another, with /y/. The probable explanation for the two different reflexes is that

---

[26] In the case of the following word, we assumed that *ai that developed in the penult became /i/:

*taseyup > *tsioka* (< *taiup < *tasiup)

[27] This change, *aa > *ai > /e/ took place after the monophthongization of the final diphthongs.

[28] There is a countercase *fi-voy* 'paddle' (< *pi-beɣecay), discussed in §D3.1.2. The word for 'give' is most likely the inherited form, and the word for 'paddle' is borrowed, as is the case in other languages of Kalimantan, as well.

in the second case, *iw underwent metathesis to merge with *uy (§D3.1.4), and in the first, it did not:[29]

*baliw$_1$ > *vady* 'one of a set of two, partner, spouse' *baliw$_2$ 'change' > *valo* 'change of sentiment' (< *baluy)

In the case of *kasiw 'tree', after *s was lost, /i/ became a glide and /w/ became vocalized:

*kasiw > *hazo* 'tree'

D3.3 Consonants

CHART TWO. DEVELOPMENT OF THE MALAGASY CONSONANTS FROM PAN

PAn	**weak**	**strong**	**PAn**	**weak**	**strong**
t	*t*	*t*	g	*h-, r*	*k-, dr*
k	*h*	*k*	ɣ	*Ø, z*	*Ø, j*
q	*Ø*	*Ø*	l	*l*	*d*
h, s	*Ø*	*Ø*	ɬ	*n, l*	*n, d*
c	*s- -Ø- -Ø*	*ts*	m, n	*m, n*	*m, n*
b	*v*	*b*	ŋ	*n*	*n*
d	*r*	*dr*	w	*v*	*b*
j	*r, z*	*dr, j*	y	*z*	*j*

The weak reflexes are those called 'unprotected' and the strong are those called 'protected' or 'strengthened', as discussed in §D3.1.12.

D3.3.1 Voiceless consonants

D3.3.11 *p

*p remained /p/ in protected and /f/ in unprotected position:

*palisi > *fady* 'taboo' *paqegu > *afero* 'gall, bile' *ipen > *ify* 'tooth' *sampay 'arrive' > *ampy* 'sufficient, complete' *jilap + *en > *lelaf-ina* 'be licked at'

In one case,*p is reflected by /b/ in a word that was contaminated by another form of similar meaning. However, the reflex in Mlg is secondary. This innovation was shared by Paiwan and all the MP languages:

*pukuh > *boko* 'pompon' (contaminated in PMP or earlier by *bukul 'knob shaped' Cf. Tg *búkol* 'boil, tumor', Cb *bungkul* 'bulging bones in joints')

In a couple of cases, *p- is reflected by the nasalized form of the root (§A3.7.1):

*pudul > *mondro* 'blunt' *picaw > *miso* 'knife' (not inherited from PMP)

At the end of a word, *p is reflected by /ka/, but when the root had a suffix, stem-final *p > /f/:

*taseyup > *tsioka* 'wind' *tsiof-ina* 'be blown'

[29] Adelaar (2009) suggests that *vady* was borrowed from a language in S. Sulawesi. However, it looks inherited from PMP, for it is widely attested over the range of the MP languages, and there is nothing in the semantics of Mlg *vady* to indicate a close connection with reflexes in S. Sulawesi. (Cf. the citations under *baliw$_1$ in the glossary.)

In some cases, after the loss of word-final *p, the ending *-ka* did not develop (§D3.1.11, middle):

*aŋap 'agape' > *ana* 'out of breath'

D3.3.12 *t

*t remains /t/ except before *i, in which case it is reflected by /ts/:

*tageɣaŋ > *tahezana* 'rib' *qatay > *aty* 'liver' *ɣabut > *avot-ana* 'be plucked up' *tinaqi > *tsinay* 'intestines' *betihec > *voa-vitsy* 'thighs' (< *betic)

In one case, *t- is reflected by the nasalized form of the root (§A3.7.1):

*taki 'intend' > *nahy* 'intended'

Word-final *t > *tra*, but when the *t was stem final and occurred before a suffix, *t remained /t/:

*jeket > *mi-rehitra* 'set on fire' *rehet-ana* 'be ignited from s.t. already burning'

In some cases, the after the loss of word-final *t, the ending *-tra* did not develop (§D3.1.11, middle):

*penet 'plugged up' > *feny* 'enclosure, hedge'

D3.3.13 *k

*k > /h/ when not protected and /k/ when protected:

*kasiw > *hazu* 'wood, tree' *aku > *aho* 'I' *kulit 'skin' + *kayu 'tree' (< *kasiw) > *hodikazo* 'bark'

In one unexplained case, *k- was lost. Perhaps there is a rule that *k- was lost in trisyllabic roots with initial *k-. There are no other reflexes in Mlg of trisyllabic roots with initial *k-.

*kutała > *ontany* 'ask'

In a few cases, *k is reflected with *k. These are borrowings into Mlg, mostly from Ml (see the examples at the end of §D3.1.12, end). There are a couple of other forms that have /k/ and are unexplained. They are surely borrowings, but the source is unknown:

*łuka 'wound' > *lokana* 'be struck by a spear'[30] *bikac > *ma-vika* 'strong, athletic'

At the end of a word, *k is reflected by /ka/, but when the root had a suffix stem-final *k > /h/:

*tałek > *mi-tanika* 'boil, cook' *taneh-ina* 'be boiled'

In some cases, after the loss of word-final *k, the ending *-ka* did not develop (§D3.1.11, middle):

*lemek > *lemy* 'supple, tender, weak'

D3.3.14 *q

*q > ∅ in all positions.

*qaselu > *alo* 'pestle' *baqeɣuh > *vao* 'new' *paqit > *faitra* 'bitter' *pełuq > *feno* 'full'

---

[30] Ml forms with /k/ are usually borrowed into Mlg with /h/—i.e., they were borrowed at a time before medial *-k- became /h/ or at a time that /k/ had not been reintroduced into medial position. Perhaps *lokana* is a late borrowing from Ml.

*q was lost without a trace, with one exception, where *q left a trace: when *q closed a syllable ending in /a/, the /a/ did not change to /i/ (§D3.2.3):

*bagaq 'inform, report' > *am-bara* 'told' *ludaq > *rora* 'spit, spittle'

D3.3.2 *h, *s, *c

D3.3.21 *h, *s

*h was lost without a trace:

*lahuj 'seaward' > *laotra* 'sea' *kukuh > *hoho* 'finger-nail'

*s was also lost without a trace:

*salac > *ala* 'forest' *qaselu > *alo* 'pestle' *tuqas > *ma-toy* 'old'

D3.3.22 *c

*c had two reflexes: Ø and /s/. In initial position *c > /s/:

*ceŋ 'stopped up' > *esina* 'breathe hard'[31] *capuh > *safo* 'pass hand over lightly' *ciwa > *sify* 'nine'

Medially and finally, *c > Ø:

*puceg > *foitra* 'navel' *mic > *ma-my* 'sweet'

In the following cases, an initial *c is reflected with Ø. The explanation may be that *c was lost after a prefix ending in a vowel, and that the form with Ø was generalized. Most likely, however, these words were borrowed from Ml:

*campay 'arrive' > *ampy* 'be sufficient and complete' (Ml *sampai* 'arrive, up to a certain point') *cukat > *ohatra* 'measure' (Ml *sukat* 'measure') *cumpaq 'oath' > *ompa* 'opprobrious language' (Ml *sumpah* 'curse')

In reduplicated or doubled monosyllabic roots beginning with *c, *c > /s/ in both occurrences of the root:

*cucuɬ 'stack up'> *sosona* 'folded, doubled layer'

In reduplicated monosyllables, if the second occurrence of the root was strengthened to /ts/, the first is also strengthened:

*ceŋeceŋ (< *ceŋ 'stopped up') > *tsentsina* 'stopper, cork'

In a number of forms, medial *c is reflected as /s/. Some of these are borrowings from Ml. Others are probably borrowings from a language with which pre-Mlg was in contact in Kalimantan.

*sacaq > *asa-ina* 'sharpened' *qabucan 'large grouping' > *avosa* 'heap' *paciɣ > *fasika* 'sand' *sicaŋ 'jawbone' > *hisana* 'gills' (/h-/ initial is additional evidence of borrowing) *iseci 'contents' > *isy* 'there is' *gucuk > *kosoka* 'rub' *qaciɬ > *m-asina* 'salty' *cak > *masaka* 'cooked' (< Ml)[32] *qucuŋ 'for two or more to carry s.t. in cloth' > *osona* 'accompany' *picaw > *miso* 'knife' *nuca > *nosy* 'island' *tacik 'sea' > *tasy* 'lake'[33]

---

[31] The rule of intervocalic *c loss was prior to the rule of disyllabization by addition of prothetic /e/.

[32] It cannot be ruled out that this root occurred without the prefix *ma-* at the time the loss of medial *-c- took place—i.e, when *c was initial. In that case /s/ would be the normal reflex.

[33] Adelaar (1988:14) also quotes *taiky* 'sea' (eastern dialect), which manifests Ø, the inherited reflex.

Final *-c is normally lost before a suffix, as well as in absolute final position. However, in several cases it has been retained and reflected with /s/. The explanation must be influence from a language with which pre-Mlg was in contact, as is the case of the forms cited immediately preceding:

*ɫicebic > *ma-nify* 'thin' + *ha-ana* > *hanifisana* 'thinness' *kicekic 'grate' > *voa-hihi* 'scraped' + *-ana* > *hihisana* 'be scraped' *lepac 'free' > *lefa* 'freeing of s.t.' *fandefasana* 'action of letting go' *pules 'twist > *foly* 'thread' *folesina* 'be spun'

Compare these two examples with the normal affixational process of *-c loss with roots ending historically in *-c:

*balec > *valy* 'answer, reply' + *-ana* > *valiana* 'be answered'

If *c closed a final syllable with /a/, the *c left a trace in that the /a/ did not change to /i/ (§D3.2.3):

*ɫimac > *dima* 'dipper for bailing' *suɣac > *oza* 'wash (body)'

In three other cases, initial *c is reflected with /ts/. Since /ts/ is the strengthened reflex of *c after a nasal or a stem-final consonant (§D3.1.12, 3rd¶ it is possible that these cases are a generalization of a now-lost form that occurred after a nasal:

*cudup 'enter with some force' > *tsorof-aka* 'rush in without permission' (< *cudup-an)
*culuq 'torch' >*voa-tsolo* 'burnt'

In a few cases, *c is reflected in its nasalized alternant (§A3.7.1):

*celecel > *nenina* 'regret' *iceŋit 'stinger' > *fa-nenitra* 'k.o. wasp'

D3.3.3 Voiced consonants stops in Mlg

Spirantization of *b and *d took place early in Mlg, but there are examples of forms with unchanged *b and *d. We assume them to be borrowings, and some at least cannot have been borrowed from Ml. This proves that the change of *b and *d to continuants occurred while Mlg was still spoken in Kalimantan. (Cf. examples in §D3.3.31, and D3.3.32, below.)

D3.3.31 *b

*b > /b/ when protected and /v/ when unprotected:

*baga 'inform' > *am-bara* 'told, revealed *baqeɣu > *vao* 'new' *ɣabut 'uproot' < *avot-ana* 'be plucked up' *dabuk > *ravoka* 'pound (rice)'

In final position, the /v/ that developed was devoiced and merged with *k (§D3.1.11), but remained /f/ before suffixes:

*kubekub > *mi-hohoka* 'covering s.t. over' *hohof-ana* 'be covered over'

Borrowing led to a reflex of /b/ in unprotected position. The source is unknown, but this example cannot have been borrowed from Ml *bawa* 'carry':

*ba + R- > *baby* 'carry on the back'

In one case, *b is reflected with /f/. This is probably the result of a back formation. Both *b and *p were changed to *m when the affix *um- was added. Thus, there was occasion for back formations to develop from the nasalized allomorph—that is, *um- + *batay > *matay; subsequently, *matay was replaced by *patay on analogy with other forms that alternate initial *m- and *p-, and the initial *p became /f/:

*batay 'profit' > *faty*, as in *faty dina* 'fine for failing to do what one has promised' also *maty*, as in *maty antoka* 'lose in selling s.t.'

By the same process, the following vowel-initial root developed an /f-/;

*weliq 'do again' > *ma-ody* 'go home' *voa-fody* 'returned' *ma-mody* 'return s.t. bought' (< *maN-* + *fody*)

Reflexes of *sebic 'thin' are reflected with *pic, as in all languages apart from Bunun:

*ɬisebic > *ify* 'thin' (< *ipic < *impic < *siɬpic < *ɬispic)

D3.3.32 *d *j

*d and *j merged and became /dr/ when strengthened and /r/ when not strengthened:

*daɣaq > *ra* 'blood' *ludaq > *rora* 'spit' *sadiɣi > *andry* 'pillar, post' *isejam > *indram-ina* 'be borrowed' (< *ijam < *sijam [§A3.5.4]) *jeket > *rehet-ana* 'be ignited from s.t. already burning' *qujaɬ > *orana* 'rain'

In word-final position, /d/ merges with /t/ (> *tra*), but when stem-final before an affix ,*d > /r/:[34]

*sated > *man-atitra* 'convey' *ater-ina* 'be conveyed'

In some cases, after the loss of word-final *d, the ending *-tra* did not develop (§D3.1.11, middle):

*waɣed > *vahy* 'liana'

The *r reflex of *d and *j was assimilated to an /l/ on the right:[35]

*dalem 'inside' > *lalina* 'deep' (< *ralem) *jalan > *lalana* 'road' (< *ralan) *jilap > *lelaf-ana* 'licked'

There are two cases where *d is reflected by /d/. The first form is probably borrowed from Ml, and the second was likely borrowed into Mlg from a neighboring language after the change of *d > /r/:

*dabuk 'pound' > *daboka* 'beat, thump' (< Ml *debuk* 'thump') *dicedic 'slice' > *didy* 'cut' (cf. *lily* 'cut' (dialectal) [Adelaar 2009])

In some cases, *j is reflected with /z/ or /j/ when strengthened. These are probably borrowings from neighboring languages or Ml in which *j and *d are not merged:

*jaqit > *zaitra* 'sew' *jabi > *zavy* '*Ficus* sp.' *jawa 'daylight' > *javanjavana* 'illumination' (initial strengthened reflex /j/ imported from the second part of the compound where /z/ was strengthened) *juɣu > *zoro* 'corner' (/r/ < *ɣ is also evidence of borrowing) *juluk 'stick inside' > *mi-joloka* 'enter' (/j/ instead of /z/ is unexplained) *tinjak 'step on' > *tsinjaka* 'a foot-stomping dance'

There are two cases in which *d- is reflected with /tr/. The first case is probably a borrowing from Ml *dada* 'chest. Ml /d/ is normally borrowed with /tr/ in Mlg. The second case is probably a fortuitous resemblance (cf. Adelaar 1989:18):

*dasdas > *tratra* 'chest' *debedeb 'chest' > *tritry* 'suck' (not connected with *debedeb)

---

[34] Word final *-j also merged with /-t/. There are no attestations of stem-final *j before a suffix.

[35] Cf. the assimilation of *l to /r/ on the right §D3.3.42, end.

D3.3.33 *g

*g onset of the penult or earlier merged with *k (> /h/ in unprotected and /k/ in protected position):

*gatel 'itch' > *hatina* 'eczema' *tageɣaŋ > *tahezana* 'ribs'

In one case, root-initial *g- is reflected with /k. It is probably borrowed from Ml *gosok* 'rub':

*gucuk > *kosoka* 'rub'

As onset of the root-final syllable, *g merged with *d and *j (> /r/ in unstrengthened position and /dr/ when strengthened):

*piga > *firy* 'how many?' *paqegu > *afero* 'gall' *qałegaw > *andro* 'day' (< *angaw)

In word-final position, *g merged with with *t (> /tra/), but when stem-final before an affix, *g > /r/ (as is the case of *d):

*belag > *velatra* 'spreading out' *velar-ana* 'place on which s.t. is spread out'

D3.3.4 Voiced consonants, continuants

D3.3.41 *ɣ

*ɣ > /z/ (and /j/ when strengthened) before *a, except when *a > /i/ (§D3.2.3):

*ɣabun > *zavona* 'mist, fog' *ɣakit > *zahitra* 'raft' *ɣaya 'great' > *jay* 'pride'[36] *baqeɣaŋ > *vazana* 'molar' *tageɣaŋ > *tahezana* 'ribs' *uɣat > *ozatra* 'sinew, vein' *teɣac 'k.o. hard wood' > *teza* 'hard inside of wood that remains when the outside is worm eaten'

In other environments, *ɣ > ∅:

*beɣay + *um- > *ome* 'give' *sadiɣi > *andry* 'pillar, post' *duɣi 'thorn' > *roy* 'prickly shrubs' *juɣuq > *ro* 'sauce, gravy' *kaɣuc > *haotra* 'scratching' *paɣis > *fay* 'rayfish' *quɣut 'massage deeply' > *otra* 'rubbed, pressed' *seqeɣet 'tight' > *etra* 'girdle, belt' *kawiɣi > *havi-a* 'left side' *deŋeɣ > *reny* 'heard' *layaɣ > *lay* 'sail'

*ɣ was also lost when preceding a final *-a that had become /i/ (§D3.2.3)—i.e., the loss of *ɣ everywhere except before /a/ took place after the final *-a had become /i/:

*baɣah > *vai-nafu* 'glowing coals'

In the following cases, *ɣ > ∅, even though it was before /a/ in the final syllable. There is no explanation:

*daɣaq > *ra* 'blood' *iɣaq + ma- > *mena* red' (< *maia- + *-na < *maiɣa)

In one case, *ɣ is reflected with /z/ between two *u's. The form is probably not a reflex of the entry quoted:

*buɣuk 'rotten' > *vozo* 'lazy' (probably unconnected)

There are many cases where *ɣ is reflected with /r/. Almost all of these forms correspond to Ml forms with /r/. They are undoubtedly borrowed from Ml. Here are a few of them:

*aɣak 'lead by the hand' > *araka* 'following, according to' *sabaɣat 'monsoon wind' > *avaratra* 'north' *baɣu > *varo* 'a shrub: *Hibiscus tiliaceus*' *buɣit 'rear end of a person' > *voritra* 'perineum of cattle' *guɣita > *horita* 'octopus' *juɣu > *zoro* 'corner, angle'

---

[36] The initial /j/ probably arose as a generalization of the form that occurred after a prefix ending in a nasal.

In one case, *ɣ is reflected by /h/. This may be a loan word from a language in which *ɣ > /h/:

*ɣudaŋ 'be grown' > *horana* 'augmented'

In a few cases, the endings *-na, -tra,* or *-ka* are found in reflexes of PAn forms that had final *-ɣ. These forms are not directly inherited but are borrowed from Ml or OJv:[37]

*dataɣ > *ratana* 'plain' (Ml *rata* 'level') *muɣ < *ho-moka* 'gargle' (Ml *kumur* 'gargle') *pasiɣ > *fasika* (dialectal: *fasina*) 'sand' (Ml *pasir* 'sand') *qiliɣ 'flow downstream' > *idina* 'pour down, descend' (Ml *hilir* 'downriver') *sapaɣ 'spread out' > *ampatra* 'stretched out' (Ml *hampar* 'spread')

D3.3.42 *l

*l > /d/ before *i:

*lima > *dimy* 'five' *kulit > *hoditra* 'skin'[38]

Otherwise (including before /i/ that had developed), *l > /l/ when not strengthened:

*laleg > *lalitra* 'fly' *balec > *valy* 'revenge'

When *l was strengthened, it became /d/:

*qulun+an > *ondana* 'pillow'

At the end of a word, *l fell together with the nasals and is reflected as /-na/ in word-final position. Before a suffix, *l became /n/:

*gatel 'itch' > *hatina* 'eczema' *tebel > *tevina* 'thickness' *ha-teven-ina* 'be made thick'

In one case, a root with final *-l, which occurs in a loan word with a suffix, retains the final -l:

*caŋkal 'handle of a tool' + *-an > *akalana* 'cutting board' (< Ml *sengkalan* 'board used in food preparation')

In some cases, the after the loss of word-final *l, the ending *-na* did not develop (§D3.1.11, middle):

*pudul > *mondro* 'blunt'

*l was was assimilated an /r/ (< *d or *j) on the right—i.e., it is reflected as /r/:[39]

*laga 'weave mats' > *rary* 'plaiting' *ludaq > *rora* 'spittle'

In one case, *l- is reflected with /j/. There is no explanation:

*luseq > *joy* 'tears'

---

[37] Adelaar (1989:22) suggests that the endings in these cases are indications of borrowing from Ml, and indeed these words all have Ml cognates. The form *homoka* has a shape that can only be borrowed from Ml *kumur* 'gargle' and *fasika* must be a borrowing because of the /s/ (§D3.3.22). Further, the passive of *ampatra*, *ampar-ina* with stem-final /r/ indicates that the form is borrowed from Ml. There is nothing in the make-up of *ratana* and *idina* that would show them to be loanwords, except for the ending *-na*, and they may in fact be inherited from PMP or earlier.

[38] There are two cases where an /i/ that developed also caused *l to become /d/. This is indicates that the change of *l > /d/ took place after the change of *e to /i/ had begun but before this change had been completed, for in most cases, *l remains /l/ before *e, even when it was destined to change to /i/ (see the following paragraph):

*lepit 'fold' > *dify* 'a fold, seam'*qiteluɣ < *atody* 'egg' (< *qatuleɣ)

[39] Cf. the assimilation of *r to an /l/ on the right §D3.3.32.

D3.3.43 *ɬ

*ɬ becomes /n/ and /l/ as described in §A3.3.4:
(1) *ɬ merged with *l when onset of an unstressed (short)[40] penult or earlier syllable—i.e., *ɬ > /l/ and /d/ before *i:

*qaɬimatek > *dimaty* 'leech' *ɬitéq > *dity* 'sap' *ɬaŋúy > *lano* 'swim'

(2) *ɬ > /n/ otherwise—i.e., when onset of a stressed (long) penult, when onset of a final syllable (including onset of monosyllabic roots), and in stem-final position (that is, *-na* in word-final position):

*ɬatu > *nato* 'k.o. tree' *aɬák > *anaka* 'son, daughter' *bulaɬ > *volana* 'moon'

In two cases, *ɬ in the onset of an unstressed (short) penult is reflected as /n/. The second example is borrowed from Ml, but in any case these two forms show that the change of *ɬ > /l/ (number (1), above, and §A3.3.4) was not completed:

*qaɬegaw > *andro* 'day' (< *angaw) *ɬisebíc > *ma-nify* 'thin' (< Ml *nipis* 'thin')[41]

In some cases, a final *-na* did not develop from *-ɬ, and *-ɬ was lost (§D3.1.11, middle):

*capiɬ 'padding' < *safy* 'cloth added to lengthen a garment'

D3.3.44 *m, *n, *ŋ

*m and *n remained unchanged in initial and medial positions. *ŋ merged with *n in Merina, but remained *ŋ in other dialects:

*matay > *maty* 'die' *lima > *dimy* 'five'' *naɬaq < *nana* 'pus' *enem > *enina* 'six' *laŋit > *lanitra* 'sky

The nasals merged in final position and usually were replaced by *-na* (§D3.1.11):

*salem > *alina* 'night' *pakan > *fahana* 'feed, weft' *lebeŋ > *mi-levina* 'be buried'

In a few cases, final *-na* did not develop from a final nasal, and the final nasal was lost (§D3.1.11, middle):

*qitem > *ma-inty* 'black' (also *ma-intina* 'black')

D3.3.45 *w and *y

*w is reflected by /v/ in initial and medial positions and /b/ when strengthened:

*walu > *valo* 'eight' *ciwa > *sivy* 'nine' *kawit > *havitra* 'hook' *taolana* 'bone' + *valo* 'eight' > *taolambalo* 'the eight bones (that have to be buried after death)'

A glide [w] between /u/ and /a/ was lost.

*buwaq > *voa* 'fruit'

After *u, *w >/v/ in the sequence *we, and *u was lost:

*dasuwen > *ravina* 'leaf' (< *dawen)

Otherwise, the sequence *we merged with the reflex of *u (> /o/), as in many MP languages:

*weliq >*m-ody* 'go home'

---

[40] That is, unstressed in pre-Mlg. The change to /l/ or /n/ took place when Mlg still retained the PAn contrastive stress.

[41] The *ɬ was lost in *ify* 'thin', the inherited reflex of *ɬisebic (§D3.1.4, end).

In the following form, *w did not become /v/ because it is a loan word from Ml:

*taquweɬ > *taona* 'year'

In final position, *-w was lost. (The PAn diphthongs were monophhtongized [cf. §D3.2.4].) However, stem-final *w before a suffix became /v/. Note that the *a preceding the *-w was changed to /o/ on analogy with the unsuffixed allomorph of the root:[42]

*liŋaw 'bewildered' > *ha-dino* 'forgotten' *hadinov-ina* 'be forgotten, neglected' *tiqadaw > *tsinjo* 'gazed at from a distaince' *tsinjov-ina* 'be gazed at'

*y > /z/ in medial position and /j/ when strengthened:

*bayaq 'leave' > *vaza* 'disdain' *duyan 'shake' > *mi-roza-roza* 'suspend' *paya > *fanja* 'swamp'

*y disappears before a final /i/ (< *a or *i)[43] except when preceded by *i:

*buqáya > *voay* 'crocodile' *layaɣ > *lay* 'sail' *iya > *izy* 'he, she, it'

In final position, *-y was lost (the PAn diphthongs were monophthongized [cf. §D3.2.4]). However, stem-final *ay before a suffix > /az/:[44]

*cahebay > *mi-sampy* 'hang' *sampaz-ana* 'clothesline, place to hang things' *calay 'preserve by drying' > *saly* 'roasting spit' *salaz-ana* 'be roasted on a spit'[45] *sukay > *mi-ohy* 'dig up' *ohaz-ana* 'be dug up'

Stem final *uy is reflected with /os/ in one case. Why it is reflected with /os/ rather than with *oz is not explained:

*ɬaŋuy > *lano* 'swim' + *-ina* > *lanosina* 'be swum through, over'[46]

In another case stem final *uy is treated analogically as if the stem ended in /o/. These forms are not inherited but were created after final *uy had fallen together with *u (§D3.2.4):

*anduy < *m-andro* 'bathe' *f-andro-ana* 'bathing festival'

---

[42] In some cases, the final /-o/ is treated as if it had developed from a final vowel—i.e., as if it had developed from *-u rather than *-aw. In those cases, no /v/ developed. These forms are not inherited but were created after final *aw had fallen together with *u (§D3.2.4):

avo 'high' + doubling + *-ina* > *avo-avo-ina* 'be made important (lit., 'raised') by words of another' *andro 'day' + *fan-ana* > *fanandroana* 'determination of lucky or unlucky days'

[43] However, the earlier *y left a trace in that /ai/ that developed from *ayi did not monophthongize to /e/ (§D3.2.4). Compare *lay* 'sail < *layi < *layaɣ and *fe* 'thigh' < *pai < *paqa.

[44] In the case of *tetezana* 'bridge' < *taytay-an, the penultimate *a was replaced by /e/ on analogy wit the first syllable.

[45] Dempwolff (1938: ¶104c) derived *salazana* 'gridiron, mast of a ship' from *layaɣ 'sail', but this is not likely, for an affix *sa-ana* (or *ca-an) is not otherwise attested.

[46] Cf. the passive of *reny* 'hear' (< *deŋeɣ), which also has an unexplained stem-final /-s/: *renesina* 'be heard'.

Chapter Four
Malay

D4.0 Background and cultural factors that influenced the history of Malay

Malay (Ml) is spoken over a wide area in Indonesia, Malaysia, and Brunei, and where it is not spoken as the native language, it is widely used as a second language. In Indonesia, it is the native language of much of the east and west coasts of Sumatra, Jakarta, eastern Kalimantan and southwest Kalimantan, northern Sulawesi, Larantuka on Flores, Kupang on Timor, and much of the Moluccas and parts of Irian Jaya. It is also spoken as a native language on the Malay peninsula reaching as far north as both coasts of the Isthmus of Kera in Thailand. Further, it is spoken natively in parts of Sarawak and Sabah, and in the metropolitan Brunei area. The Malay homeland is most likely eastern Kalimantan (Collins and Sariyan 2006). It was in conjunction with trade and empire building that Ml spread widely. Ml has a great deal of variation and consists of many dialects, some of which are mutually intelligible, but the majority of which are not. The variation is so great that it is possible to refer the whole as 'the Malayic group of languages' and by comparing them, it is possible to reconstruct proto-Malay (Adelaar 1992). Here, when we talk of Ml, we refer to the standardized Ml that functions as the national language of Malaysia, Indonesia, and Brunei. In Malaysia, the language is known as *Bahasa Malaysia*; in Indonesia, as *Bahasa Indonesia*; and in Brunei, as *Bahasa Melayu.* The standardized Ml varieties of Malaysia, Indonesia, and Brunei differ in small ways among themselves, mostly in phonology and vocabulary, but they are similar enough to be mutually intelligible. The various other dialects of Ml are confined to certain regions, and some of them have become regional lingua francas. The most important of these regional lingua francas are Banjarese (Bjr) from southwest Kalimantan, Manadonese from northern Sulawesi, Ambonese from the southern and central Molucas and Irian Jaya, and Ternate spoken in the northern Moluccas. There are also dialects in eastern Kalimantan that are used as lingua francas. In addition, Minangkabau, from eastern Sumatra, and Iban and Kendaya, from Sarawak, are not more different from standardized Ml than some very aberrant the dialects that are considered Ml dialects in the literature, and for that reason, they could be viewed as kinds of Ml. In any event, they are within the Malayic group of languages (Adelaar 1992).

Malay's closest relative is Cham. The Chamic languages, spoken mainly in Vietnam and Cambodia, derive from Old Cham, which was brought to mainland southeast Asia from the Malay homeland in the first millennium BC and is an off-shoot of Ml (Sidwell 2005: 212).[1] Most of the phonological innovations made by Ml are shared by Old Cham.

Ml has functioned as a lingua franca throughout Indonesia and even parts of the Philippines since well before European contact and has had a profound effect on the languages of these

[1] Grant (2005: 101) estimates that Cham split off from Malay at 100BC(±100 years).

areas. In recent years, the influence of Ml has strengthened at a geometric pace, and at this point Ml, standardized or regional varieties, are supplanting local languages in most parts of Indonesia. Ml has been in contact with Jv since Sri-Vijayan times, and perhaps earlier, and has itself been influenced by Jv. This influence was most profound historically in the Ml dialects spoken on Java, but currently, NJv exerts influence on the Ml spoken throughout Indonesia.

Ml is attested from a small number of inscriptions dating from the seventh century onwards. From the sixteenth century forward, Ml is well attested by a rich poetical and prose literature and by sundry nonliterary documents. Although the original composition of some of them dates back as much as six hundred years, the only extant copies of almost all of them are manuscripts made within the last two hundred years. The earliest inscriptions are in a dialect that is not likely to be the ancestor of the dialect from which standardized Ml developed, and the belletristic documents reflect a language that has features of syntax and morphology not found in any of the current spoken varieties of Ml. For all that, these older forms of Ml reflect a variety that is remarkably close to current varieties of Ml, and aside from the heavy Sanskrit loan words of the inscriptions and the Arabisms of the early literary works, they are largely interpretable from a knowledge of present-day Ml.

The best source of information on Ml lexicography is Wilkinson (1932), a dictionary composed on philological principles by classifying the contents of much of the Ml literary heritage. When a citation is available from Wilkinson, that is what is given here. There are some forms, not cited by Wilkinson, that reflect PAn forms, and we cite them, listing the source. In a few cases, Wilkinson does not cite forms with /h/ that historically had an /h/ (§§D4.3.21, D4.3.22). If we can find an attestation of such a form in a dialect that preserves the /h/, we quote that.

The Ml dialects have the same consonant inventory, but they differ among themselves as to the vowel inventory. Many of the regional dialects have merged *e with *a,[2] but the standardized dialects, which we quote here, maintain the distinction in most environments. Most Ml dialects, but not all,[3] have split the high vowels *i and *u into two each: /i/and /ɛ/ and /u/ and /o/. A few conservative dialects did not make this split and reflect the PAn *i, *a, and *u as /i/, /a/, and /u/.[4] The following chart shows the phonemes of Ml. The phonemes in parentheses do not reflect PAn phonemes, although they are of high frequency and are attested in the earliest inscriptions.

---

[2] Manadonese from N. Sulawesi lost *e, but not in the same way: it assimilated *e of the penult to the vowel of the final syllable and otherwise merged *e with *a.

[3] The dialect of inland Bjr in southwest Kalimantan, for example, has failed to split the high vowels. It has also merged *e and *a. This dialect, thus, has an inventory of only three vowels: /i/, /a/, and /u/.

[4] In fact, some of the current Indonesian dialects that are strongly influenced by Jv have further split the high vowels creating a three-way height distinction: /i/, /e/, /ɛ/ and /u/, /o/, /ɔ/. In this study we ignore this localized development.

CHART ONE. PHONEMES OF MALAY

Consonants

voiceless	p	t	(c)	k	
voiced	b	d	j	(g)	
spirants		s			h
liquids	w	l, r	y		
nasals	m	n	ñ	ng [ŋ]	

Vowels and Diphthongs

high	i		u
mid	ɛ	e [ə]	o
low		a	
diphthongs		ai	au

/c/ and /g/ do not regularly reflect any PAn phonemes. Current orthography uses *e* to transcribe both the central vowel /ə/ and /ɛ/. Here, we use *e* only to transcribe /ə/ and use *ɛ* to transcribe /ɛ/. Further, /ñ/ is written *ny* in current orthography. Here we use *ñ* to transcribe /ñ/. Otherwise, the transcription here matches current orthography. Stress is predictable: it occurs on the penult of the word unless the penult has /e/ as nucleus, in which case stress is on the final syllable.

D4.1 Processes affecting the development of Ml from PAn

D4.1.1 Syncopation of trisyllabic roots

In trisyllabic roots, contrastive PAn stress left traces in the form of syllable loss or centralization of unstressed vowels. Unstressed penults were syncopated with subsequent CC simplification (§D4.1.12) or vowel contraction (§D4.1.13). PAn stress left no traces in disyllabic roots.

D4.1.11 Syncopation of trisyllabic roots

The following rules reflect changes that took place in proto-Malay or earlier, for they hold for all Ml dialects.[5] The process of nasal-coda increment may block the effect of these rules. (Cf. the examples under the rule of §D4.1.111, following.) Other forms with exceptions to these rules are secondary in Ml and often exhibit exceptions in their other phonemes as well.[6]

D4.1.111 The first rule affects antepenults that consisted of a vowel alone or with *q or *s onset. In these cases, the antepenult was lost unless the vowel of the penult had contracted with the vowel of the final syllable.

*inum + *um- > *minum* 'drink' *qaɣicam > *resam* 'a reed: *Gleichenia* sp.' (< PMP †qaɣecam [change to *e unexplained]) *qapúcuk 'tip, top' > *pucuk* 'young leaf' *qiseguŋ > *hidung* 'nose' (< *esiguŋ) *qisuwab > *huap* 'yawn' *qiteluɣ > *telur* 'egg' *quɬuɬaŋ > *nunang* 'k.o. tree' *sabáɣat 'strong monsoon wind' > *barat* 'west'[7] *sehapúy > *api* 'fire' *sijeɣaq 'weary' > *jerah* 'sick and tired of s.t.'

---

[5] Blust 1982 discusses this matter and its historical development in the MP languages in general.

[6] Names of flora and fauna are in many cases spread by borrowing, although they may have a PAn etymology. In the following examples, the first probably originates in Oceania or eastern Indonesia, as the that is the origin of the plant:

*ɣambiya > *rumbia* 'sago palm' *kanuhec > *nus* 'squid'

[7] The following form is an exception in that it underwent metathesis, after which the antepenult was weakened: *sináwa > *nisáwa > *niháwa > *ñawa* 'breath'

If the penult had contracted with the final syllable, the first syllable is reflected with /e/:

*aɣúsuq > *eru* 'the Australian pine: *Causarina* sp.'

If the penult consisted of *se, this was lost (by the rules of §D4.3.23 and by contraction [§D4.1.13]) rather than the antepenult (unless the penult and the antepenult metathesized (§D4.1.3):

*isecí > *isi* 'contents' *isekán > *ikan* 'fish' *qiseɬép 'sleep' > *inap* 'spend the night'

Development of a nasal coda in the antepenult (§D4.14) blocked its loss. The onset is reflected, but the vowel nucleus was weakened:

*ikasu > *engkau* ([əŋkaw—disyllable]) 'you (sg)' (< *iŋkáu [trisyllable]) *paqegu > *hempedu* 'gall'[8] (< *qapegu) *qajelay > *henjelai* 'a grain: job's tears' (not inherited)

D4.1.112 The second rule affects trisyllabic roots with stressed penult not having an antepenult consisting of a vowel or a vowel preceded by *s or *q. Stressed penults are never lost. If the nucleus of the antepenult was *a, it was weakened to /e/. Other vowels in the antepenult were not weakened when the penult was stressed:

*balíga > *belira* 'weaver's sword' *taŋíla > *telinga* 'ear' (< *taliŋa)

In words that are not directly inherited, the rules §D4.1.111 and the rules of this section, do not hold. In neither of the following two cases is the source known, but the forms are secondary in Ml, as they are in most of the languages that have cognates. In the first example, the antepenult was not lost, for Ml borrowed this word after the rule of §D4.1.111 had ceased to operate. In the second case, the form was borrowed with a lost antepenult:

*laqeya > *halia* 'ginger' (< *qaliya < *qalya) *tambuɣi 'triton shell' > *buri* 'trumpet'

Stems of four syllables turn into trisyllabics, losing an unstressed syllable. This developed trisyllabic roots with a stressed penult. In those cases, the rule the first paragraph of this section took effect variably: in some roots the antepenult was lost entirely, in others it was lost only dialectally:

*qaɬisípec > *qalípas > *lipas* 'roach' (< *qalipas < *qaɬípec [§D4.3.23]) *qaɬimatéq > *halintah/lintah* 'leech' (< *qaɬintaq) *qusalipan > *halipan/lipan* 'milleped' (< *salipan)[9]

D4.1.113 Rule three concerns trisyllabic roots with unstressed penults.

D4.1.113a If stress was on the antepenult, the penult was syncopated, and the antepenult was not weakened:

*báqeɣuh > *baru* 'new' (with loss *q in standard Ml [§D4.3.23]) *dásuwen > *daun* 'leaf' (cf. §D4.3.23 for loss of *s] *qáqiyut > *ayut* 'sexual intercourse'[10] *míniyak > *miñak* 'grease' *qáɬitu > *hantu* 'supernatural being'

If the onset of the final syllable was lost, the vowel of the penult contracted with the vowel of the final syllable:

*pálisi + *paN- > *pemali* 'taboo'[11] (< *pamali [§D4.1.12])

---

[8] Standard dialects also have a variant *hampedu,* which developed under the influence of *hampadu* attested in the dialects that merged *e and *a.

[9] It is also possible that this form developed by another route—by the loss of *s (§D4.3.23) followed by contraction of the first two syllables to /a/ (§D4.1.13, 2nd ¶): *qusalipan > * qualipan > *qalipan > *halipan*

[10] A form with /h-/ is not attested, but probably it exists in an undocumented dialect.

Roots that developed the shape CV́C(w,y)V(C) after the medial syllable was syncopated (i.e., had stress on the leftmost vowel), developed /u/ or /i/before the glide and simultaneously shifted the stress to the /u/ or /i/. This caused the rule of (§D4.1.112), above, to take effect, whereby the initial syllable was weakened:

*bánuwa 'land, place where s.t. is' > *benua* 'large expanse of land' (< *banúwa < *banwa)

D4.1.113b If stress was on the final syllable, the antepenult was weakened (developed an /e/ nucleus):

*binesíq 'seed for next planting' *benih* 'seed' (< *bensiq < *benesiq) *busekáɣ > *bengkar* 'open out (like a flower)' (< *besekaɣ) *tinewún > *tenun* 'weave' *sijeɣáq > *jerah* 'sick and tired'[12]

The following form developed according to the rule and also developed a by-form that lost the first syllable and had a new meaning. I assume that end-stressed trisyllabic roots developed variants in which the first syllable was lost entirely, and in this case, the variant that lost the antepenult survived as a by-form, as well as the variant that followed the rule.

*baɣeqáŋ > *geraham* 'molar (<*beɣaqaŋ, with idiosyncratic initial /g/ and final /m/) and also *rahang* 'jawbone' (< *beɣaqaŋ, with unexplained loss of the first syllable)

The following form underwent metathesis of the antepenult and the penult after this rule ceased to operate, and the penult (which now had the *e nucleus of the former antepenult) was elided:

*leqacém > *asem* (dial., *hasem*) 'sour' (< *qáclem < *qacelem [§D4.1.3])

This rule also accounts for the weakening of the antepenult in reduplicated monosyllables, which are assumed to have developed *e between the two reduplicated roots (§A3.6.1, 2nd¶):

*dapedáp > *dedap* 'a tree: *Erythrina* sp.' *paɣatepát > *perepat* 'a tree of tidal swamp: *Sonneratia* sp.'

D4.1.113c If the antepenult nucleus was *u, it was not weakened (as long as there was an onset other than *s or *q).

*buqáya > *buaya* 'crocodile' *guɣíta > *gurita* 'octopus'[13]

---

[11] We reconstruct *pálisi and *qáɬitu even though the Philippine languages, which for the most part reflect the original PAn stress, manifest final or penultimate stress in their reflexes, Cb *lihí* 'prohibitions observed upon inaugurating s.t.' *anítu* 'k.o. benign supernatural being'. Philippine languages shifted the stress on roots with antepenultimate stress (§A3.5.3).

[12] The first syllable of reduplicated monosyllables with *i is not weakened. However in one case it is weakened. The explanation for the discrepancy probably lies in dialect mixture—that is, there were dialects in which the /i/ of the antepenult in doubled monosyllables was weakened to /e/:

*bitebit > *bitbit > *bibit* 'carry in fingers' *dicedic > *dedis (*alternatively, *didis*) 'cut into fine slices'

The form *bini* 'woman' (< *bahi + -in-) looks like an exception, in that the antepenult was not weakened. This is because this stem never was trisyllabic. After the loss of *h the first two syllables were diphthongized, forming a monosyllabic root, which was disyllabized (§D4.1.2) by infixing *-in-*:

*bahi > *bay > *binay > *bini*

[13] There are exceptions, and that is probably because dialectally, antepenultimate *u was also weakened when unstressed. An alternative form is *gerita* with a weakened antepenult. The antepenult is lost entirely in the reflex

If the onset of the penult was lost (i.e., was *s or *q [§D4.3.23]), the antepenultimate vowel contracted with the penultimate vowel:

*busekaɣ > *bengkar* 'open out like a flower' *ɣuqáɬay 'male' > *be-rani* 'brave' *tuqeláɬ > *tulang* 'bone'

D4.1.12 Simplification of CC's

Ml allows only CC's consisting of (a) a homorganic nasal and a following stop or (b) *ɣ plus a following stop. Rules for simplification of CC's that developed by syncopation (§D4.1.11, above) are as follows: (1) *h, *s or *q were lost; (2) codas of reduplicated monosyllabic roots were lost; (3) the only other cluster that developed, *tl, is simplified to /t/:

*baɣekéc > *beɣkéc > *berkas* 'bundle' *laheyu > *lahyu > *layu* 'wither' *tacetác > *tecetác > *tectác > *tetás* 'undone' *buteliɣ[14] 'cyst' > *butliɣ > *butir* 'grain'

D4.1.13 Vowel contraction and monophthongization

When a sequence of a vowel plus *e developed through the loss of a medial consonant (*s, *q, *h, *w, *y), the vowels were contracted. *e was lost.

*bacuheq > *basuh* 'wash' (< *bacuq < *bacueq) *buɣesu > *cem-buru* 'jealous' *laheyu > *layu* 'wither' *taquwéɬ > *tahun* 'year'

An exception is *uqa, which contracted to /a/:[15]

*bituqan > *bintang* 'star' (< *bituan [§D4.3.23]) *ɣuqaɬay 'male' > *be-rani* 'brave'

A penultimate *i was lost in the following form:

*jaqewis > *jauh* 'far' (< *jasuq < *jasweq < *jawiseq)

Sequences of like vowels were contracted in standard dialects except in monosyllabic roots (§D4.1.2).

*aɣusuq > *eru* 'the Australian pine' (< *eɣuu < *aɣuu [for loss of *q, see §D4.3.22, footnote] < *aɣuqus)

In monosyllabic roots and in disyllabic roots in dialects other than the standard, sequences of like vowels may develop an intervening laryngeal:

*basaq > *bah* 'flood' Bjr: *baʔah* (< *baah [§D4.3.22, footnote] < *bahah)

In trisyllabic stems with a nucleus of the penult other than *e, if a vowel sequence had developed through prefixation or loss of penult onset, the vowel of the antepenult was contracted with the vowel of the penult:

---

of *kutáɬa, *tanya* 'ask'. Cf. the comment to *baɣeqaŋ > *rahang* 'jawbone' in §D4.1.113b, above. In neither the case of *tanya* nor of *rahang* is there an explanation for the loss of the antepenult.

[14] It is impossible to determine whether stress in this root was on the antepenult or on the final syllable. (It is only clear that stress was not on the penult.)

[15] However, *usa contracted to /u/ in the following form. The explanation may be that this word historically occurred only as part of a compound (as is the case of current Ml):

*busaŋin 'sandbar' > *bungin* in *pasir bungin* 'mixture of sand and mud' *wanał + *ka- > *kanan* 'right' (< *kaanan) *wiɣi + *ka- > *kiri* 'left' *tut + *ka- > *kentut* 'break wind' (< *ka-entut < *ka-etut [§D4.1.2]) *taseyup > *tiup* 'blow on' (< *teiup < *tehiup < *tahiup)

D4.1.2 Monosyllabic roots

Ml, like most other An languages, tended to disyllabize monosyllabic roots. The most common way was by doubling the root or reduplicating it:

*biɣ > *bibir* 'lips' *kid > *kikir* 'file' *bit > *bibit* 'carry in fingers' also *bimbit* 'carry in hands' (with intercalated nasal coda of the penult)

Petrifaction of a prefix is also a very widespread method of disyllabization:

*kuj 'back' + *i- 'locative' > *ikut* 'follow' *łam 'taste' + *-an 'adjective former' > *ñaman* 'tasty' *pan + *um- > *umpan* 'bait' *puŋ 'gather' + ka- 'passive' > *kampung* 'village' (with accretion of nasal coda to the prefix) *puc 'finished' + maN- 'active verb former' > *mampus* 'die'

Disyllabization by addition of prothetic *e is evinced by many examples:

*ceŋ 'stop up' > *esang* 'blow nose holding one nostril with the fingers' *cep 'suck' > *esap* 'suck up water with sponge or the like'

In some cases, there is nasal coda intercalation after the prothetic *e:

*peŋ > *empang* 'blocking with fence or barrier' *pu 'lord, master' > *empu-nya* 'owner'

An /h/ may be accreted to the prothetic e:

*buc > *hembus* 'blowing hard, puffing' *ɣik > *hirek* 'thresh' (< *herik)

In a couple of cases, the prothetic vowel is homophonous with the vowel of the root:[16]

*buł > *ubun-ubun* 'fontanel' *ŋaw > *angaw* 'k.o. tick' < *ŋaaw)

The root may also be disyllabized by extending the vowel nucleus to two moras. An /h/ is intercalated in the two examples attested:

*luk 'cocave, curved' > *luhuk* 'bay' (Bjr) *tan > *tahan* 'set a trap'

The following form was maintained as a monosyllabic root, perhaps because it only occurred in a set phrase:

*lum 'cooked' < *lum* (only in *masak lum* 'overripe')

D4.1.3 Metathesis

Ml evinces some of the cases of metathesis that are widespread over a wide range of languages:

*bukes > *buk* 'hair' (< *busek) (Urak Lawoi) *nakis > *naik* 'climb' *paqegu > *hampedu* 'gall' (< *paqegu) *punuq 'head (main part)' > *pohon* 'tree-trunk' (< *puqun) *taŋíla > *telinga* 'ear'

The change of roots beginning in *ise- to *esi- (§A3.5.4) is also reflected in some Ml roots:

[16] These are probably cases of disyllabization by lengthening the penult followed by metathesis, e.g., *buł > *buuł > *ubuł + doubling > *ubun-ubun*.

*iseguŋ > *hidung* 'nose' (< *siguŋ < *esiguŋ) *isepun > *himpun* 'gather' (< *sipun < *esipun)

There are a few examples of metathesis that are found only in the Malayic languages or in low-order subgroups. Some of these forms underwent the metathesis in another language and are loan words in Ml:

*aɣusuq > *eru* 'the Australian pine' (< *eɣuu < *aɣuuh [§D4.3.23] < *aɣuqus) *baɣeqáŋ > *geraham* 'molar (<*beɣaqaŋ, with idiosyncratic initial /g/ and final /m/) and also *rahang* 'jawbone' (< *beɣaqaŋ, with unexplained loss of the first syllable) *ɣínu > *ñiru* 'winnowing tray' (secondary palatalization [§D4.3.41, end]) *jaqewis > *jauh* 'far' (< *jasuq < *jasweq [§D4.1.13] < *jawiseq [§D4.2.4, end]) *laqeya > *halia* 'ginger' (< *qaliya < *qaleya) *qisu > *hiu* 'shark' (< *ihu [§D4.3.22, first footnote] < *hihu)

A few cases of metathesis are unique to Ml:

*baguk > *rabuk* 'touchwood' *liyan > *lain* 'other' *dilaq > *lidah* 'tongue' *qudip > *hidup* 'alive' *ulay > *luai* 'worm' (Bjr)

D4.1.4 Prenasalization of medial stop consonants

Like other MP languages, Ml evinces a tendency to add a nasal to close a penult or earlier syllable that is open (§A3.7.2). Here are a few examples of many:

*atuk 'nod head' > *meng-antuk* 'sleepy'*ikasu > *engkau* 'you (sing.)' *isepun > *himpun* 'gather' *sebaɬ > *emban* 'sash tied around the body to hold a baby or a burden' *taw buɬi > *tembuni* 'afterbirth' (< *tabuɬi)

In some cases, the prenasalized onset of the final syllable is the remnant of a petrified infix *-um-:

*tapuk > *tumpuk* 'heap' (< *túmapuk[17]) *tebuk 'hit with a thump' > *tumbuk* 'pound' (< *tumebuk) *tubuq > *tumbuh* 'grow' (< *túmubuh) *tupaŋ 'stack up' > *tumpang* 'join in with others in an activity' (< *túmupaŋ)

D4.2.0 Vowels and diphthongs

The PAn vowels aside from *e were stable in Ml. Except for the effects of stress and contraction, *i, *a, *u remained unchanged from PAn. *e remained unchanged in the standard dialect except that in root- or word-final closed syllables, *e merged with *a.

D4.2.1 *i

*i > /i/ in all positions except where weakened in trisyllabic roots (§§D4.1.11ff., passim) or when contracted (§D4.1.13):

*bígaʔ 'k.o. giant taro' > *birah* 'an arum: *Alocasia* sp.' *beliga > *belira* 'weaver's sword' *beli > *beli* 'buy' *bukij > *bukit* 'mountain, hill'

*i is sporadically lowered to /ɛ/ in standard Ml under the influence of languages with which Ml has been in contact where cognate forms with reflexes of *i are reflected with [e]. Conservative dialects continue to evince /i/ in these forms:

---

[17] I hypothesize that the stress remained on the initial syllable (i.e., moved to the /u/ of the infix) because the penult was elided (D4.1.113a).

*biluk > *bɛlok* 'veer'[18] *ikuɣ > *ɛkor* 'tail' *liqeɣ > *lɛhɛr* 'neck'

D4.2.2 *a

*a > /a/ in all positions except where weakened in trisyllabic roots (§§D4.1.11ff., passim) or when contracted (§D4.1.13).

*ałak > *anak* 'offspring'*bataŋ 'main part of tree' > *batang* 'tree trunk'

Sporadically /a/ was fronted to /ɛ/. This probably happened through dialect mixture—that is, forms from a dialect with fronted allophones of /a/ were borrowed into a dialect that did not front /a/, creating a contrast. There is variation in a few lexical items between /ɛ/ and /a/, e.g. *jɛnggot/janggot* 'beard'. There are at least two examples in inherited forms:

*labeɣ > *lɛbar* 'wide' *laket > *lɛngkɛt* 'sticky' (< *langkat)

D4.2.3 *u

*u > /u/ in all positions except where weakened in trisyllabic roots (§§D4.1.11ff., passim) or when contracted (§D4.1.13):

*aku > *aku* 'I' *bubu > *bubu* 'fish trap with spikes'

*u is sporadically lowered to /o/ in standard Ml under the influence of languages with which Ml has been in contact where cognate forms with reflexes of *u are reflected with [o]. Conservative dialects continue to evince /u/ in these forms. (Cf. §D4.2.1, above for the parallel lowering of *i.)

*ikuɣ > *ɛkor* 'tail' *cuŋecuŋ > *songsong* 'go against s.t.' (cf. NJv *songsong* 'go to meet o. of high status') *punuq 'head (main part)' > *pohon* 'tree-trunk' (< *puqun)

D4.2.4 *e

*e > /e/ ([ə]) except when in a closed final syllable or when contracted (§D4.1.13). In many dialects, including most of those in Kalimantan, the Moluccas, and the Mingkabau dialects,*e and *a merged:

*beɣay > *beri* 'give' *depa > *depa* 'fathom'

In a final closed syllable, *e merged with *a:

*deŋeɣ > *dengar* 'hear' *gatel > *gatal* 'itch'

The word for 'neck' is an unexplained exception. The *e in the final closed syllable is reflected as /ɛ/ (in harmony with the reflex /ɛ/ in the penult):

*liqeɣ > *lɛhɛr* 'neck'

A sequence *we or *ew > /u/, as in many languages:

[18] Note that there is a rule of vowel harmony: if an *i or *u (§D4.2.3) is lowered in one syllable of a root, any other *i or *u in that root will be lowered as well.

*dasuwen > *daun* 'leaf' *jaqewis > *jauh* 'far' (< *jasweq < *jawiseq) *lasuwek 'mix food into staple' > *lauk)* 'side dish eaten with staple' *taquweɬ > *taun* 'year' *weliq > *p-ulih* 'return'

The sequences *ey and *ye > /i/:

*taseyup > *tiup* [§D4.1.13] (< *taiup [§D4.3.23] < *tasiup) *wasiyeɣ > *air* 'water' (< *wahiɣ < *wasiiɣ)

D4.2.5 The diphthongs

*ay > /i/:

*beɣáy > *beri* 'give' *ɣuqáɬay 'male' > *be-rani* 'daring' *págay > *padi* 'rice in field' *qatáy > *hati* 'liver'

Many forms reconstructed with *ay have Ml reflexes ending in /ai./ These are considered here to be secondary (cf §A3.4, 2nd¶), even though they are as numerous as the forms that have the regular reflex:

*balay > *balai* 'large open house' *baŋkay > *bangkai* 'corpse' *cahebay > *sampai* 'hang loosely' *kanaway > *kenawai* 'k.o. large white bird' *lantay < *lantai* 'bamboo strips for flooring or sitting on' *punay > *punai* 'k.o. pigeon' *qajelay > *henjelai* 'job's tears' *taŋkay > *tangkai* 'stem' *tapay > *tapai* 'fermented rice' *ulay > *luai* 'worm' (Bjr)

*aw > /au/ ([aw])

*láŋaw > *langau* 'a fly' *capaw > *sapau* 'flimsy and temporary shelter' *paheɣáw > *perau* 'hoarse'

A few forms ending in *aw have Ml reflexes ending in /u/. These are probably borrowed (cf. §A.3.4, 3rd¶):

*búɣaw > *buru* 'chase' *lakáw 'walk' > *laku* 'sell well'

*uy, *iw > /i/ (merged with *ay):[19]

*bábuy > *babi* 'pig' *sehapúy > *api* 'fire' *laɣiw 'flee' > *lari* 'run'

D4.3 Consonants

Ml reflects the PAn consonants faithfully in that only a limited number of phonemic mergers and splits occurred, as detailed in the following subsections. The following chart summarizes the Ml outcomes of the PAn consonants:

[19] In the case of *kasiw 'tree', the *s > h and was subsequently lost before the change of *iw to /i/. *i that developed from *iw became a glide /y/:

*kasiw > *kahiw > *kaiw> *kayu*

CHART TWO. MALAY REFLEXES OF THE PAN CONSONANTS

PAn	Ml	PAn	Ml
p	*p*	g	*g-, -r-, -r*
t	*t*	ɣ	*r*
k	*k, -ʔ*	l	*l*
q, s	*h*	ɬ	*l-/ñ-, -ñ-/-n-, -n*
h	*∅*	m	*m*
c	*s*	n	*n*
b	*b, -p*	ŋ	*ng*
d	*d, -t*	w	*∅, w*
j	*j, -t*	y	*y*

D4.3.1 Voiceless consonants

The voiceless stops *p, *t, *k are reflected unchanged, aside from CC simplification (§D4.1.12), and with the exception that final *-k > /-ʔ/ in most dialects.

*p > /p/ in all positions:

*pakan > *pakan* 'weft' *isepí > *m-impi* 'dream' *gapegap 'feel groping' > *gagap* 'look for s.t. by groping' *ɣecep > *resap* 'soak in'

In the following case, the initial *p was substituted for by *b, as happened in all the MP languages and in Pa (see commentary under *pukuh in the glossary):

*pukuh 'knot, node' > *buku* 'knuckle, knot'

*t >/t/ in all positions:

*tebél 'thick and compact' > *tebal* 'thick' *túbuq 'grow, shoot' > *tumbuh* 'grow' *batú > *batu* 'stone' *báɣat > *barat* 'athwart'

*k > /k/ initially and medially:

*kawil > *kail* 'fishhook' *buka > *buka* 'open' *cíku > *siku* 'elbow'

In most dialects, final *-k became [ʔ]. The glottal stop from *-k merged with a phoneme *ʔ that developed in many of the Ml dialects including standard Indonesian.[20]

*aɬák > *anak* (/anaʔ/) 'son, daughter' *cekecek > *sesak (*/sesaʔ/ 'packed tight'

D4.3.11 Accretion of /p-/

Occasionally /p-/ was accreted to a root beginning with a vowel by an analogy involving the verbal conjugation. A prefix /m-/ formed verbs from roots beginning with a vowel and also from roots beginning with a /p-/, with the /p-/ lost. Thus, a verb beginning

[20] The languages of west Java and many other areas of Nusantara developed a noncontrastive [ʔ] in word-final position. Ml in contact with Sundanese and western NJv in Jakarta borrowed cognate forms with a word final glottal stop (e.g. *dua* 'two' > /duaʔ/). Not all forms with final vowel developed a final glottal stop in standard Indonesian, and thus the glottal stop became contrastive. There are other Malayic dialects (e.g. Iban) that developed a /-ʔ/ by a process analogous to that of standard Indonesian. Adelaar (1992) reconstructed a proto-Malayic phoneme *-ʔ on the basis of data from these languages. However, I believe that the final glottal stop was an accretion, developed independently in various Malayic dialects.

with /m-/ was either to a root with an initial V or with an initial /p-/, and in some cases /p-/ was added to a V-initial root by analogy:

*jak + *is- > *pijak* 'step on' (< *ijak) *sejam + *is- > *pinjam* (< *ijam) 'borrow' *weliq > *pulih* 'return'

D4.3.2 *q, *s, *h, *c

D4.3.21 *q

*q > /h/, with some exceptions (§D4.3.23). In standard Ml and Indonesian, /h/ in initial position was unstable and was lost in many words. Some words alternate variants with /h-/ and variants lacking /h-/. *-h- was not lost between like vowels[21] and was invariably lost in standard dialects between unlike vowels.[22] Dialects of Kalimantan and other areas did not lose /h/. Final /-h/ is stable. The following reflexes all have variants without /h/:

*paqegu > *hampedu* 'gall' (< *qapegu) *qiliɣ > *hilir* 'go downstream' *qepá 'husk' > *hempa* 'empty, void of grain' *qujáɬ > *hujan* 'rain'

In the following cases, /h/ is always maintained:

*daqaɬ > *dahan* 'branch' *jaqet 'bad' > jahat 'evil' *punuq 'head (main part)' > *pohon* 'tree-trunk' (< *puqun)

Here are some examples where /h/ was lost in the standard dialects but retained dialectally:

*buqáya > *buaya* 'crocodile' (dial. /buhaya/) *paqit > *pait* (dial. /pahit/) 'bitter' *taquweɬ > *taun/tahun* 'year'

Final /-h/ is normally not lost:

*baɣeq > *barah* 'abscess' *biɣaq 'giant taro' > *birah* 'an arum: *Alocasia*' *binesíq > *benih* 'seed for planting' *búluq > *buluh* 'k.o. bamboo'

D4.3.22 *s

*s > ∅ between unlike vowels and when onset of trisyllabic roots under certain conditions (specified in §D4.1.111). *s > /h/ otherwise in initial and medial position. In this way *s fell together with *q and the resultant /h/ has the same instability as the /h/ that developed from *q (§D4.3.21, above).[23] In final position *s is lost entirely (whereas *q is regularly reflected as /-h/).

*santed > *hantar* 'deliver' *seqeɣet > *herat* 'tied tight' *siɣup > *hirup* 'slurp, sip' *suɣac 'wash' > *huras* 'besprinkle'

Between like vowels the /h/ that developed from *s (like the /h/ < *q) was not lost:

---

[21] There is one exception: in trisyllables, *q onset of the final syllable was lost (§D4.3.23):

*pacaqaɬ > *pesan* 'order, commision' (< *pesahan)

[22] The dialect on which the orthography is based did not lose /h/ between unlike vowels, and /h/ is therefore written between unlike vowels in many words. Spelling pronunciations have developed, especially due to the influence of the large number of speakers who used Ml as a second language. For example, *taun* 'year' is often pronounced /tahun/.

[23] An /h/ that developed from *q or *s was lost in all dialects in words that have an /h/ to the right:

*basaq > *bah* 'flood' *pasuq > *pauh* 'wild mango' *qisu > *hiu* 'shark' (< *ihu < *hihu) *sacaq > *asah* 'whet' (< *hasah) *supiq > *upih* 'spathe, sheathe of spadix' *tasał 'remain' > *tahan* 'hold back'

Between unlike vowels, /h/ was lost in standard dialects (but in the dialects of S.W. Kalimantan and elsewhere, /h/ is maintained):

*tisaŋ > tiang 'pole' *nasik > *naik* 'climb' *busat 'lift' > *muat* 'load'

In final position, *-s was lost in all dialects:

*dasedas > *dada* 'chest'

A few forms reflecting a root reconstructed with *s are not attested with /h/.[24]

*saŋin > *angin* 'wind' *sacek 'plant with dibble stick' > *asak* 'hole made with dibble stick' *sacaŋ > *asang* (in Kalimantan dialects) 'gills' *salac < *alas* 'forest' *sawak 'waist, torso' > *awak* 'body, self' *sipaɣ 'opposite side' > *ipar* 'in-law'

D4.3.23 *q and *s in trisyllabic roots

*s and *q were lost in medial position in trisyllabic roots, whether onset of the penult or onset of the final syllable, with a very few exceptions.[25] In initial position, *q and *s > /h/ unless the antepenult is lost entirely, as discussed in §D4.1.111. In root-final position, *q > /h/, as is the case of this phoneme as coda of disyllabic roots. Here are a few examples of the very large number:

*basequ > *bau* 'smell' *qaselu > *halu* *seqeɣet > *herat* 'tight' *baŋeqeɣ > *bangar* 'putrid' *bituqan > *bintang* 'star' *quluh + *tusud > *lutut* 'knee' (< *ulutut < *ulutuhud [cf. 1st footnote to §D4.3.22])

There are a few unexplained exceptions, were the reflexes of *q and *s are not lost:

*báɣeqaŋ > *geraham* 'molar' *buqáya > *buhaya* 'crocodile' (dial.)

*s and *q were not lost in trisyllabic roots that had previously contracted the penult and the final syllable. The following forms are dialectal:

*baqeɣu > *bahru* 'new' *dasuwen > *dahun* 'leaf' *taquweł > *tahun* 'year'

D4.3.24 *h

*h disappeared entirely without a trace:

*bahałiɣ > *banir* 'butress root' *bacuheq > *basuh* 'wash' *lahuj 'seaward' > *laut* 'sea' *capuh > *sapu* 'sweep, wipe' *qumah 'cultivated field' > *huma* 'dry rice plantation'

D4.3.25 *c

*c > /s/ in all positions:

*cak > *ma-sak* 'ripe, cooked' *cekecek > *sesak* 'packed tight' *ciku > *siku* 'elbow' *cucuł > *susun* 'be stacked up' *pacek 'wedge' > *pasak* 'stake' *bucúɣ 'bow' > *busur*

[24] Some of these forms may, in fact, exist with an /h-/ in peripheral dialects (e.g. in interior Kalimantan or in Urak Lawoi, spoken at the northernmost extension of Malayic on Phuket Island in Thailand). The research has not been done to find cognates of these forms in those dialects.

[25] The rule for the loss of an /h/ that developed in a trisyllabic root from *s or *q is recent and has spread to the dialects in only some words. In the case of *geraham* 'molar', however, the /h/ that had developed was between two /a/'s, and in this environment, /h/ is never lost.

'bow for carding' *atác > *atas* 'up above' *balec > *balas* 'answer, revenge' *dicedic > *dedic* 'slice thinly' *ɣatuc > *ratus* 'hundreds'

In a few cases, *s is reflected with /c/. The replacement of /s/ by /c/ is due to sound-symbolism or contamination in most cases, and in a couple of cases, the /c/ is in loan words from an unknown source:

*qapucuk 'tip'> *pucuk* 'young leaf' (cf. *puncak* 'summit') *capak > *campak* 'smack lips' *capit > *capit* 'pincers' *cikep > *cikap* 'catch with bare hands' *cilak 'shine, ray' > *cεlak* 'shining, glistening' (the lowering of *i to /ε/ is an indication of borrowing) *cukecuk 'shove into' > *cocok* 'prick, drive small hole through' (lowering of *u to /o/ is indication of borrowing) *lecut 'slip down' > *lecut* 'squeeze out contents' (cf. *lecit* 'ooze through') *pecaq > *pecah* 'broken into pieces' *pecit > *percit* 'squirt liquid out' (cf. *percik* 'spatter')

D4.3.3 The voiced consonants

D4.3.31 The voiced stops

The voiced stops *b, *j, *d, and *g became /b/, /j/, /d/, and /g/, respectively, in initial position:[26]

*batú < *batu* 'stone' *beli > *beli* 'buy' *bítuqan > *bintang* 'star' *bubu > *bubu* 'fish trap' *jaɣum > *jarum* 'needle' *jiguc 'bathe' > *jirus* 'sprinkle' *juɣuq 'liquid material' > *juruh* 'syrup' *dágat 'open area' > *darat* 'upland area away from sea' *deŋeɣ > *dengar* 'hear' *di > *di* 'on, at' *duɣi > *duri* 'thorn' *gatel > *gatal* 'itch' *gemegem > *genggam* 'hold in fist' *gilaŋ 'brilliant, giving of light'> *gilang* 'shining'

In medial position, *b, *j, and *d became /b/, /j/, and /d/, respectively, and *g merged with *d (> /d/):

*bábuy > *babi* 'pig' *tebel > *tebal* 'thick' *qaníbuŋ > *nibung* 'k.o. palm' *qubaɬ > *huban* 'grey hair' *pejem > *pejam* 'close the eyes' *qujaɬ > *hujan* 'rain' *tujuq 'point' > *tujuh* 'seven' *wada > *ada* 'there is' *cedu 'hicough' > *sedu* 'sob' *tiduɣ > *tidur* 'sleep' *qudam > *hudam* 'dull, faded' *pagay > *padi* 'rice in field' *iseguŋ > *hidung* 'nose' (< *siguŋ)

However, between two *a's, *b > /w/:

*baba > *bawa* 'carry' *baq + R- 'put down' > *bawah* 'below' †kaban 'flock, companion' > *kawan* 'friend, herd' *laban > *lawan* 'against' *tabaɣ > *tawar* 'tasteless, without salt or seasoning' *tábaɬ 'carry away with force' > *tawan* 'booty'

In final position, *-b loses voicing; (> /p/); *-j and *-g also lose voicing and merge as /t/; *-d > /r/—in effect, merges with *ɣ.[27]

---

[26] Cf. §A3.3.2 for a discussion of the reconstruction of initial *g- and irregularity in the reflexes.

[27] The development of *-d to [-r], a tongue-tip trill, produced a merger with *-ɣ, which had also had developed a trill articulation. Contact with Jv and Sd was likely a catalyst to the development of the trill articulation of *-d. However, there are dialects of Ml that did not develop *ɣ into a tongue-tip trill (§D4.3.32). In the dialects that did not develop the tongue-tip trill, *ɣ remained a uvular spirant, [ɣ]. In those dialects *-d and *-ɣ merged, as well: final *-d also became whatever final *-ɣ became. In most dialects in word-final position, this is a devoiced [ɣ], weakly articulated and not [x]. What needs explanation is why *-d should have become [-ɣ]. The

*lebeleb 'hidden by being covered' > *lelap* 'sound asleep' *búkij > *bukit* 'hill' *lahuj > *laut* 'seaward *penéj 'plugged up' > *penat* 'tired' *sated 'bring somewhere' > *hantar* 'deliver' *cidecid 'edge, go along edge' > *pe-sisir* 'shore' *kudekud > *kukur* 'rasp' *puseg > *pusat* 'navel' *quleg > *hulat* 'worm' *belag 'spread out' < *belat* 'k.o. fish trap made of spread out bamboo slats'

In one root, *g- is reflected with /k-/. This root probably has been contaminated by another root with similar meaning:

*getil > *ketil* 'nip off' (cf. *ketip* 'nip off')

In a few forms, medial and final *g are reflected with /r/ as in OJv and Sd. It is likely that these forms were affected by or borrowed from OJv or Sd:

*balíga > *belira* 'weaver's sword'[28] *cegep > *serap* 'seep in' *qageŋ > *arang* 'coals' *busekág > *bengkar* 'open out' *gilig 'side' > *gilir* 'rotate'

D4.3.32 *ɣ

Initial and medial *ɣ remained unchanged as a voiced spirant [ɣ] in the conservative dialects. In the less conservative dialects, *ɣ developed a tongue-tip trill articulation [r] in all positions:

*ɣínu > *ñiru* (metathesis and secondary palatalization [§§D4.1.3, D4.3.41, end]) *ɣumaq > *rumah* 'house' *aɣi 'come here!' > *m-ari* [maɣi] or [mari]'let's go!' *beɣay > *beri* 'give' *biɣaq 'giant taro' > *birah* 'an arom: *Alocasia,* sp.' *buɣaw > *buru* 'chase'

In dialects retaining spirantal articulation for *ɣ in final position, *ɣ developed in one of the following ways: (1) it lost voicing and remained a spirant; or (2) it merged with /ʔ/; (2a) it merged with /h/; or (3) it was lost (if syllable final but word internal).

*baɣ- > *ber-* [ber-] or [be-] 'derivative prefix' *bibíɣ > *bibir* 'lips' [bibir] or [bibiɣ] or [bibiʔ] *biŋaɣ > *bingar* [bingar] or [bingah] 'volute shell' *ɣaŋaɣ > *rangar* [raŋar] or [ɣaŋaɣ] or [ɣaŋaʔ] (often spelled *rangak*) 'spider conch'

When a nasal came to precede *ɣ directly in an affixational process, the *ɣ became /g/:

*ɣaŋ + doubling > *ganggang* 'roast near fire' *ɣaŋ 'heat' + *paŋ- > *panggang* 'roast'

When *ɣ came to abut on a consonant due to loss of an unstressed penultimate vowel, it was not lost unless it was the coda of a reduplicated monosyllable. It was lost, however, in dialects that retained a spirantal articulation of *ɣ in other positions. (Cf. the example of *ber-*, immediately preceding.)

*beɣekec > *beɣkec > *berkas* [berkas] or [bekas] 'bundle' *buɣebuɣ 'broken into small bits' > *bubur* 'porridge' (< *buɣbuɣ)

---

explanation probably lies in analogy: the correlation in initial and medial position of spirant articulation in some dialects and trill articulation in other dialects was extended to final position.

[28] Note that *belida* 'wolf herring' (the snout of which resembles a weaver's sword) has the regular reflex of medial *-g-.

D4.3.4 The liquids and nasals

D4.3.41 *l and *ɬ

Except where *l was lost by coming to abut on a stop as a result of penultimate vowel syncopation (§D4.1.12), *l is reflected in all environments as /l/.

> *laŋit > *langit* 'heavens' *lemek 'soft' > *lemak* 'fat (meat)' *lima > *lima* 'five' *ludaq > *ludah* 'spit' *balec > *balas* 'answer, revenge' *beli > *beli* 'buy' *culuq > *suluh* 'torch' *buteliɣ 'cyst' > *butir* 'grain' *gatel > *gatal* 'itch' *kawil > *kail* 'fishhook' *bukul > *bungkul* 'knob-shaped protrusion, bump, lump'

*ɬ underwent the developments described for PMP in §A3.3.4. Namely, *ɬ became /l/ when onset of a penult or earlier syllable with a short-vowel nucleus; *ɬ became *ñ before a long vowel and in monosyllabic roots and when onset of the root-final syllable after a long vowel. *ɬ > /n/ when onset of the final syllable after a short vowel and in word-final position.

*ɬ > /l/:

> *ɬekét > *lekat* 'stick' *qaɬihípec > *lipas* 'cockroach' (> *qalípes < *qalihípec)

*ɬ > /ñ/:

> *ɬátuq > *ñatuh* 'k.o. tree' *ɬam+-an > *ñaman* 'delicious' *qáɬuj > *hañut* 'be carried by current'

*ɬ > /n/:

> *aɬák > *anak* 'son, daughter' *qutaɬ 'scrub lands and the plants on it' > *hutan* 'forest'

In some dialects, the contrast between /ñ/ and /n/ was neutralized when preceding /i/, and dialect mixture has resulted in that standard dialects have /ñi/ for earlier *ni or /ni/ for earlier *ñi in some forms. This accounts for /ñ/ in *buñi* 'noise' (< *be-uni) < *suni 'make noise') and the /n/ in *nipis* 'thin' (< *ɬisebis) and *banir* 'buttress root < *bahaɬiɣ.

D4.3.42 Nasals

Except for being assimilated to the point of articulation of the following consonant, *m, *n, and *ŋ are reflected with /m/, /n/, and /ng/, respectively, other than in a few isolated cases.

> *manuk > *manuk* 'bird' *naɬáq > *nanah* 'pus' *ŋaŋa > *nganga* 'open mouthed' *ɣumaq > *rumah* 'house' *lama > *lama* 'old, long ago' *buŋa > *bunga* 'flower' *nem > enam 'six' *dasuwen > *daun* 'leaf' *lebeŋ 'grave, bury' > *lembang* 'low-lying, trodden underfoot' *bubuŋ 'ridgepole' > *bubung* 'roof'

In two trisyllabic roots the final nasal contrasts became neutralized to /-ng/. The second example has cognates with final /ng/ in other An languages:

> *bítuqan > *bintang* 'star' *tuqelaɬ > *tulang* 'bone'

*padeŋ is reflected as *padam* 'extinguish' with unexpected /-m/. This is most likely is due to contamination with the root *dem 'dark'. The language that made this innovation is unknown. It may have been pre-Malay. In any case, the innovation has spread to many languages in Java and Sumatra and to Moken. There is another form with final /-m/ in place of /-ng/. This was an early change and is reflected in St and other languages of Formosa, as well as in other MP languages:

*baɣeqaŋ > *geraham* 'molar'

In one case, *m is dissimilated to /n/after /m/ to the left:[29]

*mic + *ma- > *manis* 'sweet' (< *mamis)

Further, *ŋ is dissimilated to /n/ before an /n/ to the right not word final:

*santay + *maN- > *men-anti* 'wait' (< *meŋ-anti)

D4.3.43 *w

Initial *w- was lost:

*wada > *ada* 'there is'

The word for 'day' lost the initial *w- and added an initial /h-/, which is not explained:

*waɣi > *hari* 'day'

Medial *-w- > /w/ when onset of the final syllable between *a's. It is also retained as the last element in a diphthong (§D4.2.5). Otherwise, *w was lost.

*sawak 'waist, torso' > *awak* 'body, self' *kawanaɬ > *kanan* (< *kaanan) *kawil > *kail* 'fishhook' *kawiɣi > *kiri* 'left'

In the following form, the rule for the *w-loss ceased to operate at the time the medial syllable was lost by syncopation:

*tibawác 'finish off' > *tiwas* 'defeated, killed'

For *we and *ew, cf. §D4.2.4, end.

D4.3.44 *y

*y is retained intervocalically. Intervocalic /y/ between /a, e, u/ and /i/ does not contrast with its absence. No example of a Ml reflex of initial *y is attested. For *y in diphthongs see §D4.2.5.

*daya 'inland' > *barat-daya* 'southwest (wind)' *laheyu > *layu* 'withered' *tiyan > *tian* 'belly'

For *ye and *ey, cf. §D4.2.4, end

[29] *Mamah* 'chew' (< *mamaq) is a countercase that proves that this change was sporadic.

PART E. LANGUAGES OF JAVA, SUMATRA, AND THE MAINLAND

The languages of Java, including Madura, Bali, and Lombok, and the languages of Sumatra together with the mainland have much in common. It is tempting to think that they form a subgroup within Malayo-Polynesian. However, no evidence to support such a hypothesis has come to light. The innovations they show in common can have come about entirely through contact. Indeed, it has been proposed that Madurese, Javanese, Sundanese, and Malay constitute a subgroup (Nothofer 1975), and a protolanguage that gave rise to these languages has been reconstructed. In fact, though, no exclusively shared innovations have been adduced to substantiate this hypothesis, and at this point, there is no evidence to contradict a hypothesis that these languages arose as a result of independent settlement of western Indonesia by Malayo-Polynesians. What is known definitively is that the Malayic languages together with Iban and Chamic, which includes Aceh, are indeed a recent subgroup and originate in Kalimantan (Collins et al: 2006).

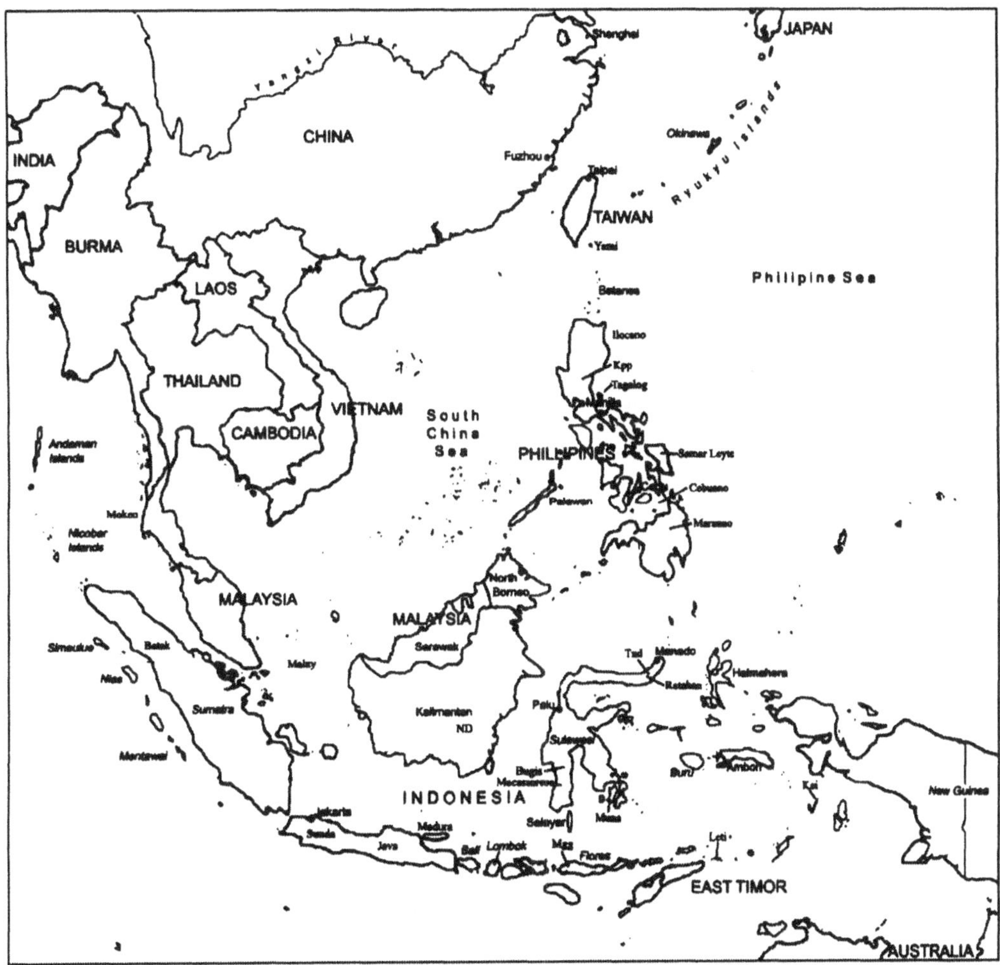

Map 8. Location of Hesperonesian languages.

CHAPTER ONE

Old Javanese

E1.0 Background and cultural factors that influenced the history of OJv

Old Javanese (OJv) is documented in inscriptions dating from the eighth century AD and in manuscripts composed from around the year 1000 AD to modern times. The language is based on dialects spoken over a period of time from the earliest inscriptions to the fifteenth century but, like most literary languages, does not reflect any spoken style faithfully. Knowledge of OJv was kept alive over the centuries in Bali, where much of the OJv literature was considered among the sacred scriptures and where OJv has remained the language of ritual and, to some of extent, of theater. OJv differs from the New Javanese dialects (NJv) mainly in vocabulary and in that it does not manifest a number of sound changes that NJv has undergone. The most accurate and most complete source for OJv is Zoetmulder 1982. Here we rely almost exclusively on Zoetmulder's work for our citations and definitions. In cases where NJv manifests a cognate for a reconstructed form where an OJv cognate is not listed in our source, we cite the NJv form with an annotation that it is only attested in NJv.

The following chart shows the inventory of segmental phonemes of OJv. The letters in parentheses represent phonemes that do not occur in forms inherited from the protolanguage.

CHART ONE. PHONEMES OF OLD JAVANESE

Consonants

voiceless	p	t	ṭ	(c)	k	
voiced	b	d	ḍ	(j)	g	
spirants		s				h
liquid	w	l,	r	y		
nasals	m	n		(ñ)	ng [ŋ]	

Vowels and Diphthongs

high	i, ī		u,ū
mid	ɛ	ə, ö	o
low		a	
diphthong	uy	ay	

The transcriptions ī and ū represent long vowels. The /d/ in NJv is an apico-dental stop. /ḍ/ is an apico-alveolar stop in NJv. We assume that the articulation was similar in OJv. The series /b, d, ḍ, j, g/ are voiceless, lenis, pharyngealized stops in NJv, but it is probably the case that in OJv they were voiced stops without the breathy quality that the current NJv pronunciation manifests.[1] OJv had lost the PAn stress contrasts. In NJv stress is predictably on the final syllable of the word, and the loss of the penult in forms shaped *(C)iyV(C) and *(C)uwV(C) is good evidence that in OJv, as well, the stress was on the final syllable (§E1.1.11).

[1] In current NJv the liquids and nasals except for /r/ may variably also be weakened and pharyngealized, but there was probably nothing like that in OJv.

E1.1 Processes affecting the development of OJv from PAn

There is a tendency to disyllabize trisyllabic roots. The penult or the antepenult was lost, depending on the make-up of the root.

E1.1.1 Loss of the penult

In trisyllabic roots, penults with *e most generally were lost. Similarly, roots with *iyV or *uwV lost *i and *u of the penult:

*baqeɣuh > *wāhu* 'new' (< *baɣhu < *baɣqu[2] < *baqɣu) *baɣiyus 'storm' > *wāyu* 'wind, air' (< *baɣyu < *baɣyus)[3] *banuwa 'place where there is s.t.' > *wanwa* 'inhabited place, village' *basequ > *a-bo* 'smell' (also *am-bö* 'stinking') *qaselu > *halu* 'pestle'

This change took place after the metathesis of *i of the antepenult and *e of the penult, a widespread process in Formosan and in MP languages, especially in roots with *(C)ise- (§A3.5.4). In roots that metathesized *i and *e, antepenultimate *e was lost (§E1.1.12), but *i remains in the penult:

*iseguŋ > *hirung* 'nose' (< *esiguŋ) *isekan > *hikan* 'fish' *qiseɬep 'sleep' > *hinep* 'spend the night'

However, in the following form, the penult was lost, and metathesis did not take place:

*isepi > *ipi* 'dream'

Two roots with *e in the penult underwent metathesis of the penultimate *e and the vowel of the final syllable or the vowel of the antepenult before disyllabization took place:

*baqeɣaŋ > *bahem* 'molar' (< *bāqem < *baɣaqem < *baɣaqeŋ) *tuqelaɬ > *tahulan* 'bone' (< *tequlan)

Two roots developed a prenasalized onset to the penult (§E1.1.4), and this prevented syncopation from taking place:

*paqegu > *hamperu* 'gall' (< *qapegu [§E1.1.3]) *qiteluɣ > *hantelu* 'egg'

E1.1.11 Loss of the penult in disyllabic roots

*i before *y and *u before *w in the penult of disyllabic roots were lost:

*liya > *lya-n* 'other' *quway > *hwi* 'rattan'

The sequences *Cw-* and *Cy-* probably did not contrast with *Cəw-* and *Cəy-*, and dialectally or stylistically they were pronounced with an [ə]. Since [ə] (/e/) > /u/ in late OJv under certain circumstances (§E1.2.2ff.), some forms are attested with /Cuy/ or /Cuw/ instead of /Cy/ and /Cw/—that is, the sub-phonemic variant with [ə] survived in these cases instead of the variant without [ə]:

---

[2] We assume that metathesis took place because of the lengthening of the *a in the OJv reflex *wāhu* (§E1.3.25).

[3] Zoetmulder (1982:230) suggests that this form derives from Skt *vāyu* 'wind, air', and certainly the meaning has changed under the influence of Skt. But the form itself is inherited: it corresponds perfectly to other reflexes of *baɣiyus.

*piyut > *puyut* 'kin of fourth ascending or descending generation' (< *peyut) *lubaŋ > *luwang* 'hole'[4]

E1.1.12 Weakening or loss of antepenult

In trisyllabic roots, the antepenult was weakened. Either the antepenult was lost entirely or the vowel of the antepenult was changed to /a/:

*juɣami > *dami* (< *jami < *jāmi < *jaɣami) *tuqelaɬ > *tahulan* 'bone' (< *tequlan [§E1.1.3]) *leqasem > *hasem* 'sour' *qatusan 'deity' < *tuhan* 'master, lord' *qiteluɣ > *hantelū* 'egg' *sapedec > *peḍes* 'hot, biting (taste)'

There are two forms with *u in the antepenult that do not weaken the *u (change it to /a/) *Wuhaya* is probably not directly inherited, and *gurita* evinces an irregular reflex of *ɣ, indicating that it is a borrowing (§E1.3.25):

*buqaya > *wuhaya* 'crocodile' *guɣita > *gurita* 'octopus'

The rules for retention of the antepenult or its entire loss depend on two factors. First is the make-up of the root: if the root contained consonants that were lost, then there was contraction between the resulting abutting vowels as listed in §§E1.1.13ff. Second, the antepenult was preserved if it was protected by intercalation of a nasal before the onset of the penult (§E1.1.4). (Cf. the rule of §E1.1.1, end, that states that the *e of the penult was not lost in such circumstances.)

*paqegu > *hamperu* 'gall' (< *qapegu) *qiteluɣ > *hantelū* 'egg'

E1.1.13 Vowel contraction and monophthongization

In trisyllabic roots, when a sequence of *i's or *u's developed after loss of a medial consonant, the two *i's or the two *u's contracted:

*palisi 'taboo' > *pali-pali* 'required ritual for ceremonial blessings' *timpusuq 'squat' > *timpuh* 'sit with feet folded under one'

In disyllabic roots, no contraction takes place, although in late OJv and NJv the long vowels were shortened:

*tusud > *tūr* 'knee' *juɣuq > *duh* 'sap, juice' (assumed to be from earlier but unattested *dūh) *wasiyeɣ > *wway* 'water' (< *way [§E1.2.1] < *wai < *waĩ [§§E1.2.21, E1.3.25] < *waiyeɣ)

When *e came to abut on a vowel because of loss of medial C, it contracted with the adjacent vowel. The following list gives the details:

E1.1.131 *e

*ae > /e/ in trisyllabic roots:

*qetaq + *ma- > *mentah* 'raw' (< maetaq)

*e also became /e/ in disyllabic roots. In disyllabic roots, the /e/ that developed from *ae was lengthened to /ö/, by the rule of §E1.1.2 that monosyllabic roots that had developed may

---

[4] Probably *luwang* developed to avoid confusion with *lwang* 'decrease'

lengthen the vowel nucleus in order to achieve a disyllabic root or a root with a nucleus of two moras (for when the *ae contracts the result is a monosyllabic root).

*baɣeq 'abscess' > *böh* 'swelling in eyes or feet' (< *baeh)

*ae that developed from *ie and *ue by the rule of §E1.1.12, that the antepenult > /a/, further changed in the same way as the *ae discussed just above. Namely, *ie and *ue that developed in the antepenult and penult of trisyllabic roots by the loss of the intervening C > /e/. In short, *ie/*ue > *ae > /e/:

*biɣeŋi > *wengi* 'night' (< *baeŋi < *baɣeŋi) *busekag > *um-ekar* 'open, unfold (flower)' (< *um + *bekag [the *m of *um- combined with the initial *b to form *m] < *buekag)

If the *e that developed from *ae in trisyllabic roots abutted on an /a/ because of the loss of the onset of the final syllable of the root, the result was *ea. This sequence then was treated in a way parallel to the development discussed under §E1.1.132, immediately following—i.e., *aea > *ea > *ua > /wa/ (§E1.1.11) This rule affects forms that originally had had *a in the antepenult as well as forms that had had *i[5] in the antepenult:

*baheɣat 'heavy' > *bwat* 'weight' (< *buat < *beat < *baeat) *tiqeɣab > *twab* 'belch' (*q before *e was lost in trisyllabic roots [§E1.3.11])

E1.1.132 *ea

*ea > /wa/ (< *ua [§E1.1.11]):

*teɣac 'k.o. hard wood' > *twas* 'hardness, hard core' (< *teas)

E1.1.133 *ee

ee > /ö/ in disyllabic roots:

*beɣek > *wök* 'hog, boar'

E1.1.134 *i or *u abutting on *e

If the onset of the final syllable was lost, *i or *u abutting on an *e contracted to /i/ and /u/, respectively:

*betihec > *wetis* 'calf' *betehus > *wetu* 'come forth, appear' *sicuheq > *isuh* 'wash'

In the following cases, *ue and *eu contracted to /e/ as well as to /u/. A possible explanation is that contraction to /e/ was dialectal):

*bacuheq > *wasuh/waseh* 'wash' *basequ > *abo/ambö*[6] 'smelling bad' (with a petrified prefix and intercalated nasal [§E1.1.4]) (< *bö [contraction to *e and lengthening in monosyllabic root] < *beu [§E1.1.31, above] < *baeu [loss of *q in onset of penult §E1.3.11, 5th¶, below] < *baqeu < *baqesu [§E1.1.3])

---

[5] The *u and *i of the antepenult became /a/ (§E1.1.12). There are no attestations of forms that had *u in the antepenult of a root that lost both the onset of the penult and the onset of the final syllable.

[6] The form *ambö* gave rise to NJv *mambu* 'smell bad'. For a discussion of the development of *abo*, see the end of this section.

In the following cases, the /u/ that resulted was lengthened to make the form disyllabic (§E1.1.24):

*luseq > *lūh* 'tears' *buhet 'squirrel' > *wūt* 'tarsier'

In one case *ue was lowered to /o/. There is no explanation:

*bukes 'hair'> *wok* 'body hair' (< *buek < *busek)

E1.1.135 *ai and *au

A sequence *ai that developed in disyllabic stems was monphthongized to /ɛ/ in two cases but remained /ay/ in two others. There is no explanation for the difference in outcome.9

*nasik > pa-nɛk 'climb' (< *pa-naik < *pa-nasik [§E1.1.3]) *paɣis > pɛ 'skate, ray' (< *pai) *waɣi 'day, sun' > *way* 'sun' *wasiyeɣ > *wway* 'water' (< *way [§E1.2.1] < *wai [§E1.1.13, 2nd¶] < *waĩ [§§E1.2.21, E1.3.25] < *waiyeɣ)

In trisyllabic stems the sequence *ai that developed became /i/, just as *ay did:

*bahi + -in- > wini 'female' (< *binay < *binai)

A sequence *au that developed (as well as inherited /aw/ [§E1.2.51]) was monophthongized to /o/, if *au had not been metathesized to *ua (§E1.1.3):

*basequ > *a-bo* 'smell bad' (< *bau [§E1.1.34, above] < *baeu [loss of *q in onset of penult [§E1.3.11, 5th¶, below]) < *baqeu < *baqesu [§E1.1.3]) *caweŋ 'protective hat' > *song* 'sunshade, cover, protection' (< *sauŋ) *jaɣum > *dom* 'needle' (< *jaum) *lahuwen 'long time' > *lon* 'slowness' *lahuj 'seaward' > *lor* 'north' *pasuq > *poh* 'mango' *taɣum > *tom* 'indigo' *taɣuq 'put down' > *toh* 'stake in betting'

E1.1.2 Monosyllabic roots

Inherited monosyllabic roots that are not enclitic or monosyllabic roots that developed in pre-OJv tend to disyllabize (but do not always do so). They disyllabized in one of four ways (as is the case of other An languages [§A3.6.2]): (1) reduplication of the first consonant and vowel (from earlier doubling followed by CC simplification); (2) petrifaction of a prefix; (3) addition of a prothetic /e/; (4) lengthening of the vowel nucleus (disyllabizing it or possibly just making it two moras).

(1) examples of root doubling:

*ba 'carry on back' > *wawa* 'take along, bring along ' *baq 'mouth' > *babah* 'opening' *cuɬ 'stack up' > *susun* 'layer, tier, storey'

(2) petrifaction of a prefix:

*cep 'suck' > *hisep* 'sucked up, absorbed' (*ise- + *cep) *deŋ 'extinguished' > *paḍem* 'extinguish' (*pa- 'causative' + *deŋ)

(3) addition of prothetic /e/:

*buɬ > *embun* 'fontantelle' (with prenasalized onset of the final syllable [§E1.1.4]) *lak 'separated' > *elak* 'with a gaping opening' *iseq > *eyeh* 'urine' (< *yeh < *ieq)

Occasionally the prothetic /e/ developed an initial /h/. This is not a sound law, but was in all likelihood a sporadic development due to the manner of articulation:

*bun > *hebun* 'dew, mist' (A form without /he/, *bun*, is also attested.)

In the following example, the prothetic /e/ that developed in disyllabization of the monosyllabic root was assimilated to the following /w/:

*wasiyeɣ > *wway* 'water' (< *way [§E1.2.1] < *wai [§E1.1.13, 2nd¶] < *waĩ [§§E1.2.21, E1.3.25] < *waiyeɣ)

(4) lengthened vowel nucleus (which in later OJv were shortened):

*luseq > *lūh* 'tears' (later OJv *luh,* NJv *eluh*—with addition of prothetic /e/) *buhet 'squirrel' > *wūt* 'tarsier, lemur' (< *wut)

E1.1.3 Metathesis

OJv evinces some of the cases of metathesis that are widespread over a wide range of languages:

*bukes 'hair' > *wok* 'hairy' (< *busek) *nakis > *pa-nɛk* 'climb' (< *pa-naik < *pa-nasik) *paqegu > *hamperu* 'gall' (< *qapegu) *taŋila > *talinga* 'ear'

There are also some cases of metathesis that only OJv evinces:

*iqebed > *iber* 'fly' (< *hibed < *qibed < *eqibed) *kudemel > *kandel* 'thick' (< *kamḍel < *kameḍel < *kaḍemel [§E1.1.12]) *qawuŋ > *ahung* 'howl' *laɣiw > *pa-layū* 'flee' (< *pa-layuɣ) *tusuq > *tuhu* 'true' (< *tuqus [§E1.3.11, middle])

A sequence *au that developed from loss of medial C sporadically metathesized to *ua and then changed to /wa/ by the rule of §E1.1.11:

*dasuwen > *rwan* 'leaf' (< *ruan < *ruan < *rahun < *dahun) *jaqewis > *dwah* 'far' (< *juah < *jauh < *jasewiq [metathesis of *s and *q] *ikasu > *kwa* 'you (sing.) (< *ikau)

After *q > /h/ (§E1.3.11), a sequence *uha > *uah:

*ɣuqaɬay 'male' > *wāni* 'courage' (< *wahni < *uhani < *uqani)

*e in the penult in trisyllabic roots sporadically metathesized with the vowel of the antepenult or the final syllable:

*baɣeqaŋ > *bahem* 'molar' (< *bāqem < *baɣaqem < *baɣaqeŋ) *tuqelaɬ > *tahulan* 'bone' (< *tequlan)

*s and *q sporadically metathesize with a nasal, *ɣ, or *c, or with an *s or *q:

*baŋeqeɣ > *banger* 'malodorous' (< *baqeŋeɣ)[7] *basequ > *a-bo* 'smell bad' (< *bau < *baeu < *baqeu < *baqesu[7]) *deɣeqec 'moving vigorously and rapidly' > *dres* 'force,

---

[7] We assume metathesis in the case of *baŋeqeɣ, *basequ, *deɣeqec , and *liceqes in order to account for the loss of *q in these forms. By the rule of §E1.3.11, 5th¶, *q onset in the penult of trisyllabic roots was lost when followed by *e.

great velocity' (< *dedes [§E1.1.2] < *des < *deɣec < *deqeɣec[7]) *liceqes > *lingsa* 'nit' (< *liqeces [§E1.1.4])

E1.1.4 Prenasalization of medial stop consonants

Like other MP languages, OJv evinces a tendency to add a nasal to close a penult or earlier syllable that is open (§A3.7.2):

*buɬ > *embun* 'fontanelle' (disyllabization by prothetic vowel [§E1.1.2(3)]) *cabuŋ > *sambung* 'contribute' *isepun > *impun* 'gathered' *sebaɬ 'carry in cloth' > *hemban* 'that which carries or encloses' *tupaŋ 'stack up' > *tumpang* 'layer, tier' *tidec 'press flat, crush' > *tinḍes* 'trample underfoot' *puti > *punti* 'banana' *takeb 'be covered' > *tangkeb* 'closing two spaces off from each other (door, curtain)'

In some cases the prenasalized final syllable is the remnant of a petrified infix *-um-:

*tebuk 'hit with a thump' > *tumbuk* 'pound' (< *tumebuk)

E1.2.0 Vowels and diphthongs

OJv reflects the PAn vowels faithfully except in cases where vowel contraction took place (§§E1.1.1ff.) and a few other places noted in the subsections below.

E1.2.1 *i

*i is reflected with /i/ in most cases:

*piliq > *pilih* 'choose'

When loss of a consonant caused unstressed *i to abut on a vowel, *i is reflected with /y/ (cf. §E1.1.11):

*íseq > *eyeh* 'urine' (< *yeh[8] < *iéh < *ieq) *wasiyeɣ > *wway* 'water' (< *way [§E1.2.1] < *wai [§E1.1.13, 2nd¶] < *waĩ [§§E1.2.21, E1.3.25] < *waiyeɣ)

E1.2.2 *e

*e > /e/ in the penult of disyllabic roots and in all final syllables with exceptions as listed below:

*sagek 'kiss, sniff' > *arek* 'kiss' *depa > *repa* 'fathom'

The following rules give the exceptions: (1) *we/*ew > /u/[9] and *ye/*ey > /i/, (2) *eɣ > /ö/ (3) *eCe > /ö/ when the medial consonant was lost (§E.1.1.133):

E1.2.21

*we/*ew > /u/ and *ye/*ey > /i/:

---

[8] We assume a shift of the stress in pre-OJv to the final syllable in order to account for the loss of the penult (§E1.0, end).

[9] The change of *ew > /u/ was on-going in OJv. After *b > /w/ (§E1.3.21) a sequence of /ew/ that developed could dialectally or in later OJv change to /uw/:

*tebek 'pierce' > *tewek/tuwek* 'a pointed weapon for stabbing' *dasuwen > *rwan* 'leaf' (< *ruan < *ruhan < *rahun < *dahun) *jaqewis > *dwah* 'far' (< *juah < *jauh < *jasewiq [metathesis of *s and *q]) *weliq 'do again' > *ulih* 'reaching destination, going home' *taquweɬ > *tahun* 'year' *taseyup > *tyup* 'blow on s.t. (trumpet)' *waseyeɣ > *wway* 'water'

However, *eyu > /uyu/:

*piyut > *puyut* 'kin of the fourth ascending or descending generations' (< *peyut [§E.1.1.11]

E1.2.22

*eɣ > /ö/[10]

*deŋeɣ > *ḍengö* 'hear'

E1.2.23

When two *e's came to abut on one another they contracted to /ö/:[11]

*beɣek 'domesticated pig' > *wök* 'hog, boar'

An *e in the antepenult or which came to be in the antepenult > /a/:

*juɣami > *dami* 'straw' (< *jāmi < *jaɣami [§E.1.1.12]) *tuqelaɬ > *tahulan* 'bone' (< *tequlan)

Root final *-es > /a/:

*liceqes > *lingsa* 'nit' (< *liqeces [§§E1.1.3, E1.1.4])

In trisyllabic roots with *e in the penult, *e was lost, and contraction took place (§E1.1.12).

E.1.2.3 *u

*u remained unchanged except when contracted, in diphthongs (§E1.1.13), and in the antepenult (where *u > /a/ [§1.1.12]).

*tuɬuh 'roast' > *a-tunu* 'ablaze' *dekuŋ 'bent' > *ḍekung* 'knee' *qaɬitu 'evil spirit' > *hanitu* 'evil powers' *qujaɬ > *hudan* 'rain'

E1.2.4 *a

*a remained unchanged except when contracted and in diphthongs (§§E1.1.13, E1.2.51):

*jalan > *dalan* 'road, way' *qaselu > *halu* 'pestle' *qelag >*helar* 'wing' *qudaŋ > *hurang* 'shrimp, lobster'

---

[10] Phonologically /ö/ is a long /ə/. Thus the change of *əɣ > /ö/ is an example of the rule that loss of a ɣ-coda causes compensatory lengthening of the preceding vowel. Cf. the footnote to §E.1.3.25)

[11] Cf. the preceding footnote, where we say that /ö/ a long /ə/. OJv /ö/ became /u/ in NJv:

rengö > *rungu* 'hear'

Similarly, OJv /eh/ > /uh/:

eyeh > *uyuh* 'urinate'

In later OJv, the sequence /wa/ > became /o/.

OJv *wwalu* > NJv *wolu* 'eight'

This process was on-going, as attested by the following forms, where one of the occurrences of /wa/ was monophtongized and the other was not:

*uɣat > *otwat* 'nerve, vein' (< *watwat—loss of *ɣ and subsequent disyllabization by doubling [§§E1.1.2, E1.3.25]) *waɣed > *odwad* 'creeper'[12]

E1.2.5 Diphthongs

E1.2.51 *ay, *aw

*ay > /i/ in most cases:

*qatay > *hati* 'liver' *quway > *hwi* 'rattan'

In a few cases, *ay > /ɛ/. These are probably cases of loan words, and not the reflex of a contrasting diphthong in PAn (cf. the discussion in §A3.4). Note that *ay that arose in pre-OJv from consonant loss between *a and *i became /ɛ/ (§E1.1.135).

*abay 'wave arms' > *awɛ* 'beckon' *balay 'building or part of building' > *balɛ* 'open building, pavillion' *lantay 'bamboo lathes' > *lantɛ* 'rattan mat' *labay > *lawɛ* 'thread, yarn' *calay 'preserve by drying' > *salɛ punti* 'banana preserves' *tapay > *tapɛ* 'fermented glutinous rice'

*aw > /u/ (parallel to the change of *ay > /i/ above):

*danaw > *ranu* 'lake, pond' *panaw > *panu* 'white spots on skin'

In a few cases *aw is reflected with /o/. These are not directly inherited (and in some cases have other sound irregularities):

*baŋaw < *bango* 'heron' *sijaw > *hijo* 'green' *qanasaw > *hano* '*Arenga* palm'

E1.2.52 *uy, *iw

*uy > /i/ in two cases and /uy/ in two others. Possibly the /i/ reflex is due to Ml influence:[13] *anduy > *m-anḍi* 'bathe' *babuy > *bawi* 'pig' *laŋuy > *langhuy* 'swim' (/h/ unexplained[14]) *sehapuy > *apuy* 'fire'
*iw > /uy/ if no consonant was lost before *iw:

*baliw 'return to previous state' > *waluy* 'return, come back'

If a consonant was lost before *iw, *i > /y/ and /w/ > /u/:

---

[12] Monophthongization first took place in unstressed position and only later affected sequences in stressed position.

[13] Both the forms with /i/ reflex have Ml cognates with /i/. The form *bawi* 'pig' shows two different reflexes for PAn *b and for this reason I hypothesize that *bawi* is influenced by Ml *babi* 'pig'. The form *manḍi* 'bathe' is probably a borrowing from Ml for it shows the petrified prefix *m-* also found in the Ml cognate *mandi* 'bathe'. Further there is another OJv word for 'bathe' *dyus* (< *jiɣuc 'bathe'), which survives in NJv *a-dus* 'bathe'.

[14] The *h* may be purely orthographic. Forms without *h* are also attested: *languy* and *langwi*.

*kasiw > *kayu* 'tree, wood' *laɣiw > *pa-layū* 'flee' (< *pa-layuɣ [§E1.1.3, E1.3.25])

E1.3 Consonants

The following chart shows the OJv reflexes of the PAn consonants:

CHART TWO. DEVELOPMENT OF THE OJV CONSONANTS FROM PAN

PAn	OJv	PAn	OJv
p	*p*	j	*d*
t	*t*	g	*g-, -r-, -r*
k	*k*	ɣ	*Ø*
q	*h*	l	*l*
s	*h*	ɬ	*n*
h	*Ø*	m, n	*m,n*
c	*s*	ŋ	*ng*
b	*b, w*	w	*w*
d	*ḍ, r*	y	*y*

E1.3.1 Voiceless consonants

*p, *t, *k were stable and remained unchanged in all positions.
*p > /p/ in all positions:

*puluq > *puluh* 'groups of ten' *sehapuy > *apuy* 'fire' *alap > *alap* 'take, fetch'

In the following case, the initial *p was substituted for by *b, as happened in all the MP languages and in Pa (see commentary under *pukuh in the glossary). This *b later became /w/ (§E1.3.21):

*pukuh 'knot, node' > *wuku* 'section of bamboo'

*t >/t/ in all positions:

talis > *tali* 'rope' *mata > *mata* 'eye' *laŋit > *langit* 'sky'

*k > /k/ in all positions:

*kasiw >*kayu* 'wood, tree' *isekan > *hikan* 'fish' *sagek > *arek* 'kiss'

E1.3.11 *q, *s

*q and *s both became /h/ in initial and medial positions with exceptions detailed below:

*saŋin > *hangin* 'wind' *cusan > *suhan* 'dibble stick' *qalun > *halun* 'long rolling wave' *paqit > *pahit* 'bitter'

However, the /h/ that developed began to be lost in pre-OJv and was lost entirely in certain environments by OJv times. The change of *s > /h/ and *q > /h/ are two unconnected developments. The change of *s > /h/ took place earlier than the change of *q > /h/ (cf. the sequence of events assumed, listed in the last paragraph of this section). Thus, environments in which /h/ became lost are not the same if the /h/ originated from *s as when the /h/ originated from *q. First, in final position, *q > /h/, and *s was lost:

*aliq > *alih* 'move to another place' *baq 'mouth' > *babah* 'opening, gate' *dasedas > *ḍaḍa* 'chest' (< *dasdas)

*s-onset in a trisyllabic root was lost:

*baŋesis > *wangi* 'fragrant' *basequ > *a-bo* 'smelly' *binesiq > *winih* 'seed, seedling' *dasuwen > *rwan* 'leaf' *ikasu > *kwa* 'you' (with loss of the antepenult and metathesis [§E1.1.3]) *qaselu > *halu* 'pestle'

*dusa 'two' which most frequently occurred as a proclitic also lost the *s by this rule: *rwa.* An exceptions is the reflex of *qatusan > *tuhan* 'lord', which lost the antepenult before the rule took effect.
*q in trisyllabic roots was lost before *e of the penult and before *uw and *iy:

*qetaq + ma- > *mentah* 'raw' (< *metaq < *maetaq) *seqeɣet 'tight' > *höt* 'narrow, confined in space' *tiqeɣab > *twab* 'belch' (< *tuab < *tieab < *tieɣab)

Exceptions are *laqeya 'ginger', *taquweɬ 'year' and *tuqelaɬ 'bone'. *laqeya is not directly inherited and also exhibits other irregularities. The form *taquweɬ disyllabized by contracting *uwe > /u/ before the rule of *q- loss in trisyllabics went into effect. The form *tuqelaɬ underwent vocalic metathesis before this rule went into effect—that is, it became *tequlaɬ).

*laqeya > *jahya* 'ginger' (< *jahiya) *taquweɬ > *tahun* 'year' (< *taqun) *tuqelaɬ > *tahulan* 'bone' (< *taqulan < *tequlan)

The following form seems to follow the rule of *q-loss (that is, *iqebed > *iber* 'fly'), but in fact, the history is more complex as the Sd cognate *hiber* 'fly' shows:

*iqebed > *eqibed (metathesis [§E1.1.3]) > *qibed > *hiber > *iber* (by the loss of /h/ in late OJv)

Note that *q onset of the penult before *a was not lost by this rule. However, in the following form metathesis caused the *h that developed to abut on a C, and in this environment, *h was lost sporadically, but caused compensatory lengthening on the preceding vowel:

*ɣuqaɬay 'male' > *wāni* 'courage' (< *wahni < *uhani < *uqani)

In roots having both *s and *q, the *s was lost:[15]

*jaqewis > *dwah* 'far' (< *juah < *jauh < *jasewiq [metathesis of *s and *q]) *iseq > *eyeh* 'urine' (< *yeh < *ieh) *luseq > *lūh* 'tears' (< *luh) *pasuq > *poh* 'mango' *qisu > *hyu* 'shark' *sacaq > *asah* 'sharpen' *sicuheq > *isuh* 'wash' *tuqas > *tuha* 'old' *tusuq > *tuhu* 'true' (< *tuqus [§E1.1.3])

This change gave rise to the phonological rule that no root could have two /h/'s. The rule that no root can have two /h/'s did not motivate the loss of the laryngeal, for in roots that have both *s and *q, it is only *s that gets lost, not *q. The sequence of events was probably as

[15] The only roots that have two *q's or two *s's are trisyllabic. They lost the *q or *s by the rules given in the 3rd and 5th ¶ of this section.

follows: *s > [h] in a stage of pre-OJv in which *q had not become [h], possibly *q had become *x. Then a root containing [h] and an *x lost the [h]. Subsequently, *x > /h/. OJv initial and medial /h/ was lost in late OJv, and there is no trace of /h/ in any NJv dialect. OJv is known only from written sources or as a dead liturgical language, and attested forms come from documents created over a period of several centuries, during which time the /h/ was lost. Many of the forms with /h/ are also attested without /h/. Some forms that have an /h/ etymologically are attested only without /h/.[16] In some cases there is evidence from the cognate in Sd or Ml that a given OJv form without /h/ must have lost an earlier /h/:[17]

> *busat$_1$ > *bwat* 'made' *busat$_2$ > *wwat* 'lift' *busat$_3$ 'perform harvest, etc. sacrifice' > *wwat* 'offering' *bukes 'hair' > *wok* 'hairy' (< *busek) *isepun > *impun* 'gathered' (cf. Ml *himpun* 'gather') *qacu > *asu* 'draw water' *quleg > 'worm' > *uler* 'caterpiler, grub' *quli 'knead' > *uli* 'trample on' *quciɣ 'chase away' > *usĩ* 'pursue' *qucuŋ > *usung* 'carry jointly' *qutek > *utek* 'brains' (cf. Ml *hutak* 'brains') *sacep 'smoke' > *asep* 'incense' *sagek > *arek* 'kiss' *sated > *ater* 'accompany, escort' (Cf. Ml *hantar* 'deliver') *sawak > *awak* 'body' *siket > *iket* 'band, tie' *sipaɣ 'other side' > *ipɛ* 'brother-, sister-in-law' *sulaɣ > *ulā* 'snake' *túsud > *tūr* 'kee'

E1.3.12 *h

*h disappeared entirely without a trace:

> *bahi + -in- > *wini* 'female' (< *winay < *winai) *betihec > *wetis* 'calif' *buhet 'squirrel' > *wūt* 'tarsier, lemur' *laheyu > *layu* 'withered' *quluh > *hulu* 'head, headwaters'

E1.3.13 *c

*c > /s/ in all positions:

> *capuh > *sapu* 'broom, wipe' *acu > *asu* 'dog' *diɣuc > *dyus* 'bathe'

E1.3.2 Voiced stops and *ɣ

*b and *d have double reflexes: one a weakened liquid and the other a voiced stop (/b,w/ and /ḍ,r/ respectively).[18] *j remained a voiced stop (/d/), and *g became weakened to

---

[16] I have only checked with Zoetmulder 1982. There are other sources for OJv attestations, and some of the forms listed here may in fact be attested with /h/ in a source other than Zoetmulder 1982.

[17] There are few examples of intervocalic *s that are reflected with /h/. Also final *-s left no trace in OJv. This is in contrast to intervocalic *q, which also became /h/. /h/ from this source tends to be attested in OJv. Cf. the 7th¶ of this section that discusses the time frame of the loss of *q and *s.

[18] The double reflex results from dialect mixture: apparently some dialects weakened the *b and *d and others did not. This is indicated by the appearance of doublets in OJv and NJv with weakened and unweakened reflexes. There may be influence from the languages with which OJv was (and NJv is) in contact, Sd and Ml, which have unweakened reflexes of these phonemes. This existence of doublets, however, cannot be attributed to borrowing from Ml or Sd for two reasons: (1) some of the forms with unweakened reflexes have no cognates in either Sd or Ml, and (2) some of the forms with unweakened reflexes show purely OJv innovations that are not shared by Sd or Ml, e.g. *ḍengö* 'hear' < *deŋeɣ, which shows the /ö/-reflex of *eɣ, not found outside OJv, but has the unweakened reflex of *d. The weakened reflexes were most likely the result of the predominant change, predominant in the sense that these were the influential changes that were spreading through the dialects. For this reason variants existed for many roots in the dialect that was the basis of the written forms in OJv.

liquid /r/ as a syllable coda or as onset of a final syllable. Otherwise (i.e., as onset to the penult or earlier or as onset to a monosyllabic root), *g remained a voiced stop. *ɣ was lost, but in some environments left traces.

E1.3.21 *b

*b > /w/and /b/ in initial and medial position. Some roots are attested with /w/ and others with /b/ and some with both /b/ and /w/. Some roots are attested with /w/ in OJv but /b/ in NJv and vice versa. In final position and when abutting on a nasal, *b > /b/

With /b/:

*basequ > *a-bo* 'smell bad' *cabuk 'belt' > *sabuk* 'sash' *qeɬeb 'shut' + *si- > *hineb* 'bring shut, door panel' *tebuk > *tumbuk* 'pound' (< *t-um-ebuk)

With /w/:

*baliw 'return to former state' > *ma-waluy* 'come back' (but NJv *bali*) *qabu > *hawu* 'ashes'

With /b/ and /w/:

*babuy > *bawi* 'pig' *baɣiyus > *bāyu/wāyu* 'wind, air' *bahi 'female' > *bi* 'wife'/*b-in-ahi > *wini* 'female'

In sporadic cases *b became [b] and then replaced by /g/ (as is also the case in NJv dialects):

*belag > *gelar* 'spread out' (also *welar* 'broadness')

E1.3.22 *d

*d > /r/ and /ḍ/ in initial and medial position. Some roots are attested with /r/ and others with /ḍ/ and some with both /r/ and /ḍ/. Some roots are attested with /r/ in OJv but /ḍ/ in NJv and vice versa:

With *r:

*danaw > *ranu* 'lake, pond' *demedem > *remrem* 'cloudy, veiled, obscure' *tuduq 'leak, drip' > *ka-turuh-an* 'be dripped on'

With *ḍ:

*dasedas > *ḍaḍa* 'chest' *deŋ 'extinguish' > *pa-ḍem* 'extinguish' *tidem 'dark' > *tiḍem* 'losing its luster, dimmed'

With both *r and *ḍ:

*deŋeɣ > *ḍengö/rengö* 'hear' *depa > *ḍepa/repa* 'fathom'

If the root developed nasalization before a medial *d, the reflex of *d is /ḍ/:

*tidec 'press flat, crush' > *tinḍes* 'trampled underfoot'

However, if a sequence *mḍ developed, the *ḍ was pulled forward to /d/ and the /m/ assimilated to the the /d/:

*kudemel > *kandel* 'thick' < (< *kamḍel < *kameḍel [§E1.1.3] < *kaḍemel [§E1.1.12])

In final position, *-d > /r/:

*tusud > *tūr* 'knee'

In one case, the final *-d was lost. There is no explanation:[19]

*cidecid > *pa-sisi* 'seashore'

In two cases, final *-d is reflected as /d/. There is no explanation:

*padud 'rasp' > *parud* 'grater' *waɣed > *odwad* 'creeper'

E1.3.23 *j

Initially and medially, *j > /d/.

*jalan > *dalan* 'road, way' *tujuq 'point' > *tuduh* 'instruction, directive'

There are some exceptions. The forms that show /j/ from *j are probably Ml borrowings or influenced by Ml:

*sijaw > *hijo* 'green' *jabat > *jawat* 'touch' *qajelay > *jaheli* 'job's tears' *tajem > *tajem* 'sharp'

The following example was probably contaminated with a root ending in *dem meaning 'close the eyes', not attested. Cf. Sd *kireum* 'close the eyes' < *kidem)

*pejem 'close eyes' > *prem* 'sleep'

In final position, *-j merged with *-d (> /-r/).

*bukij > *wukir* 'mountain' *likuj > *likuran* 'side'

There are exceptions in the case of final *-j. They evince /-t/. Two of them are unexplained[20] and a third one, *hanyut,* is clearly a Ml borrowing, as it also has an irregular medial reflex /ny/ < *ɬ:

*qaɬuj > *hanyut* 'be carried by the current' *pejepej 'pressed together'> *pepet* 'blocked off, jammed' *qubuj 'pith' > *humbut* 'shoot' (meaning uncertain [Zoetmulder 1982: 651])'

The articulation of /d/ and/ḍ/ are and probably were very similar, and there are cases of /d/ instead of /ḍ/ or doublets of wrong reflexes (cf. Wolff 1997):[21]

*daŋ 'heat near fire' > *ḍang/dang* 'cooking pot' NJv *dang* 'steam rice' *deqeɣec 'move vigorously and rapidly' > *dres* 'hurried' *jukut > *ḍukut/dukut* 'grass'

E1.3.24 *g

As onset of the penult or earlier and of monosyllabic roots, *g- > /g-/:

---

[19] Note that the Ml cognate *pesisir* 'shore' does have /-r/, the normal reflex of *-d.

[20] They could be Ml borrowings, as cognates with /-t/and with similar meanings occur in Ml.

[21] In fact, there are dialects currently in Jv, in which the contrast between /ḍ/ and /d/ has been lost. A hallmark of the Peranakan dialect in Central Java (the dialect of the creolized Chinese) is the merger of /ḍ/ and /d/. It is quite possible that there were speakers in the OJv speech community who similarly merged these two phonemes, a situation that would account for these doublets.

*gatel > *gatel* 'itchy' *gemegem 'hold in fist' > *gegem* 'hold fast' *gilaŋ 'brilliant, giving off light' > *gilang* 'shining'

The following forms reflect /k-/. They are probably borrowings, but the source is unknown:

*galih 'dig' > *kali* 'riverbed, canal' *gumic 'down, body hair' > *kumis* 'mustache'

As onset or coda of the root-final syllable, *-g-/-g > /r/:

*iseguŋ > *hirung* 'nose' *paqegu > *hamperu* 'gall' *qagan > *haran* 'name' *puceg > *puser* 'navel' *quleg > *uler* 'worm'

E1.3.25 *ɣ

*ɣ was lost, usually without a trace, but if *ɣ was the coda (either word final or internally when a following vowel was elided), it caused compensatory lengthening on the vowel preceding it:

*baqeɣuh > *wāhu* 'new' (< *baɣhu[22] < *bahɣu < *baqɣu) *baɣiyus 'storm' > *wāyu* 'wind, air' *laɣiw > *pa-layū* 'run away' (< *pa-layuɣ [§E1.1.3]) *qapuɣ > *hapū* 'lime' *qiliɣ 'flow downstream' > *hilī* 'flowing current' *ikuɣ > *ikū* 'tail' *muɣ > *ke-mū* 'rinse out mouth' *linuɣ > *lindū* 'earthquake' *ɬuɣ > *nyū* 'coconut'

Syllable-final *-eɣ > /ö/:[23]

*deŋeɣ > *rengö* 'hear'

In later OJv and NJv, the compensatory lengthening was lost. Many of the roots with *-ɣ are attested only in the later OJv or NJv shape—that is, without compensatory lengthening (or with /u/ in the case of forms with *eɣ):

*cuɣecuɣ 'follow up from behind' > *susu* 'hurry on' *dapaɣ 'be flat' > *ḍampa* 'palenquin' *layaɣ 'sail' > *laya* 'expand, stretch' *qijuɣ > *hidu* ' spittle'

In one case final *aɣ is reflected as /-ɛ/. This could well have been borrowed from one of the Sd dialects:

*sipaɣ 'other side' > *ipɛ* 'brother-, sister-in-law'

A large number of forms reflect /r/ in place of Ø. Almost all of them have Ml cognates with /r/ (the normal reflex in Ml from *ɣ). Many of them refer to flora or fauna or otherwise have the semantic character of forms that are frequently borrowed. Here are few examples:

*suluɣ 'lower slowly' > *ang-ulur* 'lower on rope' (Ml *hulur* 'drop') *sabaɣat 'strong mosoon wind' > *barat* 'strong wind' *ka-barat* 'west' (Ml *barat* 'west') *damaɣ 'light, torch' > *damar* 'lamp' (Ml *damar* 'k.o. resin') (Note /d/ is not the normal OJv reflex of

---

[22] We assume metathesis here (§E1.1.3) in order to account for the long vowel in the penult. It is not likely that the vowel of the penult would have been lengthened if the penult had had a [q] or [h] coda.

[23] It is probable that the symbol that is transcribed as *ö* is phonologically a lengthened /ə/. That means that the rule for compensatory lengthening held also for *e as well as for the other vowels. However, it is to be noted that in later OJv and NJv /ö/ does not behave in a way analogous to the other long vowels: it merges with /u/.

*d) *ka-wiɣi > *kiri/kəri* 'left' (Ml *kiri* 'left') *timuɣ 'rainy wind' > *timur* 'east' (Ml *timur* 'east')

In two cases, final *-ɣ > /-h/. In one case the form with the /-h/ varies with an allomorph that has a long final vowel. The explanation probably lies in dialect borrowing:

*buliɣ > *wulih* 'stalk' *ɬuɣ > *nyuh/nyū* 'coconut'

E1.3.3 The liquids and nasals in OJv

E1.3.31 *l and *ɬ

*l > /l/ in all environments:

*lepac > *lepas* 'free (from bonds)' *baluɬ 'rolled up, bundle' > *walun* 'cloth for wrapping' *beli > *weli* 'buy' *uleg 'worm' > *uler* 'caterpillar' *gatel > *gatel* 'itch' *tapel 'patch' > *tapel* 'closely linked, joined'

In a cluster that developed by elision of a vowel consisting of a consonant other than /h/ plus *l, the *l was lost:

*caleŋaɣ 'cook without oil' > *sangā* 'roast' (< *caŋaɣ < *caŋlaɣ) *celecel > *sesel* 'regret'[24]

*ɬ developed to [ny], [n], and [l] in Pre OJv, as in the other MP languages depending on the stress pattern of the PAn root (§A3.3.4). The [ny] became depalatalized by OJv times—i.e., fell together with the reflex /n/. Thus Pan *ɬ > /l/ and /n/ in OJv, depending on the rules given in §A3.3.4. The /l/ reflex only occurs as the onset of a penult with short vowel or earlier syllable. Otherwise, /n/ is reflected.
*ɬ > /l/:

*ɬaŋúy > *languy* 'swim' *ɬecúŋ > *lesung* 'mortar' *ɬuwáŋ 'opening' > *luwang* 'hole'

*ɬ > n:

*ɬátad 'grounds around a house' > *natar* 'grounds, surface of cloth on which a pattern is drawn' *aɬák > *anak* 'child' *cíɬaɣ 'ray of light' > *sinā* 'shine, radiate' *bulaɬ > *wulan* 'moon'

In some cases OJv attests /ny/ instead of /n/ as a reflex of *ɬ. These are cases of borrowing from Ml. NJv evinces many more cases of /ny/ instead of /n/ as the result of the uninterrupted period of contact with Ml from OJv times to the present.

*qaɬuj > *hanyut* 'carried by the current'

In some cases, the influence does not come from Ml. The source of the following form is unknown:

*ɬam 'taste' > *ki-nyam* 'taste'

---

[24] There were dialects that were not affected by this rule. A variant *celcel* 'regret' is also attested.

E1.3.32 Nasals

*m, *n, *ŋ remained unchanged in all positions.

*mata > *mata* 'eye' *lima > *lima* 'five' *gemegem 'hold in fist' > *gegem* 'hold fast' *enem > *enem* 'six' *jalan > *dalan* 'way, path' *nakis 'going up' > *pa-nɛk* 'climb' *ŋilu 'teeth on edge' > *ngelu* 'headache' *deŋeɣ > *rengö* 'hear' *iseguŋ > *hirung* 'nose'

However, OJv only allowed homorganic nasals to be the first element of a nasal + C sequence, and when syncopation or another process took place that caused a nasal cluster to develop, the nasal is assimilated to the following C:

*kudemel > *kandel* 'thick' (< *kamḍel < *kameḍel [§E1.1.3] < *kaḍemel [§E1.1.12])

The following form developed a voiced stop release after a medial nasal (as in several MP languages). This is not a normal process in OJv, and the form is secondary (although the root can be reconstructed for PAn on the basis of other languages):

*linuɣ > *lindū* 'earthquake'

In a few cases the final nasal is reflected as /m/ in place of /ng/, where the PAn etymon probably had *-ŋ. Cf. the commentary in the glossary to the following two words:

*baqeɣaŋ > *bahem* 'molar' *deŋ > *pa-ḍem* 'extinguish'

In one case *-ŋ is reflected with *-n, as in all MP languages:

*baqesiŋ > *wahin* 'sneeze'

E1.3.33 *w

*w contracted with preceding and following *e (§E1.2.21). Further, PAn diphthongs ending in *w were monophthongized in OJv—that is, *w contracted with the preceding vowel to form a monophthong (§§E1.2.51, E1.2.52). Otherwise, *w > /w/—i.e., initially and intervocalically, but not before or after *e.[25]

*waɣi > *way* 'sun' *buwaq > *wwah* 'fruit' *kiwa > *kiwa* 'left (side)' *ławáŋ 'gate' > *lawang* 'door' *quway > *hwi* 'rattan' *sáwak 'waist, torso' > *awak* 'body'

In later OJv and NJv, /wa/ monophthongized to /o/ (§E1.2.4, 2nd¶), and some forms with etymological *wa are attested only in monophthongal shape:

*qacuwal 'pry up' > *ma-sol* 'uprooted' *ɣuwaŋ > *roŋ* 'hole, depression'

In a few cases, initial *w is reflected with /ww/. The first /w/ is the reflex of a reduplicated syllable consisting of *w plus the vowel of the penult (which was subsequently lost):[26]

---

[25] I believe this to be the rule, but in fact there is no evidence for the reflexes of *w in the following environments: *awi, * uwi, *iwi, *awu, *uwu, and *iwu.

[26] Reduplication is a widely attested morpheme in An languages, where numbers and forms in a restricted list of other form-classes are reduplicated when standing as the head of a the predicate of a clause. When the syntactic category that was marked by the morphological process of reduplication became bleached in pre-OJv, the reduplicated form of a few words became generalized everywhere, replacing the unreduplicated forms (which formerly had been confined to attributive position).

*walu > *wwalu* 'eight' (< *wawalu) *wada > *wwada* 'there is' (< *wawada) *wasiyeɣ > *wway* 'water' (< *way [§E1.2.1] < *wai [§E1.1.13, 2nd ¶] < *wai̯ [§§E1.2.21, E1.3.25] < *waiyeɣ)

The forms *kānan* 'right' (< *ka-wanał) and *kεri/kiri* 'left' (< *ka-wiɣi) show loss of *w. Neither of these two forms is directly inherited.

E1.3.34 *y

*y is attested only in diphthongs and intervocalically after *i and in the sequences *aya, *ayu and *uyu:

*liya > *lya-n* 'be different' *baɣiyus 'storm' > *wāyu* 'wind, air' *qayam 'pet' > *hayam* 'chicken, cock' *laheyu > *layu* 'withered' *qayuyu 'k.o. crab' > *hayuyu* 'crab'

For *y in diphthongs see §E1.2.51.

CHAPTER TWO
Toba Batak

E2.0 Background

The name "Batak" is given to seven related communities, each of which has a separate language or dialect, located in north Sumatra. The seven Batak languages are close, but the differences among them are such that they are considered separate languages and are documented in separate dictionaries and grammars: Toba Batak, Mandailing, and Angkola, which are close to one another, Simalungun, Karo, Dairi-Pakpak, and Alas-Kluet. Here we treat Toba Batak (TB) but quote other Batak languages when TB fails to evince a cognate or when the other languages elucidate the history of the form by some feature that TB lacks. Although they are seven language communities, they consider themselves to be one ethnicity and have a family tree that explains how the seven Batak tribes are related to each other. They share a large portion of their traditional customs and beliefs, had similar alphabets, and produced similar types of literature.

TB was one of the three languages that Dempwolff chose to use for his basic reconstruction of PAn (Dempwolff 1934: 23). Adelaar (1981) reconstructed proto-Batak on the basis of the Batak languages excepting Alas. This reconstruction substantiates many of the rules cited here and is more fully exemplified, citing forms that are found only within Batak, as well as those that have cognates outside of Batak. Citations from TB figure in a great portion the literature dealing with the reconstruction of PAn and PMP. The other Batak languages are less thoroughly studied. Simalungun and Alas are the least documented Batak languages. The primary source for the TB citations here is the draft dictionary by Tindi Raja Manik (1987), checked against Warneck 1977 and on occasion the against H. van der Tuuk 1861.

CHART ONE. PHONEMES OF TOBA-BATAK

Consonants

Voiceless	p	t	(c)	k	
Voiced	b	d	(j)	g	
Spirants		s			h
Liquids	w	l, r	(y)		
Nasals	m	n	(ñ)	ng, [ŋ]	

Vowels and Diphthongs

high	i		u
mid	ɛ		o
low		a	

The voiceless consonants occur doubled in TB. In TB, /k/ only occurs doubled and in final position. In inherited forms in Simalungun, Angkola, and Mandailing, /k/ occurs only in clusters and in final position. In the other Batak languages, /k/ is free to occur anywhere. /c/, /j/, /y/, and /ñ/ only occur in loan words in TB. TB lacks /e/ [ə], but this phoneme is found in the other Batak languages. DPB and KB have long and short vowels. In TB, stress falls most commonly on the penult. However, it is not predictable: adjectives have end stress (probably a feature inherited from PMP and possibly from PAn), and other individual forms also have stress on the final syllable. The Batak languages have been in contact with Ml for more than a thousand years, and Ml has exerted a strong influence on them.

E2.1 Processes affecting the development of TB from PAn

E2.1.1 Syncopation of trisyllabic roots

In trisyllabic roots, contrastive PAn stress left traces in the form of syllable loss or centralization of unstressed vowels. Unstressed penults were syncopated.

E2.1.11 Loss or weakening of the antepenult

In some trisyllabic roots, the antepenult was lost or the vowel of the antepenult was centralized (and then became /o/ in TB [§E2.2.4]). The antepenult is lost if it had vowel onset or onset with *q or *s:

> *aluga > *luga* 'to paddle' *paqegu > *pogu* 'gall' (< *qapegu) *qaciɣah > *sira* 'salt' *qapucuk 'tip, top' > *pusuk* 'palm sprout' *sabaɣat > *barat* 'west' *saɣejaɬ > *redan* 'ladder' (KB) *sapegiq 'causing sharp pain > *pegih* 'unpleasant to the taste' (KB) *sehapuy > *api* 'fire' *seqaɬi > *ani* 'spin' *isepi + *-in- > *nipi* (< *sinipi < *esinipi)

The following examples show centralization of the antepenultimate vowel. It is probable that this change took place very early. It is shared in most cases by Ml, OJv, Moken, and other Hesperonesian languages, where these have cognates. In any case, the weakening of the antepenult can only have taken place before elision of *e (§E2.1.12) because antepenultimate weakening was motivated by the location of the stress on two syllables to the right (cf. §A3.5.3):

> *biɣeŋí > *borngin* 'night' *berngi* (KB) *binesíq > *boni* 'seed, semen' *baheɣát > *borat* 'heavy' *ɣábihi 'evening' > *robi* 'for a longer time' (< *ɣabihí) *pacaqáɬ > *porsan* 'carry over shoulder' (for /r/, cf. §E2.1.42) *paheɣáw > *poro* 'hoarse' (< *peheɣaw) *tineún > *tonun* 'weave' *tiqeɣáb > *terap* 'belch'

E2.1.12 Trisyllabic roots that lost the penultimate *e

A penult with *e was elided if it had *s or *q onset or was before a final syllable with *s or *q onset:

> *bakesaw 'k.o. mangrove' > *baho* 'k.o. tree' *baqeɣu > *im-baru* 'new' *basequ > *bau* 'a smell' *buɣesu > *im-buru* 'jealous' *isecí > *isi* 'contents' *iseguŋ > *igung* 'nose' *isekán > *ihan* 'fish' *isepi > *ipi* 'dream' *kasepal > *hapal* 'thick' *qaselu > *and-alu* 'pestle' *qetaq + *ma- > *ata* 'eat raw' (< *mata[1] < *maqetaq)

The same is true for penults with *e before or after an *l or *ɣ:

---

[1] *ata developed from *mata by analogy: the root was taken to be *ata and the prefix *m- after *qe had been lost.

*beɣekec > *borhos* 'bundle' *buteliɣ 'cyst' > *butir* 'mosquito bite' *leqacem > *asom* 'sour' (< *aslem < *qalsem < *qalecem) *qaɣicam > *arsam* 'reed-like fern' (< *qaɣecam[2])

*i before *y and *u before *u in the penult of trisyllabics were also elided:

*dasuwen > *daon* 'leaf' (< *dawen < *daswen) *peniyu > *ponu* 'sea tortoise' *taquweɬ > *taon* 'year' (< *tawen)

In one case, probably because the penult developed a stress, the /u/ before /w/ in the penult was not lost. (The cognates in other languages show the same development. Cf. *bánuwa in the glossary.)

*bánuwa 'land, place where there is s.t.' > *banua* 'land' (< *banúwa)

E2.1.13 Trisyllabic roots that underwent contraction of the penult and final syllables

The vowel contractions listed in §E2.1.16, below, caused trisyllabic roots to disyllabize. Here are some examples:

*betihec > *bitis* 'calf' *jaqewis > *dao* 'far' (< *jaweq < *jasiweq[3]) *deɣeqec > *doras* 'quick, rapid' *ɣabihi 'evening' > *robi* 'for a longer time'

E2.1.14 Trisyllabic roots that retained all three syllables without weakening

If the root did not have any of the phonemic sequences listed above (§§E2.1.11–E2.1.13), all three syllables were preserved, with the exception of those roots listed at the end of §E2.1.11, which underwent weakening of the antepenult.[4] Here are a few examples:

*balaŋa 'jug' > *balanga* 'iron pan' *balíga > *baliga* 'weaver's sword' *baŋkuwaŋ 'thorny pandanus' > *bakkuang* 'pandanus' *bitáquɣ > *bitangur* 'a tree: *Calophyllum inophyllum*' *buqáya > *buea* 'crocodile' *jalikan > *dalihan* 'trivet' *juɣámi > *durami* 'straw' *qabáɣa > *abara* 'shoulder' *qaɬimeqec 'invisible' > *alimos* 'visible for only an instant' *qatípa > *antipa* 'sea turtle' (Simalungun) *taɣutuŋ 'puffer fish' > *tarutung* 'durian'

Two forms do not follow the rules. These forms were borrowed or influenced by Ml:

*qaɬítu > *hantu* 'nature spirit' (KB) (Ml *hantu* 'ghost') *tiqadaw > *tindo* 'look in distance' (cf. Ml *tinjau*)

E2.1.15 Simplification of CC's

Batak tolerates CC's with few exceptions. The sequences *tl and *cl, which developed with elision of *e, were simplified (cf. examples in §E2.3.41), and other clusters consisting of *t followed by voiceless stops also were simplified (§E2.3.12). *c was lost in a cluster *cb that developed (§E2.3.24). Finally, in TB, clusters consisting of nasals followed by a voiceless stop were simplified to sequences of voiceless consonants (§E2.3.43).

---

[2] The change of *qaɣicam > *qaɣecam took place before MP times, and is unexplained. Cf. *qaɣicam in the glossary.

[3] We assume metathesis of the penult and final syllables to move the *q to final position in this form on the basis of the KB cognate *dauh* 'far', where the final /-h/ reflects *-q (§E3.2.31). This is an innovation that Batak shares with MP languages south of Luzon (including Tag).

[4] I assume that those roots that underwent weakening of the antepenult and did not have vowel or *q or *s onset had end stress in PMP or earlier and underwent this weakening as a result of the end stress (§A3.5.3). I assume that the roots cited in this section had or developed stress on the penult.

E2.1.16 Vowel contraction

Like vowels contracted to a single vowel after the loss of an intervening C:

*busuk > *ma-buk* 'drunk' *ɣabihi 'evening' > *robi* 'some time go' *pacaqáɫ > *porsan* 'carry over the shoulder' (< *pesaqaɫ) *qaɫimeqec 'invisible' > *alimos* 'showing itself only momentarily'

The sequences *ie and *ue , which developed by loss of an intervening consonant, contracted to /i/ and /u/, respectively:

*bacuheq > *basuh* 'wash' (Alas) *betihec > *bitis* 'calf' *buhet 'squirrel' > *menci but* 'k.o. squirrel' (KB) *bukes > *obuk* 'hair on head' (< *buk [§E2.1.2] < *busek)

E2.1.2 Disyllabization of monosyllabic roots

Monosyllabic roots that were inherited or those that developed in Batak by C loss and contraction of the abutting vowels tend to be disyllabized in one of the three ways that are found over the range of the An languages: (1) by doubling or reduplicating the root; (2) by stretching the nucleus to two moras or adding a pretonic *e; (3) by petrifaction of an affix. The following list gives examples of these three processes:

(1) doubling and reduplication:

*baq > *baba* 'mouth' (uncouth word) *cep > *sopsop* 'suck out' *daŋ > *dadang* 'expose to heat' *tup > *tutup* 'closed' *ket 'stick' > *marsi-hohot* 'cling, adhere to' *ketket* 'be sticky (good) in the mouth upon eating' (KB) *tusuq > *tu-tu* 'be true' (< *tuq)

(2) by addition of a pretonic *e. Roots formed this way in most cases have an intercalated nasal (§E2.1.41)

*buc > *ombus* 'blow' *bukes > *obuk* 'hair' (< *buk < *busek) *cep > *onsop* 'suck' *ɣik > *erik* 'thresh with the feet' (KB) *kal > *okkal* 'dig s.t. out' *engkal* 'dig up earth with stick or implement' (KB) *pan > *oppan* 'bait'

(2a) disyllabization by stretching the nucleus: There is only one example of this:

*ɫuɣ > *niur* 'coconut' (DPB) (< *ñuɣ)

(3) by petrifaction of an affix:

*liŋ 'turn, veer' *iling* 'turn to one side' (< *liŋ + ise- 'conveyance passive') *haling* 'be turned' (< *liŋ + ka- 'passive') *mic > *mamis* 'sweet' (< *mic + *ma- 'adjective former')

Forms that most commonly occur as enclitics or in compounds are not disyllabized:

*di > *di* 'preposition referring to location' *ci > *si* 'name marker' *buhet 'squirrel' > *menci but* 'k.o. squirrel' (KB)

In two cases, monosyllabic roots were not disyllabized. There is no clue why these were not disyllabized. Monosyllabic roots that are not clitics or parts of compounds are very rare:

*deŋ > *dom* 'extinguished' (for /m/, cf. commentary in glossary) *ɣiq > *ri* 'sword grass' *rih* (KB)

E2.1.3 Metathesis

TB evinces some of the cases of metathesis that are widespread over a wide range of languages:

*bukes > *obuk* 'hair' (< *busek) *nakis 'up' > *naɛk* 'climb' *paqegu > *pogu* 'gall' (< *qapegu)

There are a few examples of metathesis that are found in Ml and Batak:

*qaɣusuq > *oru/eru* (KB) 'the Australian pine' (< *eɣuu < *aɣuuh [§E2.1.11] < *aɣuqus)[5] *ɣínu > *ndiru* 'winnowing tray' (KB) *jaqewis > *dao* 'far' *dauh* (KB) (< *jaweq < *jasiweq)

Only two cases of metathesis unique to Batak are attested:

*laket 'viscous' > *m-alhot* 'thick, viscous' *alket* (DPB) *tusuq > *tuhu* 'true' (DPB) (< *tuqus)

E2.1.4 Intercalation of a coda in the penult

E2.1.41 Intercalation of a nasal before the onset of the final syllable

Like other MP languages, TB evinces a tendency to add a nasal to close a penult or earlier syllable that is open (§A3.7.2). (Note that TB nasals before voiceless stops became stops [§E2.3.43]). Here are a few examples of many:

*sabit 'carry in arms or in cloth around the body' > *ambit* 'carry child in arms' *tiqadaw > *tindo* 'look in distance' *cahebay > *sappɛ-sappɛ* 'cloth to hang over the shoulder' *sampɛ* 'hang' (KB) (< *sapay < *cahbay [cf. the commentary to the entry]) *pataɣ 'flat surface' > *pattar* 'shelf' *lakaq 'stride'> *lakka* 'step'

In some cases, the intercalated nasal is the remnant of a petrified affix *-um-:

*qumaq + *-um- > *umma* 'kiss' (< *qummaq < *qumemaq [§E2.2.3]) *qetut > *uttut* 'break wind' (< *umtut < *qumetut) *tukup > *tukkup* 'cover' (<*tumkup < *tumukup)[6]

E2.1.42 Intercalation of /r/ and /l/

The Batak languages sporadically insert /r/ or /l/ as a coda of the penult. I assume that these sporadic intercalations are the detritus of a morphological process akin to reduplication, similar to /-al-/ and /-ag-/ (< *aɣ) intercalation found in many of the MP languages and even in some of the Formosan languages. No semantic pattern can be associated with the /r/ or /l/ intercalation in Batak, and it is sometimes the case that only one language evinces the intercalation and that other Batak languages reflect the root without the intercalation:

*bitak > *biltak* 'crack, split' *cedu 'hiccough' > *seldu* 'exhale with a grunt' (KB) *pagay > *palge* 'special rice' *page* 'rice in field' (KB) *upak > *ulpak* 'beat, hit, chop' *ceɬeb 'immerse' > *sornop* 'extend into the water' *ceŋ 'stop up' > *m-orsong-orsong* 'wheeze' *cimpaŋ > *sirpang* 'sidetrack' *simpang* (KB) *daket 'adhere' > *darket* 'be parasitic on' (DPB) *pacaqaɬ > *porsan* 'carry over shoulder' *persan* (KB)

---

[5] The KB form is unequivocal in showing that the Batak reflex underwent metathesis, for KB reflects final *-q with /-h/ (§2.3.21). In other words the KB reflex *eru* remounts to a form with final vowel in pre-Batak.

[6] In cases of forms with /u/ in the penult which originate from a protoform with *u in the penult, it is difficult to know whether the nasal coda of the penult arose from *-um- or was the result of sporadic nasalization. If the meaning of the root is consistent with the meaning that *-um- is thought to impart, we take it for granted that the nasal intercalation arose from *-um-. That is the case of *tukkup* 'cover' and also of *ukkap* 'open'and *lukkas* 'stand open'.

E2.2.0 Vowels and diphthongs

The PAn vowels were stable in TB. Except for the effects of stress and contraction, *i, *a, *u remained unchanged from PAn. *e became /o/ in TB and Simalungun but remained unchanged in the other Batak languages.

E2.2.1 *i

*i > /i/ except in the few forms where it was lost by syncope (§E2.1.12):

*bígaq 'k.o. giant taro' > *bira* 'an arum' *baliga > *baliga* 'weaver's sword' *beli 'buy' > *boli* 'bride price' *duɣi > *duri* 'thorn'

When *i came to abut on *e as a result of loss of an intervening C, *i was lowered to /ɛ/. Further *i after *a is sporadically lowered to /ɛ/:

*iseq > *ɛo* 'urine' *juɣami > *duramɛ* 'rice straw' *nakis > *naɛk* 'rise, climb' *paqit > *paɛt* 'bitter' (also *pait*)[7] *paŋi > *pangɛ* 'a tree and its fruit: *Pangium edule*' (also *pangi* [DPB]) *paɣis > *parɛ* 'stingray' *pari* (KB)

*i is sporadically lowered to /ɛ/ in a few other unexplained cases:

*cigi 'winnow' > *sɛgɛ* 'clean rice' *qitik > *ɛtɛk* 'small' *situŋ > *ɛtong* 'count'

In one case, *i is reflected by /u/. This is a purely TB development. Other Batak languages show /i/ in this form:

*bituka > *butuha* 'intestines' *bituka* (KB)

E2.2.2 *a

*a > /a/ in all positions except where weakened in trisyllabic roots (§E2.1.11):

*ałak > *anak* 'offspring' *-an > *-an* 'locative passive ending' *sacaq > *asa* 'whet'

E2.2.3 *u

*u > /u/ in all positions.

*aku > *aku* 'I' *bubu > *bubu* 'fish trap with spikes' *banuwa > *banua* 'land' *buqaya > *buea* 'crocodile' *qisu > *iu* 'shark'

In trisyllables, unstressed penultimate *u > *e:

*qumáq + *-um- > *umma* 'kiss' (< *qummaq < *qumemaq < *qumumaq) *ema* (KB) (< *qumemaq, with loss of the antepenult [§E2.1.11] < *qumumaq) *pupul < *ta-pul* 'plucked (feathers)' (< tappel [simplification of cluster unexplained] < *tapepul < *ta-pupul)

In two forms, *u is reflected by /o/. The /o/ probably arose by contamination, but the source is unknown:

*ɣabun 'fog, mist' > *rambon* 'unclear' *rabun* 'unclear' (DPB) *tusud > *tot* 'knee'

Two other forms that reflect /o/ < *u probably were influenced by Ml:

*guci > *gosi* 'gums' (Ml *gusi*) *gucuk 'rub' > *gosok* 'polish' (Ml *gosok* 'rub')

---

[7] Failure to lower *i is probably due to Ml influence.

E2.2.4 *e

Except when lost by elision (§E2.1.12), *e > /o/ in TB and Simalungun:

*beɣekec > *borhos* 'bundle' *celecel 'regret' > *solsol* 'repent' *keɣet > *horot* 'cut a piece off' *quneg > *unok* 'pith'

In other Batak languages, *e > /e/ ([ə]).[8] Here are a few KB examples:

*dem > *endem* 'overcast' *ket > *ketket* 'stick' *pec > *pespes* 'squeeze'

Word-final *-es > /-a/:

*buɣes > *gam-bura* 'foam at a waterfall' *liceqes > *lisa* 'louse egg' *tumes 'clothes louse' > *si-tuma* 'dragon-fly larva'

In initial position, *we > /u/; otherwise, *we and *ew > /o/ in TB, Simalungun, and DPB (but /u/ in the other Batak languages):

*weliq 'repeat' > *m-uli* 'return home' *dasuwen > *daon* 'leaf' *jaqewis > *dao* 'far' *daoh* (DPB and Simalungun) *dauh* (KB) (< *jaweq < *jasiweq) *qawec > *aos* 'used up' *taquweɫ > *taon* 'year'

There is some evidence that *e > /ɛ/ before a following syllable with /ɛ/ in TB, but not in KB, DPB, and Simalungun:

*beɣay > *berɛ* 'give' (KB and DPB) *borei* (Simalungun) *semay > *ɛmɛ* 'rice in husk' *omɛ* (Simalungun)

In two cases, *e > /i/ by contamination with a root with *i of similar meaning:

*beɫaɣ 'flash of light' > *binar* 'radiance' (DPB) 'sparks' (KB) (cf. TB *sindar* 'ray of light') *kedep > *hidop* 'wink, blink' (cf. Ml *kilap* 'twinkling of an eye')

In two cases, *e > /a/ under the influence of Ml:

*deɣeqec 'move vigorously' > *doras* 'quick' (Ml *deras* 'quick') *cekecek 'stuffed full' > *sosak* 'cramped' (Ml *sesak* 'stuffed full')

In the following case, *e was elided:

*qetut > *uttut* 'flatulence' (< *umtut < *um-etut)

E2.2.5 The diphthongs

Inherited diphthongs were monophthongized except in Simalungun.

E2.2.51 *ay

*ay > /ɛ/:

*matay > *matɛ* 'die' *qatay > *atɛ-atɛ* 'liver'

*ay in the penult also became /ɛ/ when the following syllable was /a/—i.e., *aya > /ɛa/:

*buqaya > *buɛa* 'crocodile' *ɣaya > *rɛa* 'large *layaŋ 'fly' > *lɛang-lɛang* 'swallow, kite' *layaɣ > *rɛar* 'sail' *paya > *pɛa* 'swamp' *qayam 'kept animal' > *m-ɛam* 'toy'

In TB, *ay in the penult before other vowels > /a/ (cf. §E2.3.52):

---

[8] The development of *e in the various Batak languages is more complex than that summarized here. Cf Adelaar: 1981, §7.2.4.

*bayaw > *bao* 'brother-, sister-in-law' *sayun 'shake' > *mang-aun* 'swing, rock'

E2.2.52 *aw

*aw > /o/:

*buɣaw > *buro* 'chase birds away from rice' *danaw > *dano* 'lake' *paheɣáw > *poro* 'hoarse' *takaw > *takko* 'thievery'

E2.2.53 *uy and *iw

*uy, *iw > /i/. However, in Simalungun *uy is reflected as /uy/:

*bábuy > *babi* 'pig' *babuy* (Simalungun) *sehapúy > *api* 'fire' *baɣiw 'spoiled staple' > *bari* 'bad tasting (e.g. rice)'

In the case of *kasiw, after the loss of *s, syllabicity changed, as happened in most MP languages outside of the Philippines. Further, *i > *y, which was subsequently lost in TB, and *w > /u/—i.e., *kasiw > *kaiw > *kayu*[9] > *hau* 'tree wood'

E2.3 Consonants

TB reflects the PAn consonants faithfully, in that only a limited number of phonemic mergers and splits occurred, as detailed in the following subsections. The following chart summarizes the TB reflexes of the PAn consonants:

CHART TWO. DEVELOPMENT OF THE TOBA-BATAK CONSONANTS FROM PAN

PAn	TB	PAn	TB
p	*p*	l	*l*
t	*t*	ɬ	*l, n*
k	*h, -k*	m	*m*
q, s, h	*Ø*	n	*n*
c	*s*	ŋ	*ng*
b	*b, -p*	w	*u-, Ø*
d, j	*d, -t*	y	*Ø*
g	*h-,-g-, -k*	mp, nt	*pp, tt*
ɣ	*r*	ŋk	*kk*

E2.3.1 Voiceless consonants

The voiceless stops are reflected unchanged, with the exception that initial and medial *k > /h/ in TB, Mandailing, Angkola, and Simalungun (but not in the other Batak languages). In nasal clusters, the voiceless stops are doubled in TB (cf. the examples in §E2.3.4).

E2.3.11 *p

*p > /p/ in all positions:

*pakan > *pahan* 'feed' *depa > *dopa* 'fathom' *alap > *alap* 'take'

In the following case, the initial *p was substituted for by *b, as happened in all the MP languages and in Pa (cf. the commentary under *pukuh in the glossary):

*pukuh 'knot, node' > *buhu* 'knuckle, knot'

---

[9] *Kayu* is a KB form. In KB intervocalic *y was not lost (§E2.3.52).

E2.3.111 Accretion of *p and change of *p- to /m-/

Occasionally /p-/ is accreted to a root beginning with a vowel by an analogy involving the verbal conjugation. A prefix /m-/ formed verbs from roots beginning with a vowel and also from roots beginning with a /p-/ with the /p-/ lost (§A3.7.1). Thus, a verb beginning with /m-/ may have been added to a root either with an initial V or with an initial /p-/. In some cases, /p-/ has been added to a V-initial root by analogy:

*udesi 'last' > *pudi* 'behind, after'

E2.3.12 *t

*t >/t/ in all positions:

*tujuq 'point' > *tudu* 'show' *batu > *batu* 'stone' *baɣat > *barat* 'athwart'

*t- was lost when it came to abut on a voiceless consonant:[10]

*keteket > *marsi-hohot* 'stick, adhere' *paɣatepat 'tree of the mangrove swamps' > *parapat* 'k.o. bamboo' (< *paɣatpat)

In one case, *t > /s/ by contamination with an unknown word:

*tiŋadaq > *pasingada* 'with head back and face upward'

E2.3.13 *k

*k > /h/ initially and medially in TB, Mandailing, Angkola, and Simalungun. In the other Batak languages, it remained /k/.

*bituka > *bituka* 'intestines'(KB) *bituha* (Simalungun) *beɣekec > *borhos* 'bundle' *buka > *buhá* 'opened' *buka* (DPB) *cíku > *sihu* 'elbow' *kawil > *hail* 'fishhook'

Final *-k became /-k/:

*ałák > *anak* 'son, daughter'

*h (< *k) was lost after /h/ to the left, except in the case of reduplicated or doubled monosyllables—i.e., *k–*k > /k–Ø/:

*kakay 'foot, leg' > *haɛ-haɛ* 'thigh of slaughtered animal' *ket 'stick' < *marihohot* 'cling, adhere' (< *mariketket)

E2.3.2 *q, *s, *h, *c

E2.3.21 *q

*q was lost without a trace in TB. In KB, *q > /h/ finally and between like vowels in disyllabic roots, but otherwise was lost. In DPB and Alas, *q > /h/ initially, finally, and between like vowels:

*baɣeq > *baro* 'abscess' *bareh* (KB) *daqan > *dahan* 'branch' (KB) *qabu > *habu* (Alas) 'ashes' *abu* (KB) *diper-habu-arang* 'burn to ashes' (DPB) *sacaq > *asa* 'whet' *asah* (KB)

Between unlike vowels *q is lost in all Batak languages:

---

[10] A sequence *tC that developed in TB was simplified to /C/, but in the other Batak languages it was not simplified:

*ket > *ketket* 'sticky (in mouth,of some fruits)' (KB)

*baqaya > *buea* 'crocodile' *buaya* (KB) 'crocodile' *tuqas > *tua* 'old' (KB and TB) *tue* (Alas)

There are cases in which initial *q- is reflected with /h-/ in TB. At least two of these forms are borrowings from Ml:

*qaɬitu > *hantu* 'nature spirit' (Ml *hantu* 'ghost') *qepa 'hull' > *hopa-hopa* 'pulp, what is left after juice is expressed'[11] (Ml *hempa* 'grain that has nothing in it')

In other cases, there is no clear explanation for the initial *h-. These words may have been borrowed from DPB or Alas, which reflect *q- with /h-/:

*qeteŋ 'barrier' > *henteng* 'lie athwart' (KB) *qaɬiɣuwan > *harinuan* 'k.o. wild bee' (< *qaɣiɬúan) *qaɬiŋu > *halinu* 'shadow' (/n/ also unexplained) *qapuɣ > *hapur* 'lime'

E2.3.22 *s

*s disappeared entirely without a trace:

*suɣac 'wash' > *uras* 'cleanse by sprinkling' *qisu > *iu* 'shark' *tusuq > *tu-tu* 'be true' *piɣas > *pira* 'roe'

In one case, *s is reflected with /h/. This word was borrowed from Ml:

*tasaɬ 'remain' > *tahan* 'stand, bear s.t.' (Ml *tahan*)

In one case, *s is reflected by /s-/. There probably was contamination with a form that has not been identified:

*siɣup > *sirup* 'slurp' (Alas: *hirup* [Possibly, /h-/ developed under Ml influence.])

E2.3.23 *h

*h was lost. The only trace is the weakening of the antepenult in the reflexes of PAn trisyllabic roots with penults or final syllables with *h-onset (which was later lost):

*baɣehat > *borat* 'heavy' (< *beɣehat) *paheɣaw > *poro* 'hoarse' (< *peheɣaw) *lahuj 'seaward' > *laut* 'high seas' *qaciɣah > *sira* 'salt' *qumah > *uma* 'dry field'

E2.3.24 *c

*c > /s/ in all positions:

*cuŋu > *sungu* 'horn' *liceqes > *lisa* 'nit' *qapucuk 'tip, top' > *pusuk* 'palm sprout' *qaciɣah > *sira* 'salt' *taŋic > *tangis* 'cry'

The process of nasalization causes a morphophonemic alternation between /s/ and /n/ (< *ɬ [§§A3.7.1, E2.3.42]). *c- is reflected with /n/ in at least one case, where the nasalized form has been generalized:

*cilaw 'glare' > *nilo* 'glitter'

*c was lost after a cluster *cb developed:

*bucebuc 'pour out > *bubus* 'leak, allow water through'

---

[11] There has been semantic and formal contamination with *sopa-sopa* 'rest of betel nut that is spit out, residue'.

E2.3.3 The voiced consonants

E2.3.31 The voiced stops

The voiced stops remained voiced in initial and medial positions. In syllable-final position, they were devoiced in TB. In KB, the final voiced stops were replaced by nasals.The reflex of *g- is not clear. Some forms evince /g-/, but they may be borrowed from Ml. Three others show /k-/ (or /h-/ in TB). The following subsections provide the details.

E2.3.311 *b

*b > /b-/, /-b-/, and /-p/ (/-m/ in KB):

*batú < *batu* 'stone' *beli 'buy' > *boli* 'bride price' *bubu > *bubu* 'fish trap' *kubekub > *huphup* 'covered over' *lakeb 'cover over in a cupping way' > *langkem* 'lie on stomach' (KB) *luhab 'boil over' > *luam* 'bubble up violently' (KB) *tebu > *tobu* 'sugar cane' *tiqeɣab > *tɛrap* 'belch' *kab + *um- 'open by removing covering' > *ukkap* 'opened' (< *um-kab)

In one case, *b- is reflected by *g-. There is no explanation except that /b/ is sporadically replaced by /g/ in Hesperonesian languages.

*baɣah > *gara* 'glowing coal'

E2.3.312 *d, *j

*d and *j merged to become /d/ initially and medially, and /-t/ in final position (/-n/ in KB[12]). First, examples of *d:

*dakep 'catch' > *dahop* 'embrace' *depa > *dopa* 'fathom in length' *dusa > *dua* 'two' *wadaŋ 'clavicle' > *haliadang* 'collarbone' *tusud > *tot* 'knee' (/o/ not explained) *waɣed > *uaren* 'vine' (KB)

There are a few forms that show /r/ reflexes of roots reconstructed with *d. These forms are borrowed from Ml or influenced by the Ml cognate:

*caduŋ > *sarung* 'sheathe' (Ml *sarung*) *cuduŋ 'push forwards' > *surung* 'strong forceful' (Ml *sorong* 'push forwards') *kid > *hihir* 'file, rasp' (Ml *kikir*)

Examples of *j:

*jalan > *dalan* 'way' *qujał > *udan* 'rain' *tukej > *tukkot* 'stick for support'

A fair number of forms reflect /j/ from *j. These forms are borrowed or influenced by Ml. Here is a partial list:

*jak > *injak* 'step on' (Ml *injak*) *jaqet > *jat/jahat* 'bad' (Ml *jahat*) *sujuŋ > *ujung* 'end, extreminty' (Ml *hujung*)

E2.3.313 *g

It is not entirely clear how *g developed in root-initial position and as onset to the penult or earlier. /g-/ is reflected in a few forms, but these forms were most likely borrowed from or influenced by Ml, and in some, the vocalism clearly indicates that the form must be a Ml borrowing:

---

[12] I have found no attestations of reflexes of root-final *-j in KB.

*gatel > *gatal* 'itch' (Ml *gatal*) *gemegem 'hold in fist' > *gomgom* 'rule over' (cf. *hokkom,* next ¶) *gila > *gila* 'excited' (Ml *gila* 'crazy') *guci > *gosi* 'gums' (Ml *gusi*) *gucuk 'rub' > *gusuk* 'polish' (Ml *gosok* 'rub') *gusam > *guam* 'thrush' (Ml *guam*)

In a smaller number of cases, initial *g is reflected with /h-/ (/k-/ in KB and other Batak languages). These are probably the inherited forms:

*galih > *hali* 'dig' *gemel 'squeze in the hand' > *homol* 'keep for o.s. and refuse to share' *gemgem > *hokkom* 'cover the mouth' *kemkem* 'cover a flat surface with the hand' (KB)

Medially *-g- remained /g/:

*baliga > *baliga* 'weaver's sword' *isegung > *igung* 'nose' *paqegu > *pogu* 'gall'

*-g- was lost in TB in the following form,[13] but in KB it was not lost:

*kuga 'how' > *marhua* 'how, why' *kuga* 'how' (KB)

In final position, *-g > /-k/. In KB, *-g was nasalized, as is the case of the other final voiced consonants—i.e., *-g > /-ng/:

*belag 'spread out' > *bolak* 'be broad, wide' (KB *belang*) *laleg > *lanok* 'a fly' (KB *laneng* 'the blue fly') *quneg > *unok* 'pith, core'

E2.3.32 *ɣ

*ɣ > /r/ (/ɣ / in Alas) in all positions. There are practically no exceptions:

*ɣaya > *rɛa* 'large' *ɣumaq > *ruma* 'house' *buɣaw > *buro* 'chase away (birds from rice plants)' *taɣutuŋ 'puffer fish' > *tarutung* 'durian' *ikuɣ > *ihur* 'tail'

The following word is borrowed from Ml:

*wasiyeɣ > *aɛk* 'water'

E2.3.4 The liquids and nasals

E2.3.41 *l

For the most part, *l is reflected in all environments as /l/:

*lima > lima 'five' *alap > alap 'take' *kawil > hail 'fishhook'

In TB, *l assimilated to /r/ before a /r/ to the right. This change did not affect the other Batak dialects:

*caluɣ 'watercourse' > *sarur* 'diarrhea' *saluɣ* 'watercourse' (Alas) *layaɣ > *rɛar* 'sail' *layar* (KB)

In one case *l > /n/. There is no explanation:

*laleg > *lanok* 'a fly' *laneng* 'the blue fly' (KB)[14]

---

[13] The loss of *-g- in TB may be under the influence of *kuwas, which comes to mean 'thus, how' in some languages, e.g., OJv *kwa* 'thus, like this' Mlg *a-hoana* 'how?' Bugis *kua* 'thus, like'

[14] This is not a case of dissimilation. *l in the same environment in other forms remained /l/. Here are three examples:

*lilit > *lilit* 'twine, wind around' *luluŧ > *lulún* 'rolled up' *kiŧalá > *hilala* 'feel' (< *kilala)

In another form, *l is reflected with /r/. This form has other irregularities and is not inherited, although its source has not been identified:

*laŋaw 'a fly' > *rorongoan* 'full of flies' (*rongo* 'bother one')

*l was lost when a sequence *cl or *tl developed:

*buteliɣ 'cyst' > *butir* 'mosquito bite' *leqacem > *asom* 'sour' (< *qaclem < *qacelem < *qalecem)

There is some evidence that when a nasal coda developed before a final syllable beginning with /l/, the nasal assimilated to the following /l/. I assume that the following form developed from an intercalated nasal (§E22.1.41):

*cilak 'shine' > *sillak* 'be bright'

E2.3.42 *ɬ

*ɬ underwent the developments described for PMP in §A3.3.4. Namely, *ɬ became /l/ when onset of a penult or earlier syllable with a short-vowel nucleus; *ɬ became *ñ before a long vowel and in monosyllabic roots and when onset of the root-final syllable after a long vowel. Subsequently, *ñ was depalatalized (> /n/). *ɬ > /n/ when onset of the final syllable after a short vowel and in word-final position.

*ɬ > /l/:

*ɬecúŋ > *losung* 'mortar' *ɬekét > *lohot* 'stick' *qaɬimátek > *alimantek* 'leech' (KB)

*ɬ > /n/ (< †ñ):

*ɬála> *nala* 'flame *qáɬay > *anɛ-anɛ* 'termite' (KB)

*ɬ > /n/:

*aɬák > *anak* 'son, daughter' *qujaɬ 'rain > *udan* 'rain'

In one case (not reflected in TB), †ñ became /ni/ in the process of disyllabization of a monosyllabic root (§E2.1.2) before depalatalization took place:

*ɬuɣ > *niur* 'coconut' (< *ñuɣ) (DPB), *niwer* (Alas)

In the following case, we assume a shift of the stress to the penult to account for the reflex /n/ of *ɬ:

*qaɬiɣuwán > *harinuan* (< *qaɣiɬúwan [§E2.1.3])

E2.3.43 Nasals

*m, *n, and *ŋ are reflected with /m/, /n/, and /ng/, respectively:

*manuk > *manuk* 'chicken *ɣumaq > *ruma* 'house' *enem > *onom* 'six' *naɬáq > *nanah* 'pus' *pan > *oppan* 'bait' *ŋaŋa > *ngangang* 'wide open, gaping' (/-ng/ unexplained) *nganga* (KB) *bubuŋ 'ridgepole' > *bubung* 'ridge of roof'

*deŋ is reflected as *dom* 'extinguish' with unexpected /-m/. This is most likely is due to contamination with the root *dem 'dark'. This innovation is shared by many of the languages of Sumatra and Java, as well as Moken. It probably spread secondarily.

There are a few examples in the Batak languages in which *nV developed an epenthetic /d/. This change is sporadic.

*qanilaw 'a tree name' > *andilo* 'k.o. tree' *igan+ *an- > *andigan* 'when (future)' *ɣinu > *ndiru* 'winnowing tray' (< *niru < *rinu) (KB)

In TB (but not in the other Batak languages) nasals followed by voiceless stops were assimilated to the stop and became voiceless stops:

*buŋkaɣ > *bukkar* 'take apart'*cahebay > *sappɛ-sappɛ* 'cloth to hang over the shoulder' (KB: *sampɛ* 'hang') (< *sapay < *cahbay) *gemegem > *hokkom* 'cover mouth with hand' (KB: *kemkem* 'cover flat surface with hand') *pataɣ 'flat area' > *pattar* 'shelf' *qetut > *uttut* 'flatulence' (< *umtut < *qetut + *-um-) *sapaɣ 'spread out' > *appar-an* 'k.o. broad mat' (< *sampaɣan)

E2.3.51 *w

Initially,*w- > Ø in TB and most of the Batak languages, and /u-/ or /w-/ in KB and Alas:

*wada > *ada* in *so ada* 'there is none' *waɣi 'day' > *ari* 'day, weather' KB *uari* 'day, daytime' *waɣed > *uaren* 'vine' (KB)

Intervocalically, *w > Ø in TB, but /w/ between two like vowels in KB and other Batak languages:

*sawak 'waist' > *ak* 'small of the back' *awak* (KB) *tawa > *ta-tá* 'laugh' *ter-tawa* (DPB) *tawa* (Simalungun) *tawe* (Alas)

The word for 'eight' is an exception in TB:

*walu > *ualu* 'eight'

There are two possible explanations for the initial /u/: (1) the word derives from the reduplicated variant, found in many languages—i.e., *wawalu > *wewalu (§E2.1.11) > *uwalu* (§E2.2.4); or (2) it is borrowed from KB, which reflects *w- with /u/.
For *we and *ew, cf. §E2.2.4.

E2.3.52 *y

*y was lost except after *a, except that in Simalungun, final *uy is reflected as /uy/ (§E2.2.53). In TB, *y between two *a's contracted with the first *a to become /ɛ/. (Cf. the examples in §E2.2.51.) Otherwise, after *a before any vowel other than *a, *y was lost entirely in TB but was retained in other dialects:

*bayaw 'brother- or sister-in-law'> *bao* 'the wife of the wife's brother, or the husband of the husband's sister, or a woman's son-in-law' *bayo* (Mandailing, DPB)

/y/ in loan words from Ml is sometimes retained and sometimes lost, probably depending on the age of the loan:

*dayuŋ > *dayung* 'rudder' (Ml *dayung*) *payuŋ > *paung* 'umbrella' (Ml *payung*)

CHAPTER THREE
Moken

E3.0 Moken

Moken is the name given to a group of diverse dialects or closely related languages that are spoken on the islands in the Andaman Sea off the west coast of Thailand and lower Burma, from Phuket northwards to the northernmost island in the Mergui Archipelago. Moklen is the name given to dialects of the same language spoken in several villages in Phanga province in the southwest of Thailand. The Moken have traditionally been nomadic groups, domiciled in houseboats called *kabang* (< PAn *qabaŋ 'boat'). They survived by hunting and gathering and supplemented this by agriculture and fishing.[1] The Moklen are agriculturists. It is believed that they, like the Moken, formerly resided in boats and lived primarily by hunting and gathering and only came to live on the land in the nineteenth century, but the historical research to demonstrate this has not been done (Larish 1999:83). In the last half-century or so, many of the Moken also established themselves on land and settled in villages by the sea, but these people continue to make their living by hunting, gathering, and fishing, and to a minor extent agriculture. There still are communities that continue the traditional nomadic way of life, using their *kabang* their primary residence. The dialect of the Moklen is phonologically less conservative than Moken. In this study we will discuss only Moken developments. We quote Moklen forms only to shed light on the Moken attestations or where there are no Moken attestations. Our sources for citations are field data collected in 2004[2] at Rawai, Pukhet Island, Thailand, and forms found in the published sources listed in the bibliography. Because the data are spotty and attestations come from different dialects, we list the source where a cited form was not attested in our Rawai data.

The village of Rawai itself has been inhabited by Moken for some fifty years.[3] It is shared with the Malay-speaking Urak Lawoi, but the two communities keep themselves apart. The settlers in Rawai came from throughout the areas inhabited by the Moken. The Moken in Rawai still maintain ties with nomadic communities elsewhere. Accordingly, there is a great

[1] Many of the Moken in the last couple of decades have settled in villages, and have curtailed their tradition of living entirely on their boats and moving from place to place.

[2] I visited Rawai for two weeks together with Pittayawat Pittayaporn, , who completed his PhD dissertation on the history of the Tai languages, Cornell University 2009. He performed services of inestimable value, not only dealing with the Moken speakers and in interpreting the southern Thai language of communication with our informants, but also in analyzing and translating the texts we gathered and in working through the descriptive and historical information that could be inferred from our field data.

[3] Rawai was wiped out by the Tsunami of 2004, a few months after our visit. I have no information as to how many of the original Moken residents returned, whether they were able to resettle on their prime-waterfront property, and whether our informants survived the Tsunami.

deal of speech variation in the village. Much of the data we recorded came from people whose speech was clearly colored by the dialect of the area from which they originated. Not much is known about the origin of the Moken and the genetic connections between Moken and other Hesperonesian languages. In fact, aside from having made the Malayo-Polynesian innovations (§A1.1.32), there are few innovations outside of lexical innovations that connect Moken with any one Hesperonesian language. The only information regarding influence that the Moken language had on other languages that can be inferred from publications is the Mon loan word *kbang* 'boat', which, because of the /k/ initial (§E3.3.13), must originate in Moken.

Interestingly enough, Moken is moving toward the sesquisyllabic and monosyllabic canonical root form that characterizes the mainland Kra-Dai and Austroasiatic languages, as well as Cham (cf. Pittayaporn 2005). However, Moken has not advanced as far as any of these mainland languages along the road to sesquisyllabicity or monosyllabicity. Further, the monosyllabic roots that developed from inherited forms are very much in the minority. Moken roots may have one or two syllables, but no more. The disyllabic roots have a strong stress at the end of the word, as have many An languages across the entire An area. However, Moken has features that indicate a movement toward sesquisyllabicity, absent in other An language that also developed a disyllabic root structure with a strong end accent. Namely, (1) Moken has no roots of more than two syllables. Also (2) Moken developed long vowels in the second syllable—i.e., contrast between long and short developed in the Moken final root syllable, but the first syllable does not have such a contrast. Further, (3) the number of vowels that occur in the penult is smaller than the number of contrasts in the final syllable. Finally, (4) in colloquial speech the penult may be dropped altogether (Chantanakomes 1980: 10). The penult of the root will be called the MINOR SYLLABLE in this chapter.[4] The final syllable or the single syllable of a root will be called the MAJOR SYLLABLE.

CHART ONE. PHONEMES OF MOKEN

Consonants

voiceless stops	p	t	c	k	[ʔ]
voiceless aspirates	p^h	t^h	c^h	k^h	
voiced stops	b	d	j	g	
spirants		s			h
nasals	m	n	ñ	ng [ŋ]	
glides and laterals	w	l	y		

Vowels

high	i, ī		u, ū
non-high	e, ē	ə	o, ō
with off-glide	$\text{i}^{ə}$		$\text{u}^{ə}$
low-mid	ɛ, ɛ̄	a, ā	ɔ, ɔ̄
diphthongs	ew	aw, ay	uy, oy

The glottal stop [ʔ] is not contrastive. It is inserted automatically as syllable onset at the beginning of roots that have no consonant onset, medially between two abutting vowels, and at the end of a root that has no other consonant coda. All the vowels and diphthongs except /ə/ occur in the major (root-final) syllable. The minor syllable (the penult) may contain /ə/ or /i/, /ɛ/, /a/, /ɔ/, or /u/. The 'non-high' vowels, the long vowels, the off-glides, and the diphthongs do not occur in the minor syllable. A consonant may close the major syllable, but

[4] The minor syllable in Moken is not the same as what has been termed "minor syllable" in Mon-Khmer studies, for in Moken, several contrasting vowels may occur in the minor syllable, whereas in Mon-Khmer languages, there are no vowel contrasts in the minor syllable—i.e., only one vowel /ə/ occurs.

the minor syllable has no coda, except that possibly a handful of loan words that are names of places, are pronounced with a penultimate nasal coda.

E3.1 Changes that characterize Moken in general

E3.1.1 Weakening or loss of the antepenult trisyllabic roots

In a large number of PAn trisyllabic roots, the antepenult was weakened with the vowel nucleus lost or reduced to /ə/. A CC that resulted was simplified by the rules given in §§E3.1.16ff. In the other trisyllabic roots—i.e., those that did not weaken or lose the antepenult, the penult was lost with resultant simplification of CC's.[5] No trisyllabic roots remained in Moken.

E3.1.11 If the PAn stress[6] was on the penult, the antepenult was weakened or lost in Moken:

*buqáya > *kaya* 'crocodile' *sabáɣat > *balāt* 'west wind' *qapúcuk > *pɔcɔk* 'shoot (of plant)' *sináwa 'breath' > *ñawa* 'soul, spirit' (< *niawa < *nisawa) *taŋíla > *tɛngāʔ* 'ear' (< *tíŋa < *tlínga < *talíŋa [§E3.1.3])

E3.1.12 If the PAn stress was on the antepenult, the penult was weakened in Moken:[7]

*búɣesu > *mɔloy* 'jelous' *dásuwen > *daʔon* 'leaf' *dápuɣ + -an > *dapan* 'fireplace' (< *dápɣan)[8] *íceŋet > *eŋat* 'stinger' *qáselu > *kaʔɔy* 'pestle' *qáɬitu > *katoy* 'dangerous spirit'

In the following case, the penult was not lost and the final syllable lost sonority—i.e., *u > /w/. This was because *g was lost between *e and *u (§E3.3.34) and the resulting vowel sequence diphthongized to /aw/:

*páqegu > *kapaw* 'gall' (< *qapew < *qapeu < *qapegu)

E3.1.13 If the PAn stress was on the final syllable, the antepenult was weakened or lost:

*baliyán > *bəlɛn* 'shaman' *beɣecáy > *bɔcay* 'paddle' *biɣeŋí > *bəŋay* 'night' (< *beɣŋi < *beɣeŋi) *ɣuqaɬáy > *kanay* 'man, boy' *pacaqáɬ > *makʰān* 'carry over shoulder' (< *macqan < *pacqan) *qajeláy > *jəlay* 'job's tears' *qitelúɣ > *kəlūn* 'egg' (< *qetluɣ < *qeteluɣ) *sehapúy > *ʔapuy* 'fire'

---

[5] A cluster *ny, that developed, did not simplify. It became /ñ/.

*miniyak > *məñāt* 'oil' *sinawa > *ñawa/ñawā* 'soul, spirit' (< *nyawa < *niawa < *nisawa [§E3.1.3])

[6] In some forms where Moken weakened the antepenult, the evidence for reconstructing stress has not turned up from other An languages. In those cases, Moken does not provide evidence, for weakening of the PAn antepenult in Moken may reflect either penultimate or final stress.

[7] The word for 'star' is an unexplained exception: the final syllable rather than the penult was lost:

*bítuqen > *bituᵊk* 'star' (< bituqn)

Further, in the following cases, we assume a shift of stress to the final syllable in pre-Moken to explain the loss of the antepenult. In the case of *báqeɣu/*baqeɣú, languages of Sulawesi, eastern Indonesia, and Oceania also reflect final stress:

*báqeɣu > *kəloy* 'new' (< *baqeɣú) *túqelaɬ > *kəlān* 'bone' (< *tuqeláɬ)

[8] The failure of the stress to shift to the penult is an anomaly (§A3.5, 2nd¶), but there is no other way to explain *dapan*.

In the following examples, the penult was lost, rather than the antepenult. This may have been because the middle syllable was *he or *se:

> *baheɣát > *baʔāt* 'heavy' (also *bəʔat* [reflecting loss of the penult and weakening of the antepenult, as further exemplified in the paragraph immediately following]) *isepi> *lipuy* 'dream' (< *lipi < *ipi [§E3.1.51])

E3.1.14 The antepenult and the penult were sometimes (but not always) lost when the PAn stress was on the final syllable and the nucleus of the penult was *e. First, the antepenult was weakened, but not lost, and then the penultimate vowel was lost giving rise to a CC, which subsequently was simplified. Then the penultimate [ə] of the resulting form (the weakened former antepenult) was elided, and the resulting CC was simplified. Why this series of changes took place in some roots with penultimate *e but not in others is unknown.

> *baɣeqáŋ > *kang* 'jaw (< *bqaŋ < *beqɣaŋ < *beqeɣaŋ) *isegúŋ 'nose' > *yūng* 'face' (also *yung* 'nose') (< *iyung) *saɣejał > *ñān* 'ladder' (< *n-yan < *n-ejan < *n-eɣjan < *n-eɣejan < *n-aɣejan) *iseyup > *məñup* 'blow, puff air' (< *meñeyup < *maN- +*seyup < *iseyup [loss of antepenult])

E3.1.15 Weakening of the penult in disyllabic roots and monosyllabization

In a few cases, the penult of disyllabic roots was weakened (> /ə/ or was lost). This is not a general rule, but it may be a rule in some of the Moklen dialects (cf. the examples of variant Moklen forms in the glossary):

> *aliq > *məlēʔ* 'transfer residence' *dasuwen > *dəʔon* 'leaf' (Rawai: *daʔon*) *kitiŋ 'tendon in heel or wrist' > *kətɛng* 'calf' *lamun > *ləmōn/ləmun* 'sea grass'

In our data, there are only a few roots that show this weakening, although it is likely that in fact, more weakened penults occur in normal speech than we had been able to establish in our short stay in Rawai.[9] Weakening of the penult is part of a syndrome that we may term 'tendency to monosyllabization'. This movement toward monosyllabization is most prominently manifested in the tendency in colloquial styles to pronounce only the major syllable of the word. A similar syndrome is manifested in the variant pronunciation of *buwāk* 'flower' recorded by Chantanakomes (1980: appendix, 5): *būᵊk*, where the major syllable is weakened to an off-glide and the two syllables collapse into one.

E3.1.16 Simplification of consonant clusters

Moken does not allow consonant clusters, and any *C_1C_2 that developed through syncope was simplified. C_1 was lost and C_2 retained except when C_2 was *ɣ or *l, in which case C_1 was retained—i.e., *Cl (< *Cl and *Cɣ [§E3.3.41]) simplified to /C/. Also *nd and *mb were simplified to /n/ and /m/, respectively. Finally, clusters involving *q or *l (< *ɣ or *l) plus *s or *h are lost entirely.

E3.1.161 Examples of the simplification of C followed by a nasal:

---

[9] There is some evidence that weakening of the penult is a sound change in progress: Chantakomes (1980) reports a number of forms with /ə/ in the minor syllable where we recorded other vowels, and we recorded examples of variation between /ə/ and another vowel in the speech of our informants, e.g. *kəʔoy* and *kaʔoy* 'pestle', *bəʔok* and *baʔɔk* 'drunk'.

*cakit > *makɛt* (also *saket*) 'ill' (< *cmakit < *cumakit < *um-cakit) *tucuk 'pierce' > *mɔcɔk* 'thread a needle' *siket > *mɛkat* 'tie' *qucuŋ > *mɔcʰɔng* 'carry on pole between two people'

E3.1.162 The nasal was lost before a voiceless stop:

*qaɬimateq > *lɛtāk* 'leech' (< *lintaq < *limateq) *qáɬitu > *katoy* 'evil spirit' (< *qantu < *qanitú)

E3.1.163 The nasal was retained before voiced stop and the stop was lost:

*diŋediŋ > *dining* 'wall' (< *dindiŋ) *paŋudaɬ > *panan* 'pandanus' *tubuq 'grow' > *numūk* 'grow out beard' (< *tumbuq)

E3.1.164 A C followed by *l, *ɣ was retained, and *l, *ɣ were lost:

*buteliɣ > *butin* 'grain, seed' *dapuɣ + an > *dapan* 'fireplace' (< *dapɣan)

E3.1.165 Simplification of clusters with *s or *h

These two consonants were lost entirely. When they had come to abut on *q or an *l (< *ɣ or < *l), the *q and *l also disappeared.[10] The resulting abutting vowels contracted (§§E3.2.1ff.) forming a monosyllabic root. Subsequently the monosyllabic root was disyllabized by stretching the root vowel and intercalating a laryngeal between the two moras (§E3.1.4):

*baheɣat > *baʔāt* *basequ > *baʔoy* 'smell bad' *qaselu > *kaʔoy* pestle (< *qau < *qaslu)

E3.1.166 Examples of the simplification of other clusters:

*beɣecay > *bɔcay* 'paddle' *beɣeŋi > *bəŋay* 'night' (< *belŋi < *beɣŋi) *buqaya > *kayāʔ* 'crocodile' (< *bqaya) *baqeɣu > *kɛloy* 'new' (< *bqeɣu) *ma-qetaq > *mətāk* 'raw' (< *meqtaq < *meqetaq) *pacaqaɬ > *makʰān* 'carry on shoulder' (< *macqan < *pacqan) *saɣejaɬ > *ñān* 'ladder' (< *n-yan < *n-ejan < *n-eɣjan < *n-eɣejan < n-aɣejan) *tuqelaɬ > *kəlān* 'bone' (< *tqelan < *teqelan)

E3.1.2 Monosyllabization and disyllabization

Current Moken is tending to monosyllabization (cf. the comment at the end of §E3.1.15). In colloquial speech, many Moken disyllabic forms are abbreviated by dropping the penult. There are numerous cases of disyllabic forms for which the abbreviated form consisting of the major syllable alone has become generalized to all styles and the first syllable has been lost entirely (cf. the examples at the end of this section). Nevertheless, at an earlier stage, Moken shared the tendency of other An languages to disyllabize monosyllabic roots. That is, many of the disyllabic roots now attested derive from monosyllabic roots and were disyllabized by the processes of petrifaction of a prefix, doubling or reduplication, or stretching the root by adding a syllable to vowel nucleus or by adding a prothetic vowel homophonous with the root vowel (§A3.6.2).

---

[10] The following scenario may possibly explain how these changes came about:

(1) The medial penult is lost, resulting in sequence involving *q or *ɣ plus *s or *h.

(2) *s > *h (a general PMP change)

(3) *q and *ɣ assimilated to the *h with which they were in a cluster, resulting in *hh

(4) *hh was simplified and subsequently lost.

The most common process is petrifaction of a prefix. This is discussed and exemplified in §E3.1.21, immediately following.

There are a couple of examples of doubling or reduplication (it is impossible to determine which of these two processes is involved):

*biɣ > *bibīn* 'lips' *baq 'put down' > *babāk* 'short'

Examples of stretching the root:

*łuɣ > *ñiʔūn* 'coconut' (< *ñiyuɣ < *ñuɣ) *pu > *ʔopoʔ* 'master, lord' *pit > *paʔīt* 'narrow'

In some cases, disyllabic forms that became monosyllabic disyllabized subsequently by stretching the root and intercalating [?] between the two moras (§§E3.1.4, E3.2.1.11). The first mora of the stretched monosyllable was a central vowel if the monosyllabic nucleus was *u:

*busuk > *baʔɔk/bəʔok* 'drunk' (< *buk < *buuk) *tusud > *taʔɔt* 'knees' (< *tud < *tuud)
*wasiyeɣ > *uʔēn* 'water' (< *wēn* [Rawai] < *wayiɣ)

Some of the PAn monosyllabic roots are attested as monosyllabic in Moken. Some of these roots never disyllabized. In other cases, they were probably disyllabized and subsequently monosyllabized again. For example, the meaning of the following form makes it likely that it is cognate with other forms derived from *ɣuwaŋ (cf. Ml *ruang* 'ship's bilge'). However, Moken only attests the final syllable:

*waŋ 'space' > *wang* 'bottom of boat'

The nasalization of the initial consonant of the following root shows that that it was disyllabized before it became monosyllabic again:

*bun > *mun* 'dew' (< *mbun [§E3.1.16] < *embun (disyllabization and insertion of medial nasal ([§A3.7.2], cf. Ml *embun* 'dew')

In the following case, the disyllabized form is retained dialectally, and the Rawai form is probably derived from it:

*pan > *upān* 'bait' (< *um- + *pan) also *pān* (Rawai)

E3.1.21 Disyllabization by petrifaction

There were three prefixes that were productive in proto-Moken, the language that gave rise to the current Moken and Moklen dialects. These prefixes formed the verbal morphology cognate with the morphological processes that are still productive in many of the An languages. This verbal morphology was lost in all current varieties of Moken and Moklen. The reflexes of these prefixes, however, are widely attested in the current dialects as petrified minor syllables. These prefixes are as follows in the form reconstructed for PAn: *um-, *maN-, where N- represents nasal substitution for an initial C of the root (§A3.7.1), and *ni- (cf. §A3.5.4). There is a great deal of variation among the Moken and Moklen dialects: a given root may occur with two different affixes in different dialects or with prefixes in some dialects and without prefixes in others. In Moken *um- and *maN- have two different reflexes depending on whether the PAn root was monosyllabic or had more than one syllable. The prefix *ni- is reflected as a substitution of /n/ for the initial consonant of the root.

First, *um-:

E3.1.211 With monosyllabic roots *um- > *ume- in pre-Moken times:[11]

*duk + *um- > *madɔ̆k* 'sit' (< *eme-duk < *ume-duk < *um-duk) *kep + *um- > *məkap* 'embrace' (< *eme-kep < *ume-kep < *um-kep)

E3.1.212 With roots of two or more syllables, *um- became an infix, the *u was lost and the resulting *Cm was simplified to /m/ (§E3.1.162):

*cakit > *makɛt* (also *saket*) 'ill' (< *cmakit < *cumakit < *um-cakit) *tucuk 'pierce' > *mɔcɔk* 'thread a needle' *siket > *mɛkat* 'tie' *qucuŋ > *mɔcʰɔng* 'carry on pole between two people'

E3.1.213 With PAn roots of two or more syllables beginning in a vowel or *p-, *um- has the reflex /m-/ and the initial *p- is lost.

isecep > *mɛsap* 'suck water' *pasaqaɬ > *makʰān* 'carry over shoulder' *utaq > *mɔtāk* 'vomit'

E3.1.214 Next, the prefix *maN-: with monosyllabic roots this prefix has the shape /maN-/ or /məN-/.[12]

*gap + maN- > *mangāp* 'feel for, grope' *kep + maN- > *məngap* 'catch arrest' *sap + maN- > *məngap* 'grab'

E3.1.215 With PAn roots of two or more syllables, this prefix has altered to nasalization of the of the intial C of the root or addition of /ng-/ in the case of vowel-initial roots. (Cf. the examples in §E3.1.5.)

E3.1.216 The prefix *ni- is reflected as as a replacement of the initial consonant of the root by /n-/ (which varies with /l-/ [as explained in §E3.1.51]) or addition of /n-/ to a vowel-initial root:

*baŋuɬ > *nangon* (dialectally *mangon)* 'rise' *utaq > *nɔtāk* 'vomit' (Moklen) also *mɔtāk* (Rawai) *iseq > *niʔiᵊk* 'urine' (also *piʔiᵊk*, a back formation from *miʔiᵊk, which is not attested)

E3.1.3 Metathesis

Moken reflects the cases of metathesis that are common to all of the MP languages—that took place in PMP or at an earlier stage (cf. §A3.5.4):

[11] There is at least one exception. In the case of *upan* 'bait' (< *pan), the cluster simplified and did not develop an allomorph *ume-—i.e., *pan + um- > *umpan > *upan*.) The form was probably influenced by Ml or Chamic (cf. Ml *umpan* 'bait'). Further, the forms *madang* 'heat' and *makan* 'eat' look like exceptions in that they have /a/ in the penult rather than /ə/. We assume that these roots had a verbal-stem derivative *pa-, which became /ma-/ when *um- was added by the rule of §E3.1.213.

[12] There is no absolutely certain explanation for the variation in vowel quality of this petrified prefix. The best explanation is contamination. E.g. *məngap* 'catch arrest' (< *maN-+ *kep) was influenced by *mekap* 'embrace'. A catalyst for the change was the necessity to avoid homonymy with *mangāp* 'grope'. On the other hand, *məngap* 'grab' (< *sap + *maN-) was influenced its homonym *məngap* 'catch, arrest'. Another possibility is dialect mixture: note that there is sporadic weakening of the /a/ of the minor syllable derived from PAn disyllabic forms (§E3.1.15), and for this irregularity, there is no explanation other than dialect mixture or that it is a sound change in progress.

*taŋila > *tεngā?* (< *tilŋa < *tileŋa < *telinga < *taliŋa) *tilu > *tɔlī?* (not directly inherited) 'deaf' *nakis > *na?ek* 'go up' (< *nasik) *sinawa 'breath' > *ñawa* 'soul, spirit' (< *niawa < *nisawa)

Other forms show metathesis that is peculiar to Moken or Moken and closely related languages:

*aɣusuq > *la?oy* 'the Australian pine: *Casuarina equisetifolia*' (< *ɣau < *ɣaqsu < *ɣaqusu [double metathesis]) *baheɣat > *ba?āt* 'heavy' *luseq > *kelɔ?* 'tears' (< *qelus) *tusuq > *tɔkɔ̄?* 'true'

E3.1.4 Insertion of laryngeals

A noncontrastive glottal stop [?] was inserted automatically as syllable onset at the beginning of roots that had no consonant onset, medially between two vowels that came to abut through consonant loss or in the process of disyllabization (§E3.1.2), and at the end of a root that had no other consonant coda.

*busuk > *ba?ɔk* 'drunk' (< *bauk < *buk < *buuk) *basequ > *ba?oy* 'smell (of something)' *lahuj > *la?ok* 'sea' *pit > *pa?ī* 'narrow' *tusud > *ta?ot* 'knees' (< *tut < *tuut)

In some cases where two vowels came to abut through consonant loss, a glide developed. There is no explanation for why the glide should have developed in some cases but in general not:

*dusa > *duwā?* 'two' *qisu > *kiyoy* 'shark' *wasiyeɣ > *wēn* 'water' (< *wayiɣ < *waiɣ < *waiyeɣ [*iye > /i/—§E3.2.15])

E3.1.5 Nasalization and replacement of root initial consonants

Although Moken has no active inflectional morphs at this time, the remnants of earlier inflection are evident in the petrifaction of pre-nasalized reflexes or reflexes of *um-. (Cf. §A3.7.1 for a discussion of this process. This process is also discussed in §E3.1.21.) The following chart shows the non-nasalized initial and the initial of the Moken reflex evincing nasalization. In some cases the non-nasalized reflex is attested dialectally, but most cases only a nasalized form is attested.[13]

CHART TWO. ROOT-INITIAL NASALIZATION

root intitial	*p-, *b-	*t-,* d-	*c-, *j-	*g-, *k-, *q-	*∅-
nasalized	m-[14]	n-[15]/l-	ñ-	ng-	ng- or m-[16]

[13] This chart does not show the reflexes of Moken roots containing a petrified prefix *um-. This prefix always appears as *m- with stems of two or more syllables, no matter what the initial of the stem is. (See the discussion and examples in §§E3.1.21ff.)

[14] In the case of Moken roots with initial /m-/reflecting a PAn form with *p- or *b-, it is impossible to know whether the /m-/ reflects *um- or nasalization.

[15] In the case of Moken roots with initial /n-/ reflecting a PAn form with *t-, it is impossible to know whether the /n-/ reflects *ni- or nasalization.

[16] The reflex /m-/ originates as the reflex of *um- in roots with vowel onset, and it may originate as *um- or as nasalization with roots having *p or *b onset.

> *beli > *məloy* 'buy' *buka > *mukāʔ* 'open' *pacaqaɬ > *makʰān* 'carry over shoulder' *capuh > *ñapu* 'sweep' *culuq 'torch' > *ñuluk* 'shine' *cepaq > *ñəpak/nəpak/nəpāk* 'chew' *gaɣut 'comb' > *ngalɔ̄t* 'scratch, scrape' *kaɣaw < *ngalaw* 'scratch' *qubaɬ 'grey hair' > *ngɔbān* 'grey hair' (also *nɔbān*) *taŋic > *nangay* 'weep' (also *mangay* [< *um- + *taŋic]) *tawa > *nawā* 'laugh'

In some cases /n-/ is substituted for /m-/. This probably arose from an earlier past tense form (*ni-) that became generalized—that is, past tense came to be expressed by substituting initial *n for initial *m. Proto-Moken lost tense and retained the form with /m-/ in some cases and with /n-/ in others. Initial /n-/ and initial /m-/ are variable in the case of some roots, and the choice may be dialectal or may in fact be variable in the speech of individuals.

> *baŋuɬ > *nangon* (dialectally *mangon)* 'rise' *utaq > *nɔtāk* 'vomit' (Moklen) also *mɔtāk* (Rawai) *iseq > *niʔiᵊk* 'urine' (also *piʔiᵊk*, a back formation from *miʔiᵊk, which is not attested)

E3.1.51 Other initial consonant substitutions

In a fair number of cases, there is variation in the initial consonant of disyllabic roots that cannot be attributed to petrifaction of a tense morpheme.[17] There is no explanation. One of the fairly widespread changes is the substitution of /l/ for /n/. In some of these cases the /n/ was the result of nasalization of root with *t- or derived from an earlier *ŋ:

> *takut > *lakɔt, lakɔ̄t* 'fear' (the nasalized *nakɔt* is also attested) *tajem > *lajam* 'sharp' (also *tayam,* dialectally) *tepak 'slap' > *ləpak* 'pound into ground' (< *nepak) *tubuq 'grow' > *lumūk/numūk* 'grow a beard' (< *tumbuq < *-um- + *tubuq) *ŋipen > *lɛpan* 'tooth' (Moklen: *nəpan*)

The initial /l-/ of the following form is explained as a substitution of the n-initial that is not attested but is implied by a variant with *m-* (§E3.1.5, end):

> *isepi > *lipuy* 'dream' (also *lɛpoy* and *mɛpoy* <*um-ipi)

Mutatis mutandis, /l/ may also be replaced by /n/:

> *laleg > *nalay* 'fly' (dialectal) (Rawai: *lalay*) *ɬemec > *nəmōʔ* 'drown' (Rawai: *ləmōʔ*)

In several forms, *n is replaced by /ñ/, *ŋ is replaced by /n/, or *ñ is replaced by /n/. There is no explanation.

> *cepaq > *ñəpak/nəpak/nəpāk* 'chew' *nakis > *ñaʔek* 'ascend' (also *naʔek*) *ŋipen > *nɛpan* 'tooth' *qubaɬ 'grey hair' > *nɔbān* 'grey hair' (also *ngɔbān*) *takup > *ñakɔp* 'cover'

There are other cases in which Moken has a first syllable that does not correspond to those of cognates in other languages. These forms probably arose by contamination with other roots of similar meaning:

> *biliŋ > *buliŋ* 'roll over' *cicik > *cɔcik, kacik* 'fish scales' *lekuq > *bikɔʔ* 'bend' (contaminated by reflex of *biŋkuk 'crooked', not attested in Mok) also *lɛkoʔ* *wakaɣ > *jakan. yakan, dakan* 'root'

---

[17] In other words this variation in the initial consonants occurs only with minor syllables. No such variation is attested with the major syllables (i.e., with monosyllabic roots).

E3.1.52 Addition of final nasal or other phonemes

In a few cases, PAn forms with a final vowel have a nasal accretion /ng/. With terms of address for relatives, this is widespread in the Hesperonesian languages. The word for 'grandmother' has an /-m/ accreted in place of /-ng/. There is no explanation:

> *apu 'grandparent' > *apong* 'father' *ina > *ɛnɔng* 'mother' (/ɔ/ in major syllable by contamination with *apong* 'father') *bu + *i- 'particle before names or titles' > *ibūm* 'grandmother'

In the following root, the final /-ng/ accretion is possibly a petrified linker *ŋ* attested widely in the Hesperonesian languages:

> *anu > *anong* 'what'

The form *lawaq lost *-q and developed a final /-n/. There is no explanation:

> *lawaq > *lawan* 'k.o. fishing net'

The following form shows accretion of /-y/. There is no explanation:

> *ciwa > *cɛway* 'nine'

E3.2 Vowels and diphthongs

Moken has added three additional series of vowels to the PAn four-vowel system: the high, mid, and the off-glide vowels, high and low—i.e., Moken has added six additional vowels: *i split into /i/, /e/, /ɛ/, and /iᵊ/, and *u split into /u/, /o/, /ɔ/, and /uᵊ/.[18] Further, Moken has added length: four of these eight vowels and /a/ may be long or short, as well. In other words, Moken has developed /ī/, /ē/, /ū/, /ō/, and /ā/, as well as the above-listed vowels. It should be noted that all these contrasts obtain only in the major syllable. In the minor syllable a much smaller number of vowel contrasts occur (cf. the statement of §E3.0). How these developments came about is unclear. No one dialect made all these innovations, but all of these vowels have entered through dialect loans into the Moken we investigated in Rawai. A similarly large inventory probably developed in the same way in Moken dialects spoken in other areas as well. A possible scenario is that under unknown circumstances the PAn vowels split into two phonemes in various dialects, but the realization of the two phonemes was different in the different dialects. Through dialect mixture the three additional series of vowels developed. This hypothesis is born out first by the fact that we have found no environment that excludes any members of a series (in the major syllable), either in current Moken phonology or in a form reconstructed for an earlier stage. Second, it is born out by the vast amount of disjunction between our own recordings and in vowels as reported by other researchers.[19] In fact, even among the small number of people we recorded in our short stay

---

[18] Chantanakomes 1980 also reports /ūᵊ/, but we did not record it. In the form where Chatanakomes transcribes /ūᵊ/, *būᵊk* 'flower', we recorded /buwāk/. The phonemics of the syllabic nucleus of Moken has not been definitively established. The difference in the two variants of this root is probably stylistic: *buwāk* represents careful pronunciation and *būᵊk*, rapid or colloquial speech. This example shows that the vowel of the major syllable may be weakened as well as the vowel of minor syllable. (Cf. the comment at the end of §E3.1.15, above.)

[19] Chantanakomes, who conducted her research Rawai twenty-five years before we did and worked with different informants, often reports a different vowel quality and a different vowel length from those of our recordings. Her work gives all signs of having been carefully done and is based on research conducted over a fairly long period of time.

in Rawai there was a fair amount of inconsistency in regards to vowel quality. The same can be said of vowel length. In some cases, all sources and our own recordings agree in the vowel length of the major syllable, but these cases are in the minority. In many cases, our recordings differ with the length reported by published sources, the published sources differ among themselves, and even our informants differ among themselves. Some of the problems of the inconsistent data may be laid to errors of interpretation on the part of the researchers. Be that as it may, the Moken themselves very clearly hear all of the distinctions and make them. It is very likely that the phonemic variation in given roots is reflected as variables in the speech of individuals as well as across different speakers. There is less variation in the minor syllable, but only because a much smaller number of contrasts obtains in the minor syllable. *i split into /i/ and /ɛ/, *u split into /u/ and /ɔ/. There is no environment that determines whether a higher or lower reflex of *i and *u occurs, and the sources are not consistent with each other or with our recordings. *i, *u, and *a are also occasionally weakened to /ə/ (§E3.1.15). Again there is no correlation between this weakening and any other phonological characteristic of the environment. Our recordings in this case mostly, but not always, agree with the transcriptions of Chantanakomes 1980. Publications that report forms from areas other than Rawai show weakening to /ə/ in the minor syllable in a large number of forms where we did not find it.

In short, the research has not been done to enable us to give the historical or sociolinguistic basis for the vowel variation that published data evince and that exists in our data. We can do little more here than present the few rules we have been able to determine and otherwise to list the various outcomes that our data manifest and exemplify them.

E3.2.1 *i, *u

E3.2.11 *i > /i/ in the minor and major syllables:

*biɣaq > *bilāk* 'the giant taro: *Colocasia indica*' *binahi > *binay* 'woman' *saŋin > *ʔangin* 'wind' *bituqen > *bituᵊk* 'star'

There are also examples of /i/ lowering to /e/ in the major syllable:[20]

*laŋit > *langet* 'sky' *lilin > *lɛlen* (also *lɛlin*) 'candle, wax'

There are a very few examples of /i/ lowering to /ɛ/ in the major syllable:

*kitiŋ 'tendon in wrist or foot' > *kətɛng* 'calf'

There is a small number of forms that reflect *i as /iᵊ/ in the major syllable. No environment has been established to account for this outcome, but the sources with very few exceptions agree that these forms have a /iᵊ/:[21]

*iseq > *ni-ʔiᵊk* 'urine' (also *ñi-ʔiᵊk* and dialectally, *pi-iᵊk*) *piliq > *miliᵊk* 'choose' (dialectally: *mɛlek*, *məliᵊk*, and *mɛlik*) *puɬetiq > *putiᵊk* 'white' (also *pɔtiᵊk*) *sapegiq > *peyiᵊk*, *bejiᵊk* 'smarting, stinging'

E3.2.12 There are many examples of /i/ lowering to /ɛ/ in the minor syllable:[22]

[20] There is a tendency to lower vowels in closed final syllable (cf. Pittayaporn 2005: §2)

[21] Our informant Sayā who had very recently come to Rawai from Surin Island had long mid vowels in place of the off-glides /iᵊ/ and /uᵊ/—i.e., /ɛ̄/ and /ɔ̄/ respectively: *niʔɛ̄k*, *peyɛ̄k*, *milɛ̄k*, *putɛ̄k*,

*qitem > *kɛtam* 'black' *qaciɣah > *cɛlāʔ* (also *c*[h]*ɛlāʔ*) 'salt'

E3.2.13 *-i at the end of a root (or a root that became vowel final by the loss of final *-s or *-h) was diphthongized to /uy/ and /oy/. I have is discovered no rule for the occurrence of the higher or lower reflex, and the data show both outcomes for the same root.[23] Dialectally this diphthong is centralized to /əy/.

*buɬi > *munuy* 'hidden' *isepi > *lipuy* 'dream' (also *lɛpoy* and *mɛpoy*)

There are unexplained exceptions. In one case *-i is reflected as /ay/:

*biɣeŋi > *bengay* 'night'

In three cases, *-i is reflected as /ī/ or /ɛ̄/:

*daɬi > *danīʔ* 'near' *tilu > *tolī* 'deaf' (< *tuli) (dialect: *tuley*) *aqetih > *kətɛ̄ʔ* 'shallow, ebbing'

E3.2.14 In trisyllabic roots, *i of the antepenult was lost or weakened to /ə/ (cf. §§E3.1.1ff.). There are two cases where *i > /ə/ in a minor syllable of a disyllabic form. In the first example, the development is probably due to the fact that the form is often clitic (§E3.1.1), but the other case is not explained:

*kita > *əta* 'we, us' *cicik > *cəcik* 'fish scales' (dialectally *kacik*)

E3.2.15 When not word final, *iya and *ayi (or *ia and *ai that developed by loss of a medial C) were contracted to /e/; *eyi and *iye (or *ei and *ie) were contracted to /i/ (and sometimes subsequently lowered to /e/):

*baliyan > *bəlen* 'shaman' *wasiyeɣ > *wēn* 'water' (< *wayiɣ)[24]

E3.2.16 *i is irregularly reflected by /o/ in the following form, probably by contamination with a form of similar meaning, but this form has not been identified:

*buɣit 'rear' > *bulot* 'stern'

E3.2.17 *u > /u/ in the minor and major syllables, and this is the most common reflex in both syllables:

*bucuk > *busuk* 'rotten, smelly' *buŋkuk 'crooked' > *bukuk* 'hump-backed' *tujuq > *mujuk* 'point' (< *tmujuk) *butuq 'genitals' > *butūk* 'penis'

E3.2.18 There are many examples of /u/ lowering to /ɔ/ in the minor syllable:[23]

---

[22] There evidently was a rule of vowel harmony in pre-Moken, which no longer operates: high vowels in the penult were lowered before a mid or low vowel in the final syllable (cf. Pittayaporn 2005: §2).

[23] There is a tendency for vowel harmony—/uy/ occurs after the high vowels and /oy/ after the mid and low vowels.

*diɣi 'stand' > *diluy* 'classifier for people' *duɣi > *duluy* 'thorn' *waɣi > *aloy* 'sun, day'

But it is only a tendency, and there are exceptions:

*qisu > *kiyoy* 'shark' (perhaps influenced by the dialectal *kəyoy)* *bulu 'body hair' > *buloy* 'hair, fur, wool'

[24] In the following case, the development of /ɔ/ caused an *e that had arisen from *ai to lower to /ɛ/ by vowel harmony (a sporadic process [cf. the footnotes to §§E3.2.12 and E3.2.13]):

*qaciɬ 'salty' > *ɔ-kɛn* 'salt water' (< *u + qain [with loss of *-c—§E3.3.14, 5th¶])

*kulit > *kɔlet* 'skin' *qumah > *kɔma* 'planted field, to farm' *qutaɬ 'scrub lands' > *kɔtan* 'forest'

There are also examples of /u/ lowering to /o/ in a closed major syllable:[21]

*qetut > *ketot* 'break wind'

There are a few examples of /u/ lowering to /ɔ/ in a closed major syllable:[21]

*likuj > *lɛkɔt* 'back' (also *lɛkɔ̃t*) *qucuŋ > *mɔchɔ̃ng* 'carry on pole between two people' (also *mɔsɔng*) *tusuq > *tɔkɔʔ* 'true' *takut > *lakɔt* 'fear'

E3.2.19 At the end of a root (or a root that became vowel final by the loss of final *-s or *-h), *-u is diphthongized to /oy/. Dialectally this diphthong is centralized to /əy/.[25]

baqeɣuh > *kəloy* 'new' *beli > *məloy* 'buy'

E3.2.1.10 Similarly, a sequence *au that developed in final position by loss of the intervening consonant became /oy/:

*acu > *ʔoy* 'dog' *qaselu > *kəʔoy* 'pestle' (variant of *kaʔoy*) (< *koy—dissylabization[§E3.1.2] < *qau)

A sequence *au with coda that developed in a closed syllable by loss of the intervening consonant contracted to /o/. The resulting monosyllabic root was subsequently disyllabized:

*dasuwen > *dəʔon* 'leaf' (dialectal [Rawai: *daʔon*])

E3.2.1.11 In cases of root with *u in both the penult and final syllables, when an intervening C was lost, the two *u's were contracted and lowered to /ɔ/, resulting in a monosyllabic root. Subsequently, the monosyllable was disyllabized by stretching the root to two syllables by inserting a centralized penult (i.e., with /ə/ or /a/ [(§E3.1.2, 4th¶]):

*busuk > *baʔɔk/bəʔɔk* 'drunk' (< *buk < *buuk) *tusud > *taʔɔt* 'knee'

E3.2.1.12 In a couple of forms,*u in the final syllable is reflected as /uᵊ/. These forms probably reflect dialect mixture:

*bituq-an > *bituᵊk* 'star' *qanibuŋ > *nibuᵊng* 'k.o. tree'

E3.2.2 *e

*e in the PAn penult or antepenult > /ə/ if it is not lost by syncopation, as explained in §E3.1.l, above.

E3.2.21 *e in the penult in Moken remained /ə/ when the PAn antepenult was lost or elided (§E3.1.1):

*baqeɣu > *kəloy* 'new' *qajelay > *jəlay* 'job's tears' *tuqelaɬ > *kəlan* 'bone'

E3.2.22 *e in the penult of disyllabic roots remained /ə/:

*depa > *dəpāʔ* 'fathom' *ketut > *kətot* 'break wind' *qeti 'stop' > *kətoy* 'be finished' *telu > *təloy* 'three'

---

25 An exception is the following form, which failed to diphthongize the *-u. It is a borrowing from Ml and confined to the shamanic register:

*baɣiyus > *bayu* 'storm'

In the PAn final syllable, *e > /a/:

*bayeq > *balak* 'abscess' *dalem > *dalam* 'in' *laleg > *lalay* 'a fly' *qageŋ > *kayang* 'charcoal' *lem > *ka-lam, tə-lam* 'sink' *paqegu > *kapaw* 'gall' (< *qapew < *qapeu < *qapegu)

If the minor syllable had /i/ or /u/—i.e., its nucleus was from *i or *u but not lowered, *e in the major syllable becomes /iᵊ/.[26]

A small number of forms with *e do not follow these rules. They are probably borrowed but the source is not known in every case:

*deŋey 'hear' > *mεŋā?* 'listen' (probably not connected) *lemek > *lamak* 'fat' (< Ml) *ɬemec 'disappear' > *ləmō?* 'drown' *ɬecuŋ > *lūng* 'mortar'

E3.2.3 *a

*a > /a/ in both major and minor syllables:

*bayah > *balā?* 'embers' *bataŋ > *batang* '(tree) trunk, main part, origin' *tasaw 'open space' > *ta?aw* 'sea' *tulak > *nəlāk* 'push'

*a was weakened or syncopated in some cases in trisyllabic stems (cf. E3.1.1). The following form only occurs as the second member of a compound, and therefore the penultimate *a was syncopated:

*gayaŋ 'crab' > *klāng* in *iᵊk klāng* 'the ark shell'

The sequence *iya is contracted to /ε/:

*baliyan > *bəlεn* 'shaman'

The sequence *ayay is contracted to /ay/:

*pagay > *pay* 'rice plant' (< *payay)

E3.2.4 Diphthongs

The diphtongs remained unchanged except for *iw.

*aw > /aw/:

*laŋaw > *langaw* 'a fly'

In the following form, *-aw is reflected as /-o/. It is dialectal, reported by Lewis 1960:

*linaw 'calm, unroiled' > *lεno* 'sheltered, protected from weather'

*iw has several reflexes. The difference probably stems from dialect mixture. The following forms reflect this diphthong with /ew/ in some dialects and with /ē/ in Rawai:

*kasiw > *ka?ē* 'tree' (dialectally *ka?ew*) *layiw > *malē* 'flee' (Moklen *nalew*)

The following form also has an irregular reflex of *y and is a borrowing from an unknown source:

---

[26] There is only one instance of this rule, but it is not ad hoc, because in all other cases with *i in the penult of the reconstructed form, the *i is lowered to /ε/, and further /i/ in the final syllable is also changed to /iᵊ/ after /u/ in the minor syllable:

*iseq > *n-i?iᵊk* 'urine' *puɬetiq > *putiᵊk* 'white' (< *putiq) *baɣiw >*baʔew* 'go sour'

The following form shows metathesis of the *i and the *w:

waɬiw > *nanuy* (also *wanuy*) 'honey bee'

The following form has a final /-h/ and is unexplained:

*caliw > *ñɛlɛh* 'barter, exchange'

*ay > /ay/:

*beɣecay > *bəcay* 'paddle' *ɣuqaɬay > *kanay* 'man, boy, husband' *qaqay > *kakay* 'foot, leg'

*uy > /uy/, /oy/. The rules for occurrence of the higher or lower reflex are unknown:

*babuy 'wild pig' > *babuy* 'pig' *ɬaŋuy > *nangoy* 'swim' *sehapuy > *apuy* 'fire'

In one case, *ay is reflected by /oy/. The form is probably not directly inherited:

*calay 'preserve by drying' > *cʰəloy/səloy* 'dry'

E3.3 Consonants

CHART THREE. THE DEVELOPMENT OF THE MOKEN CONSONANTS FROM PAN

PAn	Mok	PAn	Mok
p	*p*	g	*g-, -y-, -y*
t	*t*	ɣ, l	*l*
k, q	*k*	ɬ	*ñ, n, l*
s, h	*Ø*	m	*m*
c	*c, s*	n	*n*
b	*b*	ŋ	*ng* [ŋ]
d	*d*	w	*w*
j	*j*	y	*y*

In addition, in a few cases, *p and *b, *k and *q, and *c have aspirated reflexes—i.e., *pʰ, *kʰ, and *cʰ, respectively. The aspirated reflexes were introduced into Moken through contact with another language, and not many of the forms inherited from PAn or PMP have aspirated stops, but a few do. In some cases, the aspirated reflexes arose when the consonant was in a cluster (examples given in the following sections). In other cases, the existence in Thai of forms with similar sounds and meaning but with an aspirated consonant makes it clear that it was contact with Thai that led to the development of aspirated initials in those forms in Moken. There are cases in which there is no explanation for the aspirated reflex. In some cases aspirated and plain reflexes of the same etymon occur in different dialects or as variables in the same dialect.

E3.3.1 Voiceless consonants

E3.3.11 *p

*p remained /p/ in all positions:

*paɣis > *paloy* 'rayfish' *papan > *papān* 'board, plank' *depa > *dəpāʔ* 'armspan' *gap + *maN- > *mangāp* 'feel for, grope'

The following form reflects *p with /pʰ/ (but there are variants with /p/, as well):

*puŋ 'gather' > *pʰūng* 'herd, flock' *ta-pʰung/ ta-pong* 'all' (cf. Thai *fūŋ* 'herd')

E3.3.12 *t

*t remains /t/ in almost all cases:

*taɬeq > *tanak* 'clay, earth' *taquweɬ > *takon* 'year' *tiyaɬ 'belly' > *tiyān* 'pregnant' *tutuŋ 'set afire' > *tutūng/tɔtūng* 'burnt' *bataŋ > *batang* 'trunk of tree' *buntut 'tail' > *butut/butūt* 'anus' *sabaɣat 'strong monsoon wind' > *balāt* 'west wind'

In forms with petrified prefixes, *t- is replaced by /m-/ (< *tm- < *tum- [§E3.1.161]) or /n-/ (§E3.1.5):

*takut > *nakot* 'fear' (also *lakɔt/lakɔ̄t*) *taɬem > *manam* 'to plant' *tawa > *nawāʔ* 'laugh' *tiduɣ > *midūn* 'sleep *tubuq 'grow' > *numūk* 'grow out beard' *tucuk > *mɔcɔk* 'to thread (needle)' *tujuq > *mujuk* 'point' *tulak > *nɔlak* 'push'

E3.3.13 *k, *q

*q and *k merge and become /k/:

*kapit 'hold by pinching' > *kapīt* 'pincer of crab' *kulit 'skin, bark' > *kɔlet* 'bark' *ikuɣ > *ʔikūn* 'tail' *isekan > *ɛkān* 'fish' *buɣuk > *bulok* 'rotten' *qabu > *kaboy* 'ashes' *quluh 'head' > *kɔlɔ* 'prow, handle' *qusalipan 'milliped' > *kɔpān* 'scorpion' *baqeɣu > *kəloy* 'new' *buqaya > *kayāʔ* 'crocodile' *qaɬimateq > *lɛtāk* 'leech' (< *lintaq < *limateq)

In a few cases, *k and *q > /kʰ/ :

*keɬa 'hit mark' > *kʰənā* 'touch, hit' *qujaɬ > *kʰujān* 'rain' (also *kɔyan*) *pacaqaɬ > *makʰān* 'carry over shoulder' (cf. Thai *khān* 'carry over shoulder') *belaq 'cleft' > *pelāʔ* 'side (right or left)'

In a few cases, *k was lost. There is no explanation.

*kaban > *ʔaban* 'flock' *kaka > *ʔakaʔ* 'elder brother or sister' *tacik 'seawater' > *tase* 'sea'[27]

Similarly, a few cases show a loss of *q, also not explained:

*qaɣa 'species of ficus' > *alāʔ* 'the sacred ficus' *aliq 'move' > *məlē* 'move (to a new dwelling)'

In one example, the cluster *cq that developed was replaced by /tʰ/. The replacement is probably due to Thai influence:

*cequɬ > *mə-tʰūn* 'carry on head' (< *me-cquɬ) (cf. Thai *thūn* 'carry on the head')

In one case, *q is lost. This form may have been influenced by Ml:

*qutek > *ʔɔtak* 'brains'

In another unexplained case, *k- is replaced by *g-:[28]

---

[27]Our informants were unfamiliar with this form. Possibly it is a borrowing from Ml. Our source is Ivanoff 1981, which contains texts in shamanic registers as well as normal styles. The everyday word for 'sea' is *taʔaw* < *tasaw 'open space'

[28] The dialect form *geyey* 'shark' (Rawai: *kiyoy*) also shows /g/ in place of /k/.

kutu > *gutoy* 'head louse'

In final position, *-k is reflected by /-t/ in three forms:

*ałak > *anāt* 'son, daughter' *miniyak > *məñāt* 'oil' *tacak 'cooked' > *tāt* 'ripe, cooked' (dialectal)

Final *-q is also occasionally reflected by /-t/:

*baɣeq > *balat* 'abscess' (Rawai: *balak*)

In final position, *-q is reflected with /-h/ in a few cases. These forms are borrowed from Cham or Ml (both of which reflect *-q with /h/ [§D4.3.21]):

*ca-puluq > *cəpoh* 'ten' *nipaq 'k.o. palm of tidal swamps' > *ñɛpah* 'thatch'

Final *k is reflected by /h/ in one case (perhaps a hypercorrection):

*balik < *balɛh* 'return'

*k- and *q- are occasionally replaced by nasal consonants (§E3.1.5):

*kapit 'hold by pinching' > *ngapīt* 'grip' *qubał < *ngɔbān* 'grey hair'

E3.3.14 *c

*c has two reflexes: /c/ and /s/. /c/ is currently undergoing change to /s/. In a few forms, the change has been completed (no variant with /c/ is attested), for some forms no variant with /s/ is attested, and for some forms variants with both /s/ and /c/ are attested.
Only with /c/:

*beɣecay > *bœcay* 'paddle' *cicik > *cœcik* 'fish scales' *ica > *cāʔ* 'one' *ciwa < *cɛway* 'nine' *tucuk 'pierce' > *m-œcɔk* 'thread a needle' *puceg > *pœcat/pucat* 'navel' *qapucuk 'tip' > *pœcɔk* 'shoot (of a plant)'

With /s/:

*bucuk > *busuk* 'rotten, smelly' *pacek 'wedge' > *masak* 'nail' *qacił 'salty > *m-asim* 'brackish water' *cabut > *sabūt* 'husk of coconut'

In a few cases, the reflex /c/ is aspirated. The first two cases are loan words:

*cawa > *c^{h}aba* 'python' *calay > *c^{h}əloy* 'preserve by drying' (also *səloy*) *qaciɣah > *c^{h}ɛlāʔ* (also *celāʔ* and *selāʔ*) *cucu > *cœc^{h}oy* 'milk' *leqacem > *m-ac^{h}am* 'sour' (also *kasam* 'pickle') *sacaŋ 'gills' > *ɛc^{h}ang* 'fins' (dialectal) *ɛsāng* (Rawai) *sicep > *m-ɛc^{h}ap* 'suck in water' (also *m-ɛcap* and *m-ɛsap* 'smoke [tobacco]') *ucuŋ > *m-œc^{h}ɔng* 'for two people to carry on a pole'

There are a number of cases where *c is reflected with /h/ or lost entirely. Many of these forms evince other irregularities, and they are loan words. The forms evincing /h/ are probably Chamic loans or influenced by Cham.[29] The origin of forms that have lost *c entirely is unknown. These forms are very basic vocabulary, and it is likely that a dialect of pre-Moken lost *c, but the loss of *c was not carried through, so that only a few items now reflect Ø.
*c > /h/:

[29] Classical Cham reflects *c with /h/.

*balec > *balah* 'revenge' *ɣatuc > *latɔh* 'hundred' *sapedec > *padɛh/padɛh* 'hot, sharp taste' *qacu > *kahoy* 'smoke' *ɬisebic > *ñipih* 'thin' (also *lipih* and *nipih*)

*c > ∅:

*acu > *ʔoy* (< *au) 'dog' *atac > *d-atāʔ* 'on, above' *bacaq > *pʰāk* 'wet' *ciku > *ɛkoy* 'elbow' *ɬecuŋ > *lūng* 'mortar' *ɬemec 'disappear' > *ləmōʔ* 'drown, sink' (also *nəmōʔ*) *qaciɬ 'salty' *ɔ-kɛn* 'salt water' (< *u- + qain) *sipec > *ɛpā* 'cockroach' *tacak > *tāt* 'ripe, cooked' *tiɣic > *tilī* 'leak'

In one case, *ic > /ay/—i.e., *-c > ∅, and the *-i diphthongized to /ay/ (but not to /oy/ or /uy/ [§E3.2.13]):

*taŋic > *nangay/mangay* 'weep' (also *nangoy*)

Nasalized forms of roots with initial *c- also occur (§E3.1.5):

*calin 'transfer' > *ñalen* 'change clothes' (also *salin* 'transfer) *capuh > *ñapu* 'sweep, brush' *culuq 'torch' > *ñulūk* 'shine'

E3.3.2 *h, *s

Both *h and *s disappeared and left little trace in Moken. Although it is probably the case the *h was lost before *s, for loss of *h began long before PMP split off from the other An languages, Moken offers no evidence for that and treats both consonants in the same way. The following list gives some examples of the loss of *h and *s:

*binahi > *binay* 'woman' *sehapuy > *ʔapuy* 'fire' *kukuh > *kɔkoy* 'fingernail' *dusa > *duwāʔ* 'two' *isekan > *ɛkān* 'fish' *luseq > *kəlɔ* 'tears' (< *qelus) *sulaɣ > *ɔlān* 'snake' *tebus > *təboy* 'sugar cane'

In some environments, the loss of *h or *s caused hiatus—i.e., the abutting vowels that developed contracted, but subsequently they were disyllabized with intercalation of /ʔ/ (§E3.1.2):[30]

*dasuwen > *daʔon* 'leaf' (also *daʔən* *kasiw > *kaʔẽ* 'wood, tree' *lahuj > *laʔok* 'seaward' *nakis > *naʔek* (< *nasik) *pasuq > *paʔɔ̃k* 'wild mango' *tasaw 'open space' > *taʔaw* 'the sea'

When a cluster developed with *s or *h, *s and*h were lost and the other consonants were retained, except when the cluster was with *ɣ or *q (cf. the examples in §E3.1.165).

E3.3.3 Voiced stops

The voiced stops remain in Moken in initial and medial position, but in final position, they were devoiced.

E3.3.31 *b

Initial and medial *b remained unchanged for the most part (unless in syllables lost by syncopation [§E3.1.1]):

---

[30] There are two reasons I assume contraction and subsequent disyllabization: first, contraction occurred in other cases of abutting vowels; second, in some cases the penult has an /ə/ nucleus, a phenomenon that can be best explained as a product of disyllabization (cf. the examples in §§E3.1.2, 4th¶, E3.2.1.11).

*babuy > *babuy* 'pig' *beɣecay > *bəcay* 'paddle' *bubu > *buboy* 'fish trap' *qabaŋ > *kabang* 'boat'

In final position, *-b becomes devoiced (> /-p/):

*qisuwab > *kɔwap* 'yawn'

Nasalized forms of initial *b occur in many roots (§E3.1.5):

*belaq > *məlāk* 'split' *beli > *məloy* 'buy' *buɣesu > *moloy* jealous' *bunuq > *munūk* 'kill' (*bunok* is also attested)

Reflexes of *sebic 'thin' are reflected with *pic as in all languages apart from Bunun, but the Moken form is probably influenced by Chamic *lipih*.

*ɬisebic > *ñipih* 'thin' (also *lipih*)

In two cases, initial *b- is reflected by /pʰ/. There is no explanation.[31] These forms also evince other irregularities:

*bacaq > *pʰāk* 'wet' *beɣac > *pʰəlāʔ* 'hulled rice' (also *bəlāʔ*)

In one case, initial *b- is reflected by /p/. This root was probably reshaped by sound symbolism:

*baqesiŋ > *pakan* 'sneeze'

In one case, *b is replaced by /h/. There is no explanation:

*dabuq > *dahɔk* 'fall'

E3.3.32 *d

Initially and medially, *d > /d/ with very few exceptions:

*daya > *dayāʔ* 'inland' *depa > *depāʔ* 'arm span' *duɣi > *duluy* 'thorn' *tuduq > *tudūk* 'leak' *tiduɣ > *midūn* 'sleep'

A *d that came to be in a cluster with a nasal was lost (§E3.1.163):

*diŋediŋ > *dining* 'wall'

At least three items evince initial /t/ or /tʰ/. Perhaps these are borrowings from a Chamic language that had developed pharyngealization of the initial voiced consonants:

*depa > *təpāʔ* 'fathom' (dialectal [Rawai: *depāʔ*]) *diŋediŋ > *tingin* 'cold' *dusa > *tʰəwā* (dialectal), *tʰuwā* (Moklen) (Rawai: *duwāʔ*)

Final *-d is devoiced (> /-t/):

*sated > *m-atat* 'deliver'

The following two forms show exceptions. In the first case, contamination with a word of similar meaning is the probable explanation, but for the other one, there is no explanation:

*kedep > *kelip* 'blink' *padeŋ > *payam* 'extinguish'[32]

---

[31] It is very possible that these roots were influenced by Chamic. These roots contained *c. The reflex of *c in classical Cham is /h/, and the *c of these roots, which became lost, may in fact be reflected in the aspiration of the initial consonant of the root.

[32] Variation between /y/ and /d/ is also evinced by the reflexes of *jaɣum 'needle', *dalum* and *yalum,* neither of which is regular.

E3.3.33 *j

*j > /j/ in initial and medial positions. Some forms with /j/ vary with forms having /y/. It may be that in some dialects, *j became /y,/ but this change was not carried through. In any case, not all PAn forms with *j that are attested in Moken have reflexes with /y, but all PAn forms with *j that are reflected in Moken evince /j/ in some dialect.[33]

*jalan > *jalān* (also *yalān*) 'way' *qujaɬ > *kujān* (also *kʰujān* and *kɔyān*) 'rain' *tujuq > *mujuk* 'point' (no variant with /y/ attested)

In final position, *-j is reflected in one root with /-k/, and this is probably the inherited reflex:

*lahuj > *laʔok* 'sea'

There are three other froms which reflect *-j, but they are likely borrowings from Ml or, in the case of the first two examples, they may possibly be early Chamic borrowings. They show /-t/:

*bukij > *bukit* 'mountain, hill' *likuj > *lɛkɔt* 'back' *tukej 'prop, support' > *tɔkat* 'walking stick' (Cf. Ml *tongkat* 'walking stick')[34]

E3.3.34 *g

*g > /g/ initially and /y/ medially and finally:

*galaŋ 'wedge' > *galang* 'piece of wood used as support in dragging a boat onto land' *gatel > *gatan* 'itch' *giliŋ > *gilin* 'roll up' *qageŋ > *kayang* 'charcoal' *pagay > *pay* 'rice plant' (< *payay) *sapegiq > *pəyiˀk* 'smarting' *laleg > *lalay* 'fly' *quleg 'worm' > *kɔlay* 'maggot'

There are examples of nasalized initial *g- (§E3.1.5):

*gaɣut 'comb' > *ngalɔ̃t* 'scratch, scrape' *galih > *ngaloy* 'dig' *gap > *mangāp* 'grope'

The following example shows prenasalization of the medial C (§A3.7.2):

*qagan > *ngañān* 'name' (< *ŋagan [§A3.7.1])

In the following case, /y/ did not develop from medial *g. Instead *g was lost. This is probably due to the environment (between *e and *u), but we have only one example:

*paqegu > *kapaw* 'gall' (< *qapew < *qapeu < *qapegu)

There are other exceptions. The first example is probably a loan word. The second is influenced by another word of similar meaning:

*puceg > *pɔcat* 'navel' (also *pucat*) *tebug < *təbung* 'well' (cf. *təbung* 'hole')

In the following form, which is attested only in a compound, initial *g- may have assimilated to the preceding /k/:

*gaɣaŋ 'crab > *iˀk klāng* 'ark shell'

---

[33] Pittayaporn (p.c.) suggests that the alternation between [j] and [y] has nothing to do with Moken but is an artifact of the transcriptions made by Thai speaking researchers who have difficulty in hearing the distinction.
[34] Possibly *tɔkat* was influnced by *tɔkat* 'stump' (< *tuqed).

E3.3.4 Voiced continuants

E3.3.41 *ɣ, *l

*ɣ and *l merged. They became /l/ initially[35] and medially:

*baɣah > *balāʔ* 'embers, hot charcoal' *biɣaq > *bilāk* 'giant taro' *buɣuk > *bulok* 'rotten' *aɣusuq > *laʔoy* 'the Australian pine: *Casuarina equisetifolia*' (< *ɣau < *ɣaqsu < *ɣaqusu [double metathesis]) *laleg > *lalay* 'fly' *lima > *lɛmaʔ* 'five' *bulaɬ > *bulān* 'moon' *kulit > *kɔlet* 'skin, bark'

In final position, *-ɣ and *-l > /-n/:

*bibiɣ > *bibīn* 'lips' *ikuɣ > *ikūn* 'tail' *layaɣ > *layān* 'sail' *gatel > *gatan* 'itch' *tebel > *təban* 'thick'

In clusters, *ɣ and *l are lost in many combinations. (Cf. §§E3.1.16ff. for specifics and for examples.) There are other forms reconstructed with a *ɣ that does not come to be in a cluster but is lost. There is no explanation for the lost *ɣ.

*qaliɣ 'flow'> *loy* 'trickle down' *baɣiw 'spoil (food)' > *baʔew* 'go sour' *ɣumaq > *ʔɔmak* 'house'

The following form underwent an idiosyncratic change. There is no explanation, but it is consistent with the direction of developments that Moken forms took. The penult lost syllabicity and the resulting cluster developed into [j]:

*iluɣ 'stream' > *jon* 'saliva' (< *yluɣ)

E3.3.42 *ɬ

*ɬ in Moken reflects the changes made by PMP as described in in §A3.3.4 (*ɬ > /ñ/, /n/, and /l/):

(1) *ɬ > /l/ as onset to a penultimate or earlier syllable with a short vowel:

*qaɬimatéq > *lɛtak* 'leech' *ɬepúq > *ləpūk* 'lion fish'

(2) *ɬ > /n/ when root final and when onset to the final syllable after a short vowel penult:

*ɣuqaɬáy > *kanay* 'man, husband' *aɬák > *anāt* 'son, daughter' *buláɬ > *bulān* 'moon' *peɬúq > *penōk* (also *penuk*) 'full'

(3) *ɬ > /ñ/ before or after a long vowel in the penult or as onset to monosyllabic root.

*ñam > *ñam* 'eat', *ñam-an* 'tasty' *iseɬaw > *ma-ñaw* (< *ɬaw[36]) *ɬámuk > *ñamok* 'mosquito, sandfly'

---

[35] There is only one Moken attestation of a form reconstructed with *ɣ- onset of the penult that does not evince irregularities.

[36] We reconstruct *iseɬaw in the glossary, but it is likely that Moken *ma-ñaw* reflects a monosyllabic root *ɬaw, and the reconstruction *iseɬaw consists of the monosyllabic root plus a petrified prefix *ise-. An alternative explanation is that the PAn root that gave rise to the Moken reflex was *iseɬaw, and that the antepenult and penult were lost by syncopation (§A3.5.1).

The following form shows a reflex /n/ instead of the expected /l/. This is a case of /n-/ substitution for /l-/ (cf. §E3.1.51) (and has nothing to do with the development of /ñ/ or /n/ in cognate reflexes in languages of E. Indonesia):

*łangúy > *nanguy* 'swim'

E3.3.43 *m, *n, *ŋ

*m, *n, *ŋ remained unchanged in all positions:

*manuk 'bird' > *manok* 'chicken' *qumah > *kɔmā?* 'cultivated field' *kami > *kamoy* 'we (exclusive)' *enem > *nam* 'six' *nałaq > *nanāk* 'pus' *pan > *pan* 'bait' *ŋaŋa 'mouth open' > *nganga?* 'agape' *saŋin > *ʔangin* 'wind' *qabaŋ > *kabāng* 'houseboat'

In one case, *-n was lost. There is no explanation:

*ɣabun > *labū?* 'fog'

In at least two cases, final *-ŋ is reflected with *-n. There is no explanation:

*giliŋ > *gilin* 'roll up' *baqesiŋ > *pakan* 'sneeze'

Mutatis mutandis, also *-n (< PAn *n or *ł) may be reflected by /ng/:

*daqał > *dakang* 'branch'

In one case, *ŋ- is replaced by /m/. This form must have arisen by contamination, but the model is not known:

*ŋaw 'bug' > *ma-maw* 'gnat'

E3.3.44 *w and *y

*w was retained as /w/ initially and medially:

*buwaq > *buwāk* 'fruit' *ciwa > *cɛway* 'nine' *qisuwab > *kɔwāp* 'yawn' *quway > *kuway* 'rattan' *lawaq > *lawan* 'k.o. fish net' *tawa > *nawa?* 'laugh' *walu > *waloy* 'eight' *waŋ 'space' > *wang* 'bottom of the boat' *wasiyeɣ > *wēn* 'water'

*w was lost in a few forms.[37] There is no explanation.

*waɣi > *aloy* 'day' (also dialectally *waloy*) *wiɣi > *ʔɛloy* 'left' *qawuɣ > *kaʔūn* 'bamboo'

In some dialects, /w/-onset to a minor syllable is assimilated to an /n/-onset of the major syllable:

*wałiw > *nanuy* 'bee' (dialectally, *wanuy*) *wanał > *nanān* 'right' (dialectally, *wanan*)

In a couple of instances, *w is reflected as /b/. These are undoubtedly loan words, but the source is unknown:

*cawa > *c^{h}abā?* 'python' *tewi > *təbuy* 'tree of seashore'

In intervocalic position, *-y- > /-y-/. There are no attestations of Moken reflexes of *y in initial position.

*buqaya > *kayā?* 'crocodile' *daya > *dayā?* 'inland, go to market' *duyung > *duyung* 'manatee' *tiyał 'belly' > *tiyān* 'pregnant'

---

[37] Similarly, *iw is sometimes reflected as /ē/ and sometimes as /ew/ (§E3.2.4).

www.ingramcontent.com/pod-product-compliance
Lightning Source LLC
Chambersburg PA
CBHW080116020526
44112CB00037B/2755
9780877275329